AUTHENTICITY AS SELF-TRANSCENDENCE

AUTHENTICITY AS SELF-TRANSCENDENCE

The Enduring Insights of Bernard Lonergan

MICHAEL H. MCCARTHY

University of Notre Dame Press
Notre Dame, Indiana

University of Notre Dame Press
Notre Dame, Indiana 46556
www.undpress.nd.edu
All Rights Reserved

Published in the United States of America

Copyright © 2015 by the University of Notre Dame

Library of Congress Cataloging-in-Publication Data

McCarthy, Michael H., 1942–
Authenticity as self-transcendence : the enduring insights of Bernard Lonergan / Michael H. McCarthy.
    pages cm
Includes bibliographical references and index.
ISBN 978-0-268-03537-2 (pbk. : alk. paper) —
ISBN 0-268-03537-7 (pbk. : alk. paper)
1. Lonergan, Bernard J. F.   I. Title.
B995.L654M33   2015
191—dc23

2015031817

∞ *The paper in this book meets the guidelines for permanence and durability of the Committee on Production Guidelines for Book Longevity of the Council on Library Resources.*

CONTENTS

Preface *vii*

CHAPTER ONE

The Tangled Knot of Old and New:
Lonergan's Project of Critical Appropriation   1

The Tangled Knot   5
Where Are We Now?   11
A Critical Cultural Center   24
The *Vetera*   51
The *Nova*   83

CHAPTER TWO

Objective Knowing and Authentic Living   107

The Defining Revolutions of Modernity   109
The Anthropological Turn: Human Nature and History   117
The Critique of Objectivity and Truth   130
The Polymorphic Subject   135
Cognitional Theory: From Logic to Method   142
The Centrality of Insight   149
Critical Realism   156
Objectivity Reconsidered   166
Authenticity as Self-Transcendence   171
Maturity Is Comprehensive   180

CHAPTER THREE

Authentic Faith in a Secular Age 181

Our Secular Age 182
Rising to the Challenge of Our Time 207
Enlightenment, Science, and Faith 219
Exclusive and Religious Humanism 230
Religious Authenticity 248

CHAPTER FOUR

The Chill Winds of Modernity: The Profound Challenge of Catholic Renewal 259

Critical Christian Humanism 261
The Catholic Struggle with Modernity 265
Aggiornamento 271
The Second Vatican Council 275
Critical *Aggiornamento* 283
Critical Reason and Religious Truth 286
An Ethics of Authenticity: Personal and Communal 323
Realism, Repentance, Reform, and Renewal 351

Epilogue 353

Notes 359

Bibliography 373

Index 403

PREFACE

Bernard Lonergan is one of the great, unheralded thinkers of the twentieth century. Ample evidence of his intellectual greatness can be found in his writing. But critical recognition of his philosophical and cultural importance has been remarkably limited. In secular academic circles he remains largely unknown. And even within Christian centers of learning, familiarity with his name far exceeds familiarity with his work.

My own respect for Lonergan has only deepened since reading *Insight* as a doctoral student at Yale in the 1960s. After graduating from Yale, I continued to study Lonergan during several decades teaching philosophy at Vassar College. The more philosophers I read and taught, ancient, medieval, modern, and contemporary, the more impressed I became with the quality of Lonergan's mind and the great relevance of his methodological work in philosophy and theology. I had been interested in metaphilosophical questions since writing my Yale dissertation. The more I compared Lonergan's distinctive conception of philosophy with that of several great contemporary metaphilosophers—Frege, Cassirer, Husserl, Wittgenstein, Carnap, Sellars, and Rorty—the more impressed I became. This sustained intellectual engagement led me to write *The Crisis of Philosophy*, where I argued for the superiority of Lonergan's philosophical program to those of his analytic and phenomenological rivals. In the present volume, I develop and expand that earlier argument with four new essays, designed to show Lonergan's exceptional relevance to the cultural situation of late modernity. My purpose is not to gain belated recognition for the dead, but to exhibit the power and vitality of Lonergan's thought for the living.

My hope is that these essays will serve as a bridge between Lonergan and a much broader contemporary audience, whose members stand only to benefit from a sustained encounter with a mind of such clarity, relevance, and depth.

Lonergan was a foundational thinker committed to discovering the basic principles of knowledge, being, and value. He was also an integrative thinker committed to unifying the intellectual and moral achievements of the West. A genuinely learned man, he recognized the historical dangers of both foundational and integrative thought. But his critical knowledge of history did not deter him from embracing the cultural project that defined his personal life and career as a Christian humanist: raising Christian philosophy and theology to meet the challenges and standards of his time. In undertaking a project of this magnitude, Lonergan was explicitly attempting to do for the twentieth century what Thomas Aquinas had done for medieval philosophy and theology in thirteenth-century Paris. But Lonergan was acutely aware that the cultural challenges and critical standards of his time were markedly different from those of Aquinas, his traditional mentor and guide.

My description of Lonergan as a critical Christian humanist corresponds closely to his own account of the three dynamic vectors operative in human history. Because Lonergan was a humanist, he believed in the native human aspiration to and capacity for self-transcendence. Because he was a critical humanist, he explicitly acknowledged the power of bias and sin to prevent or obstruct self-transcendence, as well as the repeated resort to ideology to justify that prevention or obstruction. And because he was a faithful Christian, he relied on the power of divine grace to *sublate* the personal quest for self-transcendence and to heal the destructive consequences of bias and sin. Lonergan's Christian humanism was interpreted and transmitted through the lens of a developed historical consciousness. He had a profound sense of the cultural challenges of his time and a clear strategy for meeting and overcoming them. He combined a synoptic vision of cultural history with a deep sense of historical responsibility, believing that the work of redeeming the world was part of the mission Christ entrusted to his apostles. But it was also part of Lonergan's mission as a Jesuit specifically called to meet the crises of his age (*Second Collection*, 183).

Lonergan claimed that the cultural crisis of the late modern West had at least three interrelated dimensions. Intellectually, the great discoveries of modern science and scholarship have transformed our understanding of nature and history. These enduring epistemic achievements, however, have come at a price. Because modern learning is specialized and highly differentiated, we know vastly more than our classical and medieval predecessors, but we no longer know how the various parts of our knowledge fit together. The fragmentation of our knowledge is particularly striking with respect to our understanding of human existence, where it has generated a disabling paradox. Despite our highly specialized knowledge of human nature and history, we are no longer confident, as a society and culture, that our most important factual and evaluative judgments are objectively true.

Our common moral situation is also paradoxical. Contemporary societies are far more ethically ambitious than the cities and empires of antiquity, and even than medieval Christendom. Inspired by the democratic revolutions of the eighteenth century, we seek liberty, equality, and justice for all people; and we accept personal and collective responsibility for advancing these utopian ideals. At the level of shared moral advocacy, our aspirations are unprecedented. At the same time, we conspicuously lack a unifying moral philosophy to clarify and justify these demanding moral ideals. This troubling gap between moral ontology and moral advocacy helps explain the instability of our culture, which vacillates uneasily between uncritical idealism and inordinate suspicion.

Contemporary religious pluralism now extends from the three Abrahamic faiths, Judaism, Christianity, and Islam, to the traditional religions of the East and the indigenous faiths of the Americas and Africa. In the midst of this unsettling pluralism, "the masters of suspicion" and their cultural allies have mounted a frontal assault on religious knowledge, morality, and hope. In many sectors of our culture, particularly in the secular academy, ontological naturalists and exclusive humanists have rejected traditional religious allegiances and experimented in living without God. Though Lonergan firmly believes that the deepest currents of modernity are compatible with religious authenticity, the cultural challenges facing mature believers today are more formidable than ever before.

All three of these crises—epistemic, moral, and spiritual—are particularly challenging for the Roman Catholic Church, to which Lonergan dedicated his life. Intellectually, the church had struggled with the discoveries of Copernicus, Galileo, Newton, and Darwin. Morally and politically, it had resisted the democratic revolutions in Europe and North America and belatedly responded to the historical projects of secular liberalism and Marxism. Because its philosophical and theological allegiances were closely tied to medieval models, the church remained critically aloof from the philosophical turn to human subjectivity and the transformation of dogmatic theology by biblical hermeneutics and critical historiography. While Lonergan never wavered in his loyalty to the church, he recognized that an important part of its cultural mission was no longer being credibly fulfilled.

To address these several crises effectively, to respond to them persuasively at the exigent level of our time, Lonergan called for the creation of collaborative intercultural centers, composed of scientists, scholars, philosophers, theologians, and educated citizens, "big enough to be at home in the old and the new, painstaking enough to work out one by one the transitions to be made, strong enough to refuse half measures and insist on complete solutions even though it has to wait" (CWL, 4:245). Lonergan's personal contribution to this collaborative project was twofold. First, as a philosophical scholar, he offered masterful interpretations of Aristotle, Augustine, and Aquinas, as well as discerning critical commentary on Kant, Hegel, Marx, and Husserl, among others. Second, as a brilliant and exacting methodologist, he clarified the normative requirements on individual thinkers hoping to diagnose and remedy the cultural predicaments he had identified. These requirements include sustained personal development, comprehensive self-appropriation, and intellectual, moral, and religious conversion. The daunting realism of these requirements and the personal and cultural obstacles that impede their realization serve to confirm both the importance of Lonergan's project and the great difficulty of successfully advancing it.

When Lonergan spoke of the old (the *vetera*), he meant primarily the philosophical culture of ancient Greece and the theological culture of medieval Christendom. When he spoke of the new (the *nova*), he meant primarily the scientific and scholarly cultures of the first and second Enlightenment and the postmodern culture of suspicion. The four long essays that compose this book are designed to reveal the strategic unfolding of Lonergan's cultural mission. Chapter 1, "The Tangled Knot of Old and New," establishes the orienting framework for the entire project, for critical appropriation of the *vetera* and the *nova* is essential to understanding, appraising, and resolving the different cultural crises we share. Chapter 2, "Objective Knowing and Authentic Living," locates Lonergan's philosophical anthropology within the historical problematic created by Descartes, Kant, Hegel, Darwin, Nietzsche, and Wittgenstein. Through his profound analysis of human subjectivity, Lonergan identified a striking paradox at the heart of modern culture and sought to unravel it by a forceful defense of the human capacity for self-transcendence. Chapter 3, "Authentic Faith in a Secular Age," attempts to clarify the nature and origins of modern secularity and the unprecedented challenges it creates for religious faith. Two related questions emerge as this chapter unfolds: what are the merits and limitations of the atheistic project of exclusive humanism, and what are the intellectual, moral, and spiritual requirements of religious authenticity today? Chapter 4, "The Chill Winds of Modernity," explains why Catholic Christianity has especially struggled with the demise of Latin Christendom, and appraises Lonergan's philosophical and theological contributions to the critical renewal of the Catholic Church. The challenge of critical renewal, as he saw it, can be simply stated. How can the church rise to meet the cultural challenges of the modern age while remaining faithful to its historic message and mission? How can it be faithful to the *vetera* and critically responsive to the *nova*? Finally, in the epilogue, I draw the substantive conclusions of the four chapters together by identifying and intelligibly relating Lonergan's most important and enduring discoveries. My governing purpose in writing this book is to show that these discoveries are so basic in nature, so fertile in their implications, and so relevant to our cultural crises that they establish Bernard Lonergan as one of the truly great minds of the twentieth century.

The organizational pattern of the four chapters tends to be similar. In each case it's essential to establish that there is a significant cultural challenge to be addressed. So the chapters begin with cultural diagnosis. Where are we now, culturally speaking, and what special predicaments—intellectual, moral, spiritual, and religious—do we commonly face? Diagnostic analysis is then followed by explanatory historical narrative. How did we gradually arrive at this tangled cultural impasse? Taken together, the diagnostic and genealogical accounts set the stage for Lonergan's remedial prescriptions. What dialectical strategies and philosophical and theological insights does Lonergan advance to clarify and unravel these unsettling cultural predicaments? The final stage involves critical appraisal. What enduring philosophical and theological contributions emerge from Lonergan's concerted attempt to meet the cultural challenges of our time at the exigent level of our time?

It is reasonable to ask at the outset for whom these interrelated essays were written. Lonergan once said that his work was intended for every serious person who really wanted to think things through. My initial attraction to Lonergan when I was beginning to study philosophy was based on just such an appeal. Though I really wanted "to think things through," I was very unclear about how to proceed. And I sensed, from an initial reading of *Insight*, that Lonergan would be a reliable guide on this interminable journey. Now, nearly fifty years later, let me respond to this straightforward query with a more complex and roundabout answer.

Bernard Lonergan was a Canadian Jesuit who studied and taught in Catholic institutions in North America and Europe. Deeply loyal to the church, he was openly critical of its intellectual stance toward modernity. By and large, the church had distanced itself from the momentous developments in modern science, philosophy, and scholarship. It had criticized their deviation from the classical and medieval models of inquiry developed in premodern culture. It had adhered to a traditional cosmology and anthropology that no longer commanded the assent of educated people. Lonergan's philosophical and theological project began as a belated effort to raise the thought and discourse of his church to the level of the time (CWL, 17:354–58, 365–66).

But Lonergan was also a genuine humanist who respected the relative autonomy of contemporary social and cultural practices. In his seminal philosophical work *Insight* and in many of his subsequent papers and lectures, he wrote as a humanist, addressing all of his educated contemporaries, not only his fellow Christians. He believed, I think correctly, that the cultural crises confronting the West are not confined to Christians, Catholics, or even educated persons of faith. The unprecedented challenges posed by our uneven cultural heritage, by the new understanding of science and culture, by the philosophical turn to the polymorphic subject, by the critical standards of research, hermeneutics, and history, and by the awesome demands of existential and collective responsibility affect all educated men and women whatever their religious allegiance. These cultural crises are more acute for Catholics because of their prolonged disengagement from modernity. But the inescapable legacy of modernity, its tangled blending of achievement and aberration, has left every serious thinker confused and uncertain.

Lonergan's ambitious cultural project, therefore, is relevant and accessible to both reflective humanists and Christians. Written in a similar ecumenical spirit, the four chapters comprising this work are deliberately intended for a comprehensive educated audience struggling, as most of us are, with our uneven cultural legacy. Chapter 1 has particular relevance for all undergraduate and graduate teachers who must sympathetically understand the past in order to make sense of the present and future. Chapter 2 makes a fundamental contribution to philosophical anthropology. By carefully exploring and articulating the foundations of human interiority, it attempts to establish the inseparable connection between intellectual and moral self-transcendence, between objective knowing and authentic living. The two concluding chapters are primarily, though not exclusively, addressed to the global community of religious believers, both Christian and non-Christian, belatedly coming to terms with the singular complexity of the modern enterprise. The cross-pressures of our secular age make the question of religious authenticity a nearly universal concern, and the global presence of Catholic Christianity makes its continuing struggle for *aggiornamento* a topic of nearly comparable interest.

I am grateful to everyone who helped me with this work but especially to my wife, Barbara, my closest friend and companion during the long years reaching up to the "mind of Lonergan."

Michael H. McCarthy
Vassar College

CHAPTER ONE

The Tangled Knot of Old and New

Lonergan's Project of Critical Appropriation

This is the first of four interrelated essays devoted to understanding and appraising the project of Bernard Lonergan. That project, I believe, has exceptional relevance to the intellectual and cultural situation of our time. But to date, its depth and importance are recognized by only a few of our contemporaries. There are multiple reasons for this oversight, both institutional and cultural, that have made it difficult for Lonergan's work to receive the critical attention it deserves.

    These essays are written, in part, to address that neglect by articulating the questions and concerns at the center of Lonergan's inquiry. Lonergan began his career as a philosopher-theologian seeking to determine what was valid and enduring in the achievement of the past. But he was profoundly aware that the modern era, shaped by the critical revolutions in natural science and historiography, was radically different from its classical and medieval predecessors. Unlike many of his contemporaries who believed that these differences obviated the need for critical attention to the past, Lonergan deliberately attempted to become at home "in both the old and the new."[1] This becoming at home is best understood as critical belonging, for both the *vetera* and the *nova* constitute tangled knots of achievement and aberration. Neither can be embraced uncritically or comprehensively. But this warranted caution serves only as a caveat, for the real challenge is to understand both the *vetera* and the *nova* well enough to discover and appraise their distinctive merits and limitations.

Lonergan frequently cited the Leonine adage *vetera novis augere et perficere*, to augment and perfect the old with the new (CWL, 3:768; CWL, 2:222–24). But critical appropriation is actually more complicated than the adage suggests. The old and the new are both complementary and contradictory. Critical aspects of the new are incompatible with the convictions of the past, and the deepest insights of our classical predecessors can challenge and overturn the unexamined prejudices of our time.

Lonergan's model in this work of appropriation was Thomas Aquinas. In thirteenth-century Paris, Aquinas confronted an extremely complex cultural heritage. That heritage included Hebrew and Christian scripture, the writings of the great Greek and Latin fathers, particularly Augustine, the doctrinal teachings of the early church councils, the dialectical theology emanating from Anselm and Abelard, and the newly translated Aristotelian corpus together with the influential Jewish and Islamic commentaries on Aristotle. As a professor of theology teaching in a European university where these diverse cultural currents were in conflict, Aquinas faced a major dialectical challenge. To meet that challenge successfully, he needed deeply to understand each of the different elements in that heritage, to distinguish their respective merits and limitations, and to integrate their enduring insights in his great works of synoptic theology.

For Lonergan, Aquinas exemplified the critical Christian thinker rising to the challenge of his time.[2] Aquinas gradually assimilated what was best in the old and the new; he learned how to integrate Augustinian insights into Aristotle's comprehensive metaphysical framework; he eventually developed and articulated a theology, cosmology, and anthropology responsive to the critical challenges and concerns of his day (*Second Collection*, 43–47).

Yet his day and time are not ours, as Lonergan was acutely aware. This contrastive awareness was heightened by Lonergan's prolonged study of Aquinas and the medieval context in which his thinking and writing developed. After years reaching up to the mind of Aquinas, after critically appropriating his theory of grace and his analysis of human understanding, Lonergan turned his attention to the even more complex cultural heritage of the twentieth century.³ This was the scientific heritage of Galileo and Newton, of Darwin, Einstein, and Planck; the philosophical heritage of Descartes and Hume, Kant and Hegel, Marx and Nietzsche, Wittgenstein, Husserl, and Heidegger; the critical historical heritage of Vico, Ranke, Schleiermacher, Dilthey, and Toynbee; the economic and political heritage of Hobbes, Locke, Smith, Mill, Jefferson, Keynes, and Schumpeter. I cite only a few of the great modern thinkers to indicate the scope and scale of Lonergan's theoretical concerns.

Yet, is it still possible to do for the twentieth century what Aquinas did so well for the thirteenth? The answer will clearly depend on how Lonergan's historical analogy is conceived and implemented. Given the specialized nature of modern science and scholarship, the symbiotic dependence of modern theory and practice, and the exigent demands of critical hermeneutics and historiography, no individual, however gifted and persevering, can hope to achieve competence, much less mastery, in these diverse fields of inquiry and conduct.

Lonergan explicitly recognized that the intellectual specialization of modernity had undermined the humanistic ideal of the Renaissance man (*Second Collection*, 182; *Method*, 301). The great centers of contemporary inquiry are scientific and scholarly communities, united by their methodological commitments and their mastery of the technical and scholarly languages and paradigms essential to their research. This communal research is ongoing and dynamic; its results are provisional and open to critical revision; its ultimate heuristic goal is the complete explanation of all empirical data both natural and human (CWL, 4:241).

Lonergan approached these dynamic and communal intellectual practices by concentrating on their constants rather than their variables. While the objects of scientific and scholarly inquiry are boundless and regularly changing, while the results of that inquiry are provisional and subject to correction and refinement, the dynamic methods of science and scholarship are unifying and relatively constant. It is these methods of discovery and verification that provide the collaborative framework for the specialized inquiry of scientists and scholars (*Method*, xi–xii).

Still, these modern methods of critical inquiry are several, and they undergo their own revision and alteration with time. So, Lonergan's search for foundational principles continued to deepen. He asked whether there existed intellectual constants, more fundamental than these specialized methods and languages, that provided their common core and critical ground. Did there exist a generalized empirical method grounded in the basic nature and aspirations of the human mind itself? If such a fundamental method existed, of what did it consist concretely, and how could we discover and credibly verify it? Finally, if discovered and verified, could it provide the shared evaluative standpoint required by Lonergan's collaborative project of critical appropriation?

These elemental questions led to several others. Were the enduring epistemic achievements of the ancients and moderns specific applications of this generalized method in the intellectual and cultural contexts of their times? Did recurrent failures to observe the method's normative requirements produce the aberrant results that compromised past and present inquiry? Can we develop and employ an effective dialectical strategy enabling us to determine what is valid and enduring in the massive and tangled knot of our cultural inheritance? Could such a dialectical method and strategy provide a collaborative framework in which scientists, scholars, philosophers, and theologians could responsibly cooperate in coordinating the diverse fruits of their inquiry? These are the ambitious and defining questions at the heart of Lonergan's philosophical-theological project.[4]

The ancient Aristotelian ideal of unifying and integrating knowledge did not survive the rise of modern science and scholarship (*Third Collection*, 41–47). Modern inquiry is specialized and differentiated; epistemic plurality and difference consistently take precedence over identity and unity. Moreover, the most influential modern strategies for unifying knowledge have tended to be reductive and imperial, often relying on an exclusive language, an exclusive method, an exclusive ontological and conceptual scheme. The manifest failure of these several integrative efforts has generated a suspicion of unity and a celebration of difference for its own sake. Intellectual imperialism is no more acceptable today than its discredited political analogue. If integrative epistemic strategies are inherently procrustean, then it's wiser and sounder to live without them.

How does Lonergan's project fit within this vigorous modern-postmodern debate? He shares the ancient and modern aspiration for the unity of knowledge; he also deeply respects the different specialized methods, discoveries, and languages that inform modern inquiry; he readily acknowledges that earlier metaphysical, logical, and linguistic attempts to unify knowledge are unsatisfactory. Lonergan explicitly believes that we've reached a stage in the history of inquiry where the most significant epistemic plurality is methodological and heuristic, and where the underlying unity we seek must be grounded in a generalized empirical method whose several specialized applications are intrinsically open to difference and change (CWL, 3:95–96; *Method*, 14–25).

Lonergan's is a remarkably ambitious cultural project founded on a synoptic historical vision that is respectful of the old but critically responsive to the new. It rejects the early modern dismissal of ancient traditions but recognizes the extraordinary achievements of modernity. It is wary of postmodern skepticism and relativism but sensitive to the pluralist demands of contemporary historical consciousness. While deeply attuned to the intellectual and moral crises of our time, Lonergan understands these crises in the light of our rich and uneven cultural history. His dialectical project is executed with a clarity, rigor, and depth that merit our attentive respect and engagement, whether or not we finally assent to his claims. In the course of the following chapters, we'll explore and appraise his critical effort to identify and preserve what is true and enduring in the tangled cultural legacy our predecessors have bequeathed us.

The Tangled Knot

All things human are under the dialectic of progress and decline.
—CWL, 17:269

There are many ways of understanding human existence. We can focus on what is universal and invariant about human beings, about what makes them always and everywhere the same. From this heuristic perspective, the historicity of human existence appears accidental and unimportant, for time and history do not change the essence of human nature.[5] However, when we think about human beings empirically and concretely, the heuristic emphasis begins to alter. Each person is a situated individual born into a particular community at a determinate stage of its cultural history. It is within that community that the person is educated, gradually acquiring the beliefs and convictions that constitute the common cultural heritage. Those convictions, in turn, shape the individual's pattern of learning and living, creating the operative intentional horizon within which each particular life unfolds.

Historicity applies not only to distinct individuals, but also to the social institutions that form and protect them, and to the evolving cultural heritage that gives the social order its meaning and purpose. These contrasting heuristic emphases, universal and historical, are not contradictory, however, for it is the universal and invariant properties of human nature that make human history intelligible and open to normative appraisal. Still, this assurance of heuristic complementarity does not determine concretely what those structural invariants actually are and how they perform their vital normative function in reliably assessing the past and the present.

The rise of modern historical consciousness in the nineteenth century did not constitute the origin of human historicity, for historicity has always been with us. What Hegel made prominent in his teaching and writing, what Tocqueville and Marx distinctively carried forward, what Ranke and the critical historians refined and revised, was a new historical mindedness, an unprecedented intellectual recognition of the constitutive role of history in understanding human existence. What did this new anthropological perspective concretely entail? That to comprehend human affairs, at the individual, social, and cultural levels, we had to understand their origin and genesis, the particular social contexts in which they emerged, the sources of their uneven, often conflicted, development, the roots of their decline, and the specific challenges they confronted and had to surmount in the course of their unfolding histories.

The new historical mindedness was emphatically empirical and critical.[6] Following the example of Ranke in Prussia, the new breed of historical scholars wanted to learn what had actually happened in the past. They were distrustful of traditional legends and myths; they were equally wary of the a priori dialectics practiced by Hegel and Marx. Critical history was to be an explicitly empirical discipline whose data and evidence consisted in the surviving remains of the past. Just as the new sciences of nature insisted on the methodological importance of empirical data and evidence, so did the critical historiography Ranke and his disciples espoused.

There was, however, an important though contested difference between the critical study of nature and history. Historical data are invariably bearers of meaning and value unlike the relevant sensible data of the natural sciences. The actual agents, actions, and events of history, as well as the institutional and cultural contexts in which they appear, are open to critical interpretation (meaning) and eventually to normative appraisal (value). Like all things human, they are characterized by progress and decline, by development and breakdown, by achievement and failure. While human beings cannot mature without the social and cultural heritage of the communal past, this historical legacy is inherently ambiguous. It is a tangled knot of insights and oversights, of justified beliefs and prejudices, of moral breakthroughs and breakdowns, of legitimate and despotic exercises of power. Although no one can escape the power of the past, we are not helpless captives of its influence. For we have the ability to understand and judge the past, and to act responsibly in the light of that critical knowledge and appraisal.

The very different stories we tell about the past reflect the complexity of human existence. The thematic center of our narratives can be technological, economic, social, political, cultural, or religious. We can emphasize the practical, theoretical, artistic, or moral changes that occur over time. These narrative differences of perspective and topical emphasis are usually complementary, for the human mind is finite and the intelligible dimensions of human existence are manifold. Although historians can differ in their heuristic methods, their factual judgments, and their causal accounts of particular events and movements, their disagreements are often most striking at the evaluative level. In their narrative assessments of the past and the present, the old and the new, do they emphasize tradition or innovation, continuity or rupture, historical progress or decline?

In contrast to classical thinkers like Aristotle and Aquinas, who emphasized the continuity of the traditions they inherited, Descartes radicalized the modern emphasis on temporal rupture. His hyperbolic doubt sought to undermine the credibility of the past and the authority of our ancient and medieval predecessors. The intellectual leaders of modern science and philosophy repeatedly stressed the sterility of medieval Scholasticism and the restrictive import of Aristotle's teaching. Nietzsche's critical genealogy of morals set the tone for postmodern hermeneutics. While

Cartesian doubt had undermined the epistemic authority of the classical tradition, Nietzsche attempted to discredit the entire moral and religious heritage of the West. His influential hermeneutics of suspicion is more unsparing than Cartesian doubt for it challenges the intellectual and moral integrity of both ancient and modern traditions.[7]

Lonergan's project of critical appropriation differs significantly from each of these interpretive models. He places greater emphasis on innovation than Aristotle and Aquinas, greater emphasis on continuity than Descartes, and greater emphasis on critically retrieving the past than Nietzsche. While Lonergan accepts, in principle, the postmodern critique of ideology, he conceives the cultural function of ideology very differently from the celebrated masters of suspicion.[8]

Lonergan repeatedly stresses the vast labor required in actually understanding the past. Both Cartesian doubt and Nietzschean suspicion are too facile in their critique of the tradition. Moreover, the past and the tradition may not be the same, as Lonergan discovered in his study of Aquinas. Traditional Thomistic accounts of Aquinas's substantive teaching could not be reconciled with the richness of his writing on grace and cognition. To understand what the *vetera* and the *nova* really were, therefore, critical interpreters have to raise their own thinking to the level of the authors and texts they are trying to understand; and the more profound and insightful the author, the greater the need for personal transformation in the developing mind of the reader and critic.[9]

Lonergan's interpretive humility did not silence his capacity for criticism. Once you have really understood the past, you are in a reasonable position to appraise it. To judge a work without sympathetically understanding it is rash; but to understand without eventually judging is unreasonably timid. This hermeneutic caution applies to exegetes of all stripes: classicist defenders of tradition, modern apostles of progress, and deliberately subversive genealogical critics. All regularly oversimplify the momentous intellectual and cultural task we commonly face: to understand the old and the new sufficiently well to disentangle their enduring achievements from their inadequacies, limitations, distortions, and errors.

But what specific aspects of the old and the new particularly engaged Lonergan's philosophical attention? Lonergan was primarily a cognitional theorist who believed that the cultural assimilation of cumulative intellectual discoveries was the principal source of historical progress. He identified three intersecting vectors in his dynamic and dialectical theory of history: a vector of progress, a vector of decline, and a vector of redemption (*Second Collection*, 271–72; CWL, 3:765). For him, progressive and cumulative discoveries, both theoretical and practical, were the chief source of human progress; the distorting effects of bias and sin on human thinking, feeling, speaking, and acting were the primary cause of decline; and the gift of divine grace, both operative and cooperative, was the effective basis of redemptive recovery. The dynamic interweaving of these distinct causal forces in history, in the lives of individuals, societies, and cultures, yields the tangled knot of human existence and makes critical appropriation an indispensable educational task for each generation of teachers and scholars.

New intellectual discoveries, of course, are not restricted to the realms of science and scholarship. They occur in all fields of human endeavor: practical, dramatic, aesthetic, artistic, moral, and religious. They serve many purposes beyond the expansion and transmission of knowledge. They arise in response to a myriad of human concerns and desires. As a cognitional theorist, however, Lonergan specifically emphasized a distinctive and salient human desire, the unrestricted desire to know, and the intellectual pattern of experience in which that epistemic desire normatively unfolds (CWL, 3:209–10).[10] He gradually discovered that the intellectual pattern of inquiry has a normative dynamic structure that remains constant through variations in human learning. As human intelligence developed historically, it created specialized methods of investigation and equally specialized research communities. Eventually, the natural and human sciences liberated themselves from the guidance and control of philosophy. Critical hermeneutics and historiography, in turn, became independent of religion and theology. Distinct realms of cognitive meaning emerged responsive to different intellectual concerns and standards of heuristic relevance (*Method*, 81–85).

Lonergan believed that this dynamic process of epistemic specialization was irreversible, that there was no credible return to earlier strategies of achieving cognitive unity. And yet, the intellectual desire for unity persists in the mind of each individual. We not only desire to know what exists; we also strive to understand how all that we know collectively fits together in a comprehensive intelligible pattern. The human desire for knowledge is inseparable, finally, from the desire for wisdom, the reflectively ordered knowledge of the whole and its parts. But the extraordinary progress of modern scientific and scholarly inquiry has made the quest for wisdom seem archaic. Specialized research has yielded numerous cognitive parts without wholes and epistemic diversity without intelligible order and unity. Has the desire for wisdom, then, become a futile passion? If it has, what does this imply for the contemporary practice of philosophy, the traditional name for the love and pursuit of wisdom, and for systematic theology, the understanding of all things in their intelligible relations to God?[11]

In these inescapable existential questions, ancient epistemic aspirations and modern scientific and scholarly developments appear to conflict. Lonergan deliberately sought to do justice to both. But he clearly recognized that classical philosophy and theology would have to be transformed in the light of modernity's intellectual progress. He began that daunting transformation with a dialectical appraisal of our impressive but uneven cognitive heritage. The ancients and the moderns shared a common desire to know, a common passion for inquiry, a common set of normative exigencies grounded in the intrinsic demands of human intelligence and rationality. Yet, they responded to these epistemic constants in the very different cultural contexts that the dynamism of human inquiry had created. To understand the specific cultural context in which we live today, we need to grasp how our highly fragmented secular culture actually emerged from the intellectual and moral history of the West.

Lonergan's narrative account of that history is based on his comprehensive theory of cognition.[12] Its critical landmarks are complex but largely familiar historical events: the remarkable rise of classical Hellenism, culminating in the metaphysics of Aristotle; the apex of medieval Scholasticism in the systematic theology of Aquinas; the eventual decline of Scholastic theology in the fourteenth and fifteenth centuries, resulting in a period of skeptical decadence; the late medieval and early modern repudiation of Aristotle's cosmology, anthropology, and metaphysics; the successive phases of the European Enlightenment, the first culminating in Newtonian physics and Kantian philosophy, the second in the rise of historical consciousness and the related development of the human sciences.

For Lonergan, these intellectual landmarks constitute distinct stages in the history of human inquiry (*Third Collection*, 63–65; *Method*, 85–99, 314–17). In Aristotle and Aquinas the cognitive demand for systematic theory transformed the practice of philosophy and theology. In Newton the scientific demand for a unified physical theory brought systematic order to the early modern understanding of nature. The historical consciousness of the nineteenth century significantly altered the classical understanding of both science and culture. Natural science was liberated from its traditional association with causal necessity; the human sciences became grounded in hermeneutics and highly responsive to cultural pluralism. After Kant's attempt at a second Copernican Revolution, his philosophic successors increasingly directed their attention to the human subject and the study of intentional consciousness. Even contemporary theologians begin their scholarly reflections on God through the study of linguistics, archaeology, anthropology, and critical history. Inherited certainties have surrendered to new questions and challenges; enduring convictions have been shaken by new experiences and discoveries. Thus we find ourselves wandering between past and future, unable to go back, unsure of the way forward, uncertain of where we are now.

Where Are We Now?

The crisis I have been attempting to depict
is a crisis not of faith but of culture.
—CWL, 4:244

The present age is not lacking in self-reflection. We have multiple ways to characterize the particular historical period in which we live. Ours is an era of digital technology, of global communications, finance, and commerce; of diminished national sovereignty and ineffective international institutions; of opposition to racism and patriarchy, and support for universal human rights; of passionate moral and political advocacy, and skepticism about the sources and justification of evaluative judgments; of heightened religious consciousness among Muslims, evangelical Christians, and orthodox Jews alongside the increasing secularization of the West.[13]

Each of these descriptions captures an important aspect of our present situation. The different aspects themselves are often interdependent, for global capitalism is an important factor in weakening the nation-state, and secularization is one source of modern moral uncertainty. We no longer trust the universal relevance of sweeping historical metanarratives like the Hegelian theory of Absolute Spirit or the Marxist appeal to unending class struggle. Our historical perspectives tend to be selective and partial, reflecting the complex intelligibility of human history itself. The many available narratives of "where we are now" may not all be true, but the fact that there are many narratives is not itself cause for concern.

Lonergan was a philosopher-theologian with a special interest in the history of these ancient disciplines. He was also a cognitional theorist whose narrative accounts of philosophical and theological history have a decidedly methodological cast. While he recognized the importance of technological, economic, social, and political change, he often interpreted these changes in the light of his comprehensive theory of meaning.[14] As they mature and develop, human beings move beyond the prelinguistic world of sensible immediacy (the world of the nursery and the domestic habitat) into a larger world mediated by meaning and motivated by value. They enter this larger world primarily through education, through assimilating different parts of their society's cultural heritage. As that heritage is internally differentiated, so is their education, with its practical, dramatic, artistic, aesthetic, and theoretical dimensions. They learn how to play different language games; they learn how to navigate different realms of meaning. They quietly assimilate (or reject) the moral beliefs and convictions of their family, the social groups with which they identify, the more inclusive culture in which family and society are embedded.[15]

The cultural heritage we assimilate through education is geographically and historically variable. Every society has an operative commonsense culture, a common set of practical ideas, beliefs, and convictions that underlies its coordinated social activities. The more isolated a given society, the more limited its members' awareness of other ways of thinking, speaking, and acting. Such societies are likely to be static, as well, both institutionally and culturally. They stand in marked contrast to self-reflective cultures that not only transmit their received historical heritage, but repeatedly subject it to critical scrutiny and appraisal. When self-reflective cultures also become historically conscious, they become acutely aware of social and cultural pluralism: of the diverse ways human beings have lived together, of the different beliefs and convictions that have shaped their common patterns of thinking, acting, and living.

A community's shared awareness of social and cultural diversity raises a series of inescapable questions.[16] Why are their ways of thinking and living so different from ours? What are we to make of their religious myths and rituals, their trusted maps of the cosmos, their ways of ordering time, their hierarchical social structures, their patterns of marriage, governance, and trade? And which of the many cultural beliefs, convictions, and privileged stories that we discover are actually true? The educational process becomes increasingly complicated for teachers and students, as our awareness of pluralism and diversity expands, and our most basic cultural questions no longer receive uncontested traditional answers.

The critical cultural challenge to tradition can also arise from within. This happened dramatically in classical Greece when pre-Socratic cosmology undermined the traditional Olympian religion and the moral and political convictions that depended upon it. The philosophical speculations of the pre-Socratics made ancient Greek citizens uncertain of their gods and their heroes. The emerging cultural crisis in the independent Greek *poleis* was intensified by the popular teachings of the sophists who stressed the relativity of Greek moral and political practices. The profound political unease created by cosmology and sophistry is vividly reflected in the trial of Socrates.[17] Socrates was indirectly accused of being a cosmologist and sophist, and directly accused of civic disloyalty for subverting traditional Athenian piety and undermining the political allegiance of the young. The historical emergence of Socratic-Platonic philosophy is inseparable from this Greek cultural crisis, as first Socrates and then Plato sought to rethink and revise the shaken foundations of Greek moral and political life.[18]

The advent of Christianity and the missionary journeys of Paul created another cultural crisis in the West. One way of expressing this crisis is through the rhetorical challenge of Tertullian, an early Christian apologist, "What has Athens to do with Jerusalem?" What relevance do Greek philosophy, mathematics, and science have for the Christian religion and the gospel of Jesus of Nazareth? Early Christian and medieval thought struggled with this intercultural challenge, under the opposing rubrics of faith and reason. Were the traditional teachings of Christian orthodoxy reconcilable with the independent discoveries of natural reason? Could the moral and religious heritage of Judaism and Christianity coexist with the self-critical intellectual heritage of the classical Greeks?[19]

In thirteenth-century Paris, Thomas Aquinas confronted this intercultural crisis in its most complex historical form. As we noted earlier, he sought to create a systematic synoptic theology that integrated the best elements of Aristotle's metaphysics, Augustinian psychology, and the scriptural and conciliar heritage of medieval Christianity. Aquinas did not simply combine the different legacies of Athens and Jerusalem. He critically appropriated both of these complex cultural traditions, carefully distinguishing their merits from their limitations. He explicitly asserted the complementarity of grace and nature, faith and reason, theology and philosophy, of the supernatural and cardinal virtues. Despite Aquinas's brilliance, his remarkable theological synthesis did not survive the condemnations of 1277 and the skeptical nominalism and hyper-Augustinianism of the fourteenth and fifteenth centuries.[20]

Lonergan was deeply influenced by each of these premodern examples. Both Greek philosophy and patristic and medieval theology emerged and flourished in times of cultural crisis. In both cases, the crises were precipitated by major intellectual developments that the traditional culture was unable to assimilate. There were, then as now, cultural conservatives who clung to the old and rejected the new; and fashionable "progressives" who embraced the new uncritically at the expense of what was valid in the tradition. For Lonergan, the most impressive Western thinkers belong to neither of these antithetical camps. Aristotle critically appropriated the opinions (*endoxa*) of his predecessors, both the many and the wise, both naturalists and Platonists. He tried to discern and preserve the truth in both popular and learned opinion. Aquinas found room in his synoptic theology for the law and the prophets of Judaism as well as the Christian gospel, the theological insights of the patristic tradition, Greek ethics, metaphysics, and psychology, and the Jewish and Islamic commentaries on Aristotle.

Today we live in a new age of cultural crisis, the crisis of late modernity. It bears analogy to the classical and medieval examples, though the actual challenges of our time are markedly different from theirs. It is analogous because once again major theoretical discoveries and developments have undermined settled cultural convictions; and because the distinctive contributions of philosophy and theology are needed if the crisis is to be addressed in its full complexity. For Lonergan, raising Christian philosophy and theology to the critical standards of our time is essential if we are to untangle the educational and cultural predicaments we commonly face.

It is natural to assume that historical crises result from breakdown or disintegration, like the collapse of the Roman Empire, the destruction of the ancien régime, or the end of the Soviet Union. Traditional political frameworks dissolve when they are no longer able to contain destabilizing forces. If the destabilizing forces are viewed unfavorably, the civilized Romans failing to repel the marauding Goths, for example, then the loss of inherited order will be explicitly emphasized (we reluctantly enter the "Dark Ages"). But if the traditional institutions had lost their legitimacy, then their collapse will be welcomed as a requirement of historical progress ("the rebirth of democracy" in the political revolutions of the eighteenth century). The historical situation is more complicated, however, when cultural crises result from the complex interweaving of growth and decline, when new discoveries undermine ancient beliefs and convictions, but fail to preserve what was valid in the traditions they swept away. The unstable cultural situation will then be a tangled knot of gain and loss, of insight and blindness, rightfully eliciting both praise and criticism *à la fois*.[21]

Lonergan's critical assessment of late modernity emphasizes this uneven and discordant pattern. The principal source of modern cultural progress is the wave of new learning that emerged from the Italian Renaissance (CWL, 10:16–17). Over the next several centuries, the European sciences gradually emancipated themselves from the powerful influence of Aristotle's philosophy.[22] Originally in physics, and then later in chemistry and biology, modern science asserted its disciplinary autonomy. The new natural sciences slowly developed their own fields of investigation, their distinctive methods and research vocabularies, their specialized communities of inquiry, their accepted hypotheses, theories, and heuristic paradigms. Even more important than the novel results of modern scientific inquiry was the new intellectual outlook it created. Whitehead considers that critical mentality the most enduring legacy of the Scientific Revolution:

"The new tinge to modern minds is a vehement and passionate interest in the relation of general principles to irreducible and stubborn facts" (*Science and the Modern World*, 16). The explanatory general principles are the distinctive mark of theoretical inquiry; the careful attention to concrete facts makes abstract theory responsive to empirical observation and criticism. That responsiveness also makes modern science dynamic, critically revising its results in the face of recalcitrant data and evidence. This critical, dynamic revisionary process is clearly at work in the history of modern physics as the successive discoveries of Copernicus, Kepler, Galileo, Newton, Einstein, and Planck both augment and amend the achievements of their predecessors.[23]

For Lonergan, the most important cultural consequence of the continuing Scientific Revolution was a transformed understanding of science itself. Despite their explicit criticism of Aristotle's physics and cosmology, both modern scientists and philosophers tacitly accepted the theory of science he outlined in the *Posterior Analytics*. According to that theory, epistemic judgments become scientific when they express true, certain knowledge of causal necessity (CWL, 4:238–39). For Aristotle, the ontological source of that necessity was the invariant structure of formal and final causality. For Galileo and Kant, it was the invariance of classical physical laws. While this dramatic change in the physicist's heuristic expectations is certainly significant, it should not obscure the fact that the leading ancients and early moderns made the *telos* of science the certain knowledge of causal necessity.[24]

The actual record of scientific inquiry reveals that this epistemic ideal is illusory. The provisional results of science are not permanent truths but the best available opinions to emerge from the communal exercise of scientific methods. Because those methods are empirical and critical, their tentative conclusions are not certain but probable, and subject to careful revision and amendment by the relevant community of scientific investigators. What modern scientists discover and verify is not causal necessity but contingent patterns of intelligible order that organize and unify vast arrays of empirical data and evidence (*Third Collection*, 41–44).

Lonergan believes that the best way to understand the complexity of modern science is to focus on its heuristic *methods* rather than on its provisional *results*. While the theoretical results of science are important but revisable, their operative methods are relatively constant and ongoing. By *method* he refers "to the normative pattern of recurrent and related operations" that yield science's legacy of progressive and cumulative results (*Method*, 4). These intellectual operations are of different kinds and occur at different levels of the normative cognitional structure.

> In the natural sciences method inculcates a spirit of inquiry and inquiries recur. It insists on accurate observation and description: both observations, and descriptions recur. Above all, it praises discovery and discoveries recur. It requires the deduction of the implications of hypotheses, and deductions recur. It keeps urging that experiments be devised and performed to check the implications of hypotheses against observable fact, and such processes of experimentation recur.
>
> These distinct and recurrent operations are related. Inquiry transforms mere experiencing into the scrutiny of observation. What is observed is pinned down by description. Contrasting descriptions give rise to problems, and problems are solved by discoveries. What is discovered is expressed in a hypothesis. From the hypothesis are deduced its implications, and these suggest experiments to be performed. So the many operations are related; the relations form a pattern, and the pattern defines the right way of going about scientific investigation. (*Method*, 4–5)

Despite its theoretical greatness and immense practical importance, the cultural legacy of modern science is decidedly uneven. Contemporary critics of science point to its ambiguous alliance with technology, a symbiotic alliance that has extended human longevity and transformed modern standards of living. But it has also yielded the bitter fruits of atomic weapons, industrial pollution, global warming, unrestricted surveillance, and nuclear waste. While Lonergan acknowledges this line of social and political criticism, it's not the dialectical stance he personally adopts. His repeated challenge is rather to the epistemic confusions created by the extrascientific assertions of many practicing scientists and their popularizing disciples.

Lonergan explicitly objects to the mechanistic cosmology often attributed to modern physics; to the universal determinism alleged to follow from its necessary laws; to the cavalier reduction of the human to the natural sciences; to the positivist bias that denies epistemic legitimacy to metaphysics, ethics, and theology; to the theoretical hubris that blindly dismisses the factual judgments of common sense; to the behaviorist prejudice that confines psychological inquiry to sensible data; to the exclusive ontological naturalism that precludes divine transcendence by fiat.[25]

Lonergan's recurrent criticism is that these influential claims are not scientific discoveries verified by the empirical canons of scientific method. Rather, they are philosophical or popular interpretations of science that enjoy extensive but unwarranted support. The needed remedy, he believes, is to pay much greater heed to what scientists actually *do* than to what they periodically *say* (CWL, 4:133; *Second Collection*, 106). Careful attention to the history and practice of science effectively undercuts many of these extrascientific claims. Such interpretive scrutiny reveals, for example, the abstractness of classical laws, science's increasing heuristic reliance on statistical methods of inquiry, the dynamic, developmental character of most natural systems, the constitutive role of meaning and value in human affairs, the dialectical dimension of the human sciences, the conscious intentionality inseparable from human subjectivity, the inescapable importance and limits of common sense.[26]

While the modern Scientific Revolution is an unparalleled human achievement, its broader cultural significance remains open to critical scrutiny. We are commonly disposed to accept its often startling but provisional results because they are the cumulative fruit of the disciplined exercise of human intelligence and reasonableness, of unrestricted intellectual inquiry and detached critical reflection. These basic cognitive principles are the underlying human factors that make the discoveries of science possible and its epistemic achievements important and credible. Any putative interpretation of empirical science that is inconsistent with the free and responsible exercise of human intelligence by practicing scientists, as well as by those who critically receive and appraise their findings, is performatively inconsistent. We cannot coherently appeal to reductive interpretations of science that deny or omit the very intellectual and rational capacities of scientific inquirers which make scientific achievement and progress possible.[27]

What then, according to Lonergan, is the genuine cultural legacy of the ongoing Scientific Revolution? We have created a plurality of autonomous specialized disciplines. These disciplines have developed novel and important heuristic structures, methods, concepts, theories, and practical applications. A correlative result of scientific progress is a transformed understanding of the nature and history of science itself. But as the natural sciences have become the paradigm of successful human cognition, their dominance has created uncertainty about the epistemic legitimacy of other ways of knowing: philosophical, theological, artistic, religious, and practical. Moreover, the specialized nature of the several different sciences has either left the human need for cognitive integration and unity unsatisfied or encouraged integrative models that can't withstand critical scrutiny.

The modern natural sciences have undermined the ancient Aristotelian cosmology and the physical and biological principles on which it depended. Most of the proposed cosmological replacements, however, the numerous versions of scientific materialism, mechanism, determinism, and reductionism, have been seriously flawed. As a critical, self-reflective culture, we profoundly need a contemporary cosmology that does justice to both the ongoing discoveries of the natural sciences and to the dignity, freedom, and responsibility of each individual human being (*Method*, 102–5, 315). At the end of the Enlightenment's first phase, Kant clearly recognized that this was the inescapable intellectual and moral challenge created by the triumph of Newtonian physics. In the post-Kantian, post-Newtonian era of the "second Enlightenment," the cultural demand for a credible comprehensive cosmology is no less acute.[28]

Another important cultural legacy of the Scientific Revolution is the empirical and critical mentality it fosters. This intellectual orientation is not limited to the practice of science. It affects the way we think and speak in nearly every domain of human knowledge and activity. This pervasive critical mentality is particularly relevant for contemporary philosophy and theology. If they are to respond effectively to the momentous challenges posed by the new learning, they will need to embody this demanding cultural *exigence* in their revised self-conception and practice.

By the mid-nineteenth century, the scientific mentality had also created a new perspective on human affairs. Lonergan called this emerging heuristic perspective the rise of historical consciousness, the application of the critical scientific spirit to the study of society and history (CWL,

17:354). Traditional historical narratives were soon subjected to the same critical scrutiny as the cosmological beliefs of the ancients had been. The heuristic focus of the new historiography was on the particular and the concrete, on what had really happened in the past. A correlative focus was on the pervasiveness of historical change, changes in institutional and social patterns, changes in the cultural assumptions embodied in both inherited and evolving forms of governance and social order. Conflicting accounts of the past were now judged on the basis of linguistic, archaeological, and documentary evidence. New forms of autonomous scholarship emerged with specialized research and verification procedures. As the natural sciences had effectively detached themselves from the governing assumptions of Aristotelian philosophy, the new human studies asserted their independence of prevailing religious and political control. Their scholarly purpose was to uncover the past as it actually was, and not as traditional institutions had used it in order to legitimate their authority and power.

The empirical study of human affairs fostered a heightened awareness of social and cultural pluralism. Throughout their long and discordant history, human beings have embraced different cosmological and religious beliefs, different moral codes and ideals, different forms of symbolic and artistic expression, different patterns of social organization and governance. Even today, this institutional and cultural pluralism persists, despite the homogenizing effects of globalized communication and commerce.

This close attention to historical differences, changes, and conflicts has shaped a new and more flexible understanding of culture. Culture is now understood empirically rather than normatively, as the operative set of ideas, beliefs, and convictions that inform a particular society's way of life (*Method*, xi, 300–302). The canonical status once accorded by European educators to Western cultural traditions, whether classical, medieval, or modern, can no longer be taken for granted. These traditions have not lost their historical importance, but they have lost their status as cultural paradigms or norms. And yet, what are the normative implications of this often bewildering social and cultural diversity? And what remains of the classical distinction between nature and convention (*physis* and *nomos*), where nature's transcultural invariance effectively served as the normative standard for the critical appraisal of marked social differences? Will the cultural legacy of the new historical consciousness be a pervasive and intractable relativism once *nature* loses its normative measuring function, as it does in the Scientific Revolution?

The critical stance of the new hermeneutics was also destabilizing.[29] Marx, Nietzsche, and Freud subversively interpreted the central religious and ethical convictions of the West. The unmasking genealogies of "the masters of suspicion" were deliberately designed to undermine faith in God and the basic moral imperatives of Judaism and Christianity. As Charles Taylor has noted, a new ethics of unbelief has gradually emerged, especially in the academy, in which pervasive suspicion of the past seems more genuine than trust, and detached skepticism more credible than genuine moral conviction (*Sources of the Self*, 404–5). There is no authentic retreat from the effects of modern critical consciousness; they are an enduring aspect of our common Enlightenment heritage. But does the responsible exercise of rational criticism really entail the death of God and the erosion of our substantive moral inheritance? Can we think and live today as authentic adults, men and women at the level of our time, while still preserving what is true and enduring in the premodern past?

The autonomy and specialization of the natural and human sciences have also created a new situation for philosophy. How is philosophy intelligibly related to the new forms of specialized learning? What distinctive epistemic contributions can it make in an age of autonomous empirical inquiry? Critical hermeneutics and historiography have created a parallel challenge for Christian theology. For how is theology to communicate the Christian religion effectively to a skeptical and secular culture whose faith has been shaken by the fierce winds of radical criticism? Lonergan dedicated much of his life as a philosopher-theologian to answering these urgent and difficult questions.[30]

Lonergan claimed that classical philosophy and medieval theology were structurally grounded in metaphysics, which sought to provide a comprehensive account of the whole of being. Metaphysical categories were assumed to be theoretically basic and universal in scope; specialized categories for different regions of being, physical, biological, psychological, and moral, were treated as specific applications of metaphysical terms and relations. In the systematic hierarchy of knowledge, metaphysical principles were viewed as foundational and unrestricted in their range of application; by contrast, the discoveries of the special sciences were seen as derivative and limited to beings of a particular ontological kind (CWL, 2:3–4).

When the modern sciences asserted their independence of metaphysical assumptions and categories, the traditional mission of philosophy had to be reconceived. The focus of attention then shifted from things (beings) to ideas, where "ideas" referred to the semantic bearers of truth within the human mind. Epistemology gradually displaced metaphysics as the basic philosophical discipline. Its original goal was to reconstruct logically the deductive order of scientific ideas so that scientific truth could be exhibited as systematic and certain. Early modern epistemologists, however, uncritically presupposed the classical conception of science as true certain knowledge of causal necessity. When that influential conception was undermined by empirical studies in the history of science, and the quest for scientific certainty was gradually abandoned, then the distinctive nature and purpose of philosophy were again cast into doubt.[31]

Classical metaphysics had emphasized the objects of knowledge (the *known*), modern epistemology the intelligible concepts and propositional truths in which human *knowledge* is logically expressed. Lonergan believed that we have entered a third stage of cognitional history, in which the heuristic focus of philosophy must shift once again, this time from logic to method, from the deductive order of propositional *knowledge* to the invariant structure of human *knowing* (CWL, 17:201–3; *Method*, 94, 304–5). Philosophy must now become a specialized form of empirical inquiry that takes the *methods* of common sense, of the natural and human sciences, of critical hermeneutics and historiography, and of an empirically based and historically sensitive theology as its principal subject matter. Within this heuristic transformation, philosophy would still retain its traditional integrative mission, but its distinctive theoretical contribution would be to distinguish and coordinate the specialized methods and provisional results of the principal forms of contemporary inquiry.

In endorsing the heuristic transition from logic to method (from reconstructive epistemology to cognitional theory), Lonergan explicitly allied himself with the post-Kantian turn to the study of human subjectivity (*Second Collection*, 69–86; *Third Collection*, 27–31). But if that heuristic turn is to be fully empirical and critical, it will need to take the whole of human consciousness (the full interiority of the human subject) into account. To do that requires a generalized conception of empirical method that treats the data of human consciousness on a par with the data of sense perception (CWL, 3:95–96, 268). As the scope of the natural and human sciences has been extended to the entire range of sensible data and evidence, so the entire field of human consciousness will fall within the investigative scope of a subject-centered intentionality analysis.

And careful intentionality analysis reveals that human consciousness is inherently polymorphic (CWL, 3:410–12, 451–52). It unfolds in distinct patterns of experience, intellectual, practical, aesthetic, artistic, dramatic, existential, and religious, depending on the governing desires or concerns that shape its orderly flow (CWL, 3:204–12). The phenomenological (or intentional) study of human consciousness, therefore, should not be restricted to the study of cognitional experience. However, the richness and complexity of human subjectivity does not lessen the philosophical importance of cognition. Many of the cultural crises we have mentioned have their source in epistemic developments that appear irreconcilable with traditional beliefs and commitments. To determine the enduring cultural significance of the scientific and scholarly discoveries of modernity, we need a critical comprehensive philosophy that is able to answer the following series of questions convincingly.[32]

What are we actually *doing* when we are pursuing and achieving knowledge in mathematics, the empirical sciences, the diverse regions of common sense, hermeneutics and historiography, philosophy and theology? This is the defining question for a comprehensive cognitional theory carefully attuned to the different forms of contemporary learning.

Why does authentically performing these cognitional operations actually lead to true and objective *knowledge* in these complementary cognitive realms? This is the central question for a critical epistemology fully responsive to the skeptical challenges of contemporary idealism and relativism.

What do we really *know* if we achieve objective knowledge in these ways? Can the heterogeneous results of the different ways of knowing reality be credibly integrated into a coherent and comprehensive theory of *being*? And can a suitably revised metaphysics respect the disciplinary autonomy and relentless dynamism of the different empirical sciences while remaining committed to a unified account of reality? These are the inescapable questions facing a critical *metaphysics* in an era of specialized inquiry and historical pluralism.

What must we do, in our personal and communal lives, to advance beyond objective knowledge of the world and achieve moral and religious authenticity? And what is the intrinsic connection between our personal and communal commitment to free and responsible action, and the disinterested pursuit of universally valid knowledge? These are the daunting questions at the core of existential ethics and of an emerging ethics of historical responsibility.

In articulating and dynamically ordering these interrelated questions, Lonergan has outlined a credible epistemic project for philosophy in the third stage of cognitive meaning. It is a sequential and cumulative project that begins with cognitional analysis (knowing), expands into epistemology (knowledge) and metaphysics (being), and culminates in existential and social ethics (living and doing). As our reflective study of Lonergan's project unfolds and develops, we shall examine and evaluate his answers to these questions, testing their power to illumine and resolve the cultural confusions and dilemmas of our time.

A Critical Cultural Center

> *What will count is a perhaps not numerous center big enough to be at home in the old and the new, painstaking enough to work out one by one the transitions to be made, strong enough to refuse half answers and insist on complete solutions even though it has to wait.*
> —CWL, 4:245

The cultural crisis Lonergan identified has intellectual, moral, and religious dimensions. Intellectually, we have witnessed a striking loss of confidence in the human capacity for achieving objective knowledge; morally, a heightened skepticism about discovering and doing what is inherently good and worthwhile; religiously, a broadly shared though often tacit conviction that the biblical God of our ancestors is no longer spiritually credible. This subversive irreligious conviction becomes explicit when ontological naturalism effectively excludes divine transcendence, and when exclusive humanism asserts God's irrelevance to the understanding and conduct of human affairs. There is, of course, countercultural resistance to each of these pervasive secular trends, but it tends to be diffuse and ineffective.

Despite the intellectual and moral progress achieved in modernity, its evolving history has yielded a "succession of descending cultural syntheses" (CWL, 10:64–65). To clarify this important normative appraisal, consider the cumulative cultural impact of the following series of landmark events. The scandalous practices of the Renaissance papacy provoked the original rupture of Latin Christendom. As the Reformation unfolded on several fronts, Luther and Calvin explicitly rejected Aquinas's complex theological synthesis of grace and nature, faith and reason, Athens and Jerusalem. The bloody wars of religion sparked by the Reformation devastated Europe and heightened demands for religious toleration. The subsequent separation of faith and reason, in the service of public peace, had divisive if unintended results; it tended to promote a one-sided rationalism openly hostile to divine revelation and a pious fideism deeply suspicious of critical reason in all its forms. Eventually, the rationalists' inability to resolve serious moral, political, and religious disagreements served to diminish the prestige of reason and strengthened skeptical doubts about the scope of legitimate knowledge. And skeptical tolerance, though it preserved civic peace for a time, proved impotent in the face of the urgent *social question*, the scandalous inequities of wealth and power created by industrial capitalism. The important limits of tolerance were also revealed by the evident racism animating Europe's imperialist enterprise. Conflicting imperial ambitions in Asia and Africa precipitated the outbreak of the Great War and the terrible slaughter to which it led. Then the economic and political crises triggered by World War I undermined the czarist regime in Russia, the Hapsburg imperium, and the Weimar republic in Germany. In the wake of their collapse, the Bolsheviks and Nazis relied on ideology and terror to impose totalitarian control on Central and Eastern Europe. The death camps of Hitler, the gulags of Stalin, and the colonial revolt against imperialism shocked the European conscience, arousing profound second thoughts about the whole modern project of mastering nature and history. What we now call the "postmodern" outlook is an intelligible reaction to the terrible excesses of modernity.[33] For all its merits as a corrective to European arrogance, its strengths tend to be critical rather than constructive, iconoclastic rather than unifying. Postmodernism is fully attuned to historical pluralism and moral ambiguity (it explicitly opposes regimes of domination in their several institutional forms). But the subversive genealogies it favors fall short of true critical appropriation, while deconstructive irony leaves our integrative aspirations unsatisfied.

What provisional historical lessons should we draw from this highly compressed account of successive cultural contractions? We cannot return to the well-ordered world of Aquinas where both reason and revelation were strongly and broadly affirmed. Nor can we restore the lost unity of Latin Christendom in our ecumenical and secular age. We live now in an era of cultural pluralism and heightened historical consciousness, of passionate moral advocacy and pervasive uncertainty about the ontological sources of genuine meaning and value. Our divided, highly contentious culture provides no common answer to very basic and inescapable questions: What sort of unity, epistemic, moral, and religious, is compatible with the contemporary emphasis on plurality and difference? What kinds of objectivity, epistemic, moral, and religious, does historically sensitive criticism permit? What enduring achievements are retrievable from the "discredited" past, and can they help to illumine the confusions and instability of the fragmented present?

These are among the profound cultural challenges facing critical appropriation today. To meet them effectively, Lonergan called for the creation of a new type of cultural association, a collaborative center of scientists, thinkers, scholars, and citizens willing to become critically at home in the old and the new (CWL, 4:245). But this willingness, though itself in short supply, is clearly insufficient. Human inquiry has traditionally focused on exploring the as yet unknown. The critical appropriation of our tangled cultural knot, by contrast, essentially requires a prior transformation in the mind and heart of the knower. What sort of persons must we become to meet the exigent demands of Lonergan's "not too numerous center"?

Intellectual, Moral, and Spiritual Development

In an era of disciplinary specialization and historical consciousness, critical appropriation is a project for a collaborative team rather than a single individual. But viable teams depend on their individual members and their personal contributions to the cooperative effort. To evaluate the past responsibly, we need first to understand the concrete historical contexts of earlier events, conflicts, achievements, and failures. We also need to discover what the old and the new really are, for the historical past and the inherited traditions that preserve it may not be the same (CWL, 3:769). To distinguish them effectively requires a long and sustained process of personal study and learning. To use Lonergan's insightful phrase, it requires "reaching up" to the minds of our predecessors in a spirit of humility and patience. Our own minds are often transformed in this arduous interpretive effort, as we sympathetically enter cultural, institutional, and textual contexts very different from our own. In credibly passing over to other minds, societies, and cultures, we need to be particularly attentive to bias and prejudice, to the personal and cultural obstacles that preclude sympathetic understanding and fair-minded appraisal. We also need to be alert to the existential factors, rooted in the human condition itself, that dispose all thinkers and scholars to serious oversights and misunderstandings. We cannot responsibly evaluate what we don't sympathetically understand; and the prior process of deep, nuanced, and generous understanding takes time, patience, devotion, and skill. This principle applies, *mutatis mutandis*, to the genuine understanding of the sciences and critical historiography, as well as to philosophical and theological thought.

Critical Self-Appropriation

Why is it that genuine intellectual discoveries are often interpreted and popularized in a reductive manner; that epistemic progress and decline are so strangely entangled together? For part of the answer, we must turn our reflective attention to the intentional subject, the center and source of all learning and teaching. As previously noted, the consciousness of the subject is inherently polymorphic; it tends to flow in distinct experiential patterns that reflect the diverse range of human desires and concerns. At birth and through infancy, the growing child lives in a world of sensible immediacy, a world confined to the sensible here and now of the nursery, the home, and the neighborhood. With language acquisition comes a bewildering entry into the larger world mediated by meaning and motivated by value. The operative world of the language-using subject gradually expands to include the realms of nature and history as well as the complex array of interpersonal relations. We slowly and painfully learn of truth and error, desire and duty, good and evil, holiness and sin. Parental and communal education, formal and informal, becomes the principal source of the subject's personal development; we assimilate, for good or ill, the beliefs and convictions, the insights and oversights, the loyalties and prejudices of our parents, teachers, and peers. Any intellectual and practical discoveries we later make on our own are functionally dependent on this fiduciary framework we originally acquired with the help of so many others.[34]

But if the cultural legacy we receive through education is inevitably flawed, why not find a way to think and live without it? Descartes attempted to do just this through his strategy of hyperbolic doubt. Although Descartes's philosophical claims were highly inflated and we no longer endorse his quest for epistemic certainty, we openly recognize the tangled legacy that our prolonged education creates. Our existential dilemma is basic and inescapable. We can't think, act, and live without the ambiguous transmission of the past, so that an essential condition of all human development is also a source of confusion, prejudice, and error.

Our incapacity for sustained personal development is due not only to our ambiguous cultural heritage. An important part of the problem rests with who we are. But what does genuine self-knowledge teach us about ourselves? We are alternatively intelligent and foolish, reasonable and biased, responsible and morally stubborn and blind. The tangled cultural knot we inherit is a public reflection of the more fundamental mix of order and disorder within the conscious developing subject. Before we can effectively unravel the massive cultural knot we inherit, we must first address the existential knot within ourselves.

It is important to be as precise as we can here. The polymorphic complexity of the intentional subject should not be confused with our common disposition to distorting bias and sin. We are not twisted and disordered beings because we are consciously complex and multidimensional. The internal pluralism of the subject, though daunting in its own right, is not the existential heart of the matter. It is rather that bias and sin can compromise every aspect of our subjectivity, penetrate every pattern of conscious experience, and effectively obstruct our developing capacities to think, know, choose, act, and love.

Critical self-appropriation, therefore, requires a twofold dialectic. The first step is to learn to distinguish the sources and patterns of our conscious experience, intellectual, moral, practical, dramatic, artistic, and religious. The second is to acknowledge how the normative unfolding of these patterns can be disturbed and distorted by dramatic, egoistic, group, and general bias.[35] The intrinsic thrust of the human spirit is toward sustained *self-transcendence* (*Method*, 35, 104–5). The inherent function of the biases is to block that thrust, thereby frustrating the deepest aspirations of the developing self. The inwardly divided subject, simultaneously seeking and refusing self-transcendence, constitutes the tangled personal knot, the radical surd that the great religions call sin.

Critical self-appropriation, therefore, is the very opposite of a rationalizing ideology. The purpose of ideology, in its many different forms, is to justify bias and sin and the effective refusal of self-transcendence to which they regularly contribute (*Method*, 55, 357–59). Ideologies uncritically identify the divinely created subject striving for self-transcendence with the sinful self. They treat the tangled knot of conflicted subjectivity as the authentic person. They reject or ignore the dialectical distinctions between created nature and disruptive sin, and between disabling sin and redemptive grace. For self-justifying ideologues, there is no sinful fall from grace and no credible hope for authentic redemption. We simply are and will always remain the way we appear at our disordered worst; end of story.

Critical self-appropriation, by contrast, seeks a normative foundation within the conscious intentional subject, a reliable rock where we can provisionally stand and responsibly judge (*Method*, 19–20). Once again, precision is required. It is critical to distinguish (a) the immanent and operative normative foundation within us, experientially conscious but cognitively unknown; (b) that same foundation as reflexively interrogated, provisionally grasped, and conceptually articulated; (c) the constitutive core of our subjectivity as objectively affirmed and personally appropriated. Self-appropriation is a critical form of self-knowledge, in which we discover, articulate, and affirm within ourselves the constitutive principles of our authentic and inauthentic existence.

But here is the performative dialectical twist (CWL, 3:353–57). We rely on these constitutive principles in the very process of coming to know and affirm them. The reflexive intentional subject cannot escape the foundational core of her own subjectivity. While we regularly fail in the demanding effort to know ourselves, these failures of self-knowledge leave the constitutive core of our subjectivity intact. For it is the constitutive principles as immanent and consciously operative, rather than as provisionally thematized and articulated, that constitute the basis of who we are as intellectual, moral, and spiritual beings. Still, a very important part of who we are is who we take ourselves to be. So, when we truncate or misunderstand the normative foundations of our own subjectivity, we further complicate the tangled knot and heighten the difficulty of finally unraveling it.

But what are these constitutive principles at the core of our common humanity? And how do they manifest themselves both within the consciousness of the individual subject and in the greater history of human affairs? Lonergan refers to them as *transcendental* principles, in both the Scholastic and Kantian senses of the term (*Second Collection*, 207). They are unrestricted in their scope and application (the traditional Scholastic sense). They serve as concrete conditions of enabling possibility for all intellectual, moral, and spiritual achievement (the Kantian sense). But their authentic operation and exercise is in no sense automatic or guaranteed, for human subjectivity is polymorphic and fragile, and constantly prone to the disruption of bias, ideology, and sin.

The first transcendental principles are erotic and dynamic: the unrestricted human desire to know all that exists (the transcendental *notion* of being); the unrestricted desire to discover and actualize whatever is genuinely good and worthwhile (the transcendental *notion* of value) (*Method*, 11–13).[36] Though human achievement is invariably finite and imperfect, our natural desires for knowledge and value are boundless. They account for the relentless dynamism of intellectual and moral inquiry; they explain our recurrent dissatisfaction with personal and public achievement, however impressive and admirable. The shared intellectual commitment of countless generations of scientists, scholars, and philosophers to understanding the endless flow of empirical data, including the data of consciousness, offers powerful testimony to the unrestricted *desire to know*. The tireless individual and collective efforts to preserve, promote, and augment what is good and to correct or repair what is harmful and broken give correlative expression, socially, politically, and globally, to the transcendental notion of value. These basic dynamic spiritual desires undergird and sustain the intellectual and moral life of humankind. They also provide a transcultural, transhistorical bond uniting the past, the present, and the future, for these constitutive desires are present and operative wherever and whenever human beings exist, inquire, act, and respond to the initiatives of others.

Lonergan refers to the second set of foundational principles as generalized empirical method (or transcendental method) (CWL, 3:268; *Method*, 14–16). We have frequently noted that human inquiry is specialized and differentiated; that it assumes different forms in natural science, critical scholarship, human studies, theology, philosophy, and common sense. And that these specialized forms of inquiry themselves evolve in the course of cognitional history. Though deeply attentive to this dynamic heuristic and cognitive pluralism, Lonergan also believed[37] that there is a universal empirical method (a transcendental method) underlying these specialized modes of inquiry, that there is a normative and recurrent pattern of conscious and intentional operations at the core of all human learning and knowing. Effectively motivated and sustained by the unrestricted desire to know (the intellectual *eros* of mind), this normative pattern is dynamically structured and consciously self-assembling. The normative unfolding of inquiry occurs on three complementary levels, the sequentially ascending levels of experience, understanding, and judgment, with the higher levels of cognitional process presupposing and completing the operations and contents of the lower. For Lonergan, human cognitional process is essentially discursive rather than intuitive in nature; it fundamentally consists of asking intelligent questions about experience and producing and verifying reasonable answers to those questions. The basic questions that give inquiry its substantive focus are of two kinds, questions for intelligence (who, what, why, how often, etc.), and questions for reflection (is it so, is it true) that are critically posed to the explicit answers offered to these questions for intelligence. The intelligent and reasonable grounds for answering these complementary questions are the conscious occurrence of numerous acts of insight, direct and reflective. To understand these complementary forms of human insight, in their enabling conditions, their functional operation, and the provisional epistemic results they progressively yield, is to confer a "basic yet startling unity" on the whole field of human cognition (CWL, 3). But like other normative patterns of intentional activity, cognitional process can easily go awry. It is the interference of bias, dramatic, egoistic, group, or general, that distorts and obstructs human inquiry, by circumscribing relevant questions, neglecting or excluding unwelcome data, resisting the occurrence of corrective insights, affirming or rejecting answers without sufficient evidence or corroboration, inwardly preventing the process of inquiry from reaching its self-transcendent goal.

There are unrestricted *transcendental norms* as well as unrestricted intentional *desires* (the transcendental notions). These norms are immanent and operative within human consciousness whether or not they are explicitly recognized and articulated by the subject or by others. Their critical regulative function is the internal ordering and disciplining of the whole of our knowing, choosing, acting, and living. When we fail to comply with their exigent demands, we violate our own intelligence and reasonableness, and our personal commitment to morally responsible choices and conduct. Lonergan articulates these immanent exigent regulatory norms in his series of transcendental precepts. We should note once again that these exigent interior norms are themselves the foundational principles (*archai*) of human subjectivity rather than the articulated precepts that publicly objectify their imperative demands and requirements (*Method*, 20, 53, 55).

But what are these transcendental precepts that prescriptively govern every human being's intentional life from within? They can be expressed as a series of ascending universal imperatives. Be *attentive* to whatever human experience reveals.[38] Be *intelligent* in asking and answering questions in every realm of human inquiry and action. Be *reasonable* in giving or withholding assent to all factual and evaluative judgments. Be *responsible* in accepting or rejecting proposed courses of practical action, and in deciding the basic direction and priorities of both personal and communal life. Be *wholeheartedly loving* in responding to the enduring biblical command to love God above all things and our neighbor as ourselves.

These universal and invariant normative precepts constitute a transcendental and historically sensitive expression of what was traditionally called the *natural law*. They do not formulate an intelligible law governing the order of natural events in the material realms of physics or biology;

rather, they articulate normative laws prescriptively governing the comprehensive activity of the human spirit (CWL, 3:640–41). To violate an immanent spiritual law of this kind is to act in opposition to one's deepest human identity; it is to be internally divided against oneself as a conscious intentional subject. It is to live in conflict with our created and dynamic nature as intentional beings striving for self-transcendence.

A natural and normative law of this kind credibly restores the ancient *physis-nomos* distinction in an era of historical mindedness and cultural pluralism (*Third Collection*, 171–82). It serves as a transcultural, transhistorical standard by which the operative beliefs, convictions, and practices of concrete and particular societies can be critically appraised. Of course, it requires careful and detailed historical inquiry to determine whether or not the particular beliefs (*doxai*) and convictions (*nomoi*) of a given society satisfy or diverge from these interior norms. The truth or adequacy of evaluative cultural judgments cannot be reasonably appraised in a contextual vacuum. But Lonergan insists that these exigent spiritual norms, this dynamically revised articulation of the natural law, provide the cognitive basis for an objective morality that is critical, dynamic, and dialectically sensitive to historical and cultural pluralism.

What are the dialectical benefits of the intentional subject's critical self-appropriation? Lonergan emphasizes two extremely valuable cultural benefits. Self-appropriation provides the individual participants in the "critical center" with the necessary spiritual resources for a dialectical response to the mounting challenges of historicity and pluralism (CWL, 17:70–104). It also provides the historical community of actual philosophers with a critical method for resolving recurrent and demoralizing disagreements in cognitional theory, epistemology, metaphysics, and ethics (CWL, 3: chap. 14). Let us briefly examine these distinct but related cultural benefits.

The specter of relativism, epistemic, moral, and religious, haunts our pluralistic secular age (CWL, 3:366–71; *Method*, 259; *Second Collection*, 207–8). The central issue turns on the deeply disputed question of truth. Can there be contradictory truths, contradictory answers to the same set of intelligent questions (conceptually formulated within the same heuristic context), equally grounded in the relevant and available evidence. It is not cognitive plurality itself that threatens the attainment of discernible truth, but a plurality of antithetical judgments equally claiming our reasonable assent and acceptance. Kant's famous antinomies illustrate this important epistemic dilemma; for it was their discovery and apparent persistence that led Kant to argue for the epistemic limits of theoretical reason and to circumscribe human reason's capacity for achieving objective knowledge (*Critique of Pure Reason*, A406–A567).

One of Lonergan's basic dialectical objectives is to rescue the many forms of legitimate pluralism from the relativist threat. To achieve this end he distinguishes three types of epistemic pluralism: complementary, genetic, and antithetical (*Method*, 271–81; CWL, 17:72–88). We find complementary pluralism in the historical varieties of commonsense knowledge, in the different realms of cognitive inquiry, in the multiple heuristic structures within the empirical sciences, in the different functions and expressions of meaning, in the multiple languages and symbols that can be used to communicate a common set of affirmable truths.

We find genetic pluralism in the dynamic process of personal and intellectual development: we must learn to crawl before we can walk, walk before we can run, run slowly before we can compete successfully in competitive races and marathons. Conversely, we must master the alphabet before we can read, read before we can write, write simple sentences before we can artfully compose novels and scholarly treatises.

We find antithetical pluralism in contradictory answers to the basic philosophical questions Lonergan outlined: what are we doing when we are knowing; why is doing that knowledge; what do we know when we do that; what are we morally obliged to do and avoid; what are the basic requirements of an authentic and meaningful life? Thus, the first dialectical challenge, the challenge of epistemic and moral relativism, eventually gives rise to the second. The scandal of unresolved philosophical conflicts led modern philosophers to search for a reliable critical method to adjudicate their differences impartially. We can track this recurrent heuristic quest through Descartes, Spinoza, Hume, Kant, Hegel, Nietzsche, Husserl, Russell, Dewey, and the logical positivists, among others. Though Lonergan did not find any of the solutions they advanced compelling, he recognized that the persistent methodological problem these thinkers confronted was an inescapable challenge for contemporary philosophy.[39]

In *Insight*, Lonergan developed an original *dialectical method* for critically adjudicating philosophical disputes (CWL, 3:268–69, 421–54).

Philosophical judgments, the specific answers given to the defining philosophical questions, he argued, can be divided into positions and counterpositions. The *positions* affirm matters of cognitional and moral fact; the *counterpositions* fail to meet this critical demand. The facts in question are the set of foundational principles, erotic, methodological, and normative, at the constitutive core of the intentional subject. To discover these constitutive facts intelligently and to articulate and affirm them reasonably is to apply the operative principles to themselves in a critical instance of reflexive self-knowledge. But we cannot coherently rely on the very operation of these principles to deny, distort, or ignore their own reality without being caught in a performative contradiction (CWL, 3:353–57). This is the inescapable existential dilemma of philosophers who deny the positions and affirm the counterpositions. It's not that the counterpositions can't be meaningfully asserted; it's rather that they can't be intelligently grasped and reasonably affirmed. For, in order to affirm them reasonably, individual philosophers must violate one or more of the transcendental principles constitutive of their own intellectual and moral existence. The central purpose of critical self-appropriation, then, is to discover, articulate, and affirm these constitutive principles within our own being and then to recognize and embrace the wealth of their normative and dialectical implications (*Method*, 20–25). Lonergan's *Insight* was written deliberately to assist this demanding process of fundamental self-knowledge (CWL, 3:14–24).

Conversion

Our unifying theme in this chapter has been the cultural crises of modernity, and the contemporary need for a critical center of scholars and thinkers epistemically at home in both the old and the new. Following Lonergan, we have argued that this interdisciplinary community will be equal to the cultural challenges of our time only if its individual members undergo a profound transformation. We have identified two requirements of that transformative process: sustained intellectual and moral development in mastering the thought of our predecessors and contemporaries; and the critical self-appropriation of the polymorphic intentional subject. We shall now turn to a third requirement, distinct from though clearly related to these prior existential demands.

Conversion is an important and recurrent theme in the history of religion and philosophy. *Metanoia*, a fundamental change in the mind and heart of a person, is central to both the gospel of Jesus of Nazareth (Mark 1:14–15; Matt. 4:17) and the maieutic method of Socrates and Plato (*Republic*, 7.515–16). The need for intellectual conversion appears in muted form in Aristotle's cognitive distinction between what is first for us as sentient animals and what is first in reality (*Metaphysics*, 2.993b, 8–11). It reappears emphatically in existential thinkers like Augustine, Pascal, and Kierkegaard, and in Heidegger's critique of the forgetfulness of being.

Jesus commands his disciples to repent so that they might enter the kingdom of heaven (Matt. 4:17; *Method*, 271). Socrates requires a moral conversion of his sophistic interlocutors before they can understand what he says to them: "For if you are serious and what you say is true, then surely the life of us mortals must be turned upside down, and apparently we are everywhere doing the opposite of what we should" (*Gorgias*, 481b–c). In the dialogues, the sophists and their pupils implicitly assume that the good is pleasure, the satisfaction of somatic or social desire. Socrates, by contrast, appears to believe that justice, the ordered harmony of the dynamic soul, is the true good of the human being, and that we must discipline our appetites and even accept bodily harm and social rejection in order to achieve it. Nearly all the dialogues end in impasse, because the moral conversion of the Socratic interlocutors regularly fails to occur.

In the *Republic* the Platonic Socrates calls for an intellectual conversion on the part of aspiring philosophers (*Republic*, books 6 and 7). Nonphilosophical mortals implicitly assume that sensible things are the final measure of reality, and that we know these things by sensibly perceiving them in space and time. In books 6 and 7 of the *Republic*, Socrates outlines the turning around (the *periagoge*) true philosophers must undergo. They must climb up and through the epistemic and ontological levels of the divided line; they must gradually ascend from the sensible darkness of the cave to the immediate noetic vision of the Good; they must master the intellectually transformative curriculum of mathematics and dialectic. In the course of this long and demanding ascent, their ontological allegiances shift from sensible things to intelligible forms. They learn to understand the sensible through the intelligible, the ontological source of each thing's specific identity and enduring unity. For the true philosopher it is *nous*, the power of intellect, rather than our sensory and imaginative capacities, that becomes the measure of what is real and what is known.

Augustine, who was deeply influenced by Neoplatonism, identifies three distinct but related conversions in his *Confessions*: the intellectual conversion to philosophy that begins with his reading of Cicero's *Hortentius*; the moral conversion to a life of chastity and ascetic virtue that he believes true philosophy and Christianity commonly require; and the religious conversion to a life of *caritas* in which the redemptive grace of God enables wholehearted devotion to the love of God and neighbor.[40]

In Augustine's case, as in the Socratic dialogues, there is a constant temptation to draw back from the stern demands of conversion. For although the converted subject is existentially transformed, the lure of pleasure and social ambition, the practical attachment to sensible objects, the counterpull of *cupiditas* remain at work. For Augustine, true and lasting conversion is impossible without God's grace; for Plato, it seems to require the pedagogical inspiration and personal example of a great maieutic teacher. Both thinkers recognize, however, that grace and inspiring examples often prove insufficient.

Effective and enduring conversion transforms more than the soul of the individual subject. It also transforms the environing world in which the subject thinks, acts, and lives (*Method*, 130–32). To use a phenomenological idiom, it transforms the intellectual and moral *horizon* of the philosopher and the Christian, so that the true philosopher's life becomes centered on *the invisible and intelligible Good*, and the genuine Christian's life on the mysterious God of Abraham, Moses, the prophets, and Jesus.

Lonergan's notion of existential conversion is clearly influenced by Plato, Augustine, and the gospel. In *Insight* he focuses primarily on intellectual conversion, a radical shift in our habitual understanding of knowing, objectivity, and being. In *Method in Theology*, he follows Augustine in requiring a threefold conversion, intellectual, moral, and religious, of the practicing theologian (*Method*, 267–71). He is also significantly influenced by his study of phenomenology and existentialism (CWL, 18). After his philosophical turn to the intentional subject, he recognizes the dialectical importance of each person's operative horizon and insists on the radical difference between the horizons of existentially converted and unconverted subjects. Although ontologically they both exist within the comprehensive universe of being, phenomenologically they live in different worlds with different centers of attention, allegiance, and concern.

What is it about human existence that makes these three conversions necessary, and for what strategic ends are they required? Answering the first question clearly should help us in responding persuasively to the second. We humans are embodied, developing, polymorphic subjects with a marked disposition to bias and sin. Because we are incarnate subjects, we have bodily needs and desires that remain with us throughout our lives. As gradually developing subjects, we must pass through infancy, childhood, and adolescence on the way to becoming mature adults. In this critical formative process, whose enduring results are always uncertain, our organic, neural, perceptual, and linguistic development largely precedes our intellectual and moral maturity, a maturity that itself depends heavily on the ambiguous cultural heritage of the communities to which we belong (CWL, 3:485–504).

Because we are polymorphic subjects we regularly respond to a multiplicity of desires and concerns. The unrestricted desires for knowledge and value coexist with more urgent, immediate, and concrete demands centered on the needs of the incarnate self. This broad range of competing concerns shapes the different patterns of conscious experience of which the intellectual pattern is but one among many. Very few people make the *eros* of mind the effective center of their lives, and the intellectual development of those who do is often not complemented by self-appropriation (CWL, 3:209–10). At the same time, the transcendental notions of intelligibility, truth, and value are singularly important to our existence. Together with the other foundational principles we identified, they repeatedly summon us to self-transcendence and demand that we actually achieve it. Our authenticity as human beings depends on the consistent pursuit of self-transcendence, intellectually through objective knowing, morally through authentic living, religiously through the wholehearted love of God and neighbor (*Method*, 104–5).

It is the relentless desire to know that draws us beyond the worlds of immediacy and common sense into the unrestricted universe of being. It is the unrestricted *eros* for value that reverses our customary moral and practical priorities. Transformed by that moral reversal or conversion, we no longer measure the good by the satisfaction of individual or group desires, but by detached and disinterested judgments of value, our authentic appraisals of what is really worthwhile. Because the transcendental notions are unrestricted in their scope and intention, they also summon us to know and love God, the ontological source of the created universe, the supreme good (the *summum bonum*) in the order of value. Our natural human desire and yearning for God are effectively strengthened and fortified by divine grace, the unmerited gift of God's love, the ultimate ground of self-transcendence within us.

Thus we humans are inherently self-centered and summoned to self-transcendence. As biological and sensitive subjects, we have a subjective horizon that is confined to a universe of objects capable of satisfying our elemental desires and needs. As practical subjects immersed in the concerns of ordinary life, we largely confine our attention to the world of common sense. As social beings, we're normally centered on the dramatic interplay of interpersonal relations. As aesthetic and artistic beings, we delight in the free play of the senses and the creative imagination. Each of these conscious patterns of experience is correlated with its own intentional *world*, its distinctive horizon of interest, relevance, and concern. This is also true of the intellectual pattern of experience in which the unrestricted desire to know unfolds. The normative unfolding of that desire intends the knowledge of all that exists, the unrestricted universe of being. As finite temporal creatures, we seek gradually to actualize that dynamic intention, one step at a time, through the specialized forms of empirical method, the natural and human sciences, historical scholarship, philosophy, and theology.

These specialized forms of learning and teaching have their own epistemic horizons, the specific regions of being they seek to investigate. As the intellectual pattern of experience becomes differentiated, so does our awareness of the regional *ontologies* that jointly constitute reality as an intelligible whole (*Method*, 81–84). This highly dynamic pluralism of knowing and being heightens the perplexity of the existential subject who alternately lives in different patterns of experience and in phenomenologically quite different worlds.

From the competing intentional perspectives of the biological, practical, dramatic, and aesthetic subject, the world of natural science seems unreal and the concerns of the historical scholar largely irrelevant. From the critical scientific perspective, scholarly discoveries seem too closely tied to common sense, while the judgments of philosophers and theologians appear to lack empirical support. Even within the intellectual pattern of experience we are tempted to restrict the range of legitimate inquiry and of epistemic and ontological possibility. We are constantly tempted to generalize from the limited heuristic pattern with which we are most familiar, thereby denying the full complexity of the intentional subject and the far greater complexity of being. But is there a way to check these reductive temptations, to do justice to the whole of our conscious selves and to the unrestricted range of our transcendental concerns? Lonergan believes that there is, but to be effective, it requires the subject's intellectual, moral, and religious conversion.

Let us test this strategic belief by first clarifying *intellectual conversion*. In discussing the intentional subject we constantly need to distinguish between prereflexive experiential consciousness, thematized self-reflective analysis, and explicit self-knowledge (CWL, 3:344–57; *Method*, 8–20). These important distinctions also apply to the required conversions as well. The intellectually converted subject has made the pure desire to know the effective center of her life. She is at home in the intellectual pattern of experience and in the specialized applications of empirical method. She is habitually faithful to the transcendental precepts with their invariant demand for self-transcendence. She is oriented intellectually to the universe of being in its full concreteness. She knows tacitly, *implicitly*, through considerable cognitive experience, of what knowing consists, what objective knowledge requires, and the internal complexity and interconnection of whatever is knowable and known. Hers is the existential stance of *conscious intellectual conversion*.[41]

To become self-reflective, the converted subject must *explicitly* address the series of philosophical questions that Lonergan has carefully outlined. This thematic shift from implicit awareness to explicit self-reflexion effectively extends the focus of inquiry from the world of cognitive objects to the desires, operations, and norms of the intentional subject. In this process of self-reflection, we thematize and objectify our own complex interiority, both our habitual self-centeredness and our converted commitment to comprehensive self-transcendence. While we recognize that objective knowing is not the exclusive purpose of human living, we affirm that it is an essential aspect of our full authenticity. The consciously converted subject gradually achieves philosophical self-knowledge (critical self-appropriation) when she can correctly answer and verify on the basis of her own cognitive experience Lonergan's basic questions about knowing, knowledge, and the known.

When intellectual conversion is raised to the level of explicit self-knowledge, the intentional subject can also clarify and repudiate mistaken accounts of cognition, objectivity, and being. She can show why the basic counterpositions in philosophy are truncated expressions of the defective self-knowledge of existentially unconverted subjects.[42] To put the most basic counterpositions briefly but clearly: the naive realist in philosophy identifies knowing with sensing, knowledge with veridical sense perception, and the real with the totality of the sensible. The different forms of philosophical idealism, by contrast, identify knowing with logical conceiving, knowledge with verified conception, and objective reality with what human concepts and propositions are, in principle, unable to attain. In marked opposition to these highly schematized counterpositions, critical realists (like Lonergan) identify human knowing with the dynamic normative process of experience, understanding, and judgment; objective knowledge with the affirmation of true judgments reflectively grasped as virtually unconditioned; and reality or being with the unrestricted object of the human desire to know that becomes known concretely through intellectual grasp and reasonable affirmation (*Second Collection*, 240–44; *Method*, 76, 262–65).

Without sustained intellectual development, critical self-appropriation, and fully actualized intellectual conversion, the existential subject cannot execute this philosophical dialectic effectively. For the verifiable philosophical *positions* are reasonably affirmed on the basis of comprehensive self-knowledge, while the numerous *counterpositions* are sympathetically understood as truncated accounts of human subjectivity, right in what they affirm, wrong in what they exclude or omit.[43]

What is *moral conversion* and why is it practically necessary for Lonergan's dialectical project (*Method*, 240–44; CWL, 17:86–87)? Though the genuine conversion of the subject depends on her prior intellectual, moral, and spiritual development, conversion's existential effects are far more profound. Through the lifelong process of teaching and learning, the intellect and character of the subject are substantially formed; through intellectual and moral conversion, the human mind and heart are profoundly transformed. This transformation extends to the subject's existential horizon, the effective range of her vital interests, evaluative standards, and central concerns. At the core of intellectual conversion is the growing existential importance of the unrestricted *eros* of mind. The converted subject becomes effectively oriented to the universe of being as an intelligible whole. At the core of moral conversion is the transcendental notion of value, the unrestricted desire to discover and actualize all that is truly worthwhile (*Method*, 11–13; CWL, 17:142–43, 337–38). Just as the dynamic and unrestricted desire to know takes us beyond the familiar horizon of common sense into the specialized realms of science, scholarship, philosophy, and theology, so the desire for what is genuinely good takes us beyond our limited concerns for individual and group satisfactions into the concrete universe of value in its full sweep and structured complexity.

But what is value and how do we learn to discover and actualize it?[44] Lonergan's answer to this question builds on the preceding account of intellectual conversion. The foundational principles within the subject are the center and source of cognitional and moral life. As the pure desire to know normatively unfolds in a dynamic pattern of recurrent operations, so does the unrestricted desire for what is good. To use Lonergan's technical language, the *eros* for value *sublates* the *eros* of mind (*Method*, 241–43). It preserves and complements the pure desire to know while raising its achievements to a higher level of importance and difficulty. The intellectual self-transcendence gradually achieved in objective knowledge is augmented and perfected by the moral self-transcendence of a genuinely good life.

As we have seen, the human knowing of reality is chiefly a matter of consistently asking and answering questions for intelligence and reflection. To discover and actualize what is genuinely good we build on the prior attainment of knowledge by raising a new set of questions, questions for moral deliberation (*Method*, 9, 34–36). What practical course(s) of action should we pursue and avoid, what sort of persons and communities should we actively strive to become? The thoughtfully considered answers we personally give to deliberative questions are evaluative practical judgments. To reach true evaluative judgments in particular contexts of action or living, we must carefully attend to the relevant situation; understand the concrete possibilities for change that it offers, as well as the enabling conditions such change effectively requires; and through a series of deliberative insights determine which of the relevant practical possibilities is best under these concrete circumstances. Since the human good is always concrete, our practical knowledge of value must be equally concrete.

But the concrete good is also dynamic.[45] Particular courses of action create new practical situations that require new questions, insights, judgments, and decisions. The concreteness of the good is also inseparable from human historicity. The moral agent is always a situated subject, living in a particular culture, participating in a network of social institutions, actively seeking a good that is simultaneously personal and social. Within the subject's social and cultural embeddedness, functional differentiation is increasingly at work. Individual agents perform different practical tasks and bear different responsibilities. Because of their distinct social roles, they are responsible for different kinds of knowledge; they master different arts and skills. Although there is a common fund of virtues moral subjects should gradually acquire, they exercise those virtues in different ways depending on their particular roles, responsibilities, and obligations.

To discover and actualize the common good in a complex modern society requires a vast amount of objective knowledge. Since this knowledge is differentially distributed, the many subjects who possess it must operate in concert, coordinating their insights, deliberations, decisions, and actions so that the appropriate goods are actually achieved. But high levels of knowledge and skill, even orderly social cooperation, are not enough. As Aristotle trenchantly observed, the skilled physician can kill as well as cure.

So while objective knowledge is clearly necessary, it is not sufficient for responsible choices, virtuous actions, and laudable outcomes. Individually and collectively we must be as deeply committed to enacting the good as we are to discovering what it is. And since there are many levels and types of value, many genuine goods—vital, social, cultural, personal, and religious—we must recognize all of them and their hierarchical relations and functional interdependencies (*Method*, 30–34; CWL, 17:14–15, 140–42, 336–37). Based on this comparative knowledge of the universe of value, we must also be willing to subordinate lesser to greater goods, partial to comprehensive goods, transient to lasting goods as concrete circumstances require. This normative willingness is fortified by the development and refinement of our moral feelings. Both moral knowledge and moral choice are deeply enriched by our *intentional responses* to value, the developing knowledge of the heart that complements the practical insights of the mind. Under the sway of moral conversion, as a result of consistent fidelity to the transcendental precepts, the whole person, at all levels of consciousness, becomes committed to the actualization of value and deeply distressed at each personal or communal failure to achieve it.

The normative picture we have just described, however, is unrealistic, for it omits the tangled knot of our human condition. Our unrestricted desires for knowledge and value invariably compete with self-centered desires and needs. The knowledge required to discover and actualize the good is hard to achieve and often pursued for quite different ends. Fidelity to the transcendental precepts is invariably compromised by bias and societal pressure. Our cultural heritage is morally ambiguous and frequently prejudiced against the active pursuit of the highest values. And our moral feelings can be twisted and corrupted in subtle and devious ways. Sustained moral self-transcendence appears to be beyond our limited grasp (CWL, 3:652–54).

Given our personal frailty, our common susceptibility to bias and sin, and the uneven effects of our social and cultural belonging, we invariably fail as individuals, and even more frequently in our collective endeavors. Of even greater concern, we are persistently tempted to rationalize our failures by justifying their repeated occurrence. These ideological justifications extend beyond our personal sins to the structural injustices of whole societies, and to the distorted priorities of a decadent culture (*Method*, 40, 117). Thus a first condition of achieving authenticity is candid acknowledgment of our moral failures and an explicit unmasking and repudiation of all ideological arguments. Inevitable failures of self-transcendence can be remedied if they are openly acknowledged and responsibly addressed. Both human learning and living are continually self-correcting processes based on correcting acknowledged mistakes. In stark contrast, moral aberration easily becomes habitual and entrenched when fortified by self-deception and seductive ideological excuses.

In the authentic subject, intellectual and moral development are profoundly strengthened and deepened by moral conversion: by the existential commitment to orient our lives by the unrestricted *eros* for value, by consistent fidelity to the transcendental precepts, by an habitual willingness to decide and act on the basis of true evaluative judgments, by the candid acknowledgment of our various moral failings and flaws. Moral self-transcendence requires repeated withdrawal from the many sources of inauthenticity and critical attention to the existential and social factors that promote their occurrence.

Lonergan bases his existential and social ethics on the existential priority of moral conversion, on our personal and communal commitment to actualizing all that is really worthwhile (*Method*, 51–52). The *terminal values* of ethics are discovered through true evaluative judgments and actualized through responsible decisions and actions. They are the objective ends or goods that authentic subjects and communities deliberately and consistently pursue. The *originating ethical values* include the foundational principles in the self-transcendent subject, the enduring fruits of the subject's intellectual and moral development, and the existential conversion of her intellectual and moral being. It is originating values that make the discovery, achievement, and preservation of terminal values possible. When this transcendental dependence of actualized value on the moral subject's authentic reality and performance becomes clearly recognized, then originating values should properly be included among the shared terminal values that we actively seek to promote both personally and communally.

The subject's personal appropriation of moral conversion has an added dialectical benefit. It enables her to understand and appraise the several counterpositions in ethics and value theory. The central obstacle to knowing and doing what is good is the implicit or explicit refusal of moral self-transcendence. When this refusal is compounded by persuasive ideologies justifying moral aberration, then the factual evidence appears to suggest that the leading moral counterpositions in our culture, skepticism, emotivism, and moral relativism, are probably true. But this appearance of truth depends on the prevailing outlook and conduct of morally unconverted subjects whose philosophical judgments violate one or more of the foundational principles at the core of their own being. Without the corrective insights elicited by genuine moral conversion, this performative incoherence goes largely unnoticed and metaethical disagreements seem permanently intractable.

Religious conversion is particularly important in an ecumenical and secular age like our own (*Method*, 243–44). The ecumenical spirit heightens our awareness of religious pluralism. Those who embrace it become increasingly aware of the varieties of religious experience and expression, both now and in centuries past. In our increasingly secular age, particularly in the North Atlantic world, believers and nonbelievers live and work side by side.[46] They marry, raise children, participate in common activities, promote and pursue common ends. In numerous social settings, they show mutual respect and affection for each other, though, in an important sense, they live in different worlds. Or better, they orient themselves within different subjective horizons that only partly overlap and coincide.[47]

In such an openly secular society, religious faith cannot be taken for granted. To use Charles Taylor's illuminating phrase, the underlying conditions of religious belief are substantially changed (*Secular Age*, 3). The public critics of religion become increasingly assertive. The masters of suspicion deny the authenticity of religious faith. Ontological naturalists exclude even the possibility of transcendent being. Exclusive humanists assert the irrelevance of God in the conduct of human affairs. Religious differences among believing communities appear to defy rational resolution. The complementary relations between faith and reason, divine grace and created nature, charity and justice become sharply disputed, particularly within the many fragmented communities of faith. Even coreligionists cannot agree whether the intellectual and moral achievements of modernity strengthen or weaken the prospects of religion in our time.

What is *religious conversion* and how is it relevant to our comprehensive cultural crisis? Lonergan emphasizes the foundational principles that shape the converted subject's expanding horizon. Intellectual conversion puts the unrestricted *eros of mind* at the center of our cognitive life. Moral conversion makes our evaluative judgments and practical and existential decisions answerable to the unrestricted desire for value. As already noted, moral conversion sublates its intellectual counterpart. The unrestricted pursuit of knowledge and truth, though intrinsically good and in fact indispensable, does not exhaust the universe of value. Objective knowing remains a critical part but not the whole of authentic living (CWL, 4:219–21).

Is the human quest for self-transcendence completely fulfilled within the horizon of these core foundational principles? It is essential to remember that the transcendental principles are unrestricted in their intended scope. We desire to know all that exists; we long to actualize all that is good. Though our actual knowledge and achievement are always finite and imperfect, our intellectual and moral aspirations are limitless. We long to know God, if there is a God. We long to do God's will, if the divine will is good and can be credibly discerned and enacted (*Method*, 101–3).

Despite their critical importance, the philosophical quest for truth and the practical quest for value yield uneven results, as the tangled knot of history makes clear. Lonergan has shown a way, in principle, to resolve the dialectical conflict of positions and counterpositions, but the existential demands of his solution are daunting. Though we have a natural capacity for self-transcendence, and are universally called to authenticity, we are invariably prone to bias and sin. Exclusively human responses to the reality of error and evil, though clearly laudable, are of limited efficacy (CWL, 3:710–15, 749–50).

In our previous discussion of human subjectivity, we have omitted any reference to *being in love*. We have acknowledged the transcendental desires of the subject, its unrestricted longing for knowledge and value. But we have neglected the concreteness and singularity of falling-in-love, of being-in-love with a particular person, a particular family, intimate friends, our native land (*Method*, 105). These powerful forms of being-in-love are also horizon shaping. As long as they remain consciously vital and effective, they shape the dramatic and existential horizon in which we live. These identity-defining loves also summon us to self-transcendence. The well-being of our spouse, our parents, our children, our friends, our country becomes central to our personal moral concern. We are ready to sacrifice ourselves, freely and generously, for all that we authentically love.

We can also love God in an analogous manner, though the God whom we love is surrounded in infinite mystery. Lonergan repeatedly insists that our human love of God has its conscious origin in God's prior love for us (*Method*, 105–12). By nature, we have an *eros* for union with God; through divine grace we can fall in love with God in an unrestricted manner. The interior gift of God's love, freely given to all, is a *supernatural* principle consciously operating within the life of the incarnate subject. In theological terms, it is an operative grace that perfects and completes our created nature, sublating its natural capacities and aspirations (*Method*, 241). In biblical language, operative grace turns the fallen sinner's heart of stone into a heart of flesh (Ezek. 11:19, 36:26). The heart of stone is basically in love with itself (Augustine's *cupiditas*); its effective horizon is restricted to the narrow concerns of the "fat Ego."[48] The heart of flesh (*caritas*), by contrast, is in love with an unknown God whom it faithfully serves but cannot see.

The gift of God's love fully respects human freedom. Each of us responds to its interior call in a uniquely personal way. But when human nature and divine grace cooperate and love's operative power lessens the counterpull of bias and sin, then the love of God can become more important than any other reality or value in our life. Our intellectual and moral horizons dramatically expand beyond the realm of created nature and human achievement. We enter in awe and silence the mysterious realm of divine transcendence in which God is both known and unknown. Known in and through the religious experience of unrestricted love, unknown in essence, power, and glory.

Religious conversion occurs when the existential subject responds to the gift of God's love in a wholehearted way, when being in love with God becomes the orienting principle of her life (*Method*, 105–7, 242–44). But God's infinite love for created being is generous and all-embracing. God wills us to know and love all that is genuinely good. Through religious conversion, our profound love of God *sublates* the other forms of being-in-love. We now can love spouse, parents, children, friends, and country both in themselves and as created gifts entrusted to us by God for their care and protection. Nothing that God has created, nothing that is humanly authentic, nothing that is genuinely good is incompatible with religious conversion, which summons us to love God, our neighbors, and the whole of creation to the best of our power in the light of their intrinsic worth.

From the enlarged perspective of religious conversion, the intellectual pursuit of truth, the moral pursuit of value, and the authentic achievements they yield are blessed by God as good and holy. The created gifts we receive are intended for the stewardship of nature, the benefit of humankind, and the glory of God. Divine grace cooperates with human nature and strengthens its operation; grace conflicts only with bias and sin, which do violence to nature and limit its intended efficacy. However, grace can lessen the power of sin by healing the subjective and objective wounds that it causes. Sin inherently resists the operation of grace, as violence resists the working of nature and art, and as bias resists the quest for self-transcendence. Grace is creative, redemptive, and horizon expanding; sin is destructive, resistant, and horizon confining. And we are the tangled dramatic knots in whom the dynamic vectors of nature, sin, and grace concretely and repeatedly converge.

The pull and counterpull of grace and sin highlight another aspect of religious conversion. In the history of religion the language of conversion is inseparable from the divine call to repentance (Matt. 3:2, 4:17). The prophets call Israel to repent of its sins against the imperatives of the law and the covenant. Jesus commands his disciples to repent, to fast, pray, and give alms, for the spirit is willing but the flesh is weak. The stricken Saul is called to repent for his pharisaic hatred of Christ and the early church. In writing his *Confessions*, Augustine sees the need to repent whenever he fails to love God with his whole heart, mind, and strength. As he humbly acknowledges, full religious conversion is effectively resisted by the rival and powerful loves of our past life. Our sinful self-centeredness makes it nearly impossible to devote our selves wholly to God. Even the lives of the saints reflect this intense and ongoing personal struggle between *caritas* and *cupiditas*, between holiness and sin.

In all three forms of conversion, authenticity requires the constant withdrawal from inauthenticity (*Method*, 52, 110). We can understand the divine command to love God and neighbor; we can see the rightness of faithfully obeying this basic imperative. Yet we repeatedly fail to honor our knowledge and prior commitment. "The good that we would we do not; the evil that we would not we do" (Rom. 7:19). But the providential God whom we seek is merciful as well as exigent, forgiving as well as commanding. And if we, despite our evident personal knottedness, are willing to forgive those who trespass against us, how much more compassionately will God forgive us, men and women of contrite heart, whom God has created and loves unconditionally.

But if the gift of God's love is given to all, then why is unbelief so prevalent? Some further distinctions are necessary to clarify this important and inescapable question. Like the unrestricted desires for knowledge and value, the religious experience of God's love first occurs at the level of consciousness. Like the transcendental notions, it is immanent and operative but not yet thematized or objectively known. As a spiritual principle, it orients our being in an unrestricted manner, but it gives us no sensible or imaginable object on which to focus our attention. We can see and touch our spouse, embrace our children and our parents, enjoy the physical presence of our friends and companions. In each case we love them in and through their sensible presence to us. But the God whom we love in faith cannot be seen, heard, or touched with our senses. Nor can God be fully understood with our mind and our judgment. At the level of religious experience we know God through the gift of divine love, a love that is singularly strange and mysterious, unrestricted in nature, indeterminate in content. This love draws us into wonder and silence; it fills us with awe and repentance; it calls us to personal holiness and transformation of life.

I have been describing religious experience as a reality in the individual subject. Because God's love is given to all, it also draws human beings into communities and into the rites, myths, and creeds of communal expression (*Method*, 118–19). Our intellectual, moral, and religious experience is always historically situated. But the common features of our spiritual life are interpreted differently in different societies and cultures, and transmitted across the generations in strikingly different religious traditions. In our contemporary Western culture, profoundly shaped by the critical revolutions in natural science and historiography, by a heightened sense of cultural pluralism, by a deep repugnance for the sins and violence committed and justified in the name of religion, by unresolved disagreements on philosophical and moral questions, and by a shared attachment to individual rights, democratic liberty, technological power, and the benefits of ordinary life, religious phenomena receive, not surprisingly, markedly different personal and cultural interpretations. Atheism, agnosticism, religious skepticism, a vague and occasional sympathy for our common spiritual longings, as well as a bewildering array of religious beliefs, modes of worship, and confessions, compete openly for our allegiance and commitment.

The existential dialectic of religious positions and counterpositions is particularly intense because the personal stakes are so high. Nothing matters more ontologically than the existence or nonexistence of God. Nothing matters more epistemically than the truth or error of our religious beliefs. Nothing matters more existentially than the personal resolve or refusal to love God and our neighbor with the whole of our being. The hermeneutics of suspicion, the ethics of unbelief, the disenchantment of nature and history, the ambiguous histories of the great religions, the apparent intractability of religious disagreements, the unprecedented evil of the twentieth century—these cultural realities deeply affect us all, believer and nonbeliever alike. The institutional and cultural conditions of religious belief, as Taylor has argued, are strikingly different in our secular age. Although they certainly do not preclude religious faith and commitment, they make personal authenticity and religious conversion more challenging than ever before.[49]

THE *VETERA*

Let us turn now from the existential demands on the critical interpreter to the task of interpretation itself. For the sake of simplicity and economy, we shall divide that task into two parts: critically appropriating the *vetera*, critically appropriating the *nova*. We shall start with the *vetera*, the classical and medieval traditions in philosophy and theology. To keep things even simpler we shall limit the scope of our project to four seminal thinkers, Plato, Aristotle, Augustine, and Aquinas, the premodern authors whose intellectual influence on Lonergan was most profound and enduring. What did Lonergan appropriate from these thinkers in the course of reaching up to their minds?

The first thing he learned was to distinguish the past from the received tradition (CWL, 2:222–27). The sympathetic interpreter of the *vetera* must be alert to the recurrent contrast between Plato and Platonism, Augustine and hyper-Augustinianism, Thomas and traditional Thomism. To substantiate this contrast the interpreter must understand not only the ancient texts but also the realities the texts are about (*Method*, 156–58; CWL, 3:769). This requires significant intellectual and moral development, even personal conversion, for when we begin the interpretive process our minds are normally on a radically different plane from the minds of the authors we seek to understand.

The philosophical and theological exegesis of important texts is of more than scholarly interest. While respecting the exigencies of critical hermeneutics and historiography, Lonergan's principal interpretive purpose is *critical retrieval*: to determine what is intellectually enduring, what is still valid and relevant, in the discoveries of our great antecedents. The modern emphasis on intellectual innovation needs to be balanced by respect for epistemic continuity, especially when the cultural context and vocabulary of our predecessors are significantly different from our own. But sympathetic interpretation does not preclude critical appraisal. The dialectical contrast between positions and counterpositions applies to the ancients as well as the moderns. Their implicit or explicit answers to the questions of cognitional theory, epistemology, metaphysics, ethics, and theology must be judged on the basis of the interpreter's personal development, self-appropriation, and existential conversion. This is simply to repeat, in a new expository context, the substantive claims of the preceding section.

Important Contrasts

Two recurrent contrasts appear regularly in Lonergan's metalevel criticism. First, he insists that we carefully distinguish the enduring discoveries of earlier thinkers from a *classicist* interpretation of their achievement (CWL, 17:73–75). Second, he contrasts two very different accounts of human cognition: intellectualism and conceptualism (*Second Collection*, 74–75). Let me briefly elaborate on the nature and purpose of these important normative contrasts.

Classicism. How does the enduring classical tradition differ from classicism? Classicism is an ahistorical interpretation of the retrievable past. Because it is ahistorical it tends to treat earlier human achievements as static rather than dynamic, as final and permanent rather than as significant but provisional stages in an ongoing intellectual and moral process. When viewed in this ahistorical light, classical achievements become normative for all of history. But this is a burden the past cannot bear without blocking future development. Thus, as Lonergan consistently argued in his post-*Insight* lectures, the classicist interpreter uncritically embraces the Aristotelian theory of science, a normative and timeless concept of education and culture, an abstract metaphysical anthropology, a propositional model of intellectual and moral foundations, a deductive approach to epistemic integration (*Second Collection*, 1–9, 98–99, 110).

Classicist thinkers are certainly justified in emphasizing normativity and principle. As we've already noted, Lonergan explicitly shares these traditional heuristic concerns. But classicism locates the sources of normativity in abstract essences and immutable propositional truths, rather than in the concrete structural invariants of the intentional subject (the dynamic transcendental principles we have identified). Lonergan's normative principles, by contrast, are erotic and exigent, dynamic and unrestricted, open to continuous development, dialectically capable of distinguishing growth from decline. They provide an immanent, operative transcultural basis for a critical encounter with cultural pluralism.

Intellectualism vs. Conceptualism. Classicists bring an ahistorical perspective to the understanding and appraisal of human achievement. The needed corrective to classicism is critical historical mindedness. Conceptualism is a specific version of classicism in the fields of cognitional theory and epistemology. According to Lonergan, it is one of the recurrent counterpositions that regularly surfaces in the history of philosophy. He first discovered conceptualism's critical importance in studying traditional accounts of Aquinas's theory of cognition. Lonergan's independent study of Aquinas convinced him that Thomas is an intellectualist rather than a conceptualist, as many Thomistic commentators had claimed. But what is the philosophical import of this pointed dialectical contrast? What does an intellectualist affirm that a conceptualist denies or omits? I shall quote Lonergan liberally on this matter, since I'm unable to improve on his concise formulations. The intellectualist believes:

> That there exists an act of understanding (*intelligere*), 2) that rational consciousness (*dicere*) is the act of understanding as the ground and origin of inner words of conceptualization and judgment, and 3) that inner words proceed from acts of understanding, not on some obscure analogy of the emergence of terminal states at the end of material processes, but as act from act. Thus the center of the Thomist analysis of intellect is held, not by such products of intelligence in act, as concepts, nexus, judgments, syllogisms, but by intelligence in act itself. Even reasoning for Aquinas is not simply a matter of concepts and judgments, but principally a progress from a less to a more complete act of understanding. (CWL, 2:152–53)

Against this view of intellect, there stands only its privation. Conceptualists conceive human intellect only in terms of what it does; but their neglect of what intellect *is* prior to what it *does* has a variety of causes.

Most commonly, they do not advert to the act of understanding. They take concepts for granted; they are busy working out arguments to produce certitudes; they prolong their spontaneous tendencies to extroversion into philosophy, where they concentrate on metaphysics and neglect gnoseology. (CWL, 2:194)

When philosophers approach cognitional theory through the heuristic perspective of *logic* rather than *method*, they tend to overlook the importance of insights. Logical analysis deals with concepts, propositions, arguments, the intelligible *products* of acts of understanding. Methodological analysis (intentionality analysis) deals with all the data of intentional consciousness: the unrestricted desire to know, the intellectual and critical questions it generates, the acts of direct and reflective insight to which questioning may lead, the propositional answers and judgments that flow from these insights, the exigent norms to which reasonable judgments are critically held. "It is only by close attention to the data of consciousness that one can discover insights, acts of understanding with the triple role of responding to inquiry, grasping intelligible form in sensible presentations, and grounding the formation of concepts. So complex a matter will never be noticed as long as the subject is neglected, and so there arises conceptualism: a strong affirmation of concepts, and a skeptical disregard of insights" (*Second Collection*, 74).

As insights fulfill three cognitive functions, so conceptualism has three basic defects: (1) an antihistorical immobilism: "while concepts do not change on their own, still they are changed as the mind that forms them (develops)" (*Second Collection*, 74); (2) an excessive abstractness: "conceptualism ignores human understanding and so it overlooks the concrete mode of understanding that grasps (intelligible form) in the sensible (data) itself. Conceptualism is confined to a world of abstract universals, and so its only link with the concrete is the relation of universal concepts to intuited particulars" (*Second Collection*, 75); (3) conceptualists recognize an abstract concept of being, but overlook the concrete *notion* of being, the unrestricted desire to know. "To advert to this (transcendental notion) clearly and distinctly, one must note not only that concepts express acts of understanding but also that both acts of understanding and concepts respond to questions. The notion of being first appears in questioning. Being is the unknown that questioning intends to know, that answers partly reveal, that further questioning presses on to know more fully" (*Second Collection*, 75).

In these critical passages from *Verbum* and "The Subject" (in *Second Collection*), Lonergan draws on important discoveries from the past to illumine and criticize philosophical assumptions still powerful in the present. The intellectualism he discovered in Aquinas occurred in a medieval heuristic context. In *Insight*, Lonergan carefully extended Thomas's intellectualism into the complex domains of contemporary inquiry. This notable transposition was an exemplary case of Lonergan's mission, *vetera novis augere et perficere*. The acts of direct and reflective understanding thematized in *Insight* occur in the context of modern mathematics, the natural sciences, common sense, textual exegesis, and philosophy. They respond to different questions from the philosophical discoveries Aquinas achieved, and they express themselves in very different concepts and theories. But the philosophical conclusions of *Verbum* and *Insight* are isomorphic in nature (CWL, 4:133–41). Both Lonergan and Aquinas rely on the same foundational principles; both support similar cognitional theories (*mutatis mutandis*); both affirm analogous versions of critical realism in epistemology and metaphysics.

Still, there is an important difference between Aquinas's and Lonergan's theories of human understanding. Following Aristotle, Aquinas developed and expounded his cognitional theory in metaphysical categories (CWL, 2: chap. 3). His rational psychology applied Aristotelian concepts and principles to the cognitive life of the soul. Lonergan believed that the subtlety and acuteness of Thomas's discoveries could not have occurred without close attention to the data of intellectual and rational consciousness (CWL, 2:56). But while Thomas's cognitional theory may have actually depended on a nuanced phenomenology of the subject, Aquinas himself did not thematize his method of discovery. He explicitly relied on a faculty psychology borrowed from Aristotle and Augustine, which he then developed and refined in a truly exceptional manner. Despite Aquinas's systematic brilliance, his intellectualist conclusions are expressed in metaphysical terms and relations that can no longer be taken for granted by a contemporary cognitional theorist.

For Lonergan, in contrast to Aristotle and Aquinas, metaphysics is no longer the basic philosophical discipline. In the third stage of cognitive meaning, when the empirical sciences and historical scholarship have become relatively autonomous and specialized, philosophers must develop their own specialized method and vocabulary (*Method*, 83 and 95). In Lonergan's judgment, philosophy must now become the empirical and critical study of the polymorphic data of consciousness. Its distinctive method is the intentional analysis of conscious subjectivity. Its fundamental questions concern the desires, operations, norms, and patterns of human consciousness as well as their epistemological, ontological, and moral implications. Its basic terms and relations refer to intentional operations and their normative unfolding in the authentic subject's conscious experience.

What does this significant heuristic contrast imply for the critical appropriation of Aquinas's intellectualism? Historically, Thomas's philosophy must be understood in its own terms, and in its own cultural context. This is what Lonergan's *Verbum* does so well. But to retrieve Aquinas's discoveries and show their relevance for contemporary philosophical debates, they have to be *transposed* from medieval faculty psychology into contemporary intentionality analysis. This is what *Insight* and Lonergan's post-*Insight* writings do superbly. That many of Aquinas's discoveries can survive this transposition with their illuminatory power intact is a sign of their enduring epistemic validity.

Plato

What did Lonergan philosophically appropriate from his study of Plato? What noteworthy and enduring contributions did he attribute to the master of the philosophical dialogue? What criticisms did he make of Plato's cognitional theory and metaphysics? I shall be deliberately brief and selective in answering these exegetical questions.[50]

Enduring Contributions. Plato recognized the philosophical importance of self-appropriation and conversion (*periagoge*). The pedagogical purpose of the written dialogues is psychagogic, to mediate in their readers the intellectual and moral conversions that Socrates's dramatic interlocutors typically resist. The climactic myths in the middle dialogues summon both interlocutors and readers to a basic existential decision on the right way, the just way, to live.[51]

Plato attributes unrestricted desires for knowledge and goodness to the human soul. The intellectual and moral desires of the soul internally conflict with its sensitive appetites and social ambitions. The individual soul is shown to be open, dynamic, restless, conflicted, and oriented in its vertical ascent toward higher levels of being and value. As the dialogues unfold, the psychagogic drama highlights the existential difficulties of sustaining and completing this demanding erotic ascent. Because the intellectual and moral desires of the soul are unrestricted, human inquiry is never final and complete. The highest attainable wisdom may be *learned ignorance*, in which we discover that we do not know what we desire to know most profoundly. Socrates deliberately chose to define his own "wisdom" in these provocative paradoxical terms.[52]

The drama of human knowing and living is fundamentally dialogical. In our shared inquiry with others, in the internal dialogue we conduct with ourselves, we grow and develop by asking and answering questions. The animating spirit with which we inquire reflects our psychological complexity, as the *eristic* spirit of the sophist is bent on dialogical victory over his rivals, while the Socratic *dialectical* spirit is devoted to attaining comprehensive truth, even when that truth is personally or politically unwelcome.[53] Plato's written dialogues effectively blend existential and political drama with complex philosophical arguments. Frequently, the key to the argumentative *aporia* on the dialogue's textual surface is a performative inconsistency between what Socrates's interlocutors *say* and what their dramatic conduct (what they *do*) actually reveals. Unresolved philosophical disagreements tend to have their source in deeper existential and cultural conflicts that only moral and intellectual conversion can unravel. When these conversions regularly fail to occur, philosophical *aporia* results.

In the dialogues, Socrates is the question man *par excellence*. Each answer to a Socratic question is followed by a further question that, potentially, carries the dialogue to a higher epistemic and moral level (though the dramatic interlocutors frequently refuse the vertical ascent to which Socrates artfully invites them).[54] Lonergan treats Socrates's relentless search for intensional definitions of the virtues (definitions true *soli et omni*) as the historical prelude to Aristotle's ethical and political reflections, which introduce the systematic exigence into classical moral theory (CWL, 4:235–36; *Method*, 82).

Following the Pythagoreans and Parmenides, Plato clearly distinguished sense perception (*aisthesis*) from intellection (*noesis*) as intentional operations, and sensible things from intelligible forms (*eide*) as intentional objects. But Lonergan criticized Plato's treatment of this critical psychological distinction at both the cognitional and ontological levels of analysis. From Lonergan's perspective, Plato failed to appreciate the full implications of his own philosophical discoveries.[55] What did Plato fail to see?

Important Limitations. Lonergan credits Plato with recognizing the unrestricted intellectual and moral desires of the soul, the process of relentless dialogical questioning, the provisional nature of our answers to the most important questions, the conflicted soul's enduring need for existential conversion. However, Lonergan is troubled by other aspects of Plato's gnoseology, particularly the cognitional myths and metaphors presented in the dialogues. To be specific, he explicitly criticizes the celebrated myth of the immortal soul recollecting the eternal intelligible forms, and the influential metaphor of the mind's intellectual eye directly intuiting the intelligible realm of being.[56]

To counter the myth of recollection, Lonergan proposes his own intellectualist account of insight into sensible or imaginable data.[57] The intelligible object of a direct act of insight is not an eternal and immutable form, but a determinate formal cause that may or may not be operative within the sensible thing being investigated. To know whether the apprehended cause is actually constitutive of the particular thing requires a further reflective insight that reasonably culminates in an affirmative or negative judgment about the proposed causal claim. Just as direct insights are not intellectual intuitions of abstract intelligible entities, they are also not self-authenticating cognitional episodes. Acts of direct understanding must be completed and confirmed by true reflective judgments for the human knowledge of being to occur.

Pace Plato, the process of intellectual abstraction (*aphairesis*) is explicitly not recollection (*anamnesis*) (CWL, 2:27). In human cognition, the mode of knowing is fundamentally different from the mode of being (from what is actually known). We know concrete sensible things by means of abstract concepts in the soul. But these logical concepts are not eternally present in the soul of the knower waiting to be temporally recalled; rather, they gradually emerge in the temporal course of inquiry as the intelligible products of particular acts of direct insight into sensible or imaginable data. Following Aristotle, Lonergan believes that the human soul at birth desires to achieve comprehensive knowledge but, at the beginning, possesses none of the knowledge it longs for.[58] Only the recurrent and successful completion of the dynamic cognitional process advances the human soul from cognitive potency to actuality.

Though Plato clearly distinguishes sense perception from intellection, Lonergan criticizes his tendency to clarify the nature of noetic acts using visual metaphors.[59] According to Lonergan, human knowledge of reality is based on identity, not the visual confrontation of mind with its object (CWL, 2:142–96). In divine self-knowledge, there is a perfect identity of knower and known. In human knowing, by contrast, a modified identity exists. The intelligible form of the sensible thing to be known is *received* into the soul of the knower according to the immaterial mode of the human intellect. But the same intelligible form exists in the thing known according to its material mode of being. Thus we mortals know the concrete universe of sensible things through abstract concepts and judgments that are intentionally grounded in acts of direct and reflective insight that arise in response to specific questions for intelligence and reflection. We cannot know the intelligible order by looking at it. In fact, we can't know anything (sensible or intelligible) merely by looking.

What are the ontological implications of these pointed cognitional criticisms? On Lonergan's account, Plato sharply separates the epistemic objects of knowledge (*episteme*) and opinion (*doxa*). Opinion is based on our changing perceptions of mutable sensible things, knowledge on our nonsensory intellection of invariant intelligible forms. But how are sensible things and intelligible forms distinguished and related? The ontological separation (*chorismos*) of things and forms is balanced by Plato's insistence on participation (*methexis*). The existence, unity, and intelligible structure of particular things are based on their ontological "participation" in eternal and immutable forms.

Plato correctly insists that intelligible forms are not sensible things; rather, they are immanent ontological principles constitutive of a thing's unity and enduring identity. But Lonergan argues that Plato mistakenly conflates the "formal cause" immanent and operative within the sensible thing (the intentional *object* of direct insight) with the abstract universal essence, "the inner word" within the soul (the conceptual *product* of direct insight) by means of which the sensible thing is known. The formal causes of sensible things are not to be confused with the logical concepts through which those things are known.

Plato's justified epistemic distinction between opinion and knowledge does not require two separate ontological realms, the sensible and the intelligible. In Lonergan's cognitional theory, opinion corresponds to what is thought or conceived by the cognitive subject but not yet reasonably affirmed. For subjects to advance from opinion to knowledge, they must proceed from direct to reflective insights, from intellectual understanding and conception to rationally verified judgment. The critical cognitional distinction between understanding and judgment does not require the ontological separation of form and thing, but the ontological complementarity of intelligible form and act of existence in the constitution of actual things.[60]

It is important to emphasize in concluding these brief but pointed criticisms that Lonergan deeply admires Plato's philosophical greatness and brilliance. He is equally intent, however, on converting Plato's philosophical myths and metaphors into articulate affirmations of psychological and metaphysical fact.

Aristotle

Enduring Contributions. Lonergan identifies Aristotle's spirit of wonder (*thauma*) with the unrestricted desire to know, the *eros* of mind (CWL, 3:34). The intellectual soul, the form of forms, as Aristotle calls it, is radically open and capacious, able to *become* all things in an intentional and immaterial way. *Nous*, intellect, is the godlike capacity of the human soul; empty of forms at birth, it is able, in principle, to *receive* all intelligible forms through the developing process of unrestricted intellectual inquiry.

Intellectual wonder about sensible experience invariably gives rise to questioning. For Aristotle, philosophical questions are of two kinds: questions of essence and essential predication (what, why) whose answers take the form of logical definitions and demonstrations; and questions of existence (whether) whose answers take the form of affirmative and negative judgments about what is (CWL, 2:26–29). As a result, human knowledge is also of two kinds: commonsense knowledge, knowledge that this sensible thing is an X and that this X has property Z; and theoretical or causal knowledge, knowledge why this thing is an X and why it has property Z as an essential attribute of its being (*Metaphysics*, 1.981a15–981b13).

Aristotle recognizes the cognitive transition from experiential knowledge (that) to theoretical science (why) as a significant intellectual development. Theoretical inquiry regularly occurs within the heuristic matrix of the four causes: matter, form, agent, and end (*Physics*, 2.3–5; *Metaphysics*, 1.3–7). These complementary causes are gradually discovered as the relevant answers to the "what" and "why" questions that are asked about sensible substances. Ontologically, the four causes account for the existence, unity, identity, intelligibility, and development of sensible things. Aristotle derives his causal matrix from the critical appropriation of pre-Socratic and Platonic inquiry. On Aristotle's dialectical analysis of the causes, the Ionian naturalists discovered the material cause of being, the Pythagoreans and Platonists the formal cause. None of his predecessors, however, adequately accounted for the agent and final cause or the intelligible interdependence of the causal matrix as a whole (*Metaphysics*, 1, 7).

For Lonergan, Aristotle's discovery and affirmation of direct insights into illuminated phantasms or images is his greatest contribution to cognitional theory (*De Anima*, 3.7.431a16–431b2). Aristotle revealed the functional complementarity of sense perception and intellectual understanding in the cognitional order, and the correlative complementarity of sensible matter and intelligible form in the order of being. These were momentous discoveries of enduring epistemic and ontological importance; they constitute a major philosophical advance over all of Aristotle's antecedents and nearly all of his ancient and modern successors.

Aristotle implicitly recognizes the causal priority of rational psychology (method) over logic. Logic deals with the definition of theoretical terms and the demonstration of essential properties. But definitions and demonstrations are explicit answers to specific theoretical questions, and it is direct insights into the relevant intelligible causes that effectively mediate the cognitional transition from scientific questions (what and why) to explanatory answers. In Lonergan's judgment, Aristotle's comprehensive logical theory, his celebrated *Organon*, despite its enduring historical influence, contains a striking blend of psychological and linguistic insights and oversights.

Although Aristotle articulates his rational psychology in metaphysical categories, Lonergan believes that the key to understanding Aristotle's metaphysics is actually found in his cognitional theory (CWL, 3:700). Thus the sensible matter of substances corresponds to the intentional objects of acts of sense perception and their intelligible forms to the intentional objects of acts of direct understanding (insights). The composite sensible substance, the concretely existing thing, is ontologically distinct from, though causally dependent on, its constitutive matter and form.

Aristotle's philosophical insights are not limited to cognitional theory, epistemology, and metaphysics. In his practical philosophy, he recognizes a fundamental distinction between natural right and convention, between what is just by nature (*physei*) and what is just according to conventional custom or law (*nomos*). But how is this critical normative distinction to be verified in human affairs? Aristotle makes the practical judgments of the genuinely virtuous person the effective criterion of ethical truth (*Nicomachean Ethics*, 2.3, 4). It is the consistently virtuous person, gradually perfected by the intellectual and moral virtues, who is the normative source of reliable evaluative judgments as well as of the virtuous conduct that is objectively worthy of emulation and praise. Lonergan's intentional analysis of evaluative judgments and responsible decisions is largely modeled on Aristotle's "virtuous person" account, though he transposes Aristotle's "virtue ethics" into his own transcendental ethics of authenticity (*Method*, 104–5).

Aristotle's philosophical theology is based on his identity theory of knowledge. In the human knowledge of composite substances, there exists a *modified* intentional identity between knower and known. Thus the sense in act is identical with the sensible in act, the intellect in act is identical with the intelligible in act. But in the case of separate substances that are without matter there is a strict and *perfect* identity of knower and known. Thus, Aristotle's divinity is conceived as an eternal act of perfect self-understanding (*noesis noeseos*). "As Aristotle's metaphysics of matter and form corresponds to a psychology of sense and insight, so Aristotle's separate forms are not Platonic ideas without intelligence but identities of the intelligible in act with intelligence in act" (CWL, 3:700). Though Lonergan's developed philosophy of God is significantly different from that of Aristotle, he does consistently affirm the Aristotelian principle of knowledge by identity for both human and divine knowing.

Important Limitations. Aristotle's cognitional and ethical theories are articulated in metaphysical categories. This is equally true of his sensitive and rational psychology, his theory of human sensibility and intelligence. Lonergan believes that these explanatory theories are heuristically based on the introspective study of human consciousness, but this methodological dependence is never acknowledged or thematized in Aristotle's texts. Instead, Aristotle explicitly relies on a single causal method for the study of plant, animal, and human life. This methodological monism blurs the important distinction between the study of *soul* as the first principle of organic life and the intentional analysis of the conscious human *subject* (CWL, 2:4–6).

With respect to the human soul, Aristotle clearly distinguishes the order of knowing from the order of being. In the order of discovery, psychological inquiry proceeds from objects to operations, operations to habits, habits to natural potencies, and potencies to the determinate essence of souls of a particular kind. At the causal level of being, the order of dependence is reversed. It is the soul's essence that grounds its potencies, its potencies that ground its habits, its habits that ground its operations, and its operations that ground its appropriate objects (*De Anima*, 2.4.415a14–20).

The methodological ambiguity Lonergan criticizes in Aristotle's psychology resurfaces at the level of objects. In a phenomenology of the subject the relevant objects are the intentional contents of the subject's intentional acts, and these acts themselves are first experienced by the subject as prereflexive data of consciousness. But for Aristotle, the relevant cognitive objects are not intentional but causal. They are either efficient causes that bring about psychological acts, or final causes for the sake of which these acts occur (CWL, 2:45).

Although Lonergan is clearly indebted to several aspects of Aristotle's rational psychology and cognitional theory, he wants to preserve Aristotle's seminal insights without relying on his metaphysical principles and presuppositions. This notable heuristic contrast does not mean, however, that Lonergan rejects Aristotle's metaphysics whole cloth. Rather, he wants to augment and critically ground Aristotelian hylomorphism (the ontological complementarity of sensible matter and intelligible form) by basing it on a richer and more dynamic cognitional theory and epistemology.

Aristotle clearly distinguishes questions of essence (what) and questions of existence (whether). And he recognizes the critical role of direct insights in arriving at plausible definitions of natural essences. But he overlooks the equally critical role of reflective insights in grounding true judgments of fact. A result of this oversight is a systemic lacuna in his cognitional theory, a failure to account for the mind's rational transition from tentative and provisional definitions to their warranted assertion in subsequent epistemic judgments. This oversight has deeper implications for Aristotle's theory of science, which overlooks the hypothetical nature of explanatory understanding and the critical need to confirm putative scientific discoveries in the relevant array of empirical evidence. Because scientific judgments, even when confirmed by the presently available evidence, remain open to revision and refinement in the face of new empirical data, the provisional conclusions of science are not permanent truths, and the theoretical systems in which those conclusions are embedded are dynamic, not static, in nature (*Third Collection*, 41–43).

In the *Nicomachean Ethics*, Aristotle sharply distinguishes the virtues of the speculative and practical intellect (6.1139a1–15). The speculative intellect deals with ontological necessity, with universal and invariant causation. The practical intellect deals with contingent human affairs, whose proximate causes are particular and variable. Practical understanding is epistemically subordinate to theoretical insight, as the contingent situations it apprehends are ontologically subordinated to causal necessity. The supreme intellectual virtue is philosophical wisdom (*sophia*), theoretical knowledge of the first causes and principles of being. It is a godlike virtue, which, when actualized, makes mortals analogous to gods. *Phronesis*, the highest virtue of the practical intellect, is restricted to human affairs (*Nicomachean Ethics*, 3.5). While it is the distinctive virtue of statesmen and excellent political leaders, it has no application to the divine.

Aristotle's strict separation of theory and practice, and his ethical subordination of *phronesis* to *sophia*, are ultimately based on mistaken accounts of science and God (CWL, 4:238–40; 3:699–701). *Pace* Aristotle, empirical science does not deal with ontological necessity but with empirically verified contingent possibility. And although human reason knows God to be eternal and necessary, the God of Jewish and Christian revelation acts decisively in history, transforming the conduct of human affairs and providing faith-inspired mortals with an exemplary model of how they should actually live.

Critical Defects. Despite Aristotle's evident intellectual greatness, there are serious problems with particular aspects of his comprehensive philosophy. He lacked an adequate understanding of human historicity and the provisional nature of both personal and communal achievement.[61] Relying uncritically on a normative understanding of culture, he sharply distinguished Greeks from barbarians (non-Greeks), while assigning a privileged and definitive status to the artistic, educational, and political achievements of the classical Hellenes. In this way, Aristotle indirectly contributed to the interpretive outlook that Lonergan designated as classicism.

The influential theory of science outlined in his *Posterior Analytics* is also seriously flawed. For Aristotle, science, *episteme*, was true, certain knowledge of causal necessity (*Posterior Analytics*, 1.2.71b9–161). But empirical science, as we know from its dynamic and continuing history, is: not true, but always on the way to truth; not certain, but probable; not knowledge, but the best available opinion of the relevant scientific community; not based on Aristotle's four causes, but on empirically verified relations of intelligible dependence; not concerned with ontological necessity, but with contingent matters of fact (CWL, 4:238–40).

Moreover, Aristotle conceived of science as an intellectual virtue gradually acquired by an individual mind. But modern science is increasingly specialized and differentiated. Particular sciences define themselves by their distinctive methods and problems; they develop and revise their own research vocabularies; they operate independently of philosophical and metaphysical oversight; they educate and accredit their own selective membership and generate their cumulative knowledge in a collaborative manner. The locus of scientific knowledge today is the ongoing research community, rather than the individual scientist, however eminent and laudable her epistemic contributions (*Third Collection*, 14–15; CWL, 17:222).

An analogous point can be made about modern scholarship and historiography and even for the celebrated Aristotelian virtue of *phronesis*.

The epistemic requirements of practical wisdom today exceed the capacity and insight of any single individual however virtuous and praiseworthy her conduct and judgment.[62] Where Aristotle emphasized individual epistemic achievement, both theoretical and practical, the contemporary emphasis is on communal and collaborative research, collective deliberation, and responsible action in concert.

Aristotle's metaphysics is also significantly flawed. He correctly emphasizes the importance of substantial forms in the constitution of sensible things. But Aristotle's forms are of two distinct kinds: the sensible forms apprehended in sensory intentional acts (Lonergan's *experiential conjugates*), and the intelligible forms grasped in acts of direct understanding (Lonergan's *central* and *explanatory conjugates*) (CWL, 3:458–60). Aristotle's unstable conflation of sensible and intelligible forms blurs the important heuristic distinction between *descriptive* and *explanatory* knowledge, between the knowledge of things in their sensory relations to human perceivers and the knowledge of things in their intelligible relations with one another (CWL, 3:316–17, 320–21). At the advent of modern science, this epistemic and metaphysical confusion led traditional defenders of Aristotle unwisely to oppose the explanatory understanding of important sensible properties like color, heat, and sound.

By failing to acknowledge acts of reflective insight, Aristotle overlooked the cognitional ground of reasonable epistemic judgments. This cognitional oversight had direct metaphysical implications. Aristotle recognized the constitutive ontological role of matter and form in the constitution of sensible substances, but he failed to discover the cognitional basis of the equally important metaphysical distinction between essence and existence, between intelligible possibility (what may be the case) and concretely verified fact (what actually is) (CWL, 3:390–91).

Aristotle's geocentric cosmology suffers from the same defects as his classicist theory of science (CWL, 3:151–52). He divided the natural universe into eternal and mortal substances. The celestial substances are ungenerated and indestructible, moving eternally in perfect cyclical patterns. Terrestrial substances, by contrast, are mortal, though the biological species they instantiate are not. These substances come into being and pass away; they grow and diminish; they change and move in unpredictable patterns that lack the lawful regularity of the heavenly bodies. For Aristotle, the different sciences of nature reflect this basic ontological dualism.

Celestial physics is the scientific study of eternal and necessary substances. Terrestrial physics, however, is limited to the eternality of species and their eternal and necessary properties.

Aristotle's cosmological oversights are structural. He failed to grasp the abstract character of the classical laws of motion; he explicitly repudiated a theoretical science of probability and contingency. He did not realize that the celestial motions themselves occur within provisional schemes of recurrence that emerge and survive in accord with changing schedules of probability. Nor did he realize that the explanatory genera and species on earth emerge and decline through a similar but far more complex evolutionary process (CWL, 3:151–52).

The collaborative dynamism of modern empirical science, the constant revision and refinement of scientific theories, the multiple heuristic structures that contemporary scientists learn to employ are an epistemic reflection of the contingent and emergent character of both natural systems and natural processes. Neither the verified results of science nor the intelligible patterns within the natural universe that they seek to explain are final and permanent. Though Aristotle remains for his many admirers *il maestro di color che sanno* (the master of those who know), Lonergan's critical appropriation of his thought recognizes its singular merits and substantial limitations.

Augustine

Enduring Contributions. Lonergan considered Augustine the greatest of the early Latin fathers. He described Augustine as a brilliant but nonsystematic thinker, who relied on commonsense terms and scriptural idioms to express important philosophical and theological insights (*Method*, 261; CWL, 2:6–9). Many of these insights are reached in the course of Augustine's existential and historical reflections: existential reflection on the concrete events and experiences of his own life, historical reflection on a scripturally based narrative of God's role in human salvation.

Augustine's method of intellectual discovery closely tracks his rational psychology. For Augustine, the human soul has three distinct faculties: memory, the faculty of recollection; intellect, the faculty of understanding and judgment; will, the faculty of choice and love. In his existential reflection, Augustine recalls the complexity and disorder of his life before his religious conversion; in historical reflection, the turbulent history of the human race beginning with the creation and fall of Adam and Eve. Then he relentlessly interrogates what he has personally remembered or recalled, seeking to understand and eventually appraise what has been. His explicit goal is to discover the light memory sheds on the causal presence of God in personal and historical time. The Augustinian understanding of the past is always accompanied by an evaluative judgment on the goodness or evil, the order or disorder, the holiness or sinfulness of what has been remembered and then understood. But moral evaluation is ultimately subordinate to existential choice. Authentic recollection obliges us as chastened sinners to give thanks for God's goodness and mercy; to repent of our sins and our sinfulness; to resolve anew to love God with the whole of our being. Philosophical, even theological, insights are ultimately in the service of deepening religious knowledge and love.

Augustine's reflective knowledge of the human soul is often profound. His most important psychological insights emerge from sustained inquiry into the human capacities of memory, intellect, and will. The seat of the human mind is in memory (*Confessions*, 10.25). Remembrance, recollection, plays an indispensable role in the introspective process that leads to self-knowledge and the knowledge of God.[63] Relentless intellectual questioning and responsive answering are the properly human way to reach a deeper understanding of what is previously sensed and remembered. Though human intellect and will are involved in a pattern of reciprocal causation, the will freely exercises its own power of moral decision and choice. While the three capacities and operations of the soul are distinct, Augustine clearly assigns the greatest existential importance to the will, the faculty of love.

Because the mind's evaluative judgments provide the substantive content of its choices, the human will is an inherently rational capacity; but, as Saint Paul insisted in his letter to the Romans, we can know what is right and still fail to will it and do it (Rom. 7:14–24). This troubling psychological fact is essential to Augustine's nuanced account of the will's freedom. The human will, as created by God, is essentially spiritual and free. But due to Adam's original sin and our own personal sinfulness, the unconverted will of the sinner eventually becomes captive and carnal. With the merciful gift of God's unmerited grace, this captive will can be liberated from sin and proximately restored to its basic goodness. But the good will of the fallen creature remains weak and imperfect. Additional graces are needed to convert a good will into good deeds on a consistent basis (CWL, 1:201–5).

The human will, in all three of these distinguishable phases, as created, as captive, as mercifully liberated by grace, is a free will responsible for its choices. But the created freedom of the captive will, and the imperfect freedom of the liberated will, both require the unmerited support of divine grace and aid: first, to make the captive will good; second, to make the ethical choices of the good will reliable and sound.

As a consequence of Adam's primordial disobedience and our own sinful history, we are all the fallen captives of sin. The harmful consequences of sin affect the human soul as a whole, making us intellectually blind, morally weak, and religiously proud and complacent. Burdened and weakened as we are, the sinful soul requires a threefold conversion to recover a state of good order and good operation. Divine graces are necessary if these complementary forms of psychic conversion are to be effective and enduring in the individual's subsequent life.

Intellectual conversion: Augustine originally identified the real with the sensible and corporeal.[64] He even thought of God and the soul as highly refined physical entities. Through his intellectual conversion, which was mediated by his study of "the Platonists," he learned to distinguish the intelligible from the sensible order, spiritual from corporeal operations, eternal from temporal realities. In each of these different regions of being, the ontological distinctions are hierarchical, so that the defining loves of the well-ordered soul subordinate the lesser mode of being (sensible, corporeal, temporal) to the greater (intelligible, spiritual, eternal). All types of being, created and creative, temporal and eternal, corporeal and spiritual, are intrinsically good, though created goodness is wholly dependent on its divine causal origin, the ontological perfection of God, the eternal creator of all things.[65]

Moral conversion is necessary because the sinful soul is disordered in its evaluative judgments and choices. When this moral disorder becomes habitual and entrenched, the unconverted soul becomes captive to sin. As a divinely created soul, it still longs, at some level, to know and do what is good, but as a habitually sinful soul it regularly confuses good and evil, as well as lesser and greater goods. The captive soul becomes proud and attached to its habitual priorities and choices and stubbornly resists all human efforts to reverse them. Only the merciful grace of God, working through the created longings of the soul, can bring about moral conversion, which unfolds in two complementary stages: through God's operative grace, the bad will again becomes good (the heart of stone becomes a heart of flesh); through cooperative grace, the now liberated good will gradually becomes stronger and capable of consistently good performance.[66]

The human will is the spiritual faculty of choice and love. What we love and how we love are the deepest measures of our identity as spiritual beings.[67] The dominant loves of the religiously unconverted soul are spiritual expressions of *cupiditas*, the disordered love of the sinful self to the neglect or contempt of God. *Caritas* is the spiritual antithesis of *cupiditas*. It is the wholehearted love of God and neighbor joined to interior contempt for the disordered and sinful self. *Caritas* is the unmerited gift of God perfecting the human will and reordering the whole life of the soul to the knowledge, love, and service of God and neighbor.

Religious conversion is a long, difficult, inconsistent process, never to be completed in this life. Only Jesus of Nazareth, the incarnate Son of God, reveals the fullness of *caritas* in human form. The critical distinction between *cupiditas* and *caritas* is the central theme not only in Augustine's *Confessions* but also in *De Civitate Dei*, *The City of God*, his eschatological narrative of the ongoing historical conflict between the two antithetical loves and the two warring cities they serve to define (*City of God*, 14.28).

In the course of experiencing his three conversions, Augustine became a deeply faithful Christian. But, as the *Confessions* consistently reveal, he regularly sought to understand and articulate the intelligible content of his Christian faith. His protracted and painful conversion convinced him that in spiritual and eternal matters, he first needed to believe in order to understand (*crede ut intelligas*) (CWL, 1:10, 2:219). However, that hard-won conviction did not lessen his effort to understand what he slowly came to believe. Augustine always acknowledged that his human understanding was imperfect and limited, and that the mystery of God was profound and inexhaustible. Still, he regularly attempted to find spiritual analogies based on his own self-knowledge to illuminate the divine mystery, however imperfectly. Lonergan was particularly impressed by Augustine's account of the soul's inner word, on which Augustine explicitly relied in trying to understand the mystery of the Trinity. In Lonergan's judgment, Augustine's Trinitarian reflections based on the analogy of the tripartite soul represent the high-water mark in early Christian attempts to understand the intelligible content of their traditional faith (CWL, 2:9).

Important Limitations. Despite his intellectual greatness, Augustine was not a systematic theologian. In contrast to Aquinas, he did not develop a comprehensive Christian theology, intelligibly unified and ordered in theoretical terms and relations. This epistemic limitation clarifies but does not lessen the importance of his numerous insights, many of which were developed to meet the polemical controversies of his age.

Although Augustine effectively distinguished the goodness of creation, the corruptive force of sin, and the healing power of grace, he lacked a clearly articulated distinction between the *natural* and *supernatural orders of being* (CWL, 1:17–20). In particular, he failed to distinguish clearly between natural and supernatural causes, habits, and operations. As a result, in his very important account of grace and freedom, he sharply opposes sin and grace, *cupiditas* and *caritas*, but is much less clear about the enduring powers of created nature, even when weakened by sin, and about the perfecting as well as healing powers of divine aid. The Augustinian dualism of sin and grace is explicit and prominent in his theology. Aquinas's subsequent dialectical account of the complex causal interplay of created nature, sin, and grace remains implicit but largely undeveloped in Augustine's remarkable analysis of God and the soul.

Lonergan gives Augustine high praise for his persistent and energetic questioning and for his nonlinguistic conception of the mind's inner word. At the same time, he is explicitly critical of Augustine's cognitional theory and metaphysics. To what oversights and errors does Lonergan object? Augustine fails to correlate the inner words of conception and judgment with the direct and reflective insights that are their intentional causes (CWL, 2:9). He repeatedly relies, as did Plato in the dialogues, on visual metaphors to account for human knowledge of truth and being.[68] To be specific, he believes that objectively valid knowledge requires a direct intuition of the eternal reasons in the divine mind, a human intuition causally enabled by God's power of illumination. For Lonergan, this postulated intellectual intuition of divine ideas is an epistemic fiction, a refined example of what he calls Augustine's "rational empiricism" (CWL, 2:192, 3:437). In addition to criticizing these visual metaphors of intuitive cognition, Lonergan rejects any role in human knowing for a Neoplatonic metaphysics of eternal reasons and divine light.

On Lonergan's alternative cognitional account, the inner word of truth as it functions in human knowledge is not eternal; it is the immanent cognitional product of the reflective insights of the human intellect as they respond to critical questions of reflection. We have no intellectual intuitions of these inner words, whether they are concepts or judgments, or of the enabling divine light, much less a direct spiritual intuition of the mind of God. Human knowledge, Lonergan insists, is ultimately based on perfection and identity, not psychic confrontation and intellectual intuition (CWL, 2:192–99). Moreover the proper objects of our knowledge in this life are the essences or natures of sensible things. When we do gain knowledge of spiritual creatures like ourselves, it is not through internal intuitions of the soul by the soul, but by sustained intellectual reflection (questioning, understanding, and judging) on the experiential data of consciousness.

There are important philosophical distinctions to be drawn between the sensible and the intelligible orders, between intelligible forms and propositional truths, between verifiable judgments and the realities they make known, between corporeal and spiritual operations, and temporal and eternal realities. But none of these ontological distinctions can be understood or confirmed on the basis of the soul's immediate intuitions of nonsensible realities. Augustine's genuine philosophical discoveries, when they occur, are based on the discursive interrogation of his own conscious experience rather than direct intellectual visions of God, the soul, and the timeless order of truth.

Although Lonergan shows profound respect for Augustine in his exegetical commentary and dialectical criticism, his deepest philosophical loyalties are clearly with Aquinas rather than Thomas's great Latin predecessor and teacher.

Aquinas

Enduring Contributions. As Lonergan repeatedly acknowledged, his intellectual debts to Aquinas are immense (CWL, 3:769–70). For reasons of economy, we shall treat these debts concisely under five headings: cultural project; cognitional theory; epistemology and metaphysics; grace and freedom; Trinitarian analogies.

Cultural project: Aquinas taught at the University of Paris in the first half of the thirteenth century. Within that international center of learning, he encountered a diverse set of intellectual and cultural traditions: biblical, patristic, Greek, Roman, Arabic, and Jewish. In his teaching and writing he critically appropriated these inherited sources of knowledge and belief, critically distinguishing their merits from their limitations, integrating their insights, where possible, into his own synoptic theology. For example, he inserted Augustinian insights on the inner word and divine grace into an Aristotelian metaphysical framework, while developing his own original theories of knowing, being, freedom, and the divine (CWL, 1 and 2). Aquinas was a systematic theologian who faithfully expounded traditional Christian teaching on God and creation. In articulating this theology, he regularly attempted to provide an imperfect analogical understanding of the core Christian mysteries. His theological writings refine and develop the inherited medieval distinctions between created nature and grace, created reason and faith, the classical virtues and Christian charity.

Lonergan's cultural project of critical appropriation is modeled on the analogy of Aquinas's dialectical achievement (CWL, 17:293). But Lonergan repeatedly insisted that we live in a very different cultural and historical context from that of Thomas, a context he designated the third stage of cognitive meaning (*Method*, 94–97). This important contextual difference highlights the inescapable question of continuity and discontinuity between the *vetera* and the *nova*. What can we authentically preserve from the past in the face of irreversible modern developments; what must we critically let go? Lonergan believed that the substantive content of Aquinas's thought is still largely valid. However, the technical language for expressing that content and the methods for validating its truth and importance will need to be carefully transposed to meet the specific cultural exigencies of our time (CWL, 17:410; *Second Collection*, 29–53).

Cognitional theory: Aquinas develops his theory of knowledge by relying explicitly on a metaphysical psychology of the soul. Though Aquinas did not thematize his method of discovery in studying the soul, Lonergan believed that he implicitly relied on the introspective examination of his own intellectual and rational consciousness (CWL, 2:5–60). What specifically did Thomas discover and affirm that Lonergan critically appropriated for his own cognitional theory?[69] Both thinkers emphasized the unrestricted human desire to know; a powerful sign of this unlimited dynamic *eros* is that humans naturally desire to know the existence and essence of God. Although the created potential of the human intellect is unrestricted, our intellectual achievement is always finite. Relying on our own powers, we can, in principle, know the existence but not the nature of God. Moreover, human knowledge is essentially discursive rather than intuitive; it gradually develops through asking and answering questions about the disclosures of common experience. But since the stream of our questions always exceeds our capacity to answer responsibly, we humans live in a complex state of knowledge, ignorance, and learned ignorance.

Intellectual acts of understanding, direct and reflective insights, causally mediate between the asking and answering of questions. Acts of direct understanding respond to questions for intelligence; acts of reflective understanding to questions for critical reflection. The enabling conditions, working and epistemic results of these two distinct kinds of intellectual act, correspond to the three stages of intellectual abstraction on which human knowledge depends (CWL, 2:186–90). *Objective* abstraction provides the enabling conditions of insights; *apprehensive* abstraction the operative working of insights; *formative* abstraction expresses the intelligible results of insights. Lonergan models the development and articulation of his own cognitional theory on Aquinas's three stages of intellectual abstraction. Inner words of conception and definition intelligently flow from acts of direct insight as their primary intentional cause; the complementary inner words of judgment and truth flow rationally from acts of reflective insight. For both Aquinas and Lonergan, the logical order of concepts, propositions, and deductive arguments is causally dependent on these prior intentional acts in the unfolding cognitional process. The linguistic order of spoken and written epistemic expressions, in turn, is directly dependent on the mediating logical order for its intelligible meaning and truth, and indirectly dependent on the developing process of cognition from which the entities of logic intentionally flow.

Epistemology and metaphysics: Aquinas is a critical realist in epistemology. True judgments are the epistemic medium through which reality or being is known (*Second Collection*, 17). Human knowing is essentially different from the knowing of animals and infants. Animals know reality immediately through sensing it; the potential scope of their knowledge is thus confined to the sensible order. Human beings, once they have acquired and mastered language, know reality by asking and answering questions about it. Their natural desire to know is unrestricted, as is the scope of the knowledge they inherently seek. But the substantive content of their knowing, as opposed to their unrestricted heuristic intending, is confined to the true judgments they can reasonably defend and affirm.

Aquinas's metaphysics, his comprehensive theory of being, is isomorphic in structure with the core principles of his cognitional theory (CWL, 3:393–96, 4:133–41). Being or reality is heuristically defined as the unrestricted aim of the human desire to know. The order of created nature (what Lonergan calls "proportionate being") is known through a process of human experience, understanding, and judgment. To the degree that it is knowable by humans, the supernatural or divine order (Lonergan's "transcendent being") is known through intellectual grasp and reasonable affirmation. Human knowledge of the supernatural is inherently limited and partial, for the proper objects of our knowledge in this life are the essential natures of sensible things (CWL, 4:136–37).

Natural substances admit of two distinct metaphysical analyses. Individual natural substances are ontologically composed of three metaphysical principles: sensible matter, intelligible form, and existential act (CWL, 4:137). Sensible matter is the intentional content of perceptual acts, intelligible form of acts of direct understanding, and existential act of rational judgments correctly affirmed. Scientific knowledge concerns the essence and existence of sensible substances, where their essence corresponds to what is known through inner words of intelligent definition, and their existence to what is known through inner words of rationally affirmed judgment.

Although Aquinas articulates his cognitional theory and epistemology in metaphysical categories, Lonergan shows how the expository order of Thomas's philosophy can be effectively reversed. When metaphysical discoveries are intentionally correlated with cognitional acts and relations, the true meaning of Aquinas's metaphysical principles is clarified, and the evidential basis for affirming their interdependent existence is made known. By basing philosophical logic, epistemology, and metaphysics on a comprehensive cognitional theory, we also gain a clearer insight into the complex causal and semantic relationships among these distinct but interdependent modal orders: the cognitional, the logical, the linguistic, and the real.[70]

Grace and freedom: Aquinas was a Christian appropriator of Aristotle who deftly inserted Augustinian insights into Aristotle's metaphysical framework. In cognitional theory, he developed an intellectualist interpretation of Augustine's inner words, making them the intelligible products of acts of direct and reflective insight. Aquinas's intellectualism is also apparent in his theology of grace and freedom (CWL, 1:96–98). Here, the rival position to be corrected and amended is *voluntarism* rather than *conceptualism*. If conceptualists affirm the existence of concepts but neglect or deny their causal origin in insights, voluntarists make the exercise of the will's created freedom appear irrational and arbitrary. The central issues in this perennial moral controversy are the intelligible relations among human knowing, choosing, and doing.[71]

In his theory of practical deliberation and choice, Aquinas again found a way to synthesize the discoveries of Augustine and Aristotle. Aristotle had focused his practical philosophy on the virtues, operations, and objects required for laudable moral and political decisions; in his moral psychology, Augustine had emphasized the freedom of the created will, the captivity of the sinful will, and the good will's effective dependence on operative and cooperative graces. Aristotle provided Aquinas with a metaphysical account of human nature and moral development, Augustine with penetrating insights into the crippling effects of sin on created order and both the liberating and healing powers of divine grace. Aquinas's theoretical challenge in synthesizing their very different discoveries was to distinguish the specific contributions of created nature, disruptive sin, and redemptive grace to a credible theory of voluntary action while articulating the internal relations and causal dependencies among these distinct operational principles (CWL, 1:143–49).

Augustine focused his thematic attention on the concrete relations between sin and grace. Sin is the spiritual creature's abuse of the created gift of free will. Grace is God's voluntary gift of unmerited aid to the fallen sinner. Operative grace makes the carnal or sinful will good (its remedial effect is to restore a proportionate order to the objects we love); cooperative grace makes the good will more effective and reliable in its subsequent choices and actions (CWL, 1:4–7). Aquinas adopted these important Augustinian insights, but his theory of moral psychology markedly differed from that of his patristic predecessor. Thomas tended to emphasize the intelligible distinctions and working relations between created nature and grace, between natural reason and faith, between the natural and supernatural virtues.

The core principle of Aquinas's theological anthropology is that divine grace perfects and completes human nature; it does not abolish nature's created integrity (CWL, 3:767; *Method*, 288). Thus, before we can properly understand the power and operation of grace, as well as the crippling effects of sin on human existence, we first have to understand the powers and operations of created nature. What does this important heuristic requirement concretely entail for Aquinas's theoretical treatment of grace and freedom?

Both human reason and will are *natural* powers, powers with their distinctive operations, virtues, and objects. Practical reason, when perfected by the relevant cardinal virtues, can reach true evaluative judgments about the human good and about the best ways to achieve and protect it. Deliberative reason naturally communicates these judgments to the will as the normative basis for its rational choices. Though the substantive content of the will's decisions is specified by the judgments of practical reason, these judgments, by themselves, do not determine the will's actual choices. As both Paul and Augustine correctly concluded, human beings can know what is good and still fail to do it (Rom. 7:19). Although the intentional objects of human choice are dependent on the practical judgments of reason, the free will remains the effective principle of its own operations (CWL, 1:96–98). The will can choose to follow or ignore the counsel of practical reason.

As the intellectual virtues perfect the theoretical and practical judgments of reason, the virtuous habits of the will perfect its recurrent decisions and choices. And as practical reason seeks to discover the full range of goods required for comprehensive well-being, so the *good will* habitually chooses what the concrete attainment of these various goods actually requires. The specific vices of intellect and will, by contrast, habitually distort the reflective judgments of reason and the free decisions and choices of the will.

How then does divine grace perfect and complete the natural operations of human reason and will? Aquinas's answer is nuanced and complex. He believes that divine grace is a free gift of God to the human soul. There are habitual and actual graces freely given to humans; there are also operative and cooperative graces that can be either habitual or actual (CWL, 1:442–50). Habitual graces instill in the appropriate faculties of the human soul the *supernatural* virtues of faith, hope, and charity. Faith enables humans to assent to divine truths we don't fully understand; hope enables us to persevere courageously in living our faith when challenged by the violence of sin, evil, suffering, and death; charity enables us to share in the perfect love, *caritas* or *agape*, of God, and in response to that supreme spiritual gift, to love God wholeheartedly and our neighbor as ourselves (CWL, 3:742–50; Method, 117–18). As the natural virtues, moral and intellectual, help us to discover and achieve natural goods and temporal ends, so the supernatural virtues enable us to share in the goods and blessings of eternal life.

Divine grace elevates human powers, virtues, operations, objects, and ends to a supernatural plane. While respecting human freedom, grace enables us to achieve what human nature, limited to its original created capacities, could never attain. But where does this partial causal analysis leave the reality of sin and its concrete interplay with human nature and grace? For Aquinas, sin does violence to the created goodness of nature; it cripples our native capacities without wholly destroying their power to act. The harmful effects of sin are pervasive. Sin darkens the mind, making the discovery of truth more difficult. It weakens the will, making good and wise choices rarer and harder. When repeated patterns of sin become habitual and entrenched in the personal life of the sinner, then evaluative reason becomes blind and confused in discerning the good, and the sinful will becomes carnal and captive to disordered loves. Habitual sin corrupts the operations of the soul, depriving human beings of their complementary spiritual ends, natural and supernatural.

In the state of habitual sin, the human soul remains *essentially* free (it retains its created nature, desires, and powers) but *effectively* captive (its operative capacities to discern the truth and enact and preserve the good are enslaved and corrupted).[72] To live in habitual sin is the existential condition of intellectual and moral impotence (CWL, 3:650–53). It is a demoralizing and destructive condition from which humans cannot escape through the exercise of their native capacities, for habitual sin severely reduces their operative power and effectiveness. This is the fallen human condition to which the Augustinian analysis concretely applies. The operative grace of God is needed to liberate the captive soul by giving divine light to the mind and divine love to the will. Cooperative grace, in turn, is needed to sustain the struggling mind in its search for truth and to strengthen the wavering will in its daily decisions and choices. Aquinas explicitly affirms the Augustinian analysis of freedom, sin, and grace, but he clarifies and deepens Augustine's moral psychology by situating it within the complementary ontological framework of created nature and elevating grace.

For Aquinas, then, divine grace has many distinguishable aspects: it is perfecting and healing, habitual and actual, operative and cooperative. In all of its distinguishable forms and contributions, grace respects the created freedom and integrity of human beings, each of whom is created in the image and likeness of God. Although sin darkens and distorts that original created image, it cannot ultimately destroy it. In the end, the power of divine grace is stronger than both sin and death.

The Trinitarian analogies: Aquinas was a systematic and synoptic theologian; for all of his remarkable brilliance and insight, Augustine was not. They both actively embraced (though in Augustine's case by anticipation) Anselm's theological project of faith seeking understanding (*Method*, 336–40). They both knew that the mysteries hidden in God were far beyond the reach of the human intellect. Although humans naturally desire to know the essence of God, they lack the intellectual capacity to achieve what they ardently long for.

The divine gift of faith, the inspired revelation of Christ and the Holy Spirit, and the traditional teaching of the church in its doctrinal councils affirm that the God of Abraham, Moses, and Jesus is three in one: three distinct persons in one divine nature. This is the ancient orthodox doctrine that Christians continue to confess in their traditional creeds. But what does this core Christian belief really mean? How can God be three and one at the same time?

Augustine and Aquinas believed that, even with the aid of grace, humans are unable to comprehend this divine mystery fully. Faithful Christians accept and affirm the truth of Trinitarian doctrine without fully understanding its meaning. At the same time, they desire to understand, as well as they can, this central mystery of their faith, and so, in their quest for understanding, they resort to created analogies. Both Augustine and Aquinas also believed that the relevant analogies for thinking helpfully about God are spiritual rather than material in nature. The whole created order is ontologically good, but only spiritual creatures are expressly created in God's own image and likeness (CWL, 2:224).

In searching for spiritual analogies that might offer insight into the Trinity, Augustine developed his account of the inner word. He may have been guided in his thinking by the Johannine symbol of Christ as the eternal Logos, the Divine Word who is in the beginning with God (John 1:1–5). Though God is eternally one, the three persons in God are eternally distinct. As the Son is eternally begotten of the Father, so the Spirit is eternally begotten of the perfect love between Father and Son.

Aquinas adopted and developed this striking Augustinian insight. He found the relevant Trinitarian analogies in the intellectual procession of the inner word from the act of direct understanding, and the rational procession of love from the apprehended truth of the inner word.[73] In human beings, these critical spiritual processions are naturally finite, contingent, complex, and temporal. We reason discursively in order to understand; we understand and conceive in order to judge; and we make careful evaluative judgments in order to decide and act responsibly. We often fail in these demanding endeavors, and even when we succeed our success is always provisional and partial. Since God is eternal and perfect, infinite and ontologically necessary, triune yet indivisibly one, none of these critical human limitations apply to the divine nature. Yet, since God is infinite, eternal, and immaterial spirit and we are finite, temporal, embodied spirits, created in God's image, we may reasonably hypothesize that God's eternal act of perfect and unrestricted understanding perfectly understands God together with all that God does and can create. We may further hypothesize that this perfect and eternal act of understanding perfectly expresses itself in the eternal truth of the Divine Word (the Logos); and that the perfect unity between unrestricted intellectual act and unrestricted intellectual expression is a unity of love eternally begetting the Spirit, the third person of the Trinity (CWL, 3: chap. 19). These intellectual and moral analogies, based on the spiritual operations of human understanding, articulate conception, and generative love, offer a partial and limited apprehension of the divine mystery. They allow us to "see," through a glass darkly, how God may be intelligibly related to us, and how we, in our deeply flawed ways, may be related to the infinite eternal perfection of God. The rest is silent wonder, thankful worship, and loving service.[74]

Our very compressed account of Lonergan's enduring debts to Aquinas emphasizes the deep connections among the various parts of Thomas's philosophical and theological legacy. His cognitional theory, his epistemology and metaphysics, his detailed analysis of will, grace, and freedom, his ethical synthesis of knowledge, action, and love, can stand on their own, of course. But in Aquinas's comprehensive theology, they also contribute, in essential and important ways, to our imperfect and partial understanding of the great Christian mysteries: the creation, the incarnation, the redemption, the resurrection, and the Trinitarian nature of God (*Method*, chaps. 12 and 13).

Limitations of Thomas and Thomism. Lonergan's prolonged study of Aquinas led him to distinguish the enduring insights of Thomas from the important limitations of classical Thomism. This explicit interpretive distinction governs his critical treatment of Aquinas's strengths and weaknesses. Lonergan's dialectical analysis of the Angelic Doctor is based on a two-part strategy: to augment and perfect the achievements of Aquinas, to disengage Thomas's insights from the classicist presuppositions of Thomism.

Aquinas was a philosophical theologian, a Christian interpreter of Aristotle, operating in a medieval theoretical context. In his expository commentaries on Aristotle and scripture, he repeatedly relied on Aristotle's metaphysical categories. In his great theological *Summa*s, he attempted to synthesize traditional Christian teaching with Aristotle's major discoveries in philosophy and natural science. Even his systematic theology draws its theoretical categories from Aristotle's theory of being. Neither Aristotle nor Thomas, however, fully appreciated the importance of history for the theoretical enterprise. While Lonergan praises the systematic character of Aquinas's theology, he criticizes Thomas's metaphysical synthesis of distinct and relatively autonomous theoretical disciplines.[75]

Lonergan's historically minded appropriation of Aquinas emphasizes the following contextual differences between the High Middle Ages and late modernity. In the third stage of cognitive meaning to which we belong, the sciences have become autonomous and highly specialized. They determine their own methods and explanatory categories; they regularly refine and revise their theoretical discoveries and provisional syntheses. Their relative autonomy makes them effectively independent of both philosophical and theological control. Philosophy (in Lonergan's own case) has responded to the disciplinary autonomy of empirical science and scholarship by becoming a new type of specialized inquiry: the intentional analysis of the data of human consciousness. While Lonergan's philosophy respects the mind's natural aspiration for cognitive unity, he resists any *logical* effort to unify the diverse realms of cognitive meaning. The differentiated categories of common sense, the natural and human sciences, philosophy, and theology are logically distinct and irreducible. Theology itself is slowly becoming a historically grounded empirical discipline based on functional specialization. The comprehensive metaphysical syntheses first attempted by Aristotle and later by Aquinas are no longer viable.

Lonergan insists, however, that these critical contextual differences do not invalidate Aquinas's enduring achievements. The relevant integrative strategy today must be based on generalized empirical method rather than logic, but logic remains an important part of that method and not its antagonist (*Second Collection*, 5; CWL, 17:201–3). Contemporary philosophy begins with the intentional analysis of the polymorphic subject, not a metaphysical account of the rational soul, but this specialized focus on human consciousness provides the cognitional basis for a dynamic and critical metaphysics of being. Though Lonergan's ethics of authentic subjectivity differs in important respects from classical theories of the virtues, both natural and supernatural virtues are still essential to the concrete realization of the human good. And while Aquinas's incarnational theology focuses on Jesus, the unique divine person with two distinct natures, human and divine, Lonergan's careful transposition of Aquinas also highlights the uniqueness of Christ and the real distinction between his two forms of consciousness (CWL, 4:179–84). Rather than repudiating Aquinas's notable discoveries, Lonergan recognizes their contextual limitations and deliberately transposes Thomas's enduring insights into the integrative framework of his own transcendental method.

There are substantive limitations to Thomas's achievement as well. Aquinas's account of reflective insight needs to be sharpened and deepened. His modified identity theory of knowledge needs to be more fully developed if the critical problem of epistemic objectivity is to be persuasively addressed (CWL, 2:86–87, 97–99). His ontological analysis of the intelligible structure of being needs to be augmented by the explanatory conjugates and acts of a more comprehensive metaphysics grounded in the dynamic pursuit of explanatory knowledge. The ethical primacy he explicitly accorded the speculative intellect needs to be revisited. While it is true that personal and communal authenticity require a firm basis in objective knowledge, this epistemic dependence is not the last word (CWL, 4:219–21). Authentic living, both personal and communal, sublates and perfects the pursuit of knowledge and constitutes a higher level of human achievement. Finally, the philosophical expression of the great Christian mysteries needs to be freed from its medieval dependence on Aristotelian metaphysics and given a new cognitive basis in the intentional analysis of human subjectivity.

Although Aquinas lacked a developed appreciation of human historicity, his consistent intellectualism made the spirit of his philosophy open, dynamic, and flexible. Traditional Thomism, by contrast, has tended to embrace an immobile conceptualism, with its one-sided emphasis on logical entities, concepts, definitions, and deductive arguments, and its oversight or denial of direct and reflective insights. Unlike Thomas's capacious intellectualism, Thomistic conceptualism tends to be restrictive and static, and drawn to classicist assumptions (*Second Collection*, 2–9; CWL, 17:160). A credible Thomism that is relevant for today and tomorrow must liberate itself from the confining strictures of both classicist and conceptualist prejudices. After years reaching up to the "mind of Aquinas," Lonergan concluded that Saint Thomas, at his best, gave ample evidence of achieving this needed liberation.

The *Nova*

Lonergan's epistemic narrative of modernity is divided into two distinct periods: the first phase of the Enlightenment, which culminates in the projects of Newton and Kant; the second phase, which originates with the discovery of non-Euclidean geometries and the steady rise of historical consciousness (*Third Collection*, 63–65). The first phase is dominated by the heuristic demand for invariant law and necessity, the second phase by the evolutionary emphasis on genetic development and the contingency of verified fact. Important intellectual discoveries occurred in both phases of modernity, but Lonergan views the historically minded second phase as a needed corrective to the oversights and distortions of the first.

In both periods of modernity, Lonergan continues to distinguish between enduring contributions and significant limitations. Since he tends to offer discerning critical comments on the great modern thinkers rather than developed interpretive accounts of their texts, I have chosen a different expository strategy for this final section, relying on an overview of broad intellectual movements rather than a critical exegesis of individual thinkers and works. This strategy provides, I believe, the most faithful account of Lonergan's dialectical critique of modernity.

Lonergan attributed the deepest novelty of the modern age to four momentous intellectual developments: the new empirical sciences of nature; the rise of historical consciousness and critical history; the philosophical turn to the polymorphic subject; the hermeneutic turn to the different functions and expressions of meaning. What were the specific merits and limitations of these great modern cognitive breakthroughs?

Enduring Contributions

The New Sciences of Nature. The most dynamic factor shaping the intellectual history of modernity was the development of the new sciences of nature, particularly Newtonian mechanics and Darwin's evolutionary biology.[76] Scientific progress, in turn, was dependent on parallel breakthroughs in mathematics, the discovery of the integral calculus, the emerging science of statistics and probability. Groundbreaking achievements in axiomatics and mathematical logic, like Riemannian geometry and Gödel's incompleteness theorem, eventually promoted a new understanding of mathematical knowledge and its critical role in the development of the empirical sciences. After Riemann and Gödel, mathematical activity was no longer conceived as the discovery and logical expression of eternal and necessary truth, but as the free creation of abstract systems of intelligible possibility. A comparable process occurs in the evolving history of the natural sciences, where several centuries of progressive and cumulative discoveries also promote a revised understanding of the scientific enterprise as a whole.

In Lonergan's reflective appraisal, what lasting theoretical contributions emerged from the new scientific learning? At the level of first-order theory, there was a critical heuristic shift from descriptive to explanatory knowledge.[77] Descriptive knowledge characterizes things in terms of their observable relations to us as sensory perceivers; explanatory knowledge characterizes the same things in terms of their intelligible relations to one another. An important limitation of the physics defended by Aristotle's early modern successors was its failure to recognize and implement this critical heuristic distinction. The heuristic commitment to achieving explanatory knowledge became the methodological basis for scientific and philosophical inquiry from the mid-seventeenth century onward.

Because the modern sciences are empirical, they are also committed to an explanatory account of all sensible data. To satisfy this demanding commitment, an evolving and complementary series of heuristic strategies had to be gradually developed by the different sciences:[78] classical method in Newtonian physics to deal with systematic natural processes; statistical method in quantum mechanics to deal with natural processes that are nonsystematic in character; genetic method in evolutionary biology to deal with the emergence, survival, and eventual decline of concrete schemes of intelligible recurrence. The methodological complexity of the natural sciences became increasingly attuned to the ontological complexity of nature itself, though reductionist tendencies continued to influence the many fashionable popularizations of science.

The complementarity of these new and distinct heuristic structures (classical, statistical, and genetic) has important implications for modern cosmology. Lonergan articulated several of these implications in his original theory of emergent probability. The leading idea of Lonergan's cosmology is complex: the dynamic and evolving universe gradually revealed by the empirical sciences should be intelligibly understood as the "successive realization in accord with successive schedules of probability of an emerging series of schemes of recurrence" (CWL, 3:144–51). The genuinely emergent character of these concrete intelligible schemes helps to explain the relative autonomy of the different sciences with their distinctive methods of inquiry, their irreducible theoretical vocabularies, and their specialized communities of research and teaching.[79] Emphasizing the ontological implications of heuristic complementarity is Lonergan's antidote to cosmological reductionism.

The belated emergence of critical historiography in the second phase of the Enlightenment gradually undermined the classical theory of science inherited from Aristotle. Despite their explicit repudiation of Aristotle's physics, leading modern scientists and philosophers continued to accept his normative conception of science as true, certain knowledge of causal necessity. But this static account of scientific knowledge and truth could not withstand critical study of the actual history of science. In response to this cumulative historical research, modern science is now understood to be a dynamic process of collaborative inquiry based on the critical communal control of rationally informed but fallible belief (*Method*, 42–43; CWL, 3:727–28). Due to the discoveries of historical inquiry, our prevailing theory of science more closely corresponds to the actual practice of the scientific community.

Perhaps the most enduring legacy of the new sciences is the empirical, critical, and methodical mentality they fostered. The normative influence of this pervasive scientific mentality now affects every serious intellectual endeavor, including philosophy and theology (CWL, 3:6; *Science and the Modern World*, 16). The broad and deep influence of the Scientific Revolution on the modern world becomes abundantly clear when we recognize that this exigent critical outlook dominates the cultural superstructure of theoretical inquiry, while the technical and practical applications of scientific theories largely dominate the cultural infrastructure of the economy, society, and politics.

The Rise of Historical Consciousness. The first phase of the Enlightenment was dominated by revolutionary developments in physics. A remarkable series of intellectual discoveries stretching from Copernicus to Newton overturned the traditional Ptolemaic cosmology and promoted a new world picture based on invariant mathematical laws. Immanuel Kant gave philosophical expression to the dominance of the Newtonian outlook when he described the project of theoretical reason as the discovery and verification of universal and necessary natural laws and the project of practical reason as the legislation of categorical moral imperatives.

The second phase of the Enlightenment witnessed the emergence and acceptance of a critical historical mentality (CWL, 17:354). Eventually, historical methods and heuristic perspectives were extended to the whole of natural as well as human reality. It gradually became clear that the cosmos itself has a history, as do the biological species that inhabit the earth, as do human beings and the social institutions and cultural practices within which they live and develop. Although Hegel contributed greatly to the new historical mindedness, the critical study of history that developed in the late nineteenth century explicitly rejected his a priori approach to the past. Ranke's critical historical method emphasized empirical sources of discovery and verification. The epistemic results of historical scholarship, like those of modern scientific research, were now treated as provisional and fallible. The community of historical investigators also became increasingly specialized and differentiated; scholarly monographs now dealt, for example, with economic, social, and political history, or the history of science and technology, or the history of religion and art.[80] Scholarly progress increasingly depended on intellectual restraint and collaborative effort.

The heightened sensitivity to historical change also contributed to a new understanding of culture. The classicist notion of culture as a permanent normative achievement by "advanced" societies for less developed societies to honor and imitate was effectively reconceived as the shared beliefs, values, and practices that shape different forms of historical life (*Method*, xi). Even in the West, the cultural ideals and pedagogical models of the classical Greeks and Romans lost their timeless normative authority. The indigenous cultures shaping each particular human society were now to be understood and evaluated on their own terms. This increased emphasis on cultural pluralism did not logically entail the loss of transcultural normativity, but it tended, in fact, to promote a rising tide of moral and religious relativism.

Augustine's theological narrative of salvation history in *The City of God* was deliberately challenged by a series of formidable secular rivals: Hegel's dialectical history of spirit, Marx's historical materialism, the liberal theory of irreversible progress through continuous advances in science, technology, and education (CWL, 17:366–70). Whether the historical process was heuristically conceived as lawful and necessary or as free, contingent, and unpredictable, these influential metanarratives highlighted the critical role of particular individuals, societies, and cultures in shaping the development of secular history. Even when these grand metanarratives were no longer widely embraced, the modern imperative of collective social responsibility remained in force (*Third Collection*, 169–82). Human beings, whether acting in concert or more often in conflict, bear a common responsibility for the character and direction of history and the achievement of its practical outcomes.

The Philosophical Turn to the Subject. The most influential philosophers in the Enlightenment's first phase were Descartes and Kant. Their theories of human existence were commonly based on sharp ontological dualisms. Descartes divided the whole of reality into two incompatible modes of being: *res cogitans*, nonextended mind, and *res extensa*, unthinking matter. Given this stark ontological separation, Descartes was unable to explain how the two modes of being causally interacted in the case of the human mind and body. Although Kant openly criticized Cartesian metaphysics and refined and revised Descartes's rational psychology, his own dualistic metaphysics of nature and morals also divides reality into radically self-enclosed realms.

Kant assigned pure practical reason to the ontological domain of freedom and moral responsibility, and Newtonian nature to the parallel but opposite domain of invariant law and causal necessity. Despite the important philosophical differences between their respective positions, both Descartes and Kant endorsed a highly abstract, ahistorical anthropology in which disembodied reason exercises technical and moral control over disenchanted nature.

In the nineteenth century, the Cartesian and Kantian anthropological pictures are frontally challenged.[81] Hegel restores the finite human spirit to an essential place within society and history. The great Romantic poets insist on the embodiment of human beings and their emotional affinity with and connection to the vital forces and energies of nature. Both the Hegelian emphasis on human sociality and historicity and the Romantic insistence on affective human embodiment are incompatible with both the Cartesian ideal of the ego's epistemic self-sufficiency and the Kantian insistence on practical reason's radical moral autonomy.

The rapid development of the empirical human sciences in the nineteenth century brought these philosophical conflicts into sharp focus. Should the new human sciences model themselves on physics and biology, the conspicuously successful natural sciences, or should they develop a distinctive methodology of their own? But if the sciences of nature and spirit are treated as, in principle, distinct, does this imply a tacit acceptance of the Cartesian and Kantian dualisms? And if these ontological dualisms have been largely discredited, how should an empirical investigation of the naturally embodied and historically embedded human subject correctly proceed?

What late modernity urgently required was a clarification and deepening of the notion of empirical method (CWL, 3:93–125). The empirical study of any subject matter begins with the data of experience. But the relevant data on human existence are of two distinct kinds: data of sense and data of consciousness. Among the data of sense a further distinction needs to be drawn between sensible data that are bearers of meaning and value and those that are not. The empirical data of the natural sciences are not treated heuristically as intentional carriers of meaning, but the relevant data of the human sciences invariably are (*Method*, 80–81; *Second Collection*, 104–5). This critical methodological difference highlights the hermeneutical character of the human sciences, and their essential reliance on the interpretation and appraisal of meaning. Moreover, the polymorphic data of intentional consciousness, perceptual, affective, intellectual, rational, moral, and religious, include an even deeper stratum of meaning than its diverse sensible expressions: namely, the causal sources, formulating acts, exigent norms, and propositional terms of meaning underlying those expressions. A comprehensive study of human existence, therefore, must effectively combine an intentional analysis of the subject's polymorphic consciousness with a hermeneutic investigation of all intentional bearers and expressions of meaning.[82]

Brentano and Husserl deliberately emphasized the intentionality of consciousness. Heidegger stressed the finite, temporal, situated character of mortal *Dasein*, whose being is being unto death. The German and French phenomenologists focused attention on human affectivity and mood; the European existentialists, on the inescapable demand for personal decision and choice; Rudolf Otto and Mircea Eliade, on the religious dimension of human existence.[83] Slowly but inexorably, the polymorphism of the human subject became a central philosophical concern. The concrete intentional subject, as we have noted, operates within different patterns of experience, is consciously oriented by varied interests and concerns, and is powerfully shaped by social and cultural belonging. Personally confronted with the inevitability of death, constantly prone to bias and sin, this polymorphic being expresses itself symbolically and linguistically in an equally polymorphic manner. The richness of existential reflection, the explicit rejection of philosophy's traditional focus on knowledge and truth, however, has its own intellectual dangers. For the symbolic, dramatic, mortal, expressive animal is also an intellectual and moral being with unrestricted desires for knowledge and value, and an equally unrestricted exigence for authenticity and truth.

Lonergan welcomes this greatly enlarged understanding of the situated symbolic subject, this comprehensive expansion of philosophical anthropology beyond the restricted parameters of Descartes and Kant. But he emphatically insists that the enduring philosophical concerns with cognition, truth, objectivity, and being remain permanently valid, for the situated subject's authentic existence is impossible without the sustained intellectual and moral development of the whole human person (*Second Collection*, 79–86).

The Hermeneutic Turn to Language and Meaning. In the first phase of the Enlightenment, modern philosophers largely operated within the rubric of ideas. For both Descartes and Kant, ideas were epistemic representations in the mind of the cognitive subject.[84] Kant clarified misleading ambiguities in Cartesian psychology by distinguishing pure from empirical representations, and intuitions and concepts from his technically designated ideas of reason. Descartes treated mind-dependent ideas as the primary bearers of truth value. Kant insisted that only propositional judgments could actually be true or false. He divided meaningful judgments into analytic and synthetic; he further divided knowledge of truth into a priori and a posteriori truth claims.[85]

But how were these private mind-dependent ideas to be properly studied and publicly discussed? How were epistemic claims about their nature and existence to be reliably confirmed? Descartes's intuition-based account of the introspective process proved deeply problematic and confusing. And subsequent descriptions of the introspective method and of what it reliably disclosed were so often incoherent that they made the truth claims of both rationalist and empiricist defenders of ideas increasingly suspect.

Growing disenchantment with the "way of ideas" led Anglo-American and Continental philosophers to take what Richard Rorty has called "the linguistic turn."[86] At the origin of this powerful metaphilosophical movement, analytic philosophers like Frege, Russell, and Carnap were primarily interested in language as the carrier of systematic meaning. They focused philosophical attention on the formal languages used to express mathematical, logical, and scientific truth. Eventually, under the influence of the later Wittgenstein and Austin, their philosophical successors began to study the diverse uses of ordinary language, and the variety of speech acts native language users are able to perform. Twentieth-century philosophy of language tended to vacillate between the syntactical study of abstract formal structures (*langue*) and the concrete employment of the diverse linguistic resources of ordinary speech (*parole*). Wilfrid Sellars, one of the ablest proponents of the new "way of words," has argued persuasively that a comprehensive semiotics must include syntax, semantics, and pragmatics, the three irreducible dimensions of any genuine natural language.[87]

Continental philosophy of language has been deeply influenced by Romantic hermeneutics. The Romantic conception of language tends to be *expressive* rather than *representational*.[88] This alternative conception of how human language operates correlates with a radically non-Cartesian anthropology, in which the human spirit naturally expresses its rich inner life in rite, myth, symbol, and art, as well as philosophy and science.[89] These public expressions of human subjectivity are not representations of an antecedently given reality. The human subject regularly actualizes itself through its varied expressive activities, and then comes to know its interior complexity, less by unmediated introspection than by hermeneutic reflection on these meaningful expressive embodiments of its own spiritual life. Moreover, these sensible expressions of meaning and value constantly change as human beings develop and as they cooperate with others in the drama of interpersonal living. In stark contrast to the disengaged Cartesian ego, the symbolic, expressive, self-interpreting animal is a dynamic, embodied, and historically situated being. Human self-knowledge, within this romantically inspired anthropology, is essentially mediated by hermeneutic reflection on society, history, culture, and language.

Does the philosophical turn to language and meaning undermine Lonergan's repeated emphasis on the importance of intentional consciousness and reflexive self-appropriation? I don't think that it does, for the following reasons.[90] Lonergan's methodological *turn* to intentionality analysis is not a *return* to the discredited way of ideas because his reflexive phenomenology of experiential consciousness is radically different from the Cartesian account of introspection as the ego's intuitive perception of its private mental states. Moreover, Lonergan's dynamic, pluralistic intellectualism undercuts the static nature of the Kantian a priori, while his candid acknowledgment of polymorphic subjectivity gives full recognition to the noncognitive dimensions of the embodied self.

The phenomenology of the intentional subject and the hermeneutics of expressive meaning are complementary sources of human self-knowledge. While there are multiple functions and expressions of meaning beyond the cognitional, the cognitive function of meaning remains critically important for the abiding concerns of philosophy. To avoid irremediable epistemic confusion, it is essential to distinguish four distinct realms of cognitive meaning: common sense, systematic theory, interiority, and transcendence. It is equally critical to recognize three distinct stages in the history of cognitive meaning. The first phase is primarily symbolic and practical and confined to the realm of commonsense meaning. In the second stage systematic theory emerges from common sense, but its substantive discoveries are linguistically articulated in metaphysical terms and relations (Aristotle and Aquinas). In the third stage to which we belong, the theoretical enterprise in both the natural and human sciences has become relatively autonomous and specialized, but the fragmented knowledge it yields is noticeably lacking in epistemic integration and unity.

Ordinary language philosophy (inspired by Austin and the later Wittgenstein) has directed attention to linguistic diversity and change in the practical realm of common sense. The logical reconstruction of theoretical meaning (Carnap and Hempel) has tended to operate within a heuristic framework of static deductive systems that cannot intelligibly account for theoretical innovation and change. But now that the empirical sciences, natural and human, have become specialized, dynamic, and highly differentiated, Lonergan's transcendental method must replace rational (logical) reconstruction as the appropriate strategy for pursuing cognitive integration in the third stage of meaning.

The irreducible pluralism of linguistic meaning corresponds to the multiple differentiations of human consciousness. Thus the uses of language can be practical, literary, systematic, scholarly, and so forth, depending on the polymorphic subject's pattern of experience and the cultural level of a community's epistemic development (*Method*, 86–99; CWL, 17:107–18). While a comprehensive philosophy of *language* must be fully attentive to symbolic pluralism and linguistic innovation and change, it must also respect the perennial *philosophical* commitment to pursuing epistemic integration and unity. Although the hermeneutic turn to language and meaning constitutes a genuine philosophical advance, it will remain incomplete and one-sided without an equally explicit commitment to comprehensive self-appropriation by the polymorphic subject (*Method*, chap. 3).

Significant Limitations

Modern Philosophy and the New Sciences of Nature. Why did a remarkable series of scientific discoveries often lead to erroneous judgments about their broad philosophical and cultural import? I shall offer a very abbreviated version of what is in fact a long, complicated, and very important story.

In the first phase of the Enlightenment, the leading modern philosophers embraced the new science of nature but interpreted its startling discoveries through the distorting lens of the classical theory of science. This traditional theory required genuine science to be certain knowledge of causal necessity, logically ordered in an axiomatic deductive system. But what normative method of inquiry could reliably guarantee the achievement of this ancient epistemic ideal? This methodological question dominated the history of modern philosophy from Descartes to Kant. The Cartesian method outlined in the *Rules* and the *Discourse* was explicitly designed to satisfy the epistemic demand for necessity and certainty. Descartes relied on hyperbolic doubt to discredit the authority of inherited beliefs; self-authenticating intuitions to provide the indubitable premises on which an axiomatic science was supposedly based; and rigorous logical deduction to ensure that the conclusions drawn from these premises were equally certain and necessary.[91]

Within the opposing empiricist tradition, Hume tacitly accepted the Newtonian laws of nature, and he modeled his new "science of man" on

Newtonian principles. But he skeptically concluded, on the basis of his empiricist convictions, that the epistemic claims of modern physics could not really be justified. For Hume, the ultimate barrier to genuine science was logical. Specifically, there was no valid logical inference from sensibly intuited particular impressions to allegedly invariant general laws. As a practical matter (as an engaged participant in the everyday world), Hume accepted the Newtonian world-picture, but as an academic skeptic (as a solitary critical thinker in his study), he could no longer endorse the new physics as genuine science.[92]

Kant explicitly criticized the epistemological dogmatism of Descartes and the rationalists (Spinoza and Wolff). At the same time, he believed Humean skepticism severely truncated the boundaries of scientific knowledge. Kant wanted to defend the epistemic claims of mathematics and physics, while ontologically circumscribing the limits of theoretical reason. He also wanted to secure the normative legitimacy of ethics against the challenge of natural necessity and invariant law. Transcendental or critical idealism was Kant's ingenious solution to this profound cultural dilemma. By confining theoretical reason and scientific knowledge to the phenomenal order (the order of lawful sensible appearances), Kant thought he had created a pure ethical space for his critical noumenal faith.[93]

Lyell's discoveries in geology, Darwin's evolutionary biology, Mendel's foundational work in genetics, and the emerging historical and human sciences gradually led to the rejection of the classical scientific ideal. A new understanding of scientific inquiry developed which was critically based on the actual history of the sciences. Empirical science is presently understood to be a fallible, communal endeavor methodically devoted to the critical control of socially transmitted belief. Its operative truth claims are not certain but probable; they refer to verifiable matters of fact, not to invariant patterns of causal necessity. And while abstract mathematical laws continue to play a major role in classical physics, statistical, genetic, and dialectical heuristic structures are equally legitimate and important dimensions of contemporary scientific inquiry (CWL, 3: chaps. 14, 15).

Rationality and logic are related but not identical features of the empirical sciences. Modern scientific practice effectively coordinates both logical and nonlogical operations. This normative and recurrent coordination makes the provisional results of scientific inquiry cumulative, progressive, and revisable (*Method*, 4–6). As an empirical inquiry, science begins with experiential data (the partial truth of empiricism), but then proceeds to ask heuristically framed questions for intelligence and critical reflection. Direct and reflective insights (both regularly overlooked in modern cognitional theories) causally mediate the pivotal transition from investigative questions to articulate answers. Direct insights are the intentional source of science's explanatory hypotheses and theories; reflective insights play an analogous role for affirmative and negative judgments about a theory's probable truth. The provisional acceptance of a theory by the relevant scientific community leads only to further observations and experiments and the critical refinement and revision of earlier epistemic results.

Scientific inquiry is *empirical* because its data and evidence are based on experience and observation. It is *intelligent and explanatory* because it seeks to discover the intelligibly patterned verifiable relations among the data experience discloses. It is *rational and critical* because it bases its claim to epistemic objectivity on effectively coordinating the three complementary strands of cognitional process: experience, understanding, and judgment.[94] This normative coordination can never be taken for granted, for genuine objectivity is always the fruit of authentic subjectivity and intersubjectivity (*Method*, 265). It is only by personal and communal fidelity to the transcendental precepts, and the individual and collective overcoming of distorting bias, that the collaborative quest for objective knowledge and the achievement of epistemic self-transcendence can be reliably assured.

The early modern philosophers were justified in insisting on the singular importance of scientific method. But they were seriously mistaken in basing their conceptions of method on the classical theory of science. As the evolving history of modern inquiry has shown, a limited number of empirical and critical methods actually exist; these different methods ground a corresponding plurality of distinct but complementary realms of cognitive meaning: common sense, explanatory science, philosophic interiority, divine transcendence. The several heuristic methods of the natural sciences, though extremely important, are limited in their epistemic scope. The specialized sciences of nature, despite their unrivaled epistemic prestige, do not exhaust the range of legitimate knowledge. The influential ontology of exclusive naturalism modeled on the latest discoveries of modern physics and biology is deeply reductive and arbitrary.

While the intellectual and practical importance of modern science is undeniable, the prevailing interpretations of its philosophical and human significance have lacked a critical grounding in cognitional fact. The *scientistic* bias of exclusive naturalism has distorted the public's understanding of science and, in some quarters, generated a humanistic backlash against it. Science is, however, a profoundly important human enterprise. What we urgently require today is an equally profound philosophical account of its nature, scope, limits, and importance.

Historiography and Hermeneutics. The emergence of modern historical consciousness was also shadowed by illusions of necessity. Both Hegel and Marx hoped to discover the dialectical laws of history. Although they jointly believed that the *telos* of history was the achievement of freedom, they uncritically assumed that the dialectical process culminating in freedom was lawful and necessary.[95] These early prophets of historical teleology clearly distinguished the laws of history from those of nature. Their dialectical accounts of freedom assign a prominent causal role to human agency, and openly reinstate the final causality rejected by Newtonian physics. Yet in their common aspiration to make the study of history scientific, Marx and Hegel sacrificed particular events and individual and social agents to universal laws, and contingent occurrences to allegedly necessary dialectical processes. The new philosophies of history, like the new sciences of nature, struggled to disengage themselves from the classical notion of science.

When modern historiography became empirical and critical, as it did in the late nineteenth century, its heuristic focus shifted to concreteness and fact. Historians were committed to discovering what had actually happened in the past, not only in Europe but throughout the world. Working in conjunction with cultural anthropologists, European and American historians began to discover the great variety of human cultures and societies. They confronted the remarkable diversity of cultural beliefs and social practices, the striking contrasts in moral conduct and political governance, the very different ways human beings have successfully lived together. The eventual acceptance of cultural pluralism, intellectual, moral, political, and religious, was the direct result of their expanding historical discoveries.

Just as the new historians wanted to uncover historical facts independent of inherited assumptions and traditional narratives, cultural anthropologists wanted to study non-European cultures without antecedent bias and prejudice. But what were modern European thinkers and scholars, as well as the educated Western public, to make of non-Christian religions and rites, of non-Western codes of sexuality and conduct, of radically different cosmologies and social structures? Should they simply be compared unfavorably with contemporary European intellectual, moral, and religious models? And if they should, did this assume that modern Europe provided credible cultural norms against which all non-European societies should be critically measured? There were powerful reasons to challenge these complacent Eurocentric assumptions.

Nineteenth-century Europe was inwardly torn by industrial and political conflict, and by the fierce struggle for overseas empires. Institutional Christianity was rapidly losing the loyalty of both intellectual elites and the urban and industrial working class. New biological and social sciences were emerging that broke with the heuristic assumptions of Newtonian physics. And secular accounts of morality were openly challenging the biblical basis of traditional European ethics. Given these grave and deepening cultural tensions, the moral, political, and religious traditions of Europe could no longer be taken for granted.[96] But if the inherited traditions of Europe could not serve as a critical evaluative standard for non-European societies and cultures, then what were the available alternatives? The important classical distinction between nature and convention (*physis* and *nomos*), between natural right and positive law, no longer appeared to help. For the dominant modern conceptions of nature, Newtonian and Darwinian, conspicuously lack normative import, and human nature viewed through the pluralistic perspectives of critical history seemed increasingly amorphous and fluid.

Human beings obviously need to make evaluative judgments in order to choose, act, and live. To be confident in their moral convictions, especially in the face of newly compelling alternatives, they need to trust that their basic orienting beliefs are impartially true. The growing public awareness of cultural diversity, the instability of Europe's traditional moral culture, and the moral neutrality of the natural sciences heightened ethical skepticism and relativism, particularly among the educated classes. The critical study of nature and history seemed to entail the loss of universal normative standards. Without a transcultural, transhistorical basis for our moral convictions, our evaluative life and conduct appear to lack objectivity and truth. What Alasdair MacIntyre later called "the emotivist age" had discordantly arrived.[97]

Nietzsche radicalized the cultural instability of nineteenth-century Europe. His subversive genealogy of morals severely challenged traditional ethics by making envy and weakness the basis of biblical morality. His deliberate transvaluation of values sought to replace the submissive "virtues" of Christianity with a revitalized warrior ethics in which the healthy and strong were ascendant and masterful. Together with Marx and Freud, Nietzsche cultivated a hermeneutics of suspicion, a radically subversive way of interpreting Europe's religious and moral inheritance. This seductive, destabilizing hermeneutics now affects our entire attitude toward the past. It supports a stance of ironic detachment toward all historical texts and traditions and offers the most powerful contemporary rival to Lonergan's project of critical appropriation.[98]

What does Lonergan hope to preserve from the uneven legacy of the modern historical revolution? Like Hegel, he affirms the philosophical importance of spirit, society, and history but rejects the necessitarian bias of Hegelian dialectic. In fact, Lonergan develops a critical dialectical method of his own specifically designed to avoid the limitations of Hegel's dynamic conceptualism (CWL, 3:396–98, 446–48).

He also affirms the Marxian emphasis on collective responsibility and the critique of ideology, but rejects Marx's theory of class struggle, his embrace of revolutionary violence, and his inflated Promethean humanism (CWL, 17:367–70). Though Lonergan endorses critical historiography and the expanded cultural awareness it creates, he carefully distinguishes cultural pluralism from all forms of normative relativism and articulates a transcultural, transhistorical basis for both individual and social ethics.

Finally, he recognizes the rhetorical power and salience of Nietzschean criticism. The cultural and political legacy of Europe, particularly Western religion, morality, and politics, is clearly susceptible to the distorting biases Nietzsche gleefully uncovers. At the same time, Lonergan rejects Nietzsche's transvaluation of values, defends the authenticity of Christian faith and practice, and clarifies the interpretive limits of the hermeneutics of suspicion, while insisting on a sympathetic and critical retrieval of the enduring insights of the *vetera* and the *nova* (*Third Collection*, 155–61).

Authentic Subjectivity. In his seminal essay "The Subject," Lonergan sketches a critical narrative account of the several philosophical responses to human subjectivity. I shall follow the clarifying contours of his outline in this section.[99]

The neglected subject: Premodern philosophy focused on metaphysics, the study of being, and logic, the formal study of theoretical terms, propositions, and arguments. Even after classical philosophers turned their heuristic attention to the human soul, they continued to cast their discoveries in metaphysical and logical categories. Prior to the modern era, philosophy's heuristic emphasis remained on the objects of knowledge and the truth vehicles constitutive of science.

The truncated subject: When he deliberately shifted philosophy's attention to "the way of ideas," Descartes proceeded to thematize their subjective bearer, the Cartesian *ego*. He pictured *res cogitans* as a disembodied rational substance, ontologically separate from the geometricized realm of extended nature. Kant's far richer picture of the transcendental subject was still ahistorical and atomistic. In fact, Kant insisted that the asocial atomism of practical reason was needed to preserve its vaunted moral autonomy.

When the new way of ideas ran its course, philosophical inquiry turned back to the sensible order. Post-Kantian philosophers, seeking to make their discipline scientific, chose to base its controversial truth claims on intersubjective data and evidence. For this reason, they methodically excluded the data of consciousness in their concerted attempt to develop a reliable science of the mind.[100] The unwelcome result of this exclusion was a further truncation of the richness of human subjectivity. Substantive behaviorists denied the causal relevance of intentional consciousness. Methodological behaviorists systematically excluded explanatory reference to intentional desires, operations, and norms. Logical empiricists limited the epistemic sources of knowledge to sense perceptions and logical inference; pragmatists emphasized the tangible practical results of human cognition and action. The polymorphic complexity of the subject's interior life remained largely unexplored and unacknowledged (*Second Collection*, 73–75).

The Epistemological Bog. Modern epistemology has repeatedly struggled with the problem of immanence.[101] If subjective ideas, the immediate objects of conscious awareness, are mind-dependent intentional states, then how is objective knowledge of reality possible? To use the problematic language this cognitive picture encouraged, how can the individual knower get outside her own mind to "the external world," to the "already out there now real."[102] Inspired by developments in scientific optics and neurology, Descartes's successors explicitly rejected naive realism, the belief that we know reality directly by sensing it. As a substitute for naive realism, they frequently embraced the representative theory of perception. According to that causal theory of perceiving, all the direct objects of conscious operations are immanent or mind-dependent entities. But if objective reality exists "outside the mind," and human awareness is confined to its own internal states, what reliable philosophical strategy can take us from epistemic immanence to the intended knowledge of being? And without such a strategy, how can human knowledge hope to be objective, how can true and false judgments be effectively distinguished?

This "epistemological bog" is created by a truncated dialectic of counterpositions. Within the narrow constraints of this dialectic, it's widely assumed that if naive realism is false, then some version of epistemic idealism must be true. Lonergan deliberately develops his *critical realism* as a way of avoiding the bog of immanence and the counterpositions on which it depends. Critical realism is a complex epistemological theory based on the following truth claims:[103] Reality or being is the unrestricted intentional object of the transcendental desire to know. We humans can know being objectively through the reasonable affirmation of true judgments. We can know that these judgments are true by reflectively grasping their propositional content as virtually unconditioned. This critical grasp occurs in reflective insights that causally mediate the intentional transition between explicit questions for reflection (is proposition P true?) and the reasonable affirmation of P's truth. Lonergan's *intellectualist* notion of being, where being is epistemically intended in intellectual and rational questioning and objectively known by answering those questions correctly, needs to be consistently and critically distinguished from the *empiricist* notion of being as the "already out there now real," the anticipated sensible object of biological extroversion. It is true existential judgments critically and reasonably affirmed, rather than veridical intuitions of the given, that serve as the rational criterion for demarcating the scope of reality. And the objectivity of these judgments results from the subject's effectively coordinating the experiential, normative, and absolute aspects of cognitional process. In making factual and evaluative judgments, epistemic objectivity, cognitive self-transcendence, is the genuine intentional fruit of authentic subjectivity and intersubjectivity (CWL, 17:204).

The partial truth of naive realism is that the intentional contents of perceptual acts are the sensible data from which human inquiry begins. The partial truth of idealism is that sense experience, by itself, is insufficient for knowledge of being. The error of naive realism is that it reduces human knowing to veridical acts of perceiving and reduces knowable reality to the intentional contents of sense perceptions or intellectual and rational intuitions. The central error of idealism is that it overlooks direct and reflective insights and the constitutive role they play in achieving knowledge of reality. Rationally defensible epistemological theories are critically grounded in comprehensive self-appropriation. The counterpositions in philosophy are based on the inadequate accounts of interiority offered by intellectually unconverted subjects. Until the basic philosophical positions and counterpositions are dialectically distinguished and then traced to their source in the polymorphic subject, the challenge of epistemic immanence remains unresolved (*Second Collection*, 75–79).

Existential Engagement.[104] Modern scientists regularly celebrated their groundbreaking discoveries as objective knowledge of things in themselves. Modern philosophers frequently raised skeptical doubts about these scientific claims to objectivity. Lonergan insisted that only intellectual conversion and critical self-appropriation could reliably lead to a defensible account of human knowing, knowledge, and the known. But the arduous dialectical process he proposed is difficult, protracted, and internally demanding. Isn't there a quicker, less complicated path out of the bog of immanence?

Several existentialist thinkers in war-ravaged Europe insisted that there is. They deliberately rejected the Cartesian picture of the disengaged ego and the perceptual model of human subjectivity Descartes defended. They insisted that human beings are fundamentally practical agents, moral and political subjects confronted with decisions and demands for action. The reliable human encounter with reality does not depend on problematic inferences from immanent ideas. Rather, humans engage the real world routinely and directly in ordinary practice and action. Traditional philosophers have been seriously mistaken in privileging cognition as the fundamental human activity. The subject's spectatorial stance, the ostensibly cognitive stance, arises only when habitual practice unexpectedly breaks down. We humans are users and makers of things long before and after we are knowers, and genuinely reliable knowledge is always instrumental to making and doing.[105]

These pragmatic existentialists offer a welcome validation of common sense against the imperial claims of philosophy and the sciences. They restore dignity and worth to *ponos* (labor), *poiesis* (making), and *praxis* (action), the modes of the *vita activa* fundamentally dependent on commonsense knowledge.[106] They rightly emphasize human freedom and responsibility, and repudiate distorted accounts of the subject based on perceptual models of cognition and consciousness. Despite these undeniable strengths, the existential tradition is burdened by its own forms of bias and prejudice. It tends to be biased against the intellectual pattern of experience, against the pursuit of theoretical knowledge and disinterested scholarship, against the critical philosophical concern for objectivity and truth, against a comprehensive anthropology fully committed to intellectual, moral, and religious self-transcendence (*Second Collection*, 79–86; CWL, 18).

Lonergan's holistic account of the human subject clearly depends on the insights of phenomenology and existentialism.[107] In his philosophical anthropology, he explicitly affirms the following: the situated existence of the subject, the critical importance of intentional consciousness, the constitutive role in the subject's development of existential horizons and fiduciary frameworks, the operative contrast between "my world" and "the world," the demand for existential and historical authenticity, and the practical need to sublate objective knowing with responsible decisions and actions. At the same time, he emphatically insists that the core philosophical disciplines of cognitional theory, epistemology, and metaphysics are still indispensable. There can be no authentic subjectivity without epistemic and moral objectivity, for the objective knowledge of being and value underlies and sustains all credible forms of authentic human existence.

With regard to the functions and dimensions of meaning, Lonergan affirms the following: When the human subject is conceived polymorphically as an incarnate spiritual being, constituted by social and historical belonging, the importance of language and symbolism comes sharply into focus. Human infants initially live in a world of sensible immediacy; as they gradually master their mother tongue they enter a larger world mediated by meaning and motivated by value. Their conscious intentionality is molded by the language(s) they speak; their operative personal horizons are structured by linguistic distinctions and contrasts. From birth until death, human beings are meaning-centered creatures.[108] They express and encounter meaning in multiple forms: in bodily gestures and tone of voice, in artistic expression and symbolism, in interpersonal exchanges, both linguistic and nonlinguistic, in the richness and diversity of spoken and written language. The comprehensive study of meaning and language is inseparable from the study of human existence itself.

In his post-*Insight* lectures and writing, Lonergan repeatedly emphasized the multiple dimensions of meaning (*Method*, chap. 3; CWL, 17: chap. 6). He also distinguished four specific *functions* of meaning: cognitive, constitutive, effective, and communicative. These complementary functions correspond to different aspects of the subject's intentional life. Through cognitive meaning we actively seek to know the whole of reality; through constitutive meaning individuals gradually develop into unique and identifiable persons belonging to distinct historical communities; through effective meaning we causally transform the natural and human world through the practical activities of cooperative making and doing; through communicative meaning we create, sustain, critique, and reform the many-layered intentional communities to which we actually belong. Each of these distinct functions of meaning relies on the subject's intentional consciousness: its unrestricted desires and demands, its distinctive operations and norms, its dynamic and creative energy, its vulnerability to bias and sin, its radical openness to grace and redemption.

As a philosopher-theologian, Lonergan concentrated his theoretical inquiry on the cognitive function of meaning, on the normative process of human cognition, on the epistemic requirements of objective knowledge, on the complementary heuristic structures through which the complexity of being is known. He recognized four distinct realms of cognitive meaning. Each of these cognitive realms depends on specifically differentiated methods of inquiry; each expresses its epistemic discoveries in an equally differentiated linguistic pattern. For example, the ordinary language of practical common sense differs significantly from the technical and systematic language of the explanatory sciences. The theoretical terms and relations of self-reflexive interiority refer directly to the desires, operations, and normative relational patterns of intentional consciousness. The varieties of religious and theological discourse are inherently analogical. They draw on all three realms of meaning, but especially common sense and appropriated interiority, as the primary analogical sources for their ways of speaking about God (*Method*, 84; CWL, 2: chap. 5).

As human history develops and as human consciousness becomes increasingly differentiated, the intelligible relations among the four realms of meaning evolve. The technical language of explanatory theory gradually distinguishes itself from the practical discourse of common sense. With Aristotle, the special sciences are treated as specific branches of metaphysics, and deductive logic serves as the preferred method of epistemic integration. In the third stage of cognitive meaning, the empirical sciences and historical scholarship have become autonomous disciplines; philosophy thematizes the specialized methods and discursive practices of the different realms of meaning; philosophy also articulates a generalized empirical method that serves as the critical basis for achieving epistemic and ontological integration; and theology becomes an empirical and critical discipline, in its own right, based on eight collaborative functional specialties (*Method*, 84–99).

In the light of this contextual background, what are the relevant counterpositions to be avoided in the philosophical treatment of language and meaning? We can easily overlook or ignore the multiple carriers of meaning. A comprehensive philosophical hermeneutics must be attuned to the full polymorphism of meaningful human expressions, both linguistic and nonlinguistic. In the domain of linguistic meaning, the focus should not be exclusively cognitive, for the meaningful uses of language and speech are clearly not restricted to articulating and justifying truth claims. At the same time, the critical distinction between the commonsense meaning of ordinary language and the systematic meaning of technical discourse should not be obscured or denied. This semantic obscurity underlies Eddington's famous paradox of the two tables (*Method*, 84, 258, 274) and contributes to the illusions of scientism.

The *prelinguistic sources* of meaning and the *extralinguistic reference* of cognitive meaning should be explicitly recognized. Unless the causal genesis of meaning in intentional operations is acknowledged, human language is assigned an ontological autonomy it does not enjoy; and without a secure basis in critical realism, truth-bearing language loses its essential function of epistemically referring to being (CWL, 3:380–83). The later Wittgenstein was right to insist on the public character of language, its dependence on intersubjective criteria of use (*Method*, 254–57). But Wittgenstein's valuable insight into ordinary linguistic meaning cannot account for significant linguistic innovation and originality without recognizing equally innovative intellectual discoveries (insights) on the part of intentional subjects.

Though clearly important, the logical analysis of language has definite limits. The meaning of commonsense language is largely a function of its regular use and should not be submitted to the specialized demands of a logical system. And though theoretical systems can be logically tested for their clarity, coherence, and rigor, the provisional results of scientific inquiry are constantly subject to amendment and revision. Only transcendental method, not logical analysis alone, can keep pace with the dynamism of the sciences and their endless succession of theoretical discoveries and provisional syntheses.

As Plato's dialogues memorably reveal, the drama of human conversation is not synonymous with discursive argument.[109] Conversations occur between concretely situated persons. Arguments result from epistemic conflicts among opposing propositional truth claims (*Third Collection*, 182). Significant propositional disagreement, of course, does not preclude conversational civility and respect. In fact, in the absence of good will and civility among the discursive interlocutors, opposing arguments easily become biased, shrill, and interminable.

Lonergan's dialectical method divides philosophical propositions into positions and counterpositions. The positions invite intelligent and reasonable development. The counterpositions, because they are performatively inconsistent, call for intelligent and reasonable reversal. To recognize and acknowledge this personal incoherence, however, takes intellectual honesty and patience; it frequently requires a protracted process of self-appropriation and personal conversion. For this reason, a critical philosophical dialectic, even if it is intellectually compelling, is often existentially inadequate. For our philosophical interlocutors, whether ancient, medieval, modern, or contemporary, should never be reduced to their explicit philosophical assertions. Individual philosophers, both living and dead, are particular persons to whom we owe friendship and sympathy. We should humbly and patiently reach up to their minds in the hope of enlarging our own. The impartial criticism we eventually apply to their truth claims needs to be balanced by the openness and hermeneutic generosity we show them as our dialogical partners in inquiry.

The fellowship of inquiry that connects human history includes ancient philosophers, medieval theologians, modern scientists, and scholars and postmodern masters of suspicion. Despite the singular importance of this extraordinary fellowship, it has yielded an uneven legacy, a tangled knot of insights and oversights, which invites us, as it did Lonergan, to the shared task of critical appropriation.

CHAPTER TWO

Objective Knowing and Authentic Living

Classical culture has given way to a modern culture, and ...
the crisis of our age is in no small measure the fact that
modern culture has not yet reached its maturity.
—CWL, 4:238

Bernard Lonergan believed that personal and cultural maturity should be comprehensive.[1] He often cited Cardinal Newman's pedagogical theorem about respecting the whole of being and knowledge (*Second Collection*, 141–42, 148). If essential parts of an ordered whole are excluded or omitted, the remaining parts tend to be inflated or badly distorted. In the third stage of cognitive meaning, when the natural and human sciences have become highly specialized and historical scholarship emphasizes cultural variation and difference, Newman's theorem is especially relevant. In chapter 2 we explore this continuing relevance by asking, what are the essential parts of human reality that we presently tend to exclude or omit; why have we regularly neglected or ignored them; and what are the consequent distortions that flow from these strategic omissions?

Lonergan openly celebrated the intellectual achievements of the modern age: the new theoretical discoveries, the heightened historical mindedness, the birth of the human sciences, the symbiotic conjunction of theory and practice, the understanding and appraisal of human beings as situated symbolic animals. These remarkable epistemic advances, however, have not been complemented by a parallel advance in human self-knowledge. While the scope of the known has been greatly expanded, the interior life of the knower remains largely dismissed or ignored. As a result, modern culture is internally compromised by a striking and unsettling paradox. Its inquiry and learning, its science and scholarship, its technological prowess and economic power are truly unprecedented; but its self-interpretation, its dominant account of human reality, tends to be shallow and often demoralizing. From Lonergan's critical perspective, the deepest modern failure is philosophical and theological. Modern philosophy and theology have not yet risen to the exigent level of the empirical sciences and critical history. Until they achieve this necessary but belated advance, the cultural crises of our age will remain unresolved.

As a critical Christian humanist, Lonergan's primary cultural mission was to reconceive philosophy and theology in the light of what is best in the modern achievement. In his judgment, this achievement was largely the fruit of new methods of inquiry that had been successfully applied to the study of nature and history. Lonergan believed that the empirical and critical core of these methods could be fruitfully extended to exploring the intentional consciousness of the human subject and the diverse historical expressions of human religious activity. He made the interior life of the polymorphic subject the thematic focus of his philosophy; he made the critical interpretation of religious phenomena the methodical basis of a revised ecumenical theology (CWL, 17:353–83).

Lonergan's most important philosophical discoveries revealed the spiritual roots of our cultural predicament. In the troubled and uneven course of modernity, we have gradually lost confidence in our collective capacity to achieve objective knowledge, to make responsible moral choices, and to lead lives of authenticity and truth. While we humans cannot live without judging and choosing, we cannot live authentically without reasonable judgments and responsible choices. Pervasive skeptical doubts about the truth of our judgments and the value of our choices have profoundly affected our self-understanding and appraisal. They have also affected our understanding of God and of God's relation to natural and historical reality.

If modern culture is to become mature, it must also become comprehensive. The contemporary understanding of nature and history must be complemented by a parallel development in self-knowledge and knowledge of the divine. Such a momentous and belated development, Lonergan believed, was critical to restoring the cultural integrity of the West. How successful was Lonergan in advancing this challenging cultural mission? That is the central question to which these chapters are devoted. But before we can fairly appraise his success or failure, we must first understand the complexity of the modern age: its intellectual origins; its deliberate break with the past; its defining discoveries and developments; its philosophical and cultural failures; the reductive nature of its self-interpretation; the paradoxical crisis of confidence to which these reductions gave rise.

The Defining Revolutions of Modernity

Revolutions in theory and practice tend to have a common structure. They begin by liberating themselves from traditional beliefs and inherited institutions. The break with the past, however, is rarely as comprehensive as the revolutionary leaders intend. They were formed, after all, in the very traditions and institutions they now seek to destroy. It is only in retrospect that we can accurately distinguish what was abandoned, what was retained, and what was newly established in the place of the earlier order.

The modern world has been effectively shaped by four interdependent revolutions:[2] the Copernican Revolution in natural science, the nineteenth-century revolution in critical historiography, the democratic revolutions that began in Western Europe and North America, and the technological revolution that regularly converted theoretical discoveries into new sources of instrumental power. In each case the moderns turned explicitly against their classical and medieval predecessors. But this emancipatory effort was partial and not complete. For the ancients had also developed a science of nature, written great works in political and ecclesiastical history, created small-scale democratic republics, and applied their scientific insights effectively in architecture, engineering, and medicine.

In the light of this significant continuity, what was the famous quarrel between the ancients and the moderns really about? A helpful way to understand that quarrel is to reflect on the cultural authority of Aristotle, *il maestro di color che sanno*.³ Toward the close of the Hellenic era, Aristotle consolidated pre-Socratic and Platonic intellectual discoveries into a comprehensive and unified philosophy. His deeply influential texts, devoted to a broad range of theoretical and practical topics, contain both first-order statements about being and metatheoretical statements about inquiry and knowledge. The first-order statements are framed in Aristotle's metaphysical categories of matter and form, potency and actuality, essence and accident, categories meant to apply to all sensible substances. Aristotle's metaphysics investigates the essential attributes of being as such. Specific kinds of being are then treated in the special sciences. Thus physics studies changing being, biology living being, sensitive psychology sentient being, to cite three prominent examples. For Aristotle, physics, biology, and psychology are special cases of metaphysics. Their inquiries presuppose metaphysical principles; their discoveries are articulated in metaphysical terms and relations (CWL, 2:1–6; *Third Collection*, 41–44).

Aristotle's comprehensive cosmology occupies the heart of his philosophy.⁴ Sensible substances are divided into exhaustive and exclusive classes: natural substances that have their principle of motion and rest within themselves; artifacts whose principle of motion and rest is either in the craftsmen who made them or the human beings who put them to use. Natural substances are themselves divided into two separate classes: celestial substances, ungenerated and indestructible, which move in invariant circular patterns; terrestrial substances, which come into being and pass away, which grow and diminish, which gain and lose qualitative attributes, and which move in irregular and variable patterns.

The cosmos as a whole is eternal, as are its celestial substances and the terrestrial species whose individual members undergo generation and corruption. It is also hierarchically organized into different kinds of being having different levels of ontological value. At the base of the cosmic hierarchy are terrestrial substances that are graded ontologically in terms of their essence and powers. The hierarchy of being progressively ascends from stones to plants, to animals, to human beings. A structural and important ontological gap exists between terrestrial and celestial substances: while the former are mortal, the latter are immortal and therefore divine. At the peak of the metaphysical hierarchy is Aristotle's god(s), ungenerated and indestructible like the celestial substances, but immaterial and immobile as they are not.[5]

The immobile earth resides at the center of Aristotle's cosmos. The celestial substances, except for the fixed stars, move in orbit around the earth in perfect circular patterns. The ontological separation of terrestrial and celestial substances is reflected in Aristotle's physics. Celestial physics investigates the invariant motions of the heavenly bodies; terrestrial physics, the variable motions and changes of terrestrial substances whose behavior is influenced by art and violence as well as their own immanent natures.

The understanding of sensible substances, both artifacts and natural beings, is based on the four causes, matter, form, agent, and end. In the order of human discovery, inquiry regularly proceeds from effects to causes, from *that* to *why*, but in the order of actual causation from *why* to *that*.[6] Aristotle's causal matrix is intended to account for the whole of being, though Aristotle's divinity is immaterial and, as pure actuality (*energeia*), enjoys a perfect identity of form and end. As causal principles, both nature and art are inherently teleological; unlike the principle of violence (*bia*), they reliably operate to actualize natural potencies. The final causes of being are really explanatory and play an essential role in explaining both natural and artifactual change. In fact, Aristotle treats God as the proximate final cause of all celestial motion and the remote final cause of the natural development of terrestrial beings.

I have presented Aristotle's ontological beliefs in some detail in order to clarify the modern revolt against his intellectual authority.[7] The Copernican Revolution in astronomy and physics, which culminated in Newton's *Principia*, repudiated nearly all of Aristotle's cosmology. Copernicus explicitly rejected Aristotle's geocentrism. Kepler discovered the elliptical pattern of planetary orbits. Galileo proposed a unified account of nature (celestial and terrestrial) based on invariant mathematical laws. While the Newtonian laws of motion apply equally to the heavens and the earth, Newton's principle of inertia undermined the basis of Aristotle's physics, making the acceleration of motion rather than its constant velocity the natural phenomenon to be causally explained.

Galileo and Newton helped to create a new heuristic structure for natural science based on invariant classical laws rather than Aristotelian causes. Newton also insisted on the disciplinary autonomy of modern physics and its effective independence of metaphysical principles and categories. The teleological explanations of natural phenomena favored by Aristotle were deliberately excluded from the new science of nature and replaced by mechanical models of motion and change.[8]

In the nineteenth century, Darwin's evolutionary theory broke sharply with Aristotle's biology by affirming the genesis and perishing of species. The Darwinian principles of random variation and natural selection were also intended to preclude teleological explanations of species development and decline. Continuing advances in physics revealed that the cosmos itself has a dynamic history: that celestial substances and terrestrial species are not immortal but share in the universal processes of birth and death. Later in the century, Freud's depth psychology challenged the governing role assigned to reason (*nous*) by Aristotle and his philosophical descendants. Both Darwin and Freud, and their naturalistic successors, insisted on the enduring influence of our animal origins on all aspects of human psychology and culture.

The modern revolt against Aristotle's intellectual authority also extended to his metatheoretical principles.[9] Aristotle sharply distinguished the theoretical from the practical intellect and the theoretical from the practical life. Theoretical inquiry, he claimed, seeks to discover universal and invariant truths. It treats exclusively of objects subject to causal necessity; it is pursued for its own sake, culminating in certain knowledge of what cannot be otherwise. The virtues of the theoretical intellect (*episteme*, science, and *sophia*, philosophical wisdom) represent the summit of human achievement. When human beings participate in the theoretical life, they become mortal gods and achieve the highest degree of *eudaimonia* available to mortals.

By contrast, practical inquiry in the arts, ethics, and politics seeks truths that are particular and context dependent. Its intentional objects are contingent substances, exhibiting a high degree of diversity and variation. Moreover, practical inquiry is pursued for the sake of ends that lie beyond the knowledge it achieves. The explicit goal of art and politics is for the artifact to be made well or for the personal or communal action to be done well. Practical knowledge noticeably lacks the precision and finality of theoretical science. This limitation also applies to the practical intellectual virtues (*techne*, craftsmanship, and *phronesis*, practical wisdom). The political activities of the citizen and statesman are the highest forms of the practical life. Although the *Bios Politikos* is good in itself, its ultimate purpose is to support and protect the *Bios Theoretikos*, the truly godlike way for mortals to live.[10]

The leading early interpreters of modern science, like Francis Bacon and Descartes, deliberately reversed these Aristotelian ethical hierarchies. Bacon made the practical "fruits and works" that flow from scientific inquiry the pragmatic test of its truth and utility. Descartes made the governing purpose of the new science the "lordship and mastery" of nature. For both Descartes and Bacon, theoretical knowledge is ultimately a source of technical or instrumental power, power over the natural world, power that compels natural processes to serve human purposes and ends.[11] Both thinkers anticipated the critical alliance of *episteme* and *techne*, of scientific insight and technological power, which would transform medicine, engineering, agriculture, war, and morality in the modern era.

Could theoretical science also become the basis of more enlightened and effective political action? Many of the leading modern thinkers were inclined to believe so.[12] But genuine political activity occurs in a realm of freedom, plurality, and deliberative persuasion and choice. Its integrity is violated by assumptions of scientific necessity and by the artisan's reliance on manipulative material techniques. For manipulation in politics, whether physical or psychological, typically serves as an instrument of despotism and terror, while belief in historical necessity leads invariably to rigid ideologies, the cultural antithesis of genuine political thinking. The leading European theorists of social and political revolution, Hegel, Marx, and Lenin, succumbed to the illusion of historical necessity, with disastrous political consequences for the West.[13] One reason the democratic revolution in North America was so different from the terror-driven upheavals in France and Russia is that the founding fathers were political thinkers of the first rank who knew from their direct experience of self-government the practical requirements of enduring liberty.

Although the leading modern thinkers explicitly devalued the contemplative life and made scientific theory subordinate to its technical applications, they failed to break cleanly with Aristotle's theory of science. In the *Posterior Analytics* Aristotle defined science (*episteme*) as true certain knowledge of causal necessity.[14] While recognizing other forms of genuine knowledge—art and practical wisdom, for example—Aristotle's epistemic hierarchy placed science and philosophical wisdom at its peak. The philosophical interpreters of modern physics rejected Aristotle's geocentric cosmology and his metaphysically based science of nature, but they uncritically retained his demonstrative theory of science. They regarded scientific discoveries as permanent truths about universal and invariant natural processes. They designed their epistemological theories to explain how these logically ordered truths could be known with apodictic assurance. They used the inherited criteria of ontological necessity and epistemic certainty to separate genuine science from ordinary belief and opinion. They used the growing prestige of modern science and technology to challenge the epistemic legitimacy of common sense, metaphysics, theology, rhetoric, and poetry. Ironically, the leading moderns retained the most problematic part of Aristotle's legacy, his apodictic theory of science, while ignoring or rejecting his insightful accounts of common sense, practical wisdom, and the linguistic arts. Though Aristotle explicitly subordinated contingency to necessity, both ontologically and epistemically, his two-level universe of immortal and mortal substances left room for both modalities of being. The invariant laws of modern physics, by contrast, appeared to eliminate contingency, and therefore freedom and moral responsibility, from the whole of the cosmic order.

Toward the close of the eighteenth century, Kant reflected on the ultimate meaning and importance of the Scientific Revolution. He concluded that a revolution in philosophy must complete the historic cosmological reversal initiated by Copernicus.[15] For Kant, the interpretive key to the new cosmology was a radical shift in epistemic perspective. Instead of accepting the observable reality of the world as it appears to a geocentric perceiver, Copernicus reconceived the cosmos from the imagined perspective of a heliocentric observer. In the light of Copernicus's proposal, the unquestioned epistemic privilege of the terrestrial perspective could no longer be taken for granted. Drawing on the example of Copernicus, Kant proceeded to challenge the philosophical basis of Aristotle's scientific realism. As an epistemic realist, Aristotle had assumed that the human knower must conform him- or herself to the known. In metaphysical terms, this meant that for human knowledge to occur, the substantial form of the knowable reality must somehow come to be present in the rational soul of the knower. In the knowable substance, the relevant form exists under material conditions, but in the knower under conditions of immateriality. But since ontological forms are invariably received according to the modal condition of the recipient, human knowledge is ultimately based on a modified formal identity between the epistemic object and subject. The specific intelligibility of the object in act becomes formally identical with the actualized intellect of the cognitive subject. Thus Aristotle subtly agrees with his ancient predecessors who had cryptically claimed that "like is known by like."

What epistemological reversal did Kant propose in order to preserve the scientific status of Euclidean geometry and Newtonian physics? He accepted Aristotle's principle of epistemic conformity between subject and object. But he insisted that for scientific knowledge to occur the object of knowledge must conform to the a priori conditions present in the knower. These a priori conditions include the pure forms of sensibility, Newtonian space and time, and the pure categories of the understanding, including lawfully invariant causation. Because these transcendental conditions present in the cognitive subject serve to *constitute* the Kantian object of knowledge, Aristotle's epistemic realism must be flatly rejected. Kant called his Copernican transformation of Aristotle's theory of knowledge "critical or transcendental idealism." According to Kant, objective knowledge, scientific knowledge of causal necessity, is exclusively knowledge of sensible *appearances* (of the causally ordered *phenomenal* realm), not *noumenal* knowledge of mind-independent reality. But from Kant's distinctively modern perspective, this radical limitation of science's ontological import should actually be welcomed. For by strictly limiting scientific objects to causally ordered phenomena, Kant deliberately made room for a noumenal rational faith in moral freedom and obligation.[16]

The philosophical dilemma Kant faced was a sophisticated version of the cultural dilemma confronting his age. Kant accepted the classical theory of science as true certain knowledge of causal necessity. He also accepted the strict categorical imperatives of the traditional moral law. But the exceptionless necessity of nature seemed to leave no room for the rational freedom that Kantian morality required. How could a critical modern philosophy accommodate both natural science and disinterested moral agency, the Enlightenment's two greatest cultural achievements?

Kant's "solution" to this unsettling predicament was his theory of transcendental idealism. By limiting scientific necessity to the phenomenal realm, he could preserve the epistemic validity of Newtonian science while circumscribing its ontological import, thus blunting the threat modern science ostensibly posed to moral freedom and responsibility.

Kant's limitative theory of knowledge was based on a new type of ontological dualism: the metaphysics of nature that is governed by invariant causal laws, and the metaphysics of pure practical reason that autonomously legislates unconditional laws of moral obligation. The theoretical and practical exercises of reason are still sharply segregated, though now both have become sources of universal law. While Kant accepts the Baconian alliance of science and technology, he clearly refuses to conflate the *practical* and *technical* operations of reason. The categorical imperatives of pure practical reason are explicitly distinguished from hypothetical imperatives of skill and pragmatic counsels of prudence. Kant's autonomous moral laws are never intended to promote human power and happiness. The goal of Kantian morality is not to help us become happy, but to help us choose and act in a way that merits or deserves happiness.[17]

If Aristotle represents the philosophical climax of classical Hellenism, then Kant is his critical Enlightenment counterpart. Both thinkers embody the core convictions, assumptions, and dilemmas of their time. Aristotle's majestic and comprehensive philosophy rests on his basic cosmological principles. The cosmos is organized hierarchically into a plurality of immortal species. The metaphysical hierarchy is split between heaven and earth, between immortal and invariant, and mortal and variable substances. Human beings are at the crux of the cosmic split, sharing attributes with animals and gods. Aristotle's epistemological and ethical dualism between theory and practice corresponds to his ontological division between necessary and contingent causation. A similar though not identical dichotomy appears in the sharp political contrast he draws between free citizens and the noncitizen members of the *polis*. Teleological causation is omnipresent in Aristotle's universe. All things, in accordance with their specific natures, strive to imitate Aristotle's God, the first principle and cause of being.

Kant's architectonic philosophy is based on his reading of the Copernican Revolution, the defining theoretical event of the modern Enlightenment. The Newtonian world order is uniform, mechanical, and egalitarian. It is an order of invariant law and causal necessity that leaves no room for freedom and meaningful choice. But personal freedom and responsibility are the basis of authentic morality and the foundation of all human dignity. To preserve their essential legitimacy Kant resorts to a new set of ontological and anthropological separations between nature and reason, theory and practice, science and morality. Kant's metaphysical dichotomy is not a division within the uniform Newtonian cosmos, but rather a strict separation between the phenomenal and noumenal orders of being, the sharply segregated realms of causal necessity and practical freedom. For Kant, philosophy's critical cultural role is to validate rationally these important and indispensable dichotomies. For as Kant proudly declares, our enlightened age is an age of criticism, and to criticism everything, including the operations of reason itself, must submit.[18]

The structural dualisms at the heart of Kant's critical philosophy proved as unstable as the ontological divisions within Aristotle's cosmos. While Aristotle's cosmology could not survive the theoretical discoveries of the new physics, the static Kantian world-picture of timeless natural and moral laws was eventually undermined by the emerging historical consciousness that marked the second phase of the European Enlightenment.

The Anthropological Turn: Human Nature and History

Four major topics dominate the inquiry of classical philosophy: the *cosmos*, the comprehensive order of being; the *polis*, the voluntary association of citizens for the sake of the good life (*eudaimonia*); the rational *psyche*, the center and source of distinctively human activity; *theion*, the divine being(s) at the summit of the ontological hierarchy. Corresponding to these four ontological themes are the major subdivisions within classical thought: cosmology, political science, rational psychology, and theology. Because the cosmos is assumed to be comprehensive in scope, the other kinds of being are believed to exist and act within it. Aristotle's cosmos, as we saw, was hierarchically ordered, with gods at the summit of the ontological hierarchy and inanimate matter at the base. Human beings, as rational political animals, occupied a complex position in the cosmic order. They shared the mortality of the terrestrial substances and the noetic capacity of the divine. Humans are, by nature, political animals because they cannot actualize their natural *telos* apart from a thriving political community. Only by exercising the full range of virtues, deliberately cultivated and acquired in the civic life of the *polis*, can they become mortal gods.

For Aristotle, theoretical inquiry is identical with philosophy. Metaphysics is the basic philosophical discipline, and the categories and principles of metaphysics apply to the whole of being. As a result, natural substances, human agents, and divine beings are all conceived metaphysically: natural substances in terms of matter and form; humans in terms of body and soul; the divine in terms of eternal, immaterial actuality. Aristotle's philosophy is majestic in its comprehensiveness and internal order. Because of this inner coherence, however, a fundamental revision of Aristotle's cosmology will have destabilizing effects on his anthropology and theology as well.

The Scientific Revolution of the seventeenth and eighteenth centuries constituted a major theoretical and cultural advance on premodern achievement.[19] Although Aristotle had implicitly distinguished common sense from theory by contrasting what is first for us as sentient beings and what is first in the causal order, modern physics introduced a much sharper separation between descriptive and explanatory knowledge. Descriptive knowledge characterizes things in terms of their observable relations to us as sentient perceivers. Explanatory knowledge characterizes the same things in terms of their intelligible relations with one another (CWL, 3:316–17). Aristotle's geocentric cosmology contains an unstable mixture of descriptive and explanatory categories. The mathematical physics proposed by the moderns uncouples this confusing mixture by prescinding from sensible forms altogether while focusing attention on verifiable intelligible relations expressed in functional laws.

For Aristotle, all the theoretical sciences are specialized applications of metaphysics. The modern empirical sciences, by contrast, gradually emancipate themselves from metaphysical principles and categories. They insist on their disciplinary and conceptual autonomy from philosophical, political, and theological control. As relatively autonomous disciplines, they establish their own methods of discovery and verification, their specialized heuristic structures and vocabularies, their self-governing communities of apprenticeship and certification. In the course of modernity, the specialized natural and human sciences eventually create a distinct and unique differentiation of theoretical consciousness.

We have been acknowledging important metatheoretical changes in the disciplinary relations between philosophy and the natural sciences. But modern physics represented as well a substantive transformation in our understanding of the natural universe. Having detailed essential aspects of that transformation in the preceding section, we won't repeat them here. The new mathematical physics based on universal and invariant classical laws prescinded entirely from Aristotle's formal and final causes. Only the material and efficient causes were retained from Aristotle's matrix of theoretical explanation. As a result, the dominant cosmological picture derived from modern physics tended to be materialist and mechanist in character, with valueless matter undergoing purposeless motion in accordance with blind and impersonal laws. The modern cosmos was broadly conceived as a disenchanted universe with no place within it for the operation of human or divine intelligence.[20]

Clearly, this disenchanted and valueless cosmos cannot be the whole of what exists. After all, scientific knowledge of the cosmos represents an extraordinary intellectual and cultural achievement, the very source of modern pride and self-assurance. How then to account for the intellectual and spiritual operations at the core of scientific inquiry, if nature itself provides no basis for their occurrence? Descartes became the spiritual father of modern philosophy through the answer he gave to this urgent and inescapable question.[21] He divided reality into two separate and exhaustive realms: *res extensa*, unthinking valueless nature, and *res cogitans*, immaterial purposive mind. Descartes reduced the whole of nature to valueless matter moving in accordance with impersonal mathematical laws. The Cartesian cosmos, outlined in *Le Monde*, is a determinist universe in which all of material reality, including the bodies of humans, animals, and plants, is completely contained. Nature is depicted as a meaningless and purposeless realm of motion that exists to be mastered, controlled, and exploited by the rational mind.

Res cogitans, by contrast, is the exact antithesis of Cartesian nature. It is immaterial, without extension or motion, and the ontological source of all possible meaning and value. Descartes recognizes two forms of *res cogitans*, infinite and finite. His omniscient and omnipotent God is infinite *res cogitans*. The human mind is a special case of finite *res cogitans*, initially lacking in knowledge and power, but capable of indefinite progress in both of these related domains. The ultimate purpose of Cartesian method is to discipline the finite mind through the deliberate control of the will so that *res cogitans* may steadily increase in both knowledge and power. Unless it obeys a rigorous intellectual method, Descartes contends, the human mind operates haphazardly, rashly assenting to judgments that lack certain and indubitable evidence. For Descartes, minds without scientific knowledge are inevitably minds without power, first power over themselves and their own operations, then power over the natural universe they were created by God to understand and subdue for the benefit of humankind.

The finite Cartesian mind has two fundamental capacities: understanding and will. Understanding is the faculty of perceptual and intellectual awareness, will is the faculty of judgment and choice. Human error arises when the will affirms mind-dependent ideas presented by the understanding that lack clarity and distinctness. Error can be systematically avoided and truth reliably achieved, however, when the assent of the will is reserved for indubitable ideas. These indubitable ideas can then be logically ordered in a deductive system analogous to Euclidean geometry. In Descartes's revisionary image of the newly bountiful tree of modern knowledge, the roots of the tree are metaphysical (the rational knowledge of God and the soul); the trunk of the tree is physical (the mathematical science of nature); the branches of the tree are technical (the useful arts of medicine, mechanics, and morals); and the fruits of the tree are the promised Baconian benefits of the new alliance between science and technology: extended life, augmented power, and greater terrestrial happiness.[22]

Kant's philosophical anthropology is a refined and revised version of the rational psychology Descartes proposed in the *Meditations*. While Kant denies the scientific status of Cartesian metaphysics (for Kant, there can be no *science* of God and the soul), he preserves the mathematical science of nature and the Baconian alliance between theoretical and technical reason. Kant insists, however, on a sharp separation between scientific knowledge and morality. The technical applications of science that extend human power and happiness (the Cartesian and Baconian fruits of knowledge) are fundamentally different from the autonomous operations of pure *practical reason*. Kant's categorical morality of duty never functions as a technical instrument serving human desire and fear.

Kant also refines Descartes's dualistic psychology, by identifying three distinct faculties of the soul: sensibility, the faculty of intuition; understanding, the faculty of rule-governed synthesis; reason, the faculty that seeks and demands the unconditioned. Kant then relies on these psychological distinctions to clarify systematic ambiguities in Descartes's theory of knowledge. The intuitions of sensibility, the concepts of understanding, and the ideas of reason are fundamentally different forms of mental representation. With these categorial distinctions in place, Kant proceeds to articulate his critical philosophical principles. Thus, intuitions without concepts are epistemically blind; concepts without intuitions are ontologically empty; the only intuitions available to humans are sensory (not intellectual) in character; and the synthesizing function of concepts requires a stratum of pure or empirical intuitions that conceptual rules can order and unify. Finally, because there are no human intuitions to instantiate the ideas of reason, their epistemic function, unlike the constitutive function attributed to intuitions and concepts, is exclusively regulative.[23]

Human knowledge occurs only at the level of judgment, but for judgments to be scientific, they must be synthetic and known to be true a priori. For Kant, the only judgments that satisfy these strict requirements are the judgments of mathematics and physics. Kant's limitative principles of reason, therefore, are designed to have both positive and negative import. To summarize Kant's important conclusions: metaphysics cannot be a science (*pace* Descartes); the mathematical judgments of geometry and arithmetic are scientific articulations of the invariant structures of pure space and time; the universal judgments of Newtonian physics are scientific articulations of the causal structure of nature, where nature is identified with the phenomenal order of law-governed sensible appearances, not the noumenal order of independent things in themselves.

While Kant's transcendental philosophy is clearer and more critical than Descartes's, it is no less distorted and problematic. For both of these great modern thinkers, the natural world is disenchanted, completely lacking in meaning, purpose, value, and freedom. The rational human subject is disembodied and effectively segregated from natural, social, and historical causation. In Kant's moral philosophy, both natural and historical causes are designated *heteronomous* factors that threaten to compromise the rational subject's practical *autonomy*. The disenchanted cosmology and the socially atomistic anthropology are perfectly and deliberately correlated. For Kant's radical inflation of the autonomous power of pure practical reason requires an equally radical deflation and devaluation of the ontological status of nature. To give Kant his due, he deliberately limits the importance of theoretical science to make room for morality and responsible choice. But by striving in this way to preserve human dignity and freedom, Kant radically separates human reason from nature and human knowledge from the reality of being, while reducing God's causal role to that of a regulative rational ideal.

The Newtonian world-picture that captivated Kant was essentially static. The causal laws that allegedly governed the cosmos were universal and invariant, as were the moral laws legislated by pure practical reason. Although Kant believed that significant progress had occurred in the disciplines of physics and moral philosophy, he excluded even the possibility of progress from his metaphysics of nature and morals. In directly challenging Kant's cultural authority, Hegel altered the course of Western philosophy by emphasizing the singular importance of history and spiritual development. Hegel attributed historicity and development to the natural world as well as to human society and culture. He deliberately designed his comprehensive dialectical laws to explain all ontological change, both natural and spiritual. In fact, for Hegel, the developing order of nature is a dialectical expression of Absolute Spirit and not its ontological antithesis as asserted by Descartes and Kant.

Hegel was firmly committed to overcoming the structural dualisms he had inherited from Kant: between nature and reason, necessity and freedom, desire and duty, what merely is and what ought to be. He was also committed, against the basic thrust of scientific modernity, to restoring teleological explanations to science and philosophy. In Hegel's great metaphysical synthesis, *Absolute Spirit* (the Hegelian divine principle) begets sensible nature as a required ontological condition for the subsequent temporal emergence of society and culture (Hegel's *objective spirit*). Finite human (*subjective individual*) spirits, in turn, causally depend on both nature and culture for their existence and personal development. Human beings, for Hegel, are not disengaged practical agents segregated from a disenchanted universe. Rather, they are finite, temporal, situated subjects, embodied in nature, embedded in social and cultural history, striving for personal freedom in accordance with dialectical laws. For Hegel, the emerging freedom and autonomy of God, Absolute Spirit, is the ultimate *telos* of history. Divine freedom, however, is not an eternal ontological given but an evolving historical achievement, causally dependent on the essential contributions of finite human agents. In fact, human beings fulfill their own spiritual *telos* by contributing, directly or indirectly, consciously or unconsciously, to actualizing the comprehensive purpose of God.[24]

Despite its visionary sweep, Hegel's Absolute idealism did not command the intellectual allegiance of practicing scientists and historical scholars. Different aspects of his philosophy were severely criticized by Kierkegaard, Feuerbach, Marx, and the many active disciples of Darwin and Ranke. But these pointed critical objections did not mean a wholesale repudiation of Hegel's numerous insights—not at all. By restoring human beings to nature and history, by insisting on their essential embodiment and sociocultural embeddedness, by validating the philosophical significance of art, religion, and politics, Hegel transformed anthropological thought in the nineteenth century and discredited the important Kantian dualisms he had inherited.

Though Hegel reasserted the spiritual primacy of speculative reason and contemplative knowledge, he also emphasized the ethical importance of passions and feelings. He shared this corrective emphasis on feeling with the Romantic movements in England, France, Germany, and North America. Like Hegel, the great Romantic thinkers repudiated Kant's strict bifurcation of disenchanted nature and disengaged reason. For the Romantics, the natural world is not disenchanted but alive, and imbued with meaning and value. Newton's depiction of nature as a lifeless, lawful machine is judged to be abstract and one sided, a deliberately impoverished account fashioned to justify human technical control of earth, sea, and sky. But the Romantics insisted that the theoretical stance of rational scientific detachment is a flawed way to experience the reality of nature. That objectifying stance effectively precludes a receptive openness to nature's dynamic self-disclosure through the senses, the imagination, and the heart. These receptive and affective capacities reveal, *pace* Descartes and Kant, that we humans belong to nature, that we share in its seasonal rhythms and dynamic energies, that we can learn from its economy and grace. And just as nature is organic and vital rather than mechanical and lifeless, so we humans are creatures of sensibility and responsive emotion even more than detached rationality.[25]

Karl Marx represents an especially powerful synthesis of these competing cultural and anthropological currents. Marx shares the Baconian ideal of knowledge as transforming power; he shares the Hegelian vision of a teleological history culminating in freedom; he shares the Romantic critique of the primacy of speculative reason. For Marx, human beings are essentially laboring animals who humanize themselves by producing their own means of subsistence. They are also sociohistorical animals whose productive capacities and needs develop through distinct historical stages. Marx further believes that the most credible and explanatory historical narrative is the unfinished story of dialectical struggle between the forces and relations of production. Both human production and consumption are socially organized historical processes. But since the original division of labor, socioeconomic relations have been relations of conflict, initially between ancient masters and slaves, then between medieval lords and serfs, and now between modern capitalists and the urban proletariat. Despite its violent past, history is moving dialectically toward a classless society without conflict, oppression, and division. To achieve history's immanent *telos* requires a decisive revolution led by the proletariat and practically guided by Marx's science of history. As a radical Baconian, Marx believed that his dialectical science of history could radically transform human society as the new sciences of nature had begun to transform the material face of the earth.

Marx shared Hegel's heuristic assumption that history's teleological development obeys dialectical laws. However, Marx is a Promethean humanist and atheist, who completely rejected the religious dimension of Hegelian thought. The ultimate *telos* of history, Marx insists, is the autonomy of man, not of God, a *telos* that requires the radical abolition of capitalism and the emergence of a classless society. Although the secular eschatology Marx espoused proved illusory, it resonated powerfully on several continents for more than a century and a half. How should we account for the intellectual and emotional power of Marx's radical utopian project? In hindsight, the answer seems clear. More than any other modern anthropologist, Marx combined the insights and aspirations of the radical Enlightenment and the European Romantic movement. He proposed a theoretical and practical way to overcome Kant's intractable dualisms by naturalizing spirit, humanizing nature, and dialectically justifying the tormented history of the human race.

Charles Darwin undercuts the Kantian dualisms in a substantially different way. His evolutionary biology, a genetic causal account of the origin and perishing of terrestrial species, repudiates the Aristotelian belief in species-immortality. Darwin also complicates Newtonian cosmology by introducing two novel heuristic structures into modern science. Newtonian physics is based on the search for invariant causal laws. The Darwinian explanation of the birth, survival, decline, and death of biological species relies on statistical and genetic methods of inquiry. The evolutionary process follows statistical rather than classical laws, and its contingent and provisional outcomes are powerful examples of biological emergence, survival, and decline. But the Darwinian picture of species-competition is clearly not Romantic in spirit. Biological existence, for Darwin, is a continuous struggle for survival; through random variation and natural selection the well-adapted species survive and the poorly adapted perish. If there is any moral lesson to be drawn from the relentless evolutionary process, it is the one Tennyson sharply articulates: "Nature is red in tooth and claw."[26]

What anthropological insights can be drawn from Darwinian naturalism? Though classical thinkers like Aristotle and Aquinas recognized the animal nature of human beings, they deliberately emphasized the human similarity to the divine. For Aristotle, humans are the only noetic (intelligent) animals; for Aquinas, as spiritual creatures endowed with intellect and will, humans are created in the image and likeness of God. For the ancients, the biological and spiritual dimensions of human existence are complementary, however mysterious their causal interdependence. Yet following Darwin's lead, scientific studies of the human being after the mid-nineteenth century were exclusively conducted *von unten auf*, from the bottom up. This meant deliberately emphasizing the biological and genetic similarity of humans to the higher primates. It is critical to remember that modern science was based on the explicit rejection of classical ontological hierarchies. As Newton had attempted to *reduce* all natural change to the operation of physical laws, so Darwin's generalizing disciples attempted to *reduce* all human behavior to the operation of biological principles. Though Descartes and Kant had insisted that the human operations of reason and will were different in kind from the lawful motions of matter, the forceful discrediting of their ontological dualisms and the growing theoretical prestige of evolutionary theory gave reductive naturalism a powerful boost. The comprehensive naturalization of human existence (biologism) became an increasingly important heuristic and cultural ideal.

The late nineteenth century also witnessed the emergence of the empirical human sciences, psychology, sociology, economics, and anthropology. Their belated appearance made the following methodological questions inescapable: How are these new human sciences related to the modern sciences of nature, particularly physics and biology? If they are fundamentally different in character, does this require a philosophical commitment to the discredited Kantian dualisms? But if these early modern dualisms are no longer tenable, then how should the natural and human sciences be credibly differentiated? Wilhelm Dilthey is the key figure in this important and ongoing controversy. Dilthey distinguished the sciences of nature (*Naturwissenschaften*) from the sciences of spirit (*Geisteswissenschaften*) by contrasting the causal explanation of nature (*erklären*) with the hermeneutic interpretation of the expressions of spirit (*verstehen*).[27] Dilthey emphasisized that the empirical data of the human sciences, in contrast to the sensible data of biology and physics, are intentional carriers of meaning and value. We cannot really understand these bearers of meaning without interpreting and appraising their objective significance and import.

The human sciences, according to Dilthey, are essentially interpretive and evaluative, while the natural sciences are not. The modern natural sciences are based on classical, statistical, and genetic heuristic structures; the human sciences add a new and irreducible heuristic dimension. Although human existence is clearly illuminated by natural causality (we are, undeniably, physical and biological beings), its complex and layered intelligibilty cannot be reduced to natural causes and laws. The questions we invariably ask about human existence include inescapable questions of meaning and value: interpretive questions, evaluative questions, questions of right and wrong, virtue and vice, good and evil, holiness and sin, historical progress and decline. To answer them credibly requires making interpretive distinctions and acknowledging explanatory causes that the natural sciences neglect or ignore. For humans are spiritual as well as natural beings, and among the spiritual causes we need to acknowledge are the intentional desires, operations, and exigent norms of the human subject.

No twentieth-century philosopher was more opposed to the reductive project of exclusive naturalism than Edmund Husserl.[28] Adopting the psychological insights of Brentano, Husserl emphasized the intentionality of human consciousness. When human beings are neither asleep nor unconscious, they are polymorphic intentional subjects. Their distinctively human operations are intentional in nature—that is, there is a psychological accusative or intentional content that they are inherently *of* or *about*. In fact, these recurrent psychological episodes or acts (perceiving, imagining, remembering, questioning, understanding, deciding, and judging, to name just a few) cannot be properly identified apart from their intentional contents.

Brentano and Husserl correctly insisted that the relevant data of empirical psychology are these conscious intentional episodes in the life of the human subject. While the initial focus of Husserl's phenomenological studies was on cognitional or epistemic operations, the scope of phenomenological inquiry was gradually extended to the entire range of intentional consciousness. Unfortunately, Husserl's practice of phenomenology was compromised by the Cartesian principle of immanence, the mistaken belief that the contents of intentional acts depend for their existence on the subject's intentional operations. Though Husserl advanced the reflexive study of consciousness well beyond Descartes and Kant, he uncritically adopted their immanent construal of intentional content. Their dubious assumption of cognitive immanence seemed to preclude the human being's intentional encounter with mind-independent reality. The existential critics of Husserl, beginning with Heidegger, strongly objected to the idealist strain in his philosophy. Heidegger wanted to break completely with the perceptual model of human existence that had dominated modern thought. From Descartes to Husserl, modern philosophers had regularly pictured human beings as detached perceivers, as passive spectators enclosed within the private theater of individual consciousness. The fundamental relation of human subjects to objects was taken to be perceptual. To subvert this model, Heidegger deliberately redescribed human beings as *Dasein*, as finite situated beings immersed in a *Lebenswelt* (a sociocultural life-world) with other mortals, burdened by finitude and care and faced with the inevitability of personal death. For the early Heidegger, *Dasein* is essentially being unto death, confronting or avoiding the truth and implications of its own mortality.[29]

From birth until death, therefore, human beings are immersed in a common world of meaning and value, of making and doing, of interacting with others, of responding to the demands of care and anxiety in a myriad of practical ways. Only when these primordial modes of engagement with the lifeworld are disrupted, when their common world of meaning and purpose collapses or is seriously challenged, do they adopt a posture of detachment and reflective scrutiny. The *spectatorial* stance of perceiving and observing isolated objects, traditionally privileged by philosophers, is actually a derivative and secondary mode of being human; the sensible things composing the lifeworld are not primarily objects of perception, but constitutive elements in a network of common significance and action, whose independent reality, though practically alterable, is not really in question.

Husserl was preoccupied with epistemic concerns, particularly the quest for cognitive certainty. Like Descartes before him, he structured his philosophical method to ensure the possibility of "rigorous science." The leading European existentialists, by contrast, largely ignored the quest for certainty and the epistemic concerns underlying it. Their focus instead was moral and political, on the inescapable personal demand for authentic decision and choice. The European world they inhabited was in turmoil: the slaughter and carnage of two global wars, the rise of totalitarian states, the despair created by the Great Depression, the collapse of parliamentary democracy. Faced with these urgent historical crises, the self-respect of philosophers demanded a stance of engagement rather than detachment, of active resistance rather than passive submission to the perceptual given. There was no escaping uncertainty and risk in either personal or political decisions. There was no trusted wisdom or guidance to draw upon. The urgent practical imperative was to act boldly, resisting injustice in its multiple forms without illusion or pretense. Personal integrity, manliness, courage, and loyalty were the indispensable virtues. These were the virtues of the soldier and resistance fighter rather than the disengaged scholar or laboratory scientist. The epistemic and ontological concerns of traditional philosophy, it seemed, had for now become irrelevant.[30]

Both Husserl and the leading existentialists were responding to the unfolding crisis of Europe. For Husserl, that crisis was essentially epistemic and theoretical. The human capacity for genuinely scientific knowledge had to be reaffirmed and defended. Husserl believed that only transcendental phenomenology could satisfy this critical cultural need. For his existentialist critics, the crisis was equally profound but radically different in nature. The moral and political structures of Europe were collapsing under the weight of momentous historical events. The authenticity of philosophers as human beings and citizens was directly at stake. Would they withdraw into the labyrinth of consciousness in search of an illusory and irrelevant certainty, or would they throw themselves bravely into the struggles of the human world when it seemed on the verge of destruction. To choose, to act, to commit oneself irrevocably, to risk everything in a potentially hopeless cause—this was the desperate portrait of human authenticity they frequently espoused. Authentic living, in their dramatic accounts of its urgent demands, seemed entirely separate from objective knowing (CWL, 4:219–21).

Despite its impressive intellectual achievements, modern culture has struggled to achieve a comprehensive understanding of human existence. The Cartesian turn to the isolated ego initially segregated humans from nature and history. But Darwin's reinsertion of humans within the natural order often fostered a reductive naturalism, while the Hegelian emphasis on history revealed the moral and political ambiguity of the European past. Transcendental idealism, in both Kant and Husserl, radically enlarged the powers of the rational subject; Marx inflated and deified the human species as a whole. The European existentialists desperately separated authentic existence from the quest for truth and authentic action from directive knowledge. The critical postmodern emphases on global technology and mass entertainment and on institutional and linguistic determinism have deepened our adversarial culture of suspicion. In this heated climate of pervasive suspicion, sweeping rhetorical judgments are increasingly fashionable. The "death of God" is blithely asserted, as well as the "death of the subject," and even, we are cynically assured, "the death of man."

Rhetorical inflation aside, what is the deeper meaning of these questionable public obituaries? I think the critical point at issue is basic. The Copernican Revolution led to the death of the ancient cosmology; it did not entail the death of the cosmos itself. A similar distinction can be applied to postmodern anthropology. It is not "man" or the "subject" who has died but particular ways of understanding and conceiving human existence. The most influential anthropological replacements, however, are not visions of ourselves we can live by authentically. The resulting vacuum in culturally reliable self-knowledge comes at a cost, for we humans are self-interpreting animals, and without a credible and comprehensive account of our common humanity, we no longer know who we are or what to expect of ourselves. When Lonergan emphasized the "immaturity" of modern culture, this profound personal and cultural quandary is a major part of what he meant.

The Critique of Objectivity and Truth

One abreviated way to state the cultural predicament of modernity is this: the discoveries of modern physics and biology undermined the classical Aristotelian cosmology. The Newtonian and Darwinian accounts of nature differed in fundamental respects from the hierarchical Aristotelian world-picture. However, the moderns were often more effective in destroying than creating. Despite their impressive theoretical achievements, they failed to create a credible and comprehensive cosmology of their own. Clearly, our contemporaries know more about the universe than any of their scientific predecessors. Yet we still lack a credible account of how the different parts of reality fit together to form an intelligible whole. In particular, we don't understand how the discoveries of the specialized sciences fit together with what we know about human beings from personal experience, common sense, the reflective study of history, and from carefully appropriating the insights of philosophy and theology. We have increasingly specialized knowledge of the universe without an integrative vision of how we humans actually belong to it.

One of our most profound cultural needs, then, is for a credible nonreductive cosmology. Although we clearly can't return to the discredited Aristotelian hierarchies, it is equally doubtful that we can avoid recognizing hierarchy as such.[31] The earliest modern philosophers tried to resolve this dilemma by allocating cosmology to mathematical physics and assigning anthropology to the philosophical investigation of disengaged reason. Ostensibly, they solved the demand for integration by accepting irreducible dualisms between nature and reason, necessity and freedom, science and morality. These sharp philosophical dichotomies were not affirmed arbitrarily. They were explicitly intended to preserve human dignity by affirming the powers of theoretical and practical reason: to uphold theoretical reason's claim to objective knowledge of nature; to uphold practical reason's claim to objective knowledge of the moral law. This way of preserving human dignity and freedom, however, came at a formidable price, the price of Kant's critical idealism. For the ontological bifurcation of phenomena and noumena meant the loss of our human ability to know reality or being as it is. Thus, Kant deliberately preserved scientific knowledge but diminished its ontological significance, and he preserved human freedom and responsibility by making them matters of rational faith rather than practical experience.

During the second phase of the Enlightenment through the combined influence of Hegel, Marx, Darwin, and the Romantic movement, the Kantian strategy collapsed. Human beings were conceived more holistically and deliberately reinserted into nature and history. The new heuristic emphasis was on communal belonging rather than detached isolation. Human beings, from conception until death, were fundamentally conditioned by both natural causes and sociocultural education and training. Since the mid-nineteenth century, anthropological theories based on these revised heuristic assumptions have provided a much richer and truer account of human existence, of our situated subjectivity and freedom.[32]

But the anthropological turn to nature and history created its own set of quandaries and challenges. The cultural confusions that emerged and gained traction were often philosophical in origin. Ontological naturalism made imperial claims on behalf of evolutionary biology, seeking to *reduce* all human activity to biological principles and causes. The new critical historiography properly emphasized cultural diversity and pluralism. However, the proponents of historicism interpreted cultural pluralism in an aggressively relativist manner. For the committed historicist, there are no transcultural norms by which to appraise the moral beliefs and practices of our predecessors and contemporaries. To address these different philosophical confusions persuasively, while preserving the groundbreaking insights of both phases of the modern Enlightenment, we need critically to distinguish: the empirical sciences from scientism, critical history from historicism, cultural sensitivity and respect for pluralism from moral and religious relativism.

Because the dominant mind-set in the contemporary academy often fails to acknowledge these essential distinctions, the tenets of scientism are frequently asserted as incontrovertible truths: "The earth is just one of the planets; man is just one of the brutes; God is just a projection from the psychological depths; religion is just a façade for economic and social interests" (CWL, 3:704). Faced with these reductive secularist claims, it is tempting to affirm the discredited dualisms of the Cartesian era. But the insights of reductive anthropology also tend to be more critical than constructive. The Enlightenment ideals of reason, freedom, and personal and historical responsibility were flawed, not in themselves, but in the way they were originally conceived and defended.

Both Descartes and Kant tied theoretical reason to necessity and certainty, embracing the classical theory of science. Careful study of the history of science has shown that this embrace was a serious mistake. Empirical science, in fact, is a fallible self-correcting collaborative enterprise that depends on the critical control of socially transmitted belief.[33] The liberation of science from the quest for certainty has also liberated human reason from its atomistic isolation. Empirical scientists are not detached and disembodied egos but polymorphic intentional subjects, deeply rooted in nature, society, and history. Theoretical inquiry is only one of their many important conscious activities. Actively engaged scientists are educated in specialized research communities where they learn the investigative methods and technical vocabularies of their discipline. They are finite, fallible beings, motivated by a myriad of desires and constantly vulnerable to bias and prejudice. Their scientific education is a cultural apprenticeship in a distinct but limited realm of cognitive meaning. Within that circumscribed realm, the intellectual emphasis is on theoretical desires, exigent norms, specialized methods and heuristic procedures, technical vocabularies, and critical forms of peer review and appraisal. The epistemic results of this dynamic collaborative enterprise, which transcends all national boundaries, are not permanent truths, but the best available opinions of the global research community. Truth is what practicing scientists are commonly seeking, not what they finally possess. Objective knowledge is the common epistemic goal that they strive for together through collaborative inquiry and critical methods of verification. For the global scientific community, epistemic objectivity is the fruit of authentic intersubjectivity, of their mutual fidelity to the specialized methods and norms of scientific research.[34]

The Kantian image of responsible freedom was also greatly inflated. Kant wanted to preserve the objectivity of morals as well as of science. This laudable goal led him to insist on the autonomy of pure practical reason. To secure this desired moral autonomy he segregated practical reason from the influence of nature and history. The whole range of natural human desires as well as the historical and cultural influences on responsible moral choice were declared *heteronomous*. For Kant, the sources, motives, and goals of authentic morality had to derive from pure reason alone. The metaphysical outcome Kant endorsed was an autonomous sphere of morality deliberately isolated from the practical influence of science, common sense, the emotions, historical reflection, education, art, and grace. Any of these concrete sources of moral energy and insight would supposedly compromise the autonomy of practical reason and the objective purity it was designed to ensure.

But moral agents, in fact, are never pure rational beings. They are invariably situated in nature and history, shaped by personal experience and education, guided by desire and emotion, informed or misled by factual knowledge and error, corrected and deceived by their peers, continually subject to bias, and open to the healing power of grace. Their essential freedom derives from their native intelligence and reasonableness, their inherent capacity to ask and answer questions; to think, understand, judge, choose, and act. Their effective freedom to do what is right and achieve what is genuinely good derives from the perfecting and liberating powers of virtue and grace.[35] Human beings acquire the intellectual and moral virtues through their education and habitual practice; grace, by contrast, is a free gift of God that elevates the operation of their natural powers and heals or checks the harmful effects of sin. The Kantian ideal of practical moral autonomy is an inflated and unrealistic account of human freedom. Effective freedom is attained only by consistently developing the intrinsic capacities of human subjects and overcoming through virtue and grace the formidable obstacles of bias and sin. These complementary requirements of actualized freedom invariably depend on the moral assistance of numerous realities beyond pure practical reason: the vitality and beauty of nature; the practical example, guidance, and support of parents, friends, teachers, and strangers; the goodness and mercy of God.

It must be acknowledged, however, that objective knowing and authentic living are always precarious achievements. In both the epistemic and moral domains, a sobering gap exists between human aspiration and attainment. As polymorphic subjects, human beings are inherently prone to several disabling forms of bias: dramatic psychological bias that makes waking consciousness unreceptive to unwelcome perceptions, memories, and symbolic images; egoistic and group bias that make us personally and collectively resistant to unwelcome questions, disturbing insights, penetrating criticisms, and critical evaluative judgments; the general bias of common sense that disparages the importance and value of disinterested theoretical, scholarly, and philosophical inquiry.[36] Moreover, the important personal benefits that flow from our natural and historical belonging are uneven in their effects. Belonging to nature makes us subject to its fierce biological imperatives and recurrent needs; belonging to history immerses us in the tangled knot of greatness and wretchedness that constitutes the human condition in all ages and places. Historical belonging also entails relentless exposure to seductive ideologies, rationally sophisticated justifications of error, injustice, weakness, and sin.[37]

In our adversarial culture of suspicion and debunking, the inescapable dangers of natural and historical belonging are treated as permanent barriers to objectivity and truth. But when these subversive suspicions are made explicit, performative contradictions are starkly revealed. For these highly sophisticated denials of human capacity actually rely on important discoveries in empirical science and historical scholarship to discredit the enabling conditions of their own possibility. Thus implicitly invoked knowledge claims are explicitly used to discredit epistemic objectivity, and implicit truth claims to discredit the human capacity for attaining and transmitting truth.

The sober reality of our tangled human condition is not so deflating. Biological needs and demands can be met and transcended. Our uneven historical legacy can be critically appraised and appropriated. Reigning ideologies can be unmasked and persuasively critiqued. Although we essentially belong to nature and history, we are conditioned rather than determined by this constitutive belonging. Ideological assertions of causal determinism, whether biological, historical, cultural, or linguistic, are consistently undermined by the performative incoherence of their critical proponents and advocates. The legitimate goal of philosophical anthropology is neither to inflate nor diminish human existence. The uncritical optimism of the early moderns, like Bacon and Descartes, finds its cultural counterpart in the reductive pessimism of our postmodern contemporaries. We can sympathize with the creative aspirations of the Enlightenment and the critical suspicions of our cultural peers without endorsing the anthropological claims of either group. What we urgently need, and what they both fail to provide, is a credible account of the full range of human experience: ignorance, knowledge and learned ignorance, bias and liberty, education and prejudice, virtue and vice, holiness and sin, moral impotence, despair, and the redemptive power of grace. Human reason is inherently fallible, constantly prone to bias and ideology, and yet capable of objective knowledge of being. Human freedom is biologically and historically conditioned, even more threatened by bias and ideology, and yet capable of informed and responsible choices. Critically transcending the modern and postmodern images of reason and freedom leaves their conditioned reality, thankfully, intact.

The Polymorphic Subject

The first three sections of this chapter have outlined the intellectual, moral, and cultural background of Lonergan's philosophical anthropology. To put our schematic account of this interpretive context in a nutshell: the important discoveries of the specialized empirical sciences have not yielded a credible and comprehensive modern cosmology. The anthropological turn to the natural and historical subject has not yielded a credible account of human existence. The theoretical and scholarly achievements of modernity have paradoxically strengthened a truncated picture of man-in-the-world. Despite the unprecedented richness of modern culture, we have repeatedly failed to unify and integrate the defining revolutions of the modern age. While scientific knowledge and technical power have grown immeasurably, our moral insight and practical wisdom have failed to keep pace.

There is a profound difference, however, between diagnosing a serious malady and proposing an effective cure (*Third Collection*, 102). Our contextual narrative until now has outlined Lonergan's critical diagnosis of modern culture. What was the appropriate cure he proposed in response to our cultural predicament? The intellectual advances of the modern age have been specialized and differentiated. The integrative efforts of modernity have tended to be reductive and imperial. The resulting cultural dilemma can be stated concisely: "Unity without multiplicity is tyranny; multiplicity without unity is confusion" (Pascal, *Pensées*, no. 604). Lonergan's remedial prescriptions were deliberately integrative and unifying: to develop and articulate a cosmology, anthropology, and theology at the intellectually exigent level of modern science and historical scholarship. In the remainder of this chapter, we shall limit exposition and commentary to Lonergan's philosophical anthropology.

Although Lonergan was deeply versed in the thought of both the ancients and the moderns, his philosophical anthropology did not substantially rely on either Aristotle or Kant. Aristotle had offered an abstract metaphysical account of the human soul. Kant had offered a faculty psychology of the transcendental ego. The form of self-knowledge Lonergan embraced was a concrete understanding of the naturally embodied and historically embedded human subject.

For Lonergan, a credible study of human existence must be empirical and critical. As an empirical study, it must be based on concrete human experience; as a critical study it must effectively distinguish speculative hypotheses from verifiable facts. As a philosophical study it must also be comprehensive. It must acknowledge the whole of human experience and be responsive to the full range of anthropological inquiry: the natural and human sciences; the critical study of the historical past; the commonsense insights on which practical living is based; the hermeneutic interpretation of the many human carriers of meaning; the phenomenology of intentional consciousness; the existential emphasis on mortality, political engagement, and authentic choice; the historical imperative of collective responsibility for our common world.

The historicity of human existence adds a further complicating dimension to Lonergan's ambitious project. Contemporary men and women no longer belong to classical republics, medieval kingdoms, or early modern nation-states. They are scattered across the globe on several interconnected continents. They live and work within very different social, economic, and political institutions. They are raised and educated in different cultural traditions. They practice different religions and respond unevenly to different forms of artistic expression. At the concrete level of situated historical existence, an apparently bewildering pluralism reigns.

It often appears that we have too much rather than too little knowledge of what it means to be human. How can we order and unify this wealth of experience and understanding in a comprehensive theory of human existence? Lonergan believed that this integrative task was one of the critical epistemic challenges facing contemporary philosophy: to provide the dynamic and critical heuristic framework for an integrated and inclusive anthropological theory. Since Lonergan accepted the disciplinary autonomy of the specialized sciences and historical scholarship, and clearly distinguished systematic from commonsense inquiry, he reasonably concluded that contemporary philosophy must become a specialized form of theoretical consciousness. The proper field of philosophical inquiry today is the interior life of the situated intentional subject (*Method*, 83–85). This diversified field of interiority has to be investigated empirically, methodically, and critically. As an empirical discipline, philosophy must attend to the experiential data of human consciousness; as a methodical discipline it must rigorously interrogate those data with a coordinated set of theoretical and normative questions; as a critical discipline it must effectively distinguish factual from erroneous answers to those probing questions.

But how can philosophy be empirical if it focuses intentional analysis on the data of consciousness rather than the data of sense perception? Lonergan answered this provocative methodological challenge in a decisive and breathtaking way. He insisted that the empirical methods used in science, historiography, and hermeneutics need to be augmented by the empirical study of intentional subjectivity. To achieve this required extension, he deliberately *generalized empirical method* to include both sensible data and the data of experiential consciousness.[38] Philosophers of interiority must rely on the intentional analysis of human consciousness as natural scientists rely on the explanatory analysis of sensible phenomena and historians rely on the factual analysis of the retrievable past.

The first thing to be noted about the concrete human subject is that her being is constantly becoming. As infants we live in a world of sensible immediacy.[39] Our operative awareness is limited to the here and now of the home and the nursery. With the acquisition and mastery of language the infant's world radically expands to include both here and there, now and then, the sensible present, the remembered past, the imaginable future. As the child gradually develops, her personal horizon of awareness expands to include fact and fiction, obligation and desire, transgression and punishment, holiness and sin. There is no fixed and final limit to the expansion of the subject's intellectual and moral consciousness and the correlative expansion of her mediated world. Through this dynamic intentional expansion, human beings transcend the world of sensible immediacy to enter a much greater unobservable world mediated by meaning and motivated by value. Their original undifferentiated consciousness becomes increasingly differentiated and complex. Through the long process of cultural formation, they learn to become at home, to varying degrees, in the practical realm of common sense, in the systematic realm of scientific theories, in the scholarly realm of historical research, in the mysterious transcendent realm of worship and prayer. They learn to move with different levels of ease among these different intentional worlds, but are often unable to explain how they do this, or how these contrasting worlds are intelligibly related to one another.[40]

If the stages of human cognitive development can be demarcated by these successive differentiations of consciousness and being, by these intentional mediations of immediacy, then the heuristic task of contemporary philosophy becomes clearer. Philosophy is called to mediate critically these multiple mediations of immediacy: to distinguish, order, relate, and unite the different modes and methods of inquiry and the correlated phenomenological worlds they disclose and reveal. Conceived in this deliberately synoptic fashion, philosophy would constitute a specialized form of cognitive development, distinct from but closely related to the momentous epistemic developments of the modern age.

The intentional subject, however, is not merely a cognitive being. Human consciousness is inherently polymorphic.[41] The polymorphic subject operates on many different levels of consciousness and within quite different patterns of experience. Normally, there is an ordered pattern to the flow of intentional consciousness, a pattern that reflects the operative desires and concerns of the waking subject. The polymorphism of these patterns corresponds to the correlative polymorphism of human desires and purposes. To be specific: the biological pattern of consciousness is oriented to securing the necessities of life; the dramatic pattern to our fluid and successful interactions with other people; the aesthetic pattern to the free play of the senses and the imagination; the practical pattern to meeting the insistent challenges of everyday living; the religious pattern to responding authentically to our encounter with the mystery of God (CWL, 3:204–12; Method, 105–7, 118–19).

In all of these patterns of experience, human intelligence and reasonableness are regularly at work. But the intentional operations of the subject are directed to the specific concerns and objectives that give the pattern its limited intelligible unity. The sensible expressions of our polymorphic consciousness are just as varied as their intentional sources. These expressive bearers of meaning, the empirical data of the different human sciences, give powerful testimony to the internal complexity of the subject. They provide observable data and evidence for the richness and diversity of our intentional operations, ranging as they do across the entire spectrum of institutional and cultural life. These hermeneutic carriers of meaning include, but are not limited to, the technological instruments and machines we produce and employ, our highly varied and dynamic economic transactions, the political discourse and action in which we engage, works of literature, painting, and architecture, religious rites and communities of faith, scientific laboratories and articulated theories, scholarly libraries and seminars, the great works of philosophy and theology. Close attention to social and cultural history confirms how diverse such public expressions of meaning can be from one age and group to another. Human beings are situated, symbolic, and expressive animals wherever and whenever they live.

Although it is difficult to find intelligible order and unity in this wealth of symbolic expressions, it is critical to avoid explanatory reduction, whether the reductive accounts are inspired by Marx, Darwin, Freud, or Foucault. The first requirement of a credible philosophical anthropology is to respect what human experience discloses. This requirement extends to the polymorphic data of consciousness as well as the polymorphic bearers of meaning that give these data symbolic and sensible expression. The more anthropological theorists neglect or distort the diverse desires, operations, expressions, and norms of consciousness, the more tempted they are by reductive accounts of human existence.

A further heuristic distinction needs to be emphasized. The human sciences are intrinsically normative as well as interpretive. Once we carefully interpret and understand the meaning of some human phenomenon, we invariably seek to evaluate it. While the relevant criteria of evaluation differ across patterns of experience and specific expressive domains, we must candidly recognize that human consciousness is inherently fragile, prone to ignorance, bias, vice, and sin, that it is potentially "the sport of every wind" (Pascal, *Pensées*, no. 28). For this reason, a critical anthropology must be dialectical and normative as well as empirical and interpretive. When the full concreteness and diversity of human experience and expression become the focus of philosophical inquiry, the classical heuristic structure of Newtonian physics, the statistical and genetic heuristic structures of modern biology and neuroscience, need to be augmented by the dialectical heuristic structure of philosophical anthropology. Not only must we trace human conduct and expression to their sources in intentional consciousness, we must also learn to distinguish true from false beliefs, good from evil motives, wise from foolish choices, just from unjust actions, holy from sinful habits and dispositions, to cite only the most basic categories of normative appraisal (CWL, 3:242–44).

The basic normativity of intentional analysis and the human sciences raises another source of difficulty, however. What is the ontological status and validity of the operative norms by which we appraise human existence and history? Are these norms grounded in nature, in history, in intentional consciousness, in society and culture, in the authoritative revelations of God? Are they ontologically grounded at all or are they deliberately crafted by influential individuals and social groups to serve as discursive instruments of power and domination? In the normative sphere of existence, does institutionally organized *might* ultimately make *right*, as the "masters of suspicion" contend? While human beings cannot avoid making evaluative judgments and comparative appraisals, are they really capable of achieving moral objectivity and truth?

Is the dynamic complexity of human existence a permanent barrier to a unified and comprehensive theory of this polymorphic normative animal? It is certainly a barrier to reductive models of integration, but what are the viable alternatives to reductive anthropological strategies? Lonergan claims that two basic human desires stand out from the rest: our unrestricted desire to know the whole of reality, and our equally unrestricted desire to discover and actualize whatever is genuinely good.[42] Lonergan characterizes these desires as transcendental in both the Scholastic and Kantian senses of the term. They are unrestricted in their scope of application, extending to the all-inclusive realms of being and value respectively (the traditional Scholastic sense). They also function as enabling conditions of human inquiry and action (the specifically Kantian sense), helping to account for the restless, expansive dynamism of the human spirit: our personal and communal discontent with existing limits to knowledge, our profound moral unease with the tangled knot of human greatness and wretchedness, both personal and collective, that we inherit. Just as our other constitutive desires shape the dynamic patterns of conscious experience, so do the transcendental desires for knowledge and value. "Deep within us all, emergent when the noise of other appetites is stilled, there is a drive to know, to understand, to see why, to discover the reason, to find the cause to explain. Just what is wanted has many names. In what precisely it consists is a matter of dispute. But the fact of inquiry is beyond all doubt. What better symbol could one find for this obscure, exigent, imperious desire, than a man, naked, running, excitedly crying, 'I've got it'?" (CWL, 3:28–29).

Although the mind's desire for knowledge can be imperious and all absorbing, the human desire to discover and actualize the good can be even more demanding. While procrustean strategies of integration seek the *reduction* of the higher to the lower, of spirit to nature, for example, Lonergan repeatedly emphasizes the *sublation* of the lower by the higher.[43] *Sublation*, as Lonergan uses it, is a philosophical term of art. It refers to the precise relation of functional interdependence between lower and higher forms of human activity. The higher forms preserve and respect the integrity of the lower while transcending their limited intentional scope. The lower, in turn, serve as concrete enabling conditions of the higher's possibility and emergence. Higher forms are therefore related to lower forms by what Lonergan calls functional complementarity. To illustrate functional complementarity concretely: in human cognitional process the conscious operations of experience (perceiving, imagining, remembering) are sublated by the intellectual operations of questioning, understanding, conceiving, and formulating what is conceived. These intellectual operations, in turn, are sublated by the rational operations of critical scrutiny, reflective insight, and factual judgment. But the process of intentional sublation does not end with the objective knowledge of fact. The human longing for value effectively sublates the unrestricted *eros* of mind, so that normative and evaluative judgments sublate judgments of fact, and responsible decisions and choices sublate the relevant judgments of value. Most significantly, given the skeptical challenges repeatedly posed by positivism, scientism, and emotivism, the authentic living of persons and communities perfects and completes the high achievement of objective knowledge.

For Lonergan, the functional differentiation and sublation of the different levels of intentional consciousness provide the key to a comprehensive but nonreductive theory of the polymorphic subject. Let us now examine concretely how sublation actually works in the complex field of human cognition.

Cognitional Theory: From Logic to Method

While the human desire to know is unrestricted, epistemic achievement does not keep pace with aspiration. Between the operative desire to know and the achievement of actual knowledge lies the complex process of human cognition. At the provisional term of this recurrent and cumulative process, human knowledge itself, in its multiple forms, slowly emerges. But the reflective assertion of actualized knowledge invariably leads to a critical appraisal of the alleged epistemic result: what do we actually know when we successfully complete this fallible passage from cognitive desire to provisional attainment. For Lonergan, the philosophical understanding and appraisal of human cognition is based on providing defensible answers to three sets of interlocking questions: What are we actually *doing* when we are deliberately pursuing knowledge in mathematics, empirical science, common sense, critical historiography, philosophy, and theology? This is the defining question of modern cognitional theory. Why does successfully engaging in these conscious intentional operations culminate in objective knowledge, knowledge whose results are normatively binding for all human inquirers and disciplines? This is the central question of modern epistemology. What do we actually know when we achieve objective knowledge in these several different ways? Are the different realms of human knowing that result from our inquiry complementary or inherently incompatible? And if complementary, can they be integrated coherently into a credible account of the comprehensive universe of being? These are the central questions at the core of contemporary metaphysics.[44]

Lonergan insisted that the serial order of these defining questions is highly significant. He repeatedly traced important philosophical disagreements in epistemology and metaphysics to underlying conflicts in cognitional theory. For Lonergan, the appropriate place to begin an empirical and critical study of knowledge today is with the intentional analysis of the diverse forms of modern cognitional activity. Lonergan realized that this heuristic strategy departed from both ancient and modern traditions. Aristotle had treated human knowing as a special case of being, and so he included the study of cognition within his metaphysics of the rational soul. Both Descartes and Kant explicitly made epistemology prior to metaphysics. For Descartes, we had to certify the indubitable truth of our ideas before determining their ontological relevance. For Kant, we had to certify the formal nature of our judgments, before determining the ontological relevance they actually had. While Descartes proceeded from the methodical critique of the ego's epistemic ideas to a rational metaphysics of God and the soul, Kant did just the opposite. He concluded, on the basis of his critical idealism, that metaphysics could not be a genuine science, though he acknowledged the regulative demand of reason for unattainable knowledge of the kind metaphysics desires. For Kant, we humans cannot know what we desire to know most intensely. The profound epistemic gap between rational aspiration and epistemic attainment is permanent and unbridgeable.

Despite their philosophical differences, Descartes and Kant both accepted the classical theory of science as true certain knowledge of causal necessity. Both thought of science as the permanent possession of a logically ordered set of unrevisable truths. Both identified the cognitive bearer of science with a disembodied rational ego. Late modern historians of science, from Duhem to Kuhn, have shown that scientific inquiry does not actually comply with these pervasive epistemic assumptions. The practice of modern science is now understood as a fallible, dynamic, self-correcting process of systematic communal inquiry. But acknowledging the inherent fallibility of science, its inescapably social and historical character, and its practical enactment by polymorphic subjects, susceptible to error, bias, and ideology, has raised skeptical doubts about the validity of human cognition itself. The original leaders of the Enlightenment celebrated modern science as the exemplary form of knowledge. When unfavorably compared with "the new science of nature," other epistemic claims were treated as suspect. Today, critical suspicion has been cast on the scientific enterprise itself by sociologists of knowledge, revisionary historians, and Nietzschean-inspired cultural critics. For many of these critics, the hidden and undeclared goal of science is the relentless quest for power and control rather than for disinterested truth. On this revisionary account, the limited credibility of science rests, in fact, not on its unwarranted claim to objective knowledge, but on the pragmatic benefits it brings to those who publicly support and defend its endeavors.

This postmodern critique of objectivity and truth cannot be ignored. Nor, I believe, should it be accepted at face value. It derives much of its critical import from the diminished credibility of the classical theory of science, and from the equally diminished credibility of the Cartesian and Kantian accounts of scientific cognition. But how can we advance beyond revisionary criticism and systemic debunking to a constructive account of human knowledge in its full scope and complexity? Though the contemporary cultural crisis has a potent source in epistemological criticism, such criticism is deeply paradoxical at its core. For the postmodern critics of science regularly appeal to important discoveries in sociological and historical inquiry to discredit the very possibility of objective cognition and truth.[45]

Classical and medieval thinkers, like Aristotle and Aquinas, focused philosophical attention on the objects of knowledge, the sensible substances we regularly endeavor to know. The leading modern philosophers, like Descartes and Kant, shifted epistemology's focus to the logically ordered ideas and judgments that constitute the results of scientific inquiry. For the path-breaking moderns, the critical epistemic challenge was to show how these often startling results satisfied the normative requirements of the classical theory of science. Starting from intuitively evident premises, whether empiricist or rationalist in origin, logical inference was needed to advance from axiom to deductive theorem (in Cartesian rationalism) or from immediate perceptual reports to generalized theories and laws (logical empiricism). When the classical theory of science was historically discredited and the epistemic limits of logic were revealed, critical attacks were then launched on the rationality of science itself. Because the operations of reason had been mistakenly conflated with the operations of logic, the nonlogical dimensions of science were wrongly construed as irrational and arbitrary (*Method*, 6). This was a serious, though contextually understandable, mistake. To correct this critical cognitional error requires careful attention to the whole spectrum of cognitional activity. Both modern and postmodern philosophers have unfortunately mired our culture in a demoralizing "epistemological bog" (CWL, 2:20). To liberate ourselves from this bog, we need to follow Lonergan's lead by shifting our philosophical focus from logic to method. But what does this shift actually mean?

To begin cognitional analysis with logic is to begin the investigation of knowledge with the provisional results (concepts, propositions, and inferential arguments) of human inquiry. To begin with method, by contrast, is to begin with human inquirers themselves. But who, in reality, are they? They are polymorphic situated subjects, intentionally constituted by the unrestricted desire to know being. When that dynamic orienting desire governs the flow of their consciousness, they enter the intellectual pattern of experience (CWL, 3:209–10). That distinctive experiential pattern, but one among several, consists in a normatively ordered set of intentional operations. These operations are related not by *similarity* but by *functional complementarity*. The later operations in the ordered set presuppose and complement, they *sublate*, the earlier operations, raising cognitional activity through a graduated series of intentional levels.

The first and basic level of inquiry is *empirical*.[46] Though the process of human cognition is essentially discursive rather than intuitive, it begins with sensory experience, with sense perceptions, images, and memories. But the intellectual inquirer is not content with the disclosures of experience as such. The desire to know is fundamentally a desire to understand what we experience. Human inquiry, therefore, becomes distinctly *intellectual* when we raise exploratory questions about the content of experience: who, what, why, how often, and so forth. When these questions are fresh and unscripted, we initially don't know the answers to them. So authentic intellectual questioning gives rise to original thinking, to the heuristically guided effort to understand what experience has provisionally disclosed. Often such thinking goes nowhere, and our initial questions remain largely unanswered. But informed, intelligent, sustained, and independent thinking can also be rewarded with relevant insights, by a grasp of intelligible unity or of significant intelligible relatedness in the thoughtfully examined data of experience. Because these direct insights into the intentional content of experience are the pivotal events in cognitional process, we shall examine them more closely in the next section of this chapter.

Direct insights are intellectual operations at the second level of cognitional process; they grasp the potential intelligibility (the intelligible unity or relatedness) of the disclosures of experience. Because they arise in response to explicit questions, they articulate their specific intelligible content in complementary acts of conceptual formulation. Because there are several different realms of cognitive meaning, these formulated answers range from the familiar propositions of practical common sense to the most sophisticated scientific and philosophical theories. To use Lonergan's technical vocabulary, these articulated propositions are *formal terms of meaning*, the provisional answers we give to our many probing questions about the content of experience. But the intellectual pattern of experience is governed by exigent norms as well as unrestricted desire. The human desire to understand experience is, *au fond*, a desire to understand correctly. Thus, the critical exigence of reason raises intentional consciousness to a third, more exacting level. The *rationally exigent* subject demands to know whether or not our provisional answers (our formal terms of meaning) are true. This exigent demand is expressed in the recurrent critical question "Is it true that p?" where p ranges over the entire domain of propositional terms of meaning (CWL, 3:346–48, 354–57).

But how do we reasonably determine the truth or falsity of p, how do we satisfy the exigent human demand for truth? Lonergan's answer is clear, straightforward, and groundbreaking: through a process of *reflective inquiry* in which we first articulate the complex truth conditions of p and then determine whether those conditions are satisfied by the cumulative evidence we are carefully able to assemble. The relevant evidence includes more than the empirical data of perception and memory and the credible testimony of others; it equally extends to our conscious subjective experience of the normative process of inquiry itself. It properly extends to the genuine openness of our ongoing attention to experience, the consistent intelligence of our questions, the clarity of the provisional answers we formulate, the rigor of our logical inferences, our actual responsiveness to the critical queries and objections raised by our partners in inquiry. Have we allowed inattention, bias, or ideological prejudice to distort the process of inquiry at the empirical, intellectual, or rational levels of its normative unfolding?

To satisfy the human subject's immanent norms, cognitive inquiry must be critical as well as empirical and intellectual. Before we can reasonably assent to the truth of p, we must determine whether p's truth conditions are fully satisfied in the relevant evidence we have patiently assembled. This critical grasp occurs in an act of reflective insight in which we apprehend p as virtually unconditioned (CWL, 3:305–6). For Lonergan, a truth-bearing proposition is virtually unconditioned when it has determinate truth conditions and these conditions actually obtain. Therefore, whenever the rational subject apprehends p as virtually unconditioned, the critical exigence for truth is temporarily satisfied. For while it is rash to affirm p without such reflective insights, it is unreasonable to withhold our provisional assent once such insights have actually occurred. The normative process of human cognition culminates in these acts of rational judgment. Because their propositional contents are virtually unconditioned, cognitive inquiry terminates in judgments of fact rather than necessity. And these provisional factual judgments are themselves subject to subsequent revision in the face of emerging data, questions, insights, and evidence. In this way, cognitional process remains fallible and self-correcting, even when the immanent norms constitutive of critical reflection have temporarily been met.

It is important to recognize what Lonergan has accomplished by shifting the focus of cognitional analysis from logic to method. Method is the fruit of reflection on prior performance. Without the philosopher's extensive prior engagement in cognitional process, there is nothing for intentional analysis to reflect upon. The more varied and proficient that epistemic engagement, the more forms of inquiry we have actually practiced and mastered, the richer our personal cognitive repertoire. First-order cognitional performance occurs at the level of the subject's conscious experience. Initially, our cognitional operations are directed at intentional objects quite distinct from the subject's intentional life. We regularly begin the life of inquiry by intentionally mediating sensible immediacy. But we are also capable of intentionally mediating our own mediating operations. We do this by intentionally analyzing our cognitional experience, by shifting our thematic attention from cognitive objects and propositional terms of meaning to the immanent desires, operations, and norms of the inquiring subject. Cognitional theory is the epistemic fruit of this reflexive intentional analysis of our prior cognitional activity. The more inclusive the range of cognitional performance examined, the more comprehensive and credible the resulting cognitional theory.

A further point needs to be emphasized. Human inquiry is profoundly dynamic and restless. The normative methodical process of cognition we've outlined recurs and recurs. The unrestricted desire to know is the source of relentless intellectual questioning; the critical exigence of reason treats even verified factual judgments as provisional findings subject to critical amendment and revision. Because our cognitive desires are unrestricted, because we strive to understand the whole of experience, human intelligence gradually develops in a highly differentiated manner: historically advancing from commonsense questioning to systematic theory; from descriptive to explanatory knowledge; through a series of evolving heuristic structures; through important scholarly advances in critical history and hermeneutics. Lonergan consistently sought to understand and unify this diversified set of epistemic developments within an integrative philosophy grounded in intentionality analysis, and later within a contemporary theology methodically divided into eight functional specialties.[47] Having gradually identified these important but unmet cultural needs, he set out resolutely to meet them.

Several imposing cultural barriers stand in the way of Lonergan's philosophical project: the neglect of the intentional subject by substantive and methodological behaviorists; the truncation of human subjectivity by empiricists, positivists, and pragmatists; the deficient accounts of intellectual and rational consciousness by conceptualists and idealists; the explicit denial of objective truth by relativists and historicists (*Second Collection*, 69–86). These competing philosophical strategies and theories are clearly in need of sustained dialectical criticism. The crux of Lonergan's normative dialectic is easy to state but hard to execute. Those who explicitly endorse what Lonergan calls the *positions* in cognitional theory intelligently grasp and reasonably affirm the comprehensive facts of cognitional process. Their detailed cognitional judgments can be factually verified in the data and evidence of intentional consciousness. The adherents of what he designates as *counterpositions* fail to achieve this level of explicit self-knowledge. The critical key to understanding philosophical conflict is to recognize the polymorphism of human consciousness and its full existential implications (CWL, 3:712–15). Most human beings, both philosophers and nonphilosophers, cling to some mixture of positions and counterpositions. We tend to be right in what we affirm and wrong in what we exclude or omit. But this truncated philosophical stance is inherently precarious, for the *positions*, when critically examined, invite further intellectual development, and the *counterpositions*, when fully articulated, invite systematic reversal (CWL, 3:412–15).

The Centrality of Insight

The whole problem of cognitional theory
is to make the transition from cognitional operations
as experienced to cognitional operations as known.
—*Second Collection*, 172

By insight, then, is meant . . . the supervening act of understanding . . .
its function in cognitional activity is so central that to grasp it in its
conditions, its working and its results is to confer a basic yet startling
unity on the whole field of human inquiry and human opinion.
—CWL, 3:3

The unresolved conflicts in cognitional theory illuminate the paradox we have been studying, the perplexing gap between successful intellectual performance and explicit and reliable self-knowledge. The original orientation of human inquiry is toward the sensible world: the world of nature, the world of history, the commonsense world in which we regularly live and interact with others. It requires a deliberate cognitive decision to turn away from these realms of intelligible objects and refocus our thematic attention on the inquiring subject. Lonergan's intentional analysis of the situated human subject yielded a wealth of anthropological discoveries: the polymorphism of human consciousness, the multiple patterns of conscious experience, the unrestricted character of the transcendental desires, the specifically intellectual pattern of experience, the recurrent normative structure of cognitional process, the functional complementarity of cognitional operations, the differentiated realms and stages of cognitive meaning, the exigent norms of critical reason, the human spirit's unrelenting desire for cognitive and moral self-transcendence.

Some of the human cognitional operations are hard to overlook or ignore: our acts of sense perception, the inferential operations of logic, our explicit acceptance or rejection of truth-bearing propositions. But many of the other intentional operations tend either to be neglected or conceived analogically. The most familiar operational analogues are perceptual or discursive acts. However, this easy resort to analogy regularly leads cognitional theorists to connect these functionally complementary operations by *similarity* rather than *sublation* (CWL, 4:207–8). Human knowing is then mistakenly treated as a form of looking, as an essentially intuitive or perceptual activity, with the knower immediately confronting the known through some form of ocular vision. By contrast, when the discursive aspects of cognition are emphasized, when our logical operations on formal terms of meaning are highlighted, then the *intentional sources* of concepts and propositions tend to remain in the dark. In saying they remain in the dark, I don't mean that they are actually unconscious. All of our cognitional activities are intentional and conscious. But, and this point is critical, being experientially conscious of a cognitive operation does not entail understanding its nature and structural importance. The difficult transition from conscious experience to authentic self-knowledge requires successful intentional analysis. This critical but neglected analytic requirement explains why Lonergan's heuristic shift from logic to method is so vitally important in developing a defensible cognitional theory.

What are the important cognitional operations we regularly enact but fail to acknowledge? If human knowing is essentially discursive, requiring the intellectual transition from intelligent questions to relevant and meaningful answers, and the subsequent critical transition from these provisional answers to reasonably verified judgments, what are the vital mediating operations at these successive levels of cognitional process? Lonergan's answer is both simple and philosophically profound: The central mediating operations are insights, direct insights at the level of inquiring intelligence, reflective insights at the level of critical reason.[48]

Lonergan did not claim to have personally discovered these pivotal acts of human understanding. He repeatedly acknowledged Aristotle's reference to insights in *De Anima* 3.7 and Aquinas's elaboration of Aristotle's earlier discovery in the *Summa Theologiae*. In *Verbum*, his historical study of Aquinas's theory of knowledge, Lonergan argued that Thomas had successfully integrated Augustine's notion of the inner word, the soul's interior *verbum*, into Aristotle's metaphysics of cognition (CWL, 2:3–10). Aquinas identified and articulated the intellectual procession of the inner words of concepts and definitions, formal terms of meaning, from prior acts of *intelligere*, preconceptual operations of human understanding.

In *Insight*, his greatest philosophical work, Lonergan enriched and updated the discoveries of Aristotle and Aquinas, by elaborating and affirming the central role of insights in all the modern realms of cognitive meaning: mathematics, the empirical sciences, common sense, philosophy, hermeneutics, and theology. *Insight* is deliberately written from a moving pedagogical viewpoint. The first part of the book is devoted to highlighting the occurrence of insights as intentional operations; the second part to recognizing the role of insights in constituting human knowledge of being. Two complementary forms of insight are explicitly distinguished and related: direct and reflective. Although these distinct acts of understanding differ in their nature and intentional content, they do have a *functional* similarity to one another. Both types of insight consciously respond to human inquiry and questioning; both grasp intelligible forms or sufficiency of evidence in empirical data; both ground the formulation of propositional terms of meaning, formal or full. Direct insights play the critical mediating role in the normative unfolding of intellectual consciousness; reflective insights play a comparable role in the progression of rational consciousness. Taken together, they constitute the pivotal epistemic operations within the normative structure of human cognition.

Let us now examine these complementary forms of insight in their enabling conditions, their concrete enactment, and their provisional results. Direct insights do not occur in a cognitional vacuum but within a conscious pattern of experience, practical, dramatic, intellectual, and so on. For expository purposes, we'll concentrate our intentional analysis on the intellectual pattern of experience. That distinctive pattern is governed in its several specialized applications by the unrestricted desire to know. When the intentional subject is governed by that specific desire, the contents of human experience primarily exist to be understood. But the desire to understand experience only becomes articulate in the form of specific questions or problems—who, what, why, how often, and so forth—and these questions themselves become further differentiated as new heuristic structures emerge within the history of inquiry. The deeper our intellectual background and mastery of a particular field of study, the more important and penetrating the questions we are able to ask.

Specific questions for intelligence, as already noted, give rise to exploratory thinking, to the heuristically guided effort to understand what experience discloses. In original thinking of this type we actively seek to connect the already known with the particular unknown(s) we are seeking. Drawing on our background knowledge and beliefs, we intellectually organize our experience into a patterned arrangement of perceptions, images, and memories. If we are sufficiently talented, adequately prepared epistemically, and intellectually fortunate, we can apprehend in those images and sensible presentations the intelligible content that our particular questions are seeking. Given this terse phenomenological description of intellectually patterned inquiry, what are the antecedent cognitive *conditions* required for the occurrence of direct insights? An intentional infrastructure of experiential data occurring within a patterned flow of consciousness; a guiding question or problem directed to this patterned experience in the light of the subject's antecedent knowledge and belief; an informed and inquisitive thinker who draws on her relevant memories and perceptions to form a schematic heuristic image fashioned in the light of these basic enabling conditions.[49]

But how do direct insights actually *work*, what do they actually do? Depending on the heuristic context, the epistemic background of the inquirer, and the operative question or problem, the thinking subject grasps in the schematized heuristic image a unifying intelligible form or an intelligible pattern of relations that connects the relevant unknown to the already known or believed. Either we grasp the intelligible unity of a concrete particular thing, or the pattern of functional relations among different things, or the frequency with which specific types of events actually occur, or the dynamic operators and provisional integrators that transform already unified systems into emerging systems on the move, or the complex interplay of normative intelligence and reasonableness with distorting bias and ideology in the tangled thicket of human affairs. Because human inquiry is dynamic and unrestricted, this normative pattern of experience and questioning recurs, a connected series of related insights occur and coalesce, or occasionally rise to strategic higher viewpoints in which the synoptic grasp of an entire intentional field becomes possible.[50]

Direct insights are the intentional source of provisional answers to the original questions that focus intelligent inquiry. They are the causal intellectual pivot between the concrete order of experienced and anticipated data and the abstract logical order of concepts, propositions, arguments, and theories. From the cognitional perspective of the inquiring subject, these abstract terms of meaning are not isolated logical entities. Rather, they are putative answers to the intellectual questions that drive our inquisitive thinking. When these questions are systematic in character, the logical norms appropriate to theoretical meaning come directly into play. These norms demand that systematic theoretical meaning be clear in its explanatory terms, coherent in the truth-bearing propositions it affirms, and rigorous in its deductive arguments. Logical analysis, though it requires the clarity, coherence, and rigor of propositional bearers of truth, deliberately prescinds from their actual truth or falsity.[51]

But the normative exigence of the inquiring subject is not content with propositional coherence and clarity. These logical virtues are necessary but not sufficient conditions of rational judgment. It is the reasonable inquirer's demand for truth that makes the critical question inescapable: simply stated, "Is it true that p?" where p ranges over all formal terms of meaning. Or more concretely, "Do the provisional answers we have offered to the original questions for intelligence meet the epistemic requirements of truth?" And how do we determine, as disinterested inquirers, whether or not our articulated answers rise to these normative standards?

At inquiry's third stage of critical reflection, we begin by articulating the truth conditions of p. What must be the case if p is actually true? Depending on the heuristic context and the particular semantic content of p, these truth conditions can be exceptionally complex, as they require the coherence of p with the relevant set of beliefs to which we assent. Logical coherence, as already noted, is a necessary but not a sufficient condition of truth. But the truth conditions of p also include nonpropositional evidence drawn from the domain of prior relevant experience. Reflective inquiry in the service of judging truth is the exemplary instance of critical thinking. We carefully marshal all the relevant evidence, propositional and experiential, in order to determine whether p's truth conditions are satisfied. This reflective process of evidence gathering must be consistently governed by the exigent norms of detachment and impartiality. We must not overlook, discredit, or repress evidence because it is epistemically unwelcome; we must not silence critical objections and arguments when they challenge our cherished beliefs; we must seriously examine the reasonable alternatives to p as the best answer to our original question. For our provisional assent to p to be justified, it must not be biased, premature, or rashly affirmed.

As the intellectual stage of cognitional process climaxes in direct insights and provisional answers, so the rational stage climaxes in reflective insights and considered judgments. When reason's exigent demands are met, the critical inquirer discovers that the assembled evidence is or is not *sufficient* to affirm p. Lonergan describes this decisive cognitional act as a reflective insight that apprehends p as a virtually unconditioned intelligible content. We have already explained that a proposition is virtually unconditioned when its truth conditions are fully satisfied in reality. At the stage of critical reflection, we determine whether a proposition, or ordered set of propositions, actually meets this exigent standard. As meaningful answers to our original questions flow intelligently from direct insights, so objectively verified judgments flow rationally from reflective insights. The cognitional results of such critical reflection are concrete judgments of fact, or circumscribed judgments of epistemic probability when the assembled evidence is *insufficient* to determine p's truth value (CWL, 3:324–29, 574–75).

These culminating acts of factual judgment do not add substantively to p's semantic content. They simply grant or withhold assent from the provisional answers critical reason is regularly asked to appraise. They add the decisive "yes" of affirmed truth, the "no" of recognized error, or the "perhaps" of epistemic probability to the three-leveled normative process of human cognition. But no sooner does that process provisionally conclude in a judgment of fact, than it begins anew. The unrestricted desire to know remains actively at work. The normative pattern of intelligent inquiry remains the dynamic source of continuing epistemic development. Although that pattern becomes specialized and differentiated in the several realms of cognitive meaning, the transcendental structure of human cognition is universal and invariant. For, as Lonergan gradually discovered and verified, a *generalized empirical method* is invariably operative whenever and wherever we ask intelligent questions of experience and thoughtfully assent to reasonable answers. Our common fidelity as inquirers to the transcendental core of this method, its constitutive desires, operations, and norms, guarantees the epistemic credibility of common sense, systematic theory, historical scholarship, and critical hermeneutics. It also grounds the credibility of contemporary philosophy and theology whenever they satisfy its erotic and exigent demands.

The specialized and differentiated character of modern knowledge has made the personal and cultural demand for unity imperative. But the dominant unifying strategies, frequently based on the theoretical discoveries of a particular empirical science, have tended to be reductive and imperial. To avoid such cultural imperialism, Lonergan proposes an integrative strategy that carefully respects both epistemic plurality and unity. Within the different realms of cognitive meaning, the normative structure of generalized empirical method remains constant, while the specific intentional contents of the functionally differentiated cognitional acts remain dynamic and variable. *Transcendental method*, generalized empirical method, is the intentional source of epistemic commonality and unity; the specialized and differentiated applications of that method across the full spectrum of human inquiry are the complementary sources of the resulting epistemic pluralism. Lonergan's unique combination of invariant methodological structure and variable intentional content offers a comprehensive account of human cognition that is differentiated, dynamic, and credibly unified. The epistemic unity that Lonergan affirms is not the static unity of an all-inclusive logical system, but the flexible and dynamic unity that flows from our common but specialized applications of the normative principles (foundations) of transcendental method.

Critical Realism

> Verum est medium in quo ens cognoscitur.
> *(Truth is the medium through which being is known.)*
> —*Second Collection*, 17

We have briefly answered the first question in Lonergan's ordered philosophical triad. What are we actually doing when we pursue knowledge in the several different realms of cognitive meaning? We are intellectually and rationally engaging in the three-leveled normative process of experience, understanding, and judgment. We are faithfully responding to the unrestricted desire to know; we are performing the relevant intentional operations in the appropriate normative sequence; we are honoring the critical rational demand for virtually unconditioned judgments. We are reasonably assenting to verifiable judgments of fact. In order to answer Lonergan's initial question, we reflexively applied cognitional process to our prior cognitional performance. We have examined our diverse forms of cognitive experience, discovered their recurrent normative structure, articulated those discoveries in a detailed and nuanced cognitional theory, critically examined the truth of those theoretical claims, and verified their factual accuracy in the relevant evidence of personal and public inquiry.

In doing all this, we have executed the difficult transition from cognitional process as subjectively experienced to cognitional process as understood, propositionally articulated, and rationally affirmed. In our earlier account of the dynamism of empirical science, we emphasized the provisional character of our systematic theories. They are fundamentally open to revision and amendment in the light of new data, new questions, new discoveries, clearer formulations, more rigorous testing, the actual emergence of recalcitrant evidence. Is Lonergan's complex cognitional theory revisable in the same way that the discoveries of the empirical sciences and historical scholarship are? Yes and no. Yes, because new fields of inquiry can arise, new specialized methods can develop, phenomenological descriptions of cognitional process can always become sharper and clearer. No, because any critical revision of Lonergan's cognitional theory will instantiate its fundamental claims. For such a revision, in order to be intelligent and reasonable, would have to be based on new forms of cognitional experience, deeper levels of explanatory understanding, a more exigent process of critical reflection. But any proposed revision that actually met these required conditions would confirm rather than invalidate Lonergan's theory. This is precisely what Lonergan meant when he claimed that only the *positions* in cognitional theory invite epistemic development while the *counterpositions* invite systematic reversal. We cannot coherently engage in cognitional process to overturn or invalidate an accurate account of its invariant normative structure. That normative structure is admittedly contingent and factual in nature; human inquiry did not need to follow this invariant intentional pattern. But because human cognition *really* does follow this normative pattern, we can't deviate from its critical requirements or deny their existence without undermining our epistemic credibility (CWL, 3:352–57).

Cognitional theory concentrates on the polymorphic human *knower* and the normative process of human cognition; epistemology and metaphysics, the complementary philosophical disciplines in Lonergan's triad, provide correlative accounts of human *knowledge* and the ontological scope and character of the *known*. But how does our detailed understanding of the knower and the normative process of knowing affect our subsequent analysis and interpretation of knowledge, objectivity, and truth? Human knowing normatively unfolds on three successive levels of intentional consciousness: empirical, intellectual, and rational. These different levels and their constitutive operations, we have argued, are related by sublation or functional complementarity. Intellectual questioning sublates concrete experience; direct insights sublate exploratory questioning; provisional answers sublate the occurrence of these insights; critical reflection sublates the formulation of credible answers; reflective insights sublate this critical scrutiny; and finally, verified factual judgments sublate reflective insights. The *counterpositions* in cognitional theory omit or distort one or more of these complementary intentional acts. The corresponding *counterpositions* in epistemology and metaphysics can be intelligibly derived from the specific cognitional oversights and distortions to which they appeal, explicitly or implicitly, in their defense (CWL, 3:412–15).

Naive realists, for example, treat human knowing as an essentially intuitive process, a case of the knower directly confronting the known. From their perspective, human knowing becomes truly objective when we veridically intuit all aspects of the known. On this highly truncated account of cognition, the discursive aspects of cognitional process are treated as merely supplementary concerns; so that in making a knowledge claim, we simply put into the appropriate words what we already know through a prior veridical intuition. And what we know through veridical perception is claimed to be being or reality because that is what reliable human intuitions directly experience. True judgments of reality, for the naive realist, merely confirm and express the epistemic contents of our prior intuitive acts. In the long history of philosophy, the different versions of naive realism correspond to different appraisals of human intuitive capacities. Are our human intuitions confined to sensible objects and their sensible properties and relations (empirical realism)? Or do they also include intellectual intuitions of eidetic forms and abstract entities like numbers, shapes, and logical concepts and propositions (intelligible realism)? Or do our intuitive operations even extend to the rational order of self-evident principles and truths (self-authenticating intuitions of indubitable truth)?

From Lonergan's dialectical perspective, all these versions of naive realism are seriously flawed. The universe of being is not confined to sensible objects and sensible properties. Within the intellectual pattern of experience, the intentional contents of our perceptual acts are, in fact, sensible data that have not yet been questioned, understood, and conceptually formulated as answers to questions. The direct insights at the core of cognitional process are not intellectual intuitions of intelligible forms and relations, nor can the logical order of formal terms of meaning be apprehended intuitively. And the true factual judgments in which cognitional process reasonably culminates are based on reflective insights that are also not intuitive acts. Yet it is only through such rationally verified judgments that being or reality is actually known.

Because naive realists severely truncate the three-leveled process of cognition, they badly distort the true nature of objective knowledge and being. Epistemic objectivity is not achieved through veridical intuitions of the immediately given, but by the subject's consistent fidelity to the transcendental requirements of empirical, intellectual, and rational consciousness. Such fidelity requires being fully attentive to the data of experience, fully responsive to the unrestricted drive of intellectual questioning, and critically withholding assent from proposed factual judgments until their truth conditions are reflectively grasped as virtually unconditioned. Human knowledge becomes objective and true only when the cognitive subject faithfully complies with these demanding transcendental precepts.

Moreover, the concrete universe of being that we know through affirming true judgments is not "already out there now" waiting to be directly intuited by the percipient knower. Within the intellectual pattern of experience, the uniquely relevant pattern for conducting philosophical inquiry, being is progressively defined as the intentional correlate of the unrestricted desire to know,[52] as what is known or knowable through intellectual grasp and reasonable affirmation, as what is actually known through rationally affirming verified answers to the full range of intelligent questions. The subject's intentional mediations of immediacy, the normative succession of functionally differentiated cognitional acts, are essential to human knowledge of being. Therefore, it is not direct intuition of any type but the inquirer's reasonable assent to propositional truth that serves as the critical medium through which being is known. While sense perception plays an important but limited role in human cognition, the complexity of knowing is not reducible to looking, nor is being itself reducible to what can be veridically looked at. The philosophical counterpositions tend to be right in what they affirm and wrong in what they exclude, distort, or omit. Lonergan's critical epistemology preserves the limited truth of naive realism, its legitimate empirical emphasis, while avoiding its numerous oversights and correcting its serious distortions and omissions.

The decisive shift in modern physics from descriptive to explanatory knowledge radically undermined the credibility of naive realism. Unfortunately, this momentous epistemic development was not itself well understood (CWL, 3:152–54, 177–78). Galileo, Descartes, and Locke all interpreted the startling results of modern physics through the representative theory of perception. According to that influential theory, the intentional contents of our perceptual acts are ideas, mental representations, causal effects in the mind of the perceiver of our body's physical encounter with mind-independent being. For these seminal interpreters of modern science, material being as described by mathematical physics is what already exists "outside" and independent of the perceiver's mind. But how did they conceive the determinate nature of this mind-independent causal reality? It consisted entirely of extended matter and its geometrically expressible properties—size, shape, location, duration, and so forth. In the causal account of the representational theory, when the extended matter of physical objects causally encounters the extended matter of the human perceiver's embodied senses, the epistemic result is a succession of sensible ideas in the immaterial mind of the perceiver. These internal ideas, in contrast to the real properties of matter, ontologically depend on mental acts in the knower for their reality and duration. Their being consists entirely in their being perceived or experienced (their *esse est percipi aut experii*).[53] But if the cognitive subject's direct awareness is confined to the perception of ideas, and ideas are mental representations of mind-independent reality, how can we reliably determine which of our many different ideas are true? Modern epistemology, from Descartes to Hume, attempted unsuccessfully to answer this skeptical question. The unhappy result of their efforts was a series of flawed philosophical theories, the "epistemological bog" to which Lonergan often referred. When naive realism was discredited by the progress of natural science, the proposed epistemological replacements were the various versions of modern *idealism*: perceptual (Berkeley), reductive (Hume), critical (Kant), absolute (Hegel).

Kant's critical idealism was the most sophisticated and interesting of these competing epistemological theories.[54] Kant ostensibly accepts a transcendental version of the basic "picture" proposed by Descartes and Locke: a mind-independent reality (the *Ding an sich*) somehow "causing" mental representations in the solitary mind of the transcendental ego.[55] But Kant insisted that all mental representations be carefully analyzed and clearly differentiated. First, he separated pure and empirical representations. Pure representations are innate subjective possessions in the mind of the knower; empirical representations, by contrast, are the "causal" effects of the mind's encounter with mind-independent reality. Then Kant divided mental representations into three distinct categories corresponding to the three distinct mental faculties he recognized: the intuitions of sensibility (pure and empirical); the concepts of understanding (pure and empirical); the ideas of reason (exclusively pure). He further insisted that the only human intuitions are sensory; there are no intellectual and rational intuitions of concepts and ideas. According to Kant, concepts are not intuited representations, but normative rules governing the reliable synthesis of sensible intuitions. In contrast to both Kantian intuitions and concepts, the ideas of reason are innate ideas of causally unconditioned realities—for example, the ideas of God and the rational soul. Kant repeatedly insisted that all concepts and ideas without corresponding intuitions are epistemically empty, and that all intuitions without synthesizing concepts are epistemically blind. These critical requirements, at the heart of Kant's cognitional theory, meant that intuitions were necessary but not sufficient for human knowledge, and that concepts yielded knowledge only when they reliably functioned to synthesize intuitions, pure or empirical.

Then Kant took an important but highly problematic step. He correctly insisted that knowledge and truth occurred only at the level of judgments, but he mistakenly treated judgments as the products of intellectual synthesis (overlooking and omitting the subject's reflective insights and their intentional grounding of rational acts of propositional assent or denial). Treated in isolation, no single mental representation, neither intuitions, nor concepts, nor ideas, can be true or false. For Kant, all verifiable judgments are the cognitive product of the interplay of sensibility and understanding, the epistemic result of the intellectual synthesis of intuitions by concepts (Kant also failed to recognize the subject's direct insights, the intentional source of our epistemic concepts and propositions). Finally, Kant clarified the typology of human judgments in the following manner. Analytic judgments, in which the predicate of a proposition explicates (clarifies) the intentional content of its grammatical subject, are necessarily true but lack existential import. The judgments of science, the exemplary form of human knowledge, are synthetic in character and known to be true a priori. Judgments are said to be synthetic when the predicate of a proposition augments or amplifies the intentional content of its grammatical subject (in Kantian terms, when the intuitions of sensibility augment the intentional content of the relevant concepts). Synthetic judgments are known to be true a priori when the propositional synthesis of subject and predicate, of concept and intuition, is universal, invariant, and necessary. Finally, it is important to note that for Kant there are no rational intuitions to confirm or augment the ideas of reason. Reason's exigent demand for unconditioned causes and intrinsic ends cannot be satisfied intuitively. Therefore, the ideas of reason, though they play an important regulative function in human cognition, are existentially empty.

What epistemological and metaphysical conclusions did Kant draw from his detailed and systematic critique of reason? What is the intended philosophical import of his second Copernican Revolution?[56] Human beings are not capable of knowing "things in themselves," mind-independent realities. We can know *that* such realities exist but not *what* they are or how they behave. Technically speaking, we can't coherently say that things in themselves "cause" mental representations, for causality and even existence are pure categories of the understanding, limited in their legitimate epistemic application to the phenomenal order of mind-dependent appearances.

Pace Descartes and the rationalists, there can never be human knowledge of transcendent reality, of God and the rational soul, for example. Human beings can *think*, but they cannot *know* the existence, nature, and functions of God and the soul. The knowledge claims of transcendent metaphysics, therefore, are treated by Kant as *dogmatic* (uncritical), since they violate the normative standards of critical reason. Humans can, however, achieve scientific knowledge in mathematics and physics, for their affirmative judgments in these legitimate disciplines can be shown to be synthetic and true a priori. Thus Hume and the skeptics are wrong when they unduly limit the scope of theoretical reason and science.

Since reason's demand for the unconditioned can never be cognitively satisfied, the objectivity of our judgments does not depend, as Lonergan claimed, on a reflective grasp of the virtually unconditioned and sustained fidelity to the transcendental precepts. For Kant, epistemic judgments are *objective* when they are the intersubjective results of rule-governed intellectual syntheses of intuitions and concepts. All the objects of human knowledge, both the knowable and the already known, must be objects of possible experience. But the field of human experience is confined to the field of intuition, and human intuitions are limited to phenomenal objects, synthesized mental representations, not noumenal realities. Thus Kant is an *empirical realist* (we humans can and do have objective knowledge of the phenomenal order of intuited appearances) and a *transcendental idealist* (these phenomenal objects are intrinsically constituted by the pure representations of the transcendental ego, and thus are not things in themselves). The appropriate subject (agent) of cognitional analysis, accordingly, is not the situated, symbolic, polymorphic knower of Lonergan's performance-based theory, but the pure transcendental ego, the transcendental source of space, time, and lawful causation, a postulated formal requirement of the essential unity of scientific knowledge and the objectivity of perceptual experience.

Like the adherents of the representative theory of perception, Kant rejects naive realism with its uncritical belief in the human intuition of mind-independent realities. And Kant's complex account of objective cognition is clearly not reducible to the naive realist assertion that knowing is essentially looking at the real. Still, Kant shares with perceptual realism the mistaken belief that intuitions hold the key to the truth, objectivity, and existential import of human knowledge. Lonergan's explicit defense of critical realism rests, in part, on his dialectical criticism of Kant's critical philosophy: first, his *cognitional theory* (specifically, Kant's distorted account of perceptual awareness, his consistent oversight of direct and reflective insights, his truncated analysis of the complementary intentional operations of intellectual and rational consciousness); second, his *epistemic idealism* (Kant mistakenly denies the functional role of the virtually unconditioned in objective judgments of fact, relying instead on empirical intuitions to confirm the truth of synthetic judgments); and third, his *transcendental metaphysics* of empirical (phenomenal) reality (rooted in Kant's failure to realize that objectively true judgments are the critical medium through which mind-independent being is known).

Kant's enduring philosophical legacy, particularly his rejection of transcendent metaphysics and rational theology, remains in force two centuries after his death. But human inquiry is far more dynamic and unrestricted than Kant's critical philosophy acknowledged. His transcendental aesthetic left no room for the discovery of non-Euclidean geometries; his transcendental logic is too closely tied to the heuristic assumptions of Newtonian physics. And Kant's static conception of the a priori is incompatible with the most important cognitive and moral developments of the last two centuries: the dynamic emergence of new heuristic structures and realms of meaning; the transformative discoveries of critical history and hermeneutics; the development of a methodical and comprehensive philosophy based on intentional analysis of the polymorphic subject; the viability of a functionally specialized theology that eschews the different forms of the ontological argument.

Modern historiography, as we have seen, emphasized the existence of cultural pluralism: religious, moral, political, and artistic. The interpretive human sciences stressed the heuristic importance of empirical carriers of meaning, both linguistic and nonlinguistic. Twentieth-century philosophers largely abandoned "the way of ideas," the early modern obsession with mental representations, to concentrate on language and expressive symbolism. Analytic philosophers in Britain and the United States tended to focus on the technical language of science and the ordinary language of common sense, Continental philosophers, on the heterogeneous discourse of art, politics, religion, and ethics. Historical studies of linguistic practice in both philosophical traditions confirmed the reality of discursive pluralism and change. Thomas Kuhn's study of scientific paradigm shifts revealed both the central importance (in normal science) and the significant limits (in revolutionary science) of logical procedures and arguments. As Kuhn freely acknowledged, there are no valid logical inferences from a ruling scientific paradigm to its critical replacement.[57] But the modern tendency to conflate rational operations with logical inferences, when combined with cognitional theories that ignore direct and reflective insights, has raised serious skeptical doubts about scientific objectivity and truth.

Kant's critical conception of knowledge has been radically modified to accommodate the new historical mindedness as well as the "linguistic turn." His static account of the aesthetic and analytic a priori has been replaced by a dynamic model of evolving categorical frameworks that are acquired and revised by epistemic subjects in the course of their linguistic and cultural formation. These linguistically mediated categories, which (in the spirit of Kant) are alleged to shape our experience of reality, are neither universal nor invariant in nature. They understandably vary from one cultural setting and historical period to another. Thus Kant's philosophical strategy for preserving epistemic objectivity (based on universal and invariant rules of synthesis) has lost its credibility. Epistemic objectivity and truth, to the extent they are still accepted and recognized, have now become relativized to a particular linguistic or conceptual scheme. This relativist outlook is even more pronounced in the domains of ethics and religion where cultural pluralism tends to receive an emphatically conventional interpretation. Where this openly relativist mind-set prevails, evaluative judgments are either excluded from truth altogether (in the case of emotivism), or unfavorably compared to the factual judgments of science and common sense.

A credible defense of objectivity and truth must take full account of historicity, plurality, and change. These are permanent dimensions of human existence, epistemic, moral, and religious. A credible comprehensive philosophy responsive to the needs of our time clearly requires a critical analysis of cultural pluralism and a critical understanding of historical change: When is epistemic pluralism genuinely *complementary* (in the cognitive realms of theoretical science and common sense, for example); when is it *genetically sequential* (as in the historical emergence of distinct and evolving heuristic structures, classical, statistical, and genetic); and when is it *contradictory* and incoherent (as in the simultaneous assertion of incompatible answers, the positions and counterpositions, to Lonergan's central philosophical questions)? And when philosophical claims are in fact contradictory, how should such fundamental epistemic conflicts be impartially and critically adjudicated?[58]

The most significant cognitive and moral changes are causally dependent on intentional operators and integrators (CWL, 3:555, 659–62). The most dynamic and powerful operators are the transcendental desires for knowledge and value that drive human inquiry and conduct forward. The relevant historical integrators are the provisional but imperfect resting places, theoretical and practical, of existing cognitional and moral achievement. Notable historical change, however, is always ambiguous; it can be either development or decline, progress or retreat, or some complex mixture of both. In order critically to distinguish development from decline in human affairs, we need to create a dialectical heuristic structure for historiography, the human sciences, philosophy, and theology. Such a dialectical structure would be based on these basic normative principles: the genuine source of intentional development and historical progress is sustained fidelity (personal and communal) to the transcendental precepts in inquiry and action; the principal cause of personal and communal decline is the persistent and obstructive influence of bias, ideology, and sin.

Let us now summarize briefly Lonergan's dialectical defense of critical realism. The proponents of naive realism have a truncated view of knowing, objectivity, truth, and being. The several versions of idealism share a common conviction: they effectively deny the human capacity to achieve objective knowledge of mind-independent or language-independent reality. Contemporary historicists and relativists lack a critical theory of cultural plurality and historical change. Yet, having noted Lonergan's explicit objections to these prominent philosophical counterpositions, we still need to ask: despite the discernible flaws of its rivals, does Lonergan's critical realism actually provide the epistemology and metaphysics we urgently need?

Objectivity Reconsidered

*The polymorphism of human consciousness
is the one and only key to philosophy.*
—CWL, 3:452

What did Lonergan mean by this cryptic assertion, and is this sweeping dialectical claim actually true? Let us begin our reply with an important maxim from Wittgenstein: "A picture held us captive, and we could not get outside it, for it lay in our language, and language seemed to repeat it to us inexorably" (*Philosophical Investigations*, 115). According to Lonergan, the counterpositions in philosophy are dominated by misleading *pictures* of the intentional subject. For naive realists, the cognitional subject is essentially intuitive. Human knowing occurs through an immediate intuitive encounter with a mind-independent object, an object that is "already out there now," awaiting the subject's epistemic attention. Objective knowledge allegedly occurs in and through this intuitive encounter, as long as the subject's direct intuition is actually veridical. To put the core assertions of naive realism in a nutshell: human knowing is essentially looking; objective reality is there to be looked at directly; and objective knowledge occurs through the immediate perception of reality, allowing the real to disclose itself fully to the subject without unwanted cognitive interference.

For the epistemic idealist, this highly simplified picture is far too stark. The cognitive subject is clearly discursive as well as intuitive. Moreover, human intuitions are confined to ideas, to mental representations, to mind-dependent objects of awareness. While idealists tend to agree with their naive realist rivals that being is "the already out there now real," they also insist that we have no immediate intuitive access to it. Human consciousness is confined to mind-dependent contents, both perceptual and logical (the assertion of epistemic immanence). Moreover, it is only at the logical level of discursive propositions or judgments that questions of truth and objectivity actually arise.

But how can we determine whether our truth-bearing propositions are true? Either we know this immediately through self-authenticating rational intuitions, or we know it through some reliable process of cognitive mediation.[59] Where the naive realist insists on epistemic immediacy between the knower and the known, the idealist counters with our inescapable dependence on epistemic mediation. However, because idealists regularly overlook or omit the critical cognitive contributions of direct and reflective insights, their concept of mediation is seriously flawed. The intentional mediation of experience (the intelligent and rational interrogation of empirical data) occurs through the subject's normative engagement in cognitional process. It culminates in the affirmation of true judgments reflectively grasped as virtually unconditioned. But epistemic idealists tend to recognize only two types of cognitional acts, the intuitive acts of sense perception and the logical operations of predication and inference. They typically *picture* the challenge of mediation as the subject's proceeding from the epistemic representation "in" the mind, whether that representation is perceptual or propositional, to the independent reality "outside" it. In the idealist tradition, perceptual acts can't take us from mind-dependent ideas to mind-independent being, for the intentional contents of these acts are supposedly confined to the order of ideas. It is because human consciousness cannot escape the closed circle of ideas or propositional beliefs that the realist's conception of truth as an intentional correspondence between mind and reality must be mistaken. Human knowledge is permanently confined to the circle of ideas or truth-bearing propositions, from which there is no credible epistemic escape.

The idealists' notion of correspondence is also fundamentally *pictorial*, a case of intuitively comparing truth-bearing representations "in" the mind of the knower with a mind-independent object "outside." Since there are no human intuitions that can perform this magical feat, they typically dismiss the correspondence theory of truth as incoherent (*Second Collection*, 15). But for the idealist, what alternative conception of truth remains credible? Only one: truth as logical consistency among the complete set of truth-bearing ideas or beliefs. We have argued, however, that logical coherence among our judgments is a necessary but not a sufficient condition of truth. Yet for the discursive idealist, it's the best criterion of truth that we have. The only way to adjudicate conflicting truth claims is to determine which of the propositions competing for our allegiance is logically consistent with our relevant existing beliefs, beliefs we already take (on trust) to be true.

What conception of epistemic objectivity is compatible with this reasonable but restricted insistence on logically coherent truth claims? For Kant, epistemic objectivity is achieved through universal and invariant agreement on synthetic a priori judgments. Although we humans can never know things-in-themselves, we can know the phenomenal order of intuitive appearances objectively (i.e., intersubjectively among subjects with minds like our own). But in the twentieth century, Kant's critically minded successors were acutely aware of historicity and pluralism. They were also methodologically suspicious of the Cartesian/Kantian "way of ideas." So they amended the Kantian *picture* of knowledge in the following way. Human knowledge still depends on epistemic mediation, but now the mediating entities are declarative sentences framed in the historical language of a particular and evolving cultural community. The objectivity of knowledge and truth are effectively measured by the coherence of contested propositions with the operative set of communal beliefs whose truth value the relevant community now takes for granted.[60] Where Kant treated objective knowledge as universal and unchanging for cognitive subjects like ourselves, objectivity and truth are now relativized to particular epistemic communities at particular stages in their linguistic and conceptual histories.

The dominant *picture* of knowledge has currently become behavioral and discursive. Linguistic agents acquire their fundamental beliefs through a precritical process of sociocultural education. Their mature epistemic behavior consists in the contestable public practices of asking and answering questions, of advancing, challenging, defending, and revising truth claims. The strength of this familiar cognitive *picture* consists in what it includes; its weakness in what it repeatedly excludes or omits: the unrestricted desire to know being as a whole, the distinctively intellectual pattern of experience, the direct and reflective insights at the core of cognitional process, the immanent norms of empirical, intellectual, and rational consciousness. The behavioral neglect of the polymorphic subject, in order to avoid "the bog of ideas," exacts a high philosophical price: a truncated version of cognitional process, an equally truncated account of epistemic objectivity and truth, and a general avoidance or relativization of the inescapable metaphysical concern with knowledge's ontological import.[61]

In this highly compressed dialectic of the dominant modern counterpositions, naive realism was critically defeated by idealism in its multiple forms. Then Kantian idealism and the "way of ideas" gradually surrendered to epistemic behaviorism and the "new way of words." In the "cool hour" of informed critical reflection, what enduring lessons can we draw from this centuries-long dialectical process? The naive realists were right to insist on the empirical dimension of knowledge, but they largely ignored the intellectual and rational operations required for human cognition. Kant's critical idealism was right to insist on the importance of epistemic mediation, but Kant neglected the most important mediating operations (direct and reflective insights) that objective knowledge actually requires. Linguistically oriented theorists are right to insist on the historical and sociolinguistic dimensions of human inquiry, but their behavioral biases promote a withdrawal from intentionality analysis and the cognitional, epistemological, and metaphysical insights to which the study of interiority can lead.

What has Lonergan actually discovered and verified within the historically situated intentional subject that each human inquirer is? The intentionally conscious human being is polymorphic in its desires, patterns of experience, cognitional and moral operations, immanent norms, intentional contents, and linguistic and symbolic expressions. Within the biological pattern of experience, the reliable sources of human nourishment, imminent danger, and sensory pleasure are frequently "already out there now." Within the practical pattern of experience, the epistemic concerns of commonsense inquiry are normally limited to the sensibly concrete and particular. Within the dramatic pattern of experience, the relevant cues to effective social interaction are typically linguistic and behavioral. Within the aesthetic pattern of experience, human consciousness can become completely though temporarily absorbed at the level of sensual and imaginative immediacy.

But the polymorphism of human consciousness is not restricted to the biological, practical, dramatic, and aesthetic patterns of experience. Intentional subjects are intrinsically constituted by their unrestricted desires for knowledge and value. When they actively engage in the intellectual pattern of experience, other measures of reality lose their normative force. Being is no longer conceived as "the already out there now real" of biological extroversion. Rather, being is heuristically identified with the unrestricted correlate of our equally unrestricted cognitional desire. And being, or reality, can become known, not immediately in perceptual experience, but through the intellectual and rational mediations of immediacy that constitute cognitional process as a whole. The core episodes in that mediating process are the nonlogical operations of intellectual and rational consciousness. Direct insights are the intentional cause of provisional answers to all our intelligent questions. Within the specifically theoretical realm of meaning, the norms of logic require those propositional answers to be clear, coherent, and rigorously ordered. But the rational exigence for objectivity and truth demands more than logical coherence and rigor. Critical rationality demands that our provisional answers be grasped as virtually unconditioned propositional contents. Once that grasp has occurred in reflective insights, the affirmation of truth reasonably follows. But until it occurs, the critical assent of reason to our formal terms of meaning should be thoughtfully withheld. The objectivity of human knowledge ultimately depends on intentional subjects consistently obeying the full set of transcendental precepts, the immanent normative requirements of an authentic intentional life.

Lonergan's most important philosophical insight is that epistemic and moral objectivity are not opposed to human subjectivity. Rather, they are the self-transcendent intentional fruits of authentic subjectivity and intersubjectivity (*Method*, 265, 292). The epistemic authenticity of the subject depends on her sustained attention to the data of experience, complete fidelity to the transcendental eros and exigence for knowledge, and detached and impartial critical judgments. The moral authenticity of the subject sublates her objective knowledge of being and value by adding the further existential dimension of responsible decisions, choices, and actions.

Lonergan's comprehensive and critical philosophy grounded in intentionality analysis completely eschews *picture thinking* (CWL, 4:218; *Second Collection*, 76–79). Lonergan refuses to think of the knower, knowing, knowledge, truth, objectivity, being, and value *pictorially*, and he explicitly highlights the dangers of doing so. There is no reliable pictorial image of cognitional process, of reflectively grasping the unconditioned, of satisfying the normative exigencies of consciousness, or of truth as the medium through which being is known. When being is defined heuristically within the intellectual pattern of experience as the unrestricted object of intellectual grasp and reasonable affirmation, we completely transcend the pictorial image of correspondence as an intuitive comparison of ideas (words) and things. What the correspondence theory of truth actually affirms is that any proposition p is true when its truth conditions are satisfied in reality, and that p is known to be true only when that satisfaction is rationally grasped by the subject in reflective insights into the relevant body of evidence, both experiential and propositional.

Why then does Lonergan insist that the polymorphism of consciousness provides the dialectical key to a critical philosophy? Unless we are consciously operating within the intellectual pattern of experience, it is extremely difficult to avoid picture thinking, the permanent existential source of the dominant counterpositions. Without critical self-appropriation, without detailed and explicit self-knowledge, all of us, philosophers and nonphilosophers alike, are consistently tempted: to picture the cognitive subject as essentially intuitive or discursive; to picture being as "already out there now" or "already in here now"; to picture truth as logical coherence, and correspondence as sensible similarity; to picture cognitive objects as something for subjects to look at, and epistemic objectivity, as the fruit of perfect, nonmediated looking; to picture epistemic mediation as essentially discursive or logical, and to picture our operative epistemic norms as historically variable social conventions.

The explanatory terms and relations, the basic philosophical vocabulary, of cognitional theory, epistemology, and metaphysics are historically saturated with semantic ambiguity and confusion. But without a critical dialectical analysis grounded in comprehensive self-appropriation, we shall never achieve a defensible philosophical semantics, or liberate our confused and fragmented culture from the familiar pictures that hold our minds captive.

Authenticity as Self-Transcendence

The skeptical critique of objectivity is not of course limited to epistemic achievement. An even more serious anthropological challenge is directed at the human capacity to attain moral insight and truth. Philosophical emotivists contend that evaluative judgments are misleading expressions of subjective emotions and preferences, rather than truth-bearing assertions.[62] Moral skeptics insist that even if our evaluative judgments were true, we are cognitively unable to determine their truth value. Moral relativists effectively reduce our evaluative commitments to socially acquired and transmitted cultural conventions. They explicitly reject the existence of transcultural, transhistorical values, obligations, and norms. Philosophers in the existential tradition rightly insist on our need for moral and political engagement. Personal authenticity requires that we accept responsibility for the choices we make, the lives that we lead, the disordered state of our world. But they frequently sever the essential connection between objective knowing and authentic evaluation and choice, either because they are suspicious of epistemic detachment, or uneasy about the public uses of science and scholarship.

Genealogists of morals, like Nietzsche, seek to discredit traditional values and virtues by revealing their emotional provenance. Nietzsche's postmodern descendants promote pervasive suspicion about the ideological function of morality, its role in legitimating institutional and cultural oppression. While the deep human need for evaluative judgments and responsible decisions is personally and communally unavoidable, our culture is deeply divided about the epistemological and ontological status of morality. We presently lack a working cultural consensus with respect to the following questions: Are we capable of making objectively true evaluative judgments? If we are, how can we defend those judgments reliably and fairly? What are the ontological sources that ground moral objectivity and truth? And how can we impartially adjudicate deep-seated moral disagreements?

Contemporary moral reflection also suffers from an inescapable paradox. We can state that paradox as the unresolved conflict between moral ontology and advocacy.[63] The Western world in our time has a morally ambitious agenda. We insist on universal human rights; we demand social justice and fairness; we require cultural, ethnic, social, and gender sensitivity; we deplore environmental decline; we are scandalized by famine, global poverty, and suffering, as well as many collective and individual deaths. I cite only a representative sample of our far-reaching moral aspirations. For the most part, these laudable ends and concerns are espoused with sincerity. We really believe they are good and that they ought to be actualized. We are even prepared to act, individually and communally, to promote and protect these values, and we experience genuine remorse when we fail in this perceived obligation.

This broad consensus on moral advocacy (the goods and ends to which we are practically committed) coexists with deep-rooted moral confusion about the ontological status of our values, the meaning of our evaluative terms, and the source and ground of our moral obligations. To put it bluntly, we lack a credible moral philosophy to clarify and justify our existing moral commitments. But profound disagreements among moral philosophers, and even among conscientious ordinary citizens, are not without ethical import. Knowing what is good and right is often not sufficient for reliably doing it. The morally authentic life consistently requires renewable resources of moral energy and light. By light I mean sustained moral insight at the deliberative and evaluative levels of practical inquiry; by energy I mean the motivated commitment to discovering and actualizing the good, particularly in the face of concerted resistance and opposition.

It is difficult to pursue moral insights consistently if we suspect that our moral judgments are ultimately irrational and arbitrary. It is even more difficult to do what is right and unpopular, if we believe moral conflict is actually reducible to the clash of rival and partisan interests. To be authentic moral agents and communities, in a public culture racked by doubt and suspicion, we need to articulate and affirm a credible moral philosophy that accords with our constitutive moral aspirations and norms.

What did Lonergan specifically contribute to fulfilling this profound cultural need? Let us start with an important insight of Aristotle's that Lonergan critically appropriated: "Actions . . . are called just and temperate when they are such as the just or temperate man would do; but it is not the man who does these that is just and temperate, but the man who also does them *as* just and temperate men do them" (*Nicomachean Ethics*, 3.4.1105b 5–8). Both Aristotle and Lonergan refuse to separate virtuous action from virtuous agency (*Second Collection*, 75). Both place the focus of moral philosophy on the intellect and character of the moral agent. But concrete moral agents are always in the process of human becoming, gradually advancing from the infant's world of sensible immediacy and appetitive satisfaction into the human world mediated by meaning and motivated by value. At the beginning of life, the individual's moral development is chiefly dependent on the precepts and practice of others: one's parents, teachers, neighbors, and peers, the diverse sources of a person's early moral education. The proximate goal of this lengthy, complex, and uncertain process is the moral formation of a relatively mature human being: personal desires and emotions are trained and refined, intellectual and moral insights are cultivated, genuine goods are pursued and protected, moral imperatives are enforced and obeyed until they become second nature.

The primary moral impetus is initially external. It comes from the numerous and varied moral teachers of the emerging individual. True moral maturity, however, requires a decisive shift from extrinsic to intrinsic motivation. In order to *become* virtuous, we regularly imitate what those of recognized virtue think, say, and do. The mark of genuine virtue, by contrast, the mark of actually *being* a virtuous person, is to think, act, feel, and speak virtuously: to do the right thing, for the right reason, in the right manner, in the appropriate practical context, based on personal knowledge and voluntary choice. The genuinely virtuous person enjoys the intrinsic rewards of the morally good life, and suffers the pangs of remorse and repentance when he or she lapses from what the virtues concretely demand.

Aristotle's virtue ethics, like the rest of his comprehensive philosophy, is largely expressed in metaphysical terms. The intellectual and moral virtues are described as acquired habits of the rational soul. The numerous moral virtues perfect the individual's sensibility, her inherent capacity to experience desire, fear, and a broad range of complex emotions. The intellectual virtues perfect the practical and theoretical intellect. The two sets of virtues, moral and intellectual, are complementary in nature and function, effectively disposing the virtuous individual to feel, think, choose, and do what is right.

While Lonergan never rejects the numerous Aristotelian virtues, he does shift the center of his moral philosophy from the rational soul to the intentional subject. He also transposes the language of moral philosophy from Aristotle's faculty psychology to his own intentionality analysis, from faculty-based virtues of the soul to the originating and terminal *values* of the subject (*Method*, 51–55). Authentic moral agents and communities are the principal originating values. They originate value by seeking, discovering, choosing, and actualizing what is humanly good, and by preventing, correcting, and healing whatever is not. All the genuine goods that we responsibly pursue, preserve, and protect are the correlative terminal values. The hierarchically ordered set of terminal goods includes several types of value: vital (health and strength), social (family and friends), cultural (education, art, and science), personal (developed authenticity and virtue), and religious (the wholehearted love of God and neighbor). The hierarchical structure of the human good is also based on the principle of sublation, with each higher-order good preserving and completing its lower-order functional complement. Following Aristotle's cardinal insight, Lonergan refuses to speak about *terminal* values apart from *originating* values, because it is only authentic persons and communities who can determine what goods are really worthy of serious pursuit, in what order of human importance, and what actions and policies can responsibly achieve and protect them.

How does the historically situated polymorphic subject gradually become a fully authentic human being? That is the central question at the heart of Lonergan's moral philosophy. The most compact answer he gives to that question is: by consistently achieving intellectual, moral, and spiritual self-transcendence (*Method*, 35). While I believe that brief answer is true, I also recognize that it's not self-explanatory. Like most moral claims it needs to be clarified, justified, and defended against reasonable objections and criticisms before receiving our critical assent.

The human path to authenticity, to comprehensive self-transcendence, begins with what Lonergan calls "development from above." The committed parents who raise us, the social groups that shelter and protect us, the inherited cultures that educate and sustain us, are our original intellectual and moral teachers. These communal sources of personal education, however, are the tangled outcomes of the uneven passage of human history. Both for good and ill, the developing intentional subject is rooted in nature and history. While we cannot survive and mature without these ambiguous moral teachers, we should not accept their principles, prejudices, and priorities uncritically. Our complex dependence on highly imperfect teachers constitutes an essential crux of the human dilemma. As children and young adults, we first have to accept their epistemic and moral authority, to assimilate our uneven cultural heritage before we can critically distinguish its genuine merits from its grave limitations. Precritical learning and belief must come before critical discernment.[64]

The immanent principles that promote and sustain this eventual discernment are the subject's transcendental desires for knowledge and value. Both of these desires are unrestricted in their intentional scope; both have an inescapable normative dimension. Their spiritual dynamism and intensity make us restless with the limitations of all existing cultural achievement, intellectual, moral, and spiritual. The unrestricted desire to know makes us passionate for achieving objective knowledge. The *eros and exigence* for unrestricted value effectively sublate the desire to know, demanding that we consistently advance beyond objective knowing to authentic and responsible choices. Our transcendental desires and normative exigences are complementary sources of personal self-transcendence, as are the intentional operations that recurrently respond to their call and demands.

The human desire to know is an unrestricted intellectual operator that responds to the incessant challenge of experience with intelligent and critical questions. When the process of inquiry these questions prompt and sustain culminates in true factual judgments, it enables us, in a partial and limited manner, to know the world as it actually is. However, the existing state of the world does not satisfy our unrestricted desire for value. For the human world is, and always has been, a tangled knot of good and evil, virtue and vice, holiness and sin. The transcendental desire for value is an equally unrestricted moral operator that responds to the complex challenge of objective reality with its own set of practical questions. What sort of person should I strive to become? What existing communities should I actively support and defend? What concrete actions should I (we) take here and now to promote and protect legitimate values and to avoid or repair prevailing evils and wrongs?

These are inescapable deliberative questions recurrently asked by developing subjects in the light of their emerging factual knowledge. At the fourth level of moral reflection, complementing and sublating epistemic inquiry, there is a normative intentional process that leads from deliberative questions to a series of thoughtful and tentative answers. The pivotal operations, at the heart of this normative process, are deliberative insights (the moral analogues of the direct insights in Lonergan's cognitional theory).[65] Deliberative insights grasp alternative ways of being or living, or revised courses of practical action that can lessen the troubling gap between the world as we know it concretely and the world as we believe it should be. Our growing awareness of personal and communal alternatives to the status quo, and our practical and remedial insights, are then formulated conceptually as articulated patterns of personal and communal living, as specific institutional and cultural reforms, as concrete policies and plans of action. Deliberative insights and practical proposals and projects, however, are never secure and infallible. They are repeatedly compromised by the ignorance, fear, greed, self-interest, prejudice, moral insensitivity, and blindness of moral subjects and their peers. Accordingly, impartial critical reflection is even more necessary in moral and political inquiry than it was in the realm of factual judgments.

It's very easy to fall in love with our bright ideas; it's tempting to surrender to the lure of moral idealism; it's invigorating to chafe at existing evils and to demand they be completely abolished; it's seductive to yield to wishful thinking and false consolation or complacency. The operative sources of moral error and failure are nearly unlimited. But responsible moral inquiry is exigent as well as erotic. Deliberative insights and practical proposals and policies remain incomplete without evaluative scrutiny. Because the human good is always concrete, responsible proposals, whether creative or remedial, must be equally concrete. Is this really the best course of action under these circumstances; is this really an effective social reform given the existing practical constraints; are the terminal goods that we publicly support and pursue really important and valuable; are the lives and communities we openly admire really worthy of imitation and praise? Evaluative questions, like these, are the moral analogues of the critical question of truth in the factual realm. And like factual questions of truth, they can reasonably lead to affirmative or negative evaluative judgments. The evaluative judgments that provisionally conclude the recurrent process of moral inquiry are either categorical (this originating or terminal value is genuinely good or bad) or comparative (this practical proposal and outcome is better or worse than that one) (*Method*, 36–41).

But there remains a critical difference between factual and moral inquiry. We should reasonably defer our assent to factual judgments until their propositional content is grasped as virtually unconditioned. In our moral deliberation, however, we often have to choose and act before we know what is best. We have to take risks, to decide in the dark, to act knowing that we don't know enough to act wisely and well. Even more than its factual counterpart, moral inquiry is a fallible, self-correcting process of continuous learning through deliberating, choosing, and doing. Our moral education greatly depends on correcting earlier errors and mistakes, heeding the criticism and example of others, carefully studying literature and history, acknowledging the unease and remorse that we feel when we invariably fall short of the mark.

The epistemic self-transcendence we achieve through objective knowing is exceedingly difficult. The moral self-transcendence we seek through deliberative inquiry, responsible choices, and wise and virtuous actions is even more arduous. We must know what is true before we can discern what is actually good. But we can know what is good and still fail to choose and pursue it. And we can responsibly choose the good and still falter in concretely realizing it. And we can actualize the good but then become morally complacent and careless. We habitually choose lesser goods rather than greater ones, apparent goods rather than real ones, and short-term goods rather than those that endure. We regularly detect the mote in our brother's eye while neglecting the plank in our own (Matt. 7:5).

Because the sources of potential moral failure seem limitless, we often resign ourselves to mediocre lives ("Surely, we live better than the rest of men"). Or we seek to silence and stifle the transcendental eros and exigence for value. But that dynamic desire is constitutive of our being as persons, and its unrestricted demands remain with us until we die or become permanently comatose. The operative thrust of our transcendental desires is toward self-transcendence, toward objective knowing and authentic living. The actual state of our being and living invariably falls short of these exigent demands. Thus we live and die in a permanent state of existential tension, longing for a comprehensive self-transcendence we never fully achieve.

The greatest existential and cultural danger we face is ideology, the sophisticated justification of our repeated failures to achieve authenticity

(*Method*, 54–55, 104–5, 357–60). Ideologies serve as intellectual and moral counterpositions. They seek to justify the refusal of self-transcendence in its epistemic, moral, and religious dimensions. Ideologies employ our native powers of intelligence and reason to deny rather than affirm our most important human capacities, to silence the immanent summons of conscience to remorse and repentance. To embrace or endorse an ideology is to sin against the light, to turn what is best in ourselves against the immanent norms and desires that make us genuinely human.

A comprehensive moral philosophy requires a normative account of our troubled and uneven moral development and frank recognition of the diverse moral sources on which that development actually depends: nature, society, culture, history, and the transcendental principles that constitute us as intentional subjects. It also requires an equally frank recognition of the sources of moral impotence and decline: dramatic, egoistic, group and general bias, the seductive power of ideology, the mistaken separation of objective knowing from authentic living. It also requires genuine humility and candor. Even when we partly achieve authenticity, it is extremely difficult to sustain this precarious good. Moreover, our fragile achievement, such as it is, always depends on the assistance and collaboration of others. We are never really alone, we are never self-sufficient, we are never the autonomous agents our exalted pride would like us to be. Nor are we the helpless pawns of natural, social, cultural, or linguistic determinism. The inescapable call to authenticity, to epistemic and moral self-transcendence, powerfully reminds us of the polymorphic truth of our being. Neither angels nor brutes, we are ignorant men and women who are summoned to knowledge, selfish men and women who are summoned to goodness, repentant sinners who are called to be saints. Our deepest longings and obligations are limitless; our operative powers are invariably finite. We live in the shadows while climbing uncertainly and unsteadily toward the light. And we silently wonder, in our precarious journey between birth and death, where we come from, why we're here, where we're ultimately going.

These are the most basic existential questions that lead inescapably to the question of God, a question no comprehensive anthropology can fail to address (*Method*, 101–3; CWL, 3: chaps. 19–20). Certainly, Lonergan did not fail to address it, nor shall we in our reflective appraisal of Lonergan's enduring achievement.

Maturity Is Comprehensive

He hath ever but slenderly known himself.
—William Shakespeare, *King Lear*, 1.1

The human need for self-knowledge is paradoxical. We already know much about ourselves: the physical elements that compose our bodies, the organic compounds those elements form and sustain, our complex genetic and cellular structure, our intricate and evolving neural networks, our animal drives and desires, our individual ambitions and fears, our social and cultural prejudices, the ambiguous historical record for which we are collectively responsible. All of these facts are presently known and will become known more fully in the future.

Although these important scientific and scholarly discoveries are clearly significant, they constitute, when taken in conjunction, a partial and limited account of human existence. For this profoundly ambitious but truncated anthropology fails to acknowledge our intentional subjectivity, our polymorphic and differentiated consciousness, our unrestricted desires for knowledge and value, the exigent norms that govern our search for knowledge and value, the normative structure of cognitional and moral inquiry, the existential call to authenticity, our common capacity and need for self-transcendence.

Lonergan believes that these are the most critical facts about ourselves that we need to understand, affirm, and responsibly live by. Our personal and communal reluctance to acknowledge them and their profound epistemic and moral implications is a major source of modernity's cultural crisis. For that crisis is ultimately rooted in a failure of maturity, a lack of comprehensive self-knowledge.

CHAPTER THREE

Authentic Faith in a Secular Age

An authentic humanism is profoundly religious.
—*Second Collection*, 144

Lonergan believed that to become authentic, human beings must achieve self-transcendence, cognitively, morally, and religiously. The thematic focus of chapter 2 was on intellectual and moral self-transcendence—on what they require of the developing intentional subject and on the existential and cultural barriers that impede their achievement. In chapter 3 our focus expands to include religious authenticity, on becoming a person wholeheartedly in love with God and profoundly devoted to the well-being and protection of our neighbors. As personal experience and recorded history make clear, religious self-transcendence has always been difficult, requiring the unmerited grace and assistance of God. A central argument of chapter 3 is that the difficulties confronting authentic faith are especially pronounced in the secular culture of the late modern West.

What does it mean to live authentically in our secular age? How was the shared religious culture of medieval Christendom gradually transformed into a largely secularized culture where many of our peers choose to live without God? Can we persuasively defend the critical distinction between secularization and secularism, between accepting the relative autonomy of modern social and cultural practices, and insisting, with regret or defiance, that God is dead? What particular existential and cultural challenges must be overcome to reestablish the credibility of religious faith in our time?

In answering these questions, I deliberately connect Lonergan's thought with that of Charles Taylor, his Canadian contemporary. I draw liberally on Taylor's masterworks, *Sources of the Self* and *A Secular Age*, and reveal their complementarity with the concerns and discoveries of Lonergan. In the concluding sections of chapter 3, I explore the profound challenges posed to all forms of humanism by the catastrophic events of the twentieth century. And I try to show why only chastened forms of religious humanism are able to address these challenges authentically.

Our Secular Age

What does it mean to think and live authentically at the level of our time? For Lonergan, this was the central question confronting the contemporary philosopher and theologian. This existential question, however, only generated others of equal difficulty. How should we characterize "our time" in a way that is faithful to its complexity? How should we distinguish its enduring merits from its serious limitations? How should we understand the concrete historical process that transformed an earlier era of faith, Latin Christendom, into our modern secular age? Finally, what do we mean when we call our age "secular," and what are the distinctive challenges confronting religious faith as it rises "to the level of our time"?

As Charles Taylor makes clear in his masterful account of modernity, *A Secular Age*, our answers to these questions are interdependent.[1] To know where we are and what credible choices remain open to us, we must know how we got here. Taylor argues convincingly that the dominant academic narratives of modernity and secularization are greatly oversimplified. According to these influential accounts, the decline of religious faith and practice is the inevitable result of the intellectual and moral changes that define the modern age. Empirical science, critical scholarship, and autonomous philosophical inquiry have allegedly undermined the credibility of religious belief. But the moral critique of religion is perhaps equally subversive. Religion's prohibitions are condemned as inhumane, its ideals and aspirations as unrealistic, and its practical conduct as deeply hypocritical. There is a deeper existential level common to both forms of critique. The modern imperative is to think and act like an adult, to put aside childish ways. But religious beliefs, imperatives, and hopes are fundamentally immature and regressive. They belong to an earlier psychological and historical stage of human development. To come of age, to live at the level of our time, requires putting religion definitively aside.[2]

Neither Lonergan nor Taylor endorses the adequacy of this broadly accepted account; nor does either simply reject it out of hand. The intellectual discoveries of modernity do present a new challenge to religious faith. The moral assumptions and convictions of traditional Christianity are unsettled by the shift from hierarchical to democratic institutions. The obstacles to human authenticity, existential and historical, are now greater than ever before. Though the thematic criticisms of religion need to be addressed with candor and probity, the received narratives of secularization tend to be excessively linear and one dimensional. By oversimplifying the genealogy of modernity, they promote a reductive account of our cultural condition and constrict the ways we can genuinely respond to its demands.[3]

In his two greatest works, *Sources of the Self* and *A Secular Age*, Taylor constructs a moral and religious genealogy of the modern world.[4] In *Insight*, *Method*, and a broad range of papers composed in the last decades of his life, Lonergan sketched an epistemic genealogy of modern culture.[5] Taylor's account is subtle and detailed; Lonergan's is often schematic and dialectical. I have drawn numerous insights from both thinkers in describing "our secular age" and the special difficulties it creates for religious faith. Although Taylor's response to these difficulties is deeply important, this chapter will center on Lonergan, his critical reading of modernity, his explicit distinction between secularization and secularism, his deliberate interweaving of human and religious authenticity.

Where Are We Now? A Synthesis of Lonergan and Taylor

Even in this era of global communication and trade, important cultural and political differences clearly persist. For the expository aims of this chapter, the term *we* shall refer to educated adults who live within the greater North Atlantic community. In what distinct senses is the culture of that community "secular"?[6]

Modernity is marked by the specialization and differentiation of human practices, epistemic, political, economic, and artistic. With specialization there arises a demand for practical autonomy. Scientists and scholars determine their own methods, problems, theories, and technical languages. States and governments operate independently of religious institutions in forming and executing law and policy. Global economic transactions are conducted without reference to God and religious authority. Artists in every medium freely create and display their works without religious patronage and approval. The public sphere, the social and cultural site where these diverse practices occur and intersect, is essentially secular—that is, there is no religious requirement for full participation in these constitutive forms of public life. While religious expression is legally permitted in the public realm, its occurrence tends to be marginal and episodic. This first sense of "secular," secular (1), in no way precludes scientists, artists, scholars, merchants, citizens, and statesmen from being religious, or acting from deeply held religious beliefs.[7]

A second sense of "secular," secular (2), refers to a marked decline in religious faith and observance. Religious believers no longer present a solid cultural front; agnosticism and religious skepticism are openly espoused and defended. Postulated atheism, which emerged among educated elites in the nineteenth century, now affects the whole of European society. Many academic and cultural circles are openly hostile to religion, mocking its adherents as infantile, archaic, and inherently dishonest. What originated as a posture of religious defiance has in many sectors become indifference as successive generations learn to live without God.[8]

What are the principal sources of contemporary unbelief? Religious faith is often perceived as irrational and superstitious. The biblical God is depicted as despotic and cruel, or as indifferent to human suffering and death. The moral influence of religion is also unwelcome in many parts of society. For these moral critics, religious codes seek to repress human sexuality and aggressiveness, while its leaders ally themselves submissively with the dominant powers of the earth. In addition, the promises of religion provide false consolation. They divert human energy from the urgent needs of this world, supporting childish but empty hopes for a better life after death. This critical culture of disbelief does not dominate the whole North Atlantic community. Its influence is far greater in Europe than in North America, and its subversive assumptions are embraced unevenly in the diverse subcultures of the United States. That said, Iris Murdoch's rueful judgment is hard to refute: "The disappearance or weakening of religion is the most important thing to happen to us (educated Europe) over the past hundred years."[9]

There is a third, less recognized sense in which our age is "secular." Both believers and nonbelievers share a common intellectual and moral background. Taylor calls this background "the immanent frame"; Lonergan, the "universe of proportionate being."[10] The relative autonomy of modern theory and practice (secular [1]) has created an immanent order of description, explanation, choice, and action that can be understood without reference to the supernatural or the transcendent. This shared, normally tacit, cultural background has eroded earlier bulwarks of religious belief and rendered unsustainable earlier forms of religious life.[11] We no longer think of the cosmos or of political society as our medieval predecessors did. Their hierarchical assumptions about heaven and earth, about monarchs and subjects, about sacred and profane no longer command our faithful allegiance. Our shared vision of the cosmos is lawful, disenchanted, purged of the influence of demonic spirits and supranatural forces. Our understanding of political legitimacy is grounded in the democratic principles of liberty and equality, the rule of law, the consent of the governed. Ordinary existence within marriage and the family, the common activities of work and citizenship, the creation and enjoyment of works of art, are presumably as "holy" as the consecrated lives and rituals of clerics, ministers, and rabbis.

The unsettling pluralism of our time partly results from opposing ways of interpreting and responding to "the immanent frame." For nonbelievers that enveloping frame is, in principle, closed and self-sufficient. It marks the ultimate boundary of reality and value. God's permanent absence from nature and history and from the dramas of interpersonal living is the literal meaning they assign to Nietzsche's vaunted declaration "God is dead."[12] Shared acceptance of that still provocative claim, however, does not entail a contemporary moral consensus. As Taylor argues convincingly, there are competing and irreconcilable responses to "the death of God" that morally divide the modern culture of disbelief.

Religious thinkers, by contrast, embrace an open reading of the "immanent frame." For Lonergan, the order of "proportionate being" is ultimately unintelligible without a transcendent intelligent ground; the hierarchical order of value is systematically distorted without a supreme good that surpasses moral criticism; and the unrestricted yearnings of the human spirit remain unfulfilled without reasonable assent and commitment to a benevolent Creator God.[13] Taylor also believes that the human longing for "abundant life," for enduring personal and spiritual fullness, cannot be satisfied within the ontological constraints of the "immanent frame."[14] Theirs are but two of a plethora of religious positions that claim the loyalty of reflective believers in our secular age.

In a common culture of faith, shared religious agreement is a powerful bulwark of traditional belief. But the unprecedented pluralism of our age subjects both religious believers and nonbelievers to inescapable "cross-pressures."[15] Neither group can genuinely ignore the powerful example provided by the other. The heterogeneity within each group only adds to the complexity of the cross-pressures, making it harder to parody and oversimplify the lives and outlooks of their dissenting contemporaries. Believers and nonbelievers typically live side by side, often within the same family, sharing common neighborhoods and places of work and study. They are frequently spouses, lovers, friends, colleagues, and political allies. In our secular (3) age, the social and cultural background conditions underlying belief and unbelief are broadly shared. Both existential stances are rendered unstable, even problematic, by the concretely embodied presence of their rivals.

How Did We Get Here?
Overlapping Genealogies of Secularization

Three distinct strands are distinguishable in contemporary accounts of secularization. The first is epistemic and concerns fundamental changes in belief and mentality. The second is moral-political and concerns the historic reversal of the hierarchical assumptions of Latin Christendom. The third is religious and concerns the radical modern critique of Catholicism, Christianity, and the Christian God. Let us begin with a brief and highly selective description of these interdependent cultural strands.[16]

Epistemic. Lonergan divides the European Enlightenment into two distinct phases.[17] The first phase begins with Renaissance science and culminates in the discoveries of Newton. The second phase begins with the acceptance of non-Euclidean geometries, proceeds through the emergence of critical historiography and hermeneutics, and culminates in the philosophical quandaries of our time. The cultural fruits of the Scientific Revolution are dramatic and enduring. Over the course of seven centuries, the Scientific Revolution undermined the ancient picture of the cosmos, generated new and important heuristic structures, gradually refined a normative method of empirical inquiry, and shaped a critical mentality and evaluative outlook that now affects every form of human investigation. Through their symbiotic alliance with modern technology, the empirical sciences have radically changed the way we think and live from birth until death.[18] The critical mind-set that dramatically changed the human understanding of nature also revised our conception of history. We gradually discovered our common historicity, the institutional and cultural pluralism this entails, the concrete interplay of explanatory constants and variables that shapes the realm of human affairs.[19]

As the natural and human sciences evolved, they established their disciplinary autonomy from common sense, philosophy, and religion. They generated their distinctive realms of meaning, their specialized methods of inquiry, their technical languages, their restricted communities of research and criticism. Because of their unprecedented achievements and pervasive practical influence, the empirical sciences became the paradigmatic forms of human cognition. This elevated cultural status, however, left undetermined the appropriate epistemic relations between the natural and human sciences and the other forms of human inquiry. How are the methods and discoveries of the autonomous sciences related to those of common sense, historical scholarship, contemporary philosophy, religion, and theology?[20]

This is an inescapable philosophical question to which the specialized sciences can provide no adequate response. Nor are contemporary philosophers agreed on how to answer it. Thus, the philosophical quandaries to which I referred. Still, the question is pressing, for the human mind naturally seeks unity, the critical integration of what it knows.[21] Although classical forms of integration based on Aristotelian metaphysics and the early modern forms based on deductive logic are no longer credible, alternative models of epistemic unity continue to be proposed, debated, and selectively embraced.

Lonergan's dialectical interpretation of modern science draws a sharp distinction between scientific discoveries and extrascientific affirmations.[22] Genuine scientific discoveries are verifiable by the canons of empirical method; extrascientific affirmations, by contrast, are not. Although these affirmations often gain popular acceptance, they tend to rest upon unexamined cultural prejudices, or the failure to respect critical philosophical distinctions. Lonergan cites several examples of these important epistemic errors: Galileo's influential contrast between primary and secondary qualities, the mechanistic interpretation of physical theories, the determinist construal of classical laws, the reductionist account of explanatory genera and species, the positivist search for a unified language of science, the imperial rejection of nonscientific forms of empirical inquiry (scientism), the alleged incompatibility between scientific and religious beliefs.[23]

A critical understanding of scientific inquiry is needed to determine its epistemic powers and limits. The dialectical key to that understanding is the cognitional analysis of scientific method and the normative canons governing its operation. The modern sciences, natural and human, seek a verifiable explanatory account of all sensible data. They prescind, as a matter of principle, from the polymorphic data of consciousness, which, in the third stage of cognitive meaning, become the specialized field of philosophy (the subjective realm of interiority). They also prescind, as a matter of course, from all questions about transcendent being, in particular the questions about God's existence, nature, and activity.[24] Modern scientists and their cultural epigones are guilty of obscurantism when they brush these important questions aside, because they arise beyond the limits of scientific inquiry. Only the uncritical assumption that scientific inquiry is omnicompetent can justify that exclusionary posture. But that positivist assumption is merely a cultural prejudice, not a verified conclusion based on adherence to the scientific methods they champion.

Determining the epistemic and ontological limits of science is a task for a critical philosophy. Acknowledging this fact does not legitimate questions about God, but it leaves them open for further exploration. The restrictive outlook of *exclusive naturalism*, the narrow confinement of reality within the boundaries of scientific discovery, effectively eliminates the question of God and the legitimacy of religious belief. Although exclusive naturalism is a deeply held background assumption, broadly shared in our secular age, if Lonergan's critical objections are sound, it can't withstand dialectical scrutiny.

Moral and Political. The cultural separation of the ancient and modern worlds can be partly defined by the reversal of hierarchical assumptions.[25] The Scientific Revolution overturned the Aristotelian cosmology with its explicit hierarchical division between earth and sky. For classical thinkers, these cosmic divisions had significant practical import. Thus the ethical priority accorded the contemplative life corresponded to the ontological superiority assigned to celestial substances. As the heavens are inherently greater (more perfect) than the earth, so theoretical astronomy is ethically superior to terrestrial making and doing.

Bacon and Descartes explicitly rejected the strict Aristotelian separation of theory and practice. In their polemical defenses of modern science, the new physics proved its practical benefit through the "fruits and works" it helped to produce and the sovereign mastery of nature it promised to yield.[26] The Protestant Reformers also contributed to this unsettling cultural reversal. They sharply criticized Scholastic theology, the hierarchical authority vested in Rome, the medieval emphasis on the church's mediating role in salvation, and the special dignity of the monastic life. The Reformers emphasized instead the immediate relation between the believer and God, the primacy of sacred scripture, the authority of individual conscience, and the intrinsic dignity of all human vocations. This assertion of vocational dignity was especially significant for it meant that individual callings were spiritually equal when genuinely pursued for the love and glory of God.[27]

The Baconian emphasis on technical power and terrestrial happiness and the Reformers' "affirmation of ordinary life" jointly diminished the prestige of the *vita contemplativa*. This historic reversal in ethical priorities gave a new valence to anthropological symbols as well.[28] The contemplative isolation of the monks, the mandated celibacy of the Roman clergy, the warrior *ethos* of the feudal nobility gradually lost their heroic status. The new modern cultural heroes were artisans, doctors, engineers, farmers, merchants and bankers, practical workers and laborers who increased earthly prosperity and reduced human suffering and want.

Hierarchical principles provided a foundation for medieval political thinking as well.[29] Feudalism was a stratified social order that descended from the king through his nobles and vassals down to the laboring peasant. Both political and ecclesiastical hierarchies were structured by feudal norms. At the summit of these institutional pyramids were monarchs and popes; beneath them were landed aristocrats and princes of the church; common laymen and laywomen were the religious equivalents of uneducated laborers and servants.[30] The urban bourgeoisie were the earliest critics of these hierarchical patterns of social and political order. Not surprisingly, the Protestant Reformers found their social base among the dissident urban middle class, who resented and repudiated the hierarchical principles underlying these inherited structures of power and privilege.

The rise of the nation-state and of absolute monarchy further complicated the original feudal model. Medieval monarchs had been first among equals; the new absolute monarchs centralized royal power in the court of the king and sought deliberately to crush the intermediary power of the nobility. This centralizing project created a temporary but precarious alliance between the bourgeoisie and the throne. The kings needed bankers to fund their wars of expansion and lawyers and accountants to manage their complex domestic affairs. The bourgeoisie initially saw the kings as their political allies in reducing the privileges of the nobility. The clerical leadership of the established Christian churches often supported the alliance between throne and altar in order to fortify their common claim to public authority.[31]

The ancien régime in France was a particularly striking example of these complex political alliances. The French king became the unifying symbol of the French nation, while the pope remained the ambiguous symbol of a no longer unified European Christianity. Three orders or estates were hierarchically organized under the common authority of the king: the nobility, the Catholic clergy, and the third estate, formed of the urban bourgeoisie and the peasants. In the course of the seventeenth and eighteenth centuries, as the cosmological analogue of this feudal social pattern disintegrated, the ancien régime became the target of relentless criticism. Republican thinkers criticized the monarchy and the nobility;

Protestant Reformers criticized the Bourbon kings' revocation of the Edict of Nantes (1685); the rising bourgeoisie and their intellectual allies criticized the hierarchical principles on which the whole scheme was based. Even before the great democratic revolutions in North America and France, the ancien régime had lost its inherited legitimacy, while clinging fiercely to its hold upon power.[32]

Both the American and French revolutions were preceded by intellectual ferment and public dissent. Both revolutions were justified in the name of equality and liberty: equality of rights and citizenship, intellectual, political, and religious liberty. Both swept away hereditary monarchies and replaced them, at least for a time, with constitutional republics. In North America, the colonial war of liberation was followed by the successful creation of a representative democracy. In France, the abolition of the Bourbon monarchy led ultimately to terror, Napoleonic despotism, abortive restoration, and constitutional and national division. For over 150 years, France struggled to achieve a national consensus on principles of political legitimacy.[33]

In a strict sense, neither of these revolutions was ever completed. Both granted liberty and equality selectively. Both compromised their founding principles through slavery, imperialism, anti-Semitism, class conflict, and patriarchy. But the democratic norms they clearly articulated discredited the ancien régime in its several European variations. Political legitimacy throughout the West now rests on civil liberties and human rights, on equality under the law, on the consent and participation of the governed, on the constitutional division of public power, on the ultimate political authority of the people, and on the regular accountability of public officials to the citizens they serve.[34]

The defining revolutions of modernity, scientific, political, and industrial, were sources of radical change. European thinkers and citizens overturned their background picture of the world, their shared conceptions of political legitimacy, their inherited patterns of production and commerce. The effective combination of scientific discoveries and technical inventions dramatically increased human power over nature. Concerted political action by the people and their leaders fashioned democratic constitutions and governments. Industrial capitalism rapidly augmented human wealth and productive capacity, though at a terrible social cost. The focus of public attention steadily shifted from eschatological thoughts of eternity to pressing practical reflections on the challenges and opportunities of secular time.

The nineteenth century witnessed the emergence of an unprecedented awareness of history, natural and human.[35] Hegel made the historical evolution of the West the central theme of his philosophical inquiry. He secularized the salvation narrative of Christian orthodoxy by locating the actualized *telos* of history within immanent time. Marx made class struggle the key to historical intelligibility, though he predicted its cessation with the inevitable emergence of international communism. Liberal theorists of progress appealed to advances in science and technology and the gradual adoption of Enlightenment principles in forecasting a future of public peace and prosperity. A shared belief in historical progress unified nineteenth-century thinkers and statesmen, whether the prescribed route to progress required social revolution or enlightened educational reform.

The global wars of the twentieth century, the carnage of Verdun and Hiroshima, the systematic terror of Auschwitz and the gulag, the killing fields of Cambodia, the terrible crimes of imperialists and anti-imperialists alike, have shattered the fragile optimism of these earlier apostles of progress. No version of social engineering or cultural re-education can guarantee global peace and prosperity. The sober lessons of the grim historical record are more complex than nineteenth-century theorists imagined. We humans are free moral and political agents, individually responsible for the lives that we lead and collectively responsible for the world that we share.[36] Our individual lives are tangled knots of authenticity and alienation; our collective existence is invariably a thicket of progress and decline. We can identify the principal sources of progress and distinguish them from the causes of decline; we can increase the probability of genuine development and reduce the probability of failure; but we have no credible formula to guarantee historical progress, nor a credible ideology to remedy and overcome decline. The complex intelligibility of human existence is dialectical. The relevant dialectic, however, is neither Hegelian nor Marxist.[37] The concrete unfolding of history is contingent rather than necessary, dependent on free agency rather than invariant law, distorted by sin and yet open to grace and divine support rather than closed within the limited causal parameters of the immanent frame.

I have been sketching the modern moral and political genealogy in, admittedly, very broad strokes. Taylor's subtle and detailed account is filled with concrete thinkers and cultural movements:[38] the reformist agendas of modern Protestants and Catholics; the eighteenth-century attraction to Providential Deism; Kant's insistence on autonomous moral agency; the exclusive humanism of the radical Enlightenment; the Romantic reaction against disengaged reason in the name of human wholeness and integrity; the Darwinian emphasis on our animal origins, desires, and fears; Nietzsche's transvaluation of Christian and Enlightenment values; Freud's tragic sense of pervasive conflict and struggle; the existential demand for authenticity in the face of evil, suffering, and death.

Taylor believes that all of these cultural factors continue to shape our contemporary moral consciousness. Both religious believers and nonbelievers feel the pull of these competing ontological and ethical visions. Our existing moral choices are not solely between theism, in its various forms, and exclusive humanism, in its Kantian, utilitarian, and Nietzschean variations.[39] The moral and political pluralism of our culture tends to be concealed when we focus on broad areas of practical agreement: the affirmation of ordinary life, the desired reduction of suffering and want, the importance of economic prosperity, the protection of the natural environment, the global imperative to promote and protect human rights. This broad practical consensus on matters of moral advocacy coexists with a profusion of moral *ontologies* that run the cultural gamut from orthodox theism to the antihumanism of the counter-Enlightenment. In the midst of this unprecedented ontological and moral pluralism, what does personal and historical authenticity require today?[40]

Religious. How did Latin Christendom gradually lose the allegiance and support of modern women and men? Why did a shared religious culture of faith dramatically fragment into a divided secular culture where belief and unbelief are constantly in question? We shall examine four distinct but interrelated aspects of this very complex history.[41]

Discrediting Christendom: The unity of medieval Christianity was severely undermined by the sinful practices and conduct of the church. Even before the outbreak of the Reformation, the public witness of many Catholics to the message of the gospel proved a source of scandal. The most disturbing episodes are by now familiar: the excesses of the Inquisition in France, Italy, and Spain; the Babylonian captivity of the Avignon popes; the systematic mistreatment and expulsion of European Jews; the material extravagance and martial ambitions of the Renaissance papacy; the church's repeated failure over several centuries to achieve effective institutional reform.[42]

Because the Christian community is a spiritual home for saints and sinners, because it constantly violates the precepts of its founder, its common life is permanently in need of reformation (*ecclesia semper reformanda*). In fact, Luther's fierce criticisms of abuses in Rome were shared by many of his Catholic contemporaries. They too were scandalized by the church's wealth and property, by its imperial pretensions, by the immoral conduct of its clergy, and the pious superstitions of its ordinary members. They too wanted a purer, more genuinely Christian church, closer to the original community sympathetically portrayed in the Acts of the Apostles.

But Luther's passionate insistence on institutional and doctrinal reform quickly led to religious and political schism; and schism led eventually to protracted wars that devastated Europe throughout the seventeenth century. These terrible wars of religion, ostensibly fought on behalf of the Prince of Peace, permanently destroyed European Christendom and hardened sectarian rivalries among Catholics and Protestants. Protestant Christianity also suffered internally from repeated sectarian splintering. The religious individualism at the heart of the Protestant movement made it difficult to establish lasting and inclusive communities of faith. Roman Catholicism, by contrast, suffered from the opposing tendency to centralize power in Rome. Catholic governance became more authoritarian, its teaching more doctrinaire, its morality more rigid and legalistic. Seeking to reunify the church, it discredited Protestant Christians and churches and made triumphalist claims for its supreme and exclusive authority.

After the Treaty of Westphalia (1648) concluded thirty years of scandalous warfare, European Christians generally accepted the need for religious toleration. The religious divisions of Europe, at that time, tended to follow political lines, with a largely Protestant north confronted by a solid Catholic south (*cuius regio eius religio*). The political truce between Catholics and Protestants in France ended abruptly when Louis XIV revoked the Edict of Nantes (1685). The Huguenot émigrés, driven from their homes by this divisive revocation, settled throughout northern Europe and the

Americas, bringing the resentment of involuntary exiles with them. From 1680 onward, as Paul Hazard has noted, the mounting public hostility to French Catholicism had multiple sources: the bitter Protestant reaction to Catholic intolerance, the deepening anticlericalism of the influential *philosophes*, the unyielding demand by Bishop Bossuet that Christian reconciliation occur along Tridentine lines. By actively encouraging the church's close attachment to the Bourbon monarchy, Bossuet made French Catholicism an easy target for the numerous foes of the ancien régime.[43]

The Catholic Church in Europe symbolically represented the Roman trinity of religion, tradition, and authority.[44] The intellectual and cultural innovators of modernity were moving in a completely different direction. The Copernican Revolution had subverted the epistemic authority of Aristotle and sacred scripture. Cartesian method had undercut inherited tradition as a reliable guide to truth. The scandalous violence caused by prolonged religious disputes weakened the moral and political authority of ecclesiastical leadership. The Roman Catholic Church was the weakest link in the ancien régime and the most vulnerable target of its radical opponents. As Tocqueville sadly regretted, in revolutionary France the friends of liberty became enemies of religion, and the defenders of religion became hostile to liberty. This tragic polarization poisoned the course of the French Revolution and made French Catholicism an enduring symbol of political reaction and intransigence.[45]

The close connection between Catholicism and established authority persisted into the nineteenth century. First, the church lost the allegiance of public intellectuals through its ties to discredited monarchy. Then it lost the trust of the European working class through its political support of the industrial bourgeoisie. When it finally addressed the dangers of the "social question," the scandalous coexistence of excessive wealth and economic deprivation, its public response was, in Lonergan's terms, "a little breathless and a little late."[46] On the defining issues of the modern age, the Vatican regularly placed itself behind the historical curve: its public rebuke of Galileo, its growing opposition to the methods and claims of the new science, its political resistance to democracy, its belated response to the class-based industrial order, its tacit acceptance of colonialism and imperialism, its antimodernist stance toward critical biblical studies.[47]

The critique of Christian doctrine: It is important to distinguish two forms of religious criticism: the critique of Christian practice for its divergence from the spirit and substance of the gospel; the critique of Christian doctrine, the skeptical or passionate rejection of orthodox Christian beliefs in their own right. In this section of our cultural genealogy, we recall the second strand of criticism, though it's important to note that historically the critical lines often intersect.

Orthodox Christian doctrine is chiefly based on sacred scripture and tradition. Christians accept the Bible, both the Old Testament and the New, as the revealed "Word of God." They also accept the writings of the Greek and Latin fathers, and the Trinitarian and Christological affirmations of the great councils of Nicea, Chalcedon, and Constantinople. Catholic teaching is also based on the systematic theology of Aquinas and Bonaventure, among others, though the Protestant Reformers were largely critical of this Scholastic theological heritage.

The Catholic tradition further insists on the complementarity of faith and reason. The deepest and most important Christian mysteries are made known through divine revelation: the Trinitarian nature of God, the humanity and divinity of Jesus, the Pentecostal descent of the Holy Spirit, the miraculous resurrection of the crucified Christ from the dead, the beatific vision that awaits all the saints in the Kingdom of God. Human reason can reflect on these mysteries and attain an imperfect understanding of their meaning and importance, but it cannot establish their truth through rational argument alone.[48] By contrast, human reason can, in principle, if not often in fact, discover the existence of God, the created nature of the world, the special dignity of human beings among all living creatures.[49] Protestant thinkers, generally, were less sanguine than their Catholic peers about reason's epistemic capacity, given the crippling effects of original sin on all human powers.

Although Thomas Aquinas carefully distinguished sacred theology based on divine revelation from philosophical theology based on the exercise of created reason, he did not separate these complementary forms of religious understanding. For Aquinas, philosophical *distinctions* are not ontological or epistemic *separations*, but the mind's way of classifying different but complementary sources of discovering religious truth. In modern philosophy, what Aquinas had carefully distinguished and connected soon became sharply separated. The rules of Cartesian method made both scripture and tradition irrelevant to metaphysics or first philosophy. Descartes claimed to prove God's existence, omniscience, and omnipotence through deductive arguments based on indubitable rational truths. Galileo circumscribed the scope and relevance of scriptural authority in resolving cosmological disagreements. For the Christian Galileo, while the Bible remains the revealed "Word of God" about the way to salvation, it is not a reliable source of scientific knowledge. After the emergence of Newton's intellectual hegemony in the late seventeenth century, it was clear that scientific method, the critical constant in modern physical inquiry, made no evidential appeal to scripture or Christian tradition. Of perhaps equal importance, the autonomous discovery of the three laws of motion made the Newtonian cosmos appear closed, or at best minimally open, to divine interference.[50]

Given the intellectual and cultural prestige of Newton, who was, in fact, a passionate and devoted interpreter of sacred scripture, a new conception of reality and knowledge emerged with modern physics. This new philosophical vision was accompanied by radical semantic change. The term *nature* now referred to the lawful, impersonal, and mechanical Newtonian cosmos, not to the graduated cosmic hierarchy of Aristotle and Aquinas. The term *knowledge* now chiefly referred to the "new science of nature," to the lawful discoveries verifiable by scientific method. And the term *reason* now referred to the methodical and critical process of discovering and verifying these invariant natural laws.

These significant ontological and epistemic changes did not occur in a cultural vacuum. Newtonian mechanics systematically unified more than a century of major scientific discoveries. During that period of extraordinary theoretical progress, the Christian religion was torn asunder by theological controversy: about the true nature of the church, the validity of the sacraments, the believer's personal relation to God, the legitimate forms of worship, the right path to salvation.[51] Enlightened thinkers, on both sides of the Atlantic, were revolted by these fierce, often violent religious disputes. The emerging cultural contrast between natural science and religion was deeply unflattering to Christianity. While the empirical methods of physics produced theoretical consensus and progress, conflicting religious appeals to tradition and scripture produced mounting intolerance and sectarian discord.[52]

Far more than a recovery of religious toleration was soon demanded. Why not radically refashion religious beliefs in the spirit of "nature" and "reason," in the spirit of Enlightenment science? This was the irenic impulse behind "Providential Deism," an "enlightened religion" closely modeled on Newtonian mechanics.[53] Eighteenth-century Deists wanted to liberate Christianity from all that was archaic and controversial: from the traditional appeal to divine revelation, religious authority, doctrinal mysteries and miracles, superstitious forms of piety and belief. A religion of "reason," by deliberate contrast, should be simple and lawful like Newtonian physics, its single Creator God an architect of perfect mechanical designs, its moral laws clear and straightforward, its leading teachers enlightened sages like Thomas Jefferson's Jesus. Jefferson's redacted version of the gospels perfectly illustrates the cosmopolitan mind-set of Providential Deism. Jefferson's selective portrait of Jesus is that of a wise moral teacher, who makes no claim to divinity, performs no miracles, and essentially proclaims the enlightened gospel of the golden rule.[54]

Jefferson's avowed religious adversaries were Calvinists and Papists. He rejected the Calvinist emphasis on original sin, the human dependence on redemptive grace, the strong appeal to the heart rather than the head in spiritual matters. From Jefferson's revisionary perspective, Papists and Calvinists were equally enemies of liberty, intellectual, religious, and political. They preached an authoritarian religion of fear based on a despotic and wrathful God, when the age of Newton demanded a humanistic religion of reason based on a wise and benevolent cosmic architect.[55]

Jefferson believed that his Unitarian rationalism would gradually become the common religious belief of the West. This confident expectation was not fulfilled, however, for several reasons. Evangelical forms of Christianity, deeply rooted in appeals to scripture and personal piety, became increasingly popular in North America and Europe. The more radical Enlightenment thinkers rejected Christianity altogether, finding Jefferson's Deism an unstable alternative to orthodox faith. In addition, radical doubts about divine benevolence and providence undermined Deistic confidence in God's perfect design of the natural world. The devastating Lisbon earthquake of 1755 made serene appeals to divine justice and providence look ridiculous. The sensible world contained too much evil, natural and moral, for the creative wisdom and goodness of God to remain "self-evident." In the heart of Europe, Pierre Bayle severely criticized the vindictive morality ascribed to the biblical God; Voltaire's *Candide* ridiculed a popularized version of Leibniz's influential theodicy. Hume raised skeptical doubts about all rational arguments for the divine, whether theistic or Deistic. Kant claimed that human reason was constitutionally incapable of achieving transcendent knowledge. The anticlerical *philosophes* insisted that however God was conceived, the Christian God was no friend to human progress and happiness. By the end of the eighteenth century, the traditional Catholic synthesis of faith and reason had effectively dissolved.[56]

In the nineteenth century this pattern of cultural antagonism only intensified. Enlightenment thinkers had dreamed of universal harmony and peace, of benevolent lawful design in nature and society. Their intellectual successors emphasized an opposing thematic of conflict and struggle. In Hegel, the defining struggle is philosophical and spiritual; in Marx, economic and social; in Darwin, biological and cosmic; in Freud, psychological and tragic. The whole of reality, natural, historical, social, and psychological, seemed equally red "in tooth and claw." Against this dark, conflict-ridden cultural background, Jefferson's bright religion of harmonious reason also lost credibility.[57]

A divisive split occurred within Protestant Christianity as well. Liberal Protestants sought to adapt Christian doctrines to the findings of science and critical history. Religious conservatives clung tenaciously to the authority of scripture, to the literal truth of the biblical Word. Scriptural fundamentalism became increasingly at odds with modern cosmological and anthropological discoveries. The timescale of Lyell's geology and the evolutionary theory of Darwin profoundly challenged the traditional creation narratives of Genesis. Since the divisive trial of Galileo, the leading moderns had struggled to reconcile natural science with sacred scripture, critical reason with divine revelation. These unresolved tensions only deepened with the emergence of critical historiography and hermeneutics in the nineteenth century. Both Judaism and Christianity are religions of revelation based on particular historical events, the exodus of the Jews and the resurrection of Christ, for example. The new historical scholarship raised skeptical questions about these revered religious narratives. How were the sacred scriptures to be properly read, with the receptive openness of religious faith, and/or the deliberate detachment of critical reason? What credible claims to truth do these narratives actually make? And what does it mean to claim divine authority for complex texts so clearly written by fallible human authors?[58] Because there are no easy answers to these difficult interpretive questions, polarized stances and outlooks tended to dominate public attention: biblical literalists versus scientific and scholarly skeptics; scriptural fundamentalists versus critical debunkers of the entire Judeo-Christian tradition.

Yet another important cultural development put Christian teaching into question. The colonial and imperial adventures of the European powers had exposed Christian thinkers to alien religions and cultures in Asia, Africa, and the Americas. This unsettling exposure heightened their growing awareness of religious diversity and pluralism. Great ancestral civilizations had opposing conceptions of nature, the meaning and purpose of human existence, and the character and activity of the divine. It began to seem naive, even apart from mounting scientific and historical criticism, blithely to privilege the traditional teachings of the Christian past.

The hermeneutics of suspicion:[59] In the secularized West, one can clearly be Christian without being Catholic and clearly religious without being Christian. In fact, we have been tracing the historical emergence of religious alternatives to orthodox Christianity, including Deism, pantheism, and the syncretic appropriation of different non-Western religions. Exclusive humanism, however, takes this pluralizing process a giant step further.[60] Exclusive humanists reject the entire spectrum of religious beliefs, insisting that the common intellectual background of modern secular culture, Taylor's "immanent frame," is comprehensive in scope and systematically closed to transcendent causation.

What are the defining tenets of exclusive humanism?[61] On what ontological and epistemic beliefs is it commonly based? The unaided judgments of critical reason, epistemic and moral, determine the limits of being and value. The only credible sources of human knowledge are empirical and logical, while the only causally effective sources of genuine value are natural and human. All appeals to divine authority and revelation, to divine assistance and grace, to divine action in nature and history, are not only false but fundamentally suspect. Religious beliefs and convictions are not simply mistaken interpretations of reality. They are genealogically rooted in grave intellectual, moral, and political failings. The deeper goal of religious criticism is to unmask the hidden purposes that religion secretly serves. Provocatively stated, all religious phenomena are the cultural product and expression of false consciousness.[62] The dismissive outlook of exclusive humanism is profoundly indebted to the "masters of suspicion," Marx, Nietzsche, and Freud.[63] To see why this is so, let us briefly examine their radical criticisms of religion, criticisms that still remain deeply influential.

Marx's postulated atheism is deep and uncompromising. For Marx, the critical issue facing students of religion is not the truth or falsity of religious belief, but its socioeconomic origin and function. Religion is the most powerful and effective form of *ideology*, a cultural device used by the ruling class to pacify the resistance and rebellion of the oppressed. The Christian religion, in particular, exhorts the economically and politically oppressed, whether ancient slaves, medieval serfs, or modern industrial laborers, to forgo violence, to turn the other cheek, to accept their miserable earthly condition, in the vain hope of eschatological reversal, when, in the next life, the last shall be first and the first shall be last.

Marx himself seeks an eschatological reversal of history, an end to the nightmare of class oppression, but in his revolutionary narrative, the inevitable reversal will occur within secular time through the concerted action of the proletariat and their political allies. In some striking respects, Marx resembles a messianic prophet, castigating the capitalist bourgeoisie, offering radical hope to the industrial working class, exhorting the oppressed to overthrow their inhuman masters. But Marx's messianism is exclusively humanistic. To appeal to God or the gods for deliverance is to forsake the only real sources of historical change, organized economic classes acting in concert with the dialectical laws of history. For Marx, genuine revolutionary change begins with the effective critique of religious ideology; it advances through strategic liberating violence; it culminates in the complete abolition of class struggle with the establishment of a communist society. In the classless society of the future, religion will finally disappear, for the rival economic classes who created and embraced it will have no further need of its false consolation. In Marx's judgment, the only effective solution for the religious problem of modernity is to eliminate the socioeconomic conditions that required its continuance.[64]

Marx rejected religion on the basis of sociohistorical criticism. In its unmasked reality, religion is a cultural construct designed by the strong to dominate the weak. Nietzsche explicitly reversed Marx's critical perspective. For Nietzsche, Judaism and Christianity were creations of the weak deliberately designed to repress the strong. From Nietzsche's revisionary genealogical perspective, Marx's utopian democratic socialism is a secularized version of traditional Christian ideals of equality. But inequality, Nietzsche insists, is a universal law of nature. It is natural and *good* for the strong to master the weak. It is equally natural for the weak to resent their involuntary submission to the strong. In a healthy warrior culture, this negating *ressentiment* remains ineffective, for it leaves unaltered the enduring imbalance of power and strength.

Jews and Christians, however, are not only resentful but cunning. They effectively succeed in proclaiming an inversion of natural values, denigrating the strong, privileging the weak, and bestowing the blessing of God on this historic reversal of the natural order. Such deliberate inversions are evidence of profound cultural sickness. They repress the natural health, emotions, and actions of the strong; they create distorted norms and ideals from the resentment and envy of the weak. The demoralizing result of biblical ethics is a scandalous contraction of the human potential for genuine greatness.[65]

The human greatness Nietzsche envisages is individual rather than collective. Marx's Promethean humanism was based on the anticipated greatness of the liberated species in a classless society. Nietzsche's equally Promethean humanism is based on the greatness of the *over-men*, those rare spiritual warriors strong enough to overthrow the repressive Judeo-Christian morality, independent enough to fashion their own table of virtues and values.[66] Marx was a spiritual child of the radical Enlightenment, Nietzsche a fierce critic of both Christian and Enlightenment values. Nietzsche's radical criticism, however, was tempered by restrained admiration. Christianity had taught the West the discipline of asceticism and self-overcoming, though it carried this liberating mind-set to self-destructive excess.[67] The Enlightenment's critical passion for truth had undermined faith in God, though it ended by making an idol of natural science. For Nietzsche, the morally liberated creative artist, not the truth-seeking scientist, is the true modern spiritual warrior, the shaper of salutary fictions able to restore human health and vitality in an age without God.[68]

Freud's pointed critique of religion is clearly indebted to Nietzsche's depth psychology. Both seek to unmask religious phenomena by revealing their genealogical provenance. For Nietzsche, Judaism and Christianity were born in the spirit of *ressentiment*. Their celebrated ethics of justice and love are, in reality, the opposite of what they appear. Theirs is a reactive ethics, grounded in envy and emotional bitterness. The restoration of human health and integrity requires a profound transformation, a transvaluation of values that restores the few creative over-men to their rightful dominance over the submissive herd.

Freud's depth psychology has both individual and cultural expressions.[69] Freud divides the psyche of the developing individual into three evolving parts. The psyche of the child is dominated by the *id*, the blind striving for libidinal and aggressive satisfaction. As the child develops, biologically, psychologically, and socially, the two other parts of the self emerge. The *ego* is the rational, conscious aspect of the self. In contrast to the pleasure-seeking id, the ego is governed by the sober and wary reality principle. Through practical trial and error, the ego learns that both the natural and social worlds we inhabit are at odds with individual happiness. The forces of nature are indifferent to our constitutional desire for pleasure. The surrounding society, especially through the formative instruction of our parents and teachers, inculcates the moral prohibitions and precepts meant to govern our individual conduct. Violation of these rigorous social imperatives is attended by punishment, first that of our parents and later the public sanctions of custom and law.[70]

The developing child is vulnerable to reality in every important respect. The parents, by contrast, are relatively strong and knowledgeable. The father, especially, provides physical protection for the child as well as intellectual and moral instruction. From the child's limited emotional and practical perspective, the father is a godlike figure who alternately protects, consoles, and punishes. Despite grave internal tensions, grounded in the dialectics of sexual development, children naturally seek the love and approval of their parents, though the implacable blindness of the id makes it indifferent, even hostile, to the pragmatic adaptations of the ego and the censorious stance of the socially generated superego.

The emerging adult seeks a functional equilibrium among these rival and competing aspects of the self. The emotionally mature person is governed by the ego's reality principle. But this is no easy autocracy, for the relentless demands of the irrational id and the punitive superego are never satisfied. Nature and society, as noted, are indifferent to the individual's desire for happiness. Social imperatives and moral ideals primarily serve the purpose of group survival, while natural forces are purposeless and blind to individual and social desires. Although humans profoundly desire happiness, identified by Freud with the full satisfaction of their most basic desires, they gradually learn that their condition is tragic, that their natural desires and the demands of reality are incompatible. They also painfully learn that their parents are not the gods they originally imagined, but rather complex and divided individuals, like themselves, with limited knowledge, virtue, and strength.

With this momentous recognition, humanity divides into two distinct groups: the tragic truth-tellers like Freud who realize that in reality there are no gods or God; the regressive truth-evaders who invent a fictional divine protector modeled on the childish image of their fathers. On Freud's deliberately reductive account, religious faith is a regressive psychological phenomenon, a form of emotional immaturity and dishonesty. For religious believers are biological adults who refuse to accept things as they really are and to make the best of what actually exists.

Near the end of his life, Freud framed this stark psychological contrast as the cultural rivalry between science and religion.[71] Science is the truth-telling agency of culture. It generally brings unwelcome news to humanity, for it refuses to flatter our childish need for parental approval and love. Freud cites three historic examples to drive home this unwelcome point. Copernicus removed the earth, our terrestrial home, from the center of the cosmic scheme. Darwin revealed our ancestral origins among the higher primates. Freud himself disclosed the precarious state of reason and ego within the continuing drama of the human soul. Given our emotional needs and intellectual cowardice, we humans regularly prefer flattery to truth from our cultural heroes and guides.

Traditional religions claim to answer Kant's three great anthropological questions: What can I know? What ought I to do? What may I reasonably hope for?[72] Freud declares with assurance that the religious answers to these questions are inherently suspect. It is science, not religion, scientific method, not religious faith or divine revelation, which advances human knowledge of reality. Because the truth claims of religion are false, its moral teachings are largely unrealistic. Religious prohibitions are far too strict, religious ideals far too lofty, the religious acceptance of human suffering, excessively passive, austere, and unfriendly. Finally, there are the religious hopes for personal immortality and enduring communion with God and the saints. From Freud's critical atheistic perspective, those deeply held longings are mere childish fantasies, a species of false consolation, unworthy of mature human assent.

What alternative form of life does Freud propose? To pursue knowledge of reality through the sciences, to balance dynamically the conflicting demands for individual survival and happiness, to embrace the hard disciplines of love and work, the true signs of emotional maturity, with the tragic awareness that both love and work will end irrevocably in death, from which there is no appeal.[73]

Living with and without God: Our contemporary secular age is the unstable historical product of many conflicting cultural forces: the critique of Latin Christendom, the Christian wars of religion, the Copernican Revolution, the violent overthrow of the ancien régime, the advent of liberal democracy, the persisting scandal of the "social question," the unsettling disclosures of critical historiography and hermeneutics, the growing influence of exclusive humanism, the skeptical challenge to divine benevolence and goodness. These powerful criticisms of Christianity, and religious faith generally, began among cultural elites: men of letters, practicing scientists, historical scholars, skeptical social and psychological theorists. Eventually, through a process of slow cultural assimilation, they become influential at all levels of society.[74] It seemed, if the secularist critics were right, that intellectual integrity required open disbelief or, at least, a skeptical suspension of faith.

The history of modernity has made the North Atlantic world endemically critical: critical of religious practice and doctrine, critical of religious rigidity and cowardice, critical of received images of God and the supernatural. The great modern cultural movements have also focused human attention and concern on the temporal and historical world: its immense challenges and opportunities, both epistemic and moral, its legitimate claim on our common hopes and allegiance. To the extent that religious faith seems escapist, indifferent to human greatness and misery, lacking in honesty and courage, weak, immature, and intolerant, a peddler of false consolation, it invites and deserves severe moral rebuke.

It is essential to acknowledge the existential import of this powerful religious critique. If religious beliefs are untrue, religious precepts unsound, and religious hopes inauthentic, then it's better to live without God than to support an indefensible fiction. At the same time, the cultural alternatives to religion are also manifestly unstable. Natural science leaves the great existential questions unanswered. Critical historiography cannot disprove the seminal claims of the most important religious narratives. Secular ideologies, like Marxism, fascism, and laissez-faire liberalism, have aggravated, rather than resolved persisting human conflicts. Exclusive humanists turn to science for truth and the arts for inspiration, but, at the end of the day, still confront sin, suffering, and death.[75] At the level of moral advocacy, there now exists in the West a broad though ungrounded cultural consensus. Ordinary life on this earth warrants our loyalty and support, the protection of human rights is essential, democratic communities must consistently depend on the active participation and engagement of their citizens.

Despite several centuries of sustained cultural critique, it remains unclear that the modern critical mind-set is incompatible with authentic religious faith. As human history has repeatedly shown, faith can be aberrant as well as authentic, both destructive and supportive of what is genuine and good. The great religious figures of the past, Abraham, Moses, the prophets, Jesus, the apostles and martyrs, Saint Francis, Saint Thomas, Saint Teresa, Joan of Arc, the great reformers, still command our clear-eyed admiration. The same is true of their contemporary analogues: Gandhi, Martin Luther King, Jr., Mother Teresa, Dorothy Day, Nelson Mandela, among so many others.

Those who live with the presence of God in the world must take full account of those who do not. But the converse is also true. Neither ontological naturalism nor exclusive humanism can account for the mysterious fact of an intelligible universe, the profound depths of human existence constantly revealed in birth, love, friendship, suffering, redemption, and death, and our unrestricted longing for meaning, goodness, and truth. We can deliberately enclose ourselves within the strict limits of the "immanent frame," or we can remain open to whatever lies beyond and beneath it. The contemporary demand for authenticity, a demand religious believers should fully embrace, cannot, by itself, resolve this most basic existential decision. What, if anything, could?[76]

Rising to the Challenge of Our Time

Perhaps the most striking characteristic of our secular age is the cross-pressures and tensions it creates. The principal source of these tensions is the unprecedented pluralism of late modernity. If the preceding narrative is sound, contemporary pluralism is simultaneously epistemic, moral, and religious. Distinct forms of knowledge coexist with ostensibly irreconcilable knowledge claims. A plethora of genuine goods are justified and rank ordered (prioritized) by rival and exclusive moral ontologies. And both the believers and the nonbelievers among us are increasingly bewildered by the variety of religious beliefs, practices, and communities that compete for our spiritual allegiance.

The conscientious individual is often overwhelmed by this rapidly expanding convergence of forces. He or she has to judge what is true, decide what is right, and shape a dignified life without a cultural consensus to guide and support the most critical commitments a person can make.[77] There is no shortage of competing cultural traditions, but no clear grounds for choosing among them. The most polarizing and strident alternatives seem reductive and scornful of apparently genuine truth claims. However, the arbitrary choice of a worldview or the deliberate refusal to choose one seems equally incompatible with the gravity of what is at stake.[78]

The existential crisis of the developing individual is ultimately a cultural crisis that results from the modern dialectic of progress and decline. We cannot reject the palpable fruits of modernity because our common lives are so dependent upon them. Nor can we accept modern culture uncritically because its dynamic and expansive pluralism is simultaneously rich and demoralizing. For Lonergan, the existential and cultural crises have to be confronted together, with full critical respect for the epistemic, moral, and religious pluralism that modern history has effectively generated.

How does Lonergan recommend we proceed? He believes the primary challenge we face is philosophical, since our most urgent cultural need is for discerning, nonreductive integration: to distinguish, order, and critically connect the whole of our tangled inheritance. But this is a collaborative project that no single individual can perform on her own.[79] What then can the reflective individual contribute to the daunting task of critical appropriation? What must we learn, what sort of persons must we become to achieve a critical, historically minded pluralism, in which complementary and genetically related truths and goods are clearly distinguished from their dialectical, that is, contradictory, counterparts?[80]

According to Lonergan, the dialectical critique of modernity must begin with critical self-appropriation. Through a long, slow pedagogical process, we must learn to give coherent and credible answers to five fundamental questions:[81] What am I doing when I am coming to know in mathematics, natural science, the human sciences, common sense, philosophy, and theology? (These questions form the basis of a comprehensive cognitional theory adapted to the epistemic complexity of our time.) Why does "doing that" result in objective knowledge in the several distinct but complementary realms of cognitive meaning (the culturally variable domain of practical common sense, the specialized theoretical domains of the different autonomous sciences, the polymorphic domain of intentional consciousness, the transcendent domain of divine being and agency)? What is actually known when we achieve objective knowledge in these very different ways? (This is the central question for a contemporary metaphysics that recognizes the reality of both proportionate and transcendent being.) How does our objective knowledge of being responsibly develop into an existential and social ethics grounded in the demand for personal and communal authenticity? Finally, what is the ontological, moral, and religious significance of our unrestricted longings for knowledge and value? Can these transcendental longings be satisfied within the universe of proportionate being; can they ever be satisfied, or are they ultimately futile though inescapable spiritual passions?

Lonergan's *Insight* is a highly ambitious philosophical essay designed to aid self-appropriation of this kind. The reader of *Insight* learns critically to distinguish two forms of knowing, two notions of reality, two conceptions of the good. These different forms and notions are dialectically related, for they are grounded at different levels of the reader's intentional consciousness.[82] At the empirical level of sense-experience, human knowing seems to occur through taking a look; reality is "already out there now" waiting to be looked at; and the attainable good is whatever satisfies our vital and immediate desires. At the normative and critical level of consciousness, however, on which human experience, understanding, and judgment coalesce, knowing occurs through affirming true judgments, reality is known through the intentional content of those verified judgments, and genuine goods are identified through true evaluative determinations of what is really worthwhile. The critical philosophical and personal challenge is to distinguish, rather than eliminate, these polymorphic aspects of the self and their irreducibly different intentional correlates and outlooks.[83]

Why is that epistemic achievement so critical for Lonergan's project? Authentic self-appropriation depends on deepening and broadening the operative horizon of the intentional subject. If knowing consists in taking a look, then the scope of the knowable is confined to the sensible and imaginable orders, to what is or might be "already out there now." If the human good is confined to the available sources of sensory pleasure, then the universe of value is confined to material objects and to the technical instruments needed to procure their sensible benefits. By contrast, if human knowing consists in understanding and judging correctly, then reality consists in whatever can be intelligently grasped and reasonably affirmed. And if genuine goods are known through the evaluative judgments of authentic subjects, then material goods are subordinated to spiritual goods, including, potentially, the supreme good that religious believers call God.

In *Method in Theology*, Lonergan characterizes these radical expansions of the subject's horizon as conversions.[84] Through intellectual conversion, the developing subject goes beyond the world of immediacy (the restricted horizon of sense and imagination) to the world critically mediated by meaning (the unrestricted horizon of the intrinsically intelligible and reasonable). Through moral conversion the subject's ethical horizon expands from the limited order of vital and immediate satisfactions to the richly differentiated order of originating and terminal values. And through religious conversion, the subject moves beyond the exclusive love of proportionate beings to a wholehearted love of God that can radically develop into a disinterested love of all that God loves and affirms.[85]

Lonergan's central point here is actually quite subtle. Whenever human beings achieve knowledge of the real or accomplish the truly worthwhile, they transcend the restricted horizon of epistemic and moral immediacy. The dialectical crux occurs, however, when they are asked to thematize what they are actually doing as inquirers and practical agents. Their explicit philosophical accounts of knowing, knowledge, being, value, and

God are frequently instantiations of the unconverted counterpositions. Thus they effectively truncate their own intentional complexity, along with the intellectual and moral horizons it has partly disclosed. The result is an existential and, ultimately, a cultural contradiction in which the reality of the self and its environing world is far richer and deeper than its self-interpretation. Taylor refers to this reductive process as "stifling" the deeper truth about ourselves and our values. Lonergan calls it "performative contradiction."[86] The dialectical purpose of self-appropriation is to bring our self-knowledge into explicit accord with the whole of our epistemic and moral achievement.

What is the relevance of personal to cultural self-appropriation? Lonergan believes the cultural confusions of modernity are traceable to a similar dialectic. The intellectual, moral, and spiritual history of modernity is a tangled knot of progress and decline, partly because our leading cultural theorists have consistently misinterpreted our finest epistemic and moral attainments. The result of this striking disparity is the uneven cultural heritage that, to quote Whitehead, "we can neither live with nor live without."[87] To state his dialectical convictions concretely, Lonergan believes the following:[88]

1. The pervasive achievements of practical common sense, technological, economic, and political, coexist with a general cultural bias against disinterested theoretical and scholarly inquiry. This commonsense bias promotes a shortsighted pragmatism that ignores or denies the theoretical basis of many of its own most important practical accomplishments.
2. The great discoveries of the natural sciences have been combined with extrascientific affirmations that distort their epistemic significance and ontological import. While the scientific discoveries can be critically confirmed through the appropriate empirical methods, the extrascientific assertions clearly cannot.
3. The great achievements of critical history and hermeneutics have been combined with distorted methodological accounts of historical and exegetical inquiry. The cultural legacy of this unhappy blending of genuine scholarly achievement and distorted self-interpretation is a reductive and debunking account of the past.

4. The gradual acceptance of our collective responsibility for the state of human affairs has frequently been conflated with ideological philosophies of history that greatly oversimplify the causal complexity and practical challenges of the historical process.
5. The philosophical turn to the subject has repeatedly overlooked the most important constants within human existence: our unrestricted desires for knowledge and value; the normative pattern in which these desires concretely unfold; the immanent norms that govern this recurrent unfolding; the existential biases that arrest and obstruct our compliance with these exigent norms. The confusing result of these critical oversights tends to be either an inflated or deflated humanism. Inflated humanists deliberately separate the incarnate subject from its causal dependence on nature and history, overstating its independence and autonomy. Their cultural rivals, the deflationary counter-humanists, concentrate on the dark side of natural and historical belonging, but fail to acknowledge the human subject's capacity for epistemic, moral, and religious self-transcendence (i.e., real but precarious authenticity).[89]
6. Finally, the existential demand for authenticity has been narrowly associated with unflinching attention to the most disturbing aspects of the human condition: natural and moral evil, meaningless suffering, inescapable mortality. But genuine authenticity requires far more than acknowledging the dark side of human existence. Epistemic authenticity requires a radical openness to truth and reality in all of its forms. Moral authenticity requires a comparable openness to the dialectical tangle of good and evil in nature and history. Religious authenticity requires an openness to God and to God's redemptive initiatives within the whole of creation.[90]

There is a common dialectical structure to these six areas of cultural tension. In each case, important insights are compromised by oversights, genuine progress is distorted by interpretive reduction. When human existence exhibits this contradictory pattern of greatness and wretchedness, dialectical analysis is needed to unravel the cultural tangle that leaves ordinary citizens confused and uncertain about who/what they are, or narrowly committed to partial and limited truths and goods.[91]

Lonergan's critical dialectic of modernity is primarily grounded in his theory of cognition. He distinguishes three important stages in the history of cognitive meaning.[92] In the first stage, human inquiry and discourse are confined to the level of practical common sense. The understanding of nature, human existence, even the divine, is limited to a commonsense perspective that treats all things in their practical relation to us (where *us* refers to the particular historical community we inhabit). The discourse of common sense is equally limited to the ordinary languages we regularly use in our daily communal transactions.[93] In the second stage of cognitive meaning, systematic theory effectively distinguishes itself from practical common sense. The description of things in their sensible relations to us is profoundly augmented by the explanation of things in their intelligible relations to one another. Ordinary commonsense language is also transcended by the technical discourse of the theoretical sciences. While commonsense inquiry is confined to the realm of familiar practical concerns, the theoretical aims of science are in principle unrestricted. Because the specialized sciences have not yet been clearly differentiated, the unification of developing knowledge is largely dependent on the operations of logic. Thus, in the synoptic philosophies of Aristotle and Aquinas, the basic theoretical terms and relations are metaphysical, and the different levels and orders of being are treated as special cases of metaphysical principles and truths.[94]

In the second phase of the European Enlightenment, a third stage of cognitive meaning gradually emerges. By the late nineteenth century, the natural sciences have become distinct and autonomous, while the incipient human sciences still seek to define themselves clearly. Critical scholarship has begun to claim its autonomy and historical mindedness has penetrated all fields of inquiry. Philosophy struggles to distinguish itself effectively from the natural and social sciences, historical scholarship and common sense, while questions about God's existence, nature, and activity have become deeply controversial.[95]

We now live with unprecedented epistemic pluralism without the requisite integration and unity. Logical strategies of integrating knowledge prove increasingly procrustean because the distinct realms of cognitive meaning rely on irreducibly different forms of discourse. This logical irreducibility applies not only between the judgments of common sense and theory, and between the natural and human sciences, but also among the different natural sciences themselves. Lonergan insists that this dynamic cognitive pluralism only heightens philosophy's cultural importance. For philosophers, on his conception of their cultural mission, seek the differentiated whole with respect to human knowledge—clearly not the whole of knowledge, but the critical unification of its distinct and relatively autonomous parts.[96]

The unrestricted desire to know has led historically to the specialization and differentiation of knowledge. But the human desire for epistemic integration and unity clearly persists. Once again we are confronted with the perennial philosophical challenge. How to do justice, *mutatis mutandis*, to the legitimate claims of the one and the many? Lonergan's strategic proposal is clear and unflinching. In the third stage of meaning, to which we belong, philosophy's integrative strategy must advance from logic to method.[97] This critical heuristic shift does not mean the rejection of logic, but the incorporation of logical operations into the larger whole of cognitional process. But what does Lonergan mean by appealing to method? Method is a normative pattern of recurrent and related intentional operations yielding progressive and cumulative results.[98] While metaphysics is traditionally concerned with the objects of cognitive meaning, with what is actually knowable and known, and logic is concerned with the formal terms of cognitive meaning, with the explicit articulation of knowledge's propositional content, method is concerned with the human knower, and the full range of cognitional desires, operations, and norms.[99]

What is the critical import of Lonergan's detailed cognitional analysis? The history of human inquiry is characterized by epistemic constants and variables. The foundational constants are transcultural and transhistorical principles, grounded as they are in the very nature of the human spirit.[100] The relevant epistemic variables are culturally and historically sensitive, reflecting the distinct heuristic contexts in which human inquiry has actually occurred. The foundational constants, to use Lonergan's terminology in *Method*, are transcendental; they serve as essential conditions of the possibility of all human intellectual and moral achievement.[101] They include the unrestricted desires for knowledge and value, the dynamic normative pattern of knowing, deciding, and doing, and the immanent normative exigences that effectively govern this four-leveled intentional process.

The relevant contextual variables include the three distinct stages of cognitive inquiry, the ontologically distinct realms of meaning, the complementary heuristic structures, classical, statistical, genetic, and dialectical, in which empirical method is practiced, and the inescapable cultural variability of practical common sense. The transcendental constants provide the enduring basis of epistemic unity; the categorical variables are the dynamic source of increasing epistemic pluralism. While the constants serve to unify the history of inquiry, the variables demarcate its most important landmark transitions.

Modern scientists and scholars have rightly insisted on the epistemic importance of empirical methods. But Lonergan shows how a generalized empirical method (a transcendental method) that includes both the data of sense and the data of consciousness can be comprehensive and historically nuanced at the same time.[102] The specialized differentiations of intentional consciousness effectively account for the distinct realms of cognitive meaning. Complete fidelity to the transcendental constants requires that all experiential data be acknowledged, all intelligent questions explored, all reasonable answers affirmed, all responsible choices enacted and honored. The unrestricted scope of these several transcendental demands leads directly to the fundamental question of God. Is there a transcendent realm of being and value that complements the philosophic realm of interiority as the interiority of consciousness complements the cognitive realms of nature, history, and common sense?[103]

In our era of autonomous science and scholarship, Lonergan preserves philosophy as a distinct form of empirical inquiry by making it the intentional analysis of polymorphic subjectivity. But a related epistemic question still remains to be critically addressed: What happens to religion and theology in the third stage of meaning? Can religious faith be authenticated and theology credibly developed within the normative constraints of transcendental method?[104] Lonergan agrees with the secular critics of religion that we must respond to these questions authentically, taking full account of the momentous cultural changes that constitute modernity. But he insists that these changes are inherently ambiguous, neither to be accepted nor rejected uncritically. And the critical stance we take in understanding and appraising them must be based on self-appropriation, both personal and historical. We have just outlined Lonergan's reflective appraisal of modern epistemic change, identifying what he accepts and what he rejects in this tangled cultural legacy.[105]

In the moral domain, Lonergan's position is less fully developed, but his critical orientation is clear. The fundamental moral imperative, for individuals and historical societies, is to become fully authentic. Authenticity requires deep and sustained self-transcendence, consistent adherence to the transcendental precepts in all aspects of our knowing and living. Epistemic self-transcendence results in the objective knowledge of reality, moral self-transcendence in exemplary instances of personal and communal existence. Because of human error, bias, and sin, we regularly fall short of these exigent intentional norms. The greatest personal and collective danger arises from our troubling tendency to deny and rationalize these repeated failings, covering them over or rhetorically justifying them with explicit ideological defenses.[106]

The personal and cultural effect of ideology is to blur and conceal the critical contrasts between authentic and inauthentic existence, between truth and error, justice and injustice, progress and decline, holiness and sin. The effective critique of ideology, the successful disclosure of counterpositions as counterpositions, requires, as we have argued, intellectual, moral, and religious conversion. Without these distinct but related conversions, there is no credible way to unravel the massive cultural knot that we share in this troubled secular age.[107]

To be clear, Lonergan does not advocate returning to the discredited culture of medieval Christendom. Because human history has no reverse gear, religious authenticity must rise to the level and challenge of our time. However, modern secularity must be critically appropriated, as well. Concretely, this entails a nuanced position with respect to our troubled religious inheritance. For Lonergan, there is a secularization (1) to be welcomed and a sacralization (1) that no longer applies. But there is also a secularization (2) to be resisted and a renewed sacralization (2) to be encouraged and fostered.[108] How should we understand this complex, four-sided cultural project? How responsive are Lonergan's dialectical contrasts to the three senses of *secular* Charles Taylor distinguished?

A secularization (1) to be welcomed: Lonergan accepts the fundamental cultural dynamic of a secular (1) age. A broad range of human practices, epistemic and moral, has become relatively autonomous. The empirical sciences, natural and human, historical scholarship and philosophy, the numerous enterprises of practical common sense, are largely self-governing. They operate independently of religious belief and authority; they communicate their discoveries across social, demographic, and cultural divisions, and impose no religious requirement for full participation in their activities. Believers and nonbelievers share in these practices with equal liberty and dignity. Although the public realm is still influenced by religious communities, there is no common faith or creed at the heart of our public existence. Nor is there common agreement about the religious implications of contemporary theory and practice. Secularization (1) has created this unprecedented cultural context for the development of religion and theology in the third stage of meaning.[109]

A sacralization (1) that no longer applies: To treat something as sacred is to accord it exceptional reverence, to identify it with God or with God's will for creation. In resisting modernity and secularization (1), many defenders of Christianity have argued that Latin Christendom constitutes a timeless cultural norm. To deviate from that norm is to violate a canonical order regulative for all of history. Lonergan designates this ahistorical normative outlook as classicism.[110] *Classicists*, in his critical use of the term, treat as sacred and unalterable what is historically provincial and culturally contingent.

The genuine alternative to the classicist mentality is critical historical mindedness. For Lonergan, to recognize the cultural importance of history is to acknowledge that:[111] not only do the empirical sciences develop, but our very *notion* of science changes with time; no particular historical culture can serve as a timeless norm for the many others; human cultures are inherently plural, consisting, as they do, of the contingent beliefs and convictions that undergird the diversity of human societies; because human beings are concretely situated in nature and history, our understanding and appraisal of human existence must be empirically, not metaphysically, based; the existential foundations of human knowledge and action are not located in timeless logical principles, but in the transcendental constants and precepts Lonergan has carefully articulated; finally, under secular (1) conditions, theology must become a functionally specialized empirical discipline that fully respects the autonomy of contemporary science and scholarship.

Historical mindedness, however, also needs to be critical, effectively distinguishing: genuine theoretical discoveries and developments from extrascientific assertions; a robust cultural pluralism from moral and historical relativism; genuine historical progress from institutional and cultural decline; transcendental constants from categorial variables; a critical, functionally specialized theology from the uncritical dogmatic insistence that theological knowledge is impossible.[112]

Secularization (1) has created a radically new cultural situation. Its classicist critics mistakenly merge their religious faith with the traditional culture(s) in which it once flourished. Though they believe otherwise, surrendering these older cultural allegiances does not require abandoning their faith. On the contrary: it requires raising their faith and its personal and public expressions to the level and challenge of our secular (1) age.

A secularization (2) to be resisted: The religious appraisal of modernity is especially difficult because two different aspects of secularization (1 and 2) were historically blended together. Important discoveries in physics were regularly conflated with a mechanistic cosmology; Darwin's evolutionary theory became the scientific basis of a reductive ontological naturalism; critical scholarship was alleged to exclude the divine presence from human affairs; cultural pluralism became popularly identified with moral conventionalism; the masters of suspicion made religious faith seem inauthentic and childish; exclusive humanists insisted that the affirmation of man requires the denial of God; their counterhumanist critics caustically responded that both "man" and God are better left dead. No wonder that religious believers struggle with modern cultural developments and nostalgically look toward a lost "age of faith."[113]

A secular (1) age can easily slide into a secular (2) age in which religious belief and practice sharply decline. If Lonergan and Taylor are right, religious communities themselves are partly responsible for their loss of broad public support. Their sectarian rivalries and despotic governing practices effectively discredited traditional Christendom. They seemed unable to articulate and clarify the meaning and relevance of the core Christian doctrines. They rejected the hermeneutics of suspicion without critically appraising its merits and limitations.[114] They failed to satisfy the spiritual aspirations of their contemporaries who drifted or were drawn into living without God.

And yet the modern critique of religion is often extreme and one-sided. The decline of medieval Christendom certainly does not entail the wholesale rejection of Christianity. The discoveries of modern science and scholarship, the development of novel heuristic structures, the full acceptance of empirical methods of inquiry, the adoption of a critical mentality in the study of nature and history, the enduring commitment to an authentic humanism, are fully compatible with a deep Christian faith. And, if Lonergan is right, they are also compatible with the truth claims of received Christian orthodoxy.[115]

To state Lonergan's cultural appraisal concisely: Secularization (1) intelligibly created a secular (1) age which believers of all faiths ought critically to accept. For contingent historical reasons, due to both the serious failures of religious institutions and important secular oversights and distortions, secularization (1) was conflated with secularization (2) to produce a secular (2) age of pervasive unbelief. Our global contemporaries, who live in a secular (3) age, have inherited the knotted cultural tangle this unwelcome and unnecessary conflation has presently yielded.

A sacralization (2) to be fostered: What would an authentic religious humanism be like today? It would radically embrace, in word and in deed, Lonergan's transcendental constants: the unrestricted desires for knowledge and value, the normative patterns of human knowing, choosing, and living, the transcendental precepts that govern human existence as a whole. It would also embrace critical historical mindedness, striving to think and live credibly at the level of our time. It would pursue critical self-appropriation and accept the existential demands of intellectual, moral, and religious conversion. Critically fortified in this way, it would dialectically distinguish the enduring achievements of the *vetera* and the *nova* from their equally important limitations. It would understand human existence, both personal and communal, as the dramatic nexus where created nature, disruptive sin, and redemptive grace concretely converge. It would recognize that sustained authenticity requires a radical openness not only to genuine human achievement but also to God's revelatory presence in human affairs. For human beings are receptive as well as creative intentional subjects, wounded as well as capable of healing, both needing and freely responding to the gift of divine aid.[116]

In the thirteenth century, Thomas Aquinas argued persuasively that divine grace perfects created nature, as revealed faith perfects human reason, and as charity perfects the cardinal virtues. Lonergan seeks to restore this great Thomist insight with an explicitly Augustinian twist. The ontological principles of human nature and divine grace coexist with the destructive reality of sin. Sin does violence to created nature, weakening its natural operations. Grace not only perfects nature (sublates natural operations, in Lonergan's terms), it also heals the wounds, subjective and objective, inflicted by sin.[117]

Inflated humanists tend to deny the profound reality of sin and the acute human need for redemptive grace and its blessings. Their counter-humanist critics are deeply aware of evil and its destructive consequences, but see no credible path to remedy or healing. An authentic contemporary humanism must be truly comprehensive, recognizing the dialectical interplay of these three causal principles, freely cooperating with God and each other in the great unfinished work of redeeming the world.[118]

Enlightenment, Science, and Faith

Writing at the end of the eighteenth century, Kant articulated the doctrinal core of the modern European Enlightenment.[119] An enlightened humanity, according to Kant, was a humanity that had finally come of age. Its leading cultural representatives had learned to think, act, and judge for themselves. Under the banner of rational autonomy, they had liberated their minds from the extended tutelage of the Roman trinity, religion, tradition, and authority. As mature rational beings, they refused to subordinate their judgments and decisions to ecclesiastical, political, or cultural mentors, nor did they look to traditional doctrines to decide what they thought and believed.

For Kant, the defining spirit of the Enlightenment was both constructive and critical. Critical reason was the chosen instrument of human liberation, freeing the enlightened present from the dead weight of the past. In Kant's celebrated adage, "Our age is an age of criticism and to criticism everything must submit."[120] He memorably depicted critical reason as the ultimate judicial authority, before whose impartial tribunal everything human must plead its case.[121]

The eighteenth-century Enlightenment is famous for its radical institutional and cultural critique. It discredited the legitimacy of the ancien régime even before the revolution in France. Kings were stripped of their authority, aristocrats of their hereditary privileges, ecclesiastical leaders of their authoritative control over morality and doctrine. Kant extended his critical scrutiny to the intellectual culture of the West. He brought mathematics, natural science, metaphysics, the entire theoretical enterprise before the bar of rational criticism. He asked what he believed were the most searching philosophical questions: whether and how theoretical science is possible; what can and cannot be known by the power of human reason alone.[122]

Kant's critical conclusions both strengthened and challenged the aspirations of autonomous reason. He affirmed the scientific status of Euclidean geometry and Newtonian physics. He denied the human capacity for transcendent knowledge, for knowledge that exceeded the limits of human experience. Kant acknowledged the human mind's natural desire to know the existence and essence of God. That desire naturally expresses itself in transcendent thinking and questioning; but human thinking is one thing, human knowing another. *Pace* Descartes and the ancient philosophers, we cannot know the truth about God, moral freedom, and the soul's immortality. To believe that we can is to be guilty of what Kant called transcendental illusion.[123]

Kant's critical philosophy did not treat natural science as the enemy of faith. In fact the strict epistemic and ontological limits Kant imposed upon science deliberately leave room for the rational faith that morality demands. God is part of that faith, though not in the traditional Christian manner. Kant's enlightened religion, confined within the limits of critical reason,[124] is a religion without grace, revelation, and miracles, a religion purged of the despotic punitive functions Kant critiqued in the biblical God.

The supreme principle of Kantian morality is the autonomy of pure practical reason. It is pure reason rather than God that legislates the moral law, decides which maxims of the will are, indeed, categorical, and supplies the motives and ends of our moral existence. God is no longer the sovereign moral legislator and judge, the ultimate enforcer of the law's strict commands. The Kantian God is a regulative practical and theoretical ideal, a postulated holy will, an inscrutable transcendent cause whose causal power is not itself caused by natural or human causation.[125]

In the second phase of the European Enlightenment, Kant's static notions of science and morality are gradually abandoned. A new historical consciousness emerges that alters our understanding of all forms of knowledge and culture. Non-Euclidean geometries are discovered and eventually accepted. Newtonian physics is significantly modified, first by relativity theory and then by quantum mechanics. Statistical heuristic structures are gradually introduced into scientific practice. Darwin radically revises classical biology by introducing evolutionary principles to account for the origin and disappearance of species. Soon, statistical and genetic explanations are applied to the entirety of nature, while empirical methods of inquiry are deliberately extended to the study of human affairs. The human sciences are then confronted with a heuristic dilemma: either to model themselves on the dominant sciences of nature, physics and biology, or to establish their own heuristic and methodological legitimacy.

The new historical consciousness only strengthened the Kantian metaphor of "coming of age." Before long, a positivist reading of intellectual history gained traction and currency. Comte's simplified narrative of cognitional life outlined three ascending stages of epistemic maturity. In the first stage, unenlightened humanity relied on religious explanations for its understanding of reality. In the second, philosophical criticism provisionally displaced the older religious mentality, substituting abstract metaphysical causes and ends for the earlier pantheon of fictional gods. In the fully enlightened positivist age of the future, Comte predicted that the empirical sciences would unseat philosophy as the ultimate arbiters of knowledge and truth. When the sciences alone determine what is true and real, both religion and philosophy will become relics of an archaic past.

Comte's positivist thesis that religious beliefs are historically outmoded was radicalized by the "masters of suspicion." For Marx, Nietzsche, and Freud, religious ideologies and institutions continued to exert undue influence, even in an age dominated by science. Religion, therefore, needed to be "unmasked," to be permanently and irreversibly discredited. The cumulative effect of their successive unmaskings put religious faith severely on the defensive. By the end of the nineteenth century, many enlightened Europeans widely believed that faith was archaic, incompatible with reason and science, and the chief cultural barrier to a state of continuing progressive maturity.

Many religious leaders, both Catholic and Protestant, accepted the alleged incompatibility between critical reason and faith. To preserve the substance of their ancient beliefs, they felt compelled to reject the disturbing discoveries of modern science and historical scholarship. Why did they so often react in this defensive manner? Because the judgments of modern critical reason had shattered the cosmological and anthropological pictures they inherited from tradition and scripture.[126] Both sides of this strident polemical debate, both the defenders and critics of religion, tended to conflate the substance of the Christian faith with the truth claims of premodern culture. This conflation created the regrettable impression of a divisive and permanent polarity between faith and reason, religion and science, divine revelation and autonomous human discovery.[127]

Lonergan disagrees with both sides of this heated polemic. The defenders of religion are wrong to identify the Christian faith with premodern beliefs about nature and history. That is the error of cultural "classicism." The critical opponents of religion, however, are wrong to assert that the epistemic achievements of modernity contradict the core truths of Christianity. That is the error of several versions of cultural "modernism."[128] In fact, Lonergan deliberately reverses the Kantian and positivist assumption that human maturity requires the abandonment or radical revision of Christian belief. He responds to this influential counterposition with a direct dialectical challenge: What a mature humanity requires is full authenticity, epistemic, moral, and religious. What authenticity, in turn, requires is a comprehensive conversion of the existential subject. A fully critical subject, one who has philosophically appropriated the transcendental notions, methods, and precepts, will then be able to develop their philosophical and theological implications. And those implications, if Lonergan is right, reveal the complementarity, rather than opposition, between the best of the old and the new.[129]

Lonergan agrees with one strand of the Enlightenment metanarrative. To understand modernity in depth you must first understand the Scientific Revolution, whose remote origins are traceable to the late thirteenth century and even to classical antiquity. The modern natural and human sciences are genuinely new, but in what does their actual novelty consist? We shall briefly summarize Lonergan's subtle and historically informed account.[130]

What modern science is: The classical notion of science is static and based upon the individual inquirer. According to Aristotle, science is a virtue of the theoretical intellect consisting of true, certain knowledge of causal necessity. This highly prized epistemic virtue informs the soul of an individual thinker, whose acquired capacity to define scientific terms and demonstrate scientific truths (the logical marks of classical *episteme*) is secure and invariant.[131]

Modern theoretical science, by contrast, is a specialized and differentiated communal endeavor committed to the explanation of all empirical data. It is a dynamic and relatively autonomous project that operates independently of philosophical, political, and religious control. Its formulated discoveries are not true but are, one hopes, on the way to truth. These discoveries do not express certain knowledge, but the best available opinion of the relevant portion of the scientific community.[132] The scientific notion of causality is neither Aristotelian nor Humean. Causality refers to the verifiable relations of intelligible dependence among implicitly defined theoretical terms.[133] Finally, the verified judgments of empirical science provide an explanatory account of contingent facts rather than insights into causal necessity. Because modern science is a fundamentally communal activity, the formation, transmission, and critical reception of belief play a major role in learning, teaching, articulating, and revising scientific discoveries.[134] To provide critical controls on their scientific beliefs, practicing scientists rely heavily on the canons of empirical method.[135]

The structure and norms of scientific method: Lonergan devoted an entire chapter of *Insight* to the canons of scientific method. His fundamental conclusions are fully consistent with his generalized account of cognitional structure. Scientific inquiry is empirical because it originates in sensible data and confirms its provisional conclusions with the available sensible evidence. It is intellectual because it examines the explanatory relations among those data, occasionally reaches insights into their intelligible interdependence, and formulates these insights in verifiable hypotheses and theories. It is critical, because it insists that the provisional answers practicing scientists reasonably affirm or deny are confirmed or disconfirmed by all relevant and available empirical evidence. These sciences are dynamic and progressive because new data are constantly generated by experimental tests and practical applications, eliciting new questions and eventually new hypotheses and theories. They are cumulative because the provisional conclusions yielded by earlier stages of inquiry create the operative heuristic context for ongoing research and criticism.[136]

Lonergan emphasizes several important implications of this specialized set of cognitional procedures: Scientific method deliberately prescinds from examining the data of consciousness, providing an independent field of research and discovery for philosophical inquiry.[137] It equally prescinds from raising philosophical and theological questions about transcendent being. As a result, the empirical sciences can neither confirm nor disconfirm the existence of God. Because the methodological canon of parsimony restricts scientific judgments to those that are verifiable in sensible evidence, it provides a critical standard for distinguishing genuine scientific discoveries from extrascientific opinions and prejudices.

The scientific canon of operations accounts for the distinctively symbiotic interplay between theory and practice. Modern scientific theories tend to generate numerous practical applications, and these applications in turn yield a steady flow of new data and evidence for theoretical research. The important canons of complete explanation and statistical residues require scientific inquirers to employ four complementary heuristic structures: classical, statistical, genetic, and dialectical. These distinctive heuristic orientations correspond to specific aspects of proportionate being: classical heuristic structure for the study of systematic processes as in Newtonian mechanics; statistical heuristic structure for nonsystematic processes as in quantum theory; genetic heuristic structure for the genesis, survival, and perishing of factual schemes of recurrence in both the natural and human sciences; dialectical heuristic structure for the tangled knot of progress and decline that constitutes human affairs.[138]

This heuristic and ontological plurality is extremely important for it reveals that the intelligibility of proportionate being is inherently complex. Scientific intelligibility is not therefore reducible to lawful systems, to random divergence from such systems, to stable and static schemes of intelligible recurrence, nor to simple linear patterns of historical progress and decline. While the "proportionate being" studied by science is intrinsically intelligible, its intelligibility is neither homogenous nor uniform, as reductionist theories would have us believe.

A credible cosmology for our time: The Copernican Revolution overturned the classical cosmology based on Aristotle, Ptolemy, and selected portions of scripture and tradition. The medieval understanding of space, time, and hierarchical order was radically unsettled, first by discoveries in physics, then by the evolutionary hypotheses of geology and biology, later by relativity theory, quantum mechanics, and profound breakthroughs in genetics, neurology, depth psychology, and social theory. The cosmological theories periodically proposed by the leading modern thinkers were largely extrapolations from the dominant science of their day (uncritical extrapolations for the most part). This influential but often unreliable process yielded highly questionable epistemic results: scientific materialism and mechanism, scientific determinism and reductionism, and, finally, an exclusive ontological naturalism confined within the "immanent frame."

Lonergan bases his alternative cosmology not on the most recent discoveries of the specialized sciences but on the four heuristic structures employed in modern scientific inquiry. His starting points are the relative constants of scientific method, not the changing variables of scientific theory. *Generalized emergent probability*, the dynamic cosmology whose intelligible contours he outlines, is the cosmological and ontological counterpart of Lonergan's *generalized empirical method*.[139]

Characteristically, Lonergan advances from cognitional theory through epistemology to metaphysics. Cognitional analysis confirms the operation of four distinct heuristic structures in contemporary scientific research. Epistemological reflection establishes the complementarity of these structures as discrete forms of factual knowledge. Lonergan's dynamic and explanatory metaphysics then articulates the intelligible structure of a changing universe that can be known through these four complementary methods.

On Lonergan's account, we humans belong to a dynamic intelligible universe that transcends the scope of both sense and imagination. Though we can understand the basic intelligible structure of the cosmos, we cannot picture it coherently. Ours is a universe in process, in a condition of dynamic becoming. Though not strictly and uniformly lawful in the classical sense postulated by Newton and Kant, cosmic becoming is, nevertheless, intelligible and orderly. The intelligible order of the universe consists in "the successive realization in accordance with successive schedules of probability of a conditioned series of schemes of recurrence."[140] That is Lonergan's succinct formulation of generalized emergent probability. Let us try briefly to unpack its several complementary aspects.

The core structures in Lonergan's dynamic cosmology are concrete schemes of recurrence, intelligible patterns of events exhibiting lawlike regularity.[141] These patterns can be found, *mutatis mutandis*, at the atomic, organic, genetic, cellular, neural, perceptual, intellectual, moral, and political levels of being. However, the emergence and survival of these recurrent intelligible schemes is concretely conditioned in a nonlawful manner. Let us take the developing human being as a microcosmic example of this macrocosmic pattern. The long arc of human development unfolds through the patterned emergence of a series of conditioned schemes, stretching upward from the genesis of the fertilized egg to the reliably virtuous conduct of the mature adult.[142] Each successive stage of development is conditioned by the successful functioning of the earlier stages. As intermediary stages of development emerge, the probability of later stages in the developmental series increases. Although each new stage constitutes a genuine emergence from its conditioning predecessors, it remains functionally dependent on their continued and successful operation. This patterned functional dependence explains how higher schemes of development can emerge from lower ones but fail to survive when lower schemes cease to function effectively.[143]

Our microcosmic example illustrates several macrocosmic principles corresponding to the four complementary types of heuristic structure. Emergent schemes of recurrence operate in accordance with classical laws (classical heuristic structure).[144] The actual emergence and survival of these schemes, however, occur in accordance with changing schedules of probability. As the underlying conditions of a particular scheme are realized, the probability of the higher-level scheme's emergence increases. Since these conditions normally include a whole series of prior schemes, the probability schedules of a conditioned scheme rise and fall as prior schemes emerge or decline (statistical heuristic structure).[145]

Higher schemes of recurrence emerge genetically from lower conditioning schemes by systematizing nonsystematic aggregates of events at the next lower level (genetic heuristic structure).[146] All higher schemes though conditioned by operative lower schemes are not reducible to them. This genetic irreducibility helps to explain why the different autonomous sciences discover irreducibly different sets of laws. It also helps to explain the repeated failure of logical attempts to unify the sciences using theoretical categories drawn from the discoveries of a particular scientific discipline.[147]

In the critical case of human affairs, creating and sustaining successful institutional and cultural schemes, human patterns of orderly and fruitful cooperation, primarily depends on prior intellectual and moral development across the generations. Within human history, the probability of achieving an intelligible order of terminal values greatly depends on first achieving personal and communal authenticity (the required originating values). Inversely, personal and communal order decline when bias undercuts authenticity, promoting systemic aberration and breakdown. Institutional decline and disorder become exceedingly difficult to reverse when fashionable ideologies justifying aberration become broadly accepted in the underlying culture. For this reason, effective institutional reform often begins with a trenchant critique of the reigning ideologies (dialectical heuristic structure).[148] Because humans are both natural (physical, biological, neurological, etc.) and spiritual beings, both intelligible and intelligent animals, their existence, activity, achievements, and failures can and should be studied within all four heuristic structures. A comprehensive philosophical anthropology must draw on classical, statistical, genetic, and dialectical heuristics to do justice to the complexity of its polymorphic intentional subject.

Thus human beings profoundly belong to both nature and history. They are finite, conditioned, emergent members of an immense natural universe marked by extremely large numbers and intervals of time.[149] They are very late arrivals in cosmic history who occupy a miniscule region of cosmic space. This theoretical perspective on human existence may be humbling to their traditional self-interpretation, as Freud suggested. But though cosmically small, even infinitesimal, in the grand scheme of nature, human beings' special dignity rests on their distinctive spiritual attributes: their transcendental desires for knowledge and value, their native intelligence and reasonableness, their capacity to guide their lives by the transcendental precepts, their ability to comprehend the universe in thought as the universe comprehends them spatially and temporally. Although they cannot exist apart from the dynamic cosmos they actively inhabit, credible cosmological theories, as far as we know, cannot exist without them.[150]

The verified factual judgments of common sense, the theoretical sciences, historical scholarship, and philosophy reveal the intelligible complexity of "proportionate being." Religion and theology, by contrast, are explicitly oriented to *transcendent* reality. Through prayer, worship, voluntary ministry (service), and faith, religious persons and communities strive to connect with an ontological realm that transcends the factual and contingent universe we know through experience, understanding, and judgment. Theology, in turn, strives to communicate to the historically diverse cultures in which religious communities are embedded their defining beliefs and commitments.[151] Since all human beings are constituted by the unrestricted transcendental desires, they inherently seek what is radically unconditioned both ontologically and morally. They seek to go beyond, to transcend, the virtually unconditioned universe of fact to reach the formally unconditioned realm of transcendent reality. They seek the transcendent ground or source of the proportionate being and value they already know and prize.[152] They seek that mysterious ground through knowledge, interpersonal union, and love. To be genuinely authentic, the religious quest must fully respect the integrity and dignity of all human practices. The transcendent, the divine, the supernatural, however we designate the aim of religious aspiration, clearly does not abolish proportionate being and value.[153] Rather, it serves as the intelligent ground (*arche*) and ultimate end (*telos*) of the immanent frame, the transcendent source of its being, intelligibility, and worth.

For Lonergan, the existential barriers to affirming transcendent reality in our secular (3) age are complex. Many of our contemporaries dismiss the question of God as unanswerable; others claim that the goodness of God is simply incompatible with the troubling existence of evil; or they scorn the transcendent order as the fictional creation of superstitious and immature minds; or they believe an authentic and autonomous existence requires living a life without God. From Lonergan's dialectical perspective, the personal and cultural horizons of these secular (2) critics are effectively closed to even the possibility of divine transcendence. To transform, to break open, their restricted horizons, existential conversion rather than logical proof is the primary personal requirement.[154]

Not conversion in the sense of a sudden and decisive revelation of the divine. But the threefold conversions, intellectual, moral, and religious, that Lonergan thematizes in *Method*.[155] Intellectual conversion leads the epistemic subject to identify being or reality, with the unrestricted objective of the unrestricted desire to know. It further leads the subject to define being, heuristically, in terms of its intrinsic intelligibility. Heuristically defined, being coincides with whatever is known (knowable) through intellectual grasp and reasonable affirmation. Contingent being, proportionate being, can be known through experience, understanding, and judgment. But does the universe of contingent being in its cosmic immensity coincide with the whole of reality? Does it satisfy our unrestricted desires for knowledge and value? Can it causally account for its own intelligibility and goodness? Or does its very existence and ontological value derive from a benevolent, transcendent Creator whose unrestricted wisdom and love create and sustain its conditioned reality?[156]

For Lonergan, God is the perfect and eternal act of unrestricted understanding and love.[157] Because divine understanding is unrestricted it knows itself perfectly; in knowing itself perfectly, it eternally knows all that flows from its creative understanding. God naturally loves whatever God has created so that the intelligibility and goodness of creation (proportionate being, the "immanent frame") derive from and bear witness to the supreme perfection of their transcendent Creator.

In the order of human discovery, we reason from the contingent intelligibility of proportionate being to the infinite creative power of God. In the ontological order of intelligible causation, God eternally creates and sustains the whole of the factual universe. What is last and most mysterious for us in the order of cognitive discovery is first and supremely intelligible in the order of what really exists. Because our intellects are finite, our understanding imperfect and limited, our judgments subject to error and correction, we can discover *that* God exists without knowing *what* God truly is. It is a mark of all genuine knowledge of God that we know that we don't know God's essence and nature.[158] The "learned ignorance" of Socrates, Cusanus, and Pascal continues to be existentially and culturally relevant.

Our limited knowledge of transcendent being is therefore based on analogy. The most illuminating analogues available to us are the result of our emerging self-knowledge. While our transcendental desires for knowledge and value are unrestricted, God's wisdom and goodness are actually and eternally unrestricted. While our insights are always finite and our fallible judgments revisable, God's eternal act of understanding is infinite and perfect. And while our personal love for God and for other creatures is inconstant and partial, God's creative love for the universe is complete and unconditional.

At our best, we praise what is really worthwhile and critique what is not, strive to actualize the good and repair what is harmed or corrupted. But we are constantly threatened by bias and sin, easily diverted in our inquiry, easily mistaken in our judgments, easily discouraged by our failures and weaknesses, easily demoralized by the tangled knot of the world we inherit. If God knows and loves whatever is good, then it's reasonable to ask what God is doing about evil. Why do natural and moral evil exist to mar the goodness of creation and created order, and what is God doing to transform their destructive effects?[159] These deeply important questions take us beyond the limited scope of this section, though we must and will address them in the concluding parts of this chapter.

Exclusive and Religious Humanism

When I consider thy heavens, the work of thy hands,
the moon and the stars, which thou hast ordained;
what is man that thou art mindful of him?
—Psalm 8:3–4

What a piece of work is man . . .
the beauty of the world, the paragon of animals,
and yet what to me is this quintessence of dust?
Man delights not me.
—William Shakespeare, *Hamlet*, 2.2

To understand the varieties of modern humanism, it is helpful to start with a particular medieval background. In thirteenth-century Paris, Aquinas carefully integrated the philosophical discoveries of Aristotle, the theological insights of Augustine and the fathers, and the formidable Catholic legacy of scripture and tradition. Aquinas based his theological anthropology on three causal principles: created nature, disruptive sin, and divine grace. By "nature" he meant the native capacities with which God endowed all creatures, including the natural capacities, corporal and spiritual, of human beings. By "sin," he meant the violence done to these capacities and to the human condition as a whole by transgressions of divine and natural law. By "grace," he meant the unmerited divine aid that God freely bestows on the order of fallen creation. Aquinas distinguished two forms of grace, of supernatural assistance, operative and cooperative. Operative grace affects the human creature's basic spiritual disposition, turning "the sinner's heart of stone," for example, into "the penitent's heart of flesh." Cooperative grace, in turn, affects the repentant creature's habitual performance and conduct.[160]

Operative grace heals the violent effects of sin upon human nature. Cooperative grace perfects and completes both our natural and acquired capacities. Thus, the supernatural virtue of faith perfects the natural powers and virtues of created reason, and the supernatural virtue of charity perfects the natural powers and virtues of the human will. Although Aquinas carefully distinguishes the natural and supernatural orders of being, he treats them not as rivals but as complements. In his revealing and confident formulation, grace does not abolish created nature but perfects and completes it, respecting and restoring nature's integrity, while transcending its limits and the injuries inflicted upon it by sin.[161] The great theological *Summa*s of Aquinas represent the high point, both realistic and hopeful, of medieval Christian humanism.

The carefully balanced Thomistic synthesis of nature, sin, and grace did not survive the thirteenth century. Both Aristotelians and Augustinians alike forcefully rejected Aquinas's nuanced combination of Augustinian theology and Aristotelian metaphysics. The medieval Scholastic tradition to which Aquinas belonged gradually declined into skepticism and nominalism. After the scourge of the Black Death and the prolonged scandal of the Babylonian captivity at Avignon, Christian theology became dominated by a hyper-Augustinian emphasis on sin.[162] As Hans Blumenberg has argued, the hyper-Augustinians maximized the sovereign power of God and minimized the effective capacity of sinful mortals. Divine power and purpose were then viewed as inscrutable; the created powers of humans were rendered impotent by the ravages of sin.[163] Only destructive sin and unmerited grace survived as explanatory anthropological categories.

One reasonable way to understand the spirit of Renaissance humanism is to see its renewed affirmation of man as a rejection of late medieval misanthropy. Where the hyper-Augustinians diminished human power and creativity, the Renaissance humanists exalted their potential. Part of the new cultural excitement derived from the recovery of the classical Greek and Latin traditions. Classical examples of excellence, intellectual, political, and artistic, renewed the humanistic confidence of their modern admirers. Renaissance humanism openly celebrated the beauty of the human body, the power of the human mind, the fertility of the human imagination, the creativity of human craftsmanship, the political arts of effective self-government. What a piece of work is man, indeed, the beauty of the world, the paragon of animals!

The Renaissance papacy revealed the dark and the bright sides of early modern humanism.[164] A series of worldly popes (1470–1530) proved to be exceptional patrons of the arts and of learning. But they were also martial and mercenary figures, the religious leaders of powerful armies, public devotees of splendor and wealth. An immense moral and cultural distance now separated Saint Peter, the contrite papal fisherman, from these scandalous symbols of worldly ambition, violence, and greed.

For several centuries before the Reformation, the Catholic Church struggled with the mounting demands for religious reform. But the repeated conciliar efforts to reform the church proved largely ineffective.[165] Luther's open break with the papacy, therefore, did not occur in a historical vacuum. With Luther's mounting defiance of Rome, however, institutional reform soon became schism, permanently shattering the vaunted unity of Latin Christendom. Although Luther was only the most visible of many radical Reformers, his hyper-Augustinian convictions shaped the general spirit of the Protestant Reformation.

Luther had an acute sense of his own sinfulness. He believed himself to be a captive of sin, cut off from eternal salvation. But on reading Paul's letter to the Romans, he experienced a powerful and decisive revelation.[166] It is the fallen individual's faith in Christ, not the deeds and works of sinful men, that justifies the impotent sinner. The Renaissance emphasis on human achievement and greatness was therefore gravely misplaced. Personal faith is an unmerited gift of God, not a human attainment. For without religious faith, without redemptive grace, sinful man delights not God; he is, indeed, a mere quintessence of dust. Luther further contended that the mediating works of the church lacked salvific power. Penitent sinners were not redeemed through receiving the sacraments, the grant of indulgences, or through their participation in sanctioned liturgical rites. Justification, salvation, occurred only through the individual's immediate encounter with and acceptance of the saving power of Christ.[167]

Luther's religious transformation proved deeply iconoclastic. He eventually rejected the hierarchical authority of the Roman church, the need for a celibate clergy, the primacy of the contemplative life, the theological relevance of Aristotle, the balanced synthesis of grace and nature, faith and reason, which Aquinas had carefully developed. For Luther, as for Reformation theology generally, sin and grace, rather than nature and reason, became the core principles of Christian anthropology.

The passionate rejection of Aristotle and of the teaching authority of Rome provided an important bond between the Protestant Reformers and the leaders of the Scientific Revolution. The cosmological doctrines of Aristotle and the intellectual influence of the Catholic hierarchy were important obstacles to the revolutionary initiatives of these great modern movements. Although Copernicus, Galileo, and Descartes were Catholics, Rome's critique of the new Copernican system, its public censure and rebuke of Galileo, and its general fidelity to the Aristotelian worldview meant that the new science lacked official Catholic support. This did not mean that the Protestant movement unconditionally affirmed the Copernican Revolution. In the sixteenth and seventeenth centuries, that revolution was the achievement of an intellectual elite scattered across Europe. While the Christian wars of religion devastated and demoralized the continent, radical changes in scientific theory aroused far less attention and passion.[168]

Yet there are striking parallels between the religious individualism of Luther and the epistemic individualism of Descartes. In both cases, the emancipated individual is freed from external religious or epistemic authority through the internal assurance of God. It is God's moral authority that confirms Luther's salvific faith; it is God's epistemic authority that validates Descartes's confidence in the truth of his clear and distinct ideas. Luther's hyper-Augustinian anthropology was centered on sin and grace; Descartes's philosophical anthropology was centered on unaided reason and mathematicized nature. While Descartes acknowledges the religious importance of faith, it plays no role in his radical reformation of knowledge.

For Descartes, the critical epistemic challenge is the problem of error, not the problem of evil.[169] And the elimination of error requires strict fidelity to Descartes's methodical rules, not the contrite reception of grace.

Still, when Descartes appeals to "reason" and "nature," he is not retrieving the insights of Aquinas and Aristotle. For both Thomas and his classical teacher, human reason was a part of the natural order; it was that distinctive natural capacity that enabled humans to understand the whole of being. Although reason's epistemic aspirations were unlimited, its effective capacity was finite and fallible. According to Aquinas, human reason, though subject to error and sin, requires divine grace not to perform its native operations but to achieve its supernatural goals. But for Descartes, faith and grace are not needed to know God's existence and essence, nor to discover God's will for the future. It is individual reason, purified and disciplined by adherence to Cartesian method, that will actualize the ultimate *telos* of modernity: the lordship and mastery of nature. As Descartes confidently predicts, the practical fruits of that mastery will be the tangible benefits of science, pure and applied, namely, terrestrial longevity, technological power, and increased human happiness.[170]

Kant represents the ironic climax of Enlightenment humanism. Although he accepts the Newtonian cosmology of universal and invariant classical laws, Kant is troubled by the moral implications of the Copernican Revolution. He insists that a genuinely enlightened age must be able to answer three interrelated questions about man: What can I know; what ought I to do; what may I reasonably hope for?[171]

What can I know is the central question of Kant's epistemology. Because we've already examined Kant's answer to this question, we'll bypass it here. What ought I to do is the central question of Kantian ethics.[172] Kant's answer is both traditional and radical. I ought to choose and act in accordance with the moral law, and I ought to do this out of reverence for the law itself. I ought to separate moral imperatives and the legitimate motives for obeying them from all instrumental considerations of punishment and reward. I ought to do what is right just because it is right, not because of the benefits or dangers that might flow from my actions or omissions.

But why does the moral law have this singular and compelling authority? Why does it merit the moral agent's obedience and reverence?

It is here that Kant becomes genuinely radical. On his revisionary account, the categorical imperatives that constitute the moral law do not come from God, nor does the reverence they properly elicit derive from their divine origin. Nor, it goes without saying, do they originate in the causality of nature or in the natural fears and desires human beings experience. Kant clearly believes that Newtonian nature is amoral and cannot ground our moral obligations. Rather, the moral law originates in the pure practical reason of the autonomous will. This law commands our respect and obedience because the rational will is the highest human capacity, the ontological source of our singular freedom and dignity. The legislative autonomy of pure practical reason is the supreme principle of morality:[173] it provides the origin, motive, and substantive content of the moral law. All other conceptions of morality, biblical, classical, medieval, and modern, are judged by Kant to be heteronomous and unsatisfactory.[174] Although Kant strictly limited the principle of autonomy to the exercise of pure practical reason, his late modern successors were far less circumspect in asserting this new humanistic ideal. Among cultural radicals in the nineteenth and twentieth centuries, human *freedom* and *autonomy* were regularly treated as synonymous terms.[175]

What can I reasonably hope for? Kant's measured and thoughtful answer is sober and cautious. I can hope for indefinite progress in scientific knowledge and its technical applications to nature. But this notable progress is limited in principle to the empirical or phenomenal order. Scientific theories are constitutionally incapable of answering the transcendent questions of reason with their demand for unconditioned causes and ends. Moreover, theoretical reason with its impressive scientific and technical achievements is not the basis of true human dignity. That dignity is grounded in the autonomy of each person's rational will, the legislative source of the universal moral law.

Morally, I can hope to have a good will, a will that consistently does the right thing for the right reason. Although I can rationally determine that my maxims of action are moral, I can never be certain of the purity of my actual motives. While the morally legislative will may be autonomous, the concretely choosing will is imperfectly rational. It may or may not choose to comply with the relevant categorical imperatives; its determining motives may be natural or social in origin rather than exclusively rational. In this mortal life, the agonal conflict between human desire and moral duty is unending. We have the regulative moral ideal of a holy will, a will free of the conflict between pure practical reason and natural desire, but we have no actual experience of this ideal during life upon earth.[176]

In its terrestrial existence, the good will does not receive its just reward. The example of Job is telling: the righteous man often suffers undeserved loss and unhappiness. His immoral and amoral counterparts may enjoy far greater, though unmerited, terrestrial felicity. Critical reason is understandably troubled by this scandalous deviation from the demands and expectations of justice. For although morally good people do not choose and act in order to be happy, their good choices and actions genuinely merit happiness. Thus, for Kant, in both the theoretical and practical realms of human life, the intrinsic demands of reason must be recognized without being satisfied.[177]

Does this mean that human existence is inescapably tragic? This might be true if terrestrial life were all that there is. But the ontological limits of theoretical reason and the noumenal postulates of practical reason make it reasonable to *hope* that the rational soul is immortal, that God is ultimately benevolent and just, and that in the course of the soul's everlasting life the just demands of reason are finally satisfied. For this supreme practical end, an enlightened and critical thinker can *reasonably* hope.

Kant's philosophical anthropology constitutes a landmark event in the European Enlightenment. It ostensibly does justice to the two fixed stars of modernity: "the starry heavens above" (Newton) and "the moral law within" (Rousseau). Kant celebrates the legislative autonomy of practical reason while acknowledging human finitude and weakness. And while demanding that human beings critically mature and "come of age," he explicitly accepts a regulative role for God in the moral and spiritual realms of existence.

Kant's many nineteenth-century successors, while respectful of his critical genius, did not subscribe to his comprehensive philosophical position. Hegel attempted to restore the supremacy of theoretical reason that Kant rejected. Kierkegaard wanted to recover the centrality and depth of the great Christian mysteries. Marx turned Kant's individual moral autonomy into a social and historical ideal, the ultimate goal of a classless society. Romantic poets and thinkers repudiated Kant's bifurcation of reason and nature, the crippling legacy of Descartes's ontological dualism. Utilitarian moralists rejected the transcendental dimensions of Kant's philosophy, while attempting to naturalize both his epistemology and ethics. These influential and revisionary anthropologies, though clearly not Kantian in content, were inconceivable without Kant's earlier groundbreaking thought.[178]

No modern thinker assigned greater importance to speculative philosophy than Hegel. Although he deeply respected art and religion, Hegel clearly subordinated their spiritual importance to synoptic philosophical insight. This subordination is evident in the use Hegel makes of traditional Christian concepts and doctrines. The central biblical themes of creation, fall, exile, incarnation, and redemption are preserved in Hegel's dialectical narrative, though in a distinctively modern and secularized form. Although Hegel is clearly not an orthodox Christian, he does seek to integrate the creedal affirmations of Christianity within his unique world-historical vision.

Our purpose here is not to criticize Hegel's philosophical theology, but to recognize his enduring anthropological contributions.[179] Hegel effectively reinserted the human subject into nature and history. He explicitly rejected the ontological and anthropological dualisms of Descartes and Kant. For Hegel, the dialectical life of the human spirit requires expressive embodiment in artistic productions, religious symbols and rituals, and articulate conceptual thought. Moreover, the finite human subject no longer exists within a lifeless and disenchanted cosmos, but in an expressive natural order that bears witness to its divine origin and *telos*. Finally, Hegel treats anthropology and theology as mutually illuminating sources of truth. Both God and humans are dynamic, expressive, teleological spirits, radically different in their causal capacities, it's true, but fundamentally analogous in the way that they actualize their most profound intentions and aims.

Kierkegaard explicitly rejected the supremacy Hegel accorded to speculative reason and the consequent subordination of religious faith to philosophy. Kant had confined an enlightened modern religion within the limits of critical reason. He had made religious beliefs instrumental to moral autonomy; he had made critical reason the ultimate judge of all things. Hegel's rational ambitions went far beyond Kant's. Where Kant limited the epistemic scope of reason, Hegel insisted that reason's speculative power was limitless, that it could grasp the very essence, the inner spirit, of God. Both Kant and Hegel claimed to have transcended the limitations of traditional Christianity. In his critical response to their thinking, Kierkegaard replied that each of them had failed to acknowledge the depth of the central Christian mystery, the miraculous event of the incarnation, the historical intersection of time and eternity, the unique temporal moment when God became man.[180] In the face of this mystery, Kierkegaard believed, both speculative and practical reason encountered insuperable limits. Because the incarnation transcended the power of reason, it also transcended Hegelian philosophy and Kantian morality. For the authentic Christian believer, the incarnation is not a speculative or practical problem to be solved, but an existential mystery to be entered into with humility and reverence.

What Christianity requires of the concrete existing individual is a deliberate choice, a wholehearted decision, a profound personal commitment. This choice is analogous to the irrevocable vows promised in marriage, though it is ultimately more challenging and radical. The existential turning point in each person's life, for Kierkegaard, is the decision to *become* a genuine (not a nominal) Christian, to enter ever more deeply through personal faith into the particular struggles and suffering to which Christ calls each individual: "Come, follow me ... even to death on a cross."[181]

For Kierkegaard, the very model of authentic religious faith was the biblical Abraham, the ancient Hebrew patriarch, prepared to sacrifice his only son, Isaac, when that was what God called him to do. Abraham's faith, a faith marked by acute fear and trembling, demonstrates both the limits of Kantian morality, with its insistence on universal maxims, and the limits of Hegelian philosophy, with its emphasis on universal patterns in history.[182] According to Kierkegaard, Christianity is a historical religion, but it is a religion of particular events, not of universal laws. Jesus Christ is a singular and unique person, and his incarnation and death are singular and unique events. The individual Christian's personal acceptance of the gospel is also a singular event, and the radical challenge of the Christian life cannot be lessened by belonging to a shared Christian culture. In fact, Kierkegaard believes, secure membership in the public culture of Christendom only serves as a barrier to authentic Christianity.[183]

Marx's rejection of Hegelian philosophy, though equally passionate, was profoundly different from Kierkegaard's. Kierkegaard centered his dialectical analysis on the religious faith of the finite individual. Kierkegaardian faith is existential, like the faith of Luther himself; it requires a radical personal commitment to the historical paradox of Christ's incarnation, a paradox that scandalizes reason with its demand for universal necessity.[184] Marx centered his dialectical analysis on the socioeconomic history of the human species. He explicitly rejected religion in general, and Christianity in particular, treating religion as an ideological effort to diffuse the justified anger of the oppressed.

For Marx, the scandal of the "social question," the continued existence of radical deprivation in a society of increasing abundance, was the genuine paradox of history. But this was a paradox speculative reason could understand, though not ultimately solve. As Marx repeatedly insisted, the true purpose of philosophy is practical, not contemplative; its legitimate goal is not to understand the world, but to change it.[185]

Perhaps Marx is best understood as a radical social Baconian, explicitly subordinating knowledge to world-historical action, and action to the purposive transformation of nature and society. For Marx, the ultimate *telos* of history is the actualized autonomy of the human species. In Marx's compelling historical narrative, the human race dialectically progresses from its pre-agricultural origins in nature, through the humanization of nature via productive labor, to the humanization of society and history through revolutionary *praxis*. Pace Hegel, the meaning and purpose of history is not the autonomy of God, but the liberty, equality, and fraternity of the whole human race. Marx boldly espouses a Promethean anthropology that deliberately abolishes God in order to divinize the revolutionary potential of humankind.[186]

Kierkegaard stressed the existential responsibility of the finite individual and the primacy of faith in the personal life. Marx stressed the historical responsibility of the human species, and the primacy of revolutionary action guided by scientific insight. Marx believed he had overcome the Kantian dichotomy between theory and practice.[187] Kierkegaard believed he had liberated the Christian faith from the imperial pretensions of autonomous reason. Marxian faith is a secular trust in the inevitable demise of capitalism and the emergence of a classless society. Kierkegaard's polemical treatment of reason has distinctively Kantian and Hegelian overtones. Modern reason's inherent demand for universal and necessary laws makes it singularly unsuited for the contingency, particularity, and freedom of historical existence.

Despite their serious internal disagreements, Kant, Hegel, Kierkegaard, and Marx share a common intellectual background in German philosophy. The leading anthropological idea in the modern German tradition is the idea of human *autonomy*. Kant, Hegel, and Marx, in marked contrast to the Protestant Kierkegaard, allocate to the rational individual (Kant), a privileged philosophical elite (Hegel), or the collective human species (Marx) some of the traditional prerogatives of God. By insisting on the existential primacy of religious faith and the impenetrable depth of the Christian mysteries, Kierkegaard deliberately rejected these heretical anthropological assumptions.[188]

Two other main currents in nineteenth-century anthropology point in very different directions. Darwinian naturalism approaches human existence *von unten auf*, from the bottom up. Within the ontological framework of scientific naturalism, humans are depicted as higher animals, not as lesser gods. They are fully rooted in the biological history of nature, a history marked by continuous violence and the relentless struggle for survival. Their very late emergence as a viable species follows the evolutionary principles of random variation and natural selection. The critical unit of evolutionary analysis is not the finite individual (Kierkegaard) or the privileged historical class (Marx), but the human species as a whole. The only natural *telos* of every species is survival, the continuance of biological life. All other human aims and activities are instrumentally subordinated to this unchanging biological goal. An immense cultural and moral distance, therefore, separates Darwinian naturalism from Kant's critical philosophy, as there is no credible place in Darwin's anthropology for the vaunted autonomy and dignity of the purely rational man.[189]

If Darwin transformed the modern study of nature and life with his evolutionary theory, then Ranke transformed the study of history with his empirical critical method. For the nineteenth-century disciples of Ranke, there was to be no retreat from Hegel's novel emphasis on human historicity. Human beings are undeniably historical as well as natural creatures. But how should their historical existence be properly studied? The scholarly critics of Hegel objected that his philosophy of history had been based on a priori assumptions. A more modest empirical and critical approach was required, if historiography, like physics, was to become scientific. Following the example of Newton, who had excluded metaphysical assumptions from the study of nature, Ranke made historical inquiry empirical (based on sensible data and evidence) and critical (based on the rigorous verification of historical claims and hypotheses). Moreover, Ranke insisted that historical judgments concerned contingent matters of fact, what had actually happened in the past, rather than illustrative examples of dialectical necessity. Speculative philosophy could no longer determine the teleological purpose of history; it now had to acknowledge the sober empirical constraints of historical fact.[190]

The rise of modern historiography coincided with the development of the new human sciences, psychology, sociology, anthropology, and economics. Hegel's philosophical and cultural account of world history was largely confined to the history of Europe. The human sciences, by contrast, studied individuals, societies, and cultures wherever and whenever they existed. Thus comparative anthropologists, for example, carefully examined the contrasting beliefs, social practices, and political arrangements that differentiated East and West, Europe, Asia, and Africa, imperial nations and the indigenous peoples they had forcefully subdued.

There was, however, an important heuristic difference between the natural and human sciences. Both modern physics and biology assume the uniformity of nature: the same physical laws and evolutionary principles apply throughout space and time. Although the sensible phenomena observed in nature clearly differ in jungles and deserts, in torrid, temperate, and arctic regions, the explanatory principles that account for this observable diversity are assumed to be causally identical. The sciences of nature heuristically aspire to reduce empirical plurality to lawful unity, sensible difference to explanatory sameness.

But does a comparable assumption legitimately apply to historiography and the human sciences? Do explanatory constants play the same role in human affairs as they do in the natural universe? Two distinct issues are at stake here: the relevant similarities and differences between the natural and human sciences; and the critical role of normative measures in the appraisal of human conduct and belief. Dilthey clarified the first issue by emphasizing the constitutive role of meaning and value in human affairs. The second issue is still fiercely contested within our culture. What remains indisputable is that human beings are evaluative animals, that we regularly appraise and critique the beliefs and practices of human societies, including our own. It is much less clear on what moral sources and norms we rely in making these appraisals. Most contentious of all is the metaethical question of how these evaluative principles and norms should themselves be impartially justified.[191]

Important factual trends in the nineteenth century gave these philosophical concerns public salience. The rapid expansion of industrial capitalism made concern for the social question (the scandalous coexistence of luxury for the few and deprivation for the many) inescapable. Was it just, was it right, that the wealthy owners of capital should flourish while their workers suffered mass degradation? Imperial conquests in Asia and Africa put the moral supremacy of Europe even further into question. Only explicit or implicit racism could justify the ruthless exploitation of overseas peoples and cultures. The rise of nationalist aspirations and political movements throughout Europe challenged the cosmopolitan ethos of the French Enlightenment, which came to be viewed by its nationalist critics as a concealed form of cultural imperialism. In time, the nationalist cause itself became morally tainted by the anti-Semitic prejudices it frequently encouraged. Finally, there was the momentous and unavoidable question of the just treatment of women, of their democratic rights to full citizenship, to legal, political, and social equality.[192]

No one saw the moral contradictions of modern Europe more clearly than Nietzsche. Celebrated European intellectuals had largely rejected the traditional Christian moral ontology. Critical advances in natural science and historiography had gradually undermined the Christian vision of nature, man, and God.[193] But the same intellectuals had secularized the Christian concept of paradise. They hoped to establish the kingdom of heaven on earth. The visionary dreams of the Hebrew prophets, of a world without violence and want, a world of shared abundance and harmony, had gradually become utopian political projects. Both liberal reformers and radical Marxists shared this unprecedented historical optimism, despite their intense disagreements about the appropriate route to this end.

But Nietzsche insisted that Christian anthropology and ethics could not survive their divorce from Christian theology. The psychological and cultural implications of "the death of God" were more profound than these historical optimists realized. The real danger confronting a post-Christian Europe was pervasive nihilism, a rejection of all valuation and striving, an overpowering will to negation and death. But if intellectual integrity required abandoning Christian faith and morality, and if nihilism promised only despair and destruction, what credible form(s) of humanism remained?[194]

Nietzsche defiantly rejected the secularized revolutionary ideals, whose Christian roots he believed were transparent. For Nietzsche, these egalitarian aspirations were dishonest and fraudulent, for all forms of existence are determined by a relentless struggle for power, for active or reactive self-assertion. This was not merely a struggle for biological survival, as the disciples of Darwin maintained, but a struggle for visionary spiritual creation, for creatively shaping one's own table of virtues and values.[195]

Although Kant was the first to elaborate the principle of moral autonomy, Nietzsche held that his creative aspirations had been far too conservative. The Kantian moral law is essentially the biblical Decalogue transcribed into a rational idiom. Its categorical imperatives are universal commands, normatively binding on all rational agents, obligating all individual wills to obey them. For Nietzsche, Kant's enlightened ideal of the pure rational will was a timid and restricted assertion of autonomy. True human autonomy, Nietzsche argued, is the freedom of the liberated individual to create his own charter of moral independence. To make matters worse, Kant had attributed moral autonomy to every rational being. But the untutored mass, the resentful herd, the psychologically and spiritually weak are incapable of such bold self-assertion. The great mass of humanity will always be followers, not leaders. Their true cultural superiors, the spiritually strong, the autonomous "over-men," will need to sweep away our compromised moral traditions and replace them with a new aristocratic code, a historically revised warrior ethic for the modern age. Within Nietzsche's transvalued ethics the relevant evaluative contrast is no longer between good and evil, right and wrong, just and unjust, holy and sinful, but between noble and base, strong and weak, healthy and decadent, the creative few and the reactive and resentful many.[196]

The fragile optimism pervading the century of progress could not survive "the guns of August" that began the Great War. Before World War I had ended, much of Western and Eastern Europe had been decimated. Catastrophic losses destroyed a whole generation of soldiers and civilians in England, France, Germany, Russia, and the Austro-Hungarian Empire. Under the rising pressures of war the Eastern empires dramatically collapsed. The Bolsheviks violently transformed czarist Russia into the Soviet Union; the punitive Treaty of Versailles dismembered the Hapsburg imperium.

The first war was immediately followed by profound instability: revolutionary turmoil in Europe and Asia, global economic depression, the rise of fascism and National Socialism, the Spanish Civil War, the territorial expansion of Japanese militarism, the demoralizing weakness of the war-ravaged liberal democracies, the provincial isolationism of the United States. The 1930s were a decade of mounting desperation and despair. Every critical observer knew greater catastrophes were coming. The unanswered questions were where and when they would inevitably occur.

World War II destroyed the battered hopes of Enlightenment humanism. The domination of nature celebrated by Bacon and Descartes was systematically turned against the human race itself. The technological applications of science created weapons of mass destruction on the land, in the air, and across and beneath the seas. Revolutionary ideology and propaganda were deliberately used to dehumanize whole sectors of humanity. Systematic terror was then applied to these dehumanized groups: Jews, Gypsies, Slavs, kulaks, the members of what were considered to be inferior races and classes.[197] The hardening effects of total war culminated in the allied firebombing of Dresden and Tokyo, and the annihilation of Hiroshima and Nagasaki. With the grotesque revelations of the Shoah, the death camps of Auschwitz and Treblinka, Hamlet's shaken descendants were forced to acknowledge that "the paragon of animals" could deliberately turn humans to dust—"man delights not me."

The unparalleled horrors of the twentieth century challenge all forms of humanism, exclusive and religious. The enlightened proponents of exclusive humanism had deliberately sought to live without God. They exalted the power of reason, spirit, nation, class, and history; they celebrated the prospect of unlimited human autonomy; they localized evil and violence in the dehumanized other: the reactionary priest, the mercenary Jew, the bourgeois capitalist, the property-owning kulak, the members of a subhuman tribe or class. The modern catalogue of "scapegoats" is depressingly long. With the source of evil safely localized in the dehumanized "other," fascists, communists, revolutionary nationalists, even defenders of the precarious status quo could ignore their own fallibility and sinfulness.[198] They could concentrate on destroying their ideological enemies, the final obstacles to utopian progress or to the restoration of order and security.

Of course, exclusive humanism is not always Promethean in spirit. It has bourgeois as well as radical expressions. But the European middle classes proved morally and politically impotent between the wars when fascism, Nazism, and Stalinism gained effective control of the continent. Moreover, the bourgeois parties and leaders had been deeply implicated in the injustices of capitalism and imperialism, had freely surrendered to the siren songs of nationalism and anti-Semitism, and had focused on their narrow class-interests while the great world was collapsing around them. In the desperate decades between the world wars, the free peoples of the West failed the most basic tests of citizenship and historical responsibility.[199]

Do these conspicuous historical failures exhaust the range of exclusive humanist alternatives? Not really. Besides Promethean radicals and a selfish and complacent bourgeoisie, there are the activist critics who self-consciously seek freedom from illusion. Freud and Camus are impressive rebels of this kind. Freud's postulatory atheism is explicit and unrepentant. Individuals, societies, the human race as a whole are alone in the world without God. We mortals have only our human capacities to rely on, and these capacities are finite and fallible. At the same time, the Enlightenment promise of universal harmony and happiness is not really credible. Human beings are surrounded by violence, suffering, and death. They suffer from internal as well as external conflict, for the desires of the id, the moral demands of the superego, and the fragile realism of the ego are perpetually at war.[200] The wish fulfillment offered by artworks and dreams, the false consolations of religion, and the pain-deadening power of intoxicants are ineffective responses to the tragic state humans inhabit. The precarious sanity and dignity of the human condition largely depend upon fallible reason, scientific and technical. Modern science enjoys a justified cultural authority because it honors the reality principle; it shows us the world as it is, not as we wish it to be. While the technical arts, like medicine and engineering, can enhance human power and reduce human suffering, they can't change our basic condition: that of biological animals struggling for existence in an indifferent cosmos, seeking a measure of personal happiness through sustained love and work, while facing suffering and death with illusion-less courage.[201]

Born in French Algeria, Albert Camus came of age during his country's armed resistance against Nazi occupation. With the liberation of France in 1944, he hoped for the creation of a new European order. But the impressive solidarity of the wartime resistance fighters swiftly collapsed after the war, as former allies soon became bitter political rivals.

For Camus, the supreme concern was to achieve and preserve individual integrity. Intellectual integrity, he believed, meant living without God in an absurd universe.[202] Moral integrity meant rejecting murderous lies and excuses whatever their source on the cultural and political spectrum. Though the universe we inhabit may be absurd, one great biblical commandment endures: Thou shalt not kill![203] Political integrity meant openly supporting the cause of the oppressed: the Algerian struggle for independence; the victims of Soviet despotism; the poor and the vulnerable wherever they live. The dogged heroes Camus celebrates in his writing are very revealing: the solitary Sisyphus, who defies the gods but without Promethean illusions; the activist rebel who acknowledges his own lack of innocence; the tenacious De Rieux who offers medical care to the victims of a plague he knows he's unable to cure.[204]

Camus and Freud are powerful examples of secular authenticity. Convinced that there is no God, they refuse to treat man and themselves as divine. Undeterred by their critique of false hope, they resolutely engage in the historical struggle for justice and healing. They do what they can; they think and act with sobriety and realism; they decline to wait passively and grimly for death.[205]

But where does this twisting moral genealogy leave the quest for religious humanism? We began our reflections with the Thomistic triad of nature, sin, and grace. We have witnessed the great modern difficulty of holding these three basic elements together. In Luther, sin and grace were asserted against reason and nature. In Kierkegaard, Christian faith was asserted against Kantian ethics and Hegelian philosophy. After censuring the faithful Galileo, Catholic Christianity largely withdrew into a culturally defensive position. It passionately opposed the Reformation, the central thrust of the Scientific Revolution, the democratic demand for equality and liberty. It belatedly clung to the hierarchical institutions and privileges of the ancien régime; it was scandalously slow in responding to the industrial social question; it rejected the new critical methods of hermeneutics and historiography; it branded as "modernist" and heretical faithful Catholics who struggled to engage with the challenges of modern society and culture.[206]

While Catholic Christianity never abandoned the Thomistic triad, it suffered from classicist prejudices that regarded the achievements of medieval Christendom as timeless and permanent. Its classicist clerical leadership was radically unprepared for world-historical events like the Scientific, democratic, and Industrial Revolutions; for world-historical changes in cosmology, anthropology, and theology; for the collective responsibility of Christians in a dynamic and unsettled world; and for impartial critical inquiry into the beliefs, traditions, and practices (including the personal and collective sins) of the church itself.

To regain credibility in our secular age, the Catholic Church must confront the reality of evil in its classical and modern forms, not only the individual evil of sinners and saints, but the systemic evil of social groups and institutions, and the cultural evil of ideology and criminal apologetics. To do this persuasively, Catholics must candidly acknowledge and repent their own role in the history of evil: their traditional anti-Semitism, their inquisitional violence, their suppression of liberty, their complicity in racism, their unjust treatment of women, their ambiguous silence during the horrors of the Holocaust.[207]

Although the Christian churches cannot uncritically endorse exclusive humanism, they must learn what they can from it.[208] They must acknowledge the disciplinary independence of science and historical scholarship, respect the modern commitment to equality and liberty, support the human rights of all people, and extend the full spectrum of rights to their own members. They must recognize the goodness of ordinary life, share in protecting the natural universe, participate generously in the healing of suffering, and publicly stand with the oppressed as Jesus himself did.

Learning and teaching are genuinely reciprocal activities. Over several centuries, people of faith slowly and reluctantly discovered what they could learn from the pluralistic culture of modernity. But an equally important question remains to be answered: What can believing Christians teach their secular contemporaries? What important and enduring insights does authentic Christian humanism possess?[209]

Religious Authenticity

It has been difficult for exclusive humanists to achieve a balanced and comprehensive account of human existence. They have struggled in their anthropological theories and narratives to strike a credible mean between pride and despair, historical optimism and pessimism, the greatness and misery of the human condition.[210] Enlightenment humanism was enthralled by the prospect of human autonomy. Liberated from the inherited constraints of religion, tradition, and authority, the *philosophes* placed their historical trust in the liberty, equality, and fraternity of the whole human race. They envisaged an educated secularist future of individual liberty, shared economic prosperity, and enduring international peace.

The secular gospel of continuous historical progress was radically challenged by the realities of post-Revolutionary Europe: the fierce struggles of capital and labor, the imperial conquest of Asia and Africa, the horrors of total war on a global scale, the prospect of nuclear annihilation. The postmodern critics of humanism have struck a very different rhetorical chord. They emphasize human violence, systemic domination, the hidden plight of the marginalized and excluded. They excel in the critique of false hope.[211]

What is Lonergan's reflective response to this deeply important contemporary debate? Exclusive humanists believe that a critical knowledge of nature and history invariably leads to the denial of God. Lonergan explicitly rejects this influential cultural assumption. His philosophical and theological challenge is to show how a credible, comprehensive anthropology leads directly to the opposite conclusion, namely, that the more we learn about human existence, the more we will learn about God.[212]

In an era of shared religious faith, serious cultural reflection could begin from a common creed. But we live in a secular (3) age where a religious consensus can no longer be credibly assumed. Reflective inquiry today must begin with human beings as they are, with what personal experience and centuries of history reveal about their nature and destiny. Although Lonergan's anthropology is clearly influenced by Thomas's ontological triad, his philosophical strategy differs markedly from that of Aquinas. Where Thomas developed and articulated a metaphysics of the human soul, Lonergan offers an intentional analysis of the polymorphic situated subject.[213] As Lonergan argues in *Insight* and *Method*, the deepest sources of a credible contemporary humanism are the transcendental desires and norms that constitute the human subject: the unrestricted desires for knowledge and value, the exigent norms governing the operations of intentional consciousness. To discover and acknowledge these desires and norms, the normative patterns in which they unfold, and their profound dialectical implications is the purpose of self-appropriation. Every genuine humanist committed to the anthropological turn must achieve this level of explicit self-knowledge.

Pace Descartes and Kant, the intentional subject is not an isolated rational ego. Rather, the concrete human being is embodied in the natural universe and embedded in particular historical communities. To borrow Charles Taylor's ontological description, Lonergan's polymorphic subject is a situated, holistic individual.[214] Each human being is born into a nexus of related communities, educated in their beliefs and prejudices, shaped by their aspirations and values, formed by their linguistic resources and practices. This sociocultural inheritance is invariably an uneven legacy, a tangled knot of error and truth. Although mature subjects can gain a measure of critical distance from their ambiguous cultural heritages, the Cartesian and Kantian ideal of individual autonomy (epistemic and moral self-sufficiency) is profoundly unrealistic.

Is the late modern aspiration to human authenticity equally inflated? That will greatly depend on how this influential ideal is construed.[215] For Lonergan, there are two complementary dimensions of authenticity: existential and historical.[216] Existential authenticity is achieved through the subject's epistemic and moral self-transcendence, through effectively coordinating the objective knowledge of being with his or her responsible choices and actions over the course of his or her personal life. Historical authenticity depends on a particular community's willingness to scrutinize its deepest beliefs and convictions, to submit its uneven historical record to the evaluative test of the transcendental precepts and norms. While sinless perfection is not required for authenticity, honesty, realism, humility, and repentance assuredly are. As individuals and communities, we cannot remedy or rectify what we fail to acknowledge needs correction and healing.

What are the major obstacles to sustained personal and historical development? Lonergan emphasizes four types of distorting bias:[217] dramatic bias that undermines the individual's psychological and emotional development; egoistic bias that fuels moral complacency and devotion to narrow self-interest; group bias that seeks to escape the social and political demands for impartial institutional justice; the general bias of common sense that belittles the theoretical quest for disinterested knowledge in philosophy, science, and historical scholarship. In all of these restrictive and crippling forms, bias serves as an effective barrier to authenticity, to sustained self-transcendence. But intellectual and moral failures, though common and deeply regrettable, are far less dangerous than the seductive ideologies regularly offered in their defense. For Lonergan, ideologies are sophisticated attempts to justify alienation and bias, to excuse the neglect or refusal of self-transcendence. Ideologies turn the intellectual and moral universe on its head, by justifying what needs correction and reform and debunking what deserves praise and cultural support.[218]

But how are we to identify persuasive ideologies, particularly when they enjoy broad cultural acceptance? Recall that Marx treated religion as inherently ideological, Nietzsche rejected the emotional basis of Christian morality, and Freud reduced religious convictions to symptoms of a regressive emotional pathology. For exclusive humanists, all forms of transcendent hope and belief are unworthy of rational assent. At the level of our deepest convictions and commitments, are we faced, existentially and culturally, with a Mexican standoff?

Lonergan vehemently denies that our fundamental beliefs and attachments must be arbitrarily chosen. That is why he bases his personal and cultural dialectic on three existential conversions, intellectual, moral, and religious.[219] Intellectual conversion enables the cognitive subject dialectically to distinguish epistemic positions from counterpositions. Moral conversion establishes a comparable critical standpoint in the contested field of moral philosophy. But what is religious conversion, and what transformative effect does it have on the existential subject?[220]

In intellectual and moral conversion, human beings rely on consistently developing and honoring their native intentional endowments, their transcendental desires, methods, and norms. In religious conversion, however, the causal initiative rests with God. It begins with the gift of God's love, given freely to all. This gift is a grace, as distinct from a natural desire or created capacity. Our unrestricted desires for knowledge and value are often unacknowledged desires for God, for unconditioned being and goodness. The unmerited and universal gift of God's love, by contrast, what Christians call *agape* or *caritas*, enables each person to share directly in God's very life.[221] In religious conversion, it is God's personal love for each of us that first awakens our love for God.[222]

But the presence of God's love within us is deeply mysterious. It is not an intuition of God, a clear and distinct idea, or an instance of propositional belief. It is, rather, an undertow of holiness that can draw us into loving an invisible reality that remains profoundly unknown.[223] Through God's love for us, we are drawn beyond the "universe of proportionate being," beyond the limits of "the immanent frame," into the ontological realm of divine transcendence. The personal horizon of our active love and concern becomes radically expanded. We come to see the whole of reality in a new, deeper transforming light. Lonergan calls this mysterious light faith, knowledge of the heart, an existential knowledge of being born of God's radical, unmerited gift.[224]

As divine love is freely given, so it must be freely returned. We are not compelled to respond to God's free initiative, and any response that we make is precarious and partial. Through our love of God, we are drawn to a deeply mysterious ontological source we cannot see, imagine, or comprehend. Given these constraints on our epistemic abilities, we can easily lose heart and lose faith. But in truth we are not spiritually isolated and alone.[225] The divine gift of love, freely given to all, provides the basis for religious community, for shared faith, common worship, and reciprocal neighborly fellowship. Moreover, our intellectual and moral conversions provide existential support for religious experience. Lonergan describes religious experience as an unrestricted love for an unknown and invisible reality. But our unrestricted desire for knowledge points toward such a reality as the creative intelligent ground of the intelligible universe; and our unrestricted desire for value points toward a supreme moral good that radically transcends the power of rational criticism. The ultimate thrust of the human spirit, intellectual, moral, and religious, draws us beyond proportionate being and value, important as they are and remain, into the mysterious realm of divine transcendence.[226] Although authenticity is always precarious, and our experience of the divine mystery may deepen with time, there is reason to believe Mauriac may be right: "One is never cured of God once one has known him."

All three forms of existential conversion are transformative. They profoundly change the basic orientation and horizon of the existential subject. With intellectual conversion, the epistemic subject becomes oriented to the unrestricted universe of intelligible being; with moral conversion, to the unrestricted universe of originating and terminal values. But how does the personal horizon of the exclusive humanist differ from that of the genuine religious believer?

Without religious faith, the sole originating values are human beings, and the sole terminal values are the limited goods they can achieve through their own efforts.[227] In the light of faith, however, the supreme originating value is divine wisdom and love, and the dynamic terminal value of God's benevolent power and goodness is the whole of the created universe. In the faith-grounded language of Genesis, "On the seventh day God rested and saw that it [the whole of creation] was all very good."[228]

Note that an authentic religious perspective does not undermine the genuine insights of secular humanism. Human beings are themselves originating values, and the terminal goods they achieve are worthwhile. The personal development of skills, virtues, insights, and knowledge is a great and laudable good; the interpersonal bonds of family, friendship, citizenship, and global solidarity should also be encouraged and supported. But religious faith places these many valuable efforts within a "friendly universe," a dynamic cosmological order to which we belong and for which we share partial responsibility, while revealing a deeper significance to human achievement and failure.[229]

In striving to be authentic, human beings strive to achieve comprehensive self-transcendence. But the fruit of God's self-transcendence, the authentic expression and revelation of God's benevolent power, is the dynamic order of creation itself. This profound religious insight helps to clarify the deeper meaning of the *Imago Dei*. To be created in the divine image means that human beings are capable of achieving authenticity. Really to become like God is to achieve self-transcendence through our own authentic lives and activities, discovering what is true, creating what is good, and healing what is wounded in history. For divine love not only creates and sustains the world but actively shares in its ongoing redemption and healing.[230]

Perhaps the principal source of modern unbelief is the demoralizing reality of evil. We can symbolize the traditional forms of evil through the four horsemen of the apocalypse: war, famine, pestilence, and death. To these recurrent sources of evil, modernity has added revolutionary ideology and terror and weapons of unprecedented destructive power. Without religious faith, without the knowledge born of God's gift of love, the world we inhabit appears too evil for God to be good.[231]

Since the nineteenth century, Western thinkers and writers have been captivated by the trials of Job, the unmerited suffering of the righteous and innocent man. Christianity, in particular, has been radically challenged by the failure of Christ's coming to bring about justice and peace. And the unprecedented terror of the Holocaust was deepened by God's apparent indifference to the fate of the Jews, the biblical God's chosen people. The contemporary believer, therefore, cannot escape the ancient Augustinian challenge: How can the benevolent power of the Creator and the ontological goodness of creation coexist with the reality of evil?[232]

Philosophers regularly distinguish two forms of evil, physical and moral. By physical evil, they mean the suffering, destruction, and death inflicted on the world by natural causes: earthquakes, hurricanes, floods, droughts, ice, wind, fire, and rain. These powerful causes are omnipresent in nature and their destructive consequences undeniable. But is physical evil of this kind incompatible with the originating goodness of God and the terminal goodness of the created order?

Lonergan did not think so.[233] He believed that God had freely created a factual universe intelligibly ordered by emergent probability, by the successive realization in accord with successive schedules of probability of a conditioned series of schemes of recurrence. These lawful schemes of recurrence are both natural and human. They come into being, survive, and pass away through both natural and human causes. Thus, the reality of physical evil does not undermine the *intelligibility* of nature; in fact, it illustrates the intrinsic power and limits of natural causes and the successive schemes of recurrence they support, sustain, and destroy. But does physical evil undermine the goodness of creation; does it make the universe hostile or indifferent to human aspirations and hopes?

It certainly challenges the common religious belief that God created everything for the happiness and pleasure of humans. But that complacent belief is unjustifiably anthropocentric.[234] Human beings are only very small parts, and in fact, very late parts, of the created cosmos. The ontological goodness of nonhuman creatures does not depend on their satisfying human desires or placating human fears. The limited perspective of religious common sense, which views all things in their practical relations to us, needs to be corrected and augmented by the explanatory outlook of theoretical science.[235] Each created thing is what it is. Each thing is good by virtue of being what it is within the greater cosmic order. Each thing has both constructive and destructive potential. The cosmos is not a nursery or a kindergarten deliberately designed for human protection and pleasure. Its ontological value is intrinsic, not instrumental, as Bacon, Descartes, and their many pragmatic descendants have assumed. "When I consider thy heavens, the work of thy hands, the moon and the stars, which thou hast ordained; what is man that thou art mindful of him?" (Ps. 8:3–4).

If the natural order is characterized by the intelligible genesis, survival, and perishing of conditioned schemes of recurrence, human history is characterized by the dialectic of progress and decline.[236] The sources of genuine historical progress at the individual, social, and cultural levels are authentic subjects acting as originating values by faithfully responding to the transcendental notions and precepts. The basic sources of human alienation and decline are violations of these precepts by egoistic individuals, self-serving groups, or decadent and demoralized cultures. Human history reliably operates according to a law of intelligible effects.[237] Earlier lines of genuine development create the conditions for future achievement and progress. But personal and communal alienation, though easy to sustain and enlarge, are very hard to correct. Political and social grievances multiply, habits harden and congeal, fear, pride, resentment, and suspicion accelerate the process of decline.[238]

As human history repeatedly shows, the discernible effects of decline are severe and far reaching. Institutional cooperation deteriorates, the rule of law is compromised by becoming an instrument of dominant privilege and power; group egoism treats the systemic suffering of the oppressed as the merited result of their sloth and incompetence. But economic, political, and social achievements based on group bias are always unjust and unfair, as the history of slavery, unregulated capitalism, imperial conquest, and the callous arrogance of patriarchy make clear.

Sophisticated and persuasive ideologies constitute the gravest source of historical decline. While individual and group bias promote personal and social alienation, ideology rationalizes alienation, justifies it, converting error into truth, evil into good, the causes of decline into sources of progress. Powerful modern examples of ideology include laissez-faire capitalism, Marxist Leninist orthodoxy, the anti-Semitic racism of the Nazis, the heretical dogmas of militant Islam. To paraphrase Lonergan, systematic injustice discredits genuine development; the mentality of corruption spreads from oppressive social groups into the principal organs of culture, popular and elite; ideological propaganda profoundly distorts human thinking, feeling, and conduct: "A civilization in decline digs its own grave with relentless consistency" (*Method*, 55).

What can be done to arrest the process of personal and historical decline? Radical Enlightenment humanists sought to localize evil in the ancien régime. They based their utopian hopes on the ruthless elimination of kings, nobles, and clerical princes. During the Industrial Revolution, Marxists localized evil in the capitalist bourgeoisie, basing their hopes for the classless society on the abolition of capitalist ownership. After Germany's demoralizing defeat in World War I, Hitler and the Nazis located evil in "inferior" races and peoples, whom they sought to exterminate through a process of state-organized terror.

All these "utopian" projects collapsed in the rubble of violence and war. The chastened stance of contemporary secular humanism has become far more sober and wary. In its postmodern variations, exclusive humanism has surrendered utopian dreams without losing its critical edge. The dominant voices of postmodernism emphasize the systemic injustices that invariably compromise society and culture. They stand with the marginalized victims of organized power: for women, indigenous peoples, racial minorities, immigrants, the economically and politically disinherited. They no longer believe in a messianic class, race, or cause that will permanently unravel the tangled historical knot. As previously noted, they excel in the critique of false hope.

But what remains of legitimate hope? We have returned, centuries later, to a modified version of the Kantian question: What can we authentically hope for, as persons of faith living in a secular age? Our religious faith in the goodness of creation includes faith in our human ability to become originating sources of value. Our candid acknowledgment of bias and sin extends to ourselves, the communities we love, the cultural traditions on which we rely for energy and light. Our critical knowledge of history teaches humility and redemptive sobriety, for historical change is always dialectical, a tangled mixture of progress and decline. Because authenticity is precarious, particularly at the level of historical action and reform, the demand for normative critical scrutiny is permanent. Though God has given us the gift of creative freedom, that precious gift is the source of error and truth, good and evil, authenticity and alienation.[239] Left to our own resources, we are creatures of greatness and wretchedness inexorably moving toward death.

However, religious faith assures us that God has not left us alone in the world. This is particularly true of Lonergan's Christian faith, based as it is on the historical incarnation of God in the person of Jesus Christ. The good news of the New Testament continues to be a source of legitimate hope. For God so loved the world that he sent his only begotten Son to redeem it from sin, and then sent the Holy Spirit to draw the world and its people toward holiness (John 3:15–17; Acts 2). What is the enduring meaning of these core Christian mysteries, and what is their practical relevance for reversing human decline?

The great Abrahamic faiths, Judaism, Christianity, and Islam, are religions of revelation. Faithful Jews believe in God's revelation to Moses and the prophets. Devout Muslims believe in the successive revelations to Muhammad recorded in the Koran. For Christians, the decisive divine revelation is the historical communication of God's redemptive love in the life, death, and resurrection of Jesus of Nazareth. As a critical Christian humanist, Lonergan believes that God becomes known to humanity in two distinct ways. Through rigorously developing the ontological and moral implications of our transcendental desires, God is known as the creative ground and end, the *arche* and *telos*, of the created universe. As a committed Christian, Lonergan also believes in God's historical revelation as faithfully transmitted through sacred scripture and tradition. For Lonergan, as for Aquinas, his theological guide and mentor, these are distinct but complementary ways of knowing the same God. Through Christ's incarnate revelation we learn that the awesome and mysterious God of creation is also the merciful Father (Abba!) of existential redemption and healing.[240]

Christ not only reveals God's redemptive love for the world, he actualizes its saving power through his public ministry and death. There are three key dimensions to the ministry of Jesus: teaching, healing, and confronting the reality of evil. In his teaching, Christ reaffirms the central truth of the law and the prophets. We humans are commanded to love God with our whole heart, mind, soul, and strength; and to love our neighbor as ourselves. Through his memorable and challenging parables Christ clarifies the depth and scope of this basic scriptural law. The mysterious God whom we love is a prodigal Father whose infinite goodness radically exceeds our most profound hopes, a compassionate Father whose merciful forgiveness is there for the asking.[241] And our neighbor is anyone in need of our help, whether physical or spiritual: "Whatever you do to the least of my brothers [and sisters] you do unto me."[242]

The healing ministry of Christ is responsive to the whole human person, body and mind, heart and soul. Christ repeatedly insisted that he came to cure and heal the sick, not those who are well. And because he came, the blind see, the lame walk, the deaf hear, sins are forgiven, and the poor have the good news proclaimed to them.[243]

Finally, Christ confronts the humanly unsolvable dilemmas of sin, suffering, and death. His personal example is deeply instructive. He does not withdraw from the presence of evil, surrender to its seductive appeal, or attempt to destroy it by force. Christ knows from direct experience the sins and temptations of individual men and women, of hardened religious establishments, of occupying military powers, of fair-weather followers and friends. His anthropological realism is profound and instructive.[244]

Still, moral evil existed before Jesus came, and it continues to flourish after his death. So what did his suffering and death really accomplish, if it did not destroy the reality of evil? As a Christian, Lonergan believes Christ's redemptive action and passion remain deeply significant. They teach us God's way of responding to evil, by overcoming its destructive power through fidelity to what is holy and good.[245] Christ did not abolish evil, but he showed us how to redeem it: first, by preserving and affirming the spiritual freedom that makes it possible; second, by weakening its vindictive grip on our own hardened or demoralized hearts.[246]

Death also existed before and after Christ. Yet Christ's resurrection and his enduring promise of eternal life mean that death, though it remains an essential part of human life, no longer has the last word. What Christ actually conquered is the finality and the sovereignty of sin and death: "I have come that you might have life and have it to the full."[247]

Finally, how are we to understand the sanctifying power of divine grace? Lonergan endorses the central insight of Aquinas's humanism. Grace does not abolish human nature but perfects and completes its intrinsic powers and operations. Thus, the revealed truths of faith perfect the activities of reason, just as grace perfects nature, and as heroic charity perfects the moral and intellectual virtues. Divine grace *sublates* human powers and operations, while respecting their integrity and efficacy.[248]

But human nature is also wounded by bias and sin, and by their destructive effects not only on the sinner but also on the broken world we sinners inhabit together. In addition, the reign of sin is greatly reinforced by the power of cultural ideologies, epistemic, moral, and religious. The human mind and heart are held captive by ideology. Violence and terror, resignation and despair, the steady drift into personal pleasure and profit, all claim its apologetic support.

How then does divine grace alter the powerful alliance of ideology and sin? Lonergan's unequivocal answer is striking and deep.[249] It is religious faith and not propaganda, not even reasoned philosophical argument, that can liberate the thinking of a culture in decline from its ideological prisons. It is religious hope, grounded in the benevolent mercy and forgiveness of God, not human promises or efforts alone, that can enable a society in decline to resist the pressures of historical decay, with the passivity and violence they evoke. And it is heroic charity, not Promethean pride and resentment, that can dissolve the hostility wrought by injustice, enabling former enemies to resolve their intractable differences.

Because authentic deeds always remain more persuasive than words, the light and power of religious authenticity will not transform our secular age until we and the religious communities we love and support courageously live and practice our faith at the exigent level of our time. Religious believers, in all times and seasons, have a common standard of authenticity to meet. "By their fruits you shall know them."[250]

CHAPTER FOUR

The Chill Winds of Modernity

The Profound Challenge of Catholic Renewal

> *The crisis, then, that I have been attempting to depict is a crisis not of faith but of culture. There has been no new revelation from on high to replace the revelation given through Christ Jesus. There has been written no new Bible, and there has been founded no new church, to link us with him. But Catholic philosophy and theology are matters, not merely of revelation and faith, but also of culture. Both have been fully and deeply involved in classical culture. The breakdown of classical culture and, at last in our day, the manifest comprehensiveness and exclusiveness of modern culture confront Catholic philosophy and Catholic theology with the gravest problems, impose upon them mountainous tasks, invite them to Herculean labors.*
> —CWL, 4:244–45

Since the papacy of John XXIII, the Roman Catholic Church has struggled with the demands of *aggiornamento,* the hard work of comprehensive and continuous Christian renewal. Pope John summoned his church, in Lonergan's language, to rise to the challenges and level of our time. But why had the comprehensive renewal of the church become necessary in the mid-twentieth century? Why is it still necessary today? And what important contributions did Lonergan make to ensure that Catholic renewal was critical, coherent, and deep? These are the framing questions that establish the substantive agenda for chapter 4.

Lonergan explicitly distinguished between the great and small renewal of the church. By the small renewal, he meant the development of a Catholic philosophy and theology that were empirical, critical, and comprehensive. In the preceding chapters, we explored the basic structure and content of Lonergan's historically minded philosophy. In this concluding chapter, we bring his philosophy and theology together in responding to the question of God. Though Lonergan clearly distinguishes between philosophical and revealed theology, he refuses, following the example of Aquinas, to separate them. Behind this refusal is a candid acknowledgment of the essential role intellectual, moral, and religious conversions play in theology. Following the lead of existential theologians like Augustine, Pascal, and Kierkegaard, Lonergan insists that we must become more authentic persons in order to know God as the creative origin and end of proportionate being, as the supreme good in the order of originating and terminal values, and as the redeemer and sanctifier of human existence and history.

While the three existential conversions are required of the authentic theologian, such conversions by themselves are insufficient. For a theology at the level of our time must be based on eight functional specialties that effectively mediate the traditional faith of a particular religious community to the different cultures in which that community is based. This final chapter distinguishes and relates these functional specialties and shows how they corroborate and amplify the philosophical discoveries of Lonergan's intentionality analysis. Toward the chapter's conclusion, we also explore the merits and limitations of Lonergan's ethics of personal and communal authenticity.

In chapter 4, the questions, concerns, and discoveries of the earlier chapters are brought together to reveal what critical *aggiornamento* in depth really requires. It is to be hoped that this convergence should confirm what Lonergan wished to achieve as a critical Christian humanist attuned to the struggles of his time and his church. It is because these cultural struggles are important to every contemporary thinker that Lonergan's substantive project and enduring achievement are also important for believers and nonbelievers alike.

CRITICAL CHRISTIAN HUMANISM

It is extremely difficult to strike the mean when writing about the Roman Catholic Church. External critics of the church tend to focus on its scandalous history. Loyal apologists, by contrast, tend to idealize its morally ambiguous present and past. When defenders and critics speak of the church they normally refer to its hierarchical leadership, especially the pope, the Roman curia, and the global episcopate. Although clerical leadership plays a critical role in the governance of "the church," it does not encompass the full meaning of that inclusive term. In reality, the church is the pilgrim people of God moving unsteadily through history, a community of sinners united by their common faith in Jesus of Nazareth as the lord and redeemer of the world.[1]

As a complex and changing society, governed by humans, supported by grace, confident of Christ's living presence within it, the church struggles to fulfill its historical calling: in word and in deed to carry forward Christ's work of redemption. The earliest teaching of the church provides the basis for its unfulfilled mission. For the good news of the gospel is this: God so loved the world that he sent his divine Son to redeem it from violence and sin (John 3:16–17), and then sent the Spirit of God to sanctify all who engage in this redemptive activity (John 14:26). As the Father sent the Son and the Spirit, so Jesus sent his Christian disciples to do what he had done upon earth: to proclaim the gospel, to heal the broken and afflicted, to transform sin and evil by fidelity to what is holy and good.

From the beginning, faithful Christians disagreed about the scope of Christ's message and mission. Was the gospel meant only for Jews or also for Gentiles? Must Gentiles become Jews in order to be faithful Christians? Would Christ soon return in glory to mark the end of historical time? How compatible are the Hebrew scriptures and the Christian gospel with the great discoveries of Greek philosophy and science (in the famous words of Tertullian, "What has Athens to do with Jerusalem?")? Can authentic Christians also be Roman citizens and soldiers, simultaneously loyal to God and empire? Who precisely is Jesus of Nazareth, and how is he actually related to the God of Abraham, Isaac, and Jacob? These are just some of the controversies that divided Christianity in its first five centuries of existence.

Through the long medieval period, stretching from the dissolution of the Roman Empire to the fifteenth-century Renaissance in Italy, internal divisions persisted within the church: about monasticism, poverty, heresy, the temporal power and authority of the pope and the bishops, the Crusades to the Holy Land, the recovery of Greek and Arabic learning, simony, Scholasticism, the scourge of the Black Death, among many others.

In responding to these critical controversies, great leaders emerged who shaped the church's enduring traditions: Saint Peter, who bravely proclaimed the forbidden gospel to the skeptical Jews in Jerusalem; Saint Paul, who brought the good news of salvation to the Mediterranean Gentiles; the Greek and Latin fathers, who irenically mediated the tensions among Jerusalem, Athens, and Rome; Saint Augustine, who articulated the first Christian theology of history and politics; Saint Benedict and the founders of Christian monasticism; Saint Francis of Assisi, who personally incarnated the Christian commitment to humility and poverty; Saint Thomas of Aquinas, whose synoptic theology briefly restored the contested alliance between Athens and Jerusalem, between reason and faith, the complementary sources of religious knowledge and truth; Saint Teresa of Avila, who renewed and deepened the Christian tradition of mystical prayer.

These revered Christian heroes are much clearer to us today than they were in their own time. It was Peter who repeatedly betrayed Christ, Paul who persecuted the earliest Christians, Augustine who initially scorned Christian teaching, Francis whose radical summons to poverty divided his own followers, Aquinas whose critical embrace of Aristotle's philosophy was later condemned by the bishop of Paris.

As this highly compressed summary acknowledges, idealized accounts of the Catholic past gloss over the church's immersion in controversy, idealized portraits of Catholic saints obscure the complexity of their personal development and their often wary, even hostile, reception by the church's clerical leadership. Yet exclusive attention to the scandalous failures of the church is equally one-sided. These scandals are real and worthy of remembrance: the violent treatment of Jews, women, heretics, and Muslims; the mercenary and martial ambitions of the papacy; the recurrent abuse of clerical authority and office; the pious superstitions of the laity; the continuous failure of Christians to imitate Christ. While there was no golden age in the history of the church, and although some periods of scandal were darker than others—the Avignon papacy and the expulsion of the Iberian Jews, for example—the survival and growth of the church through its first fifteen centuries is a genuine source of historical wonder.

A great strength of Catholicism has been its willingness to assimilate alien cultural forms. What began as a religion of Semites was slowly transformed into a Mediterranean faith that included Jews, Romans, and Greeks, and eventually the diverse peoples of North Africa, Continental Europe, and the British Isles. In this complex assimilative process, the church critically appropriated Greek intellectualism, Roman political culture and law, monastic discipline and piety, feudal institutional and architectural structures, the high learning and teaching of the medieval university. By the thirteenth century, in Western Europe at least, a comprehensive Christian culture had emerged that we now call Latin Christendom. It was led by the papacy, supported by a continental network of bishops, religious orders, and priests, and intellectually justified by the Scholastic theology developed in Paris, Cologne, Oxford, and Bologna.

Even within Christendom, however, Christianity was not united. For schism had ruptured the bonds between the Greek and Roman churches; there was growing opposition to the centralized power of Rome; heretical movements were spreading through Languedoc and as far east as Prague and Bohemia; and the remarkable Thomist synthesis of Aristotle, Augustine, and scripture had proved increasingly contentious and fragile. Although Catholics often nostalgically recall Latin Christendom as a unified and harmonious age, this was a unity deeply riven by fissures and conflict.[2]

In the fourteenth and fifteenth centuries, the Scholastic theological tradition declined, the crusading impulse ended in failure, the Black Death decimated Western Europe, and a hyper-Augustinian voluntarism shattered confidence in the benevolence and mercy of God. Aquinas's balanced theological synthesis of nature and grace, reason and faith, the classical virtues and heroic charity, was effectively undermined by relentless emphasis on the dark sovereignty of God and the radical sinfulness of fallen man.[3]

The stern misanthropy of late medieval culture was directly challenged by Renaissance humanism, which openly celebrated human achievement in the arts, politics, architecture, philosophy, and science. The buoyant spirit of early modern humanism is memorably expressed in Pico della Mirandola's "Oration on the Dignity of Man," a rhetorical paean to human freedom and power. Yet human power, as always, had its dark and bright sides, the brightness of high cultural achievement, the darkness of fierce political rivalry, intense martial combat, and ambition-driven clerical intrigue.

The Catholic response to the Italian Renaissance was deeply ambivalent. Many Christians welcomed the recovery of classical languages and learning, the renewed affirmation of human dignity and liberty, the restored interest in the beauty and intelligibility of the sensible world. Others were deeply troubled by the increasing worldliness of the church, the martial and mercenary ambitions of the papacy, the repeated conciliar failures to achieve fundamental reform. Erasmus and Savonarola exemplify these conflicting responses to the new humanistic culture emerging in Europe.

At the core of the conflict was an unresolved Christian division over the authentic relation of the church to the world. Should Christians withdraw from the world to protect themselves from its violence, ambition, and sin? Or should they freely enter the world as Christ did in order to sanctify and redeem it? But if they directly engage with the world, do they risk becoming ensnared in its spirit of pride and concupiscence? Yet how can they effectively redeem the world without knowing its greatness and misery, without sharing its profound joys and sorrows? The incarnation of Christ can be read in two different though compatible ways: that God so loved the world that he sent his divine Son to become one of us, to bless and affirm human existence even in its evident sinfulness; and that the martial and religious leadership of the world rejected Christ's message and condemned him to a terrible death. His death, however, was not the final chapter in the story. For Christians believe that Christ rose from the dead and commanded his disciples to continue his mission on earth. A Christian theology of history must take full account of all the great scriptural mysteries: the goodness of creation; the violence of sin; the original covenant with Abraham; the renewed covenant with Moses; the prophetic message of infidelity and hope; the incarnation, passion, and crucifixion of Christ; his miraculous resurrection; the descent of the Holy Spirit; the birth, growth, and continuing struggles of the church. Any form of humanism that fails to acknowledge the destructive consequences of sin is inevitably shallow. But a reactive antihumanism obsessed with the tragedy of sin overlooks the goodness of creation and the healing power of grace. Christian humanism, at its best, sees human history as the dialectical field where the goodness of nature, the violence of sin, and the redemptive power of grace dramatically converge. That was Aquinas's enduring vision of human existence; it was also the historical vision of Lonergan. And it is the theological perspective governing our interpretation of Lonergan, as he confronts "the chill winds of modernity" (*Second Collection*, 93).

The Catholic Struggle with Modernity

The Second Vatican Council (1962–65) can serve as a dividing line between two stages of Lonergan's career. In the four decades before the council, he entered the Jesuit order, studied in Canada, England, and Rome, and studiously "reached up to the mind of Aquinas" on the disputed topics of grace and freedom and the critical role of understanding (*intelligere*) in human cognition. He wrote his greatest philosophical work, *Insight*, taught theology to Catholic seminarians at the Gregorian University in Rome, and developed groundbreaking ideas in the philosophy of history and economics.[4] During and after the council, he reflected deeply on the true meaning of Catholic renewal and published *Method in Theology* as an important contribution to the ongoing project of *aggiornamento*. He also wrote several papers and lectures, anthologized in the *Collected Works of Lonergan*, that directly address the crisis of Catholicism in the modern age.[5]

Lonergan took a long and measured view of this crisis, a crisis that he believed was fundamentally cultural in origin (CWL, 4:244). What exactly did he mean by this important interpretive claim? He had the long history of the church and the specific example of Aquinas in mind. In Lonergan's view, Catholic Christianity, from its very beginning, had fruitfully engaged with the diverse Mediterranean cultures to which the apostles had proclaimed the gospel. When Saint Paul asserted that he "had become all things to all men," he was acknowledging the vital importance of cultural sympathy to the apostolic mission (1 Cor. 9:22). This important Pauline principle was later affirmed by the Greek and Latin fathers, by the doctrinal teaching of Nicea, Chalcedon, and Constantinople, and especially by Augustine, whose *De Civitate Dei* articulated the normative institutional and cultural relations between the Christian church and the late Roman Empire.

After the decline of imperial Rome, this interactive pattern continued, in the Carolingian Renaissance, the Anselmian project of *fides quaerens intellectum*, and the periodic founding of new religious orders to address new cultural challenges to the Christian faith. The church of Christ retained its vitality and relevance, not by abandoning the world but by attempting to understand and transform it. For Lonergan, the finest expression of this redemptive engagement occurred in the theology of Thomas Aquinas.[6] After years spent studying "the mind of Aquinas" (CWL, 3:769), Lonergan concluded that Thomas had performed his theological task with distinction. He effectively rose to the cultural level and challenges of his time, thereby setting a standard for all subsequent Christian thinkers and teachers.

Did the Christian successors of Aquinas live up to the exigent measure he set? Sadly, they often did not, with the unwelcome result that the Catholic Church became increasingly estranged from the intellectual and cultural leadership of the West. Lonergan frequently cited the decadence of late medieval Scholasticism, the errors of philosophical nominalism, and the theological shift from the quest for understanding to the quest for certainty (CWL, 17:187–88). But there were other sources of estrangement as well: the hyper-Augustinian emphasis on sin and unmerited grace; the failure of successive church councils to achieve significant ecclesiastical reform; the nepotism and greed of the Renaissance papacy; Rome's stubborn unwillingness to engage irenically with the Protestant Reformers; the largely defensive Catholic posture that accompanied the Tridentine reforms; the magisterial condemnation of Galileo's "Dialogues Concerning the Two World-Systems."[7]

There were, of course, important exceptions: Thomas More and John Fisher in England; Ignatius of Loyola, who founded the Society of Jesus, to which Lonergan belonged; the small band of original Jesuits who brought the Christian gospel to India, China, Japan, and North America; the Jesuit school of theologians in Salamanca; Blaise Pascal, who memorably articulated the tangled blending of greatness and wretchedness in the modern vision of man and the cosmos; Galileo himself, who freely acknowledged the Bible as the revealed Word of God but denied that the scriptures provided a reliable source of scientific knowledge; Teresa of Avila; Francis de Sales; Philip Neri; and Vincent de Paul; among many others.

For Lonergan, a radical shift occurred in the late seventeenth century. While early modern thinkers, like Copernicus, Descartes, and Galileo, had differed with the church, they had not publicly or personally rejected it. They remained doctrinally orthodox, even as they embraced and contributed to "the new science of nature." The French historian Paul Hazard has argued that this cooperative tension drastically changed around 1680.[8] French intellectuals, in particular, began a relentless assault on Catholic Christianity. This radical critique did not occur in a historical vacuum. Trust in the church's centralized leadership had been declining since the Renaissance began. The scandalous conduct of the papacy had helped trigger the Protestant Reformation. As the institutional unity of Christianity fragmented, politics and religion became even more closely entwined. The kingdoms and principalities of northern Europe largely aligned with the Protestant cause. Spain, much of France, and the Mediterranean powers remained loyal to Rome. The Lutheran and Calvinist schisms soon led to destructive religious wars that, for many, linked Christianity irrevocably to hatred and violence. The Treaty of Westphalia, 1648, signaled a new era of religious toleration based on the political principle that the religion of the prince should also be that of his people. But when Louis XIV revoked the Edict of Nantes (1685), the French Catholic Church became an international symbol of repressive intolerance.[9]

Religious and political warfare hardened minds and hearts throughout Europe. The clerical condemnation of Galileo symbolically connected the church with opposition to the new science during a period of unprecedented theoretical discoveries culminating in the *Principia* of Newton. The post-Constantinian alliance between throne and altar tied the fortunes of the church too closely to those of the ancien régime. Skeptical criticism was openly directed at the wisdom of scripture and the Christian tradition, as Pierre Bayle condemned the God of the Bible as a vengeful tyrant rather than a forgiving and merciful father. Bayle's stern scriptural criticism deepened the disturbing association of Christianity with violence and despotism.[10] Important efforts at reconciliation between Catholics and Protestants faltered when Catholic leaders, like Bossuet, insisted that the Reformers recant and penitently return to the true Catholic fold.[11]

Intellectual and cultural leadership decisively shifted from the Catholic South to the Protestant North. The leading scientists, philosophers, and writers of the late seventeenth and eighteenth centuries were English Protestants like Newton, Milton, and Locke, critical Scots like Hume and Adam Smith, Continental innovators like Spinoza, Leibniz, and Huygens. In France the anticlerical *philosophes*, led by Diderot and Voltaire, fiercely criticized the church as the enemy of reason and liberty, the defining principles of the modern Enlightenment. Though Catholic defensiveness was understandable in the face of this frontal assault, it had very unwelcome repercussions. By setting itself in open opposition to the Enlightenment, the church surrendered the intellectual and moral leadership of Europe to its religious rivals and cultural adversaries.[12]

To its numerous critics, the Catholic Church became a symbol and agent of reaction in an era of extravagant hope. The church looked to the past for its wisdom, while the leading moderns imagined a utopian future based upon science and technological power. In its intellectual outlook, the church was traditional, still loyal to the hierarchical theories of the ancients. Politically the church was also conservative, the firm ally of the ancien régime. But powerful democratic winds were blowing across North America and Europe. As the champions of democracy advocated liberty, equality, and inalienable rights, the church continued to defend hierarchical authority and monarchical rule. The contrasts in religious sensibility were equally striking. The Protestant ethic was individualist in piety and congregationalist in its governing philosophy. For the great Reformers, the individual Christian believer encountered God directly in the forum of conscience or through the solitary reading of scripture. The vibrant religious community was small and decentralized, with congregants choosing their own pastors and leaders. The Catholic emphasis, by contrast, was on religious mediation, the reception of grace through the seven sacraments, the reception of truth through the authoritative teaching of the universal Catholic community. That global community was governed from Rome by a succession of popes secretly elected in a consistory of cardinals. And many Catholic bishops who exercised regional control over particular dioceses were formally appointed by unaccountable Roman authorities.[13]

The democratic revolutions in North America and France marked a critical turning point. Although the Catholic presence in America was small, its leaders and people openly supported the revolutionary cause. In France, however, the Catholic leadership was closely allied with the established order. The violent murder of the king, the hostile assault on the nobility and the church, the terror and wars that the Revolution incited, created a lasting division within French society. To Tocqueville's regret and dismay, the friends of religion became enemies of liberty; the friends of liberty, in turn, became enemies of religion.[14] This enduring antagonism crippled French politics for more than a century and heightened hostility between secularists and Catholics throughout all of Europe. As the nineteenth century began, the European church found itself in open conflict with the Protestant kingdoms of the North, secular intellectuals and critics across the continent, the friends of democratic equality and liberty, and the liberal spirit of progressive individualism that educated Europeans of all classes increasingly embraced.[15]

During the next 150 years things only got worse. In the eighteenth century, the church lost the support of European intellectuals; in the nineteenth century, it lost the loyalty of the European working class. Catholic political responses to modernity were often a matter of too little too late. In the French Revolution, Catholic leaders defended the Bourbon monarchy; in the Industrial Revolution they belatedly supported the interests of labor, but by then the majority of the working class had been radicalized. Catholic social thinking remained tied to agrarian models while rural peasants and farmers were leaving the land to seek work in industrial factories and mines.[16]

In the intellectual sphere, the church generally resisted the new historical consciousness, the critical interpretation of scripture, the Darwinian emphasis on evolutionary change, the secular demand for collective democratic responsibility, the development of the new human sciences. The church was not anti-intellectual; it continued to defend the complementarity of reason and faith. But its defining models of reason and knowledge, society and labor, education and culture, fine art and leisure tended to be classical or medieval, while modernity had deliberately distanced itself from these earlier cultural paradigms (CWL, 4:228–29, 238–46).

The cultural nadir occurred during the late nineteenth and early twentieth centuries. When the *Risorgimento* in Italy threatened the territorial holdings of the papacy, Pius IX retaliated with his infamous "Syllabus of Errors," in which he openly condemned the doctrine that the pope "can and ought to reconcile himself with progress, with liberalism, and with modern civilization."[17] In 1870 the First Vatican Council formally declared the infallibility of the pope in his dogmatic teaching on faith and morals. Although the practical scope of this doctrine was relatively narrow, it tended to have lasting effects, namely, to strengthen the spiritual authority of the papacy as its temporal and political power steadily declined; to create an aura of Catholic inerrancy and magisterial certainty, just as the natural and human sciences were acknowledging their fallibility and immersion in history.

As Garry Wills has shown, the principle of papal infallibility too often led to deceit and distortion, the erroneous view that the pope and the church are always right.[18] Just when the Catholic community needed exceptional candor to acknowledge past failures and sins, church leaders sought to give the impression that its conflicts with modernity were exclusively caused by the faults of its rivals and critics. Like all forms of political propaganda, this stance was essentially dishonest. But sustained dishonesty exacts a heavy price. In this case it "led to ecclesiastical disaster, like the suppression of the modernists in 1907 and after, which stamped not only upon error and wildness, but upon the most promising and courageous ways by which Catholics of that generation might aim to meet the intellectual challenges of the age."[19]

The antimodernist culture of fear and repression affected every aspect of the church. Inwardly, Catholic leaders silenced their most original and creative theologians and thinkers. Catholic education for both clergy and laity became excessively traditional. Catholic philosophy and theology were dominated by neo-Scholasticism. With its claim to full possession of the truths that really mattered, the church prided itself on its refusal to change. In its external relations, the church lacked broad moral authority in a century defined by total war and global depression. It sided with Franco in Spain, reached a timid agreement with Mussolini in Italy, and lacked the technical competence to participate meaningfully in the great economic debates of the time. The critical test in the papacy of Pius XII concerned relations with Nazi Germany.[20] Why did the pope not publicly condemn the brutal anti-Semitism of Hitler's regime and intervene more effectively on behalf of the Jews? No one can say for certain why the pope remained silent, but one thing is clear. Rome spoke with a firm critical voice when condemning Communist regimes that openly threatened the church, but it proved far more accommodating with Fascist governments whose relations with the Vatican were less hostile. It was hard to avoid the demoralizing impression that the highest Catholic priority was protecting one's own.

AGGIORNAMENTO

Lonergan came of age in the antimodernist era. An original and independent thinker, he was never a radical or revolutionary.[21] At first, he considered himself a nominalist, perhaps because of his ontological attachment to concrete particulars, perhaps because he considered universal concepts abstract and immobile. Although he affirmed the Leonine adage *vetera novis augere et perficere* (to augment and perfect the old with the new) (CWL, 3:768), he was never fully at ease in the neo-Scholastic milieu. This unease was due partly to his independent reading of Aquinas. In both his doctoral dissertation on grace and freedom and in his groundbreaking papers on understanding and judgment, Lonergan interpreted Saint Thomas as a Christian intellectualist. On this interpretive basis, he drew a significant distinction between the actual teachings of Thomas and those of traditional Thomism. For Lonergan, Thomas's account of *intelligere* was the key to understanding his theories of God and the soul (Lonergan's primary reason for calling him an intellectualist): "The human soul understands itself by its understanding, which is its proper act perfectly demonstrating its power and its nature" (CWL, 4:143). In this critical sentence, Aquinas recognizes the centrality of insight (the human act of understanding) for a comprehensive treatise on man. The Thomist parallels are unmistakable in the signature passage defining the goal of Lonergan's *Insight*: "Thoroughly understand what it is to understand, and not only will you understand the broad lines of all there is to be understood, but you will also possess a fixed base, an invariant pattern, opening on all further developments of understanding" (CWL, 3:22). Although Lonergan later transposed Aquinas's metaphysics of the soul into his own intentional analysis of the subject, he continually recognized the immensity of his debt to the Angelic Doctor.

Perhaps, the deepest aspect of this debt was the model Aquinas provided for critically integrating the old with the new. In both his commentaries on traditional texts and his synoptic theological *Summas*, Aquinas brought the developing Christian tradition into fruitful dialogue with the advanced learning of his age. He did this patiently, thoroughly, brilliantly, and with a singular confidence in the complementarity of created reason and religious faith.

For Lonergan, Aquinas's cultural achievement served as the basis for an illuminating analogy of proportion (CWL, 17:293). Thus, Lonergan's goal was not only to retrieve the wisdom of Aquinas, but to do for the modern age what Aquinas had done for the culture of medieval Europe. There were obvious asymmetries in the situations of these two Christian thinkers. Aquinas was a systematic theologian addressing a profoundly Christian culture in which the church still played the leading intellectual role. Revealed theology was commonly regarded as the "queen of the sciences," while natural and moral philosophy were treated as theology's handmaids. Aquinas's theological goal was to demonstrate the unifying power of Aristotelian metaphysics in synthesizing the truths of both reason and faith.

Lonergan, by contrast, was a philosopher-theologian addressing a largely secular culture, shaped by historical consciousness, intellectual specialization and autonomy, the philosophical turn to subjectivity, and profound doubts about Christianity in general and Catholicism in particular. Or rather, he had two distinct audiences that partly overlapped. When Lonergan wrote as a humanist, as he did in *Insight*, he presupposed no religious allegiance or affiliation. He appealed to the concrete intellectual experience of his readers, as he led them through the field-specific insights of mathematics, natural science, common sense, philosophy, hermeneutics, and natural theology (CWL, 3:765–66). Only in chapter 20, "Special Transcendent Knowledge," did he invoke specifically Christian insights into the basic dilemmas of moral impotence and sin. *Insight*, as Lonergan emphasized, is deliberately written from a moving viewpoint, a pedagogical strategy intended to draw both secular and religious readers into intellectual and moral conversions (CWL, 3:18–20). A central purpose of *Insight* is to show that the native *eros* and exigence of human intelligence lead ultimately to a reasoned affirmation of God and of the radical human need for divine grace and aid.

However, Lonergan was also a Catholic, a Jesuit, an authentic believer in the gospel and the Christian tradition. The primary audience for many of his papers and lectures were Catholics, or Christians, or thinkers openly sympathetic to religion. In this chapter, I want to focus on his discourse with Catholic peers before, during, and after the Second Vatican Council. The first imperative Lonergan emphasized was the church's need to appropriate critically both the old and the new. Lonergan learned the importance of critical hermeneutics and history through his personal study of the Catholic tradition in philosophy and theology. Before we can responsibly appraise the *vetera* we must know what they really were. We cannot simply assume that the actual past and the received tradition are identical, for traditional accounts of the past are often incomplete or distorted (CWL, 3:769). Lonergan repeatedly found this to be the case in his critical encounter with Aquinas. The actual beliefs of Saint Thomas often fail to coincide with those of traditional Thomism. This interpretive discovery was particularly important in a clerical culture committed to the neo-Scholastic revival. For how could the church recover the genuine insights of Aquinas if Catholic scholars failed to grasp their depth and complexity?

The fruits of Lonergan's long study of Aquinas were both methodological and substantive. Substantively, he discovered the centrality of insight in human cognition and the centrality of grace in the course of sustained human development.[22] Methodologically, he discovered what critical appropriation really required on the part of responsible scholars: knowledge of the original languages in which the classical texts were written; knowledge of the several textual sites where the developing mind of the author is actually expressed; knowledge of the author's flexible use of critical technical terms in articulating a series of converging insights and claims; knowledge of the particular hermeneutic context to which the author is tacitly or explicitly responding—that is, the background framework of beliefs and assumptions, settled as well as unresolved questions and answers, that the author and his original audience commonly share; finally, a growing knowledge on the part of the interpreter of the realities to which the classical text intentionally refers.[23]

Method is the fruit of reflection on performance. When Lonergan later formulated the normative requirements of critical appropriation in *Method in Theology*, he was drawing on his own interpretive performance "reaching up to the mind of Aquinas." But methodological insights are not confined to the occasion of their discovery. They apply with equal validity to our reading of the entire Western philosophical and theological tradition: to Plato, Aristotle, scripture, Origen, Athanasius, Augustine, the neo-Platonists, Anselm, Aquinas, Bonaventure, Scotus, Ockham, Eckhart, Suarez, Molina, Pascal, de Sales, Newman, Maritain, Gilson, Rahner, and others, to cite only the most luminous figures. What Lonergan had achieved with selected topics in Aquinas, he invited his scholarly colleagues to do for the Christian tradition as a whole: to discover what the *vetera* really were; to understand the realities to which they referred; to discern where traditional thinkers were right, where they were wrong, and where they were simply incomplete or inadequate, limited, as we all are, to the cultural horizons of their particular historical context.

If by the new, the *nova*, we refer to the modern world as a whole, it is far too vast and complex to admit of a comprehensive appraisal.[24] Lonergan recognized this difficulty and avoided its pitfalls. He focused instead on the critical appropriation of what he called "modern culture." To clarify his project, he distinguished two distinct though interactive levels of culture: an intellectual *superstructure* consisting of the empirical sciences, natural and human, historical and hermeneutical scholarship, academic philosophy and theology; and a practical *infrastructure* consisting of technological innovations, economic initiatives and reversals, social institutions and practices, political, artistic, and religious changes in belief, sensibility, and conduct. He explicitly acknowledged the symbiotic connection between these two levels of culture.[25] Theoretical developments in science regularly lead to technical inventions that generate new data and problems for subsequent theory. Important changes in business practice and consumer demand can require professional economists to modify their theoretical hypotheses and models. Lonergan believed that an analogous relationship obtained between philosophy and theology (as critical parts of the superstructure) and politics, art, and religion (as important aspects of the cultural infrastructure). It is a mark of his consistent intellectualism that he identified new theoretical discoveries (in the superstructure) as the deepest source of modern novelty and progress.

The novelty of modernity, like that of any historical period, is a mixed blessing. It needs to be deeply understood before it can be fairly appraised. "The only way to understand a new differentiation of consciousness (a new form of specialized inquiry) is to bring about that differentiation in oneself" (CWL, 17:100). Intellectual and personal integrity both require no less. The more concretely we study human reality, the more deeply historical we realize it is. We cannot understand either the *vetera* or the *nova* without first understanding the historical contexts in which they emerged and the historical challenges and problems they sought to address. Careful interpretive attention to human historicity, however, does not obviate the need for critical appraisal. Although we must understand sympathetically and deeply before we can judge responsibly, we cannot escape the burden of judging, for we are normative beings who pattern our choices and direct our lives through the evaluative judgments we make.

The dialectical analysis of modernity is especially difficult. Not only must we understand the new before we can judge it responsibly, but we must personally appropriate the normative sources of sustained self-transcendence before we can convincingly critique what Lonergan calls the dominant cultural counterpositions: scientism and exclusive naturalism in cosmology; reductionism and exclusive humanism in anthropology; possessive individualism and collectivism in sociology; secularism and the Promethean rejection of God in theology.

The Second Vatican Council

Great leadership often appears in unexpected forms. This was surely the case when Angelo Roncalli became Pope John XXIII in 1958. Widely expected to be a minor transitional pope, John electrified the church and the world during his brief papacy (1958–63). His style and manner were different from those of his immediate predecessors. He was earthy, warm, and unpretentious. He had served the church diplomatically in non-Catholic countries, and had an open, ecumenical spirit. Perhaps most importantly, he was not defensive and polemical, but humble and welcoming with Catholics and non-Catholics alike.[26]

Pope John changed the atmosphere and direction of the church with his bracing call for *aggiornamento*. The Italian term he used means renewal, revitalization, bringing things up to date. To use Lonergan's favored idiom, the pope was asking his fellow Catholics to rise to the level and challenges of their time. The papal banner of comprehensive *aggiornamento* required a major shift in the Catholic stance toward modernity. The post-Tridentine church had been an unsparing critic of the Copernican Revolution, the philosophical turn to subjectivity, the democratic movements for equality and liberty, the critical study of history and scripture. In the wake of the Reformation, European Catholics felt under attack and reacted defensively. They largely maintained this defensive posture for five hundred years at a great cost to themselves and their non-Catholic peers. To put it simply, with John XXIII love and hope for the modern world replaced fear and mistrust as the governing emotions of mid-twentieth-century Catholics.

The defining event of John's papacy was the Second Vatican Council he called into being.[27] The First Vatican Council of 1870 is best remembered for its assertion of papal infallibility, for its insistence on Rome's magisterial authority and power. John wanted Vatican II to be different. It was to be a "pastoral council" in which the church sympathetically addressed the needs and concerns of its contemporaries. Like earlier church councils, it offered an occasion for reform and renewal, for reaffirming the best of the old and critically assimilating whatever is true and good in the new (CWL, 17:221–39).

The intellectual foundations for Vatican II had actually been laid in the antimodernist era, largely by French thinkers like Peguy, Congar, Danielou, de Lubac, and Teilhard de Chardin. They represented the deepening historical mindedness within the church that the Vatican had directly resisted. Although their theological efforts were often referred to as *la nouvelle théologie*, their actual mantra was *ad fontes* (return to the sources) or *ressourcement*. The sources to which they returned were essentially scriptural and patristic. They were seeking a viable alternative to the "classicist" status quo, not in modernity but in the thinking and practice of the early church. Although disciplined by the Vatican during the antimodernist period, their theological labors bore great fruit at the council itself, particularly in the liturgical reforms eventually adopted and in *Lumen Gentium*'s pastoral image of the church as "the pilgrim people of God."

In his excellent analysis of Vatican II, John O'Malley distinguishes three different ways of challenging the "classicist" prejudices of "the long nineteenth century" (extending from the turmoil of the French Revolution to the advent of John XXIII's papacy). All three ways offer practical alternatives to the "antimodernist" status quo. First, "*aggiornamento*" summons the church to rise to address the changing realities of the present. This was the rallying cry of Pope John in his initial address to the council, and it became the dominant leitmotif of the reform-minded conciliar majority. Second, "the historical development of doctrine" was a central theme of Newman's, openly embraced by Lonergan and other historically trained theologians. While informed by the study of the past, the advocates of development wanted the church of the future to show the same vitality and cultural responsiveness as the church had shown throughout the centuries. Third, the advocates of *ressourcement* argued that there were deeper traditions in the church than those canonized during the "long nineteenth century." Rather than calling for "novelty" or "modernization," they urged their colleagues to retrieve what had historically been lost: the insights, spirit, language, and symbols of the biblical texts and the Greek and Latin fathers.[28]

Although Lonergan's *Insight* was published before the council began, its direct impact, if any, on conciliar deliberations is unclear. Still, the humanist perspective from which *Insight* is written, its generous acknowledgment of modern cultural achievements, and its critical sensitivity to their grave limitations is surely in the spirit of the groundbreaking papal appeal for reform and renewal.

Substantive controversy preceded the opening of the council and continues now long after its close. Pope John himself died within the opening year of Vatican II, though Paul VI generally sought to maintain the direction charted by his predecessor.[29] The most important conciliar documents are the products of compromise between traditionalists and progressives.[30] They almost never repudiate the old, but, on balance, are open and welcoming toward the new. In some cases, by critically retrieving the *vetera* (biblical and patristic insights, symbols, and language, e.g.), they offer a perspective on the church and its history very different from that of the staunch antimodernists. Four documents in particular illustrate the contrast between the ecumenical spirit of the council and the narrow Catholicity of its immediate predecessors.[31]

Lumen Gentium, the light of the nations, proposes a biblical rather than a juridical conception of the church. It defines the church as the pilgrim people of God in history and reaffirms the redemptive mission to which all Christians are called. Without repudiating papal authority, it stresses the collegial and collaborative nature of church governance and emphasizes the particular importance of the laity in the comprehensive Christian community.

Dignitatis Humanae, of human dignity, clearly affirms the principle of religious liberty, of freedom of worship and conscience, for the residents of every country on earth. The older Catholic position that "error has no rights" is tacitly abandoned. The new emphasis is on the intrinsic dignity of each human being, divinely created in God's image and likeness, and on the intellectual, political, and religious implications entailed by such dignity.

Nostra Aetate, our age, addresses the relation of the church to non-Christian religions. Instead of treating them as rivals and adversaries, *Nostra Aetate* acknowledges the solidarity of the human race, the universal search for the meaning of life and death, and the enduring wisdom of the great world religions, including Hinduism, Buddhism, Judaism, and Islam. "The Church, therefore, urges her sons to enter with prudence and charity into discussion and collaboration with members of other religions. Let Christians, while witnessing to their own faith and way of life, acknowledge, preserve and encourage the spiritual and moral truths found among non-Christians."[32]

Gaudium et Spes, joy and hope, "the Pastoral Constitution on the Church in the Modern World," was the final conciliar document approved. Symbolically, it witnesses to the fundamental change Vatican II brought about in late modern Catholicism. In the preface to this pastoral teaching, addressed to all humankind, the church openly identifies itself with the joy and hope, the grief and anguish of the people of our time, especially those who are poor or afflicted in any way, and expresses its profound solidarity with the entire human race and its history. Whatever the substantive merits and limitations of *Gaudium et Spes*, its ultimate pastoral intention was clear. The church was reembracing an incarnational approach to the world and offering the promise of redemption and healing to all the world's people and problems.

If the basic goal of Vatican II was *aggiornamento*, the comprehensive renewal of the universal church, then Lonergan was surely its ally. In fact, he had personally embraced this goal long before the papacy of Pope John. Through his study of Aquinas, he had learned how to appropriate the *vetera* critically. In preparing to write *Insight*, he discovered the dialectical pattern of modern progress and decline. He also discovered the empirical-critical methods at the heart of modern science and scholarship and resolved to find relevant analogues of those methods for Catholic philosophy and theology. He saw clearly that if Catholic thought is to regain broad credibility, it must rise to the methodological level of the best forms of contemporary inquiry. *Insight* is explicitly written to satisfy these exigent demands while preserving the traditional philosophical goal of epistemic integration and unity. In some ways, *Insight* remains a transitional text. Although its concrete examples and critical standards are modern, its faculty psychology (intellect, reason, and will) remains largely traditional. Only later did Lonergan insist that specifically philosophical terms and relations be based on the intentional analysis of conscious desires, norms, and operations (*Second Collection*, 235, 277; CWL, 17:167–68, 372).

Lonergan also distinguished between a great and small renewal of the church (CWL, 17:282). The great renewal involved all aspects of the church's message and mission: its forms of ministry, worship, preaching, education, governance, social action, ecumenical, and intercultural outreach. His distinctive personal contribution was to the small renewal (small only by comparison to comprehensive *aggiornamento*), the critical transformation of Catholic philosophy and theology.

At both levels of *aggiornamento*, a vast and belated transition was required of contemporary Catholics (*Second Collection*, 93). By and large, the leaders and teachers of the church had remained detached from modern culture, both the superstructure of theory and the infrastructure of the economy, society, politics, and the arts. There were multiple reasons for this detachment, some warranted, some not. Lonergan treads this polemical ground carefully. The tone of his criticism is sympathetic, the substance is balanced and nuanced. He is not seeking to score points in an intramural debate, but trying to understand what actually happened and why.

Lonergan acknowledges the traditional role of the church in bringing Christ's message to initially alien cultures: Greek, Roman, Germanic, English, and French. He knows of the earlier Jesuit missions to India, Japan, and China. He has the model of Aquinas in medieval Paris to guide him. Given this long history of inculturation, why did the church essentially turn its back on modernity and forgo its redemptive ministry to modern culture?

Lonergan's answer has four parts, only two of which he develops in detail (*Second Collection*, 94, 112–15). (1) The papal immersion in the vices of Renaissance culture played a major role in provoking the Protestant schism. (2) The Catholic Counter-Reformation not only disciplined the conduct of the church, but it set Rome deeply at odds with the

Protestant movement that spread throughout Europe and North America. Intense religious and political divisions led to merciless wars that weakened respect for Christianity as a whole and subverted the intellectual and moral authority of all Christian leaders. (3) From the late seventeenth century forward, modern cultural developments became entangled with a sustained public critique of Catholicism (*Second Collection*, 112–15; *Method*, 317). In defending itself against external criticism, the church failed to acknowledge the substantive merit of these developments in their own right. Thus, it gradually associated modern science with agnosticism and atheism, even though many of the most important scientists had been Christians. And it opposed modern critical scholarship, even though the earliest proponent of biblical criticism was Richard Simon, a French Catholic. Indirectly, the church strengthened the agnostic claims of its cultural critics by treating the new learning as a primary source of unbelief.[33]

At the level of the cultural infrastructure, modern developments were also ambiguous. The new vernacular languages were not designed for devotional purposes; the new art was secular and, on occasion, irreligious; the new democratic movements often culminated in political revolutions hostile to the church; urban industrialism created new wealth, but at a terrible social cost. When Pius X, in 1907, designated the "heresy of heresies" as "modernism," he reflected the centuries-old papal distrust of the whole modern era (*Second Collection*, 94, 112–15).

Fear and defensiveness aside, the deepest reason for Catholic resistance was a set of metatheoretical assumptions and attitudes that Lonergan identified as classicism,[34] the fourth part of his answer. Throughout modernity, the dominant Catholic mind-set was classicist. What did a classicist mentality assume? It accepted the Aristotelian notion of science as true, certain knowledge of causal necessity. Not only did the church struggle with the substantive content of the new empirical sciences, it also failed to understand the very nature of the modern scientific enterprise. Catholic thinkers continued to treat "science" as a source of certain and permanent truths, when its theoretical discoveries were constantly subject to critical revision and amendment.

In the second phase of the Enlightenment, Western Europe became historically minded. Evolutionary thinking emphasized the historicity of the cosmos and of the biological species that inhabit the earth. But historicity was also understood to permeate human affairs, both theoretical and practical. The natural and human sciences continued to undergo significant historical changes, but so did philosophy and theology, as well as the ramified cultural infrastructure. What historical reflection clearly revealed was cultural plurality and difference: not only different beliefs and moral codes, but different ways of thinking and speaking, of socializing and governing, of teaching and learning, of responding to life and to death.

But the classicist mind-set tended to view history as culturally irrelevant. Classicists commonly share a normative conception of culture that treats the cultural forms of Greco-Roman antiquity or Latin Christendom, for example, as universally and permanently binding (*Method*, xii). This static notion of culture led Catholic classicists to canonize the cosmology, anthropology, sociology, and theology of the Middle Ages. If medieval Christendom had the last word on nature, humanity, society, and God, then the new learning had nothing important to offer.

Classicist anthropology and ethics are metaphysically based (*Second Collection*, 3–7). The emphasis is on the universal and invariant features of human nature and the human good. But modern inquiry is empirical, specialized, and historically minded. It treats human existence concretely, as situated in a particular society or culture, at a particular stage of personal or cultural development, and though capable of self-transcendence also subject to ideology and bias. Just as modern anthropological thinking is concrete and specialized, so is the modern study of the good in its many interrelated dimensions. The most important judgments of ethics concern what this particular person, community, or institution ought to do and avoid here and now (*Method*, 36, 366).

Clearly, Lonergan does not reject a transhistorical dimension of human existence. On the contrary; but he locates the universal and invariant core of humanity in his concrete transcendental principles: the unrestricted desires for knowledge and value, the invariant normative structure of human knowing, deciding, and doing, the constitutive norms that govern the authentic unfolding of intentional consciousness, the multiple biases that subvert the human quest for self-transcendence. Classicists also attach great importance to principles, basing philosophy and theology upon them. They tend, however, to conceive of these principles as certain and necessary truths. For them, the principles of philosophy are metaphysical truths about being; those of sacred theology are divinely revealed truths about God. And because these classicist principles are propositional in nature, they serve as the logical basis of elaborate deductive systems.

In criticizing classicism, Lonergan argues that logical systems are inherently static, while human inquiry is dynamic, progressive, and cumulative. The foundational principles of inquiry must exist at a deeper level than logical concepts and propositions (*Method*, 94–96, 304–5). They must be the originating sources of all intellectual and moral development and of the relevant judgments of fact and value in which that development expresses itself. While the logical principles favored by classicism are abstract and immutable, Lonergan's transcendental principles are concrete, dynamic, and critical (CWL, 17:201–2). Thus, they are able to serve as the foundational ground for an ongoing series of theoretical systems of increasing complexity and scope.

The reign of classicism in Catholic philosophy and theology was undermined by critical history and disciplinary specialization (*Method*, 281, 326; CWL, 17:283–84). Critical historians, like the European advocates of *ressourcement*, revealed the plurality of interpretive contexts in which philosophical and theological statements were made. Although these diverse cultural contexts can be intelligibly related, this synoptic connection cannot be accomplished by logical inferences. Nor can logical operations coherently integrate the discourse of the autonomous sciences into a single comprehensive system.

If the integrative aspirations of Catholic philosophy are to be met, Catholic thinkers, following Lonergan's lead, must shift their heuristic approach from logic to method. Concretely, this means beginning philosophy with cognitional theory, proceeding from there to epistemology and metaphysics, then advancing to existential ethics and the question of God. In theology, it means abandoning the quest for certainty and impersonal proofs of God's existence, and focusing instead on the intellectual, moral, and religious conversions of the theological inquirer.

If the existential foundations of contemporary philosophy must become concrete transcendental principles, like the intentional principles discovered, articulated, and verified by Lonergan, then what about the existential foundations of Christian theology? Since Lonergan believes that theology *sublates* philosophy, he augments his intellectual and moral principles with a more profound religious conversion to the wholehearted love of God and neighbor. Only the theologian's authentic response to the gift of God's love can create the personal horizon within which Christian doctrines and creeds are experienced as meaningful and true. In Lonergan's existential approach to theology, the personal conversions of the believer, not demonstrative proof, are the heart of the matter.

Although Lonergan insists that classicism was never more than "the shabby cultural shell" of Catholicism, its hold on Catholic scholarship and thought was considerable. Even now, the great majority of Catholics underestimate the formidable distance separating classicist assumptions from the intellectual culture of modernity. For that reason, Lonergan repeatedly emphasized the "mountainous tasks" and "Herculean labors" confronting Catholics as they struggled to master the highest theoretical and practical achievements of their time (CWL, 4:244–45; *Second Collection*, 44).

Critical *Aggiornamento*

Our disengagement from classicism and our involvement
in modernity must be open-eyed, critical, coherent and
sure footed . . . we have to take the trouble, and it is enormous,
to grasp the strength and the weakness, the power and
the limitations, the good points and the shortcomings
of both classicism and modernity.
—Second Collection, 98–99

All things human exist under the sign of contradiction. This sober and justified warning applies even to the belated Catholic struggle for reform and renewal. Given the scope and difficulty of *aggiornamento*, its actual unfolding could be expected to yield unintended results. Although Lonergan recognized the profound urgency of change in the church, he was not unaware of its dangers. For him, the most important question remained unresolved: would the needed Catholic renewal be comprehensive, critical, and deep?

In several different contexts, Lonergan outlined what critical *aggiornamento* required:[35] an assimilation of what is genuinely new in the cultural superstructure and infrastructure, in continuity with what is permanently valid in the Catholic tradition; an evenhanded dialectical appraisal of the merits and limitations of the traditional and the modern; such an appraisal demands disengagement from the limits of the old (*vetera*) and critical appropriation of the tangled knot of the new (*nova*). While classicists sought to create a dam to block the stream of modernity, Lonergan wanted to establish critical control of the underlying riverbed (*Second Collection*, 52). But how can such critical cultural control be effectively achieved?

It will be the work not of a single individual but of a well-prepared collaborative group. Lonergan referred to this imagined community of thinkers and scholars as the "not too numerous center" (CWL, 4:244). As he memorably predicted, in times of great cultural transition there is bound to emerge a classicist right determined to live in a culture and world that no longer exists. There is also bound to be formed a scattered left, sporadically attracted to a changing succession of cultural fashions and novelties. What the church urgently needed was something totally different: an emerging center of scientists, scholars, philosophers, theologians, and citizens critically at home in the old and the new, fully committed to intellectual integrity and excellence, historically minded, expertly trained, radically open to the intellectual, moral, and religious conversions that human authenticity requires.

Lonergan did not believe that the message and mission of the church were open to radical change. The gospel message could be deepened and clarified; the redemptive mission could be lived more authentically. But the cultural changes of modernity did not bring a new revelation, a new gospel, a new faith to supplant the revelation of Christ (*Second Collection*, 196; CWL, 4:244). Nor did they alter the obligation of Christians to bear witness to the good news of God's redemptive presence among us. Today, that obligatory witness means communicating the gospel as persuasively to the modern world as Paul did to the world of antiquity and as Thomas did in medieval Paris. Though the Word of God is "ever ancient and ever new," the historical cultures that receive or reject it are markedly different. For Catholic theologians to mediate the Christian faith to contemporary cultures effectively, they must profoundly understand both the substance of that faith and the spiritual complexity of those cultures (*Method*, 362).

To understand the substance of the faith requires critically appropriating a significant stratum of the *vetera*: the Hebrew scriptures, the New Testament texts, the patristic writings, the conciliar tradition, Scholastic theology, the complex history of Christian doctrine and systematics. To understand the complexity of contemporary culture requires critically appropriating the *nova*: the new theoretical superstructure, the corresponding practical infrastructure, the multiple differentiations of consciousness and language, the plurality of empirical methods and heuristic structures, the different realms and stages of meaning, the global commitment to political and religious liberty, the demand for personal and communal authenticity, the critical acceptance of cultural and religious pluralism.

The dialectical character of authenticity explains why almost any aspect of religion can be matched by its spiritual opposite: peace and violence, love and fear, liberty and coercion, humility and pride, holiness and sin (CWL, 17:44–45). The credibility of all religious traditions and communities is threatened by a "massive undertow of inauthenticity" (*Third Collection*, 121). Catholic Christianity is hardly an exception to this historical rule. But Lonergan insists that the remedy for inauthentic religion is to cure the inauthenticity, not to reject the religion (*Third Collection*, 122). Christianity has nothing to lose and everything to gain from contrite acknowledgment of its grave errors and sins. Genuine repentance is the beginning of all serious reform. The church cannot credibly criticize the mote in its brother's eye and neglect the beam in its own. This prophetic warning applies with special force to the church in modernity whose fear and defensiveness alienated both Catholic clergy and laity from the leading developments of their time.

Still, there are many ways to be inauthentic. While religious conservatives struggle to assimilate the new, progressive reformers risk undermining what is valid in the old. Lacking critical discernment and judgment, they can devalue or dilute the received tradition, while swallowing the new, warts and all. Critical appropriation of the *vetera* and *nova* takes time, patience, generosity, and an ongoing collaborative effort among the converted. There is no sure and easy path to critical *aggiornamento*. Under the heady banner of renewal, the Catholic faith can be watered down, Christian doctrines devalued, the continuity of the church's teaching denied, and its moral discipline compromised or abandoned.

Thus Lonergan could write that in the dramatic turmoil created by the council and its aftermath, many Catholics became deeply uncertain about the message and mission of the church itself. Unless Catholics learned to distinguish what was vital and enduring in their faith from what was culturally transient and parochial, the long overdue process of Christian renewal might regrettably mutate from a serious cultural crisis to a far graver crisis of faith. "Sound renewal is not yet, in my opinion, a common achievement."

In the remainder of this chapter, we shall examine and appraise two of Lonergan's most important contributions to the historic project of Catholic renewal. Each contribution responds to a critical challenge posed by modernity to the enduring Catholic tradition. The expository strategy is consistent: we will articulate the specific challenge, epistemic and moral, then present Lonergan's specific dialectical response, and conclude by appraising its effectiveness. The chapter concludes with a brief personal reflection on the requirements of authentic renewal today.

Critical Reason and Religious Truth

The Catholic tradition has consistently affirmed the complementarity of faith and reason as sources of religious knowledge. Christianity began as a Semitic religious faith based on Hebrew scripture, law, and ritual, the public ministry of Jesus of Nazareth, his climactic death and resurrection, and the apostolic proclamation of the gospel throughout the Mediterranean basin. To answer the questions and challenges posed to the gospel by Jews and Gentiles alike, Christian teachers and leaders had to rise to the cultural level of their audience. The two most powerful cultures in the ancient world were Greek and Roman. Greek culture was highly intellectual, based in part on the Socratic practice of dialectical questions and answers. The Roman tradition was deeply legal and political. While they lacked the theoretical aspirations of the Greeks, the Romans were noted for their military and administrative competence.

During the five centuries after Christ's death, important Christian teachers emerged from the fruitful encounter of the gospel with both Greek intellectualism and the Roman political mentality. Enduring evidence of this fertility can be found in the writings of the great Greek and Latin fathers, who shaped the doctrines and spiritual outlook of the early church. Noteworthy among the Greek fathers were Clement, Origen, and Basil. Augustine was the greatest of the Latin fathers, and along with Saint Paul, the most influential Christian writer in classical antiquity.

A fervent convert to the Christian faith, Augustine wanted deeply to understand the substance of his new religious beliefs. While he affirmed the causal priority of faith to reason (*crede ut intelligas*), his intellectual passion to understand what he believed was nearly equal to his passion for God. In the eleventh century, the Benedictine monk Anselm actively renewed the Augustinian tradition of faith seeking understanding, *fides quaerens intellectum*. For Anselm, rational argument is not a substitute for religious faith, but a way to articulate its meaning and truth. As he says in a deeply personal prayer to God, "Help me to understand that thou art what I already believe that thou art."[36]

At the height of medieval scholastic theology, Thomas Aquinas carefully distinguished the different sources of religious knowledge. Natural reason, unaided by faith, could achieve knowledge of the existence and attributes of God. But unaided reason could never know the essence of God, or comprehend the revealed mysteries at the heart of Christianity: the incarnation and resurrection of Christ, the redemption and sanctification of the world, the Trinitarian nature of God. Thus, Aquinas carefully distinguished the rational truths knowable by philosophy from the revealed truths known through sacred scripture, the Christian tradition, and the conciliar teachings of the church. Although Aquinas distinguished natural philosophy from sacred theology, he did not separate them, constantly relying on philosophical insights to clarify and deepen the mysteries of faith.

In the seventeenth century, the French mathematician Blaise Pascal had to overcome a somewhat different challenge. His Catholic contemporary Descartes, while not repudiating religious faith, had philosophically sought to replace it with the deductive arguments of reason. Cartesian metaphysics aspires to a philosophical demonstration of both God's existence and essence. At the same time, voluntaristic strains within Christianity had denigrated the power of reason and emphasized the sovereign inscrutability of God. Pascal was critical of both of these nominally

Christian positions.[37] Against Descartes, he argued that the radical disproportion between the infinity of God and the finitude of human reason made a clear and distinct idea of God impossible. Moreover, he insisted that true Christian faith, grounded in the humility of the believer's active love, provides a truer understanding of God than any philosophical inquiry.

Pascal's anthropology and theology are intimately connected. The truth about man and the truth about God are inseparable. The human condition, he believed, is a tangled knot of greatness and wretchedness, wretched without the love and friendship of God, great as originally created and then redeemed by Christ (*Pensées*, 75, 116, 122, 149). The mystery of God and the mystery of human knottedness are profoundly illuminated by the Christian gospel. The gospel teaches both the source of our sinful condition and the healing remedy of Christ's redemptive love. The hidden God of Pascal, the God of Abraham, Isaac, and Jacob, cannot be perceived by the senses, or understood by the ideas of proud reason. But the Christian God can be known through the heart's receptivity to love since "the heart has its reasons that reason does not know" (*Pensées*, 423, 110, 424). For Pascal, this is the essence of the Christian faith, the knowledge of God through the religious experience of the heart.[38]

Still, Pascal is both a critic and a defender of the mind. The mark of human wisdom is to know both the power and the limits of reason: when to doubt, when to assent, when to surrender the claims of reason to the knowledge of the heart. Because "tyranny is wanting to have by one means what can only be gained in some other way" (*Pensées*, 58), the reasons of the heart are no substitute for the reasons of the mind. Each human capacity has its proper scope and limitations. The chief cultural contribution of philosophy for Pascal is to demarcate the specific provinces of the several different sources of human knowledge.

As this highly compressed summary reveals, genuine witnesses to the Christian faith kept responding to the cultural challenges of history. The great Christian thinkers sought to articulate their faith at the exigent level of their time. In this way, Christian teaching evolved from the epistles of Paul to the *Pensées* of Pascal and beyond. John Henry Newman documented and affirmed this dynamic historical pattern in his seminal work, *An Essay on the Development of Christian Doctrine*.[39] Newman effectively argued for the historical unity of the Christian tradition and the evident plurality of its different cultural expressions. This was not the static unity of a logical system, but the dynamic unity of a living faith that combines a continuous kerygmatic tradition with an adaptive theological capacity for innovation and growth.

Newman's frank acceptance of the historicity of Christian doctrine ran counter to prevailing classicist assumptions. During the antimodernist period, the classicist mentality largely held sway. But, inspired by Newman's example and writing, courageous Catholic scholars began to study the concrete historical contexts in which the central texts of Christianity were written. Only with Vatican II did the richness and importance of their scholarly labors really begin to bear fruit.[40]

Modern Challenges

European confidence in the Christian faith probably reached its zenith in the era of Latin Christendom. During the High Middle Ages, the testimony of faith, reason, culture, and society appeared to converge. Christian theology was the recognized queen of the sciences, and metaphysics and logic were its willing handmaids; a common core of beliefs bound together all levels of medieval society. Seven centuries later, this collective confidence had largely disappeared. Europe had become an essentially secular continent, whose diverse populations were deeply ambivalent about their long Christian heritage. What had happened to bring this profound change about?

While the Reformation shattered the Thomistic synthesis of faith and reason, the Enlightenment changed the meaning of reason itself. Theoretical reason, according to Kant, is confined to knowledge of the phenomenal order. Although human reason desires to know what is unconditioned and transcendent, these enduring rational desires can never be satisfied. But if speculative reason cannot lead us to God, what alternate paths does Kant provide? Kant endorses a limited faith within the strict boundaries set by critical reason.[41] This is not the revealed faith of Judaism and Christianity, but a set of practical postulates, of necessary ontological beliefs, undergirding the moral requirement of personal freedom and responsibility.

The critical consciousness of the nineteenth century extended the Kantian critique of knowledge to include European history, society, politics, and the salvation narratives of the great Western religions. This intense, unsparing criticism had a destabilizing effect on Europe's institutional culture. The bourgeois family, the capitalist economy and state, the established Christian churches and the legitimating narratives that supported and justified them, were all radically challenged, especially from the cultural and political left. The new historical scholarship and biblical criticism produced unsettling results. A troubling gap ostensibly opened between the Jesus of history and the Christ of faith, between empirically verified historical facts and the traditional legends and stories so important to ordinary believers. Beyond its skeptical challenge to particular truth-claims, modern critical consciousness had a more profound cultural effect. It elevated distrust and suspicion to the status of intellectual virtues and reduced faith and belief to vices of the immature mind. As Charles Taylor has persuasively argued, educated Europeans embraced an ethics of unbelief that made doubt rather than trust the hallmark of intellectual integrity.[42]

The intellectual and moral critique of Christianity intensified with Darwinism. Evolutionary theory challenged both the scriptural account of human origins and the theological argument from created design. Could Darwinian biology be reconciled with the anthropomorphic creation narratives of Genesis? And, more comprehensively, are credible scientific theories and the divinely revealed truths of tradition intellectually compatible? With respect to the familiar argument from design, eighteenth-century thinkers had often conceived of God as the great cosmic architect. The lawful patterns of nature, the intricate beauty of natural substances, the distinctive excellences of humans were viewed as the direct result of divine craftsmanship. But the Darwinian principles of random variation, natural selection, and the biological struggle for survival told a very different story. Natural organisms, surviving species, and their sustaining environments are the products not of intelligent design, but rather of indeterminate chance and the violent and merciless struggle for existence. Intelligent purpose and rational choice do not lie at the origins of being; the world as we know it is rather the precarious, unplanned evolutionary effect of blind and impersonal processes. The critical study of nature, then, apparently leads to the denial, not the affirmation, of the biblical God.[43]

Darwin's own faith was shaken by his biological discoveries. For many of his late nineteenth-century defenders and critics, it now appeared that one must choose between science and religion, between critical reason and faith, between intellectual integrity and consoling spiritual illusion. Although there continued to be important moral and political reasons for opposing Christianity, by century's end the positivist genealogy of religious belief had become widely accepted. According to this influential cultural narrative, as the human mind developed and matured, as humanity slowly came of age, it rejected religious and metaphysical explanations of reality for exclusively scientific ones. Critical science, critical historiography, critical hermeneutics—these were the only legitimate sources of knowledge and truth. Once religion had been intellectually discredited by critical reason, it would soon become a thing of the past.[44]

Lonergan's Critical Response

As the twentieth century emphatically showed, religious believers and communities did not disappear, as their positivist critics predicted. But Christianity's hold on Western culture certainly weakened, especially in Europe. The Catholic religion belatedly came to terms with modern science and scholarship, but it lacked a convincing philosophical account of how the new learning was related to the old. Catholics continued to affirm, in principle, the compatibility of faith and reason. Classicist assumptions, however, weakened this affirmation and diminished its credibility for contemporary thinkers and scholars. The instability of the church's cultural position framed the challenge that Lonergan accepted. Could the complementarity of faith and reason be credibly reestablished at the level of our time?

Lonergan began his defense of this ancient Catholic principle by taking the anthropological turn (*Second Collection*, 276). Unlike Aristotle and Thomas, he did not base his philosophy of God on cosmology, on the study of the natural universe. He had historical reasons for adopting a strategic approach different from that of his cultural predecessors. We no longer live in the classical or medieval period, where metaphysics was accepted as the basic and universal science. But what is the legitimate epistemic mission of philosophy and theology in the third stage of meaning? Philosophy has become the intentional analysis of the polymorphic human subject. Its specialized field is the data of intentional consciousness, its defining questions are cognitional, epistemological, metaphysical, ethical, and religious (in that order). Lonergan's philosophical turn to the subject carefully balances plurality and unity, historicity and invariance. He locates the source of invariance and unity in the transcendental foundations of knowledge and action, and the source of historical plurality in the specialized differentiations of consciousness. In the course of human history, the inquiring mind develops new modes of apprehension and expression. In the modern era, theoretical science and critical scholarship developed out of premodern political and religious common sense, creating specialized communities of learning and teaching, and distinct realms of cognitive meaning. The contemporary cultural context summons philosophy and theology to a comparable methodological development, to create distinctively new patterns of differentiated consciousness. Philosophy then becomes the critical investigation of human interiority, theology, the functionally specialized study of the religious quest for divine transcendence (*Method*, 83–84, 95).

But how are philosophy and theology related in the third stage of meaning? How is human interiority related to the enduring search for God? Lonergan's answer is complex but straightforward. Theology *sublates* philosophy as religion *sublates* the whole of human living (CWL, 17:358–60). What do these terse formulas actually mean? Lonergan carefully transposes a discovery of Aquinas into our contemporary cultural context. Thomas had argued that divine grace perfects created nature, as faith perfects reason, and as charity perfects the intellectual and moral virtues. Grace does not abolish human nature but completes it, raising its performance to a level beyond nature's effective capacity. When Lonergan's philosophical anthropology heuristically shifts from the study of the soul to that of the subject, from faculty psychology to intentionality analysis, it preserves the great Thomistic discoveries in the following way. Lonergan's transcendental principles become the new dynamic core of human nature (*Third Collection*, 171–75). These principles have their own intellectual and moral integrity. They undergird the human quest for knowledge and value, they underpin the development and differentiation of human consciousness. The specialized realms of cognitive meaning have their intentional origin in these universal and invariant principles. Thus common sense, the empirical sciences, historical scholarship, philosophy, and theology, as distinct forms of knowledge, are specialized expressions and developments of the unrestricted desire to know.

Objective knowing and authentic living, however, are rare achievements. Ignorance, bias, sin, and ideology regularly undermine our intellectual and moral endeavors. They help to create the tangled knot of greatness and wretchedness that is the perennial human condition. How then does the Christian religion *sublate* this pervasive and intractable knot? It can do so in two complementary ways: the gospel *message* of divine love and redemption challenges the reigning errors of modern ideology, both conservative and progressive; the Christian *mission* of reconciliation and forgiveness, of sustained redemptive service to others, can help to dissolve the implacable hatreds and paralyzing apathy that transform fallen creation into a realm of moral impotence and sin (CWL, 3:740–50).

As divine grace does not abolish human nature, so it does not abolish personal and public liberty. How we respond to Christ's message of redemption when we listen to the gospel, and to the Christian mission of reconciliation, when we see it in action, is a matter of personal choice.[45] Familiar images of the divine notwithstanding, the Christian God is never coercive, never a tyrant, but always a true friend of liberty.[46] The same, of course, can hardly be said of the many clerics and churches claiming to speak and act in God's name. The religious sublation of concrete human living is neither magical nor mythical. Rather, it is the free, daily, uncertain, and mysterious cooperation of God with sinners in the hard work of redeeming the world.

If religion sublates human living through the redemptive power of grace, how does theology, in turn, effectively sublate philosophy? Contemporary philosophy acknowledges two distinct sources and directions of intentional development: development from below, through the normative unfolding of the core transcendental desires; and development from above, through the intentional subject's continuing education in the home, society, schools, and culture to which he or she belongs (*Second Collection*, 87–99; *Method*, 41–47; CWL, 3:725–40). In this educational context, culture refers both to the practical infrastructure of family, state, and civil society (including the relevant religious communities), and the theoretical superstructure of mathematics, the natural and human sciences, historical scholarship, philosophy, and theology.

The earliest forms of education rely on precritical belief.[47] Children and developing adults precritically embrace the lessons communicated by their teachers. They largely accept the truth of what they are taught before they can understand its meaning or examine the relevant evidence advanced in its support. As they mature intellectually, they can abandon or modify some of their earlier beliefs, but at no stage of learning can they fully dispense with them. Therefore, it needs to be stated clearly and unapologetically that the intellectual growth of the person and of the cultural community, both theoretical and practical, essentially depends on the transmission of belief and cannot occur without it.

Modern assertions of intellectual and moral autonomy tend, therefore, to be greatly inflated. While every young person is capable of independently generated knowledge, most of what we claim to know is based on belief: on what we have read, heard, or learned through communication with others. This lifelong dependence on trust and belief is not an intellectual weakness, but clear evidence of the collaborative nature of human learning and teaching. The point is not that doubt, suspicion, and distrust are never justified. They often are. But suspicion and doubt can never be the fundamental stance of the mind seeking knowledge of reality. Our apprehension of reality is always mediated by cognitive meaning, and the core of that meaning is composed of beliefs we accept on the testimony of others, living and dead.

Now our beliefs, of course, can be mistaken. And our teachers vary greatly in their epistemic authority and competence. Human learning is a self-correcting process, permeated, from beginning to end, with fallibility. But if the reliance on belief shapes every realm of cognitive meaning, from common sense to the highest levels of theoretical inquiry, then in what sense are science, scholarship, and philosophy more critical than ordinary practical reasoning? The relevant difference is the common reliance of the superstructural disciplines on generalized empirical method.

The modern theoretical superstructure depends on specialized methods that critically control the acceptance and transmission of belief. The methods of empirical science require all hypotheses to be verified, both directly by the relevant available evidence and indirectly by the systemic role of those hypotheses in the continuing scientific enterprise (*Second Collection*, 89). The methods of critical scholarship require: the certification of historical data in their linguistic and nonlinguistic forms; independent interpretations by trained scholars of the original meaning of those data; contrasting genealogical accounts of the relevant social and cultural contexts in which those data emerged; a critical dialectical process, conducted within the scholarly community, to distinguish better and worse instances of research, interpretation, and genealogical history.[48]

Perhaps Lonergan's deepest intellectual challenge was to devise analogous critical methods for contemporary philosophy and theology. In the case of philosophy, his practice of dialectical criticism depends on empirical data and evidence drawn from the subject's intentional consciousness. The basic dialectical distinction is between philosophical positions and counterpositions. Philosophical positions, because they are faithful to the facts of our intellectual and moral development, invite further expansion; while the counterpositions, because they omit or distort important aspects of intentional consciousness, invite reversal or amendment upon further critical reflection (CWL, 3:410–15).

But where does Lonergan's philosophical dialectic leave the practice of contemporary theology? How can it be transformed into an empirical and critical discipline at the exigent level of our time? And how does the human knowledge of God depend on intellectual, moral, and religious development from below and above? In approaching the study of God from below, Lonergan starts with the developing intentional subject. Like Augustine and Pascal, he believes that the philosophical path to God begins in human interiority. It is profound self-knowledge that leads philosophically to knowledge of the divine (*Method*, 101–5). Because our core transcendental desires are intentional, they are cognitively correlated with transcendental concepts that articulate what those several ascending desires actually intend: the intelligible, the real, the intrinsically good (*Method*, 11–12). Because these foundational desires are unrestricted in aspiration, the intelligibility, reality, and goodness they intend is equally unlimited. The contemporary question of God arises philosophically from unflinching reflection on these unrestricted desires and their specific intentional correlates. Is there an intelligent and reasonable ground of the comprehensive universe of being? Is there an originating source of the entire universe of value whose wisdom and goodness are radically beyond criticism (*Method*, 101–3)?

Lonergan insists that once we fully acknowledge the transcendental principles (desires, norms, and methods) in ourselves and reflect on their ontological and moral implications, we cannot authentically avoid "the question of God." To refuse that question is clearly obscurantist, because it inescapably arises from radical reflection on our own intelligence, reasonableness, freedom, and moral responsibility. But to raise religious questions is one thing, to answer them persuasively quite another.

Lonergan's affirmative answers to the several forms of the "question of God" are premised on convictions his skeptical opponents are loath to accept.[49] In what sense is the proportionate universe of being completely intelligible, and why does its comprehensive intelligibility require a transcendent intelligent ground? Is the ontological goodness of the universe really compatible with the existence of evil, both the natural evil of pervasive death and destruction, and the moral evil of deliberate violence and sin? In chapter 19 of *Insight*, Lonergan argued for the complete intelligibility of being and for a supremely intelligent creative ground of the universe. In chapters 18 and 20, he argued for the ontological goodness of being, without avoiding or denying the existence of evil (CWL, 3:628–30). In the final chapter of *Insight*, he heuristically appealed to the good news of Christianity, to the historic message and mission of Jesus proclaiming God's unlimited love for creation and God's redemptive response in Christ and the Spirit to the reality of sin and its consequences.

Insight, as Lonergan emphasized, is written from a moving viewpoint. The first eighteen chapters are intended to mediate the very difficult intellectual and moral conversions of the dedicated reader. Unless those conversions transform the interior outlook and horizon of the existential subject, Lonergan later acknowledged, religious skeptics would find the concluding arguments of *Insight* unpersuasive. In *Method in Theology*, Lonergan is completely explicit about the existential priority of personal conversion to logical argument in the acceptance or rejection of God (*Method*, 337–38).

It is not that Lonergan rejects the importance of critical argument in philosophical theology. He clearly does not. But he's now profoundly aware of the contrasting ontological and moral horizons of converted and unconverted subjects, and of the existential resistance of the unconverted to the philosophical arguments *Insight* employs. *Method* adds a further dimension that is lacking in *Insight*, the great importance of religious experience (*Method*, 105–9). The recurring emphasis in *Insight* is on the unrestricted desires for knowledge and value and their profound ontological and moral implications for the question of God. *Method* preserves Lonergan's original emphasis, but couples it with a Pascalian insight into the vital role of the heart in religious knowledge (*Method*, 115).

At least four distinct forms of religious love are acknowledged in *Method*: the unrestricted *eros* of the mind for knowledge of God; the equally unrestricted moral *eros* for God as the *arche* and *telos* of creation; the filial love of the faithful for their fellow believers and neighbors, both close and far off; the unrestricted gift of God's love (*agape* or *caritas*) that is freely given to all human beings (*Method*, 104–8). The constitutive transcendental desires create an intellectual and moral longing for God. Religious fellowship draws the people of God closer together in their common faith and practice. But it is *agape* or *caritas*, God's free and unrestricted gift, that is the core of religious experience. For Lonergan, this is not a direct experience of God, but rather a personal experience of God's immanent grace, God's gift of divine love freely given to all.

Phenomenologically, the subject experiences this gift as an unconditional love for a mysterious and unknown beloved. Initially, religious experience occurs at the level of empirical consciousness, but like all human experience it can be questioned and better understood. The fruits of that understanding can then be reasonably affirmed and its moral implications freely embraced. In this way, the religious experience of grace can gradually develop into a wholehearted love of God and creation in which authentic subjects love God above all created things and their neighbors as themselves. The twofold law of love at the core of Judaism and Christianity has its experiential origin and developing pattern in the basic phenomenon of religious conversion.

Like the intellectual and moral conversions that complement it, religious conversion radically transforms the horizon of the developing subject. A new, even more radical existential principle now orients the person's intentional life. For *agape* or *caritas* sublates both *eros* and *philia*, respecting their dynamic integrity, while perfecting and completing their recurrent operations and periodic achievements. Faith is the religious knowledge born of an authentic human response to God's gift of *agape* (*Method*, 115–18). It is the heart's knowledge of God to which Pascal referred. In the light of religious faith, the created universe, all of nature and history, the knot of human existence, the whole of proportionate being, are seen in a new way. For persons of faith, all things, except bias, sin, ideology, and their consequences, originate in divine love and are intended to return eventually, in their own time and manner, to the loving God who created and redeemed them.

In *Method*, religious experience becomes a central part of the philosophical quest for God. The interior path to divine transcendence draws not only on the transcendental principles of created nature and the fellowship of religious and human solidarity, but on the sublating grace of *agape* and the unconditional love of God to which it can lead. Religious conversion is the highest form of human self-transcendence, perfecting, healing, and grounding its epistemic and moral counterparts. Because grace sublates nature, and faith sublates reason, and *agape* sublates our deepest beliefs and moral convictions, the God of the philosophers and the God of religious experience are not two distinct Gods but one, though known in different but complementary ways. The human mind and heart may take different paths to God, but when their progress is authentic, they arrive at a common transcendent reality (*Method*, 115; CWL, 17:171).

Lonergan's philosophical theology clearly distinguishes but does not separate nature and grace, faith and reason, charity and human authenticity. It is a critical dialectical theology based on developing the full implications of the subject's intentional experience, intellectual, moral, and religious. Conceived and articulated in several complementary stages of existential development, it illuminates and clarifies the arduous and dynamic path to knowledge of God from below.

Let us now turn to Lonergan's account of the paths to God that develop from above. In what sense can sacred or revealed theology be an empirical and critical discipline? The highest source of all human development is God's unconditional love for creation. That love creates and sustains the whole of proportionate being as its eternal *arche* and ground. But the God of creation is also the God of history and historical revelation. The Hebrew scriptures commemorate God's historical engagement with the people of Israel, beginning in the covenant with Abraham and his descendants; sustained in the exodus from Egypt and the gift of the law to Moses; deepened and clarified in the teaching of the prophets. The God of Israel, of Abraham, Isaac, and Jacob, is a God of self-disclosure and fidelity, a God who never abandons his people however often they sin and turn away.

Christian scripture clearly builds on Israel's deep understanding of history. Faithful Christians believe that the supreme revelation of God's love occurs in the incarnation, in the historical reality of the divine Word made flesh. In the life, ministry, death, and resurrection of Jesus of Nazareth, the depth of God's love is most fully revealed. Jesus not only redeemed the whole of fallen creation, but he called his disciples to participate in this ongoing redemptive work. As noted at the beginning of this chapter, Christian redemption has the related dimensions of message and mission (*Second Collection*, 18–19, 244–61). Christians are called to proclaim Christ's message, the good news of the gospel, to every people and culture in history. They are also summoned to Christ's redemptive ministry of active love: to feed the hungry, heal the sick and disheartened, liberate captives, and create communities of service that can minister effectively to a broken and violent world. The Christian message and mission are mutually supporting, for the message gives meaning and purpose to the mission; and the mission when authentically lived provides the most powerful witness to the truth of the message.

The death of Christ did not end God's presence in the apostolic community. For the Spirit of God then descended on Jesus' disciples, fortifying their faith, strengthening their courage, sustaining their evangelical mission. Thus Jesus' frightened, often cowardly band brought the message of the gospel to the Mediterranean world, to Jews and Gentiles alike. As the Christian community developed, it confessed its resurrection faith and recorded its apostolic daring in the four canonical gospels, the epistles of Paul and his early Christian comrades, and in the testimony of Acts. As the gospel did not abolish the law and the prophets, so the New Testament did not abolish but built on the Old. Both Hebrew and Christian scripture record the saving actions of God in the dramatic life of God's people. But now the people of God explicitly include the whole human community, stretching from Jerusalem through Athens to Rome, and eventually to the ends of the earth.

As Christian teachers and leaders proclaimed the gospel to the diverse peoples and cultures of the Mediterranean world, they had to address the critical challenges and reservations of their non-Christian peers. Thus different gospels and epistles were written for different audiences, with different concerns about the credibility of Christ's life and teaching. For this reason, the history of Christianity is inseparable from the compositional history of sacred scripture and the subsequent development of the Christian teaching tradition. As Newman effectively argued, that tradition remains genuinely alive, and that means responsive to the cultural changes that transform human history. It is a tradition marked by continuity and innovation, as it evolves from the early evangelists through the Greek and Latin fathers, though the doctrinal councils of Nicea, Chalcedon, Ephesus, and Constantinople, through the writings of Augustine and Anselm, through the emergence of systematic theology in the High Middle Ages, through the rise in modernity of critical historiography and hermeneutics, provisionally culminating in the public documents and teaching of the Second Vatican Council.[50]

In its long, complex, and difficult history, the church has struggled to remain faithful to the supreme revelation in Christ, to the spirit and content of his original teaching, to the doctrinal developments in Christology and Trinitarian theology, to the dialectical insights of its great theologians, from Saint Paul to Cardinal Newman. But who is to decide on the authenticity and fidelity of the teaching and conduct of the church? When is needed continuity unwisely broken, when does apparent innovation constitute actual decline? There are no easy answers to these critical questions that have challenged Christianity from its inception. The answers of "classicism" are clearly not viable, for there is no simple logical test of the coherence and consistency of developing Christian doctrine. What alternative strategy does Lonergan propose?[51]

He draws on the cognitional insights of philosophy, the disciplinary methods of critical history and hermeneutics, and the transformative effects of the three existential conversions. The relevant philosophical discoveries concern different levels of religious understanding and diverse modes of religious expression and practice (*Method*, 114). The continuity of the tradition rests on the claim that the authentic Christian message can be faithfully understood and expressed at distinct cultural levels and in radically different cultural contexts. Within the New Testament itself, the symbolic narratives of the synoptic gospels are importantly different from the Gospel of John. And all four of the gospels differ significantly from Paul's epistolary reflections on the meaning of Christ's death and resurrection, while the apocalyptic imagery and rhetoric of the book of Revelation constitute a distinct scriptural genre of its own.

Both the Christian religion and Christian theology are deeply historical. As the followers of Christ pursue the work of redemption in time, they adapt, more or less authentically, to the societal and cultural changes and challenges they meet. These adaptations affect their modes of worship and prayer, their homiletic practices, their forms of education and governance, their ecumenical relations with Christians and non-Christians, their personal and collective engagement in the corporal and spiritual works of mercy. Christian theology is inescapably grounded in the dynamic history of the Christian religion. Its purpose is to mediate that religion, to communicate its meaning, value, and redemptive mission, to the diverse cultural contexts where Christianity is practiced and preached. As an intellectual discipline, Christian theology attempts to answer the questions, criticisms, and challenges that Christian preaching and practice evoke. To do this effectively, contemporary theologians must profoundly understand two interdependent historical realities: the internal complexity of the Christian religion; the institutional and cultural complexity of the societies where the gospel has been proclaimed and lived.

Just as the philosophy of God must adapt to the exigent demands of the third stage of cognitive meaning, so must Christian theology. Lonergan's *Method in Theology* is his chief contribution to the imperative of cultural adaptation. If Catholic theology is to become an empirical and critical discipline at the demanding level of our time, Lonergan believes it must become functionally specialized (*Method*, 124–25). To this end, Lonergan identifies eight functional specialties that take theologians on both an upward and a downward path through the history of the Christian religion (*Method*, 144–45). The upward path, designated as *mediating* theology, critically appropriates the *vetera*, the changing linguistic and nonlinguistic expressions of the Christian faith. These historical expressions include Hebrew and Christian scripture and tradition, Christian prayer, teaching, and liturgical rites, as well as the practical engagement of Christians at all levels of society and culture.[52]

The downward path, designated as *mediated* theology, deliberately advances from indirect discourse about the Christian past to direct discourse about the Christian message and mission today.[53] On the upward path of research, interpretation, history, and dialectics, contemporary scholars seek to identify, understand, and appraise the diverse expressions of Christian witness in history.[54]

The functional specialty *research* authenticates the empirical data that bear on the Christian religion. These historical expressions of Christian witness to the gospel include both words and deeds. The words can be either spoken or written; the deeds comprise what Christians did or suffered on behalf of their faith. Although Lonergan pays special attention to textual research, to corroborating the written testimony to Christian belief and practice, he recognizes that the history of Christian witness is far more extensive than the words written on or about the Christian religion (CWL, 17:404–8).

General research includes every form of discernible witness that is relevant to a comprehensive understanding of the Christian message and mission. Special research is confined to the relevant data on specific aspects of Christian history, like the history of doctrine, the liturgical history of the Mass and the sacraments, or the history of changing patterns of church governance.

Interpretation seeks deepening insight into the meaning of the relevant data assembled by the functional specialty *research*. It seeks to clarify and articulate what these data signify about Christian belief and practice through the ages. The scholarly exegesis of Hebrew and Christian texts, scriptural, interpretive, and doctrinal, is an important part of theological interpretation. Lonergan identifies four essential requirements of critical textual exegesis (*Method*, 155–73): linguistic competence in the original language(s) in which the text is written; sympathetic and nuanced understanding of the original meaning of the text for its author(s); developing knowledge on the part of the scholarly interpreter of the actual realities to which the text refers; the fallible interpreter's critical grasp of the limits of her own competence, understanding, and knowledge with respect to the preceding requirements.

Because the meaning of a spoken or written utterance is always relative to its particular discursive context, and because religious contexts develop and decline, statements that were *true* in their original context may no longer be *adequate* or sufficiently responsive to the challenges of a later, more developed cultural situation (CWL, 17:75–77, 93–95).

Historical narratives of the Christian past unfold on three levels. The first level concerns what actually happened within the many different Christian communities. The second level concerns the institutional and cultural histories of the many different societies where the Christian message was practiced and preached. The third level concerns the dramatic encounters between Christianity in its internally diverse expressions and conduct, and these very different societies and cultures. At all three levels, critical historiography seeks to determine the most important figures, events, movements, and institutional and cultural changes that shaped the Christian religion through its two-thousand-year history.

Although the eight functional specialties have distinct epistemic tasks to perform, their provisional conclusions are clearly interdependent. There is a particularly close connection between the specialized discoveries of *interpretation* and *history*. Every credible narrative of Christian history depends on the narrator's profound understanding of the Christian message and mission, while credible interpretations of the actual meaning and importance of Christian witness rely heavily on historical knowledge of the different contexts in which that witness originally occurred.

The fourth functional specialty, *dialectic*, explicitly acknowledges religious and theological differences, seeks their grounds in the polymorphism of intentional consciousness, and carefully distinguishes reconcilable from irreconcilable conflicts. Not all religious and theological differences are dialectical. Religious differences, as with other forms of cultural pluralism, may be complementary, genetic, or radical, depending on the fidelity or infidelity of their witness to the complex reality of the Christian faith (*Method*, 271–76; CWL, 17:70–104).

Complementary forms of Christian witness correspond to significant cultural differences at the level of religious common sense. Genetic differences correspond to successive levels of intellectual and epistemic development in the diverse audiences transmitting and receiving the Christian message. Radical differences correspond to irreconcilable conflicts of intentional standpoint and horizon among the functional specialists themselves. These differences manifest themselves in antithetical positions and counterpositions regarding the specific content of the Christian message and mission. They involve fundamental disputes about what Christ and his historical followers said and did, about what particular Christian words and deeds actually meant, about the factual and evaluative appraisal of the long Christian past. At the root of these dialectical differences is the presence or absence of existential *conversion* among real and nominal Christians and among the theological scholars who study and appraise the uneven record that Christians have historically created (*Method*, 130–31).

While the functional specialty *dialectic* can clarify religious and theological differences and conflicts, it cannot, by itself, resolve them. *Dialectic* reveals how complex and diverse the Christian *vetera* and *nova* really are and how differently they are understood and appraised by contemporary scholars. But *mediating* theology, important as it is to our knowledge and appraisal of Christian history, only serves as prologue to *mediated* theology in which living theologians decide where they personally stand on the truth, meaning, and importance of Christian belief and on the value of a distinctively Christian way of life (*Method*, 267).

Both *mediating* and *mediated* theology are intelligibly structured by Lonergan's basic philosophical discoveries. The successive levels of transcendental method originate in the data of experience, advance through intellectual inquiry, understanding, and articulation, proceed to reflective inquiry and factual judgment, and culminate in deliberative inquiry, evaluative appraisal, and personal or communal choice. *Mediating* theology reflects this normative and dynamic structure in its orderly progression from *research* (the level of experience), to *interpretation* (the level of understanding), *history* (the level of critical judgment), and *dialectic* (the level of evaluation and choice). In *mediated* theology, which constitutes theological development from above, the transcendental order is explicitly reversed. It begins with *foundations* (fundamental evaluation and choice), proceeds to *doctrines* (explicit judgments of truth and error), advances to *systematics* (the fruitful understanding of affirmed doctrines), and culminates in *communications* that thoughtfully share the spiritual fruits of the other functional specialties with the different cultures and contexts of our time. In *mediated* theology, contemporary theologians address the present and future in the light of their critical appropriation of the past (*Method*, 143–45).[55] This is the precise philosophical path Lonergan himself followed in his personal transition from *Verbum* to *Insight* and *Method*.

The functional specialty *foundations* critically distinguishes the intentional perspectives and horizons of converted and unconverted theological specialists. For intellectually and morally converted subjects, their intentional horizons of being and value are heuristically unrestricted and radically open to divine transcendence. Religious conversion transforms this radical epistemic and moral openness into the wholehearted love of God and neighbor. Distinctively Christian conversion deepens that religious openness and love by deliberately accepting God's supreme revelation in Christ, the gifts of the Holy Spirit, and the redemptive historical mission with which Christ charged his original disciples.

Because all forms of conversion are transformative, because they radically enlarge the intentional horizon of the subject, their concrete unfolding is prolonged, dynamic, and difficult. Thus, we need carefully to distinguish conversions as initially and imperfectly lived, as progressively deepened through time, and as articulately thematized and personally affirmed. The functional specialty *foundations* thematizes and affirms the three levels of mature self-transcendence, but with a special ecumenical emphasis on religious conversion (in which specifically Christian conversion then becomes a special case). For purposes of expository economy, we'll focus for now on that special case.

The genuinely converted Christian has made an existential decision to trust in Christ and in the religious community Christ established on earth. That foundational trust existentially supports a related decision to believe what Christ revealed about God and God's purposes in history. Concretely, this means accepting the divine mysteries Christ lived and taught upon earth, mysteries then communicated through the ages within the Christian tradition. It is on the basis of religious and distinctively Christian conversion that Christian believers and Christian theologians accept the authority of Christ as the incarnate expression of God's supreme authority and accept the teaching authority of the church as the religious community to which Christ entrusted his unique revelation.

While the functional specialty *dialectic* can trace religious and theological conflicts to their existential roots, it cannot critically resolve them without the theologian's intellectual, moral, and religious conversion (*Method*, 248; CWL, 17:145–47). To distinguish authentic from inauthentic Christian witness, cultural from specifically religious differences, and distinct but complementary levels of religious apprehension and expression, we must first achieve and sustain religious, moral, and intellectual self-transcendence. Thus the three personally appropriated conversions, the defining content of *foundational theology*, provide the critical theological basis for credibly responding to religious pluralism, preserving the continuity of faith under the challenge of historical innovation, and grasping the singular importance of authenticity at every level of Christian life and thought.

The functional specialty *doctrines* affirms what has been believed, taught, and confessed by the Christian community in history.[56] The Christian acceptance and affirmation of theological doctrines are rooted in religious conversion, in the faith-based decisions made at the level of *foundations* (*Method*, chap. 12). At the core of these decisions are several profoundly personal convictions: that God speaks to his people in history through divine revelation; that Jesus Christ is the authoritative source for revealed truths about God and God's presence and purpose in time; that the mysteries historically revealed by Christ are hidden from unaided reason; that we accept the revealed content of these mysteries as true without fully understanding their meaning. In this respect the truths of the Christian faith and the truths discovered by created reason are markedly different. In the case of reason, the developing understanding of formal terms of meaning and critical reflection on their truth precede the exercise of rational judgment; in the case of the Christian faith, the personal acceptance of Christ as God and trust in the revelatory power of his word precede the developed understanding of what his words actually meant.

Among the related convictions that flow from the dynamism of Christian conversion are these: that church doctrines develop historically from New Testament confessions of faith through the later doctrinal decrees on Christ and the Trinity proclaimed by the early Christian councils; that subsequent theological doctrines generally go beyond the formulations of scripture and tradition because they address new cultural questions and challenges whose primary purpose is to meet the questions of the day for the people of the day at the level of their time; that Christian *religious* and *moral* doctrines (what to believe about God and the church Christ established; how to live and act as authentic Christians situated in history), though distinct, are interrelated. Both religious and moral doctrines are based on the authority of Christ, his teachings about God, and the concrete moral and practical implications of the two great commandments of love.[57]

Though Christian doctrine clearly develops historically, earlier valid doctrinal achievements retain their enduring authority. In this respect, the evolving Christian tradition combines genuine continuity with Christ's supreme revelation and innovative and timely responses to later historical and cultural challenges.[58] What is permanently valid in earlier doctrinal claims is their substantive meaning and truth, not the contingent verbal formulas in which they were originally expressed (*Method,* 323). Not only are there developing doctrines of faith and morality, there are also meta-level doctrines about the epistemic and ontological status of Christian doctrines as such (*Method,* 295–98). Thus, first-order doctrines affirm ontological truths about God, Christ, the church, and the sacraments; while specifically second-order doctrines affirm metalevel truths about what Christian doctrines are, why they are believed, who is authorized to proclaim and preserve them, and how they develop without invalidating earlier doctrinal achievements.

Although doctrinal beliefs are personally accepted on the basis of faith, mature Christians, in the spirit of Paul, Augustine, Anselm, Aquinas, and Pascal, seek to understand the realities in which they believe (*fides quaerens intellectum*). The functional specialty *systematics* promotes a fruitful understanding in the believing community of the mysteries of faith, of the revealed truths publicly taught and affirmed in the doctrines of the church (*Method,* chap. 13). By thoughtfully engaging in *systematics,* the faithful theologian is seeking three important intellectual goods: a partial understanding of the divine mysteries on the basis of the relevant created analogies, particularly spiritual analogies drawn from the discoveries of intentionality analysis; the intellectual and moral coherence of the various doctrines taught by the church through the ages (the systematic theologian seeks to establish the intelligible continuity of the church's old and new teaching); the intellectual and moral coherence of revealed truths about God with the full spectrum of factual and evaluative knowledge achieved through the specialized applications of transcendental method. It must be emphasized that *systematics,* a deeply intellectual theological discipline, is ultimately grounded in religious conversion, in personal faith, in the theologian's loving orientation to the transcendent mystery of God whose reality surpasses all understanding (*Method,* 350).[59]

The vast majority of Christians are not religious scholars or theologians. They lack specialized knowledge of the *vetera* and the *nova* and the epistemic competence to resolve most dialectical conflicts. But they are universally called to religious conversion and existentially oriented, to varying degrees, by the transcendental principles constitutive of human subjectivity. On the basis of their common faith, they assent to the doctrines of the church, which they publicly confess in their prayers and their creeds. As intellectual and moral beings, they seek to understand the content and implications of their Christian beliefs as well as they can. What relevance do the functional specialties of theology have for them in their daily lives as genuine Christian believers?

Theological inquiry bears genuine fruit for the entire Christian community in the functional specialty *communications* (*Method*, chap. 14). It is through communications that the leaders, teachers, thinkers, and pastors of the church address the hearts and minds of contemporary Christians, members of other religious communities, as well as an extremely diverse range of agnostics and atheists. All Christians have an enduring personal responsibility to preach the gospel in word and deed, to live the gospel in their personal and communal existence, and to practice the gospel, to make it effective, in every sphere of society and culture. Profoundly informed by the spiritual fruits of both mediating and mediated theology, Christian communications proclaim Christ's message and mission anew for the diverse peoples and cultures of our time.

To be effective and credible, Christian communications must take full account of all who hear and receive the Christian message. It must be sensitive and responsive to their relevant commonsense differences, their varying levels of education and understanding, their multiple differentiations of consciousness, their progress (or lack of progress) in self-appropriation, as well as the exigent practical demands of contemporary ministry and service, particularly at the regional, national, and international levels where it occurs.[60] Faithful to the developing Christian message, drawing on the full spectrum of human achievement, sensitive to the distorting effects of bias and sin on every human initiative, grateful for the redemptive power of grace, specialists in Christian communications summon every person to the highest levels of authenticity in their knowing, living, and service. And because all genuine communication is reciprocal, the church, the pilgrim people of God in history, must listen as well as speak, learn as well as teach, deferring to the wisdom, knowledge, and experience of others when her own resources are lacking or insufficient.[61]

Four final points need to be made before concluding this section on developing and transmitting religious knowledge. Although there are eight theological specialties, each with its distinctive epistemic task, their methodological unity should also be emphasized. In each functional specialty, genuine progress is achieved only through the theologian's fidelity to transcendental method. Although that method is no substitute for personal faith, for religious and Christian conversion, consistent adherence to the transcendental precepts is essential to the intellectual and moral integrity of the theologian whatever her specialized disciplines.

The functional differences among the specialties are consistent with their collaborative contributions to epistemic unity. Lonergan's dynamic theological method advances from the diverse expressions of Christian witness in the past to the most credible and effective forms of witness in our time. To comply with Lonergan's governing cultural insight, we must critically appropriate the *vetera* so that we can respond most authentically to the *nova*.

Whether human knowledge develops from below or above, it remains discursive rather than intuitive in character, based on asking and answering questions about being (*Second Collection*, 268–69). It is by assenting to true judgments, whether humanly discovered, divinely revealed, or believed on the basis of scripture and tradition, that being or reality is known. Lonergan's critical epistemic realism applies to both proportionate and transcendent being, to the mediated knowledge of nature, history, interiority, and the divine. While there are no limits, in principle, to the rational knowledge of proportionate being, human knowledge of the mystery of God ultimately depends on religious faith, the trusting acceptance of divine revelation. Though our knowledge of God in this life will always be partial and inadequate, "we see through a glass darkly" (1 Cor. 13:12), still it is God whom we know, however imperfectly, through the truths of both reason and faith.[62]

Specifically modern insights into human historicity and culture led Lonergan to reject the assumptions of classicism. These insights, however, created a new set of challenges for Catholic philosophy and theology. Is the full acceptance of cultural pluralism really consistent with the unity of truth, both rational and revealed? Is the full acceptance of human historicity really consistent with a critical understanding of historical change able effectively to distinguish historical development from institutional and cultural decline? Lonergan responds to the first challenge by contrasting complementary, genetic, and dialectical pluralism, and by resolving dialectical differences on the basis of intellectual, moral, and religious conversion.[63] He responds to the second challenge by grounding historical development in epistemic, moral, and religious self-transcendence, and tracing historical decline to a refusal of what comprehensive self-transcendence requires. Since authenticity is rare and bias pervasive, the concrete historical record will always be a tangled blending of truth and error, virtue and vice, holiness and sin, development and decline. Unraveling that knot and its many intractable consequences is the hard work required of theology in its dialectical and foundational functions.

Reflective Appraisal of Lonergan's Achievement: Lonergan's Philosophy of God

Resistance and Suspicion. Lonergan's conviction that the existence and attributes of God can be known philosophically through the power of reason is confronted with massive resistance, historical, cultural, and existential. Historically, the leading movements in modern thought are arrayed against him. The great reformers believed that created reason had been fatally corrupted by sin. Kant, the Enlightenment's greatest thinker, insisted, on the basis of transcendental arguments, that human reason is incapable of transcendent knowledge. In the nineteenth century, the wisdom, goodness, and providence of God were denied on the basis of evil, suffering, and death. The positivist tradition deriving from Comte rejected the validity of theology and metaphysics, claiming that only the empirical sciences could achieve verifiable knowledge. The masters of suspicion led their cultural peers to view all religious and theological claims with distrust. Even Lonergan's allies in the Catholic tradition have generally approached the philosophy of God with classicist assumptions that Lonergan explicitly criticized. Existentially and culturally, Lonergan had few reliable allies to support his philosophical quest for knowledge of the divine.

With his deep knowledge of cultural history, Lonergan was acutely aware of the resistance he faced. Since he believed that critical self-appropriation and existential conversion are essential to a philosophical knowledge of God, he composed *Insight* as a pedagogical text to promote the intellectual and moral conversions of his readers. As every careful student *of Insight* knows, this is a long, slow, difficult, and uncertain dialectical task. Although the relevant conclusions of *Insight* are stated summarily in the opening chapters of *Method*, there is simply no substitute for gradually undergoing the relevant conversions oneself. While chapter 19 of *Insight* offers a rational argument for the existence of God, Lonergan acknowledges in *Method* that the existential requirement for accepting that argument depends on the antecedent conversion(s) of Lonergan's philosophical interlocutors.

Since the language of "conversion" is culturally freighted, suggesting to many readers the abandonment rather than the development of reason, Lonergan's philosophical rhetoric is an additional obstacle to overcome.[64] To meet this recurrent objection, Lonergan insists that once philosophy becomes existential and historical, once it focuses on situated subjects in their concrete reality, then the conversion of the subject's intentional horizon becomes more fundamental philosophically than logical argument and proof, just as the heuristic transition to the primacy of method becomes more basic than the philosophical reliance on logic alone.

Even if Lonergan's dialectical strategy is soundly conceived and effectively implemented, as I believe that it is, because his existential approach to philosophy and theology falls outside the horizon of the academic and cultural mainstream, his philosophical arguments will continue to meet strong resistance. In this respect his avowedly dialectical philosophy bears a striking resemblance to Plato's, where the absence of intellectual and moral conversion also accounts for persistent and intractable argumentative differences.[65]

The Notion, Question, and Affirmation of God. Lonergan's philosophy of God did not develop in a historical vacuum. It is based on his earlier philosophical insights into the realms and stages of cognitive meaning. The intellectual development of Western culture has brought us to a third stage of meaning in which the empirical sciences and historical scholarship have become relatively autonomous. Philosophy has taken the anthropological turn to the intentional subject, to the thematized realm of conscious interiority. Within the field of interiority, Lonergan discovered his great transcendental principles: the unrestricted desires for knowledge and value, the transcendental method in which those desires normatively unfold, the transcendental exigencies that govern their normative unfolding.

Lonergan's epistemology, metaphysics, and ethics critically explore the ontological and moral implications of these core foundational discoveries. Then, in an explicit reversal of Kant, Lonergan deliberately proceeds from transcendental to transcendent knowledge, basing human knowledge of God on the comprehensive self-knowledge of the intentional subject.[66]

We can see this progression at work in three interdependent ways: Lonergan's philosophical *notion* of God is based on the spiritual analogy of human intelligence, reasonableness, and moral responsibility. While human spiritual capacities are finite and restricted in their effective range, their transcendental desires are unrestricted in intention. Though our epistemic and ethical achievements are always limited, our intellectual and moral aspirations are not. We long for unrestricted wisdom and goodness, even as we constantly fail to attain them. Lonergan's *notion* of God constitutes a radical transformation of our spiritual situation. God is heuristically defined as the free and unrestricted act of creative understanding, expression, and love that ontologically grounds the created universe, and in which the human spirit finitely and imperfectly participates.[67] Even in our finitude and sinfulness, as spiritual creatures we imperfectly reflect the image and likeness of God. For Lonergan, God is in reality what we strive but fail to become in our deepest and most creative aspirations.

By radically exploring the transcendental conditions of all human inquiry, Lonergan arrived at the philosophical *question(s)* of God (*Method*, 101–3). A transcendental condition of all questions for intelligence is the unrestricted desire to know. While direct insights apprehend specific intelligible relations and intelligible unities within the data of experience, the unrestricted desire for knowledge aspires to understand complete and perfect intelligibility. Is there an unrestricted act of creative understanding that grounds the complete intelligibility that human intelligence naturally seeks and intends? That is the intellectual form of the contemporary question of God (*Method*, 101). Our recurrent questions for critical reflection intrinsically seek a grasp of the unconditioned. Before rational assent should be given to a putative judgment, the knower must apprehend the propositional content of that judgment as virtually unconditioned. All reasonable judgments are based on a reflective grasp of the unconditioned, and it is through these judgments that being or reality is known. But virtually unconditioned judgments are restricted to knowledge of proportionate or contingent being, being that exists only through the contingent fulfillment of its prior ontological conditions. But is the whole of reality limited to contingent or conditioned (proportionate) being, or does there necessarily exist a formally unconditioned being, God, whose radical ontological necessity grounds all of contingent existence? This is the distinctively rational form of the question of God (*Method*, 102).

Our deliberative practical questions seek to discover and actualize the really worthwhile, what is intrinsically good and able to satisfy the strict demands of evaluative scrutiny. But the genuine goods we humans pursue and achieve are always imperfect and limited, never fulfilling or satisfying our unrestricted desire for value. Is there an originating transcendent source of value radically beyond limitation and criticism in which the whole of creation (proportionate being) has its ultimate *arche* and *telos*? This is the explicitly moral form of the question of God (*Method*, 102–3). Between the question(s) of God and the reasonable affirmation of God stands the intellectual, moral, and religious conversion of the subject. Intellectual conversion leads us to affirm the complete intelligibility of being and the creative wisdom of God as the necessary condition of our unrestricted epistemic intention (*Method*, 238–40). But the intelligibility of the proportionate universe is inherently complex, requiring distinct but important explanatory roles for classical laws, statistical frequencies, genetic operators and integrators, and the dialectical principles of normative liberty and bias. These different types of intelligibility coalesce in the dynamic structure of the factual universe, as Lonergan recognized in developing his cosmology of emergent probability. But until that intelligible coalescence is personally understood and affirmed, the subject's intellectual conversion remains incomplete.

Moral conversion leads to a major revision in our criteria for evaluative judgments (*Method*, 240). Until we mature ethically, we tend to appraise reality by the standard of individual or group satisfaction. We treat as good what pleases me or us and as bad or evil what leaves us individually or collectively unsatisfied. We use this implicit egoistic standard in evaluating other persons, social institutions, cultural and moral disciplines, the natural universe, even the divine. With a genuine moral conversion, our criteria of evaluation radically shift from satisfaction to value, from preferences sourced in egoistic and group bias to what is genuinely and really worthwhile. Because authentic values in turn are hierarchically ranked, ascending in importance from vital and social values to cultural, personal, and religious values, full moral conversion requires that we ultimately dedicate ourselves to what is supremely valuable, namely the transcendent reality of God, the only actual good that is radically beyond criticism (*Method*, 115–17). The supreme goodness of God, however, is consistently challenged by the reality of evil, both the physical evil that occurs within the natural universe and the moral evil pervasive in human existence. Until the reality of evil is authentically confronted and persuasively addressed, faith in the unrestricted goodness of God remains existentially vulnerable to doubt and suspicion (CWL, 3: chap. 20).

If our intellectual conversion leads us to affirm God's unrestricted creative wisdom and our moral conversion, God's unrestricted goodness, then religious conversion draws us beyond affirmations of God to the wholehearted love of God and neighbor (*Method*, 240–44). It must be emphasized repeatedly how complex, dynamic, and dialectical the process of conversion actually is. All humans are constituted by their transcendental desires for knowledge and value, but very few undergo full intellectual and moral conversion. All humans receive the gift of God's love, the interior ground of the varieties of religious experience, but God's gift of love, by itself, is only the beginning of religious conversion. A mysterious beginning at that, for it draws us initially to an unrestricted beloved, unknown, invisible, otherworldly. While the mysterious donor of the gift may not change, its human recipient can be profoundly transformed when religious experience develops and deepens. This transformation is the work of grace sublating human nature, as our unrestricted desires for knowledge and value are perfected and completed by *agape, caritas*, with God's redemptive love for us awakening and sustaining our love for God in response.

Religious faith is the personal knowledge of God and creation born of this dynamic process of love, freely given, received, and responded to (*Method*, 115–18). It is an existential knowledge of the heart that complements the mind's limited and partial knowledge of God and the universe. But just as the human mind is easily confused, discouraged, and uncertain, so the sinful heart is easily divided and wounded. Though God's love for us is unflagging, our love for God is typically weak and inconstant. As religious faith allows us to "see" the terminal goodness of God's free creation, so the waning of love eclipses and darkens the vision of faith.[68] To believe and confess that God is *agape*, perfect and unrestricted love, and that the universe is the free, created expression of that love requires steadfast assent to the goodness of existence through the trials, sorrows, confusions, and disappointments of life. Such steadfast love and faith are impossible without grace, and even then they define a norm we mortals approach but never fully achieve.

In an era of suspicion, skepticism, and open disbelief, Lonergan brings the complexity of love, *eros, philia,* and *agape* into the very heart of philosophy, so that the acceptance or refusal of grace becomes necessary, though not sufficient, for the philosophical knowledge of God. In the tradition of Augustine, Pascal, and Kierkegaard, Lonergan insists that God's unconditional love for us and our imperfect but deepening love for God are existentially prior to human knowledge of the divine (*Method*, 122–23).[69]

Is Lonergan's explicit reliance on love's transforming power really consistent with the modern critical mentality? If we endorse the skeptical adage that love is inherently foolish and blind, we certainly won't think so. But mutual love, though it can be blind, can also be necessary for really knowing the heart and mind of another person. In human relationships, justified criticism effectively occurs within the interpretive context love gradually creates; and while criticism can erode and destroy that context it cannot bring it into being. The fundamental point is that both love and criticism can be either authentic or inauthentic. The wholesale appeal to the primacy of critical reason can never in itself be decisive.

Though God's infinite wisdom and goodness are radically beyond the scope of legitimate criticism, this does not mean that they silence the human desire to understand who and what we love. Our love of God is a free and imperfect surrender to infinite mystery; it is not a surrender of our intrinsic desire to understand that mystery as deeply and fully as we can. The core principle of Christian humanism applies here. Divine grace sublates human nature; it does not abolish or constrain its free operations.

Causality. All three forms of conversion are necessary for the philosophical knowledge of God. Without loving God wholeheartedly as perfect *agape*, we cannot know God as the originative source of all things. Without transcending individual, group, and anthropocentric bias, without shifting our evaluative criteria from satisfactions to values, we cannot fully assent to the goodness of God and creation. Without intellectual conversion, we cannot escape picture thinking, which effectively reduces the scope of reality to sensible and imaginable being (CWL, 4:218, 221).

Within the existential horizon of picture thinking, the whole of reality is already out there now; knowing is taking a good look at what is real; and causality is a sensible or imaginable relation among equally imaginable realities (CWL, 3:563–66). Within the contrasting horizon of intellectual conversion, reality or being is whatever is intelligently grasped and reasonably affirmed, human knowing is a matter of articulate understanding and warranted judgment, and causality is a verified relation of intelligible dependence among implicitly defined intelligible terms (CWL, 3:674–80).

In our knowledge of proportionate being, causal relations occur among conditioned realities, beings whose causal power is itself antecedently caused. In this realm of contingent or factual causes, Lonergan distinguishes between those that are material and spiritual (CWL, 3:539–41, 640–41). Material causes are concrete instances of nonintelligent intelligibility; spiritual causes, by contrast, are both intelligent and intelligible. He repeatedly insists that only spiritual causality provides the relevant created analogue for understanding transcendent causation. In his practice of intentionality analysis Lonergan focuses on the spiritual operations of understanding, conceiving, judging, loving, and deciding. As the inner words of formulated concepts and judgments are intentionally caused by direct and reflective insights, and the most profound personal decisions by sustained acts of self-transcending love, so these important spiritual dependencies in our interior lives serve imperfectly to illuminate the nature of divine causation (CWL, 2:191–222).

To be sure, there are multiple disanalogies between human and divine causality. The human spirit is finite, temporal, historically situated, and profoundly incarnate, constituted by transcendental desires and invariably subject to bias and sin. The divine spirit is infinite, eternal, immaterial, and ontologically and morally perfect. Human knowing, loving, and choosing are invariably conditioned by three causal vectors: nature, sin, and grace. Divine knowing, loving, and choosing are radically unconditioned, the unique instance of unconditioned spiritual causality. Though we can neither see nor imagine God's creative understanding, expression, and love, we can imperfectly illumine them by more deeply understanding the power and limits of our own interior life. Through this partial analogical illumination the mystery of God only deepens rather than contracts. An abiding feature of all authentic knowledge of God is the correlative recognition of how little we actually know.[70]

*Reflective Appraisal Continued:
Lonergan's Method in Theology*

The Divine Initiatives. For Lonergan, the human quest for God is essentially an imperfect response to divine initiatives.[71] God's creative Word (the divine Logos of John's gospel) brings forth and sustains the universe, the dynamic and evolving order of creation. In seeking to understand creation, both cosmic and human, we can gradually arrive at an imperfect knowledge of its creative origin and ground. God's inner word of love (*agape*) is universally addressed to the human heart. Beginning in religious experience, and deepening through religious conversion, human beings can gradually come to personal faith, the heart's knowledge of God as the creative source of all being and value. From the existential perspective of true religious faith, the heavens, the earth, and all they contain silently proclaim the greatness and glory of God.

But God also "speaks" to humans through the outer word of historical revelation: in Judaism, through the covenant with Abraham, the law given to Moses, the critical but hopeful voice of the prophets; in Christianity, which grew out of historical Judaism, in the unique incarnation of Christ, the divine Word (the Logos) made flesh. For believing Christians, like Lonergan, the life, death, and resurrection of Christ provide the supreme revelation of the unfathomable depth of God's love. "God so loved the world" that in the fullness of time he sent his divine Son and Spirit to redeem fallen creation from the crippling power of sin and to make it holy and pleasing once more.

The historical mission of faithful Christians is to proclaim the "good news" of God's redemptive love to all people and to continue Christ's holy work of redemption in time. The complex history of the Christian religion is the history of the highly flawed and imperfect witness of Christians to God's self-revelation in Christ. The history of Christian theology is the reflective interpretation and appraisal of the meaning and value of that inconstant witness to God's revealed Word.

If this reading of Lonergan is sound, then the existential importance of religious conversion becomes clearer. Without the liberating vision of religious faith, the divine Word of creation, the emerging intelligible cosmos, no longer proclaims God's greatness and glory. Without the personal faith born of love, religious experience is ambiguous, an interior longing and loneliness that may never be satisfied. Without faith in divine Providence and mercy, Israel is a minor historical nation and Jesus just another itinerant prophet. For God's self-revelation to humans to elicit an authentic response, the divine Words of creation, interior grace, and salvation history must be received into hearts of flesh, not hearts of stone. Most of us, most of the time, waver inconstantly between stone and flesh, alternately heeding and ignoring these complementary divine initiatives.[72]

Divine Revelation, Human Witness, and the Norm of Fidelity. Judaism, Christianity, and Islam are religions of revelation. They originate in a human response to God's self-disclosures in history. The three Abrahamic faiths trace their origin to the covenant between Yahweh and Abraham, a mutual promise of fidelity between God and Abraham's descendants. The Abrahamic covenant is renewed in the exodus from Egypt and in God's gift of the law to Moses in the Sinai. The deeper meaning and challenge of religious fidelity are revealed in God's message to Israel through the several generations of prophets. These successive revelations of God to the Jews create the interpretive historical context for the incarnation, for the divine Word made flesh in Jesus of Nazareth.

The Christian community of faith originates in the apostolic response to the life, death, and resurrection of Jesus. After receiving the transformative gifts of the Spirit on Pentecost, the disciples of Jesus began to bear public witness to the memory of their crucified leader. Initially, this witness is given to Jews, then to Gentiles, and eventually to the ends of the earth. What different forms does Christian witness take as it historically evolves? It begins with a memorial story, an oral account of Jesus' earthly life, his words and deeds, his passion, death, and resurrection. Across the Mediterranean basin, small communities of Christians gradually emerge, preserving the memory of Jesus in prayer, song, and worship. In his pastoral letters to these communities, Paul reflects on the deeper meaning of the gospel for both Jews and Gentiles. Within a century of Jesus' death, the oral stories and prayers are gradually transformed into written gospels, the textual basis of what became the New Testament canon.

Difficult and important questions continually emerged within these evolving communities of faith. How was the revelation of Jesus related to the Abrahamic covenant, the Mosaic law, and the prophetic teaching? How was the emerging Christian community related to the chosen people of Israel? Did Gentile converts to Christianity have to become practicing Jews? What enduring message did Jesus teach and live before he died and ascended to the Father; what historical mission did he entrust to his followers and their descendants? Of greatest importance, who is/was Jesus himself, and how is he related to the one God of Abraham, Isaac, and Jacob?

As fidelity to the covenant, the law, and the prophets became the authoritative touchstone of historical Judaism, so fidelity to "the gospel of Jesus" became the touchstone of the Christian religion. But what does it actually mean to be faithful to the gospel and to the person whose life and teaching it commemorates? Ultimately, the answer to this question depends on the identity of Jesus and on the authority attributed to his life and teaching. The constitutive theological answers that came to define Christian orthodoxy are that Jesus is the divine Son of God, the second person of the Blessed Trinity, who became fully human to redeem our sinful world and to found an enduring community of disciples to continue his redemptive work upon earth. Because Jesus is divine as well as human, his message and mission have the weight of divine authority. Because Jesus founded the church, the living community of faith, to proclaim his prophetic message and continue his redemptive mission, the church deserves our special respect and allegiance.

But the Christian church, though assured of God's continuing presence within it, is a human community bearing imperfect witness to Christ in all that it says and does. Just as the Jews were imperfectly faithful to the covenant and the law (as the prophets forcefully insisted), so Christians are imperfectly faithful to the gospel of Christ. They struggle to understand and articulate the full meaning of Christ's revelation; they struggle to obey and enact the great commandments of love. It is therefore imperative that Christians and non-Christians alike clearly distinguish between the unique example set by Christ himself and that of the imperfect pilgrim church he founded and sustains, even though the living witness of the church is the principal way the revealed Word of God is now communicated in history.

The historical importance and imperfection (sinfulness) of the church clarify the critical need for both mediating and mediated theology, and the particular need for the functional specialties of *dialectic* and *foundations*. *Dialectic* reveals the persistence of inauthenticity within the actual Christian community and among Christian pastors, theologians, and thinkers. *Foundations* provides a normative basis in existential conversion, religious, moral, and intellectual, for distinguishing authentic from inauthentic Christian witness in both the *vetera* and the *nova* of Christian history.

In retrospect, what is most striking about the history of divine revelation is the degree to which God entrusts the revealed Word to sinful mortals: Abraham, Moses, the prophets, the countless followers of Christ throughout history. The lone exception to this remarkable pattern of unmerited trust is the divine Word made flesh, for only Jesus of Nazareth was like us in all things but sin (Heb. 4:15).

The Importance of Doctrines. For Lonergan, the Catholic church of his era confronted two critical challenges related to the emergence of historical consciousness. Catholic classicists underestimate the importance of historical scholarship for critically appropriating the *vetera*. As a result, they oversimplify the unity of the Christian tradition and the constancy of the church's doctrinal teaching. They correctly stress the permanence or constancy of divine revelation, but overlook the historical struggle of Christians to understand and articulate its fuller meaning. They also underestimate the importance of cultural pluralism, and the perennial need for the church to communicate the gospel differently to different audiences, societies, and cultures. As a result, classicist conceptions of the church tend to separate Christian unity from legitimate plurality, the permanence of the gospel from the dynamic historical expression of its revelatory meaning and value.

If classicists oversimplify the historical dimension of Christianity, their "modernist" rivals tend to lack a critical perspective upon it.[73] One of Lonergan's basic aims in critically appropriating the past was to distinguish carefully between authentic and inauthentic forms of Christian witness through the ages. Having drawn this distinction concretely on the basis of foundational conversions and their discernible omission or refusal, his further aim was to preserve whatever is authentic and valid in the long Christian past (CWL, 17:259, 295).

Although the forms of authentic witness are diverse and evolving, including Christian prayers, hymns and stories, canonical scripture and tradition, and the common creeds Christians publicly confess, they also include Christian doctrines, the revealed truths about God that the church believes and teaches on the basis of God's divine Word. While critically appropriating the *vetera* establishes that these doctrines have developed historically in response to new questions, criticisms, and challenges, Lonergan emphatically insists that Christian doctrines constitute the defining beliefs of the authentic Christian community. To disregard doctrines, or to devalue and distort their meaning, is to compromise the integrity of the Christian faith and to rupture its historic continuity with the faith of the original disciples (CWL, 17:427).

While critical hermeneutics and historical scholarship overturn the ahistorical assumptions of classicism, the functional specialties of *dialectic* and *foundations* provide the required theological context for understanding and appraising Christian doctrines, which bear witness to the church's communal faith by declaring and affirming the revealed truths on which it is based.

Methodological and Theological Questions. *Insight* is a philosophical text that culminates in two chapters on transcendent knowledge. *Method in Theology* is divided into two complementary parts: a brief philosophical background that summarizes Lonergan's major transcendental discoveries in cognitional theory, ethics, hermeneutics, and the philosophy of religion; a methodological foreground that identifies eight functional specialties in theology, articulates their distinctive epistemic tasks, and explains how they coalesce in a comprehensive collaborative project. The philosophical foreground is based on the self-appropriation of human interiority. It highlights the transcultural, transhistorical principles that constitute the human being as a developing intentional subject. It emphasizes the human desires and interior demands for authenticity, for epistemic and moral self-transcendence, and reveals how these longings and norms lead inescapably to the question(s) of God.

The methodological foreground draws on these philosophical discoveries in constructing a specialized method of theological inquiry that satisfies the empirical and critical demands of our time. It is important to recognize that in *Method* Lonergan is proposing a new theological method and not a new substantive theology. Thus, the eight chapters of the second part of *Method* are essentially heuristic in nature. They explain the different types of intelligibility that are sought in the eight functional specialties and indicate how these different forms of intelligibility coalesce in a comprehensive and critical theology. But Lonergan does not commit himself, in *Method*, to specific substantive answers in either mediating or mediated theology. While it is not hard to surmise where his substantive loyalties lie as an orthodox Catholic theologian, he explicitly refuses to conflate methodological and theological questions (*Method*, 119).

The fact that these questions are distinct does not mean they can be entirely separated. To illustrate this point, consider Lonergan's treatment of the mediated phase of Christian theology. In order for his heuristic account of *foundations* and *doctrines* to be concrete, he has to employ the special theological categories of divine revelation, inspired scripture, developing doctrines, the teaching authority of the church, the plurality and unity of the Christian tradition, the normative contrast of authentic and inauthentic Christian witness.[74] Yet while Lonergan employs these categories heuristically in *Method*, he does not answer the important theological questions they raise. How do we determine the nature, scope, and content of divine revelation? What does it mean for sacred scripture to be divinely inspired? How can scripture credibly claim to be "the revealed Word of God" when it so clearly appears to be the historical handiwork of limited mortals? Granted that Jesus founded the church and gave it teaching authority, how should the church be internally organized and governed, and how should its limited authority be shared among the sinful people of God? Finally, in critically appraising the actual history of the church, when has its witness to the gospel been authentic or inauthentic, and to what extent are its teaching, leading, and governing genuinely authentic today? Pope John's important but unfinished project of *aggiornamento*, of comprehensive Catholic renewal, requires that these substantive theological questions be critically addressed. The fact that they can't be answered on methodological grounds alone does not mean that Catholics, individually or collectively, can legitimately evade the urgent moral and religious challenges they pose. Both the great and the small renewal of Catholicism remain to this day incomplete.

An Ethics of Authenticity: Personal and Communal

Man's deepest need and most prized achievement is authenticity.
—*Method*, 254

The Vetera *and the* Nova

Background. The Catholic moral tradition is highly complex. It is historically rooted in the law of Moses, especially the Decalogue, the prophetic emphasis on fidelity to the covenant, and the gospel of Jesus of Nazareth. In his public ministry Jesus insisted that his teaching completed the law and the prophets, bringing them to fulfillment not abrogation (Matt. 5:17–18). Over many centuries the followers of Christ gradually articulated the ways of being, thinking, and living that the gospel concretely required. In this way a Christian moral tradition developed, with Saint Paul, Saint Augustine, Saint Benedict, and Saint Francis of Assisi among its leading teachers and examples.

Aquinas's moral theology is a subtle blend of Hebrew, Greek, and Christian insights. From Genesis he adopts the scriptural claim that God's creation is indeed very good. He also acknowledges the importance of sin, both the original sin of Adam and the subsequent sinfulness of Adam's descendants. He tends to treat sin as a form of violence or injury to the created goodness of nature. In the case of humans, sin does not destroy their created capacities, but it darkens their minds, making knowledge more difficult, and weakens their wills, making their loves more disordered. Grace is a free exercise of God's divine art. The gifts of grace perfect and complete the created powers of nature and heal the harmful effects of sin on created order. Within Aquinas's Christian perspective, Aristotle's hierarchical order of nature becomes the order of creation; sin does violence to nature's orderly development toward maturity; and divine grace both perfects created nature and reverses the negative effects of sin upon it. Violence and sin, though very important, are subordinate moral concepts. They arrest or impede natural and supernatural development; their harmful effects can be healed and reversed by the redemptive power of grace. Aquinas's moral focus is on the goodness and wisdom of God, the integrity of the original creation, the rationality of law, the centrality of the virtues, the dual teleology of temporal and eternal felicity.

The Moral Challenge of Modernity. The moral culture of modernity is certainly not monolithic. Its formative movements—the European Renaissance, the Protestant Reformation, the scientific Enlightenment, the Romantic reaction to the "enlightened" emphasis on reason, pre- and postwar existentialism—often pull in opposing directions. Despite these important internal differences and the unresolved moral tensions they create, on five relevant axes of comparison the moral spirit of modernity differs markedly from that of Latin Christendom.

Equality and Hierarchy. The leading thinkers of modernity systematically dismantled the hierarchical orders they inherited from classical antiquity and medieval Christianity. The Scientific Revolution replaced the classical cosmos of Ptolemy and Aristotle with a disenchanted universe of inanimate matter in motion. The democratic revolutions of the late eighteenth century undermined the social and political legitimacy of the feudal order. In the moral realm, modern ethics preserves the moral pluralism but reverses the evaluative hierarchies embraced by the ancients. The moderns tend to prize palpable and earthly goods: longer life, greater material prosperity, increased security and comfort, the reduction of human suffering and pain. Individuals and societies, in freely pursuing their particular visions of happiness, innocently differ in the pleasures and satisfactions they prefer and espouse. There is no recognized hierarchy of human goods or forms of life, no clear priority assigned to eternal truths or eternal aims. While the early moderns did not reject the Christian God, radical Enlightenment thinkers severely censured Catholic Christianity, and the "masters of suspicion" fiercely criticized the political, cultural, and psychological functions of religion. In our time, both ontological naturalists and exclusive humanists firmly insist that the liberty and dignity of man require "the death of God," the ontological and moral summit of medieval culture.[75]

Autonomy and Authority. The modern concept of liberty is originally based on the dramatic experience of expanding liberation: of the individual believer from a corrupt and oppressive church; of the independent thinker from stifling intellectual traditions; of the democratic citizen from despotic monarchies; of the creative artist from established patterns of cultural authority. What medieval Christians largely accepted as legitimate and supportive social institutions, the leading moderns viewed as coercive and constrictive. But human freedom has two distinct but interrelated moments: the exhilarating act of liberation that abolishes an existing "tyranny"; and the deliberative act of constitution that establishes a viable replacement for what has been rejected and cast off.[76] These successive dimensions of enduring freedom are bound together in the distinctively modern ideal of human autonomy: epistemic, moral, historical, and spiritual.

Both Descartes and Kant emphasized the autonomy of the isolated individual, the disembodied *ego* of Descartes, Kant's noumenal moral agent. In the second phase of the Enlightenment, this atomistic conception of human existence was explicitly rejected. The human subject was resituated in nature, society, and culture, in the Darwinian struggle for survival, in the social institutions and cultural practices of nineteenth-century Europe. Despite these critical ontological changes, the ideal of autonomy retained its cultural power. Hegel celebrated the autonomy of Absolute Spirit, Marx the autonomy of the human species as a whole. Marx's Promethean humanism defiantly excluded any role for the divine in human affairs. For Marx, the French Revolutionary dreams of universal liberty, equality, and fraternity will eventually be fulfilled, not through the providence of God but through human cooperation with history's dialectical laws.

For today's exclusive humanists, because there is no God, there is also no creation, no sin, no grace, no divine law, no revealed mysteries, no providential redemption, no hope for life beyond the grave. Some contemporary secularists embrace these views defiantly; for others, living without God has become a matter of course.[77] There are profound internal differences within the secularist camp, and many of its members explicitly reject the inflated visions of autonomy that modernity has uncritically embraced. Despite their contrasting moral visions, exclusive humanists are united in accepting what Charles Taylor calls the closure of "the immanent frame":

the ontological conviction that nature and history are self-contained causal realms requiring no transcendent explanation, that human existence is a fortunate biological accident, and that we mortals must struggle and die in a world that exists without God.[78]

Virtue, Power, and Happiness. For both Aristotle and Aquinas, the middle term intelligibly linking knowledge and *eudaimonia* (*beatitudo*) was *arete* (*virtus*), human excellence. In their moral theories, though not all the virtues are reducible to knowledge, they all have an epistemic component. Aristotle refused to separate virtuous activity from the virtuous agent, a mature person guided by *phronesis* (practical wisdom), a constitutive feature of every true moral virtue (*Second Collection*, 82). The mature adult guided by *phronesis*, the Aristotelian *phronimos*, not only understands the hierarchical teleology of human flourishing, but also knows how to actualize it wisely in the contingent circumstances of practical life. Aquinas later elevated and deepened Aristotle's ethical vision with the supernatural virtues infused by divine grace, and the Christian teleology of eternal beatitude with God and the saints.

The moderns partly retained and largely reversed the ancient and medieval conceptions of *eudaimonia* (*beatitudo*). The knowledge prized by the moderns is based upon empirical science, the apprehension of nature's universal and invariant laws. For Bacon and Descartes, natural science proved its utility through the tangible fruits and works it helped to produce. From their explicitly pragmatic perspective, the key to human happiness is not acquired virtue, the right ordering of fear, desire, belief, and judgment, but continually increasing human power and control over material reality. Only when the power we command exceeds our actual desires are we effectively positioned for happiness, both individually and collectively. From this modern ethical perspective, it was because the ancients lacked technical power over nature that they focused their ethics on the moral and religious disciplining of human fear and desire. The new science and technology, by radically augmenting human power, made the traditional education of the passions no longer necessary.

The Cartesian and Baconian project is no less teleological than that of Aristotle and Aquinas. But the *telos* they advocate is divorced from virtuous activity and the ideal of normative order in the soul and the city. The vast majority of people can enjoy the palpable fruits of modern science and technology without knowing how they are discovered and produced. As Kant later realized, this "enlightened" conception of happiness has been radically democratized. Because each individual conceives the substance of happiness differently, even in ways that violate the traditional moral law, modern counsels of prudence (recommended paths to happiness) lack real normative import. Like the hypothetical imperatives of skill, these counsels carry no obligatory moral force.[79]

Subjectivity and Objectivity in Ethics. Charles Taylor draws an important distinction between moral ontology and moral advocacy.[80] Moral ontology refers to our framing conception of the moral life, the common structural features that shape the deliberative context for our moral reflection and choice. Moral advocacy refers to the specific evaluative judgments and policies we actually affirm and pursue. Although heuristically distinct, these two dimensions of morality are interconnected, for we regularly employ our moral ontology to clarify, justify, or criticize the specific moral positions we support or oppose.

Taylor's distinction is particularly useful in appraising the constitutive role of subjectivity in modern moral culture, for the competing versions of modern individualism make both ontological and advocacy claims. They offer contested ontological accounts of the moral activity of human agents, and contested substantive accounts of the moral ends it is good to pursue and the moral obligations human beings are required to fulfill. In the first phase of the Enlightenment (1600–1800), human beings were frequently depicted as disembodied, disembedded subjects (solitary egos) operating in a disenchanted universe. In the second phase (roughly 1815 to the present), the early modern moral ontology of atomistic individualism was largely rejected. Both the biological and the cultural conditioning of humans were assigned new importance. According to this revised ontological account, humans are fundamentally linguistic or symbolic animals who acquire and exercise the languages they master within an evolving matrix of social institutions and practices. This constitutive communal dependence on language and symbolism, in their dynamic and changing historical forms, undercuts the inflated aspirations to individual autonomy espoused by Descartes and Kant.

To what extent did the moral aspirations of early modernity survive the rejection of its moral ontology? The liberty, dignity, and responsibility of the individual person continue to be affirmed. Though liberty is no longer equated with radical autonomy, the existential responsibility of the person remains a bulwark of moral, political, and legal evaluation. The dignity of the individual has been legally translated into a new set of rights, both negative and positive. The negative rights guarantee freedom from interference in matters of conscience, worship, association, self-expression, economic initiative, and ownership. The positive rights, which are far more deeply contested, include guarantees of minimum security in the areas of education, health, housing, income, and the welfare of children and the elderly.[81] Though individual liberty is now defined in diverse, even contradictory ways, by libertarians and social democrats, for example, it remains the supreme moral value in the culture of modernity.

What sort of equality does human liberty require and permit? What sort of equality does democratic justice demand? The political struggles of late modernity tend to center on the relative importance and practical implementation of the value of equality. In the North Atlantic world, political conservatives and libertarians tend to argue that the demands of negative liberty, of noninterference with private initiative and ownership, clearly trump those of economic equality. Their rivals on the political left, stressing the positive rights associated with a social concept of liberty, tend to support public policies designed to reduce inequalities of every kind. Ontological differences continue to play an important role here, with the libertarian right espousing a more atomistic conception of the self, and their critics on the left focusing on the concrete socioeconomic conditions in which beleaguered individuals and families are historically situated. Another critical source of policy differences are the normative priorities accorded to unregulated capitalism and the market by economic conservatives, and to democratic equality and the general welfare by the liberal and socialist left. Even carefully regulated capitalism tends to generate significant economic, social, and political inequalities. The dramatic story of modern democracy, by contrast, has largely been the struggle for extending human equality: equality of rights, of political representation, of due process, of the opportunity to compete economically and politically on a "level playing field."[82] Tocqueville memorably argued that modern democracies face a continuing tension between the values of equality and liberty.[83] While Tocqueville's original thesis is sound, the profound moral and political tensions within contemporary democracy are more ramified than he realized. For these tensions exist among rival conceptions of liberty and equality, and among rival, even hostile accounts of what these core values permit and require.

The Right and the Good. *Eros* and exigence, desire and duty, are important factors in any credible account of morality. Is the moral life primarily an erotic quest for the *summum bonum*, the highest attainable good, or is it primarily a practical commitment to fulfill our obligations, even when they conflict with our deepest desires? Classical morality, without denying the importance of obligation, tended to emphasize the erotic quest, suitably purified and guided by the relevant virtues. Utilitarian moralists significantly reduced the importance of the virtues, while promoting the greatest happiness of the greatest number of discrete individuals. Kant explicitly challenged both classical eudaimonism and modern utilitarianism, basing his ethics on categorical imperatives that clearly subordinated personal desire to moral obligation. These metaethical differences have been recently highlighted by John Rawls's argument that the *right* (the obligatory demands of justice) takes moral priority over the *good* (the individual or collective pursuit of happiness).[84] Iris Murdoch, without privileging either *eros* (Plato) or exigence (Kant), believed that a credible account of morality must do justice to both the human quest for perfection and the inescapable demand that we do our duty in the mundane circumstances of ordinary life.[85] These unresolved metaethical debates are conducted at a very high level of generality. While they provide genuine guidance to today's ethical reflection, they leave ordinary mortals to decide for themselves the appropriate paths to the highest goods and the concrete obligations moral integrity requires them to fulfill.[86]

Lonergan's Critical Moral Response

Lonergan insisted that Catholic thinkers must critically appropriate the *vetera* in order to respond authentically to the *nova*. His nuanced response to the moral challenges of modernity clearly follows this established dialectical pattern.

Equality and Hierarchy. Lonergan's cosmological beliefs differ markedly from those of both ancients and moderns. He rejects the static, timeless hierarchies of Aristotle's cosmology, the sharp separation between celestial and terrestrial physics, and the classical theory of scientific knowledge (*episteme*). At the same time, he opposes scientific determinism and materialism, reductionist accounts of genetic emergence and evolution, and the heuristic conflation of the natural and human sciences. Lonergan's dynamic cosmology of emergent probability affirms the ontological distinction between matter and spirit, the normative unfolding of intentional consciousness, the freedom and responsibility of the human person, the intentional subject's openness to unmerited grace (CWL, 3:146–57, 290–92). Human beings are symbolic, polymorphic animals whose prolonged and uncertain development has organic, neural, perceptual, affective, intellectual, moral, and religious dimensions. Distinctively human existence is constitutively mediated by meaning and motivated by value, and must be understood and appraised by dialectical methods that respect these defining features of spiritual life.

Lonergan did not write at length about society and politics.[87] Although he recognized the great importance of economic, social, and political institutions, he tended to concentrate on their cultural underpinnings, the shared beliefs and values that animate and sustain their effective operation. In practical matters, he can be described as a normative realist, equally sensitive to the central role of both factual knowledge and moral precepts in shaping effective public policy. How did this normative outlook inform his practical judgments about the proper balance between equality and hierarchy (*Second Collection*, 189–92)?

Though Lonergan was not a reactionary seeking to reverse the democratic revolutions of modernity in order to restore some version of the ancien régime, he harbored few illusions about the conduct of modern democracy. He recognized the negative effects of bias on individual and group decisions; he emphasized the importance of specialized knowledge and competence in practical affairs; he criticized the vulgarity and shallowness that pervade popular culture and electoral politics. He supported an institutional strategy of "complex equality" based on the principle of functional differentiation.[88] Thriving and effective modern institutions are complex cooperative ventures relying on the collaboration of numerous individuals performing very different functions and tasks. While institutional tasks should be assigned on the basis of the requisite skills and competence, strong interpersonal relations and prudent practical leadership are also essential if the dynamic integration of these disparate functions is to occur. Careers, it would seem, should be open to talent and disciplined training, together with a demonstrated personal record of social cooperation and civic responsibility (*Method*, 47–49). Freedom and responsibility, however, are not solely confined to individual persons. Modern men and women are collectively responsible for the direction of history, for promoting historical progress and reversing historical decline (CWL, 10:76–78; *Third Collection*, 169). However, as responsible citizens, we must fulfill this great historical vocation without the liberal illusion of continuous progress, the Marxist illusion of Promethean revolt, or the secularist illusion of the divine absence from history. The inauthenticity with which individuals constantly struggle is even more pronounced in communal affairs. The greatest practical danger is the public's attraction to seductive ideologies justifying violence and terror in the service of utopian ends (*Method*, 55, 357–59). But there simply is no substitute for personal and public liberty as sources of human creativity and progress (CWL, 3:259–61). Although bias regularly distorts the exercise of freedom, the suppression of liberty guarantees stagnation and decline.[89] Since all forms of despotism suppress human liberty, they should be actively opposed. Given the scale and complexity of modern institutions, administrative bureaucracies should also be feared because they tend to prevent or obstruct the creative collaboration on which real human progress depends.

The legitimate exercise of power should not be confused with reliance on coercion or force. Power is generated by human cooperation across the ages, through human beings acting in concert with their contemporaries and predecessors. Genuine authority and power, however, are not coextensive, for power, like freedom, can be employed for both good and ill. Lonergan explicitly defines authority as legitimate power, power whose generation and exercise comply with the transcendental precepts (*Third Collection*, 5–12). In both Lonergan's existential and social ethics, authenticity is the essence of human legitimacy and inauthenticity the justifying ground for critical dissent and sustained opposition. Lonergan recognizes, therefore, a legitimate role for authority in the institutional life of the church, the state, the economic and educational enterprises of civil society, and, of course, the family. His normative position would be considerably clearer, however, if we knew his concrete appraisal of the historical exercise of power in these important but flawed institutions.

Practical judgments of value, both originating and terminal, are either categorical or comparative (*Method*, 36–41). In categorical judgments, we distinguish good from evil, right from wrong, benefit from harm, virtue from vice. In comparative judgments, we hierarchically rank the plurality of genuine values and the multiple evils that threaten them. For Lonergan, the supreme originating value is God, while all other originating values are created expressions of God's love in the world of creation. God is the transcendent source (*arche*) of all created goodness and the *telos* all created things ultimately seek. The ontological gulf between creator and creation does not preclude God's participation in the created order. Just as God's wisdom and goodness sustain the created universe in being, so God's compassion and mercy are revealed through divine initiatives in history: the covenant with Abraham, the gift of the law to Moses, the prophetic challenge to Hebraic fidelity, the incarnation of Jesus (the divine Word made flesh), the ongoing redemption and sanctification of the world.

The ontological transcendence of God is also the basis of radical human equality. All humans without exception are created in God's image and likeness, are subject to bias and sin, are redeemed by Christ's death and resurrection, are called to conversion, authenticity, and full self-transcendence. In Lonergan's redemptive theology, the ineffable mystery of God is balanced by God's radical generosity in sending his Son to dwell in our midst, becoming like us in all things but sin (Phil. 2:7; Heb. 4:15). The transcendence of God and the radical equality of mortals do not preclude a hierarchical structure within the order of created value (CWL, 3:624–26). In descending order of rank, originating values include authentic intentional subjects, the shared beliefs and commitments of authentic cultures, the institutional cooperation of authentic societies, the natural and social realities that underlie and condition the personal and communal quest for what is good (CWL, 17:336–77).

In the ordering of terminal values, the length and complexity of human development are the critical factors. Thus, vital, institutional, and cultural values condition the possibility of higher levels of personal distinction. However, the functional complementarity of values entails that what is first in the order of temporal development (vital and institutional values) may be last in the order of intrinsic excellence. Thus Lonergan affirms an objective hierarchy of originating and terminal values while recognizing the ongoing functional dependence of higher on lower goods.

Though Lonergan continues to distinguish between natural and supernatural values, originating and terminal, he also preserves Aquinas's core Christian insights that divine grace sublates created nature and does not abolish it; that grace heals the violence of sin by restoring the created integrity of nature that sin undermines. While Aquinas's Christian humanism emphasizes the complementarity of the different orders of value, the "law of the cross" inserts a powerful tension into his otherwise harmonious vision. It is not that suffering and death are inherently good; they clearly are not. But as the life of Christ unmistakably shows, they are often inseparable from the redemptive mission of actually bringing good out of evil. In the concrete drama of Christian humanism, Calvary must come before Easter.

Authority and Autonomy. A prolonged crisis of legitimacy in Latin Christendom spurred the rise of modernity in the West. Sincere Christian reformers lost faith in the Renaissance papacy. The leaders of the Scientific Revolution lost faith in the intellectual authority of Aristotle and the Aristotelian tradition. The spirited proponents of democratic equality and liberty lost faith in the institutions and culture of the ancien régime. The critical champions of the French Enlightenment lost faith initially in Catholic Christianity and then in the providential authority of God. Both industrial capitalists and their socialist critics lost faith in the economic models and norms of feudal society. Throughout the twentieth century, large numbers of women lost faith in the patriarchal assumptions and prejudices of Western religion and culture.

Despite significant differences among them, these powerful cultural movements shared a common response to the historical crises they faced. The dynamic pattern of that response has four distinguishable moments: increasing alienation from inherited forms of authority and tradition; decisive liberation from what they perceived as the institutional and cultural sources of their shared discontent; the constitution of new institutional orders on the basis of individual or collective autonomy; a gradual recognition that the autonomous foundations they championed were greatly inflated and that the new institutional orders could not be sustained and defended.

Lonergan was both a critic and a defender of modern assertions of autonomy. He explicitly rejected the atomistic moral ontologies that dominated the first phase of the Enlightenment. He explicitly welcomed the reconception of human existence as socially and historically embedded subjectivity. He recognized two distinct but complementary paths of human development, from above and below. But these complementary paths to personal growth are also potential sources of decline. For bias, sin, and ideology affect both the social and cultural formation of the person as well as the individual judgments and choices each person makes. Because natural and historical belonging are constitutive features of human existence, individual autonomy is always limited and partial; because our social and historical inheritance is inevitably a mixture of greatness and wretchedness, we must learn to appropriate critically the shared beliefs and convictions received from our ancestors.

The moderns were not mistaken in critiquing important parts of their medieval inheritance. But they were mistaken in believing they could radically emancipate themselves from its conditioning influence. The wholesale liberation they attempted is simply not possible. They were also mistaken in their inflated assertions of constructive autonomy, whether it was the scriptural autonomy claimed by the Protestant Reformers, the epistemic autonomy of Descartes, the moral autonomy of Kant, the Promethean humanism of Marx, or the market fundamentalism of laissez-faire liberals.

If critically appropriating the past and the present is required for authentically belonging to any society and culture, then neither obedience to "authority," nor wholesale emancipation from social and cultural imperatives, nor the autonomous constitution of new social orders, is a viable strategy for independent thinkers today. What alternative approach does Lonergan propose in the third stage of cognitive meaning? Because cognitive development occurs through specialization and differentiation, we need to recognize the relative autonomy of common sense, theoretical inquiry, and historical scholarship (*Method*, 94–95; *Third Collection*, 46). Differentiated learning, however, does not eliminate the human need and desire for cognitive integration. Thus we still need critical philosophers to integrate the specialized forms of modern knowledge and the specialized accounts of reality they provisionally offer. In addition, because the unrestricted desires and normative demands of the human spirit cannot be satisfied within the realm of proportionate being, we must also recognize the intellectual and moral legitimacy of philosophical and revealed theology.

A transitional crisis of legitimacy demands neither radical autonomy nor radical liberation. These were the revolutionary modern ideals that Lonergan openly criticized. His alternative cultural proposal is to insist on personal and communal authenticity. Although these basic forms of authenticity are conceptually distinct, they cannot be separated (CWL, 4:227–31; *Method*, 80–81). For personal authenticity is always the achievement of historically situated subjects; and communal authenticity, to the extent we attain it, is always the fruit of the creative and critical achievements of the community's authentic members and leaders. At both levels of existence, authenticity requires full and continuous fidelity to the transcendental desires and precepts, a realistic acknowledgment of personal and communal failings, and a critical alertness to the seductive influence of bias and ideology. The human path to authenticity also demands a constant readiness to withdraw from all forms of inauthentic existence as they develop within and around us.

The leading moderns mistakenly treated authority and liberty as incompatible values. But if authority is defined as legitimate power and legitimacy is conceived as self-transcending authenticity, then the alleged incompatibility cannot be defended. For if divine authority creates and respects human liberty, and commands an authenticity inseparable from responsible freedom, then legitimate human power must do the same. When institutional power is corrupt it tends toward despotism, wanting to "have by one means what can only be had in some other way."[90] (Montesquieu was right when he identified the animating spirit [*esprit*] of despotic regimes as the common fear of coercive power.)[91] But despotism in every form is inauthentic, even when it claims to be serving the highest values. Although social institutions cannot flourish without effective authority, their leaders are constantly tempted by despotism, by the suppression of liberty in the name of established order or progress. In our time, despotic practices, whether economic, political, cultural, or religious, are nearly always defended by ideology. But while the critique of ideology is necessary to "unmask" these *apologias* for tyranny, the deeper need of our time is to go beyond warranted critique to comprehensive creativity and healing (*Third Collection*, 100–109).

Eudaimonia, *Happiness, and Authenticity.* For Lonergan, a credible contemporary ethics must be concrete, existential, dynamic, and historically responsible. It will require a transposition but not a rejection of Aquinas's moral theology. Thus Lonergan preserves Thomas's insights into nature and grace, the violent consequences of sin, the hierarchical pluralism and functional complementarity of human goods, the centrality of the virtues, the vertically structured ends human beings pursue. But where Aquinas made human beatitude dependent on the natural and supernatural virtues, and the moderns made individual and collective happiness dependent on scientific knowledge and technical power, Lonergan makes personal and communal authenticity dependent on comprehensive and sustained self-transcendence (CWL, 17:313–31).

Epistemic self-transcendence, the objective knowledge of fact and value, is necessary though not sufficient for human authenticity. For while knowledge of the real supports knowledge of the good, ethical inquiry remains incomplete until its evaluative judgments are practically realized, not just here and now, but over the course of a lifetime or the longer history of a people and culture. Thus moral self-transcendence (authentic living) sublates its epistemic counterpart (objective knowing), preserving the vital importance of cognition while transcending its ethical limits.

Authenticity in ethics, however, is incompatible with blithe moral optimism. As human beings, we live under the reign of bias, ideology, and sin (CWL, 3:714–16). We regularly ignore or deny experience, truncate the scope of our most important inquiries, reject unwelcome insights and judgments, fail to do or avoid what our conscience commands, soothe an uneasy conscience with placating rationalizations. These recurrent lapses in authenticity create an objective surd, a tangled knot, for individuals and communities (CWL, 3:254–57). Our concrete moral existence, therefore, is always a complex mixture of good and evil, of achieved self-transcendence, and the careless, thoughtless, or defiant refusal of its exigent normative demands.

Religious authenticity refuses to consent to the reign of sin, however entrenched it may become in our lives or our world. But this heroic unwillingness should not be confused with moral idealism that sincerely wills the good but overlooks or ignores the serious obstacles blocking its attainment (*Second Collection*, 221; *Method*, 38). All genuine authenticity is based upon critical realism. We cannot do what is right or correct what is broken or twisted without knowing in detail what is real. Although religious authenticity sublates epistemic and moral self-transcendence, it continues to rely directly upon them in striving to bring good out of evil and in accepting the painful cost of this ongoing redemptive effort.

Subjectivity and Objectivity in Ethics. Does the late modern turn to the situated subject undermine the objectivity of ethics? And can a contemporary moral theory respect both the erotic and exigent dimensions of the human spirit? Lonergan gives affirmative answers to both of these questions, thus distinguishing his basic ethical position from that of the leading ancient and modern accounts of morality.

Why does the philosophical turn to the ethical subject not end in the loss of objective morality? Kant believed he could avoid this danger by depicting the moral subject as a *noumenal* ego, pure practical reason (*Second Collection*, 70n2). But post-Kantian ethics openly rejected Kant's moral atomism, resituating the moral agent in nature, society, and culture. For Kant, these were heteronomous moral sources that undermined the strict normativity of the moral law. Yet for many of Kant's naturalistic and historicist critics, the loss of moral objectivity should be taken in stride. *Pace* Kant, the utilitarians believed that untutored natural desires and fears were the ontological basis of ethics. Romantic thinkers believed that the uncorrupted passions of the heart took precedence over conventional moral imperatives. Marxists believed that the ruthless construction of a classless society was not subject to moral constraint. Nietzsche believed that the codes and ideals of Western morality had their affective source in *ressentiment*. Moral relativists believe that the limited validity of ethical judgments and norms is historically and culturally conditioned. Emotivists believe that evaluative judgments are disguised expressions of individual or group preferences.[92] In the post-Kantian era, an explicit belief in moral objectivity appears incompatible with the dominant anthropological counterpositions.

Lonergan countered this deep moral skepticism by deepening the reigning theories of the situated subject. Against the utilitarians he argued that the unrestricted desires for knowledge and value are *natural* to intentional subjects. Against Romantic defenders of the passions, he argued that the intentional responses of the heart both reveal and distort genuine values. Against Marxist revolutionaries, he argued that profound social injustice could be corrected only through sustained moral realism. Against Nietzsche he argued for critically appropriating our uneven moral inheritance rather than radically subverting it. Against the moral relativists he argued that true evaluative judgments have the same objectivity as reasonable judgments of fact. Against the emotivists he argued that the satisfaction of individual or group preferences is the basic moral criterion only for unconverted subjects; while for morally converted subjects the only genuine goods are the ones we reflectively determine to be really worthwhile.

By itself, the philosophical turn to the situated subject is morally ambiguous. For intentional subjects and the communities that nurture them regularly fail to achieve self-transcendence. They violate the transcendental precepts, fail to honor the transcendental desires, repeatedly succumb to bias and sin, resort to justifying ideology, and refuse the authentic demand for repentance and reform. Whenever these familiar failures occur, human subjectivity precludes objectivity and the position of the moral skeptics is ostensibly strengthened. I say ostensibly, because epistemic and moral objectivity, correctly understood, are always the intentional fruits of sustained self-transcendence, personal and communal (*Method*, 37, 338).

In epistemic objectivity, we come to know what is real by affirming what is true. However, moral objectivity sublates, goes beyond, epistemic achievement. We achieve moral objectivity in our practical inquiry and deliberative choices whenever we actualize what is good, correct and reform what is broken and flawed, and do all that we can to bring good out of evil. Rather than separating or opposing subjectivity and objectivity, Lonergan's critical realism makes all achieved objectivity intentionally dependent on authentic subjectivity and intersubjectivity. In human affairs, objectivity is no more or less rare than the personal or communal authenticity on which it causally depends (CWL, 17:202, 339, 389).

In the polemical rhetoric of enlightened modernity, the authentic individual is often opposed to the oppressive community as a critic or rebel.

The underlying fear is that communal belonging breeds social conformity and cowardice; it stifles personal uniqueness and strengthens institutional oppression. But if the developing individual is invariably dependent on community membership for her education, protection, and fellowship, how can the dangers of constitutive belonging be responsibly balanced and remedied? Lonergan achieves this very difficult balance by conceiving of the individual holistically: as a symbolic intentional animal, rooted in nature, situated in history, reciprocally dependent on others in an evolving network of human relationships. This dynamic pattern of communal interdependence is both a boon and a burden to the individual; while it is essential to personal growth and maturity, it also inevitably implicates the developing subject in the cultural biases of her time and place. How can the intentional subject achieve critical belonging within this web of deeply flawed but sustaining communities?[93] True critical belonging is possible because the modern secular community is not homogenous. The beliefs and convictions transmitted by parents, friends, teachers, colleagues, artists, statesmen, persons of faith frequently clash with each other and with the prevailing cultural biases. Moreover, modern liberal societies are often profoundly self-critical. They regularly submit their own convictions and histories to the test of internal consistency, while providing ample cultural resources for external critique as well. In the third stage of meaning, these cultural resources include the empirical sciences, natural and human, critical historiography and hermeneutics, philosophical reflection and existential conversion, the transcendent insights of religion and theology.

In late modernity, however, the primary cultural challenge is less oppressive uniformity than discordant pluralism: competing and confusing accounts of knowing, knowledge, reality, virtue, obligation, and the divine. And the chief cultural danger is not pluralism per se, but persuasive ideologies, the seductive appeal of the relevant counterpositions. Rationalizing ideologies, however, are not immune from effective critique and reversal. To this end, Lonergan critically appropriates the old and the new, stresses the importance of existential conversion, reveals the radical implications of the transcendental desires and precepts, and emphasizes the redemptive power of grace. None of these critical strategies can guarantee the authenticity of either the individual or the community. But to demand such guarantees is to misunderstand the human condition and the moral tensions inseparable from personal responsibility and freedom.

Authenticity and the Problem of Evil. The critical spirit of modernity has radically challenged both the Christian message and mission. At the heart of this challenge is the problem of evil, physical and moral (CWL, 3: chap. 20). Physical evil seems inconsistent with the comprehensive goodness of divine creation. Moral evil appears to mock the Christian message of God's redemptive and providential love. How can an omniscient and omnipotent God permit so much suffering, injustice, and violence? How can a religious community ostensibly dedicated to Christ remain credible when it authorizes violence, condones injustice, and calmly accepts the suffering of the innocent?[94]

Susan Neiman has argued persuasively that Lisbon and Auschwitz are the defining moments in this powerful moral critique.[95] The Lisbon earthquake of 1755, like other grave natural catastrophes, raised profound doubts about God's benevolent presence in the natural order. The extermination camps at Auschwitz and Treblinka became the concrete historical symbols of the Shoah, the systematic slaughter of millions in the name of ideology and racial purity. Neither religious nor secular institutions and causes fared well in the twentieth century. In the European crisis between the wars, the moral authority of the church was seriously compromised.[96] But the secular rivals of Christianity, on both the right and the left, fared even worse. The systemic terror authorized by Hitler and Stalin made the scandalous sins of the church appear modest in comparison. Revolutionary movements aspiring to create heaven on earth produced the very opposite of what they had promised. But the warranted critique of terror and the ideologies that justified it is manifestly insufficient to restore the lost credibility of the church.

How did Lonergan respond to this sequence of terrible events? He continued to affirm the importance of human liberty and historical responsibility (CWL, 3:710–15). But the gift of created liberty can obviously be used for good and evil; and when exercised collectively, the scope of its morally ambiguous power radically expands. We moderns have far more collective power than our historical predecessors, and therefore much greater responsibility for the state of the world. Illegitimate power, however, is invariably despotic and destructive. As previously noted, the cultural proponents of science/technology celebrated the expansion of power, but diminished the importance of virtue. They trusted that collective liberation from the sins of the past would be sufficient for a glorious future. This complacent trust in the inevitability of progress, as we now know, was extremely naive. For egoistic, group, and general bias did not disappear with feudalism and Latin Christendom, nor did the human capacity for sin and self-deception. If anything, the ideological movements of modernity are far more dangerous than the forces of the ancien régime because of the vast expansion of technical power they command.

Lonergan believed that the only responsible historical strategy was to legitimize the reality of power. But that requires authenticity, self-transcendence, and genuine conversion on the part of the individual, the community, and its institutional and cultural leadership. It also requires distinctively religious virtues: humility, repentance, and self-sacrificing love.[97] Sinful arrogance and pride were pervasive in the ancien régime, but they have been equally present in their capitalist, nationalist, Marxist, and liberal successors. The defensive posture of the church after Trent stifled its own willingness to repent, to engage openly and honestly with its critics, to rectify its sinful omissions and conduct, and to join, without pride or illusion, in collectively responding to the reality of evil.

Lonergan insists that a credible collective response will require both creativity and healing: the free development, with the help of God's grace, of the true human good, personal, institutional, and cultural; the belated healing, with the help of God's mercy, of the reign of evil, beginning with our own sins and their destructive consequences; and then proceeding, as well as we can, to heal the destructive effects of sin in the human communities to which we belong (*Third Collection*, 100–108). Even with divine assistance and support, this will be a fallible and uncertain process, fraught with error, setbacks, and failure. In stark contrast to the Promethean illusions of modernity, it will require humility, not *hubris*; hope, not defiance; forgiveness, not righteous indignation. Paradoxically, the greatest cultural need of late modernity is to recover the true Christian message and the redemptive mission Christ gave to his church in the world.

*Appraisal: The Upper and Lower Blade of Ethics (*Method, *293)*

In his philosophy and theology, Lonergan is consistently a "both-and" thinker. He carefully avoids the polarizing "either-ors" except in his critique of ideology and the cultural counterpositions. In ethics, his normative realism emphasizes the concreteness of the human good at the level of both originating and terminal values. He explicitly refuses, in fact, to appraise ethical actions and their consequences apart from the ethical agents who choose and enact them (*Second Collection*, 82–83). The authenticity of the agent or historical community is the explanatory cause of the goodness of the action. But this seminal claim should not be misread, for the moral subject's objective knowledge of fact and value is a necessary condition of all authentic choice.

Lonergan identifies three complementary levels of moral cognition: the upper blade of ethics, the lower blade of ethics, and the practical wisdom that is needed to integrate them. The upper blade corresponds to what we have called, following Taylor, "moral ontology" and "philosophical anthropology." It refers to the transcendental and transcendent dimensions of moral agency: the unrestricted desires for knowledge and value; the unrestricted transcendental precepts and norms; the normative pattern of intentional operations that complies with these precepts and dynamically responds to these foundational desires. It can also refer to the gift of God's grace and the divine revelations that shape the religious horizon within which the moral reflection of believers occurs. Though the upper blade of ethics is universal and invariant, it is also concrete and dynamic. The upper blade is not a set of propositions and abstract principles, but a set of immanent interior realities constitutive of the subject's being and agency. The universal moral determinants (created nature, distorting bias and sin, and operative and cooperative grace) shape the existential horizon of the subject's moral deliberation, decision, and action.

Within that heuristic moral horizon concrete practical questions and problems regularly emerge, directing the subject's attention to the lower rather than the upper blade. The ethical focus properly shifts from the universal and invariant to the particular and variable. What are the concrete goods to be actualized and the concrete evils to be avoided or remedied in this place, at this time, in this specific set of historical circumstances? And what forms of factual knowledge and commonsense insights are needed to inform and justify our determinate answers to these questions?

Depending on the scope and complexity of the ethical situation, the responsible individual and the deliberating community must draw upon the empirical sciences, natural and human, a deep knowledge of the relevant cultural history, a critical analysis of existing social institutions and practices, as well as the commonsense testimony and judgments of actual men and women on the scene.[98] Although every moral tradition circumscribes the range of legitimate ethical decisions (it is easier to specify in advance what ought *not* to be done), no set of rules, codes, or recipes can determine a priori the best thing to do, say, or suffer here and now (*Second Collection*, 83). That concrete and creative determination is the province of practical wisdom (Aristotle's *phronesis*, Aquinas's *prudentia*). The practically wise person or the community's tested political leadership is responsible for integrating the two blades of ethics. The dynamic normativity of the upper blade combines with the factual specificity of the lower blade in a self-correcting process of inquiry and action. While responsible agents and sound practical policies transform concrete situations for the better, their inauthentic rivals have the opposite effect. But human beings can learn from their failures, can acknowledge and remedy their mistakes. To do this, however, they must avoid the grave ethical traps of ideology, denial, and rationalization, the moral sources of irreversible decline. While the critique of ideology, by itself, cannot undo the process of decline, it is often the necessary first step in dismantling the objective surd and creating the conditions for effective and credible reform.

How should we responsibly evaluate Lonergan's philosophical and theological contributions to ethics? His work is extremely important but self-consciously incomplete.[99] His several insights into the upper blade of ethics are deep and enduring. He effectively grasped and articulated the functional complementarity of objective knowing and authentic living, and he affirmed the strategic importance of intellectual, moral, and religious conversions for resolving ethical and metaethical disagreements. Finally, as a critical methodologist, he recognized both the power and limits of transcendental method in ethics. Lonergan's transcendental method is clearly not designed as an imperialist instrument. While creating a heuristic framework for collaborative deliberation and action, he repeatedly stressed the practical importance of the specialized and differentiated knowledge provided by the lower blade. And Lonergan correctly insists on the need to integrate the upper and lower blades of ethics in generating wise and effective solutions to our many personal and public problems.

In both metaphysics and ethics, the upper blade provided by philosophers and theologians can only do so much. Without a robust, flexible, and realistic lower blade, the ethical scissors simply can't cut.

Thus Lonergan has provided a normative dialectical framework for confronting the central dilemmas of Christian ethics today.[100] These dilemmas include: war and peace in an age of nuclear weapons; asymmetric warfare and the ideologically driven reliance on terror; the difficulties of achieving economic, social, and political justice in an interconnected global community, while securing the needs of the poor and the vulnerable; the profound political and cultural challenge, especially for the Catholic Church, of fully respecting and supporting the equality and dignity of women; the urgent need to develop a credible and persuasive sexual ethics that draws deeply on the practical experience and insights of women and men at all stages of human development and maturity; the equally urgent need to clarify the limits and moral constraints on technological development, especially in the fields of biology, pharmacology, and medicine; and, finally, articulating a credible framework of normative principles and practical policies in the related fields of ecology, energy, and macroeconomics while responsibly protecting the increasingly vulnerable natural world.

As Lonergan openly acknowledges, devising authentic responses to these urgent moral dilemmas is beyond the competence of the most gifted methodologist. The persisting ethical need of our time is for creative collaboration in theoretical inquiry, practical deliberation, and cooperative action by all women and men of goodwill (CWL, 3:7; *Method*, xii, 361–66). Lonergan's heuristic contribution, though limited in scope, is essential to this collaborative effort.

Virtues and Values. How is Lonergan's ethics of authenticity related to the important moral tradition of virtue ethics? In his post-*Insight* writing, Lonergan clearly shifted from a faculty psychology of the soul to the intentional analysis of the subject. Although he no longer based his philosophy and theology on metaphysical terms and relations, he sought to transpose rather than reject the enduring insights of Aristotle, Augustine, and Aquinas (CWL, 17:410, 426–31).

Within the Thomist tradition, the virtues are conceived as metaphysical habits that perfect the powers and operations of the soul. This metaphysical analysis applies to both natural and supernatural virtues. Human beings acquire the natural virtues through the appropriate education and training; the supernatural virtues, by contrast, are direct gifts of God to the soul. One of the great merits of Thomism is the diversity of virtues it recognizes: the moral virtues, like courage and self-control, that perfect human sensibility; the intellectual virtues, like theoretical and practical wisdom, that perfect the inquiring mind; the associative virtues, like justice, friendship, marital and familial love, that strengthen and support interpersonal relationships; the divine gifts of faith, hope, and *caritas* (*agape*) that enable humans to share in the interior life of God.

When Lonergan turns philosophically from the soul to the subject, when he elevates authenticity to the supreme human good, does he flatten the landscape of moral appraisal by reducing all human virtues to one?[101] I don't believe that he does, but I acknowledge that he fails to answer this challenge explicitly. On my reading of Lonergan's ethics, authenticity is a transcendental virtue and inauthenticity a transcendental vice. Both are moral attributes of the intentional subject effectively measured by the transcendental principles that constitute the upper blade of ethics. It is fidelity to these principles that constitutes the subject as authentic, and their violation that has the opposite effect. Concretely, the most genuine human beings struggle to become more authentic by acknowledging and striving to withdraw from their own inauthenticity and that of the communities to which they belong.

While Lonergan's transcendental appraisal is sound and important, it is also structurally incomplete. Just as the upper and lower blades of ethics are complementary, so are the transcendental and categorial virtues.[102] By the categorial virtues, I refer to the normative dispositions of intentional subjects that enable them to feel, think, judge, deliberate, decide, act, suffer, and cooperate with others reasonably and responsibly. These virtues of the lower blade are directed to the concrete circumstances and situations of ordinary life. They include the virtues of self-restraint, tact, patience, generosity, compassion, impartiality, kindness, courage, flexibility, honesty, forgiveness, fidelity, wit, sensitivity, endurance, fairness, and practical wisdom, among countless others.

These are important virtues of the intentional subject rather than the soul which are acquired and exercised in the course of the subject's protracted personal development. They complement rather than rival the transcendental virtue of authenticity by revealing what authenticity concretely requires in the plentitude of human existence. By acknowledging these virtues and their correlative vices we profoundly enrich our understanding of the polymorphic subject and substantially augment and refine our operative moral vocabulary. This is a truth the great poets and novelists have always understood, and it helps to explain why the careful study of literature and history is such a critical part of our moral education.

All the human virtues, transcendental, categorial, and supernatural, are both originating and terminal values. As originating values they are among the concrete moral sources enabling us to discover and actualize the human good. As terminal values they are among the legitimate goods a sound education and culture should seek to inculcate. Although the supernatural virtues are divine gifts, not human attainments, only an effective moral education can create the interior conditions for their fruitful reception by the subject. Lonergan's comprehensive commitment to objective values includes everything in existence that is really worthwhile. The categorial virtues we've named should be explicitly included among the human values Lonergan prizes and seeks to promote.

Illegitimate Power. Lonergan gradually extends the ethics of authenticity from individual persons to historical communities (CWL, 4:227–28; *Method*, 80). Drawing on the results of his intentionality analysis, he distinguishes four complementary levels of human association: experiential, intellectual, rational, moral. An intentional community of persons is based on a common field of experience, a common set of operative ideas and beliefs, a shared commitment to common values and institutions. This intersubjective structural analysis helps to explain why particular communities historically flourish and decline. Without a common field of experience, the community's members become disconnected; without common ideas and beliefs they repeatedly misinterpret the world and their peers; without common values and ends they act at cross-purposes and lose trust in each other's good faith.

Intergenerational cooperation binds a historically enduring community together. Successful communities generate the practical power they require by drawing on both past achievement and existing knowledge, virtue, skill, and leadership (*Third Collection*, 5–7). While collective power is clearly preferable to impotence (since the world's work always needs to be done), the creation and exercise of power are always morally ambiguous.

Whenever human beings cooperate they generate power, and whenever power is actually used it changes the world for good or ill. The moral appraisal of power concerns the reasons why humans cooperate, the ends they pursue in concert, and the effects of their cooperative activity on both the natural and historical worlds and on the integrative bonds within the community itself. To be specific, both love and fear can be sources of human cooperation; both peace and war can be the goal of cooperative activity; both prosperity and depression can result from economic initiatives; both loyalty and resentment can emerge from cooperative action.

For Lonergan, a community's power is legitimate when it is generated and exercised authentically. Inauthentic power, by contrast, is illegitimate, warranting moral critique, public dissent, and, when necessary, concerted resistance. All historical communities exercise power through their social institutions, the functionally differentiated schemes of cooperation in which their members assume different roles, perform different tasks, exercise different skills and virtues, and make distinctive contributions to the terminal values they commonly seek. The secular world today contains an extraordinary array of such institutional arrangements: federal, state, and local governments, economic corporations both national and global, small businesses, political parties, labor unions, colleges and universities, religious institutions, the growing number of voluntary associations constituting civil society. The more comprehensive the aims of these communal institutions, the more they depend on a shared institutional culture for successful performance and outcomes.

Those who exercise leadership within these institutions concretely direct their employment of power. They are granted authority, the institutional right to issue commands and directives, which their colleagues are then expected to obey. Just as the generation and exercise of power can be morally appraised, so can the conduct of institutional leadership. This appraisal is complicated, for the existing leaders of a community may possess procedural legitimacy (they were appointed in accord with internally accepted norms), while their substantive decisions and actions are clearly unjust. At the same time, the community's institutions and procedures may be structurally flawed, while their leaders try vainly to do what is right.

All social institutions, like their individual members, are a complex mixture of the authentic and the inauthentic. There are extreme cases, of course: totalitarian regimes, terrorist groups, criminal syndicates, associations united by hatred and violence. These groups elicit no genuine loyalty; they deserve no voluntary obedience. But because there are no perfect communities, it is very important that our comparative appraisals of existing institutions be historically informed, factually nuanced, and critically free of utopian illusions. Historical communities, as well as their animating cultures, institutions, and leaders, are invariably compromised by bias, misconduct, ideology, and sin. In morally appraising these complex social realities, we need carefully to distinguish their practical merits and limitations, and rigorously to avoid any leveling moral equivalence.[103] The critique of ideology is especially important in contemporary social ethics, for while illegitimate conduct is morally troubling, its systematic justification is particularly dangerous. For this reason, institutional transparency, the personal accountability of those exercising authority, secure individual rights, and credible public forums for discussion, critique, and dissent are among the distinguishing marks of every free society.[104]

What corrective measures should be taken against illegitimate power? To answer this practical question concretely, we need to rely on the upper and lower blades of ethics, the transcendental and categorial virtues, and the exercise of practical wisdom. We need first to determine the nature, sources, and gravity of what we judge to be wrong. Then we need to articulate our dialectical analysis and appraisal persuasively both within and outside the relevant community. Finally, we need to decide, after candid and careful deliberation, what practical remedies would be most effective in correcting the wrongs and healing the harms we oppose.

A broad spectrum of prudential remedies exists, stretching from tacit dissent and noncompliance to civil disobedience, armed resistance, and open rebellion. Lonergan does not offer a remedial formula for correcting collective injustice, relying instead on the situation-specific judgments of practical wisdom. While this epistemic sobriety is contextually justified, the responsible citizen (employee, shareholder, religious believer, and others) remains unclear and uncertain just where Lonergan stands concretely on the categorial norms of legitimacy for democratic governments, economic corporations, and businesses, and especially religious communities like the Catholic Church. What their mature members really want to know is not whether these institutions are legitimate or illegitimate, *tout court*, but precisely when, how, and why they abuse their power, with what harmful consequences, and what concretely should be done to restore their legitimacy and effective authority.[105]

Redeeming the World: Sobriety and Hope

Lonergan placed comprehensive existential conversion at the center of his philosophy and theology: the intellectual conversion from the world of immediacy to the unrestricted universe of being; the moral conversion from individual and group satisfactions to the unrestricted universe of value; religious conversion from love of oneself and one's own to the wholehearted love of God and neighbor. Christian conversion, in particular, reveals the mysterious depth of God's unconditional love: revealing that the triune God who created and sustains the universe responded to human violence and sin by sending the divine Word into the world to restore its corrupted integrity. Christ founded his church to proclaim the gospel of *agape* to every nation and people, and to carry forward his mission of personal and historical redemption.

Because the three forms of conversion are complementary, they shape the intentional horizon of Christian moral reflection. They also help Christians to avoid the reduction or narrowing of the church's historic message and mission. Catholic Christianity, especially, should resist such truncation, for *catholic* (*katholou*) means comprehensive, inclusive, all embracing.[106] The virtue of Catholicity is essentially a virtue of wholeness. If the Christian church was founded for the task of comprehensive redemption, then its evangelical mission extends to the whole of creation.

From the beginning, Christians have struggled to understand the full scope of their redemptive mission. That struggle continues unabated today. Did Christ come only to "save the souls" of the faithful, or to redeem all that God originally created? The incarnational tradition to which Lonergan belongs views redemption in holistic (catholic) terms. That explains Lonergan's dual emphasis on the personal and historical responsibility of Christians. It also explains his affirmation of transcendent and immanent values, his explicit commitment to the complementary goods and ends of time and eternity. As a critical Christian humanist, Lonergan distinguishes the goodness of created nature from the violence of sin and the redemptive power of grace. His moral theology, like that of Aquinas, treats sin as an important but derivative and secondary cause, as a distortion of created nature and a recurrent occasion for grace.

This comprehensive ontological and moral stance enables Lonergan to avoid two familiar but polarizing counterpositions: the "Christian" rejection of the sinful world as beyond hope of redemption; and the secular rejection of divine transcendence and eternal life as fictional barriers to worldly allegiance and historical effort. For Lonergan, these are false and divisive choices, for it is the wholehearted love of God that leads directly to love of neighbor, and the profound love of neighbor that generously embraces the work of redeeming the world.

How should the historical responsibility of Christians be understood? First, theirs is a collaborative responsibility generously shared with them by God, a divine calling in imitation of Christ and supported by the Holy Spirit. Second, they are commanded to use all of their talents, affective, intellectual, moral, and religious, to create and protect what is good and to heal what is sinful and broken. Third, they are required to be consistently authentic in their redemptive activity, faithfully complying with the transcendental precepts, refusing to do evil in the vain hope of restoring the good. Finally, they have the abiding memory of Christ's heroic charity to teach them the high price of redemption in a sinful and broken world.

From the Enlightenment onward, secular modernity has also embraced the challenge of historical responsibility. Tragically, this laudable project was undertaken with serious illusions: that radical liberation from the past would ensure prosperity and peace; that a proletarian revolution would lead to a classless society; that the cult of the nation would redress historic injustices; that the power of technology could create a new heaven on earth. After Verdun, Auschwitz, the gulag, and Hiroshima, it was finally clear that the gods of exclusive humanism had failed, that the era of secular innocence was over.[107]

But the critique of ideology is only the first step in meeting the moral challenge of our time. While legitimate critique discredits the utopian illusions of the past, it leaves the systemic injustices of the present in place. To correct these injustices, three things are particularly needed: a concrete and comparative dialectical analysis of the merits and failings of existing institutions and cultures; authentic practical discernment, based on wisely integrating the two blades of ethics, of how best to remedy the gravest existing injustices, locally, nationally, and globally; the broadest ecumenical cooperation across religious and sectarian lines in the ongoing work of redeeming the world. To be wise and effective, these cooperative ventures will require the mature virtues of sobriety and hope. Sobriety recognizes that divine creation and grace have not eliminated bias, ideology, and sin. It also recognizes that without moral and religious conversion the demoralizing clash of individual and group egoisms will continue to prevent or obstruct every serious effort at reform. Sobriety brings an indispensible realism to the work of redemption. It fosters honesty, humility, and the slow shedding of moral illusions. In isolation, however, historical sobriety often leads to pessimism, resignation, the acceptance of systemic injustice as "the way of the world." Christian hope combines the critical realism of sobriety with the quiet confidence that we are doing God's work, that God joins us in this unending redemptive effort, and that courage, patience, and wisdom are needed to bring good out of evil.

Realism, Repentance, Reform, and Renewal

Before he died in 1984, Bernard Lonergan made a profound contribution to the renewal of the Catholic Church.[108] In his writing and teaching, he raised Catholic philosophy and theology to the exigent level of our time. He did not retreat from "the chill winds of modernity" but responsibly addressed the cultural challenges they presented to his church and its leadership. He showed how Catholic thought at its best could make the belated transition from classicism to historical mindedness while remaining faithful to Christ's message and mission.

But the *aggiornamento* envisaged by John XXIII requires that the ethics of authenticity be extended to the church as a whole, to the entire pilgrim people of God. What would an authentic contemporary Christianity faithful to the message of the gospel and Christ's mission of redemption really be like?[109]

The church's thought and speech (by that I mean ours, for we are the pilgrim people of God) would be consistently realistic and critical. We would be as truthful as we could in understanding and appraising our past, our present, and the complexity of the world that we serve. Genuinely repentant, we would not justify past failures, conceal present vices and sins, or shrink from the hard challenge of conversion and change.

Our understanding of human existence would be deeply historical. While the redemptive message of the gospel is constant, it must be proclaimed with fresh credibility to each culture and people in history. Such an ecumenical church would treat everyone with dignity and respect. Without glossing over genuine differences, its internal and external dialogues would seek mutual understanding and, where possible, consensus in judgment. It would be a continually learning and teaching church, conscious of its limits as well as its strengths.

An authentically Christian church would abandon the heavy baggage of patriarchy. Women and men are equally created in God's image, equally redeemed by Christ's sacrifice, equally inspired by the Spirit, and equally called to the service of God in the world. As a matter of basic justice, all the ministries of the church would be fully open to women.[110]

The principles of collegial governance and significant lay participation proclaimed in Vatican II would be fully and finally implemented. The unifying role of the pope is consistent with a far less centralized, bureaucratic, and secretive manner of conducting the church's affairs. The institutional practice and governance of Catholic Christianity must become a credible model of freedom and justice if the church's prophetic ministry to the world is to be taken seriously.

If the church Lonergan faithfully served becomes a credible agent of reconciliation, if it reveals by its discourse and practice that its authenticity is genuine, it will find, I believe, a troubled world hungry for its presence and ministry.[111] For the conflicted world of late modernity needs the insight, wisdom, and compassion of Christianity as much as any period in history. A humble and repentant church, a joyful and honest church, a genuinely "catholic" church, can again become a light unto the nations by consistently searching for truth, overcoming evil with good, and by charitably resolving the painful divisions within its own ranks. The profound challenge of *aggiornamento* is ours.

Epilogue

Bernard Lonergan is best understood as a critical Christian humanist seeking to raise Christian philosophy and theology to meet the cultural challenges and disciplinary standards of our time. By *cultural* he explicitly meant the theoretical superstructure of the natural and human sciences, the provisional discoveries of historical scholarship, the verified insights of a critical and comprehensive philosophy, and a functionally specialized theology based on three existential conversions able to mediate the Christian religion effectively to a diversified contemporary audience. But he also meant the particular beliefs and moral convictions that inform the several varieties of practical common sense. Meeting the standards of our time required designing and partly executing a philosophy and theology that were simultaneously critical, methodical, and credibly comprehensive.

Lonergan also believed that philosophy and theology have to become collaborative enterprises. But the collaboration they require is importantly different from that of the specialized sciences. Contemporary philosophers and theologians must learn to appropriate critically the old (the *vetera*) and the new (the *nova*) if they are to respond persuasively to the cultural crises they face. This task is very easy to state, but very hard to achieve. For what does critical appropriation demand of the individual thinker who would make a significant contribution to the interdisciplinary cultural centers Lonergan claimed were presently needed? The short answer to this question can be stated concisely: sustained personal development, comprehensive self-appropriation, and intellectual, moral, and religious conversion. Unpacking the full meaning and implications of these exigent personal requirements has been one of the central aims of this book.

Drawing on a broad range of Lonergan's writing composed before and after *Insight* and *Method in Theology*, I have identified four distinct cultural challenges that Lonergan chose to confront. The first crisis concerns the tangled knot of our Western cultural heritage. That complex heritage includes the achievements and limitations of classical and medieval culture as well as those of the defining revolutions that transformed Western modernity: scientific, historical, philosophical, and democratic. Among our peers, there are prominent cultural conservatives who generously embrace the *vetera* while rejecting the *nova*. There are equally prominent cultural liberals who tend to do just the opposite. And there are influential cultural radicals who cast suspicion on the entire Western intellectual and moral inheritance. Lonergan wisely differs from all of these divisive and partisan scholars, calling for the critical appropriation of the old and the new by a collaborative center of responsible thinkers and scholars striving to embrace critically the whole of our uneven history. He further strengthens this ecumenical appeal by explaining just how urgent and arduous a task critical appropriation actually is.

Among the personal obstacles to be overcome are the polymorphism of human consciousness, the human predilection for picture thinking, the personal difficulty of sustained intellectual and moral development, the four forms of distorting bias, and the seductive lure of the ideological counterpositions. The relevant cultural barriers include the powerful, though often tacit, influence of scientism and exclusive naturalism in cosmology; reductionism and exclusive humanism in anthropology; relativism and emotivism in moral theory; possessive individualism and collectivism in political thought; secularism and the Promethean rejection of God in theology. Given these significant personal and cultural barriers, Lonergan's nuanced distinction between dialectic and dialogue is especially relevant. The dialectical critique of philosophical and theological counterpositions is an indispensable part of Lonergan's remedial strategy. But free, open, and respectful dialogue with our fragmented cultural peers is a necessary complement to dialectical criticism, for the collaborative work of the critical center cannot wait until Lonergan's exigent standards are commonly met.

The four chapters of this book are intended to show how Lonergan's redemptive project strategically developed from the critical appropriation of our cultural heritage (chap. 1) to the dialectical defense of our common capacity for intellectual and moral self-transcendence (chap. 2). But the exigent human demand for self-transcendence is not limited to objective knowledge and responsible living. It inexorably unfolds into the profound demand for an authentic religious faith, a demand only heightened by the daunting obstacles facing religious commitment in our secular age (chap. 3). In the concluding chapter on the challenges of Catholic renewal, the central themes of Lonergan's life work are brought together. After describing the Catholic struggle with modernity and John XXIII's bracing call for *aggiornamento*, the chapter examines Lonergan's distinctive contributions to the philosophical and theological renewal of his church. Particular attention is given to his philosophy and theology of God and to the ethics of authenticity, personal and communal, that he vigorously defended and practiced.

After nearly fifty years of reading and reflecting on Lonergan's work, what do I believe are his deepest and most enduring achievements? Lonergan's *Insight* is a truly great book, comparable in philosophical importance to Aristotle's *Metaphysics*, Kant's *Critique of Pure Reason*, Hegel's *Phenomenology of Spirit*, Wittgenstein's *Tractatus*, and Heidegger's *Being and Time*. When the groundbreaking discoveries of *Insight* are combined with the synoptic historical vision outlined in *Method in Theology*, we have the critical basis for a contemporary philosophy and theology able to satisfy the exigent standards of modernity.

In *Insight*, Lonergan executed a philosophical strategy that begins in cognitional theory, expands into epistemology, metaphysics, and ethics, and climaxes in speculative theology. In *Method*, he outlined a general philosophical background based largely on the prior discoveries of *Insight*, and then articulated a detailed heuristic foreground consisting of the eight functional specialties in theology. When these complementary texts are taken together, Lonergan's foundational ideas and his most significant discoveries (and rediscoveries) become reasonably clear. In my judgment, these ideas and discoveries include the following.

Cognitional theory: At the heart of Lonergan's cognitional analysis are the transcendental principles he discovered, articulated, and affirmed: the unrestricted desires for knowledge and value (the *eros* of mind and the *eros* of the human spirit);[1] generalized empirical method, "a normative pattern of recurrent and related operations" yielding cumulative and progressive results in every field of cognition and action; direct, reflective, deliberative, and evaluative insights, the central cognitional events within generalized empirical method; the transcendental precepts that articulate the immanent normative operational requirements of objective knowing and authentic living. On the basis of these complementary principles, Lonergan was able to establish the relative autonomy of the five realms of cognitive meaning, the important distinction between descriptive and explanatory inquiry, the complementarity of the four heuristic structures, and the philosophical and cultural significance of the three stages of cognitive meaning.

Epistemology: Lonergan's epistemology is structurally grounded on his articulated cognitional theory just as human knowledge is based on the normative structure of cognitional process. This internal connection supports his original interpretation of epistemic and moral objectivity as the intentional fruits of authentic subjectivity and intersubjectivity. Lonergan further proceeds to clarify the elusive modern idiom of "authenticity" by basing genuine authenticity on the self-transcending performance of intentional subjects and communities. Among Lonergan's great epistemological achievements are his persuasive defense of critical realism, and his dialectical critique of picture thinking and the epistemological and metaphysical counterpositions to which picture thinking regularly leads.

Metaphysics: Metaphysics is traditionally described as the theory of being, but no part of philosophy has been subject to more serious criticism. By grounding his critical metaphysics in an empirically verified cognitional theory, Lonergan is able to clarify the several senses of "being" and to distinguish his specifically heuristic notion of being from the leading philosophical counterpositions. For Lonergan, philosophers should learn to conceive of being sequentially: as the unrestricted heuristic object of the transcendental desire to know; as what is knowable through intelligent grasp and reasonable affirmation; and as what is known through reasonably affirming true answers to the full range of intelligent questions.

These explicitly second-order definitions of being (based on the appropriated discoveries of cognitional theory) allow Lonergan to develop a dynamic and integrative metaphysics that fully respects the relative autonomy of the empirical sciences and the unfolding discoveries of intentionality analysis. It also allows him to address the important integrative demands of late modernity with his cosmology of emergent probability, his philosophical anthropology of the polymorphic intentional subject, and his functionally specialized theology attentive to the demands of both critical reason and religious faith.

Metaphilosophy: Kant directly criticized metaphysics by comparing it unfavorably with mathematics and natural science. While these genuine sciences had effective methods for distinguishing "sound knowledge from shallow talk," metaphysics, in Kant's judgment, did not. Kant's specific objections to transcendent metaphysics were generalized by his successors into a comprehensive critique of philosophy's knowledge claims. According to these deflationary critics, philosophy was epistemically inferior to the empirical sciences because it lacked a critical method to resolve its internal disagreements. Lonergan's greatest metaphilosophical contribution was his brilliantly conceived dialectical strategy of dividing philosophical statements into positions and counterpositions, statements formulated as answers to his highly specific philosophical questions, and then showing how only the verifiable philosophical positions invite intelligent and reasonable development while the unverifiable counterpositions do not. Later, in *Method in Theology*, Lonergan explains the critical role of intellectual, moral, and religious conversions in resolving dialectical conflicts in both the philosophy and theology of God.

Moral philosophy: In the secular culture of late modernity both ethics and metaethics are fiercely contested. The gravest human concerns are at stake here. How should we live as individual persons and as members of imperfect but indispensable human communities? What concrete goods should we pursue, in what order of rank, and what evils must we avoid, correct, and redeem? And what are our primary obligations to nature, other persons, our country, and God? These are among the central and inescapable questions of contemporary ethics.

Despite the gravity of these practical concerns, our moral disagreements extend beyond substantive ethical differences. Can our basic ethical questions be answered objectively? Can our different moral priorities and values be reconciled? Can important ethical conflicts be reasonably and responsibly resolved? These are among the critical questions in contemporary metaethics.

Lonergan's enduring contributions to moral philosophy are primarily methodological. He offers persuasive and groundbreaking answers to the difficult questions of metaethics, and articulates a normative transcendental standard, comprehensive authenticity, that every ethical agent, community, and decision should meet. His ethics of personal and communal authenticity, rooted in the human struggle for comprehensive self-transcendence, provides the critical moral realism we need at a time of unprecedented moral confusion.

Theology: Though Lonergan wrote systematic theological treatises on the incarnation and the Trinity, we have focused on his important contributions to theological method. Like his mentor Aquinas, he distinguished but refused to separate philosophical and revealed theology. His philosophical theology responds to the question(s) of God from the standpoint of self-appropriation and existential conversion. His revealed theology is based on the varying human responses to the several forms of the divine initiative in nature and history. Those transformative initiatives include the divine word of creation, the divine gift of love, *agape*, bestowed on us all, and the several divine revelations to Israel culminating historically in the person of Jesus of Nazareth. Lonergan consistently argues that revealed theology sublates the philosophy of God, preserving its insights while transcending its inherent limitations. Lonergan's important methodological distinction between mediating and mediated theology enables contemporary theological specialists to appropriate critically the relevant religious *vetera* and the *nova* before communicating the message and mission of their faith to the pluralistic cultures and communities of our day.

In concluding this brief summary of Lonergan's enduring achievements, allow me to repeat what I initially claimed in the preface. His many intellectual and moral discoveries are so basic in nature, so fertile in their implications, and so relevant to our cultural crises that they firmly establish Lonergan as one of the truly great minds of the twentieth century. I now invite you, patient reader, to examine and appraise these strong evaluative claims for yourself.

NOTES

CHAPTER ONE
The Tangled Knot of Old and New

1. The project of critically appropriating the *vetera* and the *nova* is relevant to nearly all of Lonergan's published writing. In CWL, 2:222–24, the emphasis is on appropriating the *vetera*; in CWL, 3:768–69, and in most of the post-*Insight* writings, on appropriating the *nova*. CWL is my shorthand for *The Collected Works of Bernard Lonergan*, which has been published in multiple volumes (see the bibliography). Volume 2 is entitled *Verbum*; volume 3 is *Insight*.

2. See CWL, 1:2, 4, 133–41; *A Second Collection* (Philadelphia: Westminster Press, 1974), 43–54; *A Third Collection* (New York: Paulist Press, 1985), 35–54; CWL, 17:282–87.

3. In *Insight*, the complex legacies of modern science and philosophy are explored; in *Method in Theology* (New York: Herder and Herder, 1972), close attention is given to modern historiography and hermeneutics; technological advances and activity within economic and political institutions are treated under the rubric of "common sense" in *Insight*; economic analysis receives special attention in CWL, 15 and 21.

4. Lonergan's commitment to cross-disciplinary collaboration is explicit in CWL, 3:7, and in *Method*, xi–xii.

5. *Third Collection*, 170–71.

6. Lonergan borrows the term *historical mindedness* from Alan Richardson. See *Third Collection*, 171, and CWL, 17:354. See also Frederick Crowe, *Developing the Lonergan Legacy* (Toronto: Toronto University Press, 2004), chap. 5, 78–110.

7. See Michael McCarthy, "The Critical Appropriation of Tradition," *Soundings* 82, no. 3–4 (Fall/Winter 1999).

8. "In its proper meaning the term 'ideology' includes a moral judgment of reprobation both of the system of thought that one opposes and of the system of actions that system of thought would legitimate" (CWL, 17:323). See also *Method*, 357–59.

9. Lonergan learned this lesson concretely in "reaching up to the mind of Aquinas." He acknowledged this debt in CWL, 3:769, and thematized its implications in *Method*, chap. 7.

10. In *Insight* (CWL, 3), Lonergan focuses on the unrestricted desire to know and the equally unrestricted desire to actualize the good. In *Method in Theology*, he distinguishes three transcendental notions constituting the second, third, and fourth levels of intentional consciousness respectively. In my judgment, the two accounts are complementary, for the treatment in *Method* largely makes explicit what is implicit in *Insight*. To simplify the exposition of Lonergan's thought, I have generally used his *Insight* formulations, though I recognize when relevant the greater specificity and detail provided in *Method* (11–13, 23–24, 36).

11. For the critical impact of theoretical specialization on contemporary philosophy, see Michael McCarthy, *The Crisis of Philosophy* (Albany: SUNY Press, 1990). For the impact of critical historiography and hermeneutics on theology, see Lonergan's *Method in Theology*.

12. For a compact summary, see *Method*, 85–99.

13. I have found particularly helpful in this section Charles Taylor's *Sources of the Self* (Cambridge, MA: Harvard University Press, 1989) and *A Secular Age* (Cambridge, MA: Harvard University Press, 2007); Alasdair MacIntyre's *Three Rival Versions of Moral Inquiry* (Notre Dame, IN: University of Notre Dame Press, 1990); Leszek Kolakowski's *Modernity on Endless Trial* (Chicago: University of Chicago Press, 1990); and Nicholas Boyle's *Who Are We Now?* (Notre Dame, IN: University of Notre Dame Press, 1998).

14. For the evolution of Lonergan's reflections on meaning, see CWL, 3: chaps. 10 and 17; CWL, 4: chap. 16; *Method*, chaps. 3 and 7.

15. See CWL, 3: chaps. 6 and 7, 703–18; CWL, 10; and *Method*, 50–55.

16. Lonergan explicitly addresses the challenge of pluralism in *Method*, chaps. 10–12; CWL, 17: chap. 5; and *Third Collection*, chap. 15. See Michael McCarthy, "Towards a New Critical Center," *Method* 15, no. 2 (Fall 1997).

17. In defending his "way of life" Socrates explicitly distinguishes his old accusers from his new ones. The old accusations charge him with cosmology and sophistry, the new accusations with impiety and corruption of the young. In his legal defense, Socrates shows how the new accusations implicitly depend on the older cultural criticisms. See Plato's *Apology*.

18. Eric Voegelin's *The World of the Polis* (Baton Rouge: Louisiana State University Press, 1957) is particularly illuminating on this dependence.

19. See Jaroslav Pelikan, *The Emergence of the Catholic Tradition (100–600)* (Chicago: University of Chicago Press, 1971), 27–41.

20. Although Lonergan emphasizes the fragmentation of Aquinas's thought after the condemnation of 1277, he is acutely aware of Thomas's complex historical legacy. This legacy includes the Dominican retrieval of Thomism before the Council of Trent and the assimilative work of important Jesuit thinkers like Molina, Bellarmine, and Suarez during the Counter-Reformation. In the late nineteenth century, under the explicit direction of Pope Leo XIII, there was a deliberate and extensive renewal of Thomism that produced eminent thinkers like Gilson, Maritain, and Marechal, among many others.

21. I have borrowed the metaphor of a "tangled knot" from Pascal's *Pensées*, no. 131.

22. In his important studies in the history of science (*Studies in Leonardo da Vinci* and *The System of the World*), Pierre Duhem has shown how late medieval and early Renaissance thought contain a powerful critique of both Aristotle's philosophy of nature (his physics) and his philosophy of science. Duhem also critically retrieves the important contributions of Roger Bacon, Jean Buridan, and Nicholas Oresme (the school of Paris) to the origins of modern physics. Thus Aristotle's intellectual authority was compromised well before the Copernican Revolution of the sixteenth and seventeenth centuries.

23. See Herbert Butterfield, *The Origins of Modern Science* (New York: Free Press, 1957); Alexandre Koyré, *From the Closed World to the Infinite Universe* (New York: Harper and Brothers, 1958); A. N. Whitehead, *Science and the Modern World* (New York: Macmillan, 1925); Thomas Kuhn, *The Copernican Revolution* (Cambridge, MA: Harvard University Press, 1957).

24. There is both an ontological and an epistemic dimension to Aristotle's conception of science (*episteme*). The ontological dimension refers to the scientific study of patterns of causal necessity. The epistemic dimension refers to the certainty with which these causal patterns are known to be true. In the fourteenth and fifteenth centuries, when the ontological necessity of natural causality is explicitly challenged, the corresponding epistemic challenge to scientific certainty understandably follows. Ironically, the leading modern interpreters of physics—for example, Galileo, Descartes, and Newton—retained Aristotle's classical theory of science, while consciously overturning his geocentric cosmology.

25. For Lonergan's critique of the extrascientific assertions of numerous scientists and scientific popularizers, see CWL, 3, especially chaps. 2–5; CWL, 4: chap. 14; *Second Collection*, 3, 106–8; *Third Collection*, 107–8; *Method*, 247–49.

26. See in particular CWL, 3:151–62, and CWL, 3: chaps. 6 and 7.

27. CWL, 3:353–60; *Method*, 18–20.

28. There are striking parallels between Kant's philosophical project and Lonergan's. Kant sought to answer three related questions in the light of the Copernican Revolution: What can I know? What ought I to do? What may I hope for? While Lonergan criticizes Kant's substantive answers to these questions, his own conception of philosophy in the third stage of meaning has markedly Kantian overtones. See, in particular, *Second Collection*, 75–86, and CWL, 4:192–204.

29. CWL, 4:244; *Method*, 154–55; CWL, 17:261–63, 275–76, 419, 428.

30. In highly schematic terms, *Insight* addresses the challenge to contemporary *philosophy* from the natural and human sciences, *Method* the challenge to contemporary *theology* from critical historiography and hermeneutics. Lonergan's two great constructive works are substantively complementary, as are his revised accounts of contemporary philosophy and theology.

31. See McCarthy, *Crisis of Philosophy*.

32. I have slightly modified Lonergan's actual language in articulating these questions, particularly in my use of the first person plural. See *Method*, 83–85; *Second Collection*, 85–86; CWL, 17:357.

33. See CWL, 3:250–67, 710–15; *Method*, 252–53; *Second Collection*, 113.

34. For Lonergan's persuasive defense of the reasonableness of human belief, see CWL, 3:703–18, and *Method*, 41–47.

35. For the sources and effects of bias, see CWL, 3:214–27, 244–67, and 711–15.

36. See note 10, where the expository language of *Insight* (based on two unrestricted human desires) is contrasted with the more expansive language of *Method*. The three transcendental notions of *Method* are directly correlated with the second, third, and fourth levels of intentional consciousness. Generally, I use the language of *Insight* while acknowledging, where relevant, the greater specificity provided by *Method*.

37. The following claims offer a compact summary of the central conclusions of *Insight*.

38. Whitehead, *Science and the Modern World*, 167, and Stephen Spender, *The God That Failed* (London: Hamilton, 1950), 253–54, emphasize how difficult it is to comply with this precept.

39. See McCarthy, *Crisis of Philosophy*, for the protracted search for a critical and comprehensive philosophical method.

40. See Augustine's *Confessions*, books 3, 7–8, and 10.

41. In *Insight* Lonergan emphasizes the distinction between cognitional *process* (conscious), cognitional *analysis* (self-reflexive), and verified cognitional *theory*

(self-knowledge). In *Method in Theology* the same threefold distinction applies to conversions as *experienced* (conscious), conversions as *thematized* (self-reflexive), and conversions as explicitly *affirmed*, together with their epistemic, moral, and religious implications. The functional theological specialty *foundations* thematizes the three forms of *experienced* conversion and articulates their dialectical import. In both textual contexts, Lonergan carefully distinguishes between the experiential consciousness of the subject and reflexive intentional activity. It is only in reflexive activity that the intentional subject and her operations become the objective (focal) content of intentionality analysis.

42. See CWL, 3: chap. 14, "The Method of Metaphysics"; and *Method*, chaps. 10 and 11.

43. Aristotle, *Metaphysics*, 1.993 a-11–993 b-30; CWL, 2:52.

44. See *Method*, 34–55; CWL, 17:11–19, 140–49.

45. See CWL, 3:626–56; CWL, 10:30, 50–58; *Method*, 47–55; *Third Collection*, chaps. 11–12.

46. See Taylor's *A Secular Age* for the distinct but related senses in which our age is "secular" (1–22). See also chap. 3 of this volume, "Authentic Faith in a Secular Age."

47. For the useful concept of an "overlapping consensus" within a pluralistic society, see John Rawls, *Political Liberalism* (New York: Columbia University Press, 1993), 133–72.

48. The phrase is Iris Murdoch's. See *The Sovereignty of Good* (New York: Schocken Books, 1971), 52.

49. These challenges are explored in detail in chaps. 3 and 4 of this volume.

50. Lonergan's critical references to Plato occur in CWL, 2, 3, 4; *Method*; and *Second Collection*, 264–65. In "Revisiting Insight" in *Second Collection*, 193, he pays special attention to J. A. Stewart's *Plato's Doctrine of Ideas* (Oxford: Clarendon Press, 1909).

51. See in particular Plato's *Gorgias*, *Phaedo*, and *Republic*.

52. *Apology*, 20d–23c.

53. See in particular Plato's *Gorgias*, 456b–458b.

54. In Lonergan's language, this resistance is equivalent to a refusal of conversion. In the Platonic dialogues, these refusals are the principal source of protracted *aporia*.

55. See CWL, 2:41–42, 84–85, 192–99; CWL, 3:290, 388–90, 411, 417, 438, 538.

56. *Phaedo*, 66d–67b, 73c–77; *Meno*, 81b–83c; *Republic*, 507b–509d.

57. See CWL, 2:24–46, 53–55, 168–79, 192–98.

58. *De Anima*, 3.4.

59. CWL, 2:192–96; CWL, 3:437–38.
60. CWL, 3: chap. 15, "Elements of Metaphysics."
61. *Third Collection*, 41–44, 176–82; CWL, 17:355–57. See also Alasdair MacIntyre, *After Virtue* (Notre Dame, IN: University of Notre Dame Press, 1981), 149–50.
62. See Michael McCarthy, "Practical Wisdom, Social Justice and the Global Society," *Journal of the Lonergan Workshop* 22 (2011).
63. See Augustine's *Confessions* (especially book 10) and *The City of God* for the indispensable role of memory in discerning the presence of God in existential and historical time. See also John Dunne, *A Search for God in Time and Memory* (London: Macmillan, 1969).
64. *Confessions*, 3.7, 6.5, 7.1.
65. *Confessions*, 7.10–16.
66. CWL, 1:4–7, 193–204.
67. In the *Confessions*, the original freedom of the created will is central to Augustine's understanding of evil; in the *City of God*, the defining love of the will determines to which of the two eternal cities the human creature ultimately belongs.
68. CWL, 1:85, 192, 196–97; CWL, 3:394, 437.
69. The following claims offer a compact summary of Lonergan's interpretation of Aquinas's cognitional theory in CWL, 2 and 3.
70. See McCarthy, *Crisis of Philosophy*, "The Matrix of Cognitive Meaning," 10–20.
71. The following synopsis is drawn directly from CWL, 1.
72. For the important distinction between essential and effective freedom, see CWL, 3:643–56.
73. See CWL, 2: chap. 5, "Imago Dei"; *The Triune God*; CWL, 11, 12.
74. For Lonergan's compressed account of the "psychological analogy" in Thomas, see CWL, 2: chap. 5, "Imago Dei." For his own more elaborate account, see *The Triune God, Doctrine and Systematics* (Toronto: University of Toronto Press, 2007, 2009). "We desire to know *quid sit Deus*, but in this life the only understanding we can attain is through analogy. Philosophy proceeds from pure perfections by the ways of affirmation, negation and eminence . . . Thus the Augustinian psychological analogy makes Trinitarian theology a prolongation of natural theology, a deeper insight into what God is" (CWL, 2:214–15).
75. *Second Collection*, 43–53, 58–67; *Third Collection*, 47–53; *Method*, 93–96, 309–17.
76. CWL, 3:151–57; *Third Collection*, 63–65; CWL, 17:353–57.
77. CWL, 3:273, 316–17, 320–21, 368–69.

78. CWL, 3: chaps. 2 and 15 (484–507).
79. CWL, 3:126–62.
80. CWL, 17:74, 75, 354, 378.
81. See Charles Taylor, *Hegel and Modern Society* (New York: Cambridge University Press, 1979), 1–23, 154–66, and *Sources of the Self*, chaps. 20 and 21.
82. CWL, 3: chap. 17; CWL, 4: chaps. 15–16; *Second Collection*, 69–86; *Method*, chaps. 3 and 7.
83. *Method*, 69, 96, 106, 108.
84. Kant carefully distinguishes, as Descartes does not, between the transcendental and empirical ego. Because Kant is an *empirical realist*, the objects of experience are independent of the intuitions of the empirical subject. But Kant's empirical realism is combined with *transcendental idealism*, because those same objects are dependent (constituted) by the a priori representations of the transcendental ego. From the transcendental perspective, the objects of human knowledge, therefore, are phenomenal, not noumenal in nature. See also note 36 in chap. 2.
85. Immanuel Kant, *Prolegomena to any Future Metaphysics*, Preamble.
86. Richard Rorty, *The Linguistic Turn* (Chicago: University of Chicago Press, 1967).
87. See McCarthy, *Crisis of Philosophy*, chap. 5, "The New Way of Words," for a detailed account of Sellars's position.
88. See Taylor, *Sources*, chap. 21, "The Expressivist Turn."
89. See Ernst Cassirer's *An Essay on Man* (New Haven: Yale University Press, 1962).
90. See McCarthy, *Crisis of Philosophy*, chaps. 7 and 8.
91. See Descartes's *Discourse on Method*, pt. 2.
92. For Hume's distinction between moral and academic skepticism, see *An Inquiry Concerning Human Understanding*, sec. 12, "Of the Academical or Sceptical Philosophy."
93. Kant, *Critique of Pure Reason*.
94. CWL, 3: chap. 13, "The Notion of Objectivity."
95. See Hannah Arendt, *On Revolution* (New York: Viking, 1965), 51–58.
96. Hannah Arendt, *The Origins of Totalitarianism* (New York: Harcourt Brace, 1966), 139–47, 155–57, 333–35. There are several different editions.
97. MacIntyre, *After Virtue*, 6–34.
98. See McCarthy, "The Critical Appropriation of Tradition," 481–503.
99. *Second Collection*, 69–86.
100. See Wilfrid Sellars, *Science, Perception and Reality* (New York: Humanities Press, 1963), 22.
101. See CWL, 2:20–21; CWL, 4:213–19; *Second Collection*, 75–79.

102. Cartesian skepticism about "knowledge of the external world" has its origin in a distorted "picture" of cognitional process. "A picture held us captive. And we could not get outside it." Ludwig Wittgenstein, *Philosophical Investigations* (New York: Macmillan, 1965), no. 115.

103. This synoptic account of Lonergan's "critical realism" is based on CWL, 4:192–204, 214–19; CWL, 3:22–23, 364–65, 439, 448; *Second Collection*, 218–19, 240–44; CWL, 17:119–31.

104. See CWL, 4: chaps. 15–16; CWL, 18: pt. 3; *Second Collection*, 79–86; Hannah Arendt, *Between Past and Future* (New York: Penguin, 1968), 6–9.

105. This pragmatic conception of human living and knowing unites thinkers as disparate as John Dewey, the early Heidegger, and Gilbert Ryle. From Lonergan's cognitional perspective, they all base their conception of knowing on the commonsense realm of meaning.

106. See Hannah Arendt, *The Human Condition* (Chicago: University of Chicago Press, 1998), 7–21.

107. See CWL, 18: pt. 3.

108. CWL, 4:232–45; *Method*, chap. 3; CWL, 17:107–31, 384, 390.

109. David Tracy, *Plurality and Ambiguity* (Chicago: University of Chicago Press, 1987), chap. 1, "Interpretation, Conversation and Argument."

Chapter Two
Objective Knowing and Authentic Living

1. In particular see CWL, 4:222–45; *Method in Theology* (New York: Herder and Herder, 1972), 81–99; CWL, 10:79–186; CWL, 17:282–431.

2. There are many ways of narrating the cultural history of modernity. In this highly compressed account, I have drawn liberally from the writing of Lonergan, Charles Taylor, Hannah Arendt, A. N. Whitehead, Herbert Butterfield, and Alan Richardson.

3. Dante Alighieri, *Divine Comedy, Inferno*, Canto 26.

4. For a concise summary of Aristotle's hierarchical cosmology, see *Parts of Animals*, 1.5.644b–645b.

5. *Metaphysics*, 12.7.1072a 18–1073a 13.

6. *Physics*, 2.3.194b 16–195a 27; *Metaphysics* 1.3.983a 24–993a 24.

7. The revolt against Aristotle can originally be traced to the condemnation by Bishop Tempier of Paris in 1277. It continued in the late medieval period with the explicit rejection of important aspects of Aristotle's physics and philosophy of science (see note 22 in chap. 1). The resurgent interest in Platonism in the Italian

Renaissance also lessened Aristotle's intellectual and cultural influence, setting the stage for the concerted critique of his cosmology in the Scientific Revolution.

8. This exclusion is starkly explicit in the appendix to pt. 1 of Spinoza's *Ethics*.

9. *Third Collection*, 41–47; *Method*, 93–96, 310–17.

10. *Nicomachean Ethics*, 6.3–11, 10.7–8.

11. Bacon, *Novum Organon*; Descartes, *Discourse on Method*, pt. 6.

12. While Machiavelli is often considered the father of modern political philosophy, it is Thomas Hobbes who first attempts to base political theory on the new science of nature. See especially Hobbes's *De Cive* (1642) and *Leviathan* (1651). A similar approach can also be found in Spinoza's *Tractatus Theologico-Politicus* (1670).

13. See Hannah Arendt, *On Revolution* (New York: Penguin, 1965), 51–58.

14. Aristotle, *Posterior Analytics*, 1.2.71b 9–16; *Posterior Analytics*, 1.4, 6, 8; *Nicomachean Ethics*, 6.3, 6; CWL, 4:238–40; *Third Collection*, 41–47.

15. Immanuel Kant, *Critique of Pure Reason* (New York: St. Martin's Press, 1961), preface to 2nd ed.

16. Ibid.

17. Immanuel Kant, *Groundwork of the Metaphysics of Morals*, trans. H. J. Paton (New York: Harper Torchbooks, 1964), chap. 3, p. 104: "The mere fact of deserving happiness can by itself interest us without the motive of getting a share in this happiness."

18. Kant, *Critique of Pure Reason*, preface to 1st ed.

19. For the origins, character and intellectual and cultural consequences of the Scientific Revolution, see Pierre Duhem, *The System of the World*, Alexandre Koyré, *From the Closed World to the Infinite Universe*, Thomas Kuhn, *The Copernican Revolution*, A. N. Whitehead, *Science and the Modern World*, Herbert Butterfield, *The Origins of Modern Science*, A. C. Crombie, *Styles of Scientific Thinking in the European Tradition*, James Lattis, *Between Copernicus and Galileo*, David Lindberg and Robert Westman, *Reappraisals of the Scientific Revolution*, Margaret Jacob, *The Cultural Meaning of the Scientific Revolution*.

20. See Charles Taylor, *Sources of the Self*, and A. N. Whitehead's account of the cosmology of scientific materialism in *Science and the Modern World*.

21. See Descartes's *Meditations on First Philosophy* and *Principles of Philosophy*.

22. Descartes, preface to the *Principles of Philosophy*.

23. In the *Critique of Pure Reason*, Kant sharply distinguishes the *constitutive* function of intuitions and concepts from the purely *regulative* function of ideas.

24. Although his numerous references to Hegel in *Insight* are often critical, Lonergan also explicitly recognizes Hegel's philosophical brilliance and importance.

25. See Charles Taylor's account of *Nature* as a moral source in *Sources of the Self*, pt. 4, sec. 20.

26. Alfred Lord Tennyson, *In Memoriam*, Canto 56.

27. See Wilhelm Dilthey's *Introduction to the Human Sciences*, ed. Rudolf Makreel and Frithjof Rodi (Princeton: Princeton University Press, 1989).

28. See Edmund Husserl, *Philosophy as Rigorous Science* and *The Crisis of European Sciences and Transcendental Phenomenology*. Also, CWL, 18: sec. 11–13.

29. For Heidegger's *Dasein Analytic*, see *Being and Time*, trans. John Macquarrie and Edward Robinson (New York: Harper and Row, 1962). Also, CWL, 18: sec. 7 and 8, and appendix.

30. See Hannah Arendt, *Between Past and Future* (New York: Penguin, 1968), 3–9.

31. For Lonergan's cosmological principle of "emergent probability," see CWL, 3:144–61, 287–95.

32. See Charles Taylor, *Hegel and Modern Society* (Cambridge: Cambridge University Press, 1979), 154–66.

33. In his appraisal of the epistemic and ontological import of scientific hypotheses and theories, Lonergan is a critical realist. When such theories are provisionally affirmed by the relevant scientific community after faithful adherence to the canons of empirical method, they are not true (*sans phrase*) but "are on the way to truth"; they do not constitute "certain knowledge" but "the best available opinion" of practicing scientists in that field. One reason scientific judgments will not regress from the theories of Einstein and Planck to those of Aristotle and Ptolemy is because the heuristic shift from descriptive to explanatory understanding is irreversible. A second reason is that modern science is committed to providing an explanatory account of all the data of sense.

34. *Method*, 265, 292; *Third Collection*, 144.

35. For Lonergan's contrast of essential and effective freedom, see CWL, 3:643–56.

36. For Lonergan's typology of bias, see CWL, 3:214–27, 244–67.

37. *Method*, 357–59: "Inversely, man is alienated from his true self in as much as he refuses self-transcendence, and the basic form of ideology is the self-justification of alienated man."

38. CWL, 3:95–96, 268–69; *Third Collection*, 140–44.

39. *Method*, 76–77.

40. Ibid., 82–85.

41. CWL, 3:410–12, 422, 438–40, 451–52. For an excellent study of polymorphic subjectivity, see *Lonergan on Philosophic Pluralism: The Polymorphism of Consciousness as the Key to Philosophy*, by Gerard Walmsley (Toronto: University of Toronto Press, 2008).

42. *Method*, 13, 34–36; and numerous passages in CWL, 3. Here, as in chap. 1 (notes 10 and 36), I want to acknowledge Lonergan's three transcendental notions, the transcendental desires for the intelligible, the real, and the valuable, while continuing to emphasize the two unrestricted desires, to know the real and to actualize the good, in order to simplify the textual exposition.

43. *Method*, 241–43, 316, 340; *Second Collection*, 80–82.

44. *Method*, 83, 316; *Second Collection*, 85–86. These passages summarize the comprehensive strategy Lonergan adopts in *Insight*.

45. See CWL, 3:412–15, for Lonergan's dialectical concept of performative inconsistency.

46. CWL, 3:346–52, 405–7; CWL, 4:208–11; *Third Collection*, 57–60.

47. See *Method*, 125–45.

48. See CWL, 3: pt. 1, "Insight as Activity."

49. *Second Collection*, 74; *Third Collection*, 116–17.

50. For the epistemic significance of higher viewpoints, see CWL, 3:37–43, 258–67.

51. For the merits and limitations of logic, see *Second Collection*, 50, 197–99; CWL, 3:596–600.

52. See CWL, 3: chap. 12, "The Notion of Being."

53. See George Berkeley, *Principles of Human Knowledge* (New York: Penguin, 1988), pt. 1, 3.

54. For Lonergan's critique of Kant's cognitional theory, see CWL, 3:362–66; CWL, 4:192–97; *Second Collection*, 77–79.

55. Kant's epistemological position is complicated by his systematic contrast between empirical and transcendental psychology. For the transcendental subject, the alleged bearer of the a priori intuitions and categories, the objects of human knowledge are constituted by these pure subjective representations. But for the empirical subjects whose psychological experiences are temporally and causally ordered, their cognitive objects are treated as mind independent. This distinction allows Kant to be an *empirical realist* with respect to the numerous empirical subjects of inquiry and a *transcendental idealist* with respect to the transcendental ego. In addition, because causation is a category confined to the objects of experience, and we humans have no intuitive experience of the *Ding an sich*, we can't strictly say that things in themselves "cause" representations in the transcendental ego. Thus the parallels between Kant and his rationalist and empiricist predecessors are only analogous. For a persuasive critique of the Kantian project of transcendental psychology, see Peter Strawson, *The Bounds of Sense* (New York: Routledge, 1989).

56. The following points summarize Kant's epistemological and metaphysical conclusions in the *Critique of Pure Reason* and the *Prolegomena to Any Future Metaphysics*.

57. See Thomas Kuhn, *The Structure of Scientific Revolutions*, 2nd ed. (Chicago: University of Chicago Press, 1970).

58. For a concise account of the sources and varieties of pluralism, see Michael McCarthy, "Towards a New Critical Center," *Method* 15, no. 2 (Fall 1997): 122–25.

59. For a powerful critique of "self-authenticating intuitions," see Wilfrid Sellars, *Science, Perception and Reality* (New York: Humanities Press, 1963), where Sellars explicitly criticizes the "myth of the given."

60. See Wittgenstein's *On Certainty*.

61. See W. V. O. Quine, *Ontological Relativity and Other Essays* (New York: Columbia University Press, 1969).

62. For a comprehensive critique of emotivism, see Alasdair MacIntyre, *After Virtue* (Notre Dame, IN: University of Notre Dame Press, 1981).

63. For the important but neglected moral contrast between ontology and advocacy, see Charles Taylor, *Philosophical Arguments* (Cambridge, MA: Harvard University Press, 1995), 181–86. The same contrast pervades Taylor's *Sources of the Self*.

64. For the importance of precritical belonging and learning, see Michael McCarthy, "The Critical Appropriation of Tradition," *Soundings* 82, no. 3–4 (Fall/Winter 1999): 3–4.

65. For a detailed analysis of deliberative insights, see Brian Cronin, *Value Ethics: A Lonergan Perspective* (Nairobi: Consolata Institute of Philosophy Press, 2006).

Chapter Three
Authentic Faith in a Secular Age

1. Charles Taylor, *A Secular Age* (Cambridge, MA: Harvard University Press, 2007).

2. The motif of "coming of age" has both religious and nonreligious expressions. See Paul's first letter to the Corinthians, 13:11: "When I was a child I spoke as a child, I understood as a child, I thought as a child, but when I became a man, I put away childish things."

3. See Taylor's introduction to *A Secular Age*, 1–22.

4. Charles Taylor, *Sources of the Self* (Cambridge, MA: Harvard University Press, 1989).

5. CWL, 3; *Method in Theology* (New York: Herder and Herder, 1972). See CWL, 4; *A Second Collection* (Philadelphia: Westminster Press, 1974); *A Third Collection* (New York: Paulist Press, 1985); CWL, 6 and 17.

6. Taylor, *Secular Age*, 1.
7. Ibid., 2.
8. Ibid., 2–3; *Method*, 244.
9. Peter Conradi, *Iris Murdoch: A Life* (New York: Norton, 2001), 587.
10. Taylor, *Secular Age*, 542–57; CWL, 3:391, 640.
11. *Secular Age*, 594.
12. Nietzsche; a claim first articulated by the madman in *The Gay Science* (108). The actual assertions of the madman are far more complex than popular citations of his claim.
13. CWL, chap. 19; *Method*, 101–3, 110–11, 115–18.
14. *Secular Age*, 8.
15. *Secular Age*, 584–85, 732.
16. The epistemic commentary briefly examines the intellectual sources and limitations of ontological naturalism. The moral genealogy explores the ethical and political implications of the modern critique of hierarchical structures and institutions. The religious narrative seeks to explain the disintegration of Latin Christendom and the gradual emergence of our fragmented secular age.
17. *Third Collection*, 63–65; CWL, 17:353–54.
18. Lonergan's account of the history of science tends to slight the importance of late medieval and early Renaissance thought. Pierre Duhem provides a valuable corrective to Lonergan's omission by retrieving the important contributions of Roger Bacon, Jean Buridan, Nicholas Oresme, and Nicholas of Cusa to the origins of modern physics. Where Lonergan emphasizes the philosophical and theological sterility of the late Middle Ages, Duhem emphasizes their importance for the history of modern science.
19. *Method*, 81, 325; CWL, 17:354.
20. *Method*, 93–96, 314–18.
21. CWL, 3:424: "Every mind by its inner unity demands the integration of all it knows."
22. Ibid., 79; *Method*, 317.
23. CWL, 3:130–33, 203–6, 423–30, 480–83, 653–57.
24. *Method*, "Realms of Meaning," 81–85.
25. I am well aware of the moral and political complexity of modern Europe. The story presented here applies better to England, France, and the Low Countries than it does to Spain, Italy, and the Hapsburg imperium. But an important part of my argument is the notable shift in cultural leadership from southern to northern Europe from the seventeenth century onward.
26. See Bacon's *Novum Organum* and Descartes's *Discourse on Method*.
27. See Taylor, *Sources*, chap. 13, "God Loveth Adverbs."

28. See Hannah Arendt's *The Human Condition* for the cultural elevation in modernity of *homo faber* and the *animal laborans.*

29. The feudal order did not go unchallenged even during the medieval period. Important towns and cities emerged along the trade routes of Europe, providing alternative models of economic and political organization. In *The City in History*, Lewis Mumford comments favorably on the political and economic vitality of the medieval communes. But, he regretfully notes, "the community life of the medieval cities was never quite lucidly or definitively formulated by medieval scholars."

30. The Fourth Lateran Council of 1215 marked the summit of papal power and prestige. For the next three centuries, papal authority declined due to the scandalous division of the papacy, the Babylonian captivity in Avignon, the rise of the conciliar movement, and the Vatican's loss of moral stature during the Renaissance.

31. The alliance of "throne and altar" characterized both the Protestant and Catholic states of modern Europe. The operative adage, flowing originally from the religious divisions of Germany, was *cuius regio, eius religio* (the religion of the prince is the religion of his subjects). While both Catholic and Protestant monarchs based their legitimacy on the "divine right of kings," this principle was fundamentally inconsistent with the normative political theories of Aquinas, Suarez, and Bellarmine. The principle was also repudiated by the dissenting Puritans and their parliamentary supporters during the English Civil War.

32. See Paul Hazard, *The European Mind* (New Haven: Yale University Press, 1953); *European Thought in the Eighteenth Century* (New Haven: Yale University Press, 1954).

33. For the differences between the American and French revolutions, see Hannah Arendt, *On Revolution* (Penguin: New York, 1963).

34. Charles Taylor, *Modern Social Imaginaries* (Durham, NC: Duke University Press, 2004); *Secular Age*, 171–76, 200–201.

35. See Alan Richardson, *History, Sacred and Profane* (London: SCM Press, 1964), 32–33; Hannah Arendt, *Between Past and Future* (Penguin: New York, 1968), 28–30, 37–39, 67–69.

36. CWL, 4:243–44; *Third Collection*, 169–83. "I have said that people are responsible individually for the lives they lead and collectively for the world in which they live them" (*Third Collection*, 176).

37. Lonergan introduces the notion of dialectical method in *Insight*, CWL, 3:217–44. He elaborates on its critical significance in *Method*, 235–66.

38. The critical elements and sequence of this genealogy are found in both *Sources* and *Secular Age*.

39. See Taylor, *Secular Age*, pt. 3, "The Nova Effect"; for a compressed account of contemporary moral alternatives, see Taylor, *A Catholic Modernity?* (New York: Oxford University Press, 1999), 13–37.

40. Lonergan deeply believes that human authenticity is the opposite of arbitrary choice. See *Third Collection*, "Dialectic of Authority," 4–12, and the explicit claim "arbitrariness is just unauthenticity," *Method*, 268.

41. I am heavily reliant on Taylor's *Secular Age* in this highly compressed account of religious decline. Other useful sources on which I have drawn include: Owen Chadwick, *The Reformation* (New York: Penguin, 1972), and *The Secularization of the European Mind in the Nineteenth Century* (Cambridge: Cambridge University Press, 1990); Herbert Butterfield, *The Origins of Modern Science* (New York: Free Press, 1957); Susan Neiman, *Evil in Modern Thought* (Princeton: Princeton University Press, 2002); A. N. Whitehead, *Science and the Modern World* (New York: Macmillan, 1925); Paul Hazard, *The European Mind* (New Haven: Yale University Press, 1953); Iris Murdoch, *Metaphysics as a Guide to Morals* (New York: Penguin, 1992); James Collins, *God in Modern Philosophy* (Chicago: Regnery, 1959); *The Oxford History of Christianity*; CWL, 4; *Second Collection*; *Third Collection*. In emphasizing the decline of Christendom and the critique of Christian doctrine and practice, I don't mean to preclude important forms of religious development in modernity. But these notable instances of development are not the relevant theme of this section.

42. See Barbara Tuchman's *The March of Folly* (New York: Knopf, 1984), 51–126, for the willful blindness of the papacy on the eve of the Reformation.

43. Hazard, *European Thought in the Eighteenth Century*, pt. 1, "Christianity on Trial."

44. Arendt, *Between Past and Future*, chap. 3, "What Is Authority?," 120–41.

45. Alexis de Tocqueville, *Democracy in America* (New York: Vintage Books, 1961), 1:319.

46. *Rerum Novarum* (1891) and *Quadragisimo Anno* (1931) represent serious but belated attempts to come to terms with the socioeconomic consequences of the Industrial Revolution. But in assessing their timing and influence, it's important to recall that Marx's *Communist Manifesto* was published in 1848, the year of the great urban insurrections in Europe.

47. *Second Collection*, 94–99; CWL, 17:274–76; *Method*, 317.

48. *Method*, 335–40.

49. Ibid., 320–26.

50. See the important debate between Leibniz and Clarke in Alexandre Koyré's *From the Closed World to the Infinite Universe* (New York: Harper and Brothers, 1958), chap. 11, "The Work-Day God and the God of the Sabbath."

51. See Butterfield's *Origins of Modern Science* and Hazard's *The European Mind*.

52. Kant strikes a similar note in his *Prolegomena* when contrasting genuine science and metaphysics.

53. *Secular Age*, "Providential Deism," 221–69.

54. Thomas Jefferson, *The Philosophy of Jesus of Nazareth*, ed. Dickenson W. Adams (Princeton: Princeton University Press, 1983).

55. See Garry Wills, *Head and Heart: American Christianities* (Penguin: New York, 2007).

56. See Neiman, *Evil in Modern Thought*, chap. 2, "Condemning the Architect."

57. Taylor, *Sources*, 417–18; 434–55.

58. See Richardson, *History, Sacred and Profane*; Raymond Brown, *The Critical Meaning of the Bible* (New York: Paulist Press, 1981).

59. I explicitly borrow the phrase "hermeneutics of suspicion" from Paul Ricoeur, *Freud and Philosophy: An Essay on Interpretation* (New Haven: Yale University Press, 1970).

60. For Taylor, "exclusive humanism" "is a critical term of art." See *Secular Age*; Lonergan makes a similar point when he describes "a humanism in revolt against the supernatural" (CWL, 3:728–29).

61. *Secular Age*, 19–21, 26–28, 98–99, 233–69, 636–42.

62. The origins of this critical stance are traceable to Feuerbach and Marx, and ultimately to Hegel.

63. Ricoeur, *Freud and Philosophy*.

64. *Karl Marx: Selected Writings*, ed. David McLellan (Oxford: Oxford University Press, 1977), 39–112, 131–247, 388–91.

65. Friedrich Nietzsche, *Genealogy of Morals* (New York: Doubleday Anchor, 1956), 150–299.

66. Ibid., 160–65, 170–71, 186–88, 230.

67. Ibid., essay 3, "What Do Ascetic Ideals Mean?"

68. See the genealogical triad of camel, lion, and child in Nietzsche's *Zarathustra*.

69. Sigmund Freud, *Origins and Development of Psycho-Analysis, General Introduction to Pyscho-Analysis, The Ego and the Id, Totem and Taboo, The Future of an Illusion, Civilization and Its Discontents, Moses and Monotheism*. In *Great Books of the Western World*, vol. 54, *Freud* (Chicago: Encyclopedia Britannica, 1952).

70. See in particular *Civilization and Its Discontents*, pt. 2.

71. Freud quotes Goethe in *Civilization*, pt. 2: "He who has science and has art, religion, too has he; who has not science, has not art, let him religious be."

Freud elaborates on the critical contrast between religion and science in lecture 35, "The Question of a *Weltanschauung*," in *New Introductory Lectures on Psychoanalysis* (1933).

72. See Kant's *Critique of Pure Reason* (New York: St. Martin's Press, 1961), B833.

73. Freud, *New Introductory Lectures*, lecture 35.

74. Taylor, *Secular Age*, chap. 13, "The Age of Authenticity."

75. CWL, 3:726–29.

76. For Lonergan's comprehensive response in *Insight* (CWL, 3), see chap. 20, "Special Transcendent Knowledge," and *Method*, chap. 4, "Religion."

77. CWL, 4:244.

78. CWL, 4:221: "If any authenticity we achieve is to radiate out into our troubled world, we need much more objective knowledge than men commonly feel ready to absorb." CWL, 4:227–31; *Method*, 104–10, 252, 284.

79. He therefore conceives transcendental method as a "framework for collaborative creativity." *Method*, xii; CWL, 3:xxv–xxx.

80. *Method*, 235–37.

81. I am summarizing the pedagogical strategy Lonergan follows in *Insight*. For an even more compact account, see *Second Collection*, 86; *Method*, 25.

82. CWL, 3: xvii–xxiii.

83. Ibid., 385–87, 427. "The polymorphism of human consciousness is the one and only key to philosophy." For a careful analysis and critique of this claim, see Gerard Walmsley, *Lonergan on Philosophic Pluralism: The Polymorphism of Consciousness as the Key to Philosophy* (Toronto: University of Toronto Press, 2008).

84. See *Method*, 267–71.

85. Ibid., 237–44.

86. See Taylor, *Sources*, 518–20; *Catholic Modernity*, 19, 388–89; CWL, 4:192–93.

87. Whitehead, *Science and the Modern World*, 52.

88. I am summarizing several different sections of *Insight* and *Method* in 1–6.

89. *Method*, 104–5.

90. *Second Collection*, 144: "I venture to affirm that an authentic humanism is profoundly religious."

91. "The best lack all conviction, and the worst are filled with a passionate intensity" (W. B. Yeats, "The Second Coming").

92. *Method*, 85–96, 305–18.

93. CWL, 3: chaps. 6 and 7.

94. *Method*, 93–96, 309–12; CWL, 2:vii–viii.

95. *Method*, 94–96.
96. CWL, 3:390–96, 498.
97. *Method*, 6, 94, 304–5; *Second Collection*, 50–51.
98. *Method*, 4.
99. I am summarizing in this section pt. 1 of *Insight*, "Insight as Activity"; for Lonergan's most compact summary of his cognitional theory, see *Method*, 6–25.
100. *Method*, 14.
101. See *Second Collection*, 207.
102. CWL, 3:72, 243, 423–30.
103. Ibid., chaps. 19 and 20; *Method*, 84–85.
104. This is the central question addressed in *Method in Theology*.
105. *Second Collection*, 90–99.
106. *Method*, 357–59.
107. See the complementarity of *dialectic* and *foundations* as functional specialties, chaps. 10 and 11 of *Method*.
108. CWL, 17:263–76.
109. Ibid., 274–76.
110. *Second Collection*, 98–99.
111. *Method*, 79–81; *Second Collection*, 48–52, 233.
112. *Second Collection*, 19–30, 85–86, 90–99; CWL, 3:217–43.
113. For a sympathetic critique of such nostalgia, see Taylor, *Catholic Modernity*, 16–19.
114. Paul Ricoeur, Nicholas Lash, and Taylor himself are three critical counterexamples to this pattern. See CWL, 17:261–63, 275–76.
115. *Method*, 319–29; *Second Collection*, 11–32.
116. This synoptic account of authentic religious humanism is intended as a compact summary of Lonergan's comprehensive project.
117. See CWL, 10:38–79.
118. CWL, 6: chap. 1, "Redemption."
119. Immanuel Kant, *Political Writings* (New York: Cambridge University Press, 1970), "An Answer to the Question: 'What Is Enlightenment?,'" 54–60.
120. Kant, *Critique of Pure Reason*, Axii.
121. Ibid.
122. See Kant's Introduction and Preamble to his *Prolegomena to Any Future Metaphysics*.
123. *Critique of Pure Reason*, A61–A64, A295–A309.
124. See Kant's *Religion within the Bounds of Reason Alone* (New York: Harper, 1960).
125. See Kant's *Groundwork of the Metaphysics of Morals*, trans. H. J. Paton (New York: Harper Torchbooks, 1964).

126. See Taylor's masterful exposition of this process in *Sources* and *Secular Age*.

127. I do not mean to imply that all Protestant and Catholic theologians prior to Lonergan were trying to cling to an outmoded Christendom. Among the obvious counterexamples cited in the text are: Pascal, Richard Simon, Leibniz, Kierkegaard, Newman, Schleiermacher, Tyrell, the French and German proponents of *la nouvelle theologie*, and Teilhard de Chardin. But Christian thinkers often failed to exercise the kind of intellectual and moral leadership in modernity that Saint Paul did in the first century, Augustine did in the late Roman Empire, and Aquinas did in thirteenth-century Paris.

128. For Lonergan's complex attitude toward "modernism" and "antimodernism," see his nuanced remarks in *Second Collection*, 94, 112, 264. "In brief, so far were churchmen from acknowledging the distinctive character of modern culture that they regarded it to be an aberration that had to be resisted and overcome. When they were confronted with a heresy, which they considered to be the sum and substance of all heresy, they named it modernism. So far were they from seeking to enrich modern culture with a religious interpretation that they had only mistrust for Teilhard de Chardin. Today [1968] the pendulum has swung to the opposite extreme." For Lonergan's emphatic insistence on critical *aggiornamento*, see chap. 4, in the section "Critical *Aggiornamento*."

129. I have argued in detail for this complementarity in chap. 1 of this book.

130. I draw here principally, but not exclusively, on *Insight*. Several essays in Lonergan's three *Collections* are also quite relevant.

131. CWL, 4:238–40.

132. *Third Collection*, 41–44.

133. See CWL, 3:651–57.

134. Ibid., 703–6.

135. Ibid., chap. 3, 70–102.

136. See CWL, 3: chap. 3, 574–75, 591–93; *Method*, 94–96.

137. CWL, 3:72–74; *Method*, 94–95.

138. See CWL, 3: chap. 4, "The Complementarity of Classical and Statistical Investigations," and CWL, 3:217–44, 461.

139. CWL, 3:123–28, 171–72, 264–66, 462, 698.

140. Ibid., 115–28.

141. Ibid., 117–34, 208–11, 259–60, 459–60, 533.

142. Ibid., 469–79.

143. *Second Collection*, 35–36.

144. CWL, 3:35–53.

145. Ibid., 53–69.

146. Ibid., 458–83.

147. Ibid., 607–8.

148. Ibid., 234–44.

149. See Michael Polanyi, *Personal Knowledge* (Chicago: University of Chicago Press, 1958), 5: "Objectivity does not demand that we estimate man's significance in the universe by the minute size of his body, by the brevity of his past history or his probable future career. It does not require that we see ourselves as a grain of sand in a million Saharas. It inspires us on the contrary with the hope . . . of conceiving a rational idea of the universe which can authoritatively speak for itself."

150. See Pascal's *Pensées*, no. 113, 199–200.

151. *Method*, xi: "A theology mediates between a cultural matrix and the significance and role of religion in that matrix."

152. For Lonergan's critical notion of "sublation," see *Method*, 241–43, 316, 340.

153. *Method*, 101–5; CWL, 17:204–8.

154. CWL, 17:171–73, 208–10.

155. *Method*, 167–71.

156. See CWL, 3: chap. 19; CWL, 17:160–218; *Method*, 101–24.

157. For Lonergan's definitive account, see *The Triune God: Doctrines*, CWL, vol. 11 (Toronto: University of Toronto Press, 2009), and *The Triune God: Systematics*, CWL, vol. 12 (Toronto: University of Toronto Press, 2007).

158. CWL, 3:639–44, 657–86.

159. See Lonergan's explicit transition in *Insight* from chap. 19 to chap. 20, where God's "solution" to the problem of evil is heuristically developed.

160. CWL, 1:119–49, 350–82.

161. CWL, 3:746: "Grace perfects nature both in the sense that it adds a perfection beyond nature and in the sense that it confers on nature the effective freedom to attain its own perfection. But grace is not a substitute for nature . . ." (*Summa Theologica*, pt. 1, question 1, article 8).

162. Aquinas's influence on Christian philosophy and theology did not end, of course, with the condemnation of 1277. Aquinas's writing remained an important source of inspiration and commentary for Dominican thinkers like Cajetan, the Jesuit school at Salamanca, and even for English Protestants like Richard Hooker. In the late nineteenth century Pope Leo XIII sought to reestablish Aquinas as the leading philosophical and theological teacher of the Catholic Church.

163. Hans Blumenberg, *The Legitimacy of the Modern Age* (Cambridge, MA: MIT Press, 1983).

164. See Chadwick, *Reformation*, and Tuchman, *The March of Folly*.

165. See Chadwick, "The Cry for Reformation," in *Reformation*, 11–39.

166. Paul's epistle to the Romans is a profoundly important text in both Catholic and Protestant Christianity. It deeply influenced Augustine, Luther, and Barth, among many others.

167. Justification through *faith* not *works* (fidelity to the law) is perhaps the central theme in Pauline theology.

168. Whitehead, *Science and the Modern World*, 10: "Since a babe was born in a manger, it may be doubted whether so great a thing has happened with so little stir."

169. Descartes's debt to and contrast with Augustine is striking. Both reconcile the goodness of God with the existence of evil (Augustine) and error (Descartes) by appealing to the freedom of the human will.

170. See Descartes's memorable image of the modern tree of knowledge in *The Principles of Philosophy*, "Author's Letter."

171. Kant, *Critique of Pure Reason*, A805. For Kant, the three questions can be summarized in the single question, What is man?

172. Here I am summarizing Kant's *Second Critique* and the *Grundlegung* (*Foundations of the Metaphysics of Morals*).

173. See sections 70–74 and 88 of the *Grundlegung*.

174. See the *Grundlegung*, 88–96: "*Heteronomy* of the will as the source of all spurious principles of morality."

175. See Jerome Schneewind, *The Invention of Autonomy* (New York: Cambridge University Press, 1998).

176. For Kant's regulative idea of a "holy will," see *Grundlegung*, 39, 86.

177. See Neiman, *Evil in Modern Thought*, 70–74, 325–28.

178. See Hegel's *Phenomenology of Spirit* (Oxford: Clarendon Press, 1977); for a compact account, see *Reason in History: A General Introduction to the Philosophy of History* (Indianapolis: Library of Liberal Arts, 1953).

179. See Charles Taylor, *Hegel and Modern Society* (New York: Cambridge University Press, 1979).

180. See Søren Kierkegaard's *Philosophical Fragments* (Princeton: Princeton University Press, 1941), *Concluding Unscientific Postscript* (Princeton: Princeton University Press, 1968), *Stages on Life's Way* (Princeton: Princeton University Press, 1940), *Sickness unto Death* (Princeton: Princeton University Press, 1954).

181. For Kierkegaard, the existential requirement for becoming an authentic Christian is to become personally "contemporary with Jesus of Nazareth." The cultural influence of Christendom can be a major impediment in this most demanding process.

182. Søren Kierkegaard, *Fear and Trembling* (Princeton: Princeton University Press, 1954).

183. See Kierkegaard's *Attack on Christendom* (Princeton: Princeton University Press, 1944).

184. Kierkegaard follows Hegel in accepting this modern conception of reason. Lonergan explicitly dissents from this Hegelian requirement. For Lonergan, reason demands not "necessity," but the virtually unconditioned reality of contingent fact. That contrast explains how he can treat the conclusions of faith and reason as complementary, not contradictory.

185. See the last of Marx's theses on Feuerbach.

186. For Marx, the revolutionary aspirations of 1789 will remain unfulfilled until the full historical emergence and acceptance of communism.

187. Marx follows Bacon and Descartes in treating theory as directive of practice. It is theoretical insight into the "laws of history" that must guide successful revolutionary "praxis."

188. Lonergan's notion of "grace sublating nature" allows him to acknowledge the relative autonomy of human practices without recourse to Promethean illusions about human independence.

189. Kant, as we have seen, made the autonomy of practical reason the basis for human dignity. Ontological naturalists are divided over what type of freedom and dignity their moral ontology allows for.

190. Lonergan insisted that rational judgments about both nature and history were limited to contingent matters of fact.

191. See the critique of emotivism in Alasdair MacIntyre's *After Virtue* (Notre Dame, IN: University of Notre Dame Press, 1981).

192. For the critical role of anti-Semitism and imperialism in creating the political and cultural conditions for totalitarian mass movements in the twentieth century, see Arendt's *Origins of Totalitarianism* (New York: Harcourt Brace, 1951).

193. Nietzsche, *Genealogy of Morals*, sec. 27, pt. 3: "Thus Christianity as dogma perished by its own ethics of truthfulness."

194. Ibid., sec. 5, pt. 1: "a will that had turned against life."

195. For Nietzsche, it is the mark of the noble and high-minded to decree themselves and their actions to be good.

196. See part 1 of the *Genealogy of Morals*, "good and evil," "good and bad," and *Beyond Good and Evil* (London: Allen and Unwin, 1967).

197. See chap. 13 of Arendt, *Origins*, "Ideology and Terror."

198. René Girard, *The Scapegoat* (Baltimore: Johns Hopkins University Press, 1986).

199. See Arendt's critical contrast in *Origins* between the self-serving bourgeois individual and the public-spirited citizen.

200. Freud, *Civilization and Its Discontents*, sec. 2.

201. Ibid., sec. 8: "I have no consolation to offer (my fellow men), for at bottom this is what they all demand."

202. See Albert Camus, *The Myth of Sisyphus* (New York: Knopf, 1955).

203. See Albert Camus, *The Rebel* (New York: Knopf, 1956).

204. See Albert Camus, *The Plague* (New York: Knopf, 1972).

205. See John S. Dunne, *The City of the Gods* (New York: Macmillan, 1965).

206. See Lonergan's sympathetic criticism of the Catholic resistance to modernity in "Belief: Today's Issue," *Second Collection*. For Lonergan's nuanced approach to "modernism," see note 128.

207. The relevant issue here is the conduct of Eugenio Pacelli (Pius XII) before, during, and after World War II. There are numerous credible defenders of the pope's conduct and character, but there are equally credible critics (Robert Katz, Guenter Lewy, Saul Friedlander, Walter Laquer, John Cornwall, Garry Wills). At least two related questions are at issue: *what* the pope did or failed to do about blatant Nazi anti-Semitism and the eventual extermination of European Jewry to which it led; and *why* he did what he did or failed to do. While the fact of the pope's "silence" is well documented, the reasons for his silence are open to credible dispute.

208. Taylor exemplifies this stance of sympathetic critical retrieval in *Sources* and *Secular Age*.

209. In *Gaudium et Spes*, the Pastoral Constitution on the Church in the Modern World, the Second Vatican Council embraces the reciprocity of teaching and learning between the church and the modern world it inhabits.

210. See Pascal's *Pensées*, no. 131: "Who will unravel such a tangle . . . man transcends man"; and no. 130: "If he exalts himself, I humble him, if he humbles himself, I exalt him."

211. For Taylor's account of the "immanent Counter-Enlightenment," see *Secular Age*, 369–74, 636–42, 724–26.

212. See *Second Collection*, 147–48: "Religion is intrinsic to an authentic humanism . . . in theology theocentrism and anthropocentrism coincide"; also *Second Collection*, 161 and 226, about the implications of executing "the anthropological turn."

213. See *Second Collection*, 51; *Third Collection*, 75–77; CWL, 2:vii–xv; CWL, 17:167–68, 395–98.

214. For Taylor's notion of "holistic individualism," see *Philosophical Arguments* (Cambridge, MA: Harvard University Press, 1995), 181–89; for his critique of "Atomism," see *Philosophical Papers*, vol. 2 (Cambridge: Cambridge University Press, 1992), 187–210.

215. For several conflicting versions of "authenticity" as a modern moral norm, see Lionel Trilling, *Sincerity and Authenticity* (Cambridge, MA: Harvard

University Press, 1972), as well as Taylor's *The Ethics of Authenticity* (Cambridge, MA: Harvard University Press, 1991).

216. CWL, 4:219–21, 227–31; and a slew of important references in *Method*.

217. CWL, 3:191–244.

218. *Method*, 357–64.

219. Ibid., 224, 237–53, 267–71.

220. Ibid., 107, 123, 241–43, 283–84, 338.

221. For Paul's developed account of *agape* as God's greatest spiritual gift, see 1 Cor. 13.

222. "Herein is love, not that we loved God, but that he loved us, and sent his Son to be the propitiation for our sins" (1 John 4:10).

223. *Method*, 105–7, 113; CWL, 17:168–71.

224. *Method*, 115–19. "Faith is the knowledge born of religious love."

225. Ibid., 49–55, 118–19.

226. See ibid., 101–5; for the transcendent exigence, 83–85.

227. Ibid., 116; CWL, 3:725–29.

228. I am deliberately conflating the end of Genesis 1:31 and the beginning of Genesis 2:2. See Taylor, *Sources*, 516: "There is a divine affirmation of the creature, which is captured in the repeated phrase of Genesis I . . . 'And God saw that it was good.'" *Agape* is inseparable from such a "seeing good."

229. *Method*, 117.

230. See *Third Collection*, chap. 7, "Healing and Creating in History," 100–112.

231. *Method*, 117.

232. See Neiman, *Evil in Modern Thought*; Andrew Delbanco, *The Puritan Ordeal* (Cambridge, MA: Harvard University Press, 1989), and *The Death of Satan* (New York: Farrar, Straus & Giroux, 1995); Dostoyevsky's parable of the Grand Inquisitor in *The Brothers Karamazov*; *Night*, by Elie Wiesel; Jung's *The Answer to Job*; among so many others.

233. See Lonergan's important but highly compressed account, "The Ontology of the Good," CWL, 3:604–7.

234. In fact, the egocentrism and anthropocentrism of traditional accounts of faith are a major barrier, for many, to religious belief today. See Iris Murdoch's *Metaphysics as a Guide to Morals*. Murdoch's disinterested moral stance is clearly influenced by Plato and Kant, as well as by Buddhism.

235. Common sense considers sensible things in their practical relation to our concerns; theoretical science, in their intelligible relations to one another. "To identify the good with the intelligibility of being is to identify it not with the ideal intelligibility of some postulated utopia, but with the ascertainable intelligibility of the universe that exists." CWL, 3:607; *Method*, 27 ("What is good, always is concrete"); *Method*, 116–17.

236. *Method,* 52–55.

237. CWL, 3:467, 471.

238. For the short and long cycles of decline, see CWL, 3:222–44.

239. CWL, 3:721–22, 724: "As the problem of evil exists because God respects man's freedom, so the existence of the solution leaves human freedom intact."

240. CWL, 17:171. See Pascal's *Pensées,* no. 172: "The way of God, who disposes all things with gentleness, is to instill religion into our minds with reason and argument and into our hearts with grace."

241. Luke 15:11–32.

242. Luke 10:25–37; Matt. 25:31–45.

243. Matt. 11:5; Luke 7:22.

244. John 2:25: "For he knew what was in man." See also Jer. 17:9.

245. CWL, 3:724, and *Second Collection,* 7–9. "Is the proper Christian ethic the law of the cross, i.e. the transformation of evil into good?" See also *De Verbo Incarnato,* a thesis on the "law of the cross," CWL, vol. 8 (Toronto: University of Toronto Press, 2004).

246. This extraordinary aspect of Christ is beautifully illustrated in his interaction with the Grand Inquisitor in *The Brothers Karamazov.*

247. John 10:10; see also Taylor's important reflections on "fullness of life" in *Secular Age,* 26–27, 596–97, 600–607, 729–30, 768–69.

248. *Method,* 241–43, 316–40.

249. See ibid., 117–18.

250. Matt. 7:20.

Chapter Four
The Chill Winds of Modernity

1. Chap. 2, "The People of God," *Lumen Gentium, Dogmatic Constitution on the Church,* in Vatican Council II, *The Conciliar and Post-Conciliar Documents,* ed. Austin Flannery (Northport, NY: Costello Publications, 1987).

2. Alasdair MacIntyre insists in *After Virtue* that the celebrated unity of medieval thought is more fictional than real. *After Virtue* (Notre Dame, IN: University of Notre Dame Press, 1981), 154–56.

3. See Hans Blumenberg, *The Legitimacy of the Modern Age* (Cambridge, MA: MIT Press, 1983).

4. For a detailed account of Lonergan's personal and intellectual development, see William Mathews, *Lonergan's Quest* (Toronto: University of Toronto Press, 2005). For Lonergan's own brief account of this process, see *Second Collection,* 263–78.

5. In particular, see CWL, 17, *Philosophical and Theological Papers, 1965–1980*, and the first, second, and third *Collections*.

6. For Lonergan's critical appropriation of Aquinas's theory of grace, see CWL, 1, *Grace and Freedom*; for a parallel appropriation of Aquinas's cognitional theory, see CWL, 2, *Verbum: Word and Idea in Aquinas*. See also CWL, 4: chap. 9, and *Third Collection*, chap. 4.

7. In this synoptic overview, I have drawn on multiple sources, including Owen Chadwick, *The Reformation* (New York: Penguin, 1972); Roland Bainton, *The Reformation of the Sixteenth Century* (Boston: Beacon Press, 1952); Barbara Tuchman, *The March of Folly* (New York: Knopf, 1984); Herbert Butterfield, *The Origins of Modern Science* (New York: Free Press, 1957); and A. N. Whitehead, *Science and the Modern World* (New York: New American Library, 1954).

8. Paul Hazard, *The European Mind: The Critical Years, 1680–1715* (New Haven: Yale University Press, 1953), and *European Thought in the Eighteenth Century from Montesquieu to Lessing* (New Haven: Yale University Press, 1954).

9. Hazard, *European Mind*, 69–71, 82–84. Catholic religious toleration, as exemplified by King Stephen Bathory in sixteenth-century Poland, was the exception rather than the rule.

10. See Susan Neiman, *Evil in Modern Thought* (Princeton: Princeton University Press, 2002), chap. 2, "Condemning the Architect."

11. Hazard, *European Mind*, 229–33.

12. While serious Catholic engagement in science did not cease with the rebuke of Galileo, the intellectual leadership of the Scientific Revolution clearly shifted to the Protestant North (England, the Low Countries, northern Germany, *inter alia*).

13. The primacy of Rome was challenged not only by the Reformation but also by powerful Catholic monarchies like France. The Gallican forces in France rejected Roman control of episcopal appointments in their country until the nineteenth century.

14. Alexis de Tocqueville, *Democracy in America*, vol. 1 (New York: Schocken Books, 1961), 319.

15. See Owen Chadwick, *The Secularization of the European Mind in the Nineteenth Century* (Cambridge: Cambridge University Press, 1990).

16. As noted earlier, *Rerum Novarum* (1891) and *Quadragesimo Anno* (1931) are serious but belated attempts to come to terms with the socioeconomic consequences of the Industrial Revolution, and they have had a significant impact on subsequent Catholic social teaching. But in appraising the Catholic response to "the social question," we should recall that Marx's *Communist Manifesto* was published in 1848, the year of the great urban insurrections in Europe.

17. Chadwick, *Secularization*, 111.

18. Garry Wills, *Papal Sin: Structures of Deceit* (New York: Doubleday, 2000).

19. Chadwick, *Secularization*, 251.

20. John Cornwell, *Hitler's Pope: The Secret History of Pius XII* (New York: Viking, 1999). There are numerous credible defenders of Pius XII's conduct and, in my view, equally credible critics. The fact of the pope's "silence" about Hitler's persecution of the Jews is well documented, but the reasons for his silence are open to legitimate dispute.

21. See CWL, 3:250, where Lonergan contrasts reactionaries, revolutionaries, progressives, and liberals; see also CWL, 17:236–37, where he contrasts revolutions that repudiate the past and revolutions that incorporate the original meaning of the past within a new, more inclusive perspective.

22. CWL, 1; CWL, 2.

23. See the numerous hermeneutical principles cited in CWL, 2, and CWL, 17:283–84.

24. "To make a massive judgment on the whole modern world is just impossible" (CWL, 17:29).

25. See *Second Collection*, 102–12, and *Method*, 81–99, on the different realms and stages of meaning.

26. Peter Hebblethwaite, *Pope John XXIII, Shepherd of the Modern World* (Garden City, NY: Doubleday, 1985). For Lonergan's references to Pope John, see *Third Collection*, chap. 14, "Pope John's Intention"; and CWL, 17:224–28.

27. There are numerous important studies of Vatican II. For our purposes in this chapter, I have limited the focus to four conciliar documents that explicitly depart from the antimodernist outlook that preceded the council.

28. See John O'Malley, *What Happened at Vatican II?* (Cambridge, MA: Harvard University Press, 2008), 36–43.

29. On nearly all accounts, the critical postconciliar event was Paul VI's encyclical *Humanae Vitae*, published in 1968. Did this controversial encyclical reverse the pastoral direction charted by Pope John? It's easy to speculate but very hard to answer with justified assurance. We simply don't know what John himself would have decided. We do know that the encyclical and its ecclesiastical and pastoral implications have profoundly divided the church for the last forty-five years.

30. Thomas O'Dea, *The Catholic Crisis* (Boston: Beacon Press, 1968). For the most balanced and comprehensive account of the spirit and substance of the council, see O'Malley, *What Happened at Vatican II?*

31. 1. *Dogmatic Constitution on the Church, Lumen Gentium*; 2. *Declaration on Religious Liberty, Dignitatis Humanae*; 3. *Declaration on the Relation of the Church to Non-Christian Religions, Nostra Aetate*; 4. *Pastoral Constitution on the Church in the Modern World, Gaudium et Spes.*

32. Vatican Council II, *The Conciliar and Post-Conciliar Documents*, 739.

33. See Hazard, *The European Mind*, and Alan Richardson, *History, Sacred and Profane* (Philadelphia: Westminster Press, 1964).

34. *Second Collection*, 1–7, 91–93, 110, 260; CWL, 17:73–74, 97, 160; *Method*, 29, 124, 302, 338–39.

35. *Second Collection*, 97, 112–16; CWL, 17:293–98.

36. Saint Anselm, *Proslogion*, chap. 2.

37. "If we submit everything to reason our religion will be left with nothing mysterious or supernatural. If we offend the principles of reason our religion will be absurd and ridiculous" (Pascal, *Pensées*, no. 173). See also Pascal on the power and limits of reason: "One must know when it is right to doubt, to affirm, to submit" (*Pensées*, no. 170).

38. See *Method*, 115, where Lonergan acknowledges his theological debt to Pascal.

39. John Henry Newman, *An Essay on the Development of Christian Doctrine* (Westminster, MD: Christian Classics, 1968). For Lonergan's indebtedness to Newman, see both the *Second* and *Third Collection* and *Method in Theology* (New York: Herder and Herder, 1972).

40. See note 28 for the important contributions of historically minded theologians to the central documents of Vatican II.

41. Immanuel Kant, *Religion within the Limits of Reason Alone* (La Salle, IL: Open Court, 1960).

42. Charles Taylor, *Sources of the Self* (Cambridge, MA: Harvard University Press, 1989), 401–11; *A Secular Age* (Cambridge, MA: Harvard University Press, 2007), 561–69.

43. Charles Taylor directly challenges "the mainline story" that treats the rise of science and critical reason as the major sources of modern unbelief. For Taylor the principal obstacles to religious faith in modernity are moral and spiritual not epistemic. See both *Sources* and *Secular Age*.

44. Auguste Comte was the father of modern positivism, but the positivist mind-set extended far beyond his contested historical analysis.

45. Dostoyevsky's novels vividly illustrate the exigent freedom of the Christian message. See, in particular, the myth of the Grand Inquisitor in *The Brothers Karamazov*.

46. "Religious appeal is directed . . . to excite that fear of an all-powerful arbitrary tyrant behind the unknown forces of nature." A. N. Whitehead, *Science and the Modern World* (New York: New American Library, 1954), 170.

47. See Michael McCarthy, "The Critical Appropriation of Tradition," *Soundings* 82, no. 3–4 (Fall/Winter 1999).

48. See *Method*, chaps. 6–10.

49. The "moving viewpoint" of *Insight* is deliberately designed to promote intellectual and moral conversion before the reader advances from knowledge of proportionate being to transcendent knowledge. CWL, 3: chaps. 19 and 20.

50. For the interplay of continuity and innovation in the history of Christian theology, see *Second Collection*, 239–61; CWL, 17:181–89; and Lonergan, *The Way to Nicea* (Philadelphia: Westminster Press, 1976). Particularly helpful as well is the exegetical commentary of Raymond Brown.

51. *Method in Theology* is explicitly designed to transcend the ahistorical limitations of logic. Lonergan, of course, does not reject logic but incorporates its intentional operations into the comprehensive framework of transcendental method. See *Method*, 6, and CWL, 17:199–203.

52. The mediating path takes full account of the need for comprehensive *ressourcement*. See note 28.

53. In mediated theology, *aggiornamento* is conceived as the necessary complement to *ressourcement*.

54. For a compact account of the eight functional specialties, see *Method*, 125–45.

55. In this way, O'Malley's three approaches to historical time are combined in a well-ordered unity. See note 28.

56. See Jaroslav Pelikan, *The Christian Tradition: A History of the Development of Doctrine* (Chicago: University of Chicago Press, 1978), ix; and Charles Hefling, *Why Doctrines?* (Chestnut Hill, MA: Lonergan Institute at Boston College, 2000).

57. See John T. Noonan, *A Church That Can and Cannot Change* (Notre Dame, IN: University of Notre Dame Press, 2005), 219–22. "The rule of faith is the rule of Christian love."

58. See Hefling, *Why Doctrines?*, chap. 5; and *Method*, "Continuity, Development and Revision," 351–53.

59. "When conversion is the basis of the whole theology, when religious conversion is the event that gives the name, God, its primary and fundamental meaning . . . not a little has been done to keep systematic theology in harmony with its religious origins and aims" (*Method*, 350).

60. "Never has adequately differentiated consciousness been more difficult to achieve. Never has the need to speak effectively to undifferentiated consciousness been greater" (*Method*, 99).

61. The need for a learning as well as a teaching church is recognized in *Gaudium et Spes* and highlighted in the pastoral letters of the American bishops on nuclear defense and economic justice. See also Frederick Crowe, *Developing the Lonergan Legacy* (Collegeville, MN: Liturgical Press, 1992).

62. See Lonergan's spirited defense of critical realism in *Second Collection*, "The Dehellenization of Dogma," 11–32: "Verum est medium in quo ens cogniscitur" (Truth is the medium in which being is known), *Second Collection*, 17.

63. See Michael McCarthy, "Towards a New Critical Center," *Method* 15, no. 2 (Fall 1997), and "Pluralism, Invariance and Conflict," *Review of Metaphysics* (1997).

64. See *Method*, 237–40, for the distinction between horizontal and vertical exercises of freedom. For a parallel account of the philosophical need for conversion, *periagoge*, see Plato's *Republic*, books 6 and 7.

65. Lonergan's *Insight* closely follows Plato's dialogues in the importance it assigns to philosophical pedagogy and psychic transformation. See CWL, 3:15, where Lonergan emphasizes Plato's and Augustine's recognition of the existential need for conversion.

66. This is only one of many ways in which Lonergan explicitly distances himself from Kantian "counterpositions." At the same time he deliberately honors Kant by recognizing his exceptional importance within modern philosophy and culture. See *Insight* and the three *Collection*s.

67. See CWL, 2: ch. 5; CWL, 3: ch. 19; CWL, 11 and 12.

68. "The original Christian notion of *agape* is of a love that God has for humans which is connected with their goodness as creatures . . . there is a divine affirmation of the creature, which is captured in the repeated phrase of Genesis I about each stage of creation, 'and God saw that it was good.' *Agape* is inseparable from such a 'seeing good'" (Taylor, *Sources*, 516).

69. For the revelatory power of love, see Pascal's *Pensées*, Newman's "Cor ad cor loquitor," and John Dunne's *Reasons of the Heart* (Notre Dame, IN: University of Notre Dame Press, 1979).

70. For the complementarity of *apophatic* and *kataphatic* theology, see *Method*, 341. For the theological concept of "learned ignorance," see the *Docta Ignorantia* of Nicholas of Cusa.

71. See Michael Stebbins, *The Divine Initiative* (Toronto: University of Toronto Press, 1995).

72. For Lonergan's use of Aquinas's distinction between operative and cooperative grace, see CWL, 1:107, 241, 288–89. "Operative grace is the replacement of the heart of stone by a heart of flesh" (*Method*, 241).

73. If "classicists" in this context correspond to Lonergan's "solid right," then "modernists" in this restricted usage form part of Lonergan's "scattered left." See CWL, 4:245. For Lonergan's complex attitude toward "modernism" and "antimodernism," see his nuanced remarks in *Second Collection*, 94, 112, 264.

74. For Lonergan's distinction between general and special theological categories, see *Method*, 283–92.

75. This is the crux of the disagreement between Lonergan and "exclusive humanism." For Lonergan an authentic and comprehensive humanism must be religious. See CWL, 3:747–51, and *Second Collection*, 144.

76. For the complementarity of liberation and the "foundation of freedom," see Hannah Arendt, *On Revolution* (New York: Penguin, 1965), 141–48.

77. See Taylor, *A Secular Age*, for the branching expressions of "exclusive humanism."

78. For the moral ontology of "the immanent frame," see Taylor, *Secular Age*, chap. 15, "The Immanent Frame."

79. Immanuel Kant, *Groundwork of the Metaphysics of Morals* (also known as the *Grundlegung*), trans. H. J. Paton (New York: Harper Torchbooks, 1964), 82–84. Categorical imperatives are carefully distinguished from both technical imperatives of skill and counsels of prudence. Only categorical imperatives are morally binding. This sharp Kantian separation of duty from desire underlies the distinctively modern separation of morality (the right) from ethics (the good).

80. Charles Taylor, *Philosophical Arguments* (Cambridge: Harvard University Press, 1995), 181–86.

81. See Isaiah Berlin, *Four Essays on Liberty* (Oxford: Oxford University Press, 1969), 118–72; and Charles Taylor, *Philosophical Papers*, vol. 2 (Cambridge: Cambridge University Press, 1992), 211–29.

82. See Benjamin Barber, *Strong Democracy* (Berkeley: University of California Press, 1984); and Benjamin Barber and Patrick Watson, *The Struggle for Democracy* (Boston: Little, Brown, 1988).

83. Tocqueville, *Democracy in America*, vol. 2, bk. 2, chap. 1, "Why Democratic Nations Show a More Ardent and Enduring Love of Equality Than of Liberty."

84. John Rawls, "Justice as Fairness," *Philosophical Review* 67, no. 2 (1958): 164–94. See note 81 as well.

85. Iris Murdoch, *Metaphysics as a Guide to Morals* (New York: Penguin, 1993), 177–81, 494.

86. If moral ontology corresponds to the "upper blade of ethics," then moral advocacy corresponds to the substantive policies concrete individuals and communities choose to pursue. Effectively mediating the important transition from ontology to advocacy is the "lower blade" of ethics and practical wisdom.

87. The striking counterexample to this general claim is Lonergan's important work in economics. See CWL, 15, *Macroeconomic Dynamics: An Essay in Circulation Analysis*, and CWL, 21, *For a New Political Economy*.

88. See CWL, 3:232–34, 249–50; *Method*, 48–52; *Third Collection*, 6–10.

89. For Lonergan's critical distinction between essential and effective freedom (*authenticity*), see CWL, 3:643–56. "A consideration of effective freedom is meaningless, unless essential freedom exists" (643).

90. Pascal, *Pensées*, no. 58.

91. Charles Montesquieu, *Spirit of the Laws*, trans. and ed. Anne Cohler, Basia Miller, and Harold Stone (Cambridge: Cambridge University Press, 1989), bk. 3, "Of the Principles of the Three Kinds of Government."

92. See MacIntyre, *After Virtue*, chaps. 2 and 3.

93. See CWL, 3:242–44; *Third Collection*, 176–82, 209–15; *Method*, 249–50, 358, 365.

94. Dostoyevsky captures the essential spirit of this criticism in the unforgettable conversation between Ivan and Alexei Karamazov in *The Brothers Karamazov*. Ivan encapsulates his moral critique of Christianity in the legend of the Grand Inquisitor.

95. Neiman, *Evil in Modern Thought*, "Earthquakes: Why Lisbon? Mass Murders: Why Auschwitz?"

96. See Cornwell, *Hitler's Pope*; Wills, *Papal Sin*; and Ignazio Silone's essay in *The God That Failed* (London: Hamilton, 1950).

97. Stephen Spender's testimony in *The God That Failed* is particularly striking: "Power is only saved from corruption if it is humanized with humility. Without humility, power is turned to persecutions, executions and public lies."

98. See Michael McCarthy, "Practical Wisdom, Social Justice and the Global Society," *Journal of the Lonergan Workshop* 22 (2011).

99. This incompleteness, of course, reflects the complementarity he explicitly recognized between philosophy and the other realms of cognitive meaning. In this respect, Lonergan's ethics closely resembles his metaphysics.

100. See Basil Mitchell, "The Christian Conscience," in *The Oxford History of Christianity*, ed. John McManners (New York: Oxford University Press, 2002).

101. Iris Murdoch, *The Sovereignty of Good* (New York: Schocken Books, 1971), 57–58.

102. For Lonergan's distinction between transcendental and categorial sources of meaning, see *Method*, 11, 20, 73–74. I have transferred this important distinction into the sphere of the human virtues.

103. In the evaluation of human institutions and cultures, comparative appraisals are particularly important. Since all human societies are flawed in significant ways, it's essential to distinguish the varying gravity of their failings and weaknesses.

104. In this respect, Catholic Christianity today lags far behind the best practices of the liberal democracies.

105. See Michael McCarthy, "The Loss of Effective Authority: A Crisis of Trust and Credibility," a lecture delivered at Boston College in May 2005 as part of the college's series "The Church in the Twenty-First Century."

106. See Charles Taylor, "A Catholic Modernity?," in *A Catholic Modernity?*, ed. James Heft (New York: Oxford University Press, 1999), 14: "I want to take the original word *katholou* in two related senses, comprising universality and wholeness."

107. While communism is "the god that failed" in the famous volume of that title, it is actually only one among the many gods elevated by exclusive humanism.

108. In this concluding section, I attempt to extend the principles of Lonergan's "small renewal" to the "great renewal" of Catholic Christianity. While the concrete proposals advanced for comprehensive *aggiornamento* are mine, they reflect, I believe, my own critical appropriation of Lonergan.

109. See Michael McCarthy, "Towards a Catholic Christianity," *Journal of the Lonergan Workshop* 20 (2012), and *In Search of the Whole*, ed. John C. Haughey (Washington, DC: Georgetown University Press, 2011).

110. Like many faithful Catholics, I am not persuaded by the Vatican's public arguments against the ordination of women to the priesthood. For me and for countless others, this warranted reform is a matter of basic justice, the belated correction of centuries of prejudicial attitudes, conduct, and governance.

111. The global response to the brief papacy of Pope Francis provides confirmation of this claim. The pope's public manner and bearing, the directness and humility of his speech, and his consistent emphasis on the needs of the poor and vulnerable have greatly impressed both the friends and critics of the church. Because the pope tries to speak and live in accordance with the gospel, the power of the church's traditional message is, for many, experienced anew.

Epilogue

1. I recognize that in *Method* Lonergan distinguishes three transcendental notions: the unrestricted desire for the intelligible, the unrestricted desire for truth, and the unrestricted desire for value. Throughout this work, I have deliberately compressed the first two transcendental notions into "the unrestricted desire to know." Though I've done this for reasons of expository economy, I've also acknowledged, where the distinction is relevant, the important difference between the desire for intelligibility and the more exigent desire for truth.

BIBLIOGRAPHY

Basic Works by Bernard Lonergan

Collected Works of Bernard Lonergan (hereafter CWL). Vol. 1, *Grace and Freedom: Operative Grace in the Thought of Thomas Aquinas*. Edited by Frederick Crowe and Robert Doran. Toronto: University of Toronto Press, 2000.

CWL. Vol. 2, *Verbum: Word and Idea in Aquinas*. Edited by Frederick Crowe and Robert Doran. Toronto: University of Toronto Press, 1997.

CWL. Vol. 3, *Insight*. Edited by Frederick Crowe and Robert Doran. Toronto: University of Toronto Press, 1992.

CWL. Vol. 4, *Collection*. Edited by Frederick Crowe and Robert Doran. Toronto: University of Toronto Press, 1988.

CWL. Vol. 6, *Philosophical and Theological Papers 1958–1964*. Edited by Frederick Crowe and Robert Doran. Toronto: University of Toronto Press, 1996.

CWL. Vol. 10, *Topics in Education*. Edited by Frederick Crowe and Robert Doran. Toronto: University of Toronto Press, 1993.

CWL. Vol. 17, *Philosophical and Theological Papers 1965–1980*. Edited by Robert Doran and Robert Croken. Toronto: University of Toronto Press, 2004.

CWL. Vol. 18, *Phenomenology and Logic: The Boston College Lectures on Mathematical Logic and Existentialism*. Edited by Philip McShane. Toronto: University of Toronto Press, 2001.

The Lonergan Reader. Edited by Mark Morelli and Elizabeth Morelli. Toronto: University of Toronto Press, 1997.

Method in Theology. New York: Herder and Herder, 1972.

A Second Collection. Philadelphia: Westminster Press, 1974.

A Third Collection. New York: Paulist Press, 1985.

The Way to Nicea: The Dialectical Development of Trinitarian Theology. Philadelphia: Westminster Press, 1976.

Selected Works about Lonergan

Cronin, Brian. *Value Ethics: A Lonergan Perspective*. Nairobi: Consolata Institute of Philosophy, 2006.

Crowe, Frederick. *Developing the Lonergan Legacy*. Toronto: University of Toronto Press, 2004.

———. *Lonergan*. Collegeville, MN: Liturgical Press, 1992.

Doran, Robert. *Theological Foundations*. Vol. 2. Milwaukee: Marquette University Press, 1995.

———. *Theology and the Dialectics of History*. Toronto: University of Toronto Press, 1990.

Flanagan, Joseph. *The Quest for Self-Knowledge*. Toronto: University of Toronto Press, 1996.

Hefling, Charles. *Why Doctrines?* Chestnut Hill, MA: Lonergan Institute at Boston College, 2000.

Liddy, Richard. *Transforming Light: Intellectual Conversion in the Early Lonergan*. Collegeville, MN: Liturgical Press, 1993.

Mathews, William. *Lonergan's Quest: A Study of Desire in the Authoring of Insight*. Toronto: University of Toronto Press, 2005.

McCarthy, Michael. *The Crisis of Philosophy*. Albany: SUNY Press, 1990.

McShane, Philip, ed. *Foundations of Theology: Papers from the International Lonergan Congress 1970*. Notre Dame, IN: University of Notre Dame Press, 1971.

———, ed. *Language, Truth and Meaning: Papers from the International Lonergan Congress 1970*. Notre Dame, IN: University of Notre Dame Press, 1972.

Meynell, Hugo. *An Introduction to the Philosophy of Bernard Lonergan*. Toronto: University of Toronto Press, 1991.

Roy, Louis. *Coherent Christianity*. Ottawa: Novalis, 2005.

Stebbins, Michael. *The Divine Initiative: Grace, World Order and Human Freedom in the Early Writings of Bernard Lonergan*. Toronto: University of Toronto Press, 1995.

Tracy, David. *The Achievement of Bernard Lonergan*. New York: Herder and Herder, 1970.

Walmsley, Gerard. *Lonergan on Philosophic Pluralism: The Polymorphism of Consciousness as the Key to Philosophy*. Toronto: University of Toronto Press, 2008.

Other Works Cited or Discussed

Anselm. *Proslogion*. Chicago: Open Court, 1903.

Aquinas. *Basic Writings of Thomas Aquinas*. Vols. 1 and 2. Edited by Anton Pegis. New York: Random House, 1945.

Arendt, Hannah. *Between Past and Future.* New York: Penguin, 1968.
———. *The Human Condition.* Chicago: University of Chicago Press, 1998.
———. *On Revolution.* New York: Viking, 1965.
———. *The Origins of Totalitarianism.* New York: Harcourt Brace, 1975.
Aristotle. *The Basic Works of Aristotle.* Edited by Richard McKeon. New York: Random House, 1941.
Aron, Raymond. *Main Currents in Sociological Thought.* Vol. 1. New York: Basic Books, 1965.
Augustine. *The City of God.* New York: Modern Library, 1950.
———. *Confessions.* New York: Penguin, 1961.
———. *De Trinitate.* Washington, DC: Catholic University of America Press, 1970.
———. *The Teacher. The Free Choice of the Will. Grace and Free Will.* Washington, DC: Catholic University of America Press, 1968.
Bacon, Francis. *Novum Organon.* New York: Oxford University Press, 2004.
Bainton, Roland. *The Reformation of the Sixteenth Century.* Boston: Beacon Press, 1952.
Barber, Benjamin. *Strong Democracy: Participatory Politics in a New Age.* Berkeley: University of California Press, 1984.
Bayle, Pierre. *Historical and Critical Dictionary.* Edited by Richard Popkin. Indianapolis: Bobbs-Merrill, 1965.
Bellah, Robert, et al. *Habits of the Heart: Individualism and Commitment in American Life.* Berkeley: University of California Press, 1985.
Berkeley, George. *Principles of Human Knowledge/Three Dialogues.* New York: Penguin, 1988.
Berlin, Isaiah. *Four Essays on Liberty.* New York: Oxford University Press, 1969.
Blumenberg, Hans. *The Legitimacy of the Modern Age.* Cambridge, MA: MIT Press, 1983.
Bossuet, Jacques. *Discourse on Universal History.* Chicago: University of Chicago Press, 1976.
Brown, Raymond. *The Critical Meaning of the Bible.* New York: Paulist Press, 1981.
Burtt, Edmund. *The Metaphysical Foundations of Modern Physical Science.* Garden City, NY: Doubleday, 1954.
Butterfield, Herbert. *The Origins of Modern Science 1300–1800.* New York: Free Press, 1957.
Camus, Albert. *The Myth of Sisyphus and Other Essays.* New York: Knopf, 1955.
———. *The Plague.* New York: Vintage Books, 1972.
———. *The Rebel: An Essay on Man in Revolt.* New York: Knopf, 1956.
Cassirer, Ernst. *An Essay on Man.* New Haven: Yale University Press, 1962.
Chadwick, Owen. *The Reformation.* New York: Penguin Books, 1972.

———. *The Secularization of the European Mind in the Nineteenth Century.* Cambridge: Cambridge University Press, 1990.

Cohen, J. Bernard. *Revolutions in Science.* Cambridge, MA: Harvard University Press, 1985.

Collins, James. *God in Modern Philosophy.* Chicago: Regnery, 1959.

Comte, Auguste. *Auguste Comte and Positivism: The Essential Writings.* Edited by Gertrude Lenzer. New York: Harper and Row, 1975.

Coppleston, Frederick. *Late Medieval and Renaissance Philosophy.* Garden City, NY: Image Books, 1963.

———. *Medieval Philosophy.* Garden City, NY: Image Books, 1962.

Cornwell, John. *Hitler's Pope: The Secret History of Pius XII.* New York: Viking, 1999.

Crombie, A. C. *Styles of Scientific Thinking in the European Tradition.* Vols. 1–3. London: Duckworth, 1994.

Crossman, Richard, ed. *The God That Failed.* New York: Harper and Brothers, 1949.

Darwin, Charles. *The Origin of Species.* New York: Dutton, 1928.

Dawson, Christopher. *The Age of the Gods.* Boston: Houghton Mifflin, 1928.

Descartes, René. *The Philosophical Works of Descartes.* Vols. 1 and 2. New York: Cambridge University Press, 1972.

Dewey, John. *The Influence of Darwin on Philosophy.* New York: Peter Smith, 1951.

Dilthey Wilhelm. *Introduction to the Human Sciences.* Edited by Rudolf Makreel and Frithjof Rodi. Princeton: Princeton University Press, 1989.

Dostoyevsky, Fyodor. *The Brothers Karamazov.* New York: Bantam Books, 1970.

Duhem, Pierre. *Études sur Leonardo da Vinci.* Paris: De Nobele, 1955.

———. *Système du Monde. Selections.* Chicago: University of Chicago Press, 1985.

Dunne, John. *The City of the Gods.* New York: Macmillan, 1965.

———. *Reasons of the Heart.* Notre Dame, IN: University of Notre Dame Press, 1979.

———. *A Search for God in Time and Memory.* New York: Macmillan, 1969.

———. *The Way of All the Earth.* Notre Dame, IN: University of Notre Dame Press, 1978.

Freud. Vol. 54 of *Great Books of the Western World.* Chicago: Encyclopedia Britannica, 1952.

Galilei, Galileo. *Dialogue Concerning the Two Chief World Systems, Ptolemaic & Copernican.* Translated by Stillman Drake. Berkeley: University of California Press, 1953.

Gilson, Étienne. *History of Christian Philosophy in the Middle Ages.* New York: Random House, 1955.

Girard, René. *The Scapegoat*. Translated by Yvonne Frecero. Baltimore: Johns Hopkins University Press, 1986.
Hazard, Paul. *The European Mind: The Critical Years 1680–1715*. New Haven: Yale University Press, 1953.
———. *European Thought in the Eighteenth Century, from Montesquieu to Lessing*. New Haven: Yale University Press, 1954.
Hebblethwaite, Peter. *Pope John XXIII, Shepherd of the Modern World*. Garden City, NY: Doubleday, 1985.
Hegel, G. W. F. *Lectures on the History of Philosophy*. Vols. 1–3. Lincoln: University of Nebraska Press, 1995.
———. *Phenomenology of Mind*. Translated by J. B. Bailie. London: Allen and Unwin, 1964.
———. *Reason in History*. Indianapolis: Library of Liberal Arts, 1953.
Heidegger, Martin. *Being and Time*. Translated by John Macquarrie and Edward Robinson. New York: Harper and Row, 1962.
Hobbes, Thomas. *De Cive*. Oxford: Clarendon Press, 1983.
———. *Leviathan*. London: W. W. Norton, 1997.
Humboldt, Wilhelm von. *The Limits of State Action*. Edited by J. W. Burrow. London: Cambridge University Press, 1964.
Hume, David. *An Inquiry Concerning Human Understanding*. Indianapolis: Library of Liberal Arts, 1955.
———. *A Treatise of Human Nature*. Edited by L. A. Selby-Bigge. Oxford: Clarendon Press, 1967.
Husserl, Edmund. *The Crisis of European Sciences and Transcendental Phenomenology*. Translated by David Carr. Evanston, IL: Northwestern University Press, 1970.
———. *Phenomenology and the Crisis of Philosophy*. Translated by Quentin Lauer. New York: Harper and Row, 1965.
Jefferson, Thomas. *The Philosophy of Jesus of Nazareth*. Edited by Dickinson W. Adams. Princeton: Princeton University Press, 1983.
Jung, Carl. *An Answer to Job*. Translated by R. F. C. Hull. Princeton: Princeton University Press, 1973.
Kant, Immanuel. *Critique of Practical Reason*. New York: Liberal Arts Press, 1956.
———. *Critique of Pure Reason*. New York: St. Martin's Press, 1961.
———. *Groundwork of the Metaphysics of Morals*. Translated by H. J. Paton. New York: Harper Torchbooks, 1964. This work is sometimes cited in the text as the *Grundlegung* or as *Foundations* (names commonly used for the text).
———. *Prolegomena to Any Future Metaphysics*. Translated by James Ellington. Indianapolis: Hackett, 1977.

Kierkegaard, Søren. *Attack on Christendom*. Princeton: Princeton University Press, 1944.

———. *Concluding Unscientific Postscript*. Princeton: Princeton University Press, 1968.

———. *Fear and Trembling and The Sickness unto Death*. Princeton: Princeton University Press, 1954.

———. *Philosophical Fragments*. Princeton: Princeton University Press, 1941.

Kolakowsi, Leszek. *Modernity on Endless Trial*. Chicago: University of Chicago Press, 1990.

Koyré, Alexandre. *From the Closed World to the Infinite Universe*. New York: Harper and Brothers, 1958.

Kuhn, Thomas. *The Copernican Revolution*. Cambridge, MA: Harvard University Press, 1957.

———. *The Structure of Scientific Revolutions*. Chicago: Chicago University Press, 1970.

Leibniz, Gottfried Wilhelm. *Discourse on Metaphysics; Correspondence with Arnauld, and Monadology*. Chicago: Open Court, 1937.

Lobkowicz, Nicholas. *Theory and Practice: History of a Concept from Aristotle to Marx*. Notre Dame, IN: University of Notre Dame Press, 1967.

Machiavelli, Niccolò. *The Prince and the Discourses*. New York: Modern Library, 1950.

MacIntyre, Alasdair. *After Virtue*. Notre Dame, IN: University of Notre Dame Press, 1981.

———. *Three Rival Versions of Moral Enquiry*. Notre Dame, IN: University of Notre Dame Press, 1990.

Maritain, Jacques. *The Degrees of Knowledge*. New York: Scribner's Sons, 1959.

———. *The Social and Political Philosophy of Jacques Maritain*. Edited by Joseph W. Evans and Leo R. Ward. New York: Scribner's Sons, 1955.

Marx, Karl. *Karl Marx: Selected Writings*. Edited by David McLellan. New York: Oxford University Press, 1977.

Mill, J. S. *On Liberty*. Indianapolis: Hackett, 1978.

Montesquieu, Charles. *The Spirit of Laws*. Translated and edited by Anne Cohler, Basia Miller, and Harold Stone. Cambridge: Cambridge University Press, 1989.

Mumford, Lewis. *The City in History*. New York: Harcourt Brace, 1961.

Munitz, Milton. *Theories of the Universe*. New York: Free Press, 1957.

Murdoch, Iris. *Existentialists and Mystics*. New York: Penguin, 1997.

———. *Metaphysics as a Guide to Morals*. New York: Penguin, 1992.

———. *The Sovereignty of Good*. New York: Schocken Books, 1971.

Murray, John Courtney. *We Hold These Truths*. New York: Sheed and Ward, 1960.

Neiman, Susan. *Evil in Modern Thought*. Princeton: Princeton University Press, 2002.
Newman, John Henry. *An Essay in Aid of a Grammar of Assent*. Garden City, NY: Image Books, 1958.
———. *An Essay on the Development of Christian Doctrine*. Garden City, NY: Image Books, 1960.
Niebuhr, Reinhold. *Moral Man and Immoral Society*. New York: Charles Scribner's Sons, 1960.
———. *The Nature and Destiny of Man*. Vols. 1 and 2. New York: Charles Scribner's Sons, 1964.
Nietzsche, Friedrich. *Beyond Good and Evil: Prelude to a Philosophy of the Future*. London: Allen and Unwin, 1967.
———. *Fröhliche Wissenschaft*. New York: Macmillan, 1912.
———. *The Genealogy of Morals: A Polemic*. New York: Doubleday Anchor, 1956.
———. *Thus Spake Zarathustra*. New York: Viking Press, 1966.
Noonan, John T. *A Church That Can and Cannot Change: The Development of Catholic Moral Teaching*. Notre Dame, IN: University of Notre Dame Press, 2005.
O'Dea, Thomas. *The Catholic Crisis*. Boston: Beacon Press, 1968.
O'Malley, John. *What Happened at Vatican II?* Cambridge, MA: Harvard University Press, 2008.
Oxford Illustrated History of Christianity. Edited by John McManners. Oxford: Oxford University Press, 1992.
Pascal, Blaise. *Pensées*. New York: Penguin Books, 1966.
Pelikan, Jaroslav. *The Christian Tradition: A History of the Development of Doctrine*. Vols. 1–4. Chicago: University of Chicago Press, 1978.
———. *Jesus Through the Centuries*. New Haven: Yale University Press, 1985.
Pico Della Mirandola, Giovanni. *On the Dignity of Man*. Translated by Charles G. Wallis. Indianapolis: Bobbs-Merrill, 1965.
Plato. *The Collected Dialogues*. Edited by Edith Hamilton and Huntington Cairns. Bollingen Series. 1961. Reprint, Princeton: Princeton University Press, 1996.
Polanyi, Michael. *Personal Knowledge*. Chicago: University of Chicago Press, 1958.
———. *The Tacit Dimension*. Garden City, NY: Doubleday, 1966.
Putnam, Robert. *Bowling Alone*. New York: Simon and Schuster, 2000.
Quine, Willard Van Orman. *Ontological Relativity and Other Essays*. New York: Columbia University Press, 1969.
———. *The Web of Belief*. New York: Random House, 1970.
Ranke, Leopold von. *The Secret of World History: Selected Writings on the Art and Science of History*. New York: Fordham University Press, 1981.

Rawls, John. *Political Liberalism*. New York: Columbia University Press, 1993.
———. *A Theory of Justice*. Cambridge, MA: Harvard University Press, 1971.
Richardson, Alan. *The Bible in the Age of Science*. London: SCM Press, 1961.
———. *History, Sacred and Profane*. Philadelphia: Westminster Press, 1964.
Ricoeur, Paul. *Freud and Philosophy: An Essay on Interpretation*. New Haven: Yale University Press, 1970.
Rorty, Richard. *The Linguistic Turn*. Chicago: University of Chicago Press, 1967.
———. *Philosophy and the Mirror of Nature*. Princeton: Princeton University Press, 1979.
Rousseau, Jean-Jacques. *The First and Second Discourses*. Edited by Roger Masters. New York: St. Martin's Press, 1964.
Sandel, Michael. *Democracy's Discontent*. Cambridge, MA: Harvard University Press, 1996.
———. *Liberalism and the Limits of Justice*. Cambridge: Cambridge University Press, 1995.
Schneewind, Jerome. *The Invention of Autonomy: A History of Modern Moral Philosophy*. New York: Cambridge University Press, 1998.
Sellars, Wilfrid. *Science and Metaphysics*. London: Routledge and Kegan Paul, 1968.
———. *Science, Perception and Reality*. New York: Humanities Press, 1963.
Spinoza, Baruch. *The Ethics and Selected Letters*. Indianapolis: Hackett, 1982.
———. *Tractatus Theologico-Politicus*. Translated by Samuel Shirley. Indianapolis: Hackett, 1998.
Stewart, John A. *Plato's Doctrine of Ideas*. Oxford: Clarendon Press, 1909.
Taylor, Charles. "A Catholic Modernity?" In *A Catholic Modernity?*, edited by James Heft. New York: Oxford University Press, 1999.
———. *The Ethics of Authenticity*. Cambridge, MA: Harvard University Press, 1991.
———. *Modern Social Imaginaries*. Durham, NC: Duke University Press, 2004.
———. *Philosophical Arguments*. Cambridge, MA: Harvard University Press, 1995.
———. *Philosophical Papers*. Vols. 1 and 2. Cambridge: Cambridge University Press, 1992.
———. *A Secular Age*. Cambridge, MA: Harvard University Press, 2007.
———. *Sources of the Self*. Cambridge, MA: Harvard University Press, 1989.
Tocqueville, Alexis de. *Democracy in America*. Vols. 1 and 2. New York: Schocken Books, 1961.
———. *The Old Regime and the Revolution*. Edited by François Furet and Françoise Mélonio. Chicago: University of Chicago Press, 2001.

Tracy, David. *Plurality and Ambiguity*. Chicago: University of Chicago Press, 1987.

Trilling, Lionel. *Sincerity and Authenticity*. Cambridge, MA: Harvard University Press, 1972.

Tuchman, Barbara. *The March of Folly*. New York: Knopf, 1984.

Vatican Council II. *The Conciliar and Post-Conciliar Documents*. Edited by Austin Flannery. Northport, NY: Costello Publications, 1987.

Voegelin, Eric. *Israel and Revelation*. Baton Rouge: Louisiana State University Press, 1956.

———. *The World of the Polis*. Baton Rouge: Louisiana State University Press, 1957.

Voltaire. *Candide*. Translated and edited by Peter Gay. New York: St. Martin's Press, 1963.

Walzer, Michael. *Spheres of Justice: A Defense of Pluralism and Equality*. New York: Basic Books, 1983.

Weber, Max. *The Essential Weber: A Reader*. Edited by Sam Whimster. New York: Oxford University Press, 1958.

Weinberg, Julius. *A Short History of Medieval Philosophy*. Princeton: Princeton University Press, 1964.

Whitehead A. N. *Adventures of Ideas*. New York: Macmillan, 1933.

———. *Science and the Modern World*. New York: New American Library, 1954.

Wills, Garry. *Head and Heart: American Christianities*. New York: Penguin, 2007.

———. *Papal Sin: Structures of Deceit*. New York: Doubleday, 2001.

Wittgenstein, Ludwig. *Philosophical Investigations*. New York: Macmillan, 1965.

———. *Tractatus Logico-Philosophicus*. New York: Humanities Press, 1963.

INDEX

Abelard, Peter, 2
Abraham, 206, 298, 317, 318, 319, 320, 332
absolute monarchy, 190–91
abstraction
  apprehensive abstraction, 74
  Aquinas on, 74
  formative abstraction, 74
  objective abstraction, 74
  vs. recollection, 58–59
Acts of the Apostles, 194, 256, 299
Adam and Eve, 68, 323
aesthetic pattern of experience, 29, 139, 169
aggiornamento/renewal, 259, 260, 265, 271–86, 322–23, 351–52, 355, 377n.128, 387n.53, 391n.108
agnosticism, 50, 184, 280, 308
alienation, 192, 250, 254, 255, 256, 333, 368n.37
American Revolution, 113, 191, 372n.33
Anselm, St., 2, 79, 266, 273, 287, 300, 307
  Proslogion, 386n.36
anthropology, 126, 131–32, 241, 247, 275, 281
anti-Semitism, 194, 242, 245, 255, 262, 263, 270, 380n.192, 385n.20
  Holocaust, 244, 247, 253, 340, 350, 381n.207

Aquinas, Thomas, 262, 307, 372n.31, 377n.127
  on abstraction, 74
  vs. Aristotle, 55, 76, 81, 83, 206, 230, 231, 272
  vs. Augustine, 55, 71, 76–77, 79–80, 230, 231
  on beatitude, 326
  on cardinal virtues, 14, 77
  on charity, 73, 231, 263, 292
  on cognition, 2, 8, 53, 55, 56, 73–76, 81, 83, 151, 212, 364n.69, 384n.6
  condemnation of 1277, 14, 262, 361n.20, 366n.7, 378n.162
  on cosmology, 197, 291
  as critical Christian thinker, 2, 3
  as critical realist, 74–75
  cultural heritage of, 2, 7, 14, 25, 73, 230, 271
  on divine revelation, 196, 260, 272, 287, 358
  on existential act, 75
  faculty psychology of, 55, 56
  on faith, 14, 25, 73, 76, 78, 79–80, 218–19, 231, 233, 258, 262, 263, 271, 287, 289, 292
  on grace of God, 2, 8, 14, 25, 71, 73, 76–80, 81, 218–19, 230, 231, 233, 234, 246, 258, 263, 292, 323, 323–24, 326, 333, 336, 345, 350, 378n.161, 384n.6, 388n.72

403

Aquinas, Thomas (*cont.*)
  on human freedom, 76, 79, 81
  on human intellect, 125, 271
  on human reason, 14, 25, 26, 73,
    77–78, 196, 218–19, 233, 234, 258,
    262, 263, 271, 287, 289, 292
  on human will, 76, 77–78, 81, 125
  on incarnation, 82
  on insights, 151, 271
  as intellectualist, 271
  on intelligible form, 75
  vs. Lonergan, 2–3, 8, 51, 55–56, 249,
    256–57, 260, 265, 271–72, 333,
    344, 350, 358
  Lonergan on, 2, 3, 8, 10, 11, 53,
    55–56, 72–83, 92, 151, 219, 266,
    271–72, 273–74, 278, 284, 292,
    336, 360n.9, 361n.20, 364nn.69, 74,
    384n.6, 388n.72
  on metaphysics, 14, 56, 75–76, 81, 82,
    212, 249
  on natural substances, 75
  on nature, 14, 25, 73, 76, 77, 230–31,
    233, 246, 258, 263, 292, 323–24,
    333, 336, 378n.161
  on practical wisdom (*prudentia*), 343
  on sensible matter, 75
  on sin, 71, 76, 78–79, 230, 231, 246,
    323–24, 333, 350
  on the soul, 271
  on speculative intellect, 83
  on supernatural virtues, 14, 78, 231
  on the Trinity, 79–81, 364n.74
  on truth, 74–75
  on virtue, 14, 73, 76, 77–78, 219, 231,
    263, 292, 324, 326, 336, 344–45
  See also Thomism
Arendt, Hannah, 366n.2
  Between Past and Future, 366n.104,
    368nn.30, 35, 373n.44
  The Human Condition, 366n.106,
    372n.28
  On Revolution, 365n.95, 367n.13,
    372n.33, 389n.76
  The Origins of Totalitarianism,
    365n.96, 380nn.192, 197, 199

Aristotle, 2, 4, 7, 8, 15, 20, 136, 263, 333,
    344, 368n.33
  vs. Aquinas, 14, 55, 76, 81, 83, 206,
    230, 231, 272
  on artifacts, 110, 111
  on biology, 110, 112, 125
  on causality, 16, 61, 63, 64–65, 67,
    86, 111, 112, 113–14, 116, 119,
    143–44, 223, 280, 361n.24
  on causal necessity, 16, 64–65, 86,
    112, 113–14, 116, 143–44, 223,
    280, 361n.24
  on celestial substances, 110–11
  on cognition, 60–61, 114–15, 143,
    151, 212, 223
  on cosmology, 16, 19, 66–67,
    110–11, 114, 116, 117–18, 119,
    130, 189, 197, 224, 233, 291, 324,
    330, 366nn.4, 7
  cultural authority of, 110–14, 333
  De Anima, 61, 63, 151, 363n.58
  on efficient causality, 61, 63, 111,
    119
  as epistemic realist, 114–15
  on essence and accident, 110
  on essence vs. existence, 64, 66
  on *eudaimonia*, 112, 326
  on experiential vs. theoretical
    knowledge, 60–61
  on final causality, 16, 111, 112, 116,
    119
  on form, 110, 111, 118
  on formal causality, 16, 111, 119
  on God, 110–11, 116, 117, 118
  on hierarchy of being, 110–11, 116,
    117–18, 130, 131, 189, 197,
    323–24, 324, 330, 366n.4
  on human beings as political
    animals, 118
  on human intellect (*nous*), 60, 125
  on identity of knower and known,
    62–63, 114–15
  in insights, 151
  on intellectual conversion, 36
  on intelligible form, 60, 62, 64, 66,
    114–15

on justice and temperance, 173
on logic, 61–62, 104
Lonergan on, 10, 11, 51, 55–56, 57, 60–67, 151
on matter, 62, 64, 66, 110, 111, 117, 118, 119
on metaphysics, 14, 56, 62, 63–64, 66, 81, 82, 83, 92, 104, 110, 116, 118, 151, 174, 187–88, 212, 231, 272
Metaphysics, 36, 61, 355, 363n.64, 366nn.5, 6
on natural substances, 110, 111, 118
on nature vs. convention, 62
Nicomachean Ethics, 62, 64, 173, 367nn.10, 14
Parts of Animals, 366n.4
on philosophical questions, 60–61
on *phronesis* (practical wisdom), 64, 65–66, 112–13, 114, 326, 343
on physics, 16, 86, 110, 111, 330, 361n.22, 366n.7
Physics, 61, 366n.6
on politics, 113, 116, 117, 118
Posterior Analytics, 16, 65, 113–14, 367n.14
on potency and actuality, 110
on practical intellect/inquiry, 64, 112–13, 114, 116, 174, 189
on reason (*nous*), 112, 143, 174, 234
on sense perception, 61, 64, 66
on sensible substances, 110
on skilled physicians, 43
on *sophia* vs. *phronesis*, 64, 65–66, 112–13
on the soul, 59, 60, 63, 110, 114–15, 118, 143, 174
on species-immortality, 66, 67, 116, 125
on spirit of wonder (*thauma*), 60
on terrestrial substances, 110, 111, 118
on theology, 62–63, 64–65
on theoretical intellect/inquiry, 64, 112, 116, 118–19, 174, 189, 223

theory of science, 52, 64, 65, 66–67, 86, 104, 113–14, 118–19, 132, 143–44, 223, 280, 330, 361n.22, 361n.24, 366n.7
on virtue, 62, 64, 65, 76, 112–13, 173, 174, 175, 223, 326
art, 274, 280
Athanasius of Alexandria, St., 273
atheism, 50, 184, 201, 217, 245, 246, 248, 275, 280, 308, 324–26, 331, 354
attentiveness, 32
Augustine, St., 2, 14, 36, 260, 262, 273, 295, 300, 307, 323, 344, 377n.127, 379n.166
on Adam and Eve, 68
vs. Aquinas, 55, 71, 76–77, 79–80, 230, 231
on *caritas*, 37, 70, 71
on cognition, 71–72
Confessions, 37, 49, 68, 70, 362n.39, 364nn.63–65
on conversion, 388n.65
on *cupiditas*, 48, 70, 71
De Civitate Dei, 70, 87, 265, 364n.63
on evil, 68, 253, 379n.169
on faith and reason, 287
on free will, 68–69, 76
on God and evil, 253
on God and salvation, 67
on God as Trinity, 71
on grace of God, 37, 68–69, 70, 71, 76–77, 79, 233, 266
on human will, 67, 68–69, 70, 76, 263, 379n.169
on inner words, 70–71, 73, 76, 80, 151
on intellect, 67, 68
on intellectual conversion, 37, 69
Lonergan on, 51, 67–72, 219, 364n.74
on love of God, 68, 70, 315
on memory, 67, 68, 364n.63
on metaphysics, 71, 72
on moral conversion, 37, 69–70
on moral evaluation, 68
on original sin, 68–69

Augustine, St. (*cont.*)
  on religious conversion, 37, 49,
    67–68, 70–71
  on repentance, 49
  on sin, 68–70, 71, 76–77, 79,
    231–32, 233, 266
  on the soul, 67–68, 69–71, 72, 151
  on the Trinity, 79–80, 364n.74
Austin, J. L., 91, 92
authenticity, 21, 29, 34, 47, 49, 51, 56,
    90, 99, 101, 102, 108, 129, 284,
    293, 308, 310, 323, 332, 341,
    347–48, 390n.89
  vs. arbitrary choice, 373n.40
  of Christian witness, 305, 320–21,
    322
  dialectical character of, 285
  as epistemic, 170, 211, 222, 249
  ethics of, 62, 82, 260, 331–32, 336,
    343–46, 351, 355, 358, 381n.215
  existential authenticity, 137, 193,
    211, 249
  historical authenticity, 249–50
  as moral, 24, 170, 211, 215, 222,
    249
  as personal and communal, 24,
    32, 83, 95, 208, 215, 217, 227,
    260, 285, 335, 336, 338, 355, 358
  and problem of evil, 340–41
  relationship to genuine authority,
    331–32
  relationship to moral failures, 44,
    45
  relationship to objective knowing,
    102–3, 129, 134, 170, 249, 338
  as religious, 181, 182, 183, 209, 211,
    218, 222, 228, 248–58, 285,
    295–96, 298, 337, 355, 375n.90
  secular authenticity, 246
  as self-transcendence, 38, 95,
    175–79, 180, 181, 211, 215,
    249, 250, 252–53, 336, 338,
    345–46, 356, 358
  as transcendental virtue, 345–46
authority, 325–26, 331–32, 333–36,
    341

autonomy, 240, 328, 333–36, 380n.188
  Descartes on, 249, 325, 327, 334
  Kant on, 88–89, 122, 133–34, 193,
    220, 234–36, 240, 243, 249, 325,
    327, 334, 380n.189
  Lonergan on, 334

Bacon, Francis, 135, 189, 239, 254,
    380n.187
  Novum Organon, 367n.11, 371n.26
  on science and technology, 113,
    116, 120–21, 124, 244, 326–27
Bacon, Roger, 361n.22, 371n.18
Bainton, Roland: *The Reformation of
    the Sixteenth Century*, 384n.7
Barber, Benjamin
  Strong Democracy, 389n.82
  The Struggle for Democracy,
    389n.82
Barth, Karl, 379n.166
Basil, St., 287
Bayle, Pierre, 198, 267
beatific vision, 196, 326
behaviorism, 18, 99, 148, 169
Bellarmine, St. Robert, 361n.20,
    372n.31
Benedict, St., 262, 323
Berkeley, George, 160
  Principles of Human Knowledge,
    369n.53
Berlin, Isaiah: *Four Essays on Liberty*,
    389n.81
bias, 18, 47, 48, 90, 97, 102, 132,
    133, 135, 144, 154, 256, 335,
    351
  distorting effects of, 9, 28, 29, 30,
    32, 44, 49, 95, 96, 98, 147, 153,
    250, 308, 331, 342, 354
  dramatic bias, 29, 32, 134, 179,
    250, 354
  egoistic bias, 29, 32, 134, 179, 250,
    313–14, 316, 341, 354
  general bias, 29, 32, 134, 179, 250,
    316, 341, 354
  group bias, 29, 32, 134, 179, 250,
    255, 313–14, 316, 341, 354

Lonergan on, 9, 27, 28, 29, 30, 32, 95, 103, 165, 210, 215, 224, 227, 230, 250, 255, 258, 281, 293, 308, 310, 313–14, 316, 330, 331, 332, 334, 335, 336, 338, 339, 341, 342, 348, 354, 362n.35, 368n.36
scientistic bias, 96
Bible, 196, 197, 199–200, 273, 286
biblical studies, critical, 195, 199–200, 275, 280, 290
biological pattern of experience, 139, 169
biologism, 126
Black Death, 262, 263
Blumenberg, Hans, 231, 378n.163
  The Legitimacy of the Modern Age, 383n.3
Bonaventure, St., 196, 273
Bossuet, Bishop Jacques-Bénigne, 195, 267
bourgeoisie, 190, 191, 195, 201, 245, 255, 290
Boyle, Nicholas: *Who Are We Now?*, 360n.13
Brentano, Franz, 89, 127
Brown, Raymond, 387n.50
Buddhism, 278, 382n.234
Buridan, Jean, 361n.22, 371n.18
Butterfield, Herbert, 366n.2
  The Origins of Modern Science, 361n.23, 367n.19, 373n.41, 374n.51, 384n.7

Cajetan, Thomas, 378n.162
Calvin, John, 25, 198, 267
Camus, Albert, 245, 246, 381nn.202–4
capitalism, 12, 25, 124, 191, 201, 239, 242, 245, 248, 255, 290, 328, 333, 334, 341
Carnap, Rudolf, 91, 92
Cassirer, Ernst: *An Essay on Man*, 365n.89
Catholicism, 190, 222, 230, 344, 349, 390n.104
  aggiornamento/renewal, 259–60, 265, 271–86, 320–21, 322–23, 351–52, 355, 377n.128, 387n.53, 391n.108
  antimodernist era, 247, 265–70, 275–76, 277, 279–80, 285, 289
  and classicism, 216, 247, 276, 280–82, 283, 289, 291, 300, 310, 320, 351
  Council of Chalcedon, 196, 265, 300
  Council of Constantinople, 196, 265, 300
  Council of Ephesus, 300
  Council of Nicea, 196, 265, 300
  Council of Trent, 195, 266, 275, 341, 361n.20
  Counter-Reformation, 279–80
  doctrine of papal infallibility, 269–70, 276
  First Vatican Council, 176, 269–70, 276
  hierarchical leadership, 261, 267, 268, 269–70, 352
  Latin Christendom, 25, 26, 182, 186, 193–95, 198, 199, 205, 216, 232, 263, 281, 289, 300, 341, 371n.16, 373n.41
  Mass, 302
  moral tradition in, 323
  papacy, 25, 194, 195, 231, 232, 262, 263, 264, 266, 267, 268, 269–70, 276, 277, 279, 333, 352, 372n.30, 373n.42, 384n.13
  periods of scandal, 25, 193–95, 231, 247, 261, 262–63, 266, 267, 372n.30
  sacraments, 268, 302
  saints, 262
  See also Second Vatican Council
causality
  Aristotle on, 16, 61, 63, 64–65, 67, 86, 111, 112, 113–14, 116, 119, 143–44, 223, 280, 361n.24
  causal contingency, 64–65, 67
  causal necessity, 11, 16, 22, 86, 88, 93, 94, 96, 112, 113–14, 115–16, 117, 143–44, 223, 280
  divine vs. human, 316–17
  efficient causality, 61, 63, 111, 119
  final causality, 16, 61, 111, 112, 116, 119
  formal causality, 16, 58, 59–60, 61, 63, 111, 119
  Kant on, 115–16, 143–44, 162–63, 369n.55

causality (*cont.*)
   Lonergan on, 215–17
   spiritual vs. material, 316–17
Chadwick, Owen
   The Reformation, 373n.41,
      378nn.164, 165, 384n.7
   The Secularization of the European Mind in the Nineteenth Century,
      373n.41, 384nn.15, 17, 385n.18
charity, 37, 46, 49, 258, 297, 298, 314, 350, 382n.221
   Aquinas on, 73, 231, 263, 292
   as supernatural virtue, 78, 345
   See also love
Christianity
   Athens and Jerusalem, 13–14, 25, 261, 262
   church councils, 2, 14, 79, 195, 196
   church fathers, 2, 14, 67, 196, 230, 262, 265, 287, 300
   critique of Christian doctrine, 195–200, 205, 267–68, 289–91, 324, 373n.41
   critique of Christian practice, 193–96, 205, 217–18, 232, 267–68, 279–80, 373n.41
   cultural adaptations, 301, 306, 320, 352
   as evangelical, 11, 198
   prayer, 301
   scripture, 2, 14, 196, 197, 199–200
   teaching tradition of, 299–300
   wars of religion, 194–95, 205, 233, 267, 280
   See also Catholicism; Jesus Christ; Protestantism
Cicero's *Hortentius*, 37
classical heuristic structure, 85, 94, 126, 140, 165, 214, 221, 224, 226, 227, 313
classicism
   and Catholicism, 216, 247, 276, 280–82, 283, 289, 291, 300, 310, 320, 351
   Lonergan on, 52–53, 65, 81, 83, 87, 216, 222, 280, 281–82, 283, 284, 309, 310, 320, 321, 351, 388n.73

Clement of Alexandria, 287
cognition
   Aquinas on, 2, 8, 53, 55, 56, 73–76, 81, 83, 151, 212, 364n.69, 384n.6
   Aristotle on, 60–61, 114–15, 143, 151, 212, 223
   conceptualism, 52, 53–55, 76, 83, 98, 149
   direct insights, 54, 58, 59, 60, 61–62, 64, 74, 76, 83, 95, 101, 146, 151–53, 157, 158, 161, 163, 164, 167, 169, 170, 177, 316, 356
   functional complementarity in, 61, 142, 145, 150, 157
   identity theory of, 59, 62–63, 72, 83, 114–15
   intellectualism, 52, 53–56, 58, 76, 83, 92, 100, 271
   levels of cognitive process, 31–32, 145–46, 149–55, 156–57, 158–59, 168
   Lonergan on, 8–11, 12, 21–24, 31–32, 34, 40–41, 52, 53–56, 58–59, 60–61, 62–63, 71–72, 73–76, 90, 94–95, 100–101, 102, 103–4, 108, 138–39, 142–55, 156–57, 162, 169–71, 177, 208–9, 212–14, 222–24, 225, 271, 273, 281, 282, 300, 336, 338, 342–43, 355, 356, 357, 362n.41, 366n.105, 375n.78, 384n.6
   normative structure of, 9, 17, 29, 30, 31, 32, 39, 42, 103, 104, 140–41, 145, 146, 147, 148, 150, 151–52, 153, 154, 155, 156, 157, 159, 168, 170, 171, 180, 208, 211, 213, 218, 256, 281, 356
   provisional/fallible results in, 3, 16–17, 18, 22, 31–32, 64, 82, 86, 87, 94–95, 105, 132, 133, 144, 147, 148, 153–55, 156, 223–24, 270, 280, 353, 368n.33
   reflective insights, 54, 58, 60, 64, 66, 74, 76, 82–83, 95, 100, 101, 147, 151–52, 154, 157, 158, 162, 163, 164, 167, 169, 170, 171, 316, 356

role of generalized empirical method in, 3–4, 5, 23, 31–32, 82, 104, 137–38, 155, 214, 225, 294–95, 356

role of insights in, 31–32, 43, 45, 54, 58–59, 60, 61–62, 64, 66, 71, 74, 76, 82–83, 95, 100–101, 146, 147, 149–55, 273, 356

stages of cognitive development, 138–39

and virtually unconditioned judgments, 41, 100, 147, 154, 156, 158–59, 162, 163, 167, 170, 178, 312–13, 380n.184

See also cognitive meaning; epistemology; heuristic structures; knowledge; questions and answers

cognitive meaning
realms of, 92, 95, 103–4, 146, 150, 151, 155, 156, 187, 208, 214, 285, 292, 294, 311, 356, 385n.25

stages of, 92, 150, 212–13, 214, 285, 311, 356, 385n.25

third stage of, 73, 81–82, 92, 107, 188, 212, 213, 214, 292, 301, 311, 334–35, 339, 362n.28

collectivism, 275

Collins, James
God in Modern Philosophy, 373n.41
The Oxford History of Christianity, 373n.41

colonialism, 25, 195, 200

common sense, 18, 22, 23, 31, 39, 42, 61, 82, 102, 105, 114, 118, 130, 137, 143, 155, 164, 187, 210, 214, 227–28, 272, 292, 334, 343, 353, 359n.3, 366n.105

general bias of, 29, 32, 134, 179, 250, 316, 341, 354

language of, 92, 104, 164, 212

as realm of cognitive meaning, 92, 95, 138, 151, 165, 208, 212–13, 294

religious common sense, 254, 292, 303

vs. theory, 118, 382n.235

communism, 25, 270, 391n.107

Comte, Auguste, 221, 310, 386n.44

concepts, 74, 83

Congar, Yves, 276

Conradi, Peter: *Iris Murdoch*, 371n.9

consciousness
data of, 23, 30, 54, 55, 56, 63, 72, 82, 89, 99, 127, 137–38, 140, 188, 214, 224, 291–92, 295

intentionality of, 11, 18, 23, 27, 32, 33, 37–38, 55, 56, 63, 71, 82, 83, 89–90, 92, 100–101, 102, 103, 104, 105, 108, 127, 132, 137–38, 140, 142, 148, 149, 150, 163, 166, 169–70, 174–75, 179, 180, 188, 208–9, 214, 249, 271, 279, 281, 291–92, 295, 303, 316, 321, 330, 338, 342, 344, 345, 356, 357, 360n.10, 362nn.36, 41

patterns of conscious experience, 9, 23, 27, 28, 29, 31, 38, 39, 40, 56, 88–89, 93, 102, 104, 139, 140, 141, 145, 150, 152, 169–70, 171

as polymorphic, 23, 27, 28, 30, 35, 37, 56, 82, 89–90, 92, 93, 103, 108, 127, 132, 134, 139–41, 142, 144, 145, 149, 150, 157, 162, 163, 166, 168–70, 171, 175, 179, 180, 188, 208, 209, 214, 227, 249, 291, 303, 330, 346, 354, 357, 368n.41, 375n.83

See also human subjectivity

conversions, existential, 35–51, 52, 105, 222, 228, 303, 332, 339, 341, 358, 362n.41, 388nn.64, 65

intellectual conversion, 36–37, 40–42, 46, 49, 57, 69, 101, 209, 215, 218, 228–29, 250–51, 252, 260, 272, 282, 284, 296, 297, 298, 300, 304, 309, 310, 313, 315–16, 320, 343, 349, 353, 354, 357, 387n.49

moral conversion, 36, 37, 38–39, 40, 41–45, 49, 57, 69–70, 209, 215, 218, 228, 229, 250–51, 252, 260, 272, 282, 284, 296, 297, 298, 300, 304, 309, 310–11, 313–14, 315, 320, 338, 343, 349, 351, 353, 354, 357, 387n.49

relationship to knowledge of God, 315–17

conversions, existential (*cont.*)
  religious conversion, 37, 40, 46–51, 67–68, 70–71, 215, 218, 228, 229, 250–52, 260, 282–83, 284, 296–98, 300, 304–5, 306, 307, 309, 310–11, 313, 314–16, 317, 318, 320, 343, 349, 351, 353, 354, 357, 387nn.49, 59
cooperative grace, 9, 70, 76–77, 78, 79, 231, 342, 388n.72
1 Corinthians
  9:22, 265
  13:11, 370n.2
  13:12, 309
Cornwall, John, 381n.207
  Hitler's Pope, 385n.20, 390n.96
cosmology, 13, 130–31, 185, 199, 247, 281, 354
  Aquinas on, 197, 291
  Aristotle on, 16, 19, 66–67, 110–11, 114, 116, 117–18, 119, 130, 189, 197, 224, 233, 291, 324, 330, 366nn.4, 7
  Copernican Revolution, 11, 16, 86, 109, 111, 114, 116–17, 130, 162, 195, 204, 205, 224–25, 233, 234, 267, 275, 361n.22, 362n.28
  Lonergan on, 17, 19, 85–86, 136, 224–27, 253–54, 313, 330, 357, 368n.31
  as mechanistic, 17, 19, 119, 188, 197, 198, 217, 225
Council of Chalcedon, 196, 265, 300
Council of Constantinople, 196, 265, 300
Council of Ephesus, 300
Council of Nicea, 196, 265, 300
Council of Trent, 195, 266, 275, 341, 361n.20
critical mentality, 19, 20–21, 86
critical retrieval, 51–52
Crombie, A. C.: *Styles of Scientific Thinking in the European Tradition*, 367n.19
Cronin, Brian: *Value Ethics*, 370n.65
Crowe, Frederick: *Developing the Lonergan Legacy*, 359n.6, 387n.61

cultural centers, interdisciplinary, 24, 26, 33, 35, 284, 353–55
cultural crises, 13–15, 23, 35
  Lonergan on, 11, 14–15, 24–26, 108, 129, 180, 207, 259, 265–70, 353, 358
cultural diversity
  Athens and Jerusalem, 13–14, 25, 261, 262
  cultural pluralism, 11, 13–14, 20–21, 26, 33, 50, 53, 87, 96–97, 98, 132, 163–64, 166, 168, 187, 193, 207, 216, 217, 248, 281, 303, 309, 320, 339
  Lonergan on, 13, 20–21, 107, 320, 360n.16
cultural heritage, 2–3, 6, 10, 14–15, 28, 38, 44
  of Aquinas, 2, 7, 14, 25, 73, 230, 271
  critical appropriation of, 2, 4, 8–9, 12–13, 26–27, 51–83, 98, 105, 106, 210–11, 214–15, 218, 249, 273–75, 285, 309, 320–21, 329, 334, 353–54, 355
culture
  intellectual superstructure vs. practical infrastructure, 274, 279, 284, 285, 293–95, 353
  self-reflective cultures, 11–14, 19
Cusanus, Nicholas, 229

Daniélou, Jean, 276
Dante Alighieri: *Inferno*, Canto 26, 366n.3
Darwin, Charles, 3, 97, 123, 130, 131, 140, 243
  evolutionary biology of, 84, 94, 112, 125–26, 129, 193, 199, 204, 217, 221, 240, 269, 290–91, 325
  naturalism of, 129, 217, 240
  on natural selection, 112, 125, 240, 290
  on random variation, 112, 125, 240, 290
Day, Dorothy, 206
death, 89, 90, 128, 137, 206, 211, 246, 257, 258

Decalogue, 323
deconstruction, 26
Deism, 193, 198–99, 200
Delbanco, Andrew
  The Death of Satan, 382n.232
  The Puritan Ordeal, 382n.232
democracy, 183, 205, 206, 325, 330–31, 348–49, 390n.104
  democratic revolutions, 109, 191, 268–69, 324
  equality in, 185, 191, 247, 268, 269, 275, 328–29, 333
Descartes, René, 3, 34, 91, 92, 94, 100, 129, 135, 244, 254, 267, 380n.187
  on autonomy, 249, 325, 327, 334
  on certainty, 143
  on cosmology, 119
  Discourse on Method, 93, 365n.91, 367n.11, 371n.26
  on doubt, 7–8, 28, 93, 195
  on error, 379n.169
  on God, 120, 143, 162, 196–97, 220, 233–34, 287–88
  on happiness, 326
  on human reason, 88, 126, 233, 234, 249, 287
  on human will, 120, 126, 379n.169
  on ideas, 90, 99, 143, 160, 233–34, 288
  on indubitable ideas, 120
  on intellectual method, 93, 120
  on knowledge, 120–21, 233–34
  on matter (*res extensa*), 88–89, 99, 101, 119–20, 159–60, 237
  Meditations, 120, 367n.21
  on mind (*res cogitans*), 88–89, 99, 101, 119–20, 143, 144, 160, 237, 249, 325
  Le Monde, 119
  on principle of immanence, 127
  Principles of Philosophy, 367n.21, 379n.170
  Rules, 93
  on science, 113, 128, 132, 143–44, 159, 189, 234, 326–27, 361n.24
  on tree of knowledge, 379n.170

despotism, 335–36, 340
destabilizing forces, 15, 19–21
determinism, 17–18, 19, 119, 135, 179, 188, 225, 330
Dewey, John, 34, 366n.105
dialectic, 4, 29–30, 219
  and critical self-appropriation, 33–35, 208, 209–10
  dialectical character of authenticity, 285
  dialectical heuristic structure, 94, 140, 165, 224, 227, 313
  vs. dialogue, 354–55
  as functional specialty in theology, 303–4, 305, 310, 320, 321, 376n.107
  Hegel on, 96, 98, 122, 192, 237
  in history, 5, 9, 96, 122, 192, 256, 325
  Lonergan on, 9, 10, 18, 34–35, 98, 101, 105–6, 149, 158, 165–71, 183, 188–89, 208, 209–12, 218, 222, 228, 250, 275, 278, 284, 285, 286, 295, 298, 309–11, 330, 341–42, 344, 350–51, 354–55, 356, 357, 372n.37
  Plato on, 35, 57, 58
  positions vs. counterpositions, 35, 41, 45, 47, 50–51, 52, 100, 101, 104, 105–6, 149, 157, 159, 165, 166–71, 179, 209–10, 250, 275, 295, 303, 337–38, 339, 342, 356, 357, 388n.66
  of progress and decline, 5, 9, 256
  and self-appropriation, 29–30, 33–35, 208, 209–10, 249
Diderot, Denis, 268
Dilthey, Wilhelm, 3
  Introduction to the Human Sciences, 368n.27
  on meaning and value, 126, 241–42
  on sciences of nature vs. sciences of spirit, 126–27
Dostoyevsky, Fyodor: Grand Inquisitor in *The Brothers Karamazov*, 382n.232, 383n.246, 386n.45, 390n.94

dramatic pattern of experience, 29, 139, 152, 169
Duhem, Pierre, 143, 371n.18
   Studies in Leonardo da Vinci, 361n.22
   The System of the World, 361n.22, 367n.19
Dunne, John S.
   The City of the Gods, 381n.205
   Reasons of the Heart, 388n.69
   A Search for God in Time and Memory, 364n.63

Eckhart, Meister, 273
economic conditions, 128, 193, 195
economics, 126, 241, 274
ecumenism, 26, 46, 301, 351, 352, 354
Eddington, Arthur, 104
education, 52, 65, 87, 131, 134, 168, 175–77, 192, 203, 293–94, 328, 339
   Catholic education, 270
   and cultural heritage, 12, 13, 20, 28, 137
   moral education, 174, 178, 345, 346
   scientific education, 132–33
efficient causality, 61, 63, 111, 119
Einstein, Albert, 3, 16, 368n.33
Eliade, Mircea, 89
emergent probability, 85–86, 313, 330, 357, 368n.32
emotivism, 142, 164, 172, 337, 338, 354, 370n.62, 380n.191
empiricism, 6, 87, 96–97, 100–101, 148
   empirical realism, 158, 365n.84
   generalized empirical method, 3–4, 5, 23, 31–32, 82, 104, 137–38, 155, 214, 225, 294–95, 356
   logical empiricism, 99, 145
   modern science as empirical, 16, 19–20, 55–56, 64–65, 67, 85, 88–89, 93–95, 118–19, 151, 187, 210, 218, 221, 223, 241, 278, 280, 292, 294–95, 311, 326, 339, 343, 357
English Civil War, 372n.31

Enlightenment, 115–17, 125, 135, 192, 202, 242, 245, 324, 333
   first vs. second phases, 10, 19, 83–90, 93–94, 131, 132, 187, 212, 219–22, 280–81, 325, 327–28, 334
   humanism during, 193, 234–37, 244, 248, 255
   Kant on, 219–20
   Lonergan on, 19, 83–84, 86–87, 88, 90, 93–94, 117, 131, 187
   reason during, 21, 197–99, 243, 268, 289, 310, 324
epistemic pluralism, 4, 5, 34–35, 39, 155, 207, 212–13, 214, 285
   antithetical, 34, 165
   complementary, 34, 165
   genetic, 34, 165
   See also specialization, intellectual
epistemology, 22, 23, 33, 52, 53, 73, 102, 114, 144, 145, 160, 225
   critical realism in, 41, 55, 74–75, 100–101, 105, 163, 165–66, 309, 337, 338, 356, 358, 366n.103, 368n.33, 388n.62
   naive realism in, 41, 100–101, 157–59, 163, 165, 166, 167, 169, 171
   relationship to metaphysics, 22, 24, 74–76, 143, 157, 225, 282, 291–92, 356–57
   See also cognition; knowledge
equality, 202, 239, 248, 324–26, 332, 344
   in democracy, 185, 191, 247, 268, 269, 275, 328–29, 333
   of women, 242, 344, 352
Erasmus, Desiderius, 264
ethics, 18, 45, 52, 62, 281, 282
   of authenticity, 62, 82, 260, 331–32, 336, 343–46, 351, 355, 358, 381n.215
   evaluative principles and norms, 241–42
   of historical responsibility, 24
   Lonergan on, 98, 337–49, 357–58, 390n.99
   subjectivity and objectivity in, 327–29, 337–41

upper and lower blades of, 341–44, 345, 348, 350–51, 389n.86
See also moral responsibility
Euclidean geometry, 115, 120, 220
Eurocentrism, 97
evil, 49, 78, 177, 193, 211, 219, 247, 255
  Augustine on, 68, 253, 379n.169
  and authenticity, 340–41
  and existence of God, 198, 228, 230
  Lonergan on, 253–54, 257–58, 296, 314, 340–41, 378n.159, 383nn.239, 245
  natural vs. moral, 253, 296, 340
  reality of, 47, 247, 253–54
  in twentieth century, 51, 244–45
evolutionary biology, 3, 67, 85, 97, 131–32, 225, 241, 243, 280–81, 330
  of Darwin, 84, 94, 112, 125–26, 129, 193, 199, 204, 217, 221, 240, 269, 290–91, 325
existential engagement, 101–6, 172
existentialism, 37, 89, 101–2, 128–29, 172, 193, 324
exodus from Egypt, 199, 298, 318
Ezekiel
  11:19, 48
  36:26, 48

faculty psychology, 55, 56, 279, 292, 344
faith
  Aquinas on, 14, 25, 73, 76, 78, 79–80, 218–19, 231, 233, 258, 262, 263, 271, 287, 289, 292
  as authentic, 24, 181–82, 206
  and divine grace, 232
  Kierkegaard on, 238–40, 246–47, 379n.181
  Lonergan on, 217, 218, 222, 251, 252, 256, 284–85, 292, 297–98, 299, 306, 307–8, 309, 314–15, 317, 318, 355, 357, 380n.184
  and reason, 14, 25, 46, 73, 77, 196, 199, 218–19, 221–22, 233, 258, 262, 269, 271, 286, 287–88, 290–91, 292, 298, 306, 309, 357, 383n.240, 386n.37

  and secularization, 181–83, 184–86, 193–206, 228, 289
  as supernatural virtue, 78, 231, 345
  and works, 379n.167
fascism, 206, 244, 270
feudalism, 190, 372n.29
Feuerbach, Ludwig, 123, 374n.62
final causality, 16, 61, 111, 112, 116, 119
Fisher, John, 266
formal causality, 16, 58, 59–60, 61, 63, 111, 119
Foucault, Michel, 140
Fourth Lateran Council, 372n.30
France
  ancien régime, 190–91, 195, 205, 219–20, 247, 255, 267, 268–69, 333, 341
  anticlericalism in, 195, 199, 268
  Edict of Nantes, 191, 194, 267
  Inquisition in, 194
  Louis XIV, 194, 267
  philosophes in, 195, 199, 248, 268
  and primacy of Rome, 384n.13
  Revolution of 1789, 113, 191, 195, 205, 268–69, 276, 325, 372n.33, 380n.186
Francis de Sales, St., 266, 273
Francis of Assisi, St., 206, 262, 323
Francis I, 391n.111
Franco, Francisco, 270
Frege, Gottlob, 91
Freud, Sigmund, 21, 98, 112, 140, 193, 199, 227, 374n.69
  atheism of, 245
  Civilization and Its Discontents, 374nn.70, 71, 380nn.200, 201
  on happiness, 204
  on id and ego, 203–4, 245
  New Introductory Lectures, 375n.73
  on religion, 202–3, 204–5, 221, 245, 250, 374n.71
  on science, 204, 205
  on superego, 203–4, 245
  on wish fulfillment, 245
Friedlander, Saul, 381n.207
functional complementarity, 61, 142, 145, 150, 157, 333, 336, 343

functional specialties in theology, 217, 260, 292, 301–10, 322, 353, 355, 357, 387n.54
   communications, 304, 308, 387n.60
   dialectic, 303–4, 305, 310, 320, 321, 376n.107
   doctrines, 304, 306–7, 320–21, 322
   foundations, 304–5, 306, 310, 320, 322, 362n.41, 376n.107
   history, 302–3, 304
   interpretation, 302, 303, 304
   research, 302, 304
   systematics, 304, 307

Galileo Galilei, 3, 197, 361n.24
   condemnation of, 195, 199, 233, 247, 266, 267, 384n.12
   on physical laws, 16, 111–12
   on primary and secondary qualities, 159–60, 188
Gandhi, Mohandas K., 206
gender, 242, 247, 344, 352
Genesis, 252, 290
   1:31, 382n.228
   2:2, 382n.228
genetic heuristic structure, 85, 94, 125, 140, 165, 214, 221, 224, 226, 227, 313
genetics, 225
geology, 225
Gilson, Étienne, 273, 361n.20
Girard, René: *The Scapegoat*, 380n.198
globalization, 12, 20
God
   as creator, 39, 69, 79, 80, 81, 125, 186, 196, 198, 229–30, 237, 252–53, 254, 256, 260, 290, 295, 296, 297, 298, 312, 314–16, 317, 323, 332, 349, 351, 358, 382n.228
   essence of, 220, 229, 234, 238, 287
   existence of, 50, 74, 188–89, 196–97, 198–99, 212, 220, 224, 228, 229, 230, 234, 282, 287, 290, 296, 310, 311–13
   as Father, 80, 257, 261
   forgiveness of, 49, 257, 258, 293
   goodness/benevolence of, 186, 198, 205, 228, 230, 236, 252, 253, 257, 258, 263, 295, 310, 314–15, 316, 324, 332, 340
   human beings as image and likeness of, 79, 80, 125, 252–53, 278, 312, 332, 352
   infinity of, 288
   knowledge of, 39, 47, 68, 74, 79, 108, 109, 287–88, 295, 297–98, 309, 310–11, 312, 314–17
   love of, 32, 37, 39, 47–48, 49, 50, 68, 78, 175, 229–30, 251, 257, 283, 304, 306, 312, 314–15, 316–17, 319, 340, 349, 350
   as loving, 251, 253, 264, 293, 296, 297–98, 299, 314, 315, 316–17, 340, 349, 358, 382nn.222, 228, 388n.68
   mercy of, 258, 263, 318, 332, 341
   as omnipotent, 120, 197, 340
   as omniscient, 120, 196–97, 340
   openness to, 211, 218
   perfection of, 69, 81, 229
   providence of, 198, 310, 318, 333
   revelation of, 26, 65, 79, 140, 196, 197, 198, 199, 200, 218, 222, 256–57, 260, 272, 282, 284, 287, 290, 298–300, 305, 306, 307, 309, 317–18, 320, 321, 322, 332, 342, 358
   spiritual causality of, 316–17
   as supreme good (*summum bonum*), 39, 209, 260, 314
   transcendence of, 18, 24, 48, 95, 104, 208, 228, 251–52, 292, 298, 304, 307, 316, 350
   as Trinity, 71, 79–81, 196, 287, 300, 306, 319, 358
   union with, 47
   will of, 47, 234
   wisdom of, 310, 313, 314, 315, 324, 332
   Word of, 299, 317, 318, 320, 321, 322
   See also grace of God; Jesus Christ
Gödel's incompleteness theorem, 84

grace of God, 39, 103, 133–34, 135, 181, 192, 198, 200, 232, 251, 253, 264–65, 268, 308, 351, 382n.221
  Aquinas on, 2, 8, 14, 25, 71, 73, 76–80, 81, 218–19, 230, 231, 233, 234, 246, 258, 263, 292, 323–24, 326, 333, 336, 345, 350, 378n.161, 384n.6, 388n.72
  Augustine on, 37, 68–69, 70, 71, 76–77, 79, 233, 266
  cooperative grace, 9, 70, 76–77, 78, 79, 231, 342, 388n.72
  Lonergan on, 9, 29, 46, 47–50, 219, 258, 272, 273, 283, 297, 298, 314, 315, 330, 336, 339, 341, 342, 349–50, 380n.188, 384n.6, 388n.72
  operative grace, 9, 47–48, 70, 76–77, 78, 79, 231, 342, 388n.72
  relationship to nature, 14, 25, 46, 73, 76, 77, 230–31, 233, 258, 263, 292, 293, 323–24, 333, 336, 378n.161
Great Depression, 128
Greek culture, 10, 13–14, 25, 261, 262, 286
Greek Orthodox Church, 263

habit, 77, 78–79, 134, 174, 344–45
happiness, 324, 326, 329, 336
Haughey, John C.: *In Search of the Whole*, 391n.109
Hazard, Paul, 195, 267
  The European Mind, 372n.32, 373n.41, 384nn.8, 9, 11, 386n.33
  European Thought in the Eighteenth Century, 372n.32, 373n.43, 384n.8
Hebblethwaite, Peter: *Pope John XXIII*, 385n.26
Hebrews 4:15, 320, 332
Hebrew scripture, 2, 14, 298, 299, 301, 302
Hefling, Charles: *Why Doctrines?*, 387nn.56, 58
Hegel, G.W.F., 3, 6, 34, 199, 367n.24, 374n.62
  on Absolute Spirit, 12, 122, 123, 325
  on Christianity, 237
  on dialectic, 96, 98, 122, 192, 237
  on history, 12, 87, 88, 96, 98, 113, 122, 123, 129, 131, 192, 238, 239, 240–41
  on human beings, 122–23
  idealism of, 160
  vs. Kant, 236, 237–38, 240
  on nature, 122, 123
  on passions and feelings, 123
  Phenomenology of Spirit, 355, 379n.178
  on reason, 380n.184
  Reason in History, 379n.178
  on teleological explanations, 122, 123, 124
  on theology, 237
  on theoretical reason, 236, 237–38
Heidegger, Martin, 3, 366n.105
  Being and Time, 355, 368n.29
  on *Dasein*, 89, 128, 368n.29
  on death, 89, 128
  on forgetfulness of being, 36
  on *Lebenswelt*, 128
  on perceptual model of human existence, 127–28
Hempel, Carl, 92
heresies, 263, 280
hermeneutics, 3, 9, 22, 23, 51, 84, 90–93, 138, 148, 151, 155, 163, 187, 210, 247, 272–73, 274, 291, 300, 321, 339
  critical biblical studies, 195, 199–200, 275, 280, 290
  and human sciences, 11, 89
  of suspicion, 7–8, 21, 50, 98–99, 200–205, 217, 374n.59
heuristic structures, 225, 226–27, 285, 356
  classical, 85, 94, 126, 140, 165, 214, 221, 224, 226, 227, 313
  dialectical, 94, 140, 165, 224, 227, 313
  genetic, 85, 94, 125, 140, 165, 214, 221, 224, 226, 227, 313
  statistical, 18, 85, 94, 125, 126, 140, 165, 214, 221, 224, 226, 227, 313

hierarchy, 371n.16
  and Christianity, 183, 186
  of value, 43, 175, 186, 189–90, 209, 314, 324, 332–33
Hinduism, 278
history, 5–7, 137, 380n.190
  critical historiography, 1, 3, 6–7, 9, 19–20, 21, 22, 23, 27, 39, 50, 51, 65–66, 86, 96–98, 107, 109, 132, 138, 143, 155, 163–64, 165, 187, 199, 205, 206, 210, 212, 216, 240–42, 247, 275, 291, 300, 302–3, 309, 339, 360n.11
  dialectic in, 5, 96, 122, 192, 256, 325
  Hegel on, 12, 87, 88, 96, 98, 113, 122, 123, 129, 131, 192, 238, 239, 240–41
  historical change, 20, 87, 165, 166, 171, 216
  historical consciousness, 6, 10, 11, 13, 19–21, 26, 33, 83–84, 86–88, 107, 216–17, 218, 221, 272, 276–77, 280–81, 320, 359n.6
  historical necessity, 113
  historical scholarship, 39–40, 55–56, 87, 104, 107, 134–35, 136, 137, 155, 156, 187, 199, 212, 216, 222, 227–28, 247, 250, 274, 290, 292, 293, 294–95, 311, 320, 334, 353
  historicism, 132, 149, 165–66
  and human nature, 117–30
  Marx on, 12, 87, 96, 113, 124–25, 131, 201, 239, 325, 380n.187
  progress in, 8–9, 87, 165, 192, 210, 217, 221, 224, 248, 254–55, 256, 331, 340–41
  of science, 144, 371n.18
Hitler, Adolf, 25, 255, 340
Hobbes, Thomas, 3
  De Cive, 367n.12
  Leviathan, 367n.12
Holocaust, 244, 247, 253, 340, 350, 381n.207
Holy Spirit, 79, 80, 196, 256, 261, 296, 299, 305, 318, 352
Hooker, Richard, 378n.162

hope, 201, 248, 250, 254, 255–56, 341
  Kant on, 204, 234, 235–36, 256
  religious hope, 78, 205, 206, 258, 345, 351
  as supernatural virtue, 78, 345
Huguenots, 194–95
human desire, unrestricted
  to discover and actualize the good, 30–31, 38–39, 42–44, 46–47, 49, 57, 58, 90, 141, 142, 150, 165, 169–70, 176, 178, 180, 208, 211, 213, 218, 227, 228, 229, 249, 251–52, 254, 256, 281, 293, 295, 296–97, 311–12, 313–14, 316, 321, 335, 338, 339, 342, 356, 360n.10, 362n.36, 369n.42, 391n.1
  to know all that exists, 30, 31, 38, 39, 40, 41, 42, 44, 46–47, 49, 54–55, 57, 58, 59, 60, 74, 75, 90, 100, 141, 142, 145, 148, 150, 152, 155, 156, 159, 165, 168, 169–70, 176, 178, 180, 208, 211, 213, 218, 227, 228, 229, 249, 251, 254, 256, 281, 292, 293, 295, 296–97, 311–13, 314, 316, 321, 335, 338, 339, 342, 356, 360n.10, 362n.36, 369n.42, 391n.1
human development, 90, 138, 226
  intellectual, 26–27, 35, 40–41, 44–45, 354
  moral, 26–27, 35, 41, 44–45, 173–74, 179, 354
  spiritual, 26–27, 41
human dignity, 19, 122, 131, 196, 227, 235, 240, 263–64, 277–78, 324, 328, 344, 380n.189
human existence
  historicity of, 5–7, 43, 50, 65, 81–82, 83, 131, 134, 135, 136–37, 165, 168, 169, 175, 187, 216, 227, 240–41, 264–65, 274–75, 281, 309, 352
  progress and decline in, 5, 7, 8–9, 165, 192, 207, 210, 217, 224, 254–55, 256, 278, 310, 331
  redemption in, 9, 218, 219

human freedom, 24, 102, 114, 124, 131, 132, 135, 192, 220, 235, 324–25, 335, 339, 379n.169, 383n.239, 386n.45
  Aquinas on, 76, 79, 81
  essential vs. effective freedom, 78–79, 364n.72, 368n.35, 390n.89
  horizontal vs. vertical exercises of freedom, 388n.64
  Kant on, 88, 115–16, 117, 122, 131, 133–34, 193, 220, 289, 325, 327
  Lonergan on, 19, 78–79, 256, 330, 331, 364n.72, 368n.35, 383n.239, 390n.89
  See also liberty
humanism, 230–48
  critical Christian humanism, 260, 261–65
  during Enlightenment, 234–37, 248, 255
  exclusive humanism, 25, 46, 193, 200–202, 205, 206, 217, 244–45, 247, 248, 250, 252, 255, 275, 324–26, 350, 354, 374n.60, 389nn.75, 77, 391n.107
  inflated vs. deflated, 211, 217, 219
  religious humanism, 181, 182, 218, 244, 246–48, 260, 261–65, 376n.116, 381n.212, 389n.75
  during Renaissance, 231–32, 263–64
human nature, 5, 6, 77, 78, 219, 292, 293
  and history, 117–30
  sublation by grace, 47–48, 258, 298, 314, 315, 333, 380n.188
human rights, 11, 172, 191, 193, 206, 247, 268, 328
human subjectivity, 11, 27–35, 53, 63, 83, 91, 92, 99–101, 272
  constitutive/foundational principles of, 29–33, 35, 45, 46
  Lonergan on, 22–23, 37–38, 99, 102–3, 108, 136, 137–41, 142, 145, 150, 162, 166, 171, 174–75, 249, 271, 279, 291–92, 295, 311–12, 316, 321, 330, 335, 338, 342, 357, 360n.10, 362nn.36, 41, 375n.83

in philosophy, 56, 82, 88–90, 89, 101, 137–38, 188, 214, 224, 291–92, 295, 311, 321, 337, 338
prereflexive experiential consciousness, 40, 63
thematized self-reflective analysis, 40–41
See also consciousness
human suffering, 78, 172, 184, 193, 205, 206, 211, 236, 246, 253, 254–55, 257, 340
human will
  Aquinas on, 76, 77–78, 81, 125
  Augustine on, 67, 68–69, 70, 76, 263, 379n.169
  Descartes on, 120
  as good will, 69, 70, 76, 77, 235
  Kant on, 126, 235–36, 243, 379n.174
  as natural power, 77
Hume, David, 3, 34, 223, 268
  skepticism of, 93–94, 160, 162, 198–99, 365n.92
humility, 341, 390n.97
Husserl, Edmund, 3, 34, 89, 127–28, 129
  The Crisis of European Sciences and Transcendental Phenomenology, 368n.28
  Philosophy as Rigorous Science, 368n.28
Huygens, Christian, 268

idealism, 23, 100, 149, 165, 166–68
  of Kant, 115–17, 121–22, 129, 131, 143, 160–63, 169, 365n.84, 369n.55
ideology, 113, 135, 144, 172, 192, 247, 253, 281, 351
  distorting effects of, 30, 147, 153, 165, 178–79, 215, 255, 293, 334, 368n.37
  as justifying sin/bias, 29, 44, 45, 134, 178–79, 215, 244, 250, 255, 258, 338, 348
  Lonergan on, 8, 29, 98, 147, 165, 178–79, 211, 215, 227, 250, 255, 258, 281, 293, 331, 334, 335–36, 338, 339, 341, 343, 348, 350, 354, 360n.8, 368n.37
  Marx on, 201, 239, 250

Ignatius of Loyola, St., 266
imagination, 58–59
imperialism, 195, 200, 242, 245, 248, 255, 380n.192
individualism, 268, 269, 275, 327
Industrial Revolution, 247, 255, 269, 280, 373n.46
inequality, 25, 242
intellectual development, 26–27, 35, 40–41, 44–45, 354
intellectual pattern of experience, 9, 29, 38, 39, 40, 102, 145, 146, 150, 152, 169–70, 171
intelligible form, 58, 59–60, 72, 75, 151, 153, 158
   Aristotle on, 60, 62, 64, 66, 114–15
intelligible realism, 158
interiority, 92, 95, 101, 103
introspection, 63, 68, 73–74, 90–91, 92
intuition, 157–59, 163, 166, 171, 370n.59
Islam, 11, 255, 256, 278, 318
isolationism, 244
Italy
   Inquisition in, 194
   Mussolini government, 270
   Risorgimento, 269

Jacob, Margaret: *The Cultural Meaning of the Scientific Revolution*, 367n.19
Japanese militarism, 244
Jefferson, Thomas, 3, 198, 199
Jeremiah 17:9, 383n.244
Jesus Christ, 36, 79, 198, 206, 247, 253, 290, 322
   healing ministry of, 257–58, 299, 383n.246
   humanity and divinity of, 196
   as incarnation, 70, 80, 81, 82, 237, 238, 239, 256, 257, 261, 264, 284, 287, 299, 305, 306, 317, 318, 319, 332, 349, 358
   on the law, 323
   message and mission, 261, 296, 299, 300, 301, 302–3, 305, 318–19, 323, 340, 341, 349, 351
   passion and death, 264, 286, 299, 300, 317, 318, 332, 333
   and reality of evil, 257–58
   as redeemer, 260, 261, 284, 288, 293, 296, 299, 317, 319, 332, 333, 349, 350, 351
   on repentance, 36, 49
   resurrection of, 81, 196, 199, 256, 258, 264, 286, 287, 299, 300, 318, 332, 333
   and spiritual freedom, 257–58, 383n.246
   teaching of, 257, 318–19
   as Word, 80, 299, 317, 318, 320, 332, 349
Joan of Arc, 206
Job's suffering, 236, 253
John
   1:1–5, 80
   2:25, 383n.244
   3:15–17, 256
   3:16–17, 261
   10:10, 383n.247
   14:26, 261
1 John 4:10, 382n.222
John XXIII, 259, 275–76, 277, 278, 322, 351, 355, 385nn.26, 29
Judaism, 11, 14, 21, 65, 199, 201–2, 256, 278, 317, 318
Jung, C. G.: *The Answer to Job*, 382n.232
justice, 36, 46, 172, 236, 242, 246

Kant, Immanuel, 3, 10, 30, 34, 83, 125, 127, 136, 141, 160
   on analytic vs. synthetic judgments, 90
   anthropological questions, 204, 234–36, 362n.28
   antimonies of, 34
   on a priori vs. a posteriori truth claims, 90
   on autonomy, 88–89, 122, 133–34, 193, 220, 234–36, 240, 243, 249, 325, 327, 334, 380n.189
   on categorical imperatives, 86, 115–16, 121, 220, 234–36, 238, 243, 329, 389n.79

on categories of the understanding, 115, 121, 160, 162, 367n.23, 369n.55
on causality, 115–16, 143–44, 162–63, 369n.55
and Copernican Revolution, 11, 116–17, 162, 234, 362n.28
on critical reason, 219, 220, 237–38, 240
Critique of Pure Reason, 34, 355, 365n.93, 367nn.15, 16, 18, 23, 369n.56, 375n.72, 376nn.120, 121, 123, 379n.171
on *Ding an sich*, 160, 162, 168
as empirical realist, 365n.84, 369n.55
on Enlightenment, 219–20
Foundations of the Metaphysics of Morals, 379nn.172–74, 176
on God, 120, 122, 161, 162, 199, 220, 222, 235, 236, 310
Groundwork of the Metaphysics of Morals, 367n.17, 376n.125, 389n.79
on happiness, 116, 326, 329, 367n.17
on hope, 204, 234, 235–36, 256
on human freedom, 88, 115–16, 117, 131, 133–34, 193, 289, 325, 327
on human will, 126, 235–36, 243, 379n.174
on ideas of reason, 90, 121, 122, 143, 160–61, 220, 235–36, 289, 367n.23, 379n.176
on immortality, 220, 236
on intuitions of sensibility, 121, 160–61, 162, 168, 367n.23
on judgments, 121, 143, 161
on justice, 236
Lonergan on, 163, 312, 362n.28, 365n.84, 369n.54, 388n.66
on mathematics, 121, 357
on metaphysics, 143, 220, 357
on moral responsibility, 88, 115–16, 117, 121, 122, 131, 133–34, 234–36, 243, 325, 326, 329, 337, 389n.79
on natural laws, 86, 235

on noumena, 94, 115, 117, 121, 131, 160, 162, 168, 236, 325, 337, 365n.84, 369n.55
on phenomena, 94, 115, 117, 121, 131, 168, 235, 289, 365n.84
on physics, 16, 19, 121, 225
on practical reason, 86, 88, 99, 116, 120–21, 122, 131, 133–34, 220, 235, 236–37, 239, 337, 380n.189
Prolegomena to Any Future Metaphysics, 369n.56, 374n.52, 376n.122
on pure vs. empirical representations, 160–61
Religion within the Bounds of Reason Alone, 376n.124, 386n.41
on science, 162, 220, 221, 235, 357
on the soul, 161, 162, 220, 236
on space and time, 115, 121, 162–63
on synthetic a priori judgments, 121, 161, 162, 168
on theoretical reason, 34, 86, 94, 116, 120–21, 131, 132, 162, 199, 220, 235, 236, 239, 289, 310
on transcendental ego, 99, 136, 143, 162–63, 249, 365n.84, 369n.55
transcendental idealism of, 115–17, 121–22, 129, 131, 143, 160–63, 169, 365n.84, 369n.55
on truth, 121, 161, 162, 168
on understanding, 115, 121
Katz, Robert, 381n.207
Kepler, Johannes, 16, 111
Keynes, John Maynard, 3
Kierkegaard, Søren, 36, 123, 236, 260, 315, 377n.127
Attack on Christendom, 380n.183
on becoming an authentic Christian, 379n.181
Concluding Unscientific Postscript, 379n.180
on faith, 238–40, 246–47, 379n.181
Fear and Trembling, 379n.182
Philosophical Fragments, 379n.180
on reason, 237, 239, 380n.184
Sickness unto Death, 379n.180
Stages on Life's Way, 379n.180

King, Martin Luther, Jr., 206
knowledge
   epistemic specialization, 3, 4–5, 9–10, 15, 18–19, 21, 22, 23–24, 31, 39, 55–56, 65, 82, 85–86, 92, 104, 107, 118–19, 130–31, 132–33, 136, 137, 155, 184, 187, 212–13, 215–16, 223, 272, 282, 285, 311, 343, 353, 360n.11
   explanatory vs. descriptive, 85, 118, 159–60, 356, 368n.33
   of God, 39, 47, 68, 74, 79, 108, 109, 287–88, 295, 297–98, 309, 310–11, 312, 314–17
   integration and unification of, 4–5, 9–10, 11, 19, 23, 52, 92, 93, 104, 130–31, 136, 143, 155, 187–88, 207, 212–13, 279, 334–35, 371n.21
   objective knowledge, 26, 33, 34, 38, 40–41, 42, 43, 46, 71, 83, 90, 95, 100–101, 102, 103, 108, 129, 131, 133, 134–35, 142, 143, 157, 158–59, 162–63, 164–71, 167–69, 170, 171, 172, 176, 178, 179, 208, 215, 249, 293, 336, 338, 343, 356, 375n.78
   as virtually unconditioned judgments, 41, 100, 147, 154, 156, 158–59, 162, 163, 167, 170, 178, 312–13, 380n.184
Kolakowski, Leszek: *Modernity on Endless Trial*, 360n.13
Koyré, Alexandre: *From the Closed World to the Infinite Universe*, 361n.23, 367n.19, 373n.50
Kuhn, Thomas, 144
   The Copernican Revolution, 361n.23, 367n.19
   on scientific paradigm shifts, 164
   The Structure of Scientific Revolutions, 370n.57

language, 27–28, 34, 75, 90–93, 103–5, 138, 327
   of common sense, 92, 104, 164, 212
   philosophy of, 91, 164, 169
   of science, 104, 164, 212
   Wittgenstein on, 91, 92, 105, 166

Laquer, Walter, 381n.207
Lash, Nicholas, 376n.114
Lattis, James: *Between Copernicus and Galileo*, 367n.19
Leibniz, Gottfried Wilhelm von, 268, 373n.50, 377n.127
Lenin, V. I., 113
Leo XIII, 361n.20, 378n.162
   adage *vetera novis augere et perficere*, 2, 55, 271
   Rerum Novarum, 373n.46, 384n.16
Lewy, Guenter, 381n.207
liberalism, 87, 206, 242, 328, 331, 334, 341
libertarianism, 328
liberty, 198, 216, 239, 248, 293, 324–26, 331, 335, 340–41, 389n.76
   in democracy, 50, 113, 185, 191, 195, 247, 268, 269, 275, 328–29, 333
   religious liberty, 25, 194, 267, 277–78, 285, 384n.9
   See also human freedom
Lindberg, David: *Reappraisals of the Scientific Revolution*, 367n.19
Lisbon earthquake of 1755, 198, 340
Locke, John, 3, 159–60, 268
logic, 64, 76, 99, 105, 158, 164, 167, 212
   Aristotle on, 61–62, 104
   deduction, 17, 22, 52, 74, 83, 93, 104, 145, 153, 188, 197, 282, 287
   logical coherence, 153, 154, 167–68, 170, 171
   vs. method, 54, 61–62, 82, 145, 147–48, 150, 213, 282, 311, 387n.51
   vs. reason, 94–95, 145
logical positivism, 34
Lonergan, Bernard
   on Aquinas, 2, 3, 8, 10, 11, 53, 55–56, 72–83, 92, 151, 219, 266, 271–72, 273–74, 278, 284, 292, 336, 360n.9, 361n.20, 364nn.69, 74, 384n.6, 388n.72
   on Aristotle, 10, 11, 57, 60–67, 92, 173, 223
   on Augustine, 51, 67–72, 219, 364n.74
   on autonomy, 334

on bias, 9, 27, 28, 29, 30, 32, 95, 103, 165, 210, 215, 224, 227, 230, 250, 255, 258, 281, 293, 308, 310, 313–14, 316, 330, 331, 332, 334, 335, 336, 338, 339, 341, 342, 348, 354, 362n.35, 368n.36
on Catholic renewal, 259–60, 265, 279, 283–86, 320–21, 351, 355, 377n.128, 391n.108
on causality, 215–17
as Christian humanist, 2, 108, 256–57, 261–65, 272–73, 277, 315, 349–50, 353
on classicism, 52–53, 65, 81, 83, 87, 216, 222, 280, 281–82, 283, 284, 309, 310, 320, 321, 351, 388n.73
on cognition, 8–11, 12, 21–24, 31–32, 34, 40–41, 52, 53–56, 58–59, 60–61, 62–63, 71–72, 73–76, 90, 94–95, 100–101, 102, 103–4, 108, 138–39, 142–55, 156–57, 162, 169–71, 177, 208–9, 212–14, 222–24, 225, 271, 273, 281, 282, 300, 336, 338, 342–43, 355, 356, 357, 362n.41, 366n.105, 384n.6
on cosmology, 17, 19, 85–86, 136, 224–27, 253–54, 313, 330, 357, 368n.31
on creative collaboration, 207, 344, 375n.79
on critical appropriation of cultural heritage, 2, 4, 8–9, 12–13, 26–27, 51–83, 98, 105, 106, 210–11, 214–15, 218, 249, 273–75, 285, 309, 320–21, 329, 334, 353–54, 355
on critical realism, 55, 100, 105, 163, 165–66, 309, 337, 338, 356, 358, 366n.103, 368n.33, 388n.62
on cultural crises, 11, 14–15, 24–26, 108, 129, 180, 207, 259, 265–70, 353, 358
as cultural diversity, 13, 20–21, 107, 320, 360n.16
on data of consciousness, 23, 30, 54, 55, 56, 63, 72, 82, 214, 224, 291–92
on democracy, 330–31

on dialectic, 9, 10, 18, 34–35, 98, 101, 105–6, 149, 158, 165–71, 183, 188–89, 208, 209–12, 218, 222, 228, 250, 275, 278, 284, 285, 286, 295, 298, 309–11, 330, 341–42, 344, 350–51, 354–55, 356, 357, 372n.37
on divine grace, 9, 29, 46, 47–50, 219, 258, 272, 273, 283, 297, 298, 314, 315, 330, 336, 339, 341, 342, 349–50, 380n.188, 384n.6, 388n.72
on divine initiatives in history, 317–18, 332, 358
on economics, 389n.87
on emergent probability, 85–86, 313, 330, 357, 368n.32
on empiricism, 145–46, 214, 218
on ethics, 98, 337–49, 357–58, 390n.99
on European Enlightenment, 19, 83–84, 86–87, 88, 90, 93–94, 117, 131, 187
on evil, 253–54, 257–58, 296, 314, 340–41, 378n.159, 383nn.239, 245
on experiential conjugates, 66
on explanatory conjugates, 66, 83
on extrascientific assertions, 17–18, 188–89, 210, 217, 224, 361n.25
on faith, 217, 218, 222, 251, 252, 256, 284–85, 292, 297–98, 299, 306, 307–8, 309, 314–15, 317, 318, 355, 357, 380n.184
on functional complementarity, 61, 142, 145, 150, 157
on functional specialties in theology, 260, 292, 301–10, 320–21, 322, 353, 355, 362n.41, 376n.107
on generalized emergent probability, 225–26, 253–54
on generalized empirical method, 3–4, 5, 23, 31–32, 82, 104, 137–38, 155, 214, 225, 294–95, 356
on genuine authority, 331–32, 335–36, 341, 347–49
on God, 109, 179, 186, 214, 219, 224, 229–30, 248–58, 260, 272, 283, 291–323, 312–13, 321, 332, 355, 357, 358, 364n.74, 387n.59

Lonergan, Bernard (*cont.*)
  on historical communities, 346–49
  on historical consciousness, 19–20, 216–17, 281
  on historical progress, 8–9, 217
  on history of science, 371n.18
  on human freedom, 19, 78–79, 256, 330, 331, 364n.72, 368n.35, 383n.239, 390n.89
  on humanism, 2, 181, 218, 219, 248–58, 260, 261–65, 374n.60, 375n.90, 376n.116, 381n.212, 389n.75
  on human reason, 150, 151, 154–55, 310, 311, 312, 315, 380nn.184, 190
  on human subjectivity, 22–23, 37–38, 99, 102–3, 108, 136, 137–41, 142, 145, 150, 162, 166, 171, 174–75, 249, 271, 279, 291–92, 295, 311–12, 316, 321, 330, 335, 338, 342, 357, 360n.10, 362nn.36, 41, 375n.83
  on human will, 77
  on ideology, 8, 29, 98, 147, 165, 178–79, 211, 215, 227, 250, 255, 258, 281, 293, 331, 334, 335, 336, 338, 339, 341, 343, 348, 350, 354, 360n.8, 368n.37
  on intellectual specialization, 4–5, 9–10, 15, 18–19, 31–32, 55–56, 65, 81–82, 85–86, 92, 104, 107, 136, 137, 152, 155, 188, 208, 212–13, 215–16, 223, 260, 282, 285, 291–92, 294, 301–10, 311, 322, 334–35, 343, 353, 355, 357, 360n.11, 387n.54
  on interdisciplinary cultural centers, 24, 26, 33, 35, 284, 353–55
  as Jesuit, 265, 266, 272
  on Jesus Christ, 256–58, 259
  on Kant, 163, 312, 362n.28, 365n.84, 369n.54, 388n.66
  on levels of culture, 274
  on levels of moral cognition, 342–43
  on meaning, 12, 18, 89, 92, 95, 103–5, 138, 139–40, 146, 209, 330, 360n.14, 366n.105, 390n.102
  on metaphysics, 21–22, 75–76, 83, 102, 143, 281, 291, 356–57
  on method vs. logic, 54, 61–62, 82, 145, 147–48, 150, 213, 282, 311, 387n.51
  on modernism, 222, 377n.128, 381n.206, 388n.73
  on modernity, 25–26, 81–82, 83–106, 107–17, 130, 136, 180, 183, 207–8, 212, 214, 222, 259, 274–75, 277, 283, 284, 320–21, 330–31, 334, 354, 377n.128, 381n.206, 385n.24
  on normative appraisal, 140
  on normative relativism, 98
  on Pascal, 386n.38
  on the past vs. tradition, 8, 27, 51, 273
  on performative contradiction, 210
  on philosophy, 11, 12, 15, 21–24, 31, 33, 34–35, 42, 51, 82, 86, 89–90, 108, 137–39, 143, 148–49, 151, 155, 165, 166, 207, 208, 213, 214, 222, 224, 259, 274, 278, 279, 281–83, 291–92, 293, 295, 300, 304, 310–11, 321–22, 335, 339, 344, 351, 353–54, 355–58, 362n.30, 390n.99
  on picture thinking, 166–68, 169–71, 316, 354, 356
  on Plato, 51, 56–60, 71, 363n.50
  on power, 331–32, 335–36, 341, 346–48
  on proportionate vs. transcendent being, 71, 75, 186, 208, 209, 224, 227–28, 229, 251, 260, 296, 298, 309, 312–13, 335, 387n.49
  on public policy, 330
  on question(s) of God, 312–13, 321
  on sacralization, 215, 216
  on scientific method, 3, 16–17, 22, 89, 137–38, 188–89, 222–24, 294–95
  on secularization, 46, 181–82, 183, 215–18
  on self-knowledge, 40, 108, 109, 136, 149–51, 171, 180, 210, 229–30, 249, 271, 295–96, 312, 362n.41

on self-transcendence, 29, 150, 170,
    175–79, 180, 215, 305, 310, 316,
    321, 335, 336–37, 338, 341,
    345–46, 355, 356, 358, 368n.37
on sense perception, 23, 58–59, 75,
    89, 137–38, 138, 158, 214
on sin, 9, 28, 29, 30, 78, 103, 165, 215,
    218, 219, 230, 258, 272, 293, 296,
    308, 314, 316, 332, 334, 336, 338,
    341, 342, 348, 349–50
on social institutions, 346–49,
    390n.103
vs. Taylor, 182, 183, 185–86, 215, 217,
    249, 342
on theology, 9, 11, 12, 15, 18, 21–22,
    31, 42, 51, 86, 104, 108, 136, 148,
    151, 155, 165, 208, 214, 216, 217,
    222, 224, 227–28, 259, 272, 274,
    278, 279, 281–83, 284–85, 291–92,
    293, 295–323, 335, 339, 344, 351,
    353–54, 354, 355, 357, 358, 362n.30,
    378n.151, 387n.59, 388nn.70, 74
on third stage of cognitive meaning,
    73, 81–82, 92, 107, 188, 212, 213,
    214, 292, 301, 311, 334–35, 339,
    362n.28
on truth, 102, 108, 146–47, 156,
    170–71, 177, 211, 223
on unification of knowledge, 4–5,
    9–10
on universe of proportionate being,
    185, 186
on value, 18, 138, 174–75, 330,
    332–33, 338, 342, 349, 382n.235
on *vetera* and *nova*, 1–2, 5, 8–9,
    10–11, 24, 26–27, 35, 55, 73, 99,
    218, 222, 272–75, 276, 278–79,
    284–85, 301, 304, 307–8, 309,
    320–21, 329, 339, 353–54, 358,
    359n.1
on virtue, 173, 174–75, 344–46,
    390n.102
See also authenticity; conversions,
    existential; self-appropriation,
    critical; sublation; transcendental
    principles

Lonergan, Bernard, works of
    Collection (CWL, 4), 3, 11, 16, 18, 24,
        26, 46, 55, 57, 65, 75, 82, 83, 107,
        129, 150, 170, 259, 265, 269, 271,
        283, 284, 316, 335, 346, 361n.25,
        362nn.28, 29, 363n.50, 365nn.82,
        101, 366nn.103, 104, 108, 1,
        367n.14, 369nn.46, 54, 372n.36,
        373n.41, 375nn.77, 78, 86,
        377nn.130, 131, 382n.216,
        384nn.5, 6, 388nn.66, 73
    De Verbo Incarnato, 383n.245
    Grace and Freedom (CWL, 1), 69, 70,
        71, 73, 76, 359n.2, 364n.68,
        378n.160, 384n.6, 385n.22, 388n.72
    Insight (CWL, 3), 2, 5, 9, 23, 27,
        29–30, 31, 32, 33, 34–35, 37, 38,
        40, 44, 47, 51, 55, 56, 60, 62, 66, 67,
        72, 77, 78, 80, 85, 86, 89, 94, 98,
        118, 132, 139, 140, 141, 146, 147,
        149, 151–55, 157, 159, 166, 179,
        183, 208–9, 210–11, 223–24, 249,
        265, 266, 271, 272–73, 277,
        278–79, 293, 295, 296–97, 304,
        311, 314, 316, 321–22, 330, 332,
        336, 340, 344, 354, 355, 359nn.3, 4,
        360nn.9, 10, 14, 15, 361n.25,
        362n.41, 362nn.30, 33–37, 41,
        363nn.42, 45, 50, 55, 364nn.68, 72,
        76, 77, 365nn.78, 79, 82, 94,
        366n.103, 367n.24, 368nn.31, 35,
        36, 38, 41, 369nn.42, 44, 45, 46, 48,
        50–52, 54, 370n.5, 371nn.10, 21,
        23, 372n.37, 374n.60, 375nn.75, 79,
        81, 88, 93, 376nn.96, 99, 102, 112,
        377nn.130, 133, 136–42, 144–46,
        378nn.147, 156, 158, 159, 161,
        382nn.217, 227, 233, 235,
        383nn.237–39, 245, 385n.21,
        387n.49, 388nn.65, 67, 389nn.75,
        88, 390nn.89, 93
    Method in Theology, 3, 5, 9, 11, 17, 19,
        20, 29, 30–31, 32, 33, 34, 35, 36,
        37, 39, 40, 41, 42, 44, 46, 47, 48, 49,
        50, 51, 56, 57, 62, 67, 73, 77, 78, 81,
        86, 87, 89, 93, 103, 104, 105, 137,

Lonergan, Bernard, works of (*cont.*)
  139, 145, 170, 175, 177, 179, 183,
  209–10, 213, 228–29, 249, 255,
  265, 273, 280, 281, 282, 284, 293,
  295, 296–98, 300, 301, 302, 303–4,
  305, 307, 308, 312–15, 321–22,
  331, 332, 334, 335, 337, 341, 344,
  346, 354, 355, 357, 359nn.3, 4,
  360nn.8–12, 15, 16, 361n.25,
  362nn.29, 30, 32, 33, 34, 36, 41,
  363nn.42, 44, 45, 50, 364n.75,
  365nn.82, 83, 366nn.108, 1,
  367n.9, 368nn.34, 37, 39,
  369nn.42, 43, 44, 47, 370nn.5,
  371nn.8, 13, 19, 20, 22, 24,
  372n.37, 373nn.40, 47, 48,
  375nn.76, 78–81, 84, 88, 89, 92, 94,
  376nn.95, 97–100, 103, 104, 106,
  107, 111, 115, 377nn.136, 137,
  378nn.151–53, 155, 156,
  382nn.216, 218–20, 223–27, 229,
  231, 235, 383nn.236, 248, 385n.25,
  386nn.34, 38, 39, 387nn.48, 51, 54,
  58–60, 388nn.63, 64, 70, 72, 74,
  389n.88, 390nn.93, 102, 391n.1
 Phenomenology and Logic (CWL, 18),
  37, 102, 366n.104, 368nn.28, 29
 *Philosophical and Theological Papers
  1965–1980* (CWL, 17), 5, 22, 33,
  34, 41, 42, 43, 52, 65, 73, 82, 83, 86,
  87, 93, 97, 101, 103, 108, 266, 271,
  274, 276, 279, 282, 285, 292, 298,
  302, 303, 305, 321, 332, 336, 338,
  344, 359nn.2, 6, 360nn.8, 16,
  362nn.29, 32, 363n.44, 364nn.61,
  76, 365n.80, 366nn.103, 108,
  366n.1, 371n.17, 373n.47,
  376nn.108, 114, 378nn.153, 154,
  156, 381n.213, 382n.223, 383n.240,
  384n.5, 385nn.21, 23, 24, 26,
  386nn.34, 35, 387nn.50, 51
 Second Collection, 2, 3, 9, 18, 22, 30,
  33, 41, 52, 54–55, 73, 75, 82, 89,
  99, 101, 102, 107, 149, 156, 167,
  173, 181, 265, 279, 280, 281, 283,
  284, 291, 293, 299, 309, 326, 330,
  337, 342, 343, 359n.2, 361n.25,
  362nn.28, 32, 33, 363n.50, 364n.75,
  365nn.99, 101, 366n.103,
  369nn.43, 44, 49, 51, 54, 370n.5,
  373nn.41, 47, 375nn.81, 90,
  376nn.97, 101, 105, 110, 111, 112,
  115, 377nn.128, 130, 143,
  381nn.206, 212, 213, 383nn.245, 4,
  384n.5, 385n.25, 386nn.34, 35, 39,
  387n.50, 388nn.62, 66, 73, 389n.75
 "The Subject" (*Second Collection*),
  99–101
 Third Collection, 4, 11, 22, 33, 64, 65,
  84, 88, 99, 105, 110, 136, 281n.213,
  285, 292, 331, 334, 341, 346,
  359nn.2, 5, 6, 360n.16, 361n.25,
  363n.45, 364nn.61, 75, 76,
  367nn.9, 14, 368nn.34, 38,
  369nn.46, 49, 370n.5, 371n.17,
  372n.36, 373nn.40, 41, 377nn.130,
  132, 381n.213, 382n.230, 384nn.5,
  6, 385n.26, 386n.39, 388n.66,
  389n.88, 390n.93
 Topics in Education (CWL, 10), 15,
  25, 331, 360nn.15, 16, 363n.45,
  366n.1, 376n.117
 The Triune God, 364nn.73, 74,
  378n.157
 Verbum (CWL, 2), 22, 51, 53–54, 55,
  56, 58, 59, 61, 63, 67, 71, 73, 74, 83,
  104, 110, 145, 151, 304, 316,
  359n.1, 363nn.50, 55, 57, 364nn.73,
  74, 365n.101, 375n.94, 381n.213,
  384n.6, 385nn.22, 23, 388n.67
 The Way to Nicea, 387n.50
love
 of God, 32, 37, 39, 47–48, 49, 50, 70,
  78, 181, 209, 229–30, 251, 257,
  283, 304, 306, 312, 314–16, 319,
  349, 350, 388n.69
 God's love for human beings, 251, 253,
  264, 293, 297–98, 299, 316–17, 340,
  349, 358, 382n.222, 388nn.68, 69
 of neighbor, 32, 37, 48, 49, 50, 70, 78,
  175, 181, 257, 283, 297, 304, 306,
  314, 319, 345, 349, 350

Lubac, Henri de, 276
Luke
  7:22, 383n.243
  10:25–37, 383n.242
  15:11–32, 383n.241
Luther, Martin, 25, 194, 232–33, 246, 267, 379n.166
Lyell, Charles, 94, 199

Machiavelli, Niccolò, 367n.12
MacIntyre, Alasdair
  After Virtue, 364n.61, 365n.97, 370n.62, 380n.191, 383n.2, 390n.92
  on emotivism, 97, 380n.191
  on medieval thought, 383n.2
  Three Rival Versions of Moral Inquiry, 360n.13
Mandela, Nelson, 206
Maréchal, Joseph, 361n.20
Maritain, Jacques, 273, 361n.20
Mark 1:14–15, 36
Marx, Karl, 3, 6, 140, 331, 374n.62, 380n.185
  atheism of, 201
  on classless society, 124, 201, 202, 236, 239, 255, 337, 350
  on class struggle, 12, 98, 192, 199, 201, 239, 240, 255, 337
  on communism, 380n.186
  Communist Manifesto, 373n.46, 384n.16
  and Hegel, 96, 123, 192, 239, 240
  on history, 12, 87, 96, 113, 124–25, 131, 201, 239, 325, 380n.187
  on human beings, 124, 129, 239
  on human freedom, 124, 325
  on ideology, 201, 239, 250
  vs. Kierkegaard, 239–40
  on philosophy, 239
  on religion, 21, 201, 221, 239, 250
  on theory and practice, 380n.187
Marxism, 206, 242, 255, 334, 337, 338, 341, 350
material causality, 61, 119
materialism, 19, 225, 330

mathematics, 23, 36, 55, 94, 143, 151, 162, 208, 272, 293
  geometry, 84, 115, 120, 220
  Kant on, 121, 357
  in physics, 111, 118, 119, 131, 159–60
Mathews, William: *Lonergan's Quest*, 383n.4
Matthew
  3:2, 49
  4:17, 36, 49
  5:17–18, 323
  7:5, 178
  7:20, 383n.250
  11:5, 383n.243
  25:31–45, 383n.242
Mauriac, François, 252
meaning, 27, 90–93, 126–27
  formal terms of, 146
  functions of, 103
  Lonergan on, 12, 18, 89, 92, 95, 103–5, 138, 139–40, 146, 209, 330, 360n.14, 366n.105, 390n.102
  See also cognitive meaning; hermeneutics
Mendel, Gregor, 94
metaphysics, 18, 23, 52, 55, 99, 114, 157, 171, 213, 216, 220, 281–82
  Aquinas on, 14, 56, 75–76, 81, 82, 212, 249
  Aristotle on, 14, 56, 62, 63–64, 66, 81, 82, 83, 104, 110, 116, 118, 151, 174, 187–88, 212, 231, 272
  Lonergan on, 21–22, 75–76, 83, 102, 143, 281, 291, 356–57
  relationship to epistemology, 22, 24, 74–76, 143, 157, 225, 282, 291–92, 356–57
Mill, John Stuart, 3
Milton, John, 268
Mitchell, Basil, 390n.100
modernity, 371n.16
  vs. antiquity, 109–17
  cultural crises of, 11, 13–15, 23, 24–26, 35, 108, 129, 180, 207, 259, 265–70, 353, 358

modernity (cont.)
    defining revolutions of, 109–17
    vs. High Middle Ages, 81–82
    intellectual progress in, 10
    Lonergan on, 25–26, 81–82,
        83–106, 107–17, 130, 136,
        180, 183, 207–8, 212, 214,
        222, 259, 274–75, 277, 283,
        284, 320–21, 330–31, 334,
        354, 377n.128, 381n.206,
        385n.24
    moral challenge of, 324–41
    See also cultural heritage
Molina, Luis de, 273, 361n.20
monasticism, 262
Montesquieu, Charles: *Spirit of the
    Laws*, 335, 390n.91
moral authenticity, 24, 170, 211, 215,
    222, 249
moral development, 26–27, 35, 41,
    44–45, 173–74, 179, 354
moral objectivity, 140–41, 171–79
moral ontology, 327, 342, 370n.63,
    389n.86
moral relativism, 45, 87, 132, 172, 217,
    337, 338, 354
moral responsibility, 19, 32, 43, 69, 80,
    102, 108, 114, 142, 247, 249, 289,
    296, 308, 312, 328, 330, 335, 339,
    350
    collective responsibility, 88, 98, 137,
        180, 192, 211, 247, 252, 269, 331,
        340
    historical responsibility, 24, 132,
        239, 245, 336, 340, 349, 350
    Kant on, 88, 115–16, 117, 121, 122,
        131, 133–34, 234–36, 243, 325,
        326, 329, 337, 389n.79
    moral aspirations, 172–73
    moral failures, 44, 178
    moral idealism, 177
moral uncertainty, 11, 12
More, Thomas, 266
Moses, 206, 298, 317, 318, 319, 320, 323,
    332
Mumford, Lewis: *The City in History*,
    372n.29

Murdoch, Iris, 185, 329
    Metaphysics as a Guide to Morals,
        373n.41, 382n.234, 389n.85
    The Sovereignty of Good, 363n.48,
        390n.101
Mussolini, Benito, 270

naive realism, 41, 100, 101, 157–59, 163,
    165, 166, 167, 169, 171
nationalism, 242, 245, 341, 350
national sovereignty, 11, 12
naturalism, exclusive ontological, 18,
    24–25, 46, 127, 188–89, 206, 225,
    275, 324–26, 354, 371n.16, 380n.189
    as reductive, 95–96, 126, 129,
        131–32, 217
natural law, 32–33
nature, 46, 134, 135, 197
    Aquinas on, 14, 25, 73, 76, 77,
        230–31, 233, 246, 258, 263, 292,
        323–24, 333, 336, 378n.161
    vs. convention, 20–21, 62, 97
    Hegel on, 122, 123
    as meaningless/purposeless, 119, 121
    physical laws, 16, 17, 18, 86, 93–94,
        111–12, 114, 118, 119, 121, 122,
        123, 125, 126, 188, 197, 225, 234
    relationship to grace, 14, 25, 46, 73,
        76, 77, 230–31, 233, 258, 263, 292,
        293, 323–24, 333, 336, 378n.161
    and Romanticism, 123–24
    and sin, 323–24
Nazism, 25, 244, 245, 246, 255, 270
Neiman, Susan, 340
    Evil in Modern Thought, 373n.41,
        374n.56, 379n.177, 382n.232,
        384n.10, 390n.95
Neoplatonism, 37, 72, 273
neo-Scholasticism, 270, 271, 273
Neri, Philip, 266
Newman, John Henry, 273, 276,
    377n.127, 388n.69
    on Christian teaching tradition, 300
    *An Essay on the Development of
        Christian Doctrine*, 288–89, 386n.39
    on respecting whole of being and
        knowledge, 107

New Testament, 196, 256, 299, 300, 301, 302, 306, 319
Nicholas of Cusa, 371n.18
   Docta Ignorantia, 388n.70
Nietzsche, Friedrich, 3, 34
   on asceticism, 202
   Beyond Good and Evil, 380n.196
   on creativity, 202, 243
   on death of God, 185, 243
   The Gay Science, 371n.12
   on genealogy of morals, 7–8, 98, 172, 201–2, 203, 337, 338, 380n.193
   Genealogy of Morals, 380nn.193, 196
   on inequality, 201–2
   on nihilism, 243
   on over-men, 202, 243
   on religion, 21, 98, 201–3, 221, 242–43, 250, 380nn.193, 194
   on *ressentiment*, 202, 203, 337
   on the strong and the weak, 201–3, 243
   Thus Spake Zarathustra, 374n.68
   on transvaluation of values, 98–99, 193, 202–3, 243, 338, 380n.195
nominalism, 14, 231, 266, 271
non-Euclidean geometries, 83, 84, 163, 187, 221
Noonan, John T.: *A Church That Can and Cannot Change*, 387n.57
normative appraisal, 6, 7, 20–21, 25–26, 275
nouvelle théologie, la, 276–77, 282

O'Dea, Thomas: *The Catholic Crisis*, 385n.30
Old Testament, 196, 286, 298, 299, 301, 302
O'Malley, John, 276–77
   What Happened at Vatican II?, 385n.28, 387n.55
ontological argument, 166
operative grace, 9, 47–48, 70, 76–77, 78, 79, 231, 342, 388n.72
Oresme, Nicholas, 361n.22, 371n.18
Origen, 273, 287
original sin, 196, 198, 237, 263, 323

orthodox Judaism, 11
Otto, Rudolf, 89

pantheism, 200
Parmenides, 58
Pascal, Blaise, 36, 140, 229, 260, 266, 273, 307, 377n.127, 386n.38
   on faith and reason, 287–88, 383n.240, 386n.37
   on God, 287–88, 295, 297, 315
   on human condition, 288, 381n.210
   on love, 388n.69
   Pensées, 288, 361n.21, 378n.150, 386n.37, 388n.69
   on unity and multiplicity, 136
patriarchy, 11, 255, 333, 352
Paul, St., 13, 232, 262, 265, 284, 287, 288, 299, 300, 307, 319, 370n.2, 377n.127, 381n.221
   conversion of, 49
   on justification through faith, 379n.167
   on knowing vs. doing what is right, 49, 68, 77
Paul VI, 277
   Humanae Vitae, 385n.29
Peguy, Charles, 276
Pelikan, Jaroslav
   The Christian Tradition, 387n.56
   The Emergence of the Catholic Tradition, 361n.19
Peter, St., 232, 262
phenomenology, 37, 89, 102, 127–28, 137
Philippians 2:7, 332
philosophy, 14, 27, 39, 130, 187, 216, 227–28, 241, 250, 261, 270, 272
   critical realism in, 41, 55, 74–75, 100, 105
   and data of consciousness, 56, 82, 89, 137–38, 224, 291–92, 295
   epistemic immanence in, 100, 101–2, 127, 166–67
   human subjectivity in, 56, 82, 88–90, 101, 137–38, 188, 214, 224, 291–92, 295, 311, 321, 337, 338

philosophy (*cont.*)
  idealism in, 41, 100, 101
  of language, 91, 164, 169
  Lonergan on, 11, 12, 15, 21–24, 31, 33, 34–35, 42, 51, 82, 86, 89–90, 108, 137–39, 143, 148–49, 151, 155, 165, 166, 207, 208, 213, 214, 222, 224, 259, 274, 278, 279, 281–83, 291–92, 293, 295, 300, 304, 310–11, 321–22, 335, 339, 344, 351, 353–54, 355–58, 362n.30, 390n.99
  as love of wisdom, 10
  and science, 9, 21–23, 55–56, 86, 93–96, 188–89, 212
  specialized method and vocabulary in, 56, 82, 104
  as sublated by theology, 283, 292, 293
  See also cognition; dialectic; epistemology; ethics; metaphysics
physics, 162, 241, 368n.33, 371n.18
  Aristotle on, 16, 86, 330, 361n.22, 366n.7
  Kant on, 121, 225
  Newtonian physics, 3, 10, 11, 16, 19, 83, 84, 85, 86, 93–94, 96, 97, 111–12, 115, 121, 122, 123, 125, 126, 130, 140, 163, 187, 197, 198, 220, 221, 224, 225, 234, 235, 236, 241, 267, 268, 361n.24
  quantum mechanics, 85, 221, 224, 225
  relativity theory, 221, 225
physis-nomos distinction, 20–21, 62, 97
Pico della Mirandola, Giovanni: "Oration on the Dignity of Man," 263–64
Pius IX: "Syllabus of Errors," 269
Pius X, 280
Pius XI: *Quadragisimo Anno*, 373n.46, 384n.16
Pius XII, 270, 381n.207, 385n.20
Planck, Max, 3, 16, 368n.33
Plato, 13, 61, 110, 273, 329, 363n.54, 366n.7, 382n.234
  Apology, 360n.17, 363n.52
  on cognition, 56, 57, 58, 59–60, 71
  and dialectic, 35, 57, 58, 105, 311
  on the Good, 36, 37
  Gorgias, 36, 363nn.51, 53
  on intellectual conversion, 36–37, 56, 388nn.64, 65
  on intelligible forms (*eide*), 58, 62
  Lonergan on, 51, 56–60, 71, 363n.50
  Meno, 363n.56
  on metaphysics, 56
  on opinion vs. knowledge, 59, 60
  Phaedo, 363nn.51, 56
  on recollection, 58–59
  Republic, 36–37, 363nn.51, 56, 388n.64
  on sense perception, 36–37, 58, 59
  on the soul, 57, 58–59, 60
Platonism, 14, 51
pleasure, 36
pluralism, 5, 24, 137, 186, 207–8, 360n.16
  as cultural, 11, 13–14, 20–21, 26, 33, 50, 53, 87, 96–97, 98, 132, 163–64, 166, 168, 187, 193, 207, 216, 217, 248, 281, 303, 309, 320, 339
  as epistemic, 4, 5, 34–35, 39, 155, 165, 207, 212–13, 214, 285
  as moral, 207, 324
  as religious, 207, 305
poetry, 114
Polanyi, Michael: *Personal Knowledge*, 378n.149
politics, 137, 274
  alliance of throne and altar, 372n.31
  Aristotle on, 113, 116, 117, 118
  hierarchy in, 190–91
  political legitimacy, 185, 191, 219–20
  and science, 113
positivism, 18, 34, 142, 148, 188, 221, 222, 291, 310, 386n.44
postmodernism, 5, 7, 8, 25–26, 105, 129–30, 135, 172, 248, 255
practical pattern of experience, 29, 139, 152, 169
practical wisdom, 136, 342, 345, 348, 389n.86
  Aristotle on, 64, 65–66, 112–13, 114, 326, 343

pragmatism, 148, 210
pre-Socratics, 13, 61, 110
principle of inertia, 111
probability, 84
prophets, 14, 37, 49, 206, 242, 256, 257, 264, 298, 299, 317, 318, 319, 320, 323, 332
Protestantism, 199, 222, 267–68, 269, 372n.31, 378n.162
  Reformation, 25, 189, 190, 191, 193, 194–95, 196, 232–33, 247, 266, 267, 268, 275–76, 279–80, 289, 324, 333, 334, 373n.42
Providential Deism, 193, 198–99, 200
Psalm 8:3–4, 230, 254
psychology, 126, 241
Ptolemy, 224–25, 324, 368n.33
Pythagoreans, 58, 61

Quadragisimo Anno, 373n.46, 384n.16
quantum mechanics, 85, 221, 224, 225
questions and answers, 57, 58, 75, 95, 100, 142–43, 146, 152–55, 157, 165, 170, 208, 309
  question(s) of God, 312–13, 321
  questions for intelligence, 31, 42, 59, 68, 74, 95, 152–53
  questions for moral deliberation, 42–43, 176–77
  questions for reflection, 31, 42–43, 59, 72, 74, 95, 100, 176–77
Quine, W. V. O.: *Ontological Relativity and Other Essays*, 370n.61

racism, 11, 25, 242, 247, 255
Rahner, Karl, 273
Ranke, Leopold von, 3, 6, 87, 123, 240–41
Rawls, John
  Political Liberalism, 363n.47
  on the right vs. the good, 329
reason, 148, 245
  Aquinas on, 14, 25, 26, 73, 77–78, 196, 218–19, 233, 234, 258, 262, 263, 271, 287, 289, 292
  Aristotle on *nous*, 112, 143, 174, 234

critical reason, 25, 146, 150, 151, 154–55, 162, 199, 200, 219, 220, 222, 286–91, 294
  during Enlightenment, 21, 197–99, 243, 268, 289, 310, 324
  and faith, 14, 25, 46, 73, 77, 196, 199, 218–19, 221–22, 233, 258, 262, 269, 271, 286, 287–88, 290–91, 292, 298, 306, 309, 357, 383n.240, 386n.37
  Kant on ideas of, 90, 121, 122, 143, 160–61, 220, 235–36, 289, 367n.23, 379n.176
  Kant on practical reason, 86, 88, 99, 116, 120–21, 122, 131, 133–34, 220, 235, 236–37, 239, 337, 380n.189
  Kant on theoretical reason, 34, 86, 94, 116, 120–21, 131, 132, 162, 220, 235, 236, 239, 289, 310
  vs. logic, 94–95, 145, 199
reasonableness, 32
reconciliation, 293
reductionism, 4, 19, 27, 40, 109, 127, 135, 136, 139–40, 141, 183, 188, 210, 211, 250, 275, 354
  of exclusive ontological naturalism, 95–96, 126, 129, 131–32, 217
  relationship to empirical sciences, 17–18, 85, 86, 95–96, 126, 129, 131–32, 155, 204, 217, 224, 225, 330
relativism
  moral, 45, 87, 132, 172, 217, 337, 338, 354
  religious, 87, 132
  regarding truth, 5, 13, 23, 33–34, 41, 45, 97–98, 132, 149, 164, 165–66, 168, 169, 217, 337, 338, 354
relativity theory, 221, 225
religious pattern of experience, 29, 139
religious toleration, 25, 194, 267, 277–78, 285, 384n.9
Renaissance, 15, 25, 231–32, 262, 263–64, 266–67, 324, 333, 366n.7, 371n.18, 372n.30

repentance, 36, 49, 50, 285, 341, 352
Rerum Novarum, 373n.46, 384n.16
research communities, 65–66, 85, 133, 187, 292
ressourcement, 276–77, 282, 387nn.52–53
Revelation, book of, 300
rhetoric, 114
Richardson, Alan, 359n.6, 366n.2
  History, Sacred and Profane, 372n.35, 374n.58, 386n.33
Ricoeur, Paul, 376n.114
  Freud and Philosophy, 374n.59
Riemannian geometry, 84
Roman Empire, 261, 265, 286
  collapse of, 15, 262, 266
Romans, 379n.166
  7:14–24, 68
  7:19, 49, 77
Romanticism, 88, 91, 123–24, 125, 131, 193, 236–37, 324, 337, 338
Rorty, Richard, 91
  The Linguistic Turn, 365n.86
Rousseau, Jean-Jacques, 236
rule of law, 185
Russell, Bertrand, 34, 91
Russian Revolution, 113
Ryle, Gilbert, 366n.105

salvation, 67, 192, 197, 232–33, 299
Savonarola, Girolamo, 264
schemes of recurrence, 225–27, 253–54
Schleiermacher, Friedrich, 3, 377n.127
Schneewind, Jerome: *The Invention of Autonomy*, 379n.175
scholarship, 3, 4, 20, 31, 42, 65–66, 106, 182, 217, 218
  biblical studies, 195, 199–200, 275, 280, 290
  historical scholarship, 39–40, 55–56, 87, 104, 107, 134–35, 136, 137, 155, 156, 187, 199, 212, 216, 222, 227–28, 247, 250, 274, 290, 292, 293, 294–95, 311, 320, 334, 353
  See also hermeneutics

Scholasticism, 7, 10, 30, 141, 189, 196, 231, 262, 263, 266, 285, 287
Schumpeter, Joseph, 3
science, 42, 182, 197, 222, 227, 247, 250, 382n.235
  Aristotle's theory of, 52, 64, 65, 66–67, 86, 104, 113–14, 118–19, 132, 143–44, 223, 280, 330, 361n.22, 361n.24, 366n.7
  as communal activity, 223
  cultural status of, 187, 245–46
  Descartes on, 113, 128, 132, 143–44, 159, 189, 234, 326–27, 361n.24
  as empirical, 16, 19–20, 55–56, 64–65, 67, 85, 88–89, 93–95, 118–19, 151, 187, 210, 218, 221, 223, 241, 278, 280, 292, 294–95, 311, 326, 339, 343, 357
  human sciences, 9, 10, 11, 18, 19–20, 21, 22, 23, 27, 31, 34, 39, 82, 88–89, 94, 97, 107, 118–19, 126–27, 137, 140, 164, 165, 187, 188, 208, 212, 213, 216, 221, 222, 225, 241–42, 269, 270, 274, 281, 293, 330, 339, 343, 353, 362n.30
  Kant on, 162, 220, 221, 235, 357
  language of, 104, 164, 212
  Lonergan on scientific method, 3, 16–17, 22, 89, 137–38, 188–89, 222–24, 294–95
  natural sciences, 1, 3, 4, 6, 7, 9, 11, 15–16, 17–19, 20, 21, 22, 23, 27, 31, 34, 39, 55–56, 67, 82, 84–86, 88–89, 92, 93–96, 97, 107, 109–17, 118–19, 125–27, 136–37, 138, 187, 188, 197, 206, 208, 210, 212, 213, 216, 220, 222, 225, 241, 242, 270, 272, 274, 281, 293, 330, 339, 343, 353, 362n.30, 367n.12, 368n.33
  paradigm shifts in, 164
  and philosophy, 9, 21–23, 86, 93–96, 188–89, 212
  provisional/fallible results in, 3, 16–17, 18, 22, 64, 82, 86, 87, 94–95, 105, 132, 133, 156, 223–24, 270, 280, 368n.33

Scientific Revolution, 15–16, 18–21,
  50, 86, 114, 118, 187, 189, 222, 233,
  247, 324, 333, 366n.7, 367n.19,
  384n.12
  and technology, 17, 113, 116, 120–21,
    124, 187, 191, 234, 235, 244, 268,
    274, 326–27, 336, 340–41, 344
  theories in, 15, 16–17, 67, 82, 86, 95,
    105, 113, 138, 223–24, 225, 274,
    290, 368n.33
scientism, 104, 132, 142, 188, 275, 354
Scotus, John Duns, 273
scriptural fundamentalism, 199, 200
Second Vatican Council, 265, 272,
    275–83, 289, 300, 352, 385nn.27,
    30, 386n.40
  Dignitatis Humanae, 277–78,
    385n.31
  Gaudium et Spes, 278, 381n.209,
    385n.31, 387n.61
  Lumen Gentium, 276, 277, 385n.31
  Nostra Aetate, 278, 385n.31
secularism, 181–82, 183, 275, 325–26,
  331, 354
secularization, 11, 12, 21, 25, 26, 50–51,
  181–206, 242, 248, 350, 355,
  371n.16
  definitions of "secular," 184–86, 215,
    363n.46
  genealogies of, 186–206
  Lonergan on, 46, 181–82, 183, 215–18
  and religious faith, 181–83, 184–86,
    193–206, 228, 289
  Taylor on, 46, 182–83
self-appropriation, critical, 27–35, 52,
  56, 93, 101, 105, 171, 208–10,
  214–15, 218, 310, 354, 358
  and dialectic, 29–30, 33–35, 208,
    209–10, 249
  vs. ideology, 29
  reflexive self-appropriation, 29–30,
    40–41, 92
  of transcendental principles, 29–33,
    35, 222, 249
  See also conversions, existential; self-
    transcendence

self-centeredness, 39, 40, 44, 49
self-deception, 44
self-knowledge, 28, 29, 68, 91, 92, 130
  Lonergan on, 40, 41, 108, 109, 136,
    149–51, 171, 180, 210, 229–30,
    249, 271, 295–96, 312, 362n.41
self-transcendence, 29, 39, 180, 275,
  316, 332, 341
  authenticity as, 38, 95, 175–79, 181,
    211, 215, 249, 250, 252–53, 336,
    338, 345–46, 356, 358
  as epistemic, 38, 42, 95, 101, 102, 150,
    170, 175, 178, 179, 181, 211, 215,
    249, 298, 305, 310, 321, 336, 355
  as moral, 38, 42, 44–45, 102, 150,
    170, 175, 178, 179, 181, 211, 215,
    249, 298, 305, 310, 321, 336, 355
  as religious, 175, 179, 181, 183, 211,
    298, 305, 310
  and transcendental principles, 40, 42,
    46–47, 95, 150, 176, 178, 215, 281,
    298
Sellars, Wilfrid, 91
  Science, Perception and Reality,
    365n.100, 370n.59
sense perception, 23, 41, 85, 99, 101,
  145–46, 150, 157–60, 163, 167,
  208
  Aristotle on, 61, 64, 66
  Lonergan on, 23, 58–59, 75, 89,
    137–38, 138, 158, 214
  Plato on, 36–37, 58, 59
  representative theory of, 159–60
  See also empiricism
sexual ethics, 344
Shakespeare, William
  Hamlet, 230, 244
  King Lear, 180
Silone, Ignazio, 390n.96
Simon, Richard, 280, 377n.127
sin, 90, 135, 193–94, 206, 247, 256, 257,
  264–65, 320
  Aquinas on, 71, 76, 78–79, 230, 231,
    246, 323–24, 333, 350
  Augustine on, 68–70, 71, 76–77, 79,
    231–32, 233, 266

sin (*cont.*)
  distorting effects of, 9, 28, 29, 30, 44, 48–49, 79, 134, 192, 308, 310, 342, 350
  Lonergan on, 9, 28, 29, 30, 47, 78, 103, 165, 215, 218, 219, 230, 258, 272, 293, 296, 308, 314, 316, 332, 334, 336, 338, 341, 342, 348, 349–50
  original sin, 196, 198, 237, 263, 323
  redemption from, 9, 29, 37, 81, 103, 135, 211, 218, 219, 237, 253, 256, 257–58, 260, 261, 277, 278, 284, 287, 288, 293, 296, 298, 299, 305, 317, 319, 332, 333, 337, 339, 340, 349–50, 351
skepticism, 5, 11, 14, 23, 97–98, 101, 134–35, 142, 231, 290, 315
  epistemic, 24, 25, 26, 144, 164
  of Hume, 93–94, 160, 162, 198–99, 365n.92
  moral, 21, 24, 26, 45, 97, 108, 171–72, 338
  religious, 24–25, 26, 50, 184–85, 198–99, 200, 205, 272, 296
  Wittgenstein on, 366n.102
slavery, 255
Smith, Adam, 3, 268
sobriety, 351
social conformity, 338–39
socialism, 328, 333
social pressure, 44
Society of Jesus, 265, 266, 279, 361n.20, 378n.162
sociology, 126, 241, 275, 281
Socrates, 229, 286
  on intellectual conversion, 36–37, 56
  on learned ignorance, 57
  trial of, 13, 360n.17
sophists, 13
Soviet Union, 244
Spanish Civil War, 244, 270
Spanish Inquisition, 194

specialization, intellectual, 21, 22, 23–24, 39, 87, 95, 118–19, 130–31, 132–33, 184, 187, 272, 282, 285, 311
  functional specialization in theology, 217, 260, 292, 301–10, 322, 353, 355, 357, 387n.54
  vs. generalized empirical method, 3–4, 31–32, 104, 155, 294–95
  Lonergan on, 4–5, 9–10, 15, 18–19, 31–32, 55–56, 65, 81–82, 85–86, 92, 104, 107, 136, 137, 152, 155, 188, 208, 212–13, 215–16, 223, 260, 282, 285, 291–92, 294, 301–10, 311, 322, 334–35, 343, 353, 355, 357, 360n.11, 387n.54
  See also epistemic pluralism
Spender, Stephen
  The God That Failed, 362n.38, 390nn.96, 97, 391n.107
  on power, 390n.97
Spinoza, Benedict de, 34, 94, 268
  Ethics, 367n.8
  Tractatus Theologico-Politicus, 367n.12
spiritual development, 26–27, 41
Stalin, Joseph, 25, 245, 340
statistical heuristic structure, 18, 85, 94, 125, 126, 140, 165, 214, 221, 224, 226, 227, 313
statistics, 84, 85, 94
Stephen Bathory, king, 384n.9
Stewart, J. A.: *Plato's Doctrine of Ideas*, 363n.50
Strawson, Peter: *The Bounds of Sense*, 369n.55
Suárez, Francisco, 273, 361n.20, 372n.31
sublation
  defined, 141–42, 378n.152
  of epistemic and moral by religious self-transcendence, 337
  of epistemic by moral self-transcendence, 83, 102, 336, 338
  of *eros* of mind by *eros* for value, 42, 46, 176
  of *eros/philia* by *agape/caritas*, 297, 298, 314

as functional complementarity, 142, 145, 150, 157, 175
of human living by religion, 292, 293
of human nature by grace, 47–48, 258, 298, 314, 315, 333, 380n.188
of philosophy by theology, 283, 292, 293
of philosophy of God by revealed theology, 358
of reason by faith, 298
suspicion, 130, 134–35, 293, 314
  hermeneutics of, 8, 21, 50, 98–99, 200–205, 217, 374n.59
  masters of, 8, 21, 46, 106, 140, 201–5, 217, 221, 310, 324
symbolism, 108, 164, 327, 330, 339
systematic theory, 11, 92, 95, 104, 105, 148, 153, 155, 156, 212

Taylor, Charles, 366n.2, 376n.114, 391n.106
  on *agape*, 388n.68
  A Catholic Modernity?, 373n.39, 375n.86, 376n.113
  on death of God, 185
  The Ethics of Authenticity, 382n.215
  on ethics of unbelief, 21, 290
  on exclusive humanism, 374n.60, 389n.77
  on fullness of life, 383n.247
  Hegel and Modern Society, 365n.81, 368n.32, 379n.179
  on holistic individualism, 249, 381n.214
  on the immanent frame, 185–86, 192–93, 200, 206, 325–26, 389n.78
  vs. Lonergan, 182, 183, 185–86, 215, 217, 249, 342
  Modern Social Imaginaries, 372n.34
  on moral advocacy, 327, 370n.63
  on moral ontology, 327, 342, 370n.63
  Philosophical Arguments, 370n.63, 381n.214, 389n.80
  Philosophical Papers, 381n.214, 389n.81
  on religious belief, 46, 51, 182–83, 386n.43
  A Secular Age, 46, 182–83, 360n.13, 363n.46, 370nn.1, 3, 371nn.6–8, 10, 11, 14, 15, 372nn.34, 38, 373nn.39, 41, 374nn.53, 60, 61, 375n.74, 377n.126, 381nn.208, 211, 383n.247, 386nn.42, 43, 389nn.77, 78
  Sources of the Self, 21, 181, 183, 360n.13, 365nn.81, 88, 368n.25, 370nn.63, 4, 371nn.27, 38, 374n.57, 375n.86, 377n.126, 381n.208, 382n.228, 386nn.42, 43, 388n.68
  on stifling deeper truth, 210
technology, 109, 114, 192, 350
  and science, 17, 113, 116, 120–21, 124, 187, 191, 234, 235, 244, 268, 274, 326–27, 336, 340–41, 344
Teilhard de Chardin, Pierre, 276, 377nn.127, 128
teleological causation. *See* final causality
Tempier, Étienne, Bishop of Paris, 366n.7
Tennyson, Alfred Lord, 125
Teresa, Mother, 206
Teresa of Avila, St., 206, 262, 266
Tertullian, 13, 261
theology, 10, 14, 23, 27, 39, 52, 82, 114, 117, 130, 143, 163, 187, 189, 212, 247, 270
  apophatic theology, 388n.70
  Aristotle on, 62–63, 64–65
  functional specialties in, 260, 292, 301–10, 320, 353, 357, 362n.41, 376n.107
  general vs. special theological categories, 388n.74
  kataphatic theology, 388n.70
  Lonergan on, 9, 11, 12, 15, 18, 21–22, 31, 42, 51, 86, 104, 108, 136, 148, 151, 155, 165, 208, 214, 216, 217, 222, 224, 227–28, 259, 272, 274, 278, 279, 281–83, 284–85, 291–92, 293, 295–323, 335, 339, 344, 351, 353–54, 354, 355, 357, 358, 362n.30, 378n.151, 387n.59, 388nn.70, 74

theology (*cont.*)
  mediated theology, 301, 304–9, 320–21, 322, 358, 387n.53
  mediating theology, 301–4, 308, 320, 322, 358
  as queen of the sciences, 289
  as sublating philosophy, 283, 292, 293
  See also Aquinas, Thomas; Augustine, St.
theoretical inquiry, 16, 61, 86, 103–4, 112, 118, 132, 294, 334, 344
Thomism, 51, 81, 83, 263, 271, 273, 344–45, 361n.20
Tocqueville, Alexis de, 6, 195, 269, 328–29, 373n.45, 389n.83
Toynbee, Arnold, 3
Tracy, David: *Plurality and Ambiguity*, 366n.109
transcendental principles, 53, 162, 213, 216, 282
  generalized empirical method/transcendental method, 3–4, 5, 23, 31–32, 82, 104, 137–38, 155, 214, 225, 294–95, 356
  relationship to self-transcendence, 40, 42, 46–47, 95, 150, 176, 178, 216, 281, 298
  self-appropriation of, 29–33, 35, 222, 249
  transcendental notion of being (*eros* of mind), 30, 31, 38–39, 40, 41, 42, 44, 46–47, 49, 54–55, 60, 90, 100, 141, 142, 145, 148, 150, 152, 155, 156, 159, 165, 168, 169–70, 176, 178, 180, 208, 211, 213, 218, 222, 227, 228, 229, 249, 251, 254, 256, 281, 292, 293, 295, 296–97, 311–13, 314, 321, 335, 338, 339, 342, 356, 360n.10, 362n.36, 369n.42, 391n.1
  transcendental notion of value (*eros* for value), 30–31, 38–39, 42–44, 46–47, 49, 90, 141, 142, 150, 165, 169–70, 176, 178, 180, 208, 211, 213, 218, 222, 227, 228, 229, 249, 251–52, 254, 256, 281, 293, 295, 296–97, 311–12, 313–14, 321, 335, 338, 339, 342, 356, 360n.10, 362n.36, 369n.42, 391n.1
  transcendental precepts/norms, 32–33, 40, 44–45, 158–59, 162, 165, 170, 215, 218, 227, 249, 254, 281, 295, 309, 311–12, 331, 335, 338, 342, 356, 360n.10
Treaty of Versailles, 244
Treaty of Westphalia, 194, 267
Trilling, Lionel: *Sincerity and Authenticity*, 381n.215
truth, 57, 99, 104, 114, 135, 140–41, 157, 176
  Aquinas on, 74–75
  coherence theory of, 167–68, 171
  correspondence theory of, 167, 171
  Kant on, 121, 161, 162, 168
  Lonergan on, 102, 108, 146–47, 156, 170–71, 211, 223
  propositional truths, 22, 53, 72, 90, 100–101, 105, 121, 146, 150, 153–54, 159, 161, 162, 167, 168, 208–9, 309
  relativism regarding, 5, 13, 23, 33–34, 41, 45, 97–98, 132, 149, 164, 165–66, 168, 169, 217, 337, 338, 354
  unrestricted desire for truth, 38, 46, 177, 360n.10, 362n.36, 369n.42, 391n.1
  See also relativism; skepticism; suspicion; transcendental principles
Tuchman, Barbara: *The March of Folly*, 373n.42, 378n.164, 384n.7

utilitarianism, 237, 329, 337, 338

value, 27, 126–27
  categorical judgments of, 332
  comparative judgments of, 332
  hierarchy of, 43, 175, 186, 189–90, 209, 314, 324, 332–33

intentional responses to, 44
Lonergan on, 18, 138, 174–75, 330, 332–33, 338, 342, 349, 382n.235
originating values, 45, 227, 260, 332, 333, 342, 346
terminal values, 45, 175, 177, 209, 227, 260, 332–33, 342, 346, 347
See also transcendental principles
Vico, Giambattista, 3
Vincent de Paul, St., 266
virtue, 43, 329, 341
Aquinas on, 14, 73, 76, 77–78, 219, 231, 263, 292, 324, 326, 336, 344–45
Aristotle on, 62, 64, 65, 76, 112–13, 173, 174, 175, 223, 326
associative virtues, 345
cardinal virtues, 14, 77
categorial virtues, 345–46, 348, 390n.102
intellectual virtues, 64, 65, 77, 78, 112–13, 174, 258, 292, 345
Lonergan on, 173, 174–75, 344–46, 390n.102
moral virtues, 62, 78, 82, 134, 171–79, 292, 345
natural virtues, 77, 78, 336, 344–45
Socrates on, 57
supernatural virtues, 14, 77, 78, 82, 231, 292, 326, 336, 344–45, 346
transcendental virtues, 345–46, 348, 390n.102
vocational dignity, 189
Vogelin, Eric: *The World of the Polis*, 361n.18
Voltaire, 268
Candide, 198
voluntarism, 76

Walmsley, Gerard: *Lonergan on Philosophic Pluralism*, 368n.41, 375n.83
Watson, Patrick: *The Struggle for Democracy*, 389n.82
Westman, Robert: *Reappraisals of the Scientific Revolution*, 367n.19
Whitehead, Alfred North, 366n.2
on critical mentality, 15–16
on cultural heritage, 210
on God, 386n.46
Science and the Modern World, 15–16, 86, 361n.23, 362n.38, 367n.19, 373n.41, 375n.87, 379n.168, 384n.7, 386n.46
Wiesel, Elie: *Night*, 382n.232
William of Ockham, 273
Wills, Garry, 270, 381n.207
Head and Heart, 374n.55
Papal Sin, 385n.18, 390n.96
Wittgenstein, Ludwig, 3
on cognition, 366n.102
on language, 91, 92, 105, 166
On Certainty, 370n.60
Philosophical Investigations, 166, 366n.102
on skepticism, 366n.102
Tractatus, 355
Wolff, Christian, 94
women
Catholicism on, 247
equality of, 242, 344, 352
ordination of, 391n.110
working class, 195, 201, 269
World War I, 192, 244, 255, 350
World War II, 25, 192, 244, 246, 381n.207, 385n.20

Yeats, W. B.: "The Second Coming," 375n.91

MICHAEL H. McCARTHY

is professor emeritus of philosophy at Vassar College.
He is the author of a number of books, including
The Political Humanism of Hannah Arendt.

www.ingramcontent.com/pod-product-compliance
Lightning Source LLC
Chambersburg PA
CBHW071234300426
44116CB00008B/1034